Dedicated to the memory of my late father.

You may be gone but you will never be forgotten.

Until we meet again.

Chasing the Dream

FOREWORD

Back in the day, whenever I was in the company of family or friends, I would sometimes make the following lighthearted comment and caveat, "be careful of what you say and/or do because somewhere in the corner of the room is my personal fly on the wall camera that has been recording every moment of my life..."

This is my life's journey over the course of my first forty eight years, a journey that from the outset, has been driven by a desire and a dream (that continues even to this day) of wanting to achieve, an ambition to succeed that is coupled with an idealistic goal of wanting to leave a legacy for others in the future to hopefully aspire to and surpass.

Some may say, with some justification, that my enduring ambition has been but a pipedream, a dream that, no matter how hard I work, no matter how successful I may become, will always be tantalisingly beyond my reach. In the real and pragmatic world, that may be true, but given the person that I am and have always been, that will never prevent me from chasing what I have always aspired to.

My life's journey has been no different from anyone else's, having encountered my own fair share of disappointment and delight along the way. As the great Seventeenth Century metaphysical poet John Donne so rightly observed, "no man is an island" and like any other journey of life, my own has not been made in isolation. There have been many, many people who have helped me (and in some cases, hindered me) along the way. Some of those people have been mentioned by name in this book, whilst others have not, but the important thing to note is that I would not be the person that I am today but for the impact (for better or for worse) that they have had in my life and that is something for which I will always be grateful.

Writing my autobiography has not been an easy exercise to have undertaken, even at the best of times, and there are a couple of people who to my mind deserve special praise, because if it were not for their unwavering support, assistance and commitment, this autobiography would never have seen the light of day. The biggest shout out of all goes out to the one and only, Fiona Fearon (aptly named the original Princess Black), who selflessly and devotedly typed the original draft after hours and hours of seemingly endless dictation, without so much as a hint of complaint. I would have been lost without your help Fee, THANK YOU! A massive shout out also goes to my eldest nephew and computer wizard-in-chief, Myles Francis, who both literally and metaphorically picked me up off the floor when I was at my lowest point after I had lost all of my work to some dreaded computer glitch that totally erased my work, meaning I had to start again from scratch (and before you say it, yes I know, I should have backed up my work, where were you when I needed you?). Myles is also responsible for inserting all of the images that are contained in this book. A big thank you also goes out to my dedicated team of proof readers: Fiona Fearon (once again), Debbie Gay, Debra Clarke and Lauren Mercurius-Taylor, for helping me dot all the "i's" and cross all the "t's" and of course their all important constructive and extremely helpful feedback along the way. In terms of the design work for the book's front cover, I would like to say a big thank you to everyone whose individual creative talent combined to turn the visions that I had in mind for the book's general design and layout into a wonderful reality. A massive, massive thank you also goes out to my long-time friend, Ken Grant, for providing the image on the back of the book. I'd also like to thank David Hahn and Kirsty Smillie, without whom this book wouldn't be on the shelves.

Finally, I want to thank you - the reader of this book. There are no words that can truly express how grateful I am for the fact that you have taken the time out to buy and read about the various ups and downs of my life and I sincerely hope that by the time you have finished reading my story, you would have found it to have been both an enjoyable and inspiring experience.

Respect and Love Always,
Shaun Wallace

CHAPTER ONE

"CONGRATULATIONS BARRY," exclaimed Dermot in a tone and manner that expressed both his excitement and delight, "YOU ARE AN EGGHEAD!"

Then the fanfare music began to play heralding not only the end of the game, but also heralding the fact that the Eggheads will never be the same again.

I paused to observe the delight on Barry's face as it began to dawn on him that it was mission accomplished so far as he was concerned. He had come out on top. We turned and faced each other, and I whispered to him, "well done, Barry," a genuine heartfelt sentiment on my part yet at the same time, I could not help but wonder how I managed to snatch such an unlikely defeat from the apparent jaws of victory. In my line of vision, I could see Dermot, who, far removed from his usual unflappable demeanour, appeared to be totally caught up in the moment. He sat propped up on his three depleted cushions, so much so I was half expecting him to bounce up and down Zebedee fashion in the way as he is so wittily parodied by the brilliant impressionist, Jon Culshaw of Dead Ringers fame.

"WHAT A ROUND, BARRY! GOING INTO THAT 4-1 BEHIND, WHAT WERE YOUR THOUGHTS?"

Barry replied, "I was confident, because I'm renowned in the quizzing world for never getting any of the easy questions right, that everybody in the world seems to know, but always knowing the hard ones, which only a few seem to know. I just must have that sort of mind. I felt that I had a good chance, but Shaun is such a great competitor, I didn't know what was going to happen. Still, I wasn't without hope."

Dermot then turned his attention to me and asked, "SHAUN, I MEAN, WHAT WENT WRONG?"

"I was beaten by the better opponent; end of story. It took an Egghead to finally send me into retirement."

"THAT'S RIGHT," Dermot continued, "YOU CAME OUT OF RETIREMENT TO COMPETE!"

"That's correct," I replied, trying to be as gracious as possible whilst at the same time trying to hold myself together even though deep inside, I was totally distraught about the manner of my defeat. "The whole experience of being on Eggheads was wonderful and I couldn't have lost to a better opponent."

Dermot then turned to the Eggheads panel for their Grand Final post-match analysis. Kevin Ashman who by common consent is not only the most outstanding member of the esteemed Eggheads panel, he is also, quite possibly, the best quizzer of all time, was extremely gracious in his assessment. He said that both Barry and I were fantastic and for the pair of us to come through four rounds to the Grand Final was a real testament to our abilities.

CJ de Mooi echoed Kevin's warm sentiments by adding, "it's not just a test of knowledge, it's a test of temperament, manner, how you hold yourself as well as holding one's nerve. This was the fifth match and they both played brilliantly to get here."

Before the show's final closing credits began to roll, Dermot as always had the last few words: "LET THE MESSAGE GO OUT TO THE WORLD, THERE'S A NEW EGGHEAD ON THE BLOCK. CONGRATULATIONS BARRY, WELCOME ON BOARD!"

I'd gone beyond empty now. I felt physically and mentally drained after my very long day in the studio and despite my obvious sense of disappointment in falling at the final hurdle, I still felt a sense of pride of what I had achieved. OK so I lost, but at least I gave it the best shot that I could, and despite my disastrous second half performance, at least I went down fighting. It was at this point that the studio set came alive with people. Some of the production assistants were making their way to both Barry and me.

I turned to him and said, "You fully deserved that, well done my son!"

Barry was equally gracious with his sentiments. "Shaun you were magnificent. That was the toughest contest that I have been in. You should be very proud of yourself!"

At this point, we were momentarily interrupted by Charlotte Gorman, a member of the Eggheads production team who turned to me and said, "Shaun you did fantastically well, are you all right?"

Before I could reply, a voice from the studio set floor said, "let's give a round of applause to Barry on his magnificent achievement and especially to Shaun for a truly, truly great effort."

Then everybody, from the production team to Dermot himself, stood up in unison and burst into applause. I was still slumped in my seat at this point, and I just about summoned up the strength to rise to my feet and whilst I was doing so, I thought, *this is really wonderful they didn't have to do that!* I responded in kind by clapping back, just like my beloved Chelsea had done during their lap of honour around The Luzhniki Stadium in Moscow after having been agonisingly beaten 6-5 in a penalty shoot-out in the Champions League Final to Manchester United six weeks previously. After the unexpected applause had died down, I stood up and moved to the side of the desk and the first member of the Eggheads panel to approach me was CJ, whose facial expression appeared to express even greater disappointment than I was feeling myself. Both CJ and I shook hands before he said to me with more than a hint of sadness in his voice, "Oh Shaun what can I say?"

"That's how it goes, CJ!" I replied somewhat ruefully. Charlotte was standing nearby and I turned to her and said, "I'm really knackered, can I go home now?" The reason I wanted to leave was not only because of the physical and mental state I was in, but also because of the simple fact that this was Barry's moment not mine. I had my golden moment back in 2004 and now I just wanted to quietly ride off into the sunset without a trace.

"Just one more thing, Shaun," Charlotte said, "could you take part in the final set of interviews?"

"Of course," I replied. I was escorted to another part of the studio set where I met the Executive Producer, John Graham, who asked me if I would do a short piece to about my reaction after the Grand Final. My words were far too incoherent to be comprehensible and in truth, all I wanted to do was to get it over and done with so that I could leave the building and go home. Once I had finished the short interview, I turned to Charlotte who was close by and asked her could she make arrangements to take me back to my Dressing Room in order for me to collect my belongings. As I was leaving, I saw Daphne Fowler and Judith Keppel, two other Eggheads panellists, standing in the middle of the studio set floor. I went up to both ladies to say my goodbyes for the last time and they each in turn gave me a warm embrace before wishing me the very best of luck in the future. As I was approaching the exit, standing close by were Kevin Ashman and the remaining member of the original Eggheads panel, Chris Hughes. Two colossal quiz legends that have both entertained and inspired me over the years and yet here we were together, three former Mastermind Champions engaged in general conversation on the studio floor.

I turned to both and said, "Gentlemen it's been my absolute pleasure to have met the pair of you," and their response was more than complimentary. I turned to Kevin and said, "That's probably the very last time I will compete as a quiz contestant."

"That's a real shame," he replied. "It would be really nice to see you at one of our Quiz League events."

I told him that I would give it some thought and we exchanged contact details before shaking hands for the final time before they left the studio floor. Just as I was making my way with Charlotte towards the exit door, I noticed Barry also leaving the studio in the company of the show's producers presumably to be formerly inducted as the new Egghead and as he disappeared from view, I could not help thinking about the bitter disappointment of a golden opportunity that was lost and what might have been.

Once in my Dressing Room, I started to gather all of my personal belongings. I retrieved my favourite pink shirts which had served me so well in my past game show triumphs and placed them in my holdall. With all my belongings safely gathered, we then made our way out of the building complex towards the turnstile exit on Wood Lane where we were greeted by the warm evening sunshine.

"Well, take care Charlotte," I said to her as I stretched out my right hand in order to shake hers.

"Goodbye Shaun," she replied before pushing the green button by the large turnstile gates for me to make my exit.

I was struggling slightly as I passed through those metal turnstiles gates because I was weighed down with all my personal belongings. Because I was not wearing a watch, I was unsure as to the time and just before I exited the turnstiles, I asked Charlotte for the time and she replied it was just after eight o'clock. With both body and mind physically and emotionally drained, I finally made my way to the Car Park's fifth floor where precisely eleven hours earlier, I had arrived on a wave of excitement and determination on my quest to become an Egghead. With my belongings deposited safely in the boot, I immediately slumped wearily into the driver's seat and soon the burden of disappointment that I was carrying on my shoulders started to feel a little less heavy.

"How did Atlas cope?" I dryly asked myself, trying to inject a little gallows humour to an already depressing situation. I reached for my packet of Consulate cigarettes from the centre console. I was dying for a cigarette as I desperately needed something to unwind and help assuage the real sense of disappointment which still had a firm hold over me and for a while I just sat there completely motionless and devoid of any real or meaningful thoughts. You would have thought that somebody had just died as opposed to coming a very commendable runner up on a TV quiz game show. I needed something, anything to steer me away from this black cloud but my general demeanour and mood was such that I felt in no real rush to get home so I decided to recline the driver's seat and take a moment to relax and reflect for a while. I switched on the car's CD player which was left on the track Babylon Sisters by Steely Dan as it was the CD that I was singing merrily along to when I set out for the BBC studios that morning, a journey filled with unlimited hope that was more than matched by expectation and I decided to play the CD from the beginning in the hope that somehow it would evoke similar feelings of the euphoria and excitement that I felt earlier on in the day and as the soothing sounds seeped through the car's speakers, it began to have the effect of gradually lifting the feelings of disappointment and defeat and shifting them to one of contemplation and reflection about everything that I had managed to achieve in my life up until this point and like Marcel Proust before me, I began to embark on my own personal recollection of things past (*a la recherché du temps perdu*) as I cast my mind back to where it all began.

My journey begins when I entered this mad, bad world in the early hours of Thursday, the 2nd June 1960, in one of the maternity wards of Central Middlesex Hospital (Park Royal) at approximately 12:10am, the two persons mainly responsible for bringing me into the world were Doctor McVitie who was assisted in my delivery by Sister Lamb. How is it, you may ask, that I know this momentous event with such detail? This is because the details of my birth are all recorded in my Baby Book, a padded 7" x 5" booklet that includes not only my first photograph, but every vital statistic surrounding my birth and my first few months in this world. It is the one true artefact that is directly connected to me. My own personal time capsule that is both priceless and unique. I was always aware of the book's existence and on my 18th birthday, I took possession of the book (albeit without my Mum's express permission!).

Other important details about me: I weighed 7lbs and 15oz, my height was twenty inches, my hair was naturally black, soft and curly and I had brown eyes. I first took notice of my surroundings at approximately seven weeks. I had my first tooth at the age of six months and although I could sit up and creep about after seven months, I took my first steps on 3rd August 1961. I was named Shaun Lynford Anthony Wallace, the first born son of Millicent Rehoda Wallace and Linford Benjamin Wallace. My mother was a State Registered Nurse who was born on the 23rd of October 1930 and came to England from the parish of St. Ann's, Jamaica sometime in 1958 and my father, born the 24th of May 1928 in Mount Prospect in the parish of Manchester, Jamaica, was a Factory worker who arrived on these shores in 1956. Dad insisted that the name Linford (which on both my Birth Certificate and Baby Book was for some inexplicable reason spelt with a "y" as opposed to an "i"), should be my middle name, but Mum had set her heart on the name Anthony. So, by way of healthy compromise, the name Anthony was somewhat haphazardly inserted after the name Lynford. To be given an old-fashioned middle name like Lynford was bad enough but that name, or indeed any name was infinitely more preferable than Timothy, the first choice Christian name Mum had initially set her heart on. Can you imagine the name Timothy Lynford Anthony Wallace? It hardly bears thinking about!

Sadly, there wasn't a section in my Baby Book which described what the weather was like on that day, but as Mum held me in her arms for the first time, I hoped she wasn't worried by the fact that I was born on a Thursday on account of the line in that well known nursery rhyme, "Thursday's Child has far to go!" A line in truth, that perfectly describes the roller coaster nature of my life as it began to take shape and I'm pretty sure that apart from thanking God for the delivery of a healthy and happy baby, Mum was both hoping and wishing for the very best for me in life and if I didn't manage to set the world alight and leave a lasting impression then at the very least I would grow up to be a decent, honest and responsible human being.

At the time of my birth, my parents were living in a three-bedroomed house at 102 Roundwood Road, London NW10. The house was owned by my parents, which was a significant achievement given the fact that black people found it hard to find decent housing for themselves and their families, especially when, every time they tried to find suitable accommodation, they were confronted with the familiar blunt and depressing response: NO BLACKS HERE! But with typical collective Caribbean spirit, the black man or woman who worked hard enough to lay down their own foundations, would always help their fellow black brother or sister by either renting a room or more usually, by grouping together to give collective financial support in the form of a partnership (or as we West Indians would say, "Pardna") which involved a group of people putting in an equal sum of money and each week, one member of that group would take the collected sum, another member of the group received his/her share the following week and so on until each member of the collective received their share.

My parents were typically West Indian in terms of the way they helped their fellow West Indians who, like my parents, were trying to establish a new life in a strange and foreign land. Occasionally, they would rent a room to one or two of their fellow West Indians who were finding it difficult to acquire their own accommodation, and some of these people became close friends with our family. One lady in particular, Aunty Dor (Dorothy Roberts), became my Godmother, and another lady, Miss Amy (Parkinson), was one of my earliest child minders who looked after me and treated me like a son. Eleven months after my arrival on 7th May, a second addition to the Wallace family arrived in the form of my sister Debra (She was actually christened Debra-Marie). I don't know any details of Debra's birth statistics as her Baby Book (that's if she ever had one) appears not have survived to tell the tale. Despite the eleven-month age gap, it's often been said that Debbie and I are a virtual carbon copy of each other although I just can't see it. We were very close during our formative years, so close in fact that any habit picked up by one sibling was always copied by the other, in particular the habit of thumb-sucking, the only difference between us in this regard was that Debbie would suck both her thumbs at the same time. We grew apart somewhat during our teenage years possibly on account of the fact that there was no room for two adolescent growing egos in the same household. There was even a time when we stopped speaking for a whole year but thankfully, that lengthy period of discord between us never caused any permanent damage to our relationship. Debbie eventually left home in her early twenties and moved as far away as possible from the family home to Forest Gate in East London, as she was determined to assert her independence. We still have our ups and downs from time to time as is the case with most sibling relationships, but on the whole we remain very close.

With an ever-expanding family, the Wallace clan left Roundwood Road and moved to 83 Purvess Road, Kensal Rise, London NW10, and even though I would have been no more than two or three at the time, it is a place where I do have a faint, albeit distant recollection. After two or so years of living in Kensal Rise, the family uprooted itself once more in February 1964, and moved to Wembley where I have lived for the last 44 years and counting and is the place where I have experienced some of my happiest and occasionally, my saddest memories but despite these highs and lows I will always consider my home to be the safe, stable and comforting environment that has played a crucial role in keeping me both sane and secure.

Not long after our move to our new home in Wembley, there was another addition to the family household. Sandra Beverley Walters was born in St. Ann's, Jamaica, on Easter Sunday, 18th April 1954 and is my Mum's first child and eldest daughter. Mum had sent for her shortly after her tenth birthday, which was not untypical in your average West Indian household at the time. When people from the Caribbean and other parts of the Commonwealth were invited to come to these shores in order to work and settle in the 1940's and 1950's, they usually left any children that they had back home in order to be raised by extended family members. Once the parents found employment after their arrival, they waited until they were sufficiently settled before sending for their children back home. The fact that I was now no longer the eldest child in the family any more didn't make me resentful or envious. On the contrary, I could not have been happier with the fact that I had an older big sister, especially a sister like Sandra. She was my first idol and role model; I loved her to bits when I was younger (and I still do I hasten to add!). Sandra was kind and loving to both myself and Debbie but on the flip side, she could be rough, tough and could be very domineering and the pair of us were overshadowed by her vast and towering personality. It was pretty clear who the top dog was amongst the siblings in the Wallace household and woe betide anyone who dared challenge her position or indeed, step out of line. Sandra was more than capable of looking after herself and she protected me too. On many occasions she would have to ride to my rescue if anyone tried to pick on or bully her little brother. But the one thing that I love Sandra for above all else, was the constant source of encouragement and support she would give me, particularly when it came to education. She used to help me a great deal with my reading, constantly encouraging me so that by the age of seven, I was capable of reading daily newspapers without too much difficulty. It was a priceless gift that she gave me and with her hands-on guidance during my formative years, I was beginning to have a little understanding of the world in which I was growing up.

The fourth Wallace sibling is by convention everyone's favourite. Stephen Omar Wallace joined us on 9th February 1967. Mum was originally going to call him Rory, but the combination of good fortune and divine intervention saved my kid brother from being forever condemned to a name clearly not suited to him. Mum stood firm however with his middle name Omar, a name chosen probably because she had the hots for Omar Sharif who was the number one pin up actor of the day. The so-called "favourite tag" bestowed on my kid brother was probably born out of slight resentment and no less envy. As the last born, it always seemed to the other siblings when we were growing up that whatever my little brother wanted, he got! He was the first to go on school trips, the first to travel abroad and even more galling, the first of the male siblings to get screw-in football boots whereas I had to make do with moulded studs from FW Woolworth's, not exactly what one would call a leading brand in sports footwear! That's not to say however that the rest of the Wallace siblings went without. The same scenario is probably true in all families, where the youngest of the litter is spoilt rotten and invariably gets all the perks and treats. Good luck to him! I can honestly say that I didn't envy Stephen one little bit! Stephen and I have always had a great relationship. Aside from your typical older brother/younger brother relationship during the formative years, the man upstairs couldn't have given me a better person to have as a brother, a fact all too evident in our later years, especially during those difficult episodes that would sometimes blight my life.

Stephen is not the last of my siblings however. Last, and by no means least, I have another older sister called Rose (nee Judith Annabel Wallace) who is my Dad's eldest daughter and was born on the 11th of January 1952 in Mount Prospect in the parish of Manchester Jamaica. I have always known of Rose's existence from a very young age. Rose spent the best part of her life growing up and living in New York and eventually she qualified as a Nurse. Aside from those basic facts, I don't know Rose's personal history in the same meticulous detail as I do with my other siblings. The first time that I had ever met Rose was in the early 1980's when she came over to visit Dad on vacation with her young daughter, my niece Sherene. That meeting, as with the subsequent two or three other times that I have met up with Rose, was warm, loving and cordial. Nowadays, our relationship amounts to telephone calls or contact by email, by virtue of the fact the pair of us are geographically separated by the vast Atlantic Ocean and one can't just simply hop on a plane from New York to London and vice versa; we all have very busy lives to lead and often I find there aren't enough hours in the day to see my siblings who live in the same city as me, let alone in New York. In saying all of that however, that doesn't mean that the bond between Rose and I has been in any way been fractured and when we do get together whether it be by phone calls, emails or a short flying visit by Rose to these shores, the sibling bond is just as strong and loving as ever.

My life growing up in Wembley was by and large happy and stable. Although the Wallace family household could hardly be described as being well off, both my parents worked as hard as they could in order to ensure that we never went hungry and that we always looked presentable. My father was not the brightest nor the most educated of men, but he was kind and loving. By and large, he has a benign and placid demeanour, but there were the odd occasions when he could really lose it when meting out physical punishment with that dreaded leather belt but only when he felt such a punishment was warranted or justified.

He worked the night shift as a Food Processor at the HJ Heinz factory in Harlesden, hardly the most stimulating job in the world but it was a job that he committed wholeheartedly to, always punctual, rarely taking a day off sick and he worked for the company for well over thirty years until his retirement in the mid to late nineties. It was his honest, unwavering dedication that not only made me proud of my Dad but had a significant impact on me in terms of appreciating the value and importance of hard work both in my student days and my adult working life.

My father cared deeply for all his children, and this was never more self-evident than in the special relation he had with my younger brother Stephen. From the day he was born, Stephen always had a very close bond with Dad and that special closeness between Father and youngest son still burns as bright to this day. I would constantly tease Stephen about this when we were growing up, especially during the time when I could easily exert a Svengali type influence over him but not even my level of control could get in the way of the real and deep love that Stephen had for his father.

Mum, by contrast, was at the opposite end of the spectrum in terms of character and temperament. Mum could be very volatile at times and did not suffer fools. But the real scary thing about my Mum was that there was no real difference between her bark and her bite and if any of her children misbehaved or indeed stepped out of line, her enforcement of discipline whether by a verbal telling off or the use of her plastic soled slipper could be a very painful experience indeed. However, despite these occasional flashes of temper, I love my mother dearly. There's an old adage that says, "you can't choose your parents", but even if the man upstairs had granted me such a choice before having entered this world, I wouldn't swap either Mum or Dad for all the riches that have existed in the world since the dawn of time. Mum has always been there for me (and all of us), through thick and through thin, the good times and the bad and when I really sit back and reflect on all the encouragement and support from all the different sources that I have had, it has been Mum's constant support that has been the most profound and I can honestly say, that if it wasn't for her then the Shaun Wallace that the public has come to know and recognise would simply not exist.

That stark clash of contrasting personalities was bound sadly in the long run to lead to cracks in the marital relationship. The breakdown was complete when the Decree Absolute was announced, finally dissolving my parent's marriage, an event which ironically occurred on the 2nd of June 1975 - my fifteenth birthday. It was sad to see two people you love so dearly go from the supposed heights of marital bliss to the depths where they became sick of the sight of each other. But it was worse for my seven year old self to witness with increasing regularity Dad semi-throttling Mum after the usual cursing and swearing between them escalating with every bad word, or the sight of Mum chasing after Dad with an old iron Dutch pot threatening to commit unrepeatable as well as unspeakable acts of violence whilst Dad just about managed to escape by locking himself in the toilet. There was many a time when Sandra, Debbie and myself would struggle to prevent either Mum or Dad from going at each other but after witnessing years of constant bickering and arguments, we as children gradually became more and more apathetic and weary, and less and less involved or concerned with our parent's private marital war. As I have already stated, I love both my parents dearly, but the one thing I learned from all of that constant marital strife during those years was, whatever the right and wrongs, and whoever was to blame: NEVER, EVER TAKE SIDES!

Although Mum could be a fearsome individual and despite Dad's general placid demeanour, it would be fair to say that my father was no different to any other typical alpha adult male during that era. He was a man who steadfastly believed that his word in the household was law and that women should obey and know their place. Also, without sounding unkind, accusatory or disrespectful, it would also be fair to say that Dad wasn't exactly generous when it came to financial matters as he was a man who wouldn't spend his money beyond what he deemed to be "absolutely necessary", a principal and philosophy that was a complete anathema so far as Mum was concerned. The occasional furious exchanges between the pair of them revolved around issues such as whether the home should have central heating, or whether to build an extension. To my Dad these were Items of luxury, but to my Mum they were a reasonable demand from the perspective of a woman who took a great deal of pride in her efforts to maintain a comfortable family home.

This wasn't the only conflict that was raging within the Wallace household. The old adage that "two hens cannot rule the roost in the same coop" was never better illustrated than in the ever-growing arguments between Mum and Sandra. But like Dad, Mum was also a woman of her times, a woman who was determined to exert total control over her eldest daughter. Although Sandra's rebelliousness and dogged determination to be treated as a woman in her own right was equally uncompromising, there was only going to be one winner in that war of attrition which resulted in Sandra leaving home at sixteen after falling pregnant and giving birth to my first niece, Melanie, on 20th March 1971. Sandra briefly moved back home for a period of about two or so months after Melanie's birth and for me it was great to have my big sister back home once more, but the fragile truce that existed between mother and daughter during this supposed happy time, was shattered almost beyond repair when on my eleventh birthday, Sandra gathered together all her possessions and announced that she was leaving home for good. I was glued to the TV watching the European Cup Final that was playing at Wembley Stadium at the time, but once I became aware of the bitter dispute between my Mum and my favourite big sister, I lost all interest in the game and immediately burst into floods of tears. I was terrified that I would never see either Sandra or Melanie again and was at my wits end about what was going to happen to them. However, before she left home for the last and final time, Sandra assured me that both herself and Melanie would be all right and that she would come and get Debbie, Stephen and me once she had found a place and was settled in. Her reassuring words didn't stop me fretting that night however, or the days and weeks that followed thereafter but true as ever to her word, Sandra did come and get all three of us. And so, during that turbulent period leading up to my parent's divorce, the three of us spent our summer holidays at Sandra's, in Bluebird Walk on the Chalk Hill Estate, always benefitting from her altruistic encouragement but not forgetting her occasional domineering ways.

The relationship between Mum and Sandra hardly improved over the forthcoming years and although there were brief periods of respite, by the mid 1990's, they were barely on speaking terms, a situation sadly that remains even to this day. However, just like the destructive warring nature of my parent's relationship, I refused to take sides in Mum and Sandra's sad and in my view wholly needless dispute and whatever relationship they may have had in the past unfortunately seems destined never to be rekindled mainly on account of the unbending and stubborn streak that both women possess.

Meanwhile, the last dying embers of my parent's disparate relationship was still heading towards its inevitable demise. The only saving grace was that the main protagonists rarely shared the same stage for any encore performances, which at times was a great relief to a reluctant observing audience. Mum decided that she was going to go to stay with relatives in New York for a while. Aside from the odd trip back home to Jamaica to see her family, this was the first time that Mum was going to be away from us children for any length of time and it seemed when she sat down and explained her reasons for going away, that there was no definite date as to her return. She tried to reassure us by telling us she loved us all very much and that she would come home as soon as she can. I would have been twelve or thirteen at the time and more than capable of understanding what was going on. I was devastated by what she told me but I was determined not to let it show and to try and deal with what was happening on my own, trying to wrap myself in some sort of emotion proof cocoon that was designed to protect me from the marital fallout but at the same time, I could understand the reasons behind Mum's decision to get away. I realised that it must have been extremely agonising for her to take her leave knowing full well that would mean she would be separated from all of her children for some considerable time but she was very unhappy and I'm sure that if she hadn't taken the decision to leave when she did, then it probably would have pushed her over the edge. Mum made sure that Dad would have the necessary help to look after the three of us and one of Mum's close nursing colleagues kept a regular watchful eye so as to ensure that any disruption to a normal family life was kept to an absolute minimum. I can't remember precisely how long Mum stayed in America for, but to me it seemed like an eternity.

Mum eventually came home and I for one was glad to see her back. The break seemed to have done her a world of good. She was a whole new, totally invigorated woman. Mum was glad to be back with her children, although I doubt whether she shared the same sentiments about the house that was the marital home. I know how close Mum came to making a new life for herself in America working as a Nurse, she confided that much to us and that would have been all well and good, but what would have happened to Debbie and Stephen and myself? Would we have gone to the United States with her? What about Dad? What about my friends? All these questions and anxieties were swirling around in my head, as the normal stable home life that I revelled and thrived in now seemed to be heading towards the realms of total uncertainty. Thankfully though, Mum's reassuring words that she would never leave us again for such a long period of time went an extremely long way to assuaging those anxieties and fears.

Not that long after Mum had returned home, Dad then had his own marital sabbatical when he too headed to New York for about nine or so months, staying at the home of my other sister Rose. Stephen who was about five years old at the time, was going to feel Dad's absence the most, even more than me, but by now I had come to terms with the whole situation and by the time Dad eventually came back, I had a pretty good idea of what was going to happen next. My parents were just two adults, living together but with totally separate lives whose different work shifts and requirements meant that daily face to face contact would have been sporadic at best. I'm not sure how long this "arrangement" was going to last for, but the one thing I did know that it wasn't going to last forever. As time went on, I noticed letters that were addressed for Mum's attention from the law firm, Alexander and Partners, which made it pretty clear that she intended to start legal proceedings with a view to obtaining a divorce. I'm not sure whether Dad had his own lawyer to assist him, but what I did know was that he put up virtually no resistance to Mum's demands. I didn't know the nature of the grounds my parents were divorcing on and if I was brutally honest, I wouldn't want to know either. All married couples have their ups and downs and Mum and Dad were no different. The answer why Mum and Dad's marriage, a union which started out with all the usual hope and promise on 23rd January 1960 and ended with a stroke of a pen at the Willesden County Court fifteen years later, had broken down is a simple one really. They were two completely different personalities who just weren't made for each other.

Mum got custody of Debbie, Steve and me as well as a maintenance order payment from the court that was to go towards our general upkeep right up until we left school. The one remaining asset to be decided upon was the home that I grew up in and the worrying issue in my mind was whether or not our home was going to be sold. The house itself at the time couldn't have been worth more than £4,000 and if sold, once the mortgage was paid off and the lawyers had taken their legal fees, there would hardly have been anything left for Mum to start again with in terms of buying her own home. Dad eventually moved out of the home and he took all his personal belongings with him together with a few of the household items that they agreed between them. He initially moved to Kensal Rise to stay with his brother, my uncle Sonny and his wife, Aunt May. He was there for some time before eventually obtaining a cosy one bedroom flat in Chapter Road, Dollis Hill where he has remained in residence ever since. Even though Dad no longer lived with us, we never lost contact with him and since the divorce, he has always tried to give us the best support that he could. Deep down, Dad didn't want to be divorced from my Mum and the loss of his castle hit him to his very core and it is a loss that, in truth, he's never really ever come to terms with. That personal loss would manifest itself from time to time by utterances of sad lamentations of what he had lost which bore all the classic hallmarks of bitterness and regret. But as they say, time is the greatest of healers and over time, Dad's lamentations of bitterness and regret were heard with all the loudness and frequency of a heart murmur. However, the battle scars of years of constant marital strife together with the divorce itself will go with him to his grave.

Mum's own journey as a forty-four year old newly divorced woman all on her own with three young children to support, feed and raise began with her somehow managing to hang onto the home that we all grew up in. Eventually, the house was sold to Brent Council who agreed that Mum could remain in our home but as a council tenant. This drop in "status" was a bitter pill for my very proud Mum to swallow, but in the circumstances what choice did she have? Her priority was to ensure that we had a roof over our heads and that we were comfortable and happy. However, *all* responsibility now rested solely upon her shoulders, a heavy burden that would test the strength of Hercules himself.

Mum by this time had given up being a full-time nurse and had got a job as a Telephonist at the GPO (now British Telecom) as it paid more and the job was less physically demanding. However, Mum's wages could only stretch so far and that meant that she had no option but to earn extra income for the family by doing Agency Nursing in addition to her normal duties at weekends. How she managed to hold our family together as well as keep her physical and mental wellbeing intact, only she and the man upstairs know. The three of us couldn't really put into words how lucky we were to have a woman like Mum in our lives because if she wasn't the woman that she was, then our lives probably would have turned out for the worst. She sacrificed a great deal for us and paid for it with her own personal happiness. I say that because by and large all three of us have turned out to be happy, well-adjusted people and despite the trials, tribulations, hardships that Mum had to go through for the sake of her children, I have no doubt that she would still say that irrespective of the cost to her own personal happiness, it was a price worth paying.

Mum eventually stopped all forms of employment in the mid 1980's when she took the redundancy package offered to her by the GPO and I suppose from her perspective, she had gone beyond her physical and mental limit and was determined to grab a slice of tranquillity and contentment in her life. But the retirement years have not been kind to my Mother. The onset of Diabetes, which coincidently, also affects my Father, has taken such a heavy toll on her both physically and to a greater extent, mentally. It has left her a pale shadow of a woman who was once beautiful, independent and proud, who has gradually declined into a virtual house bound recluse with only loneliness for company and the bitter taste of regret.

The three of us will always rally round Mum and try to give her the same love and support that she gave us over the years and although our collective love and support represents a mere fraction of what Mum has done for us, we will continue to give that love and support until the sun no longer rises in her sunset years.

Debbie, Stephen and myself have somehow managed to emerge from the emotional trauma of our parent's divorce pretty much unscathed. Stephen is now happily married with two beautiful children, Lucas and Leni and although Debbie never got married, she has done a magnificent job in raising her only son Myles virtually on her own. From my perspective in looking back at this troubled episode in my life, it would probably go a long way to answering the question as to the reason(s) why I cling so doggedly to my single marital status.

I must make it abundantly clear that I am not totally against the whole idea of the institution of marriage but as the years have gone by, I've decided that despite all the benefits a stable, loving committed relationship can bring, it's probably not the thing for me. Being single is something that I have got used to after all this time and unless there is a radical volte face in both my attitude and mindset in general, in all likelihood that is the way it will remain until the end of my days.

Despite the fact that Mum and Dad now lead totally separate and independent lives, deep down they still have a soft spot for each other. As the years have gone by, the raging mutual loathing and antipathy that they once expressed to each other appears to be all but dead and buried even though occasionally, it makes the odd encore. As they got older, they would call each other, visit each other and even more astonishing even go shopping for food with each other. They did this I suppose probably because in some strange way they still do care for each other. It appears their relationship has turned full circle.

CHAPTER TWO

My journey to becoming the barrister that I've wanted to be since I was eleven years old was a long and arduous one. It was a journey that was fraught with distractions, delays and disappointments, but I managed somehow to finally cross the finishing line and thus vindicate the ambitions of my childhood.

The first school I attended was Oakington Manor Primary School which I started in the first week of September 1965. I spent six happy years at that school, and I am lucky enough to have forged lifelong friendships that I know will last beyond the end of time. I would never claim to be the most gifted of students academically, but my one saving grace was that I did have an aptitude for learning and remembering things, a gift that was first spotted and nurtured by my big sister Sandra whose guidance and encouragement made sure that that fledgling talent didn't go to waste.

Despite the fact that both myself and my male classmates enjoyed the lessons we were taught at school, the only thing we were really interested in was the sport that my footballing hero and idol Pele so aptly labelled: The Beautiful Game.

My lifelong affair with football began some forty years ago, ignited as a result of my first ever meeting in 1967 with my cousins, Roy Walker who was sixteen and a fanatical Tottenham Hotspur fan and my favourite cousin, Paul Kitson who was a few years younger than Roy. Paul was a gifted footballer. He later forged a successful career in football in the United States and was Man United through and through. I really admired and looked up to my cousins and was impressed by not only the way they played football, but the passion with which they spoke about the game.

On the 20th of May 1967, my cousin Roy's football team Tottenham Hotspur were playing in the FA Cup Final. As we were settling down to watch the game, I remember Roy getting all excited about his team and how they were going to win the Cup. I of course, didn't have a clue who Tottenham Hotspur were, or whom they were playing against, but to get back at my older cousin, I decided to support the other team who were wearing dark shirts on the screen of my Mum's black and white TV. When I asked Roy who that team was, he told me that they were called Chelsea and throughout the entire game I cheered their every move. Tottenham won the game 2-1 much to Roy's obvious delight and even though they lost, I decided from that day Chelsea was going to be the team that I was going to support and since that seminal game, my interest in the sport and Chelsea in particular, soon turned into an unhealthy obsession. Whether playing the game with my friends in the park (despite the fact that I wasn't good enough to get into the Primary School team), reading about it or watching football programmes, everything so far as I was concerned was football, football and more football.

I started to buy all the football magazines that were around at the time, most notably, *Shoot* magazine and its memorable first edition which had a free cardboard cut-out of one of my footballing idols, the legendary Bobby Moore. Both myself and the friends that I grew up with also collected football picture cards. I was absolutely obsessed with watching football matches on TV, whether it involved the England team or my beloved Chelsea and all of my friends were totally mesmerized by the dazzling spectacle and skill on display at the 1970 World Cup Finals in Mexico when the magnificent Brazilian team that included Pele in his prime swept all before them. But out of all of the football matches that I used to love to watch, it was always FA Cup Finals that held a special place in my heart. Because I lived so close to the stadium, Cup Final day was always a special affair. I would get up early and walk up Oakington Manor Drive to the Wembley Triangle where I was always greeted by the sight of thousands upon thousands of fans intent on taking over Wembley for the day gathering in or around the nearby Greyhound Pub. After sampling some of the Cup Final atmosphere, I would then rush home to switch on my TV and enjoy the simultaneous build up to the game on both ITV and BBC, constantly flicking between channels in order to get the best coverage of all the pomp and majesty surrounding the game. Just before kick-off, I always had to undergo having to make the agonising choice as to which of the rival TV channels to watch the game on, either availing myself of listening to the commentary of either David Coleman (and later John Motson) on the BBC, or to watch the ITV coverage with the late football commentating icon, Brian Moore.

As for the Final itself, if my beloved Chelsea were not on the pitch (which in the subsequent wilderness years after our glorious 1970 triumph didn't happen very often), I would always cheer for the team who I most wanted to win on the day and my cheers would be just as loud and passionate for them as if they were my own team and after the game, both myself and my friends would head straight for the local park and try to replicate the thrilling parts of the game that we had just witnessed, pretending to be either Peter Osgood or Charlie George immediately after sticking the ball in the back of the net. Later that night, I would watch the highlights of the match all over again on *Match of the Day* at the Victor's Banquet and for the sake of completeness, watch *the Big Match Cup Final highlights* the following afternoon (Mum and Sunday School permitting!). The whole occasion showed just how important the FA Cup Final was as a national institution and as a young boy growing up, I felt extremely proud and privileged to be living a stone's throw away from such an iconic Stadium that is known throughout every city or remote village throughout the world.

Without a shadow of doubt, my greatest FA Cup Final memory was as a nine year old when Chelsea beat Leeds in that epic replay in 1970 to win the Cup for the first time. Chelsea were given the real run around in the first match and our poor performance can be partly explained by the state of the Wembley pitch, which resembled a large muddy sand pit because of The Horse of the Year Show which took place the week previously. My only disappointment in that historic and epic victory was that the great Ron Harris didn't lift the famous old pot at Wembley's Royal Box but at Manchester United's Old Trafford ground, I had to wait until 1997 to witness that unbridled joy.

My favourite Cup Final anecdote comes from the aftermath of the 1975 Final where Fulham's unfortunate Goalkeeper, Peter Mellor, having conceded West Ham's Alan Taylor's second goal through his legs turned to his wily old boss, Alec Stock, after the game and said *"Sorry about the second goal boss...I should have kept my legs closed"* to which Alec Stock immediately replied *"I wish your Mum had done so at conception!"*

In complete contrast to my obsession with the beautiful game, my attitude to school left a lot to be desired. I was always getting into trouble for being too talkative and disruptive. My antics, which usually amounted to a cheeky one liner, would bring fits of laughter from my classmates. My school reports were not very praiseworthy or flattering: "Shaun Wallace is the Clown of the Class!" wrote Mr Evans, our Form Teacher in my second year of junior school who dressed and looked like a sterner version of the World War II British General, Montgomery of El Alamein. His teaching methods and style resembled that of a Drill Sergeant Major at a military camp and my mischievous antics were a constant thorn in his side. Despite being constantly on the receiving end of Mr Evans' reprimands, there was one memorable occasion during one of his lessons where I showed much to his complete astonishment, that there was more to this Class Clown than met the eye.

During our English lessons, Mr Evans would at random ask his pupils to stand up and spell a word, an exercise which was both frightening as well as embarrassing, even more so if you spelt the word incorrectly. On this occasion, Mr Evans wanted us to spell the word *chaos*. Whilst some members of my class were standing on their feet attempting to spell the word (and failing miserably in the process!), I was mucking about as usual with my classmates, Trevor Deacon and Junior Sinclair. My disruptive antics were quickly stopped dead in their tracks when the booming voice of Mr Evans called out my name. Mr Evans barked out instructions for me to stand up and I rose nervously to my feet. I stood there in total fear and dread for a few seconds for which seemed to drag on for an eternity, but in that time I somehow managed to arrange the letters in my head that I hoped would spell the word. *Here goes!* I said to myself and after a sharp intake of breath, I began to utter the letters in a high pitched squeaky voice that seemed to go up an octave after every given letter.

"C-H-A-O-S!"

Mr Evans fixed his cold steely glaze in my direction which made me think that I was about to be shot down in flames just like the rest of my classmates but in his all too familiar gruff tone he grudgingly uttered, to my complete astonishment and joy, "that's correct...now sit down and stop talking!"

Did I do as I was told? Of course I didn't! I felt on top of the world for putting one over on my teaching nemesis. But these occasional flashes of what I was actually capable of were, so far as my teachers were concerned as well as myself, oh so few and very far between.

I left Oakington Manor in the summer of 1971, an event that from a personal view, was tinged with a great deal of sadness because my friends were about to be scattered amongst the secondary schools of Brent. Most of my classmates had chosen to go to Alperton High School whose main site was at the bottom of the Ealing Road. Naturally, I wanted to go there as well but the school that my parents chosee was Copland High School on the Wembley High Road as it was the same school that my elder sister Sandra had attended. Sandra's school career was hardly covered in glory as her frequent clashes with the teaching staff meant that she ended up leaving school at sixteen with precious little in terms of academic qualifications but left in its place an infamous but unwarranted and unfair reputation, a fact I was quick to discover in my first few tentative days of my new surroundings.

I was in class 1L in my first year at school which was in the middle stream of the six classes for that year and during our first few days when the new intake of students were being shown around the school, our first port of call was the Science Department. In the middle of that department was a tall spiral staircase that went up three floors. "I'm going to slide down those stairs when the opportunity presents itself!" I mischievously muttered to myself and when the opportunity presented itself a few days later after we had finished a lesson in a classroom on the top floor, I was determined to grab the chance. I slung my duffle bag over my shoulder and then mounted the handrail before setting off at break neck speed for my hair-raising trip to the bottom of the stairs without a moments' thought of the risks and possible danger. As I stormed past my astonished classmates at break neck speed, my unbridled sense of joy was brought to a swift and unceremonious end when all of a sudden, I felt a sharp yank at the scruff of my neck and the next thing you know, I was being held suspended in the air as if I were dangling at the end of a hangman's noose. Holding me in that manner was a tall burly man who seemed even bigger than the biblical Goliath and he immediately hauled me off towards a small corridor that lead to an office. Once inside, I was totally consumed with fear and terror about my impending fate and before I knew it, he produced from his cupboard an old trainer that was so large that it made the footwear worn by clowns look like a pair of baby booties. Within a blink of an eye, I was on the receiving end of several stout whacks on my backside which was swiftly followed by a very stern lecture on how he expected pupils at the school to behave. He asked me whether I had any brothers or sisters who had previously attended the school. "Sandra Walters," I replied somewhat hesitantly, and he reacted by arching his eyebrows skywards before uttering a reply that was laced with a hint of menace, "ahh...I see. Well I'm going to be keeping a careful eye on you!"

The man responsible for my painful introduction to life at Copland School was Dennis Rice, who was the Head of the 3rd and 4th Year School at the time. In his spare time, Mr Rice used to play rugby for Wasps RFC and although he had a zero-tolerance approach to unruly behaviour by any student at the school, he was by and large, a fair man and was one of the few approachable teachers during my time there. Mr Rice didn't strike me as being the type of person who would involve himself in gossip, but it didn't take long for word to get around the teaching grapevine that I was Sandra's brother. From now on I would have to watch my step and try to avoid being tarnished with the same brush that they used on my sister. It was up to me to knuckle down and buck the trend of that kind of thinking. However, my attitude and general behaviour at school, particularly in my first three years there, gave the school all the ammunition it needed to ear mark me as a person who wasn't going to amount to much in life and the twice yearly school reports endorsed my apparent lack of potential.

"Shaun seldom tries hard and has no aptitude for learning!" was one notable acerbic comment from my Technical Drawing teacher. His comments represented the common view of most of my form teachers (my History and French tutors excepted), which was that any academic aspirations were a long way off.

My fascination with the Law can be traced back to the early 1970's when I became engrossed watching one of my favourite programmes on ITV at the time, *Crown Court*. I was constantly gripped by the cases that were heard in the fictional Fulchester Crown Court and all of its seemingly true to life courtroom trials with the lawyers eloquently and passionately arguing the case on behalf of their respective clients. The programme seemed so real through the eyes of an impressionable eleven year old kid like myself.

I was constantly accused by my teachers of being far too talkative and argumentative in the classroom, so a career as a lawyer seemed to be the perfect choice for me. But in order to turn those childhood dreams into a reality, I had to take O Levels at the end of the two year course in the subjects that I had chosen. Both my academic prowess and attitude towards school in general had made a considerable improvement, however, I was informed by the school that aside from French, I did not qualify to sit O Levels in any of the remaining five subjects I had chosen. As you can imagine, I was bitterly disappointed by the school's decision that I was not considered academically good enough to sit more than just one O Level exam and from my perspective, It was pretty clear that the school had already made up their minds that I was already a failure. My sister Sandra had those same barriers and obstacles put in her path and it seemed from my perspective that history was repeating itself. The CSE syllabus was widely regarded at the time as the lower tier academic qualification in comparison to the O Level course. The students who enrolled on these CSE courses were to all intents and purposes, written off academically and were perceived as having no chance of pursuing a stellar professional career such as an Accountant, Doctor or Lawyer. The only real value that a CSE qualification had was that if a student obtained a Grade 1 in their chosen subject, it was recognised as being the equivalent of a Grade C pass at O Level.

Once the first year of a student's designated course had been completed, we were required to attend a mid-term review on our progress in one to one discussions with both our Form Tutor and the School's Career Advisor. My own progress on the CSE course up to that point in time could at best be described as no more than average. My less than impressive performance up to that point was something that I have to bear responsibility for and whilst it would be more than fair to say that I can have no real excuse for such failings, my lack of real effort can probably be best explained by what I perceived to be a real sense of frustration and disappointment in not being seen by the school as being good enough to take O Level examinations the following year. I was not looking forward to my own individual one to one sessions but when that day eventually came, I knew the prevailing view of the School was that my chances of succeeding in the exams the following year were very low indeed.

In those discussions with my Form Teacher, it was made clear to me in no uncertain terms that unless I showed greater dedication and application over the next twelve months, my chances of getting decent grades the following year were virtually non-existent. There was little I could say or indeed contribute to such a one-sided debate but in truth, I didn't believe that my Form Teacher really cared about what I had to say or indeed, showed any real interest in my claim that I was working as hard as I could. Throughout those discussions with my Form teacher, I felt as if I was hitting my head continuously against a concrete ceiling with no hope of a breakthrough and all I could do was to promise to show an improvement both in my attitude and effort as my Form teacher had demanded. My one to one session with the School's Career's Advisor was even more scathing as she poured nothing but scorn when I revealed to her my choice of career. I told her that I wanted to be a barrister when I grew up and showed her the letter that I had received from The Bar Council a year or so previously, the contents of which spelt out in clear and unmistakeable terms all of the qualifications I would need to obtain in order to qualify as a barrister. But instead of offering words of encouragement, her devastating response was, "Shaun, you'll probably end up stocking shelves and I wouldn't be surprised at all if you were to end up at some point in prison!"

That whole experience left me both shocked and bitterly disappointed over how dismissive the school was. It was a harsh and damning assessment but at least it had the effect for the first time in my life of making me realise how important it is to take control of your own destiny and the only way one can do this is to make sure that you are an individual who is academically educated, an individual who won't end up in some dead end job with no real hope for the future, but an individual who can be anything he or she wants to be with the relevant academic qualifications behind them.

I left those meetings with the brutal endorsements ringing in my ears, but I was neither prepared to accept them or take them lying down and as I headed back to my class, I made a solemn promise to myself that I would not allow Copland High School to turn me into another failed statistic. I thought, *that may be their prediction for my future, but that's not how I see my future. I've got to make sure that I work hard, get the right qualifications and control my own destiny.*

I was determined to make something of myself, but I knew deep down that it wasn't going to be easy. Being disciplined and focused wasn't going to happen overnight. Becoming a lawyer demands commitment and dedication together with the necessary focus and sacrifice in order to achieve those aims, but with the all the things that were happening in my life at this time, even I was beginning to have real doubts as to whether I had the right maturity, let alone the confidence, to realise those ambitions.

I put in the best effort that I possibly could in terms of preparation for my exams that took place throughout May and June of 1976 which left me virtually no time whatsoever to mark the milestone occasion of my sixteenth birthday. I would be the first to admit that I found it hard at times to sustain and maintain the focus and discipline when preparing for those exams but nevertheless, I still felt pretty confident after having sat them that I would get a healthy return of CSE grade 1's that would, with all being well, keep me on the academic track to prepare for the next stage of my academic development, the A Level course.

After the school had broken up for the long summer recess that marked the end of the academic year, I managed to get my first ever job earning a proper wage working as a builder's mate on a building site in Hendon. I was at an age where I needed to have financial independence rather than having to be constantly relying on pocket money from Mum and Dad all the time.

Whilst I was awaiting my exam results which were due to be published during the last week in August, I still hadn't decided on the place where I wanted to continue with my studies. Most of my school friends and colleagues were either applying for apprenticeships or going onto Further Education Colleges but in the end, I decided to play it safe and applied to join the Copland's Sixth Form despite being fully aware of the fact that the school still retained its low opinion of me.

I enrolled in Sixth Form in the first week of September armed with a mixed set of results that were disappointing to say the least.

The results of those examinations were as follows:

CSE Maths - Grade 1
CSE English - Grade 2
CSE History - Grade 2
CSE General Science - Grade 2
CSE Chemistry - Grade 3
'O' level French - Grade C.

Chasing the Dream

This was a very average return for someone who had set his ambitions so high. My parents and especially my sister Sandra though were extremely encouraging and supportive when I broke the news, but their unwavering support couldn't assuage the deep sense of disappointment I felt. I had let myself and everybody down. It seemed that my loud and proud boasts that one day I'd become a famous and successful lawyer were beginning to sound empty and hollow and my less than average set of results seemed to justify the school's assessment that the probable direction of my life would be one of predictable under achievement.

That first day back at school was the beginning of the school's Induction Week, where all the potential Sixth Formers would be deciding upon the courses they would be studying for over the next two years. There were quite a lot of returnees to the school. Some of those returnees did really well in their exams, others not so well, for instance a group of black students who were close friends of mine and like me, had long held dreams of pursuing a professional career but also like me, these students were perceived by the school as having ideas well above their stations.

The Sixth Form at the time was run by the formidable and extremely overbearing Miss Sayers, a teacher who was cold and by and large, not very approachable and that image hardly endeared her to the student population at large, an image my sister Sandra could whole-heartedly attest to given their regular and frequent run ins during Sandra's time at the school and Miss Sayers was all too aware of our sibling connection.

There was a welcoming address held in the Sixth Form Common Room which all the Sixth Formers were required to attend. As I sat there with my friend Glenmore Johnson who was an aspiring Economics Graduate listening to Miss Sayers drone on and on, I began to wonder whether coming back to Copland School to continue my studies was the right move. After she finished her less than inspiring address, all the students were mingling around in the Common Room chatting. The main topic for discussion during these conversations was the worthiness of the "new" qualification which was about to enter the educational mainstream, the CEE (The Certificate of Extended Education). So far as we were concerned, this new qualification was about as valuable as yesterday's news and in reading between the lines of Miss Sayers' address, that was going to be the course followed by the vast majority of the returning Sixth Formers. Well that was something that I refused to accept, but in my discussions with Miss Sayers over the subsequent few days, she made it very clear that this CEE course would be the course that I would be doing during the forthcoming academic year.

As we made our way home from school after the third torturous day, both Glenmore and I could not have felt any more demoralised and worthless. By common consent, both Glenmore and I agreed that the school was doing everything in its power to prevent us from progressing and moving on and if we remained on the CEE course, then any chance of the pair of us realising our respective professional dreams and ambitions would sink without a trace.

As we walked out of the school gates with our respective heads bowed and demeanour subdued, we noticed a former student at the school, Beverley James, walking towards us. All three of us stood and chatted for a while about how things were going in general and by the end of our brief conversation, the suggestion that Beverley had made to both Glenmore and myself was to profoundly change the spiralling direction both of our lives appeared to be heading towards.

I had known Beverley James since the aged of five. Beverley was the youngest sibling in her family and her elder brothers and sisters were very close friends with my sister Sandra. Both Beverley and I went to the same primary school and she was a very bright girl academically and when we both joined Copland in 1971, she was in the second top set throughout her secondary school years right up to the Fifth Form. Just like Glenmore and me, Beverley had her own personal ambitions blocked by the school's lack of positive support and encouragement and its concrete ceiling but unlike Glenmore and me, she had the good sense of refusing to return to the school and join the Sixth Form to endure more of the same. Beverley informed us that she had transferred to the Sixth Form at Aylestone High School as they ran Arts and Humanities subjects such as Sociology, Economics, Politics and Law that were more tailored and suited to what she wanted to do. When we told Beverley about all of the goings on at Copland, she didn't hesitate in suggesting that we should contact Aylestone and urged us to make that call straight away. Within a blink of an eye, Glenmore and I immediately headed towards the telephone box situated directly across the road from the school and armed with just a single two pence piece between us, we contacted Aylestone School. The Receptionist put us straight through to the Deputy Headmaster, Dr David Knight who to our complete surprise and astonishment, agreed to see the pair of us the following day.

Glenmore and I agreed to meet up early the following morning so as to ensure that we would not be late for our 9am appointment and arrived at the school in plenty of time. Dr Knight interviewed us separately in an environment that was both relaxed and friendly that lasted no longer than fifteen or so minutes, at the end of which both myself and Glenmore were welcomed into the school with open arms. I was overcome with a feeling of unbridled joy and relief. We both had found an educational establishment that appeared to genuinely have our best interests at heart. Glenmore and I were floating on cloud nine as we walked out of the School gates and we couldn't wait to get back to Copland to tell the school and Miss Sayers in particular, to stick the CEE syllabus in a place where the sun doesn't shine. By the time we arrived back at the Sixth Form block at Copland, our respective lessons were already under way and rather than join those classes late, Glenmore and I decided to remain in the Common Room and join our respective classes after the morning break. A couple of minutes after our arrival though, Miss Sayers entered the Common Room and when she saw both Glenmore and I lounging around on the Common Room's chairs apparently doing nothing, she immediately asked us why we were not in our lessons. We endeavoured to explain our conduct, but Miss Sayers' intolerant body language and demeanour made it abundantly clear that she was in no mood to hear what we had to say. She ordered the pair of us to go straight to our lessons immediately and made it clear that she would not tolerate our apparent lackadaisical attitude whilst we were members of the Sixth Form. We both did as we were told if only to be seen to be going through the motions of carrying out her orders.

At lunch, we informed our friends of our intentions to leave Copland and join Aylestone, urging them to do the same. They all said that they would and after saying those final goodbyes, Glenmore and I turned and headed for the Common Room's exit door and the school grounds for the last and final time. I felt as though a heavy burden had been lifted from my shoulders and felt mightily relieved that I was leaving behind such a cold, unsupportive and unforgiving establishment. As I finally stepped outside, I turned to look back at the school seemingly and as I was doing so, I vowed that I would never, ever step foot inside Copland High School again, or if I ever did it would only be if the SCHOOL ITSELF INVITED ME!

Aylestone High School was, without a shadow of a doubt, the most supportive and encouraging academic institution that I've ever been associated with. The whole ethos of the Sixth Form was geared towards nurturing and encouraging a student's long-term goals as opposed to stifling them and the students responded to that ideal by working hard, the product of which saw a healthy return in terms of examination success. I joined a Sixth Form that was blessed with very clever and talented young individuals who were bright, highly motivated who had an unflinching belief that they were going to make something of their lives. The Aylestone Sixth Form was a great place to thrive and develop as an individual on account of the fact that it was run by a group of teachers who both treated and respected the students in their care as responsible young adults and they sought to create an environment where, if you worked hard in your chosen subjects, academic success was virtually guaranteed. Teachers such as Jack Veltman, a school Deputy Head, Geoff Mott and the larger than life Head of Sixth Form, the Tottenham Hotspur loving Christine Watts, who taught Government and Politics, were the architects of that philosophy as any member of that Sixth Form would attest to. I felt both fortunate and privileged to be a member of such a special group as it offered me the chance of academic salvation and redemption that I would never hope to achieve if I had stayed on at Copland. I had been thrown an academic lifeline and now it was up to me to make the most of this chance. At least three other students from the Copland Sixth Form, Maurice Mattis, Ian Henry and my old classmate and good friend throughout my time at Copland, Julie Robinson decided to jump ship and join both Glenmore and me at Aylestone and by the end of the first week in September, all five of us were happy and settled in our respective courses that we had chosen and in making those choices, it gave each and every one of us a renewed sense of belief and purpose.

In my first year, I chose O Levels in Law, History, British Constitution, English Language and English Literature, subjects that were both interesting and relevant to my academic and career ambitions. I couldn't wait to get started on the course and I received a much cherished and confidence boosting gift the weekend before the start of the long journey on my way to becoming a barrister. I was visiting my sister Sandra and my niece Melanie, who by this time were living in a flat on Mortimer Road in Kensal Green. She wanted to see me and find out how I was getting on. When I told her that I was doing O Levels at Aylestone, she was very pleased indeed, then unexpectedly, she handed me a small pink covered book entitled The English Legal System and inscribed inside the book's main cover were the words that showed how much my big sister both loved and believed in me which said, *To Shaun, the Lawyer. Good Luck and study hard!" Love Sandra.*

That book was one of my most prized and treasured possessions, right up there with my treasured Baby Book and the letter I wrote to the Inner Temple. I kept that book for many years and I would from time to time look at those words for inspiration during the many triumphs and knock backs on that long academic road, but for now, I was at the starting line on my quest to become a barrister. The sweat, tears and sacrifice START HERE!

My results at the end of my first year at Aylestone were as follows:

O level Law - Grade B
O level History - Grade B
O level British Constitution - Grade C
O level English Language - Grade E
O level English Literature -Unclassified.

I was naturally pleased with the first three grades but not so pleased with the latter two. I'd got the equivalent of five O Levels and was therefore eligible to enrol on the 1st year A Level course in Law but my dreams of going to University would sadly have to be put back a year due to the minimum demands of Universities or Polytechnics, which stated that entrants had to pass 2 A Level exams as well as a minimum grade C pass in English Language.

The summer of 1977 was a summer that I remember with particular fondness as it was a time when everything seemed to be going my way. The first stroke of good fortune occurred when myself, Glenmore and Ian were selected to work at the UK's first Burger King restaurant on Coventry Street. After undergoing a week's training at the company's newly refurbished site prior to its grand opening, the latest edition to the fast food franchise was ready and open for business and the much anticipated deluge of eager and hungry customers meant that throughout its first two months of trading, the restaurant and its staff were always kept busy. All three of us were mainly assigned to kitchen duties making Burger King's legendary Big Whopper hamburgers where we had to place the raw hamburger meat on a slowly rotating grill for approximately five or so minutes until it was cooked before adding all the burger's ingredients such as tomatoes, onions and lettuce, then carefully wrapping the product and placing it in a heating tray ready for collection. Aside from making hamburgers, our other duties included constantly ensuring that the station where we worked was kept clean at all times as well as taking turns to clear tables and sweep the floors in the restaurant's dining area and clean the toilets. There was a great esprit de corps amongst the workers at the restaurant who were made up mostly of students from different areas of London who were only working there until the end of the summer before going back to full time study. Although the wages we received weren't exactly a King's ransom, the friendly and jovial atmosphere more than made up it. After almost eight weeks of working throughout the summer the three of us handed in our notices in preparation for a return to the Aylestone Sixth Form and the start of our own individual academic challenge of attempting to gain that first A Level.

Both Ian and myself enrolled on the one year A Level Law Course whilst Glenmore enrolled on the one year A Level Economics course. In addition to my Law studies, I decided that I would study for another O Level in Sociology as well as enrol on the courses in both English Language and Literature as I was determined to remove the stain of under achievement. The first step on the way to putting right all the previous summer's wrongdoings was to enter for the Autumn re-sit examinations that were due to take place towards the end of October and early November. Despite that determination, my preparations for those exams was side tracked considerably by a totally unforeseen opportunity that almost turned my attentions away from my ambition of wanting to qualify as a barrister.

The unexpected opportunity in question came about during the first couple of days into the new term. Wednesday afternoons was the period that was set aside for non-academic activities for example, Sport or Drama. I had absolutely no interest or inkling for Drama. Playing football was how I spent my free time. During my second year, I felt more settled within the school and therefore ready to engage in the extra-curricular activities the school had on offer, my sights firmly fixed on trying to earn a place in the Sixth Form school football team. Because the football season hadn't yet got under way during the first week of the new term, I spent the afternoon idly hanging around the Common Room whilst those students who were members of the Drama group, which included Glenmore and Beverley, were having their first lesson back with the Drama teacher, Miss Frankie Cole in the school's Main Hall. After that lesson, the students came into the Common Room with potentially exciting news. They said that Miss Cole had been contacted by a film company who were looking for young actors to appear in a feature film about an idealistic teacher trying to make a difference with a caring approach to teaching in a delinquent secondary school and that they were all going to the audition just off The Haymarket in the West End. Naturally, I was quite pleased with the Drama group's slice of good fortune but since it wouldn't benefit me in any way, their good news was neither here nor there so far as I was concerned. Glenmore then asked me what I was doing and I replied that apart from going home and do nothing more exciting than watch TV that I had nothing planned. He then suggested that I should tag along with the group to the West End for their audition and after that, the whole group could pop in at Burger King which was only around the corner to have a bite to eat and catch up with some of our old colleagues. This sounded far more appealing than simply going home and just watching TV so I agreed to tag along.

After we arrived at the venue by the appointed time, the group were escorted into a spacious room and we all instinctively headed towards the chairs that were scattered around the room, none of the Drama group having a clue as to the manner or form the actual audition was going to take. Moments later, two men with American accents walked into the room. The shorter of the two males introduced himself as Judd Bernard who was the film's Producer and a man slightly taller than Judd, the Canadian Film Director, Silvio Narizzano whose notable film credits include the much acclaimed 1960's romantic comedy film, Georgy Girl starring Lynne Redgrave and James Mason. Silvio's animated demeanour upon his entry into the room was like a tour de force and he began by thanking the group for attending the audition. Then suddenly and totally unexpectedly, Silvio looked straight in my direction and said, "I want YOU, YES YOU IN THE PICTURE!" For a split second, it seemed that the world had stopped spinning and my initial reaction was a mixture of total disbelief and sheer excitement. I don't know who was the more surprised by Silvio's totally unexpected outburst, me, or my even more astonished schoolmates whose collective innermost thoughts were probably a mixture of disappointment and envy. The drama group's unexpected loss was now my sole personal gain and over the next few weeks I was going to be involved in something that I was sure I was going to enjoy as well as treasure for a very long time.

The name of the film that I was chosen to take part in was called "The Class of Miss MacMichael", a comedy drama slightly grittier than the 60's classic, "To Sir With Love" with Glenda Jackson as a dedicated teacher at the fictional Selkirk High, a school for delinquents whose pupils were virtually uncontrollable. Miss MacMichael's attempts to make a real difference to the school are thwarted at every turn by the terrifyingly dictatorial Headmaster played by Oliver Reed. I wasn't given any star billing in the film, I was no more than an uncredited film extra, but the producers did send me a script where my character (Graham) was given spoken dialogue in a classroom scene as well as a contract for which I would receive £10 per day for my services plus travel expenses.

The film was mainly shot on location at a school in Old Ford, a stone's throw away from Bethnal Green in East London and for the next five weeks or so, I had to get up at the crack of dawn and take the train to Bethnal Green station on the Central line and then a short bus ride to the location for a prompt 8am start and during the first couple of opening scenes in the film, I can be seen quite a few times in the school assembly scene which almost descends into complete anarchy as one of the delinquent inmates runs amok   only to be thwarted in his tracks by the tyrannical Headmaster.

The main credited actors, who appeared in the film included the rising young actor Phil Daniels (of Quadrophenia and EastEnders fame), Patrick Murray (who played the character Mickey Pierce in the classic BBC sitcom in Only Fools And Horses), the American actress Rosalind Cash (whose acting film credits include the films Omega Man and Klute) and the versatile British actress Patsy Byrne (best known for playing Nursie in the cult comedy classic, Blackadder II), the American actor Michael Murphy (best known for his role as Woody Allen's duplicitous friend, Yale in the 1979 rom-com drama film, Manhattan), and last but not least the Actor and Singer with whom I became friends with on the film set, and it is a friendship which still exists until this day, Victor Romero Evans, who played a starring role in one of my favourite films about the ups and downs of the relationship of a young black couple in Ladbroke Grove, Burning An Illusion.

The five or so weeks I spent on the film set was an exciting and wonderful experience and I must admit there were times when I was awestruck at the fact that I was working alongside people as famous as Oscar winner Glenda Jackson, or hell raising acting icon Oliver Reed, and it was a real eye opener to observe the effortless ease with which everyone, from the film crew to the acting talent, went about their craft. But what made the whole experience working on the film such an enjoyable and memorable one was that, save for the odd flashes of tantrums and tempestuousness from the Director Silvio, everyone got on well and respected the contribution each individual had given to the making of the film, irrespective of whether that individual was one of the main actors or an extra like me, one was always made to feel after shooting every scene or rehearsing every dialogue that you were contributing something of real value.

The film eventually went on general release in the Spring of the following year to less than favourable reviews and in all probability, less than average takings at the Box Office, but despite its lack of critical acclaim or commercial success, it still managed to get shown quite a few times on all the major UK television stations mainly after the watershed or in the wee small hours of the morning and whenever it was shown, I would always stay up and watch it and although it would be fair to say that most of the scenes that I was involved with ended up sadly on the cutting room floor, I nevertheless felt a great pride in seeing those fleeting images of myself as a young seventeen year old with a lop sided afro hairstyle clearly having the time of his life enjoying every moment of his unlikely fifteen minutes of fame now captured forever on celluloid.

Despite the obvious benefits of having the time of my life on the film set, the down side to my full on involvement in the film meant that it left little time to focus my attention on my school studies and because I was required to be on the set virtually every single day, I was almost a month behind in terms of the courses I had enrolled on. The fact that I was some way off the pace in terms of my schoolwork did not escape the school's notice when I returned to resume my studies by the middle of October. Although the school didn't stand in my way in terms of seizing the opportunity of appearing in a feature film, that allowance didn't imply that they were particularly pleased by my prolonged absence, especially Miss Watts, who pulled no punches when it came to letting me know where my priorities should lie. "You'll stand no chance of appearing in the Old Bailey, let alone the Old Vic in the future if you don't pull your socks up!" was Miss Watts' frank yet damning assessment especially when I told her about an approach I received from a BBC producer whilst on the film set to attend an audition at the main BBC's studios in White City. There was no doubting the fact that Miss Watts' assessment of my academic efforts and studies in general were spot on. I had to re-focus my attention on my school studies and forget the pie in the sky fantasy that I was going to set the acting world alight. My fifteen minutes of fame was now a thing of the past and with the examinations less than a month away, it was imperative that I studied and worked as hard as I could to maintain and sustain an academic future.

Despite working as hard as I could in the time that I had left in preparing for those exams, the results I received the following January were even worse than the grades five months earlier. I got a **double U,** a double disappointing Unclassified. My face (if such a thing was possible!) went totally crimson after reading the results slip and all I wanted to do at that moment in time was hide somewhere in the remotest corner of the world away from all the shame and embarrassment of falling at the final hurdle yet again. This was another serious setback. The disappointment of falling short was constantly preying on my mind and I was at a total loss as to how I was going to be able to turn things around. It was as if I was in complete and total free fall, hurtling towards the ground without the aid of a safety net and it was pretty clear that if things didn't improve, then my chances of doing well five months from now at the final examinations in June were remote to say the very least.

My preparations for my A Level as well as the other exams I entered for, began a little earlier than my usual revision timetable. This was not because of any newfound sense of urgency on my part but was primarily due to the unflinching efforts and commitment of one teacher who for me, stood head and shoulders above all the great teachers who taught me at the school. A man whose attitude and dedication towards his Law students, particularly during the six week revision period leading up to those Law exams, helped shape both my attitude and philosophy over the years. The Guyanese born Gordon Small was the teacher in question who taught on the intensive one year A Level Law Course. The course itself was extremely popular with students past and present and it consistently produced good A Level results year after year. In addition to being a full time teacher, Mr Small was also a qualified barrister. That fact alone was inspiring enough from my perspective as he was the first qualified barrister that I'd ever seen in the flesh even more so in that he had the same black skin as me. It was clear from the manner in which he spoke and the manner how he taught his students that academic success and achievement wasn't simply handed to Mr Small on a plate as there were times during the teaching sessions, where he would be at pains to constantly remind the class how difficult it was for him juggling the demands of bringing up a family and studying at nights after a hard day's shift on the factory floor in his efforts to qualify as a lawyer. He would constantly drum into his students the importance of dedication to one's studies in order to progress, achieve and succeed in life. "What you sow, you reap!" was his mantra and the lectures were always delivered in such a manner and style that clearly showed his passion for the students that he taught. His commitment to his students was not, however, a one way street. From the outset of the course, Mr Small made it clear that he was prepared to give his all to ensure that his students achieved success but in return, he demanded that all the students on his courses had to match (and in some cases, surpass), his own high expectations otherwise ultimate success and achievement in his view would be nothing but a mere pipe dream.

I was very good at A Level Law, or so I thought. I had a computer like memory for reciting cases and most of the legal principles, from *Donaghue v Stephenson* (a major case in relation to persons owing a Duty of Care to others under the Law of Negligence), to the rules governing the Law of Contract, but by the time I received my examination results on the third Thursday of August 1978, my unflinching belief that I was a Grade A law student turned out to be nothing more than a total fallacy. As always, there was no shortage of effort on my part when revising and preparing for the subjects that I would be tested upon. I constantly poured over past examination papers, sat numerous timed essays as well as faithfully attending all of Mr Small's revision classes. Mr Small even made himself available after the first three hour gruelling ordeal to offer words of encouragement to all the examinees, irrespective of that student's state of confidence.

In between my Law exams, I re-sat my O Level English Language again as well as O Level Sociology for the first time but sadly as with all the exams I sat that for that year, I allowed examination jitters to get the better of me and as a consequence I ran out of time and failed to answer all of the questions on the various question papers that I sat. All of my exams were finished by the middle of June 1978 but instead of relaxing and winding down for the summer, I spent the next eight or so weeks worrying and fretting about whether or not I would get good enough grades to take me on to the next academic level.

The end of those examinations also marked the end of what was a very special time at Aylestone High. The vast majority of the Sixth Formers were leaving the school with high hopes of either going on to further education or employment, with the remaining students electing to stay at the school for the next academic year. As for my next move, I had decided to leave the Sixth Form because I felt that a change of scenery might somehow kick start a positive change in my academic fortunes and acting upon Sandra's advice, I applied to and was accepted by Sandra's former college, Southwark College based at The Cut in Waterloo.

The Sixth Formers decided to have one last big celebration together as a group at the end of the summer term before the winds of life and destiny scattered us all in different paths and directions and what a memorable celebration it turned out to be! The first part of the day was a raucous and riotous coach trip to the seaside at Littlehampton. From the start of the journey outside the school gates to our return at dusk, we all had a fantastic and wonderful time having fun on the beach as well as the funfair, taking as many photos as we could in order to record those never to be forgotten precious moments before concluding festivities back at our Common Room for what would be the last of our now legendary Common Room rave ups that lasted right up until the near midnight hour. It was a bitter sweet end to a special period in my life spent in the company of some very special people, more than half of which I will probably never lay eyes on again. That's all part of life I suppose as we all have different paths to take and I can only hope that whatever path my soon to be erstwhile fellow members of the Aylestone Sixth Form choose, that they find their hopes, dreams and lifelong ambitions at the end of them.

I spent that summer working in a small metal factory unit at the Wembley Trading Estate, which was a stone's throw away from Wembley Stadium. This stroke of good fortune was solely due Glenmore who spoke to his elder brother Gavin, who in turn had words with the Foreman of the unit about employing the pair of us on a temporary basis throughout the summer vacation. For the next seven or so weeks, Glenmore and I had to be at work from 8am to 3.30pm doing monotonous and repetitive piecemeal work by spot welding small metal components together. Although the wages I received were very modest, I was nevertheless grateful to at least be doing something with my time rather than drift aimlessly throughout the summer, worrying about my exam results and even though the nature of the work was boring and repetitive, it only served as a temporary measure until I started college in September. But the one thing that would sometimes flash through my mind was the horrifying nightmare scenario of a future fifty year old Shaun Wallace working in a similar type of factory environment having fulfilled the predictions and assessments made long ago by my Careers Teacher at Copland High School.

The third Thursday of August finally arrived and I woke up earlier than usual for work mainly due to the mixture of nervousness and excitement in what for me was a very important day. I rushed downstairs to the front door to see whether the postman had delivered that all-important letter but it hadn't arrived. Rather than go through the torturous agony of waiting for its arrival, I decided to get in early for work and wait until lunchtime which would give me plenty of time to get home to discover my fate.

When I arrived at work, I discovered that Glenmore's results hadn't arrived either and as I looked into his eyes, I could tell that he was just as nervous as I was. That morning, it was hard to concentrate. All that kept running through my mind was, *what grade was in that envelope? A, B, C, D, E…* Those letters swirled around in my mind spinning like the symbols of a one armed bandit machine and I was totally unsure as to which of the letters it was eventually going to stop at. All that constant fretting seemed to drag that morning period on for what seemed like ages but eventually, lunch time arrived and I wasted no time in rushing home to see if the envelope containing my results had too. I opened the door and there it was. The addressee's name staring up at me whilst it lay on the mat, screaming at me demanding that I pick it up. I bent down and nervously picked up the brown envelope and slowly peeled back the sticky flap before pulling out its contents to reveal the following result:

Shaun Wallace, A Level Law - Grade E.

I paused for a while after reading the slip and my first thoughts were one of considerable disappointment. OK so I passed an A Level, but only just. Although there was nothing wrong with my efforts, there was clearly something fundamentally wrong with my examination technique and if I was being brutally honest, there was something clearly amiss in terms of my overall abilities as a student. As the news of my disappointing result began to sink in, I couldn't help but think that the realisation of all my hopes and dreams of becoming a lawyer were becoming a faint and distant proposition, with a future that to all intents and purposes, was beginning to look very bleak and uncertain. By the time I arrived back at work, Glenmore was already there. I asked him what his results were and he said that he got a Grade D. I was pleased for him and even though he got a better grade in his subject than I did he was nevertheless very disappointed with the result. We then talked about what we were going to do for the forthcoming year and when I revealed to him that I intended to study at Southwark College, Glenmore told me that he decided to stay on at the Sixth Form and retake his Economic A Level again and enrol on the one year A Level Sociology so as to ensure that he could sit two A Levels at the same time. It wasn't the time for mass celebration for the pair of us but at least we both proved that we were capable of passing A Levels, something that Copland High School thought we could never achieve. The only one of the ex-Copland students who had any real cause for celebration was Ian Henry who gained a very respectable grade C in A Level Law, a result which clearly demonstrated that he was more than capable of making that step up to higher education but so far as both Glenmore and myself were concerned, we concluded our grim post mortem discussions on our less than impressive academic success with the positive declaration that we would strive to improve as students and build on our grades.

This newfound optimism however proved sadly to be yet another false dawn when a week or so later, I received the results of my 'O 'level exams:

O level English Language – Grade E
O level Sociology – Grade E

Those results completed a miserable twelve months of my academic career which had suffered yet another major setback. A setback not only in terms of my ambitions of becoming a lawyer, but also in terms of my overall confidence as an individual. By the time I arrived for enrolment at Southwark College during the first week of September, I felt woefully unprepared for the academic challenge that lay ahead of me.

CHAPTER THREE

I spent two years at Southwark College from September 1978 to the summer of 1980 and during my first year there, I found it extremely difficult adjusting to my new surroundings. It was a total culture shock for me especially in terms of the teaching styles and methods employed in lectures that were usually held in vast halls in order to cope with the dozens upon dozens of students of all different ages and abilities who were on the courses I had enrolled on. It felt far too daunting and impersonal a place for me to develop and thrive and the three hour lectures always seemed to fly by without me being any the wiser of what I was being taught. As the weeks progressed, I began to wonder whether I had made a monumental mistake in enrolling at the college and soon found myself pining for the halcyon days of the Aylestone Sixth Form. But as I quickly discovered, Aylestone's altruistic yet somewhat cossetted approach to teaching its students was in complete contrast to the way subjects were apparently taught in further educational establishments. The teaching philosophy of the College was clearly based on the premise that students were expected to study and research on their own and the role of the course tutors was simply to facilitate and guide as well as encourage students to think analytically for themselves when studying any given topic and for a student who had been mollycoddled and spoon fed all of his academic life, it was a philosophy that was a complete culture shock that sadly for me I was having major difficulties getting to grips with.

The subjects I decided to study at the college was the one year A Level course in Sociology despite the fact that I got a very low passing grade at O Level, the one year A Level course in 20th Century World History as well as another attempt to secure an acceptable passing grade in O Level English Language. However, by the time we reached half term by mid October, it was pretty clear that I was struggling to make a positive impact on the A Level courses I was studying for.

My inability in coming to terms with the teaching methods and styles in my A Level subjects were evident and reflected in the written essays I frequently had to submit which when given back, were usually accompanied with below average marks. My progress on English Language though, by strange contrast, was considerably better than my other subjects. Those lessons by the Course tutor, Ms Cullen-Bown, were delivered in a style that made me feel much more relaxed as she was far more personable and approachable than the tutors in my A Level subjects. As a result, the pieces of coursework

44

I submitted throughout the year began to show a gradual and consistent improvement but in truth, I can't claim all the credit for my gradual reversal of fortune. Some of that credit has to go to my ever faithful and reliable big sister Sandra, who would check over all of my written essays before they were submitted and would always insist that I rewrite the final draft piece in neat, legible handwriting. "The presentation of a piece of work," she would always drum into me, "… is just as important as its contents."

By mid November, I was back at Aylestone High once more in order to re-sit my exam in O Level Sociology. I had contacted the school at the beginning of September and asked Miss Watts whether I would be allowed to do so and she agreed to my request without a hint of hesitation. Once again, there was no lack of dedication or effort on my part in terms of preparation for that exam however, by the time I received the result in the middle of January 1979, it was clear that there was no real change in my overall academic development. I got a grade D this time, a slight improvement on my last efforts the previous summer, but the cold harsh reality was this was another disappointing return and with it, all of the old haunting fears of failure and under achievement resurfaced with a vengeance and another spectacular exam failure five months hence, seemed to be, so far as my flagging confidence was concerned, a certainty.

Despite my seemingly hopeless situation, I felt that I had no choice other than to bite the bullet and press ahead with preparing for and sitting those exams. But this decision was made mainly because of the unwavering encouragement and support my big sister Sandra was giving me. As always, with her pragmatic mixture of tact and tough love, she reminded me that although my exam results so far had been disappointing, I nevertheless still had to show all the necessary courage and determination if I wanted to reach my intended destination and that my ultimate goal of success would never be attainable if I was constantly wallowing in my own self-pity. Her stark but frank assessment was just what my deflated levels of confidence needed and it helped give me a renewed sense of purpose to pick myself up from my depths of despair and persevere. I had no other choice but to soldier on in preparation for the forthcoming exams in the summer.

The only way I was going to get into Higher Education this year was to take the gamble and roll the dice. *I've got to pass two A Levels this summer!* my inner voice would repeat constantly in order to prop up my floundering self-confidence and the best chance I felt that I had in achieving that goal would be to sit A Level History and re-take Law, a decision that would mean my Sociology studies would have to be set aside. I thought that if my grades were good enough, then I could always go through the UCAS clearing system and get into University via the back door. My ambitious yet fanciful plans soon gave way to the cold hard facts that, academically speaking, I wasn't good enough or indeed, mature enough to be the successful student I needed to be in order to make the transition to the next academic level.

Despite the slow but gradual improvements in my knowledge and understanding on my History course, it was still woefully short of the requirements needed to achieve at least a grade B or a C. Those grades were the absolute bottom line in terms of minimum targets and objectives that I had to aim for. The Law faculties at the various universities I had set my sights on were demanding and if I managed to meet those demands, it would at least give me the slim but fighting chance of being considered for the most competitive of degree courses.

The Easter break arrived which effectively signalled the end of all formal lectures and seminars at the college. It was also the cue that it was time to turn my attentions to my revision programme. It was vitally important that I attended a structured revision programme and the programmes that I knew would be best for me were going to be held at my old alma mata, Aylestone High School.

I contacted the Sixth Form with a considerable degree of apprehension and nervousness before speaking to the Head of Sixth Form, Miss Watts. I had no idea how she would react to my desperate cries for help and I was hoping that both she and the school would support me one last time. I told Miss Watts about my situation at the college and how difficult a time I was having with my studies and I asked her whether it was possible for me to sit in on all the revision classes for History and Law at the school even though I would be sitting these exams externally. Miss Watts never hesitated for a moment in granting her approval to my request. Miss Watts's reassuring words caused me to breathe a massive sigh of relief. I was back in familiar and comfortable surroundings with teachers who I respected and liked and the best place that I felt would get the best out of me.

With each passing lesson that I attended, I knew that I had made the right call. The classes were fully attended by students who were both keen and motivated to do well and the commitment and dedication shown both by Mr Small and Mr Cooley at such a crucial time showed no signs of relenting. Time seemed to fly by and before I knew it, we had reached the week approaching half term that signified the end of the revision classes. Those last six or so weeks I spent in those revision classes at Aylestone gave me a renewed sense of confidence and optimism, a feeling that was nigh on impossible a mere four months previously and for that, I owe the school a debt of gratitude, a debt that I could only ever repay in one way and that was to attain successful passing grades in all of my exams.

The opportunity to make the first instalment of that debt to Aylestone High School was now only ten days away and despite my cautious optimism, I knew I was still drinking in the last chance saloon, but Aylestone's support had at least given me a fighter's chance and that made me even more determined to succeed.

The day of judgement had finally arrived and I woke up feeling confident and determined. I was looking forward to getting off to a great start in the first of those exams, A Level History paper 1. The three hour exam was scheduled to start at 2pm and was going to take place at the college's main site at The Cut. The second History paper was due to be held at the same venue eight days thereafter, at 10am. The venue for the Law exams were due to be held at the college's annexe on the Blackfriars Road four days after the first History exam paper at 2pm in the afternoon, with the final paper three days thereafter in the morning and somewhere sandwiched in between all of those, was a one off written exam on that old nemesis of mine, O Level English Language. Not the most daunting of exam timetables and with all things being equal, this time there should be no excuses!

I squeezed in some lastminute revision before leaving home mid-morning and making my way on foot to Stonebridge Park train station for the forty minute journey to Waterloo, arriving at The Cut with more than an hour to spare. I double checked which room I would be in then headed to a nearby café for some food to refuel.

Not long later, I was in my seat for the all too familiar words: "you may now turn over your test papers and begin!" After that, the only sound that could be heard was the simultaneous rustling of paper as we completed the exam in total silence.

Looking at the paper, my feelings oscillated between optimism and ambivalence. Thankfully, there were just enough questions out of the four that I could manage. Before the invigilator called time, I rose from my seat and left the lecture hall cautiously optimistic that I've got off to a solid start. I headed straight towards Waterloo station for the journey home to begin preparations for my next two exams, A Level Law and attempt number five in O Level English Language.

Like most students, I was counting the days when the exams would be finally over because admittedly, it was becoming extremely difficult to retain my focus and discipline. All what was needed now was one last monumental effort and then it would be job done with nothing left to look forward to other than finding myself a temporary summer job and hopefully, carefree, stress free time. But like that old saying in football of it being the game of two halves, my last set of exams in both History and Law sadly did not go so well. The topics I was hoping to come up failed to materialise, the questions that did come up were structured in such a way that I didn't understand their meaning, and worst of all, I ran out of time.

I somehow found myself drawn to the dreaded post-exam discussions with my fellow students, and it was awful. When I talked about my performance I displayed all the classic signs of a demoralised and defeated man. My fellow students were doing everything in their power to lift my flagging spirits and told me to try and forget about the exams and put it all behind me. I nodded back half-heartedly, trying and failing miserably to give the outward impression that they were probably right with their advice but inwardly, I knew that the writing was probably on the wall.

I met up with Glenmore a day or so after all our exams were over to catch up and have our own post examination review. By the looks of things, Glenmore matched my own ambivalent assessment and like me, thought that his chances of doing well were hanging by a thread, but between us, we both arrived at the general consensus that the best thing to do was to put all talk about exams and higher education to one side and try to enjoy the summer as best we could. I asked Glenmore what his plans were for the summer as I hoped to get a job at his brother's workplace again. Glenmore though had other plans on his horizon and he told me that instead of working for the summer, he was going to Jamaica for a six week holiday and would be flying out at the end of June. He was clearly delighted at the prospect of his first visit back home since leaving to come to England as a young boy of nine. I couldn't help feeling slightly envious on hearing the news. I wished I was going with him but I didn't have any money to go especially for that length of time. I was left with no choice but to stay in England and try to find myself another temporary summer job as I needed to earn some money of my own without having to rely on hand outs from Mum all the time, as well as help to take my mind off those niggling exam anxieties.

My search for a summer job however, was not so easy this time around and after days of fruitless searching in the local Job Centres close to where I live, I signed up with a Job Recruitment Agency based on the Wembley High Road who were looking for temporary labourers. I had little choice but to take anything that was available and for the next three or so weeks, I had to get up at the crack of dawn for 7.30am starts for six or so hours of gruelling, back breaking chores at various businesses in and around the borough of Brent. However, a series of events were about to unfold that were so detrimental not only to my physical well-being, but seriously called into question the true nature and extent of my academic abilities.

I was working at one of the large warehouse units near Staples Corner by the North Circular Road Flyover and the Foreman asked me to arrange all the long radiators that were lying around the floor and stack them vertically one by one on top of another on wooden pallets along the walls. Needless to say it was back breaking work, but after having stacked the fifth radiator against the fourth, disaster struck. As I bent down to pick up the sixth radiator, the arrangement collapsed like an avalanche and I was smothered with heavy falling radiators. Almost immediately, some of the workers rushed to where I lay stricken and began pulling the radiators off me. I was ordered to lay completely still for a few minutes until they were certain that I wasn't paralysed or suffered any broken bones. Mercifully, I was spared any serious injury and eventually with the help of my colleagues, I was slowly brought to my feet. Feeling slightly dazed and disorientated, I asked to sit down as my middle and lower back was beginning to throb. The Foreman called for an ambulance, which arrived fairly quickly and I was rushed off to Edgware General Hospital where the doctor who examined me diagnosed bruising of the middle to lower back areas and I was advised not to engage in any physical or strenuous activity for the next six or so weeks. I had to spend the first three days at home virtually bedridden until I was well enough to get up and move around, the accident more or less effectively ended my chances of finding alternative temporary work which as a consequence meant that I had nothing to do to occupy my time apart from sit at home watching endless daytime television and worry and fret about that dreaded third Thursday in August that was looming large in the horizon.

The third day in August finally arrived and I soon discovered that the physical pain I got for my efforts from stacking up heavy radiators that came tumbling down upon me was nothing in comparison to the emotional pain of failure and disappointment when I finally opened the envelope containing my A Level results which read as follows:

A level Law – Grade E

A level History – O Level Pass.

The gamble had failed to pay off. I burst into floods of tears. Tears that were becoming so uncontrollable, that I began to sob out loud, babbling incoherently, *"WHAT A FAILURE I HAVE BECOME!"* Debbie and Stephen were also at home at the time and the pair of them upon hearing my cries of lamentation immediately rushed towards the hallway where I was sitting on the stairs with my head in my hands. They did their level best to get me to calm down and after a while my incessant crying and wailing began to die down and I went upstairs to my room and spent the next couple or so hours locked in my bedroom in total seclusion. All I wanted to do was hide my face from the whole world because in my mind, all the world would see would be just another failure. Intermittently throughout the remainder of the day, I would emerge from my self-imposed exile to receive telephone calls from my friends and fellow students anxious to find out how I got on. Virtually most of my friends seemed to have got the grades they were hoping for and even though I was pleased for them all, I felt as though I was the odd man out. Ian had managed to obtain a second A Level passing grade in Sociology and although he failed to match the success of the previous year, he had been offered a place to read Law at North East London Polytechnic (now East London University). Glenmore, who by this time had returned from his six week holiday in Jamaica, got two passing grades and although he couldn't get into the university of his choice, he at least got 2 A Levels in one go and as such he could start on the BSc Degree Course in the Autumn in Economics at the same Polytechnic as Ian. I was genuinely pleased for the pair of them. They made the academic quantum leap onto higher education and the only thing I craved above anything else at the time, the status of undergraduates.

There was a small silver lining that emerged from the dark clouds that had gathered all around me. At long, long last, I finally passed my O Level English Language, attaining a rather surprising **Grade B** which had the welcoming effect of lifting my spirits a little but with the onset of a new academic year just around the corner, the cold realisation suddenly dawned on me that for the first time in four years, I wouldn't have a guaranteed place at a seat of learning. That safety net was now gone and all that was left was the prospect of a bleak and uncertain future.

The start of the new academic year was already under way and my mood and general state of mind at this time can be summed up in one single sentence: drifting along aimlessly without any sense of direction or purpose and a future that appeared to be firmly behind me. It seemed that all my friends, even those who weren't studying or doing some further education course, seemed to be moving forward and doing something with their lives whereas my life in seemed to be moving backwards beyond minus square one. My grand plan lay in tatters and I had no plan B to fall back on. The options I did have at my disposal appeared to be narrowing with every passing second but the prolonged feelings of disappointment and failure were preventing me from thinking both clearly and rationally as to what should be my next move. Those limited options were either, re-enrol for another year at Southwark College, try to find a job (although given the high unemployment rate at the time coupled with my less than average qualifications, the chances of me getting a decent job were practically zero), or finally, the nightmare scenario: sign on the dotted line for the dole. I had little choice in the end but to dust myself down and try to recover and re-focus from this latest setback and re-enrolled at Southwark College for the one year A Level History course once more as well as the A Level Sociology course that I abandoned during the previous academic term.

My timetable for my lectures and seminars for the academic year meant that I had a lot of spare time on my hands. All that free time was a godsend and it enabled me to make the instant decision in the first few days back at college to apply to re-sit the A Level History exam at the earliest opportunity the following January. Realistically speaking, that seemed to be a mad decision to make given my poor showing the previous summer, a knee jerk reaction in my obsessive desire to try to recover already lost ground as quickly as possible, but whatever the rights or wrongs of that decision, I had to go for it. The odds of a successful outcome in four months' time were no different than the summer before but If I was to stand any chance of doing well, then I had to show a real and proper commitment and dedication, making sure that I did all the relevant and necessary reading and revision in preparation for those exams during those free periods. But those efforts, irrespective of how sustained and consistent they may be, wouldn't by itself provide a firm guarantee for examination success as the bitter disappointments of the last two successive summers would bear testimony to. My study methods and examination technique would have to undergo a complete dismantling and reconstruction if I really wanted to move things forward and that meant, for the umpteenth time, I would have to eat humble pie and go cap in hand to seek help and guidance from the only place I believed who would be willing to support me in this vital and long overdue transformation. I mustered up the courage to call Aylestone High School. Miss Watts said that the school and the teaching staff would always be on hand to offer what advice and help I needed and suggested that I contact Mike Cooley as she was sure that he would be more than willing to help me prepare for my A Level retake. Her extraordinary offer of allowing me back on the school premises to sit in on Mr Cooley's lessons already added to the infinite debt of gratitude I owed both to her and the school and I wasted little time in accepting her generous invitation. As soon as I ended our conversation, I contacted Mike Cooley straight away and he too was unwavering in his offer of support. He also suggested that I contact Miguel Martinez who was without doubt the cleverest student in the Sixth Form, a fact reflected in the three straight A grades he achieved as he was sure that Miguel would be more than willing to provide any help and assistance that I would need. I contacted Miguel and he was more than willing to help and so we arranged to meet up before he left for university up north. At that meeting, the first thing he did was to hand me all his class notes and written essays. Being the friend he is, he not only offered plenty of words of encouragement but was also honest and frank with me in his assessment as to why I was not producing the goods. He told me that although I knew my subject very well, the A Level History exam is a completely different beast to the O Level one, the latter which in reality, was more or less a memory test to recall dates and events.

"There was nothing wrong with your recall of historical facts and figures Shaun," Miguel remarked. "For A Level exams, it's how you analyse and interpret those events that counts. It's not that difficult a transition to make and in my view you're not that far away."

I was grateful for Miguel's honesty and I immediately took on board the wise and encouraging words of a man who had been there, seen it and most importantly, done it! With one final hug, we said our last goodbyes before going our separate ways to begin our own separate personal challenges.

Both Glenmore and Ian meanwhile were happily settling into life as a first year undergraduates at North East London Polytechnic, sampling all the trappings of what student life is all about, particularly during the celebrated undergraduate rite of passage namely, "Fresher's Week" and even though there was a difference between us with regards to our academic status, the pair of them still found the time to check up on me. Seeing the pair of them successfully make the transition into higher education acted as a symbol of inspiration for me.

In terms of my preparation, I was working to a very structured schedule that had only one aim in mind: to achieve a worthwhile passing grade in A Level History. I attended the History lectures at both Southwark College and Aylestone High School, getting the best of both worlds and over time, I began to develop both an appreciation and understanding of the subject that was sorely lacking in my first year. I used the free period in my College timetable to produce a constant stream of written essays and submit them to Mike Cooley who would look over them and give me invaluable constructive feedback on the contents. It took a while to get the hang of what was required, but the more I practiced writing those essays, the more I improved my analytical and critical understanding of the subject. Much of the credit for that considerable improvement must go down to Miguel Martinez. His priceless gift of his old history notes and essays were so clear and easy to read and it made the chore of the in depth reading from textbooks, even easier to digest, analyse and understand.

The final invaluable source of help and support in my attempt to pass that all important exam, came in the form of the pure and unadulterated selflessness of another old school mate of mine, Jacqueline Nedd, who was in the final year of her A Level History course at Aylestone. I got to know Jacquie in my second year at the school when she was part of an influx of Fifth Formers who joined the Sixth Form. In the previous academic year, Jacquie was part of Gordon Small's intensive one year A Level class that she passed with flying colours attaining a very impressive grade B. With one A Level secured and with two further exams to sit in June, she had her eyes firmly set on reading Law at Warwick University later on that year. When Jacquie heard about my History setback the previous summer and my intention to sit the exam in January, she offered, without a hint of reluctance or hesitation, to lend me all of her lecture notes and essays in the same selfless way that Miguel had done and I promised that I would return them to her the moment my exams were completed. Her kind offer in lending me her History notes wasn't the limit of her extraordinary selflessness. Jacqueline also invited me to be a part of the History study group at her large three storey family home in Kilburn. In these study sessions, the group would put me through my paces on topics on the syllabus ranging from the Fourth French Republic to China's foreign policy from the 1950's to the present. Their contribution in helping me prepare for my History re-take was just as invaluable as all of the support and encouragement I was constantly receiving.

The History re-sits were getting ever closer and with each passing day both my knowledge and examination technique in the subject was making all the necessary improvements that I needed to make. I was growing more and more confident that my time to deliver the goods had finally arrived.

The day of the first paper had arrived and I was required to be at the designated examination centre just off Gower Street for a 10am start. That morning, I woke up nice and early after a good night's rest feeling very relaxed and confident in the daunting challenge that I would have to face and headed off towards Stonebridge Park Station for the journey into town. I felt completely at ease with myself, more than ever before. The invigilator gave the order to turn over the question paper and begin the exam. After a quick scan of the questions it looked as if I would have nothing to worry about however, it wasn't a case of being merely comfortable with the set of questions, it was how I performed over the next three hours that counted.

Throughout the whole of those three hours I remained calm and in control, answering each question within the allotted time applying all that I had learnt over the previous three months. I made sure that I had more than enough time before the invigilator gave the order to stop writing to have one final thorough check of my answer sheets before they would be submitted, taking care this time in going over any spelling mistake or more importantly, poor grammar. By the time I eventually rose from my desk, I felt completely satisfied with my morning's work which was in stark contrast to the feelings of worry and anxiety the last time I sat the exam. As the candidates filed out of the examination hall, the three hours of complete and total silence was substituted for the lively post exam discussions and banter that usually accompany such an occasion. Those discussions had their usual mix of how easy or difficult the students had found the question paper but I decided to bypass those discussions and headed straight for home eventually arriving at my house in the late afternoon with my confident mood very much intact.

The day of the second paper arrived and I went through the same routine designed to keep me both calm and in control for the three hour test as both myself and my fellow exam candidates awaited the invigilator's instructions to commence writing. On my initial sighting of the questions on the paper, they once again, so far as I was concerned, held no fears. The exam went really well, so well in fact that I almost got carried away answering a question on Chinese Foreign Policy that left me very little time to answer the last question. But unlike my last unsuccessful attempt the previous summer, this time there was no feelings of panic or desperation and I completed the last answer with a detailed bullet point essay plan. I knew that I would probably lose valuable marks for my profligacy, but I had an unshakeable belief that I had still performed well enough to get a passing A Level grade.

Just after 5pm, the invigilator ordered all the examinees to stop writing and with that, my examination ordeal was finally all over. All the hard work and commitment over the previous three months had paid off and as I left the examination hall (bypassing the post exam discussions in the process once more), my mood and general state of mind was in complete contrast to the dark days of disappointment and underachievement that seemed to blight both my life and thoughts the last couple of weeks the previous August and the first few weeks of September. The History exam was now exactly as the subject says, history. The results were not due to be published until the middle of March so rather than sit and worry about a result I had no control over, it was high time to redirect my focus and energies to resuming my studies at Southwark College in the firm expectation, as opposed to forlorn hope, of completing a remarkable reversal in my fortunes.

Over the next few months, the renaissance of my inner self confidence and belief was now in full bloom. I was back at college full time, working as hard as I could in trying to make up all the lost ground in my A Level Sociology studies and with the encouragement and support of my lecturer Chris, I managed to bridge that seemingly impossible gap. I felt far more relaxed and self-assured, more than at any other time in my career as a student and with the summer examinations only three months away, this time I knew that I was ready to successfully cross the finishing line.

Sometime towards the end of March, I received my exam results for A Level History:

A Level History – Grade D.

"I've got 2 A Levels!" I shrieked aloud as if I'd come up with the magical eight score draws on the pools. I'd finally managed to achieve the one thing that I was beginning to think would remain tantalisingly beyond my grasp. I could finally look forward to next September and starting life as a Law undergraduate. There was no getting away from the stark fact that with A Level grades like D and E in the bag, places like Oxford or Cambridge would hardly be beating a path to my front door begging me to join them, but at least I had the minimum qualifications to be a Law undergraduate at some Higher Educational establishment, and to hell with the overt snobbery that a Polytechnic degree was somehow inferior to a degree awarded by a university. Nothing, absolutely nothing was going to dampen my own sense of personal achievement. Even the fact that I got a D for History didn't really seemed to matter. I believed in my heart of hearts that I could have at least got a C if not higher, had I not run out of time in the last paper, but the result was tangible proof that I had taken on board all the advice that I had been given despite the fact that my examination technique by virtue of me running out of time in the second paper was still a work in progress.

I went straight off to Aylestone High School before going off to college that morning to break the news, as well as to thank them for all the help they had given me. When I arrived at the Sixth Form block, the Common Room was alive as usual with students milling about and when I saw Jacquie and some other members of the History group, they could tell straight away by my demeanour that I was not a bearer of bad news. There were smiles and hugs all round from the group and that feel good factor was extended when I eventually got around to seeing Miss Watts and Mike Cooley. Mike Cooley was very pleased with my efforts and although we dwelt momentarily on the fact that I probably would have got a higher grade if I hadn't run out of time, that was soon swiftly swept under the carpet amid the air of congratulations and success. I also caught up with my mentor, Gordon Small, who was no less pleased by my good news. "Why don't you retake Law?" was his suggestion during our discussions. "You've proved that you've got the tools Shaun, now go and finish the job!" Mr Small's suggestion was something that I was contemplating in the aftermath of the euphoria of my results. Sitting both my Law and Sociology exams in June and aim for higher grades. *Who knows? I thought to myself. Perhaps Oxford or Cambridge could yet still be beating a path to my door after all!*

I eventually arrived at Southwark College for an afternoon seminar in Sociology. After the lesson had ended, I went up to my lecturer Chris and told him my good news.

"That's fantastic news Shaun!" Chris replied enthusiastically. "Now, let's see if we can turn those two A Levels into three."

With my levels of self-belief now at an all-time high, it was a challenge that I was not going to disagree with.

The end of the Spring term was upon us which meant that after the Easter break of about two or so weeks, the final term would mark the start of countdown towards the summer examinations which were to take place from the last week in May to the end of June. Because all formal lectures had now ended, the final term was geared towards both revision and preparation for those exams and non-attendance was simply not an option. I only had to attend Chris's revision lectures at the college which was timetabled for twice a week, thus allowing me time to attend Gordon Small's legendary revision lectures back at Aylestone to help me at one last final stab in obtaining a decent enough grade in my Law exam. The revision lectures were of the highest quality, particularly in the Sociology classes and that was in no small measure due to Chris's teaching style and enthusiasm. Chris's desire to see his students do well rubbed off on all of us and with each passing revision lecture, one couldn't help but feel that there was more than just a fighting chance of ultimate success.

The day of my first exam, A Level Sociology, had now arrived and what a day to kick start that first exam for the day itself was on my twentieth birthday. I was determined to make it a birthday to remember. I woke up that Monday morning feeling on top of the world and when I went downstairs, I was greeted by the sight of what seemed like a mountain of birthday cards. I picked them all up and placed them all unopened on the hallway table as any birthday celebrations would have to be placed on hold until after the exam in the afternoon. Once I finished my breakfast, I went upstairs to get washed and dressed before leaving home and the leisurely stroll to Stonebridge Park to wait for the Bakerloo train to Waterloo. I arrived at the Cut some two or so hours before the start of the exam and I couldn't have felt any more relaxed or at ease despite the important task that lay ahead of me. I grabbed a quick bite to eat from the sandwich bar close to the college before making my way to the examination hall. Soon afterwards, all the exam candidates had gathered outside the hall and then we were all invited to take our places.

I turned over my test paper and much to my delight, there wasn't a single question at first glance, that I either didn't know or would find extremely difficult. I immediately set about putting into practice all that I had learned from Mike, Gordon and Chris, which meant that by the time the invigilator had called time, I walked out of the examination hall feeling inwardly pleased and quietly confident with my efforts. The post mortem discussions about the exam were as usual, very much in earnest in and around the examination hall and once again, I gave them an extremely wide berth. After all, today was my birthday and I was hardly in a mood to either entertain or countenance any negative vibes. All I wanted to do was go home and relax as well as celebrate what was left of my birthday.

The remaining set of exams went well, particularly my second paper in Sociology, and even though once again I ran out of time on my second Law paper, I still felt that I had done more than enough to at least attain a passing grade. I could look forward to an anxiety free summer full of expectation as opposed to the angst ridden fragile hope of summers gone by.

I was very fortunate in finding temporary employment for the summer, a job that was a far cry from the mundane, backbreaking work I had to endure during the previous summer vacation. I was working with young children on play schemes for the Westminster Play Association as a Play Leader. I had a fantastic time working with a bright and lively set of youngsters enjoying such a wide variety of activities on offer, from day trips to museums or the seaside, that it hardly felt that I was actually employed at all.

Amidst all the fun and excitement, the third Thursday in August had arrived, a date which meant the publication of those all-important examination results. The letter had duly arrived on the doormat and after a short, sharp intake of breath, I bent down and picked it up. I quickly opened it and the slip of paper contained therein revealed the following results;

A Level Sociology – Grade C
A Level law – Grade D

I'd done it! At long last I'd finally mastered the art of passing A Level exams that a couple of years ago seemed well beyond my reach. I was the proud owner of **3 A Levels** and whilst at that point in time, I didn't know at what institution or place I was going to commence my studies, the one thing I was certain about was that come September, I was going to be an undergraduate student in Law.

Before leaving for work that morning, I contacted the UCAS clearing house system. This was the first time I had any contact with that organisation in terms of trying to find a place at University. I had refused to apply to UCAS in the past for the plain and simple reason that I was neither ready nor in truth, good enough to gain a place at University but this time armed with three A Levels, I felt that I earned the right to contact them. They took all of my details and promised that they would contact me over the next day or so to let me know whether my application for a University place had been successful. In fact, UCAS contacted me that very same day and informed me that there were a few places left at Keele University in Staffordshire on their four year course with a work placement requirement in the third year. I decided not to take it up. The course was going to run for four years instead of the usual three which didn't appeal to me. I was already two years behind with my Law studies and I didn't want to fall even further behind with the addition of another year and furthermore, I didn't feel that I was sufficiently mature enough to uproot myself and spend the next four years away from all the comforts of home. I therefore decided to apply to all of the main Polytechnics in London and the Home counties and the institution I settled upon was North London Polytechnic with its Law Faculty based at Highbury Grove.

I contacted the College who were more than happy to send me an application form, which when it arrived, I duly filled in and returned it post haste. The College then invited me to attend an interview in the first week of September at the end of which, I was offered a place on the Law course that would begin in a fortnight's time. At long last, I was a full time, fully fledged law undergraduate and ahead of me lay three more years of studying, which I hoped would be an exciting, enjoyable, and ultimately, a successful experience.

CHAPTER FOUR

It has often been said that the best three years of your life are as an undergraduate and in my case, there was never truer a phrase spoken. From the first day I walked through the front door, right up until the point when I saw my name on the Polytechnic's Noticeboard with the publication of the Degree Classification Awards in the summer of 1983, I enjoyed every minute. But that's not to say there weren't moments on the course when it was far from plain sailing.

The Law Faculty was part of the Arts and Humanities Department at the annexe Ladbroke House on Ladbroke Grove, a stone's throw away from Arsenal's Highbury Stadium. The less than spacious surroundings at the Ladbroke House annexe meant that students from other undergraduate courses shared the site's facilities and whilst on the whole the students all got on well with each other, there was a lot of friendly rivalry and banter. I remember I was using the cubicle in one of the Men's toilets when I first arrived at the College and I couldn't help but raise a smile at the anonymous but amusing graffiti written (no doubt by a Law student), just above the toilet roll which read, "BA (Hons) Sociology Degree please take a sheet!" This schoolboy acerbic humour was matched by the equally amusing yet childish retort written directly above which read, "what do you call a thousand law undergraduates at the bottom of the sea? – A start!"

In the first year of the Law Degree course, a student was required to study and pass four subject modules. The first three were main core subjects, Criminal Law, The Law of Contract and the English Legal Institutions with the fourth module being a non-law related subject. These subjects in question were, Economics, Accountancy, French, German, Sociology and finally, Politics/International Relations, which is the subject I chose. I was one of more than fifty or so students who attended that very first lecture in the College's vast lecture halls on the first floor. *How many of us are going to make it to the very end of the course?* I asked myself quietly as I sat in my seat for the very first lecture in Criminal Law. The answer to that question would depend upon how much effort and sacrifice we all were prepared to make in order to achieve that ultimate goal.

The most important part of the course was the end of year written examinations and a student wishing to progress into the next year of the course had to attain a passing grade in all subjects. A student who failed any one of those exams was given the opportunity to make amends by taking a re-sit in that exam that was usually held in the last week of August before the start of the new academic year. If a student failed two of those exams however, that student would have to re-sit all four exams but if a student failed three of the exams then that student would have to repeat the whole year from the beginning, a nightmare scenario I for one had no intention of being involved in, or at the very least would be doing my very best to try and avoid. Given the difficult time I had in trying to get my A Levels, I knew that it would be highly unlikely that I would end up as the top student in the group once the course was completed, but the one thing that I was determined to ensure, was that I would do whatever it takes to successfully get over the finishing line.

In addition to the end of year written exams, the written pieces of coursework that each student had to submit (a student had to submit a total of twelve written pieces of coursework for the academic year) were an integral and essential part on the Degree course as the average score would be added to the score attained for the end of year examinations and those marks could be the crucial difference between passing or failing any given subject. The overall grades obtained in the first year didn't count towards the Degree. It was only the second and final years that would ultimately determine a student's degree classification. My mind set and strategy so far as the way I intended to approach the law course over the next three years was both clear and uncompromising: *Do well in that first year as it will set the tone for the following years to come!*

The timetable for the first year involved daily three hour lectures which were interspersed with smaller seminar groups for a one hour tutorial. Wednesday afternoons however, were mainly free. Most students used that free time to both relax and unwind and mingle with other students and there was no better place to indulge such hedonistic activities than in the Student Common Room in the building's basement. I had contemplated going to the football trials that were being held at the College's main sporting campus in Stanmore, North London but in the end I decided that the wisest thing to do was to put those sporting ambitions on hold, at least until I was sure that I had made it into the second year. Even though I decided against playing any form of team sports during my first year, there was something which had caught my attention during those first few weeks on the course. One of the College's Notice Board had an advert which read as follows: "Looking for an adventure and fun next summer? Then apply to be a part of THE CAMP AMERICA summer STUDENT EXCHANGE PROGRAMME!" I decided straightaway to apply, imagining the possibility of leaving these shores for the very first time and, if I was lucky enough to be chosen for the programme, it would provide the perfect opportunity to see the USA without it costing me a penny!

60

After the second week in September, the Law course began in earnest and being true to my word in terms of both attitude and approach, I settled down quickly in all my subjects. By the time I was ready to sit the end of year exams in late May early June the following year, I was on course for an overall B grade provided I performed well in my written exams and even if didn't do so well in those exams, the above average marks I was getting for my written pieces of coursework would help cushion any shortfall.

But there was even better news on my horizon. The application that I submitted to be a part of the Camp America experience was successful which meant that towards the end of June, I would be going abroad for the very first time, spending two months in the summer working at an American Summer Camp as a Play leader and once those two months were completed, I would be given the remaining six weeks to go off and explore the rest of the United states before returning back to the UK by mid September. Naturally, I was excited by the whole prospect of living and working abroad in another country and I could hardly wait for the time to arrive but first, there was the small matter of preparing for the end of year examinations. I worked hard and they went fairly smoothly, which meant I could finally turn my attentions to my forthcoming trip to America and the chance to experience a whole new culture that was sure to offer something both new and exciting.

The day of my Camp America adventure had finally arrived and I woke just before the crack of dawn with all the eagerness and excitement of a child who couldn't wait to rip open all his presents on Christmas morning. Winston Davis, my old schoolmate and best friend agreed to take me to Heathrow Airport and judging by my over eagerness to get to the airport, it seemed like we were the first arrivals at Heathrow's Terminal 3 but as soon as we entered the main Terminal Hall, the place was buzzing with loads and loads of passengers criss-crossing the gigantic Terminal foyer, just as eager and excited to get to their own chosen destinations. After Winston helped me carry my luggage towards the long queue that was forming at the Check-In Desk for JFK Airport, we both did a high five before he wished me a safe trip. The long queue of passengers waiting to check in mainly consisted of the Play Scheme workers. I already knew in advance what part of America I was going to. I was going to Boston, Massachusetts, and a remote residential camp named Camp Nelson, situated some ten or so miles from Boston's main City Centre. I was hoping for a more glamorous posting to say, Los Angles on the West Coast or Miami in the sunshine State of Florida, but beggars can't be choosers I suppose and I was just grateful that I was amongst those persons selected to work on the scheme that summer and the opportunity to embark on an exciting new adventure.

Whilst I was waiting in the queue to check-in for the flight, a voice called out, "Shaun, is that you?" I turned to look around to see who was calling my name and to my complete surprise and astonishment, I saw John Jackson, an old friend I hadn't seen since my student days. I wasn't expecting to see anyone that I knew in the queue and John's unexpected presence really was a sight for sore eyes. We greeted each other like long lost brothers and it didn't take us long to discover the amazing coincidence of not only being on the same Camp America programme, but we were actually going to be on the same summer camp. John was also a first year undergraduate studying law but unlike me, he had ambitions to qualify as a Solicitor. The journey couldn't have got off to a better start. Being reunited with an old work colleague and friend for the trip couldn't have provided a better omen that the next three months were going to provide all the fun and excitement I was anticipating and hoping for.

As we waited in the Departure Lounge, John and I eventually got to meet the two other play leaders that we would be working alongside with at Camp Nelson. Rob, a slightly built bespectacled man in his early twenties who came from Holland and Sylvie, a German girl who was also similar in age. I thought straightaway that the four of us were going to get along great. Eventually, we all boarded the plane and as I strapped myself in, my initial concern apart from the natural feeling of apprehension and nervousness that goes hand in hand with being a first time flyer, was whether my tall 6ft plus gangly frame could survive the seven and a half hour journey in a seat that not even Tom Thumb himself would feel comfortable sitting in. After the initial and gradual ascent into the clear blue sky an hour or so after take off, we were allowed to move around the body of the aeroplane which gave me the opportunity to stretch my legs. It also gave me the opportunity to sit down for a while in the spare seat next to John and the pair of us chatted for what seemed like hours on areas ranging from our mutual excitement about the summer camp, to our lives as law undergraduates as well as a nostalgic trip down memory lane talking about the time we spent that summer working at Burger King only four years previously.

Eventually, the plane touched down at JFK International Airport just after 4pm in the afternoon and I emerged from my first ever plane journey pretty much unscathed before being gripped by feelings of excitement and anticipation that finally, at the ripe old age of 21, I was setting foot on foreign soil. Once we had retrieved all our luggage and undergone the rigorous and laborious processing of passengers at the US Immigration Desk, all the Camp America exchange students had to gather together with the assistance of the schemes' Staff Co-ordinators who were on hand to guide us on to the large iconic Yellow Transport Buses they had laid on in order to take us to the hotels that we would be staying in overnight in the centre of Manhattan. As we all filed out of the Terminal, I was consumed by the Big Apple's stifling summer heat that was coming from a skyline dominated by one skyscraper after another that stretched way into the horizon. This is New York City. More grand and exciting than London could ever be and as we travelled along the city's vast multi-laned freeways to Downtown Manhattan, I was utterly fascinated and at times in total awe of the sheer size of the place as I constantly gazed at the sites all around me acting as if I was a curious visitor from another world.

After a good night's rest and my first experience of breakfast American style, a breakfast that was so huge that it would take me two further sittings just to finish it, we were split into groups and met our respective Team Leaders. The Camp Leader in charge of our summer camp was a man called Art Standley, a larger than life jovial figure of a man. Art asked us to gather our belongings as there was a transportation bus waiting to take us on the five hour journey north towards the outskirts of Boston. It was a journey I can honestly say that I was not particularly looking forward to given my notorious aversion to travel sickness on coaches in years gone by. Just as I anticipated, the long journey was not a pleasant experience and it didn't take long before the smell of the bus's emission fumes caused me to suffer a double violent reaction of a nauseating queasy stomach and blinding headache. My poor state of health throughout the journey meant that I could neither enjoy, or indeed appreciate, the spectacular and breath taking scenic views as we travelled through New York State and the adjoining States in between and after almost six hours of non stop travelling, we finally arrived at our destination, a vast secluded forest which was the home of Camp Nelson.

After the team wearily unloaded our belongings in near dead of night, Art took the four of us to meet the other members of staff who we would be working alongside throughout the summer vacation and after that, Art took us to our spartan sleeping quarters. They were three separate huts on wooden plinths on the outskirts of the woods near to the Camp's Reception Centre. Sylvie took one hut to herself, which meant that out of the two remaining huts, one of them would have to be shared between two. Well, the thought of sharing a hut, even with a person that I knew was not an appealing one and I immediately said, "I'll take the hut for the single person Art", before

John or Rob could make a bid for it. I headed to the middle hut, thus leaving John and Rob to decide for themselves which side of the room in the remaining hut they were going to occupy in such a small and confined space. I opened the wooden door of what would be my home for the next two months and turned on the small light switch nearby and I was greeted by the sight of a single iron bed situated next to a small wooden table whilst on the other side of the room was a wardrobe and a solitary washbasin. The intense bright light bulb dangling on the end of a wire hanging from a wooden joist in the ceiling acted like a calling card as moths and other flying insects seemed to appear from nowhere in their droves before immediately gravitating towards the bright shining light. *Welcome to America* I muttered to myself sarcastically, before dumping my belongings in the middle of the floor and going back to the Reception Centre where Art was waiting for the four of us to return in order to show us the all-important washroom facilities. By the time Art had finished his mini tour of the camp, all four of us had a pretty good idea of the lay of the land and afterwards, Art took the four of us all back to the main Reception Centre where he told us to relax and help ourselves to the food and drink in the Kitchen area. It was the perfect opportunity for the four of us to relax and unwind. After helping ourselves to the food and drink that had been provided, Sylvie, Rob, John and I were both refreshed and relaxed and we spent the next couple of hours chatting amongst ourselves getting to know each other which proved to be a good and useful bonding exercise against the backdrop of a quiet secluded wooded paradise far removed from Boston's urban metropolis. But the travails of the arduous journey from Downtown New York to our base camp were slowly beginning to creep up on me and I was the first among the group of four to decide to call it a night. I wanted to get all of my unpacking done before getting a good night's rest. As I made the short walk to my sleeping quarters, I could hear the collective chorus of chirping crickets that shattered the still dead of night. I opened the wooden hut door and confronting my rapidly tiring mind and body were my pieces of unpacked luggage in the middle of the room. It was the last thing I wanted to attend to at that point in time but they weren't going to unpack themselves, so I decided to bite the bullet and set about the task of packing everything away neat and tidily and fairly soon, my small cramped tiny wooden hut began to look something like home from home. Once I had completed that arduous task, I eventually climbed onto the hard, single iron framed bed which just about accommodated my long gangly limbs before pressing the play button on my portable beat-box that I had placed by the side of my bed so that I could relax to some soothing soulful melodies. I reached for my packet of Benson and Hedges cigarettes which I had bought at Duty Free and that first inhalation/exhalation of the smoke from the cigarette represented the deep sigh of satisfaction and contentment of how lucky and fortunate I was for being on foreign soil for the first time in my life and how grateful I was to be so far removed from all the anxieties and uncertainties that seemed to blight my life for the past two years. Tomorrow would be the start of what promised to be two months of carefree fun in the sun and I couldn't wait to get started.

The following morning, I was awoken by the sun's rays that pierced though the various gaps of my wooden home like a crisscross matrix of laser light beams. I gathered all my things together and headed over to the Wash Room Area for a quick shower before changing into my sports gear and making my way to join John, Sylvie and Rob for breakfast. We were expecting the transportation bus carrying the hoards of energetic children just after 9am and we had just over an hour and a half to eat and set up all the equipment that would provide the day's entertainment. Whilst Sylvie and Rob were getting themselves together for the Art and Craft's and nature activities, John and I set about the task of getting out the Camp's sporting equipment for Soccer, Softball and just about everything and anything we hoped would keep the children both interested and entertained and carried them over to the areas set aside for the sporting activities. Just before 9am, the sight and sound of the iconic American Yellow School Bus finally rolled into the Camp Site and all the Camp's staff were on hand to greet the seemingly endless line of seven to ten year olds pouring off the two buses in an excitable yet orderly fashion carrying their satchels or duffle bags containing their packed lunches. The children were escorted and assembled into the main Reception Area where Art formally welcomed them to Camp Nelson before concluding his short address by wishing that everyone taking part in the Camp's activities both today, as well as the rest of the summer, to have fun and an exciting time.

For the next seven weeks, all the staff where going to have our hands full with at least eighty or so fun seeking children who wanted to be amused and entertained. It was of no surprise that most of the children favoured the sporting activities, which meant that both John and I were going to really have to prove our worth. John and I split our group into two, with John taking his group over to the area where he set up a mini soccer pitch. John was more than suitably qualified to take the first soccer session. This was due to the fact that John had acquired his football coaching badges and it was self evident that he'd taken everything in from those sessions by the meticulous way he set up the session in terms of laying out the pitch and small practice areas where the children could learn and practice a sport which even back then was barely on the radar of popular sporting American activities and pastimes.

For my first session, I decided to do something different. I divided my group into two groups, the kicking team and the fielding team, and announced much to their bewilderment, that we were playing a game called Kick Cricket, a combination of Baseball and Cricket which I used to play at my old primary school. The rules were plain and simple. The fielding team's bowler would pitch a football underarm to a kicker from the opposing team who would try to prevent the ball from striking the stumps by kicking it away and once having done so, would have to run some fifteen or so yards square of the stumps and try to make it back in time before the bowler had the chance to bowl him/her out if the kicker was not back in time. The only other way a kicker would be out was if s/he were caught and like Baseball, once three of the kicking team were out, the teams changed places. The children immediately took to both sporting activities on offer particularly the Kick Cricket which was played with all the vibrancy and raucousness of a sporting scene on a field of a typical all American High School. As we walked off with the children to have lunch at the end of the morning session, John and I gave ourselves a self-congratulatory high five on a job well done so far. Working on the premise that "if it ain't broke, don't fix it" it was a case of carrying on the afternoon's session of activities from where we left off and we rotated the children from one play scheme activity to another. Trying to keep a child's interest high in any particular activity or pastime, even for a short period of time is not an easy exercise to achieve let alone, trying to achieve that objective working in the sun's oppressive heat, a factor which didn't make that task any easier but that's what I and my fellow colleagues were hired for. It was our job for the next seven weeks if possible, to ensure that the interest and enthusiasm as play scheme workers remained high, in the range of activities that Camp Nelson had to offer.

The sporting equipment used by the children throughout the day were scattered all over the place and the children responded to the play worker's calls to pack all the equipment away neatly with the minimum of fuss. Once the Camp was tidy and ship-shape, all the children then made their way to the Camp's Reception Centre to pick up their belongings in their lockers and onwards to board the awaiting yellow school busses to take them back into the metropolis and home. The overall consensus was that the first day of the scheme was a stunning success and the hope was that the day itself would serve as the benchmark for the rest of the summer.

Two or so weeks after my arrival at camp, I received a call from my brother Stephen back home in England and he told me that I had received a letter from my Polytechnic. I knew straight away that the contents of the letter were my first year exam results and I wasted no time in demanding that he tear open the envelope and tell me the results. There was a temporary pause in the conversation due to Stephen ripping open the envelope and once he had finished doing so, he read out its following contents:

Criminal Law - Grade B

English Legal System- Grade B

Contract Law - Fail

Politics - Grade B

It goes without saying that I was disappointed by the news. Not just for the fact that it meant that I would have to do another re-sit before the start of the next academic year, but because it would mean that I would have to cut short my American adventure and fly back early at my own expense. All re-sits had to take place in the last week of August and there was no way I was going to forfeit my place on the second year for the sake of three to six weeks of sightseeing. I asked Steve to send me one of my Contract text books and Lecture notes in the post and this setback meant that I would have to organise my time constructively thus enabling me to do my revision studies during my spare free time after the day's activities and whilst the inconvenience of having to do revision for an exam during the summer wasn't something that I planned for, I was determined that I wouldn't let it pray on my mind, nor effect the job I was hired to do for the rest of my time working on the play scheme.

The remainder of the summer scheme was every bit the success that everyone working on the scheme had hoped for and by the time I said all of my fond farewells as I prepared to head back to England in the last week of August, I felt a tinge of sadness that I would be leaving behind a fantastic group of people as well as fantastic working environment that I knew all too well I would probably be seeing for the last time and the only precious thing from the whole Camp America adventure that I would be taking back home with me were the good times as well as the fond memories that will stay with me for the rest of my life.

However, of more immediate concern was the important matter of my Contract Law re-sit, an exam where I could afford no more slip ups otherwise I'd be condemned to the unthinkable nightmare scenario of having to repeat the whole of the first year all over again. A couple of days after returning from America, I contacted the College to see whether my Contract Lecturer, Judy Newton was available but I was told that she was still away on holiday and would not be back until the end of the week. I went up to see my Contract lecturer on the Friday of that week and when I arrived outside her office, it was pretty clear from the sizeable numbers of first year law students waiting around for one to one meetings with the Law lecturers on the course that I was not alone in facing that dreaded repeat exam. At least I only had to retake one exam. Some of my fellow students who were waiting anxiously to discuss their own dire performance in those summer examinations were in the unfortunate position of having to re-sit all four exams. Eventually, I managed to see Judy to discuss my own performance. Judy told me that although I was a few marks short of a passing grade, the areas I needed to work on were my analytical skills in the questions where I was asked to give advice to a fictitious client as well as my ability to use the relevant legal principles in a way so that the client knows where he stands. Judy said I had to start thinking and writing like a lawyer if I wanted to become one. She was spot on of course about my shortcomings and if I didn't take on board her firm but frank assessment, I wouldn't stand much chance of progressing beyond the first year and with the re-sit paper only five days away, I had just enough time to put into practice Judy's constructive and helpful criticisms and hopefully this time, to good effect.

In truth, it was more likely that my complacent attitude towards the subject, by virtue of the fact I studied Contract Law before, that probably cost me a passing grade as I failed to give the subject the same amount of time and effort as I did with my other modules. This setback was the wakeup call that I needed as it was patently clear that I still hadn't fully learned the lessons of all those harsh and painful setbacks of summers past when the deadly cocktail of hubris, pride and over confidence almost fatally undermined my academic ambition but now wasn't the time to dwell on such negative sentiments. I had to make those necessary adjustments both to my exam technique and analytical approach to all of my subjects, not just the forthcoming re-sit exam because if I don't manage to turn things around in time, then the haunting nightmare of academic failure and under achievement would return with a vengeance.

Those very same thoughts and sentiments ran through my mind fleetingly as myself and the seven or so other candidates were given the instruction to turn over the Law of Contract question paper in one of the small rooms in the Arts and Humanities Department on the day of the re-sit exam. I was determined to use those fleeting thoughts, not as a means of fear and terror, but as a means of inspiration and motivation when I saw the contents of the question paper which on the face of it appeared to present no real difficulties. I set about the task of putting everything that I had taken on board from my one to one session with Judy Newton into practice and with no margin for error, I had to ensure that I answered all the of questions within the time allowed. Thankfully at the end of three gruelling hours, I felt pretty confident that my objectives had been accomplished.

Three days later, the college informed me of the results of my re-sit by telephone and to my obvious delight and relief, I made it into the second year. I was extremely fortunate this time that I managed to squeeze through by the skin of my teeth and if I learned anything from the whole nerve wracking experience it was not to treat the course lightly or to take anything for granted because if I do and find myself in similar sticky situation, the next time I might not be so lucky.

CHAPTER FIVE

With the end of Fresher's week, the following Monday marked the start of the new academic term. I made all the usual well-meaning solemn promises to myself that I would work hard and show commitment in the hope that I had learned from the mistakes from the past that almost brought my continued participation on the course to a premature end. I couldn't afford any more slip ups. Out of the original fifty or so students from the first year, ten failed to make the cut as a consequence of either quitting the course altogether or having suffered the indignity of repeating the whole year. My main goals and objectives for the forthcoming academic year would be to pass and to pass well enough to set me up for one big effort in the final year and to leave the Polytechnic with my head held high and a Degree classification that I can be proud of.

The three core subjects I would have to get to grips with in the second year were Constitutional Law taught by the lecturer who interviewed me when I applied to join the course, Jeanette Harden. The Law of Tort, a subject that like the Law of Contract I covered extensively both at O Level and A level taught by Sue Knight and last, but by no means least, the legal subject that is the scourge of almost every law undergraduate, the Law of Property taught by Angela Sydenham. They weren't the most daunting subjects in the world but by the same token, they were not subjects to be taken lightly either. If I stuck to the game plan of working hard and matching that work with total commitment then I saw no reason why I couldn't achieve continued academic success.

Academic success wasn't the only objective on my agenda for the forthcoming year. The free Wednesday afternoons I had were going to provide the catalyst of a genuine but, admittedly, absurd fantasy that I was going to become Britain's first black qualified barrister to play professional football.

I wouldn't be too wide of the mark when I say that it's virtually every young boy's dream to be a professional footballer; scoring loads of goals playing for your favourite team, going on to win of International cups for England, and I was no different. But in my formative years, I could hardly be described as a budding George Best or a future Pele, that would be too farfetched to even be remotely fanciful. There could be no better illustration of that point when, at the age of fourteen, I told Mum that I had been invited by my beloved Chelsea Football Club to attend their football trials after I had written to them, and she crushed all my hopes and excitement of making the grade with her dismissive response, "Best footballer at Chelsea? You're not even the best footballer in your own household!"

I grew up in an area where most of the friends I hung around with were very good footballers. My classmates, Junior and Trevor, were part of a defensive back four in our primary school team, a team I was so desperate to be a part of but sadly wasn't good enough to be chosen. I always used to feel a great deal of both sadness and envy when Mr Thomas, our primary school PE teacher, would call some of the boys in my class for training after school whenever there were any upcoming matches against other schools, but not me. I was determined to improve my abilities as an outfield player but whenever I got together with my friends to play football in our local park right behind my back garden, my efforts to improve my skills were usually thwarted because when it came to picking teams before the start of a game, I was, more often than not, one of the last to get picked and that usually meant I had to play in goal. I would always complain that it was not fair but whenever I protested, I would be met by the immediate hollow and insincere reply that I was brilliant at saving goals and the promise that I would get my chance at some point during the game, a promise that was rarely kept. As time went on, I became quite useful as a goalkeeper, a feat achieved in no small part, to the many hours I used to spend in one or in shooting practice with my close friend and first footballing hero, Selvin Campbell. Selvin was a year older than me and he lived with his family ten houses down the road from where I lived. Selvin lived, slept and breathed football and his obsession and dedication was such he would spend day after day practicing his heading, dribbling and shooting skills relentlessly before constantly badgering me to follow him to the football pitch at the back of his garden where we would practice for hours on end (on one memorable occasion, even on Christmas Day!) where Selvin would take pot shots at me using either foot whilst I would be trying my dammed hardest to save them. Selvin was, so far as I was concerned, the most naturally gifted footballer on our street and even though he didn't play professionally (a choice of his own making having turned down the opportunity to sign for Wimbledon's Crazy Gang in the mid 1980's on account of the fact that the money they were offering at the time wasn't sufficient or enticing enough for him to give up his stable and secure full time job), he played to a good standard at non-league level for a host of both London and the Home Counties and had a two season stint in New Zealand. Only one of the original Monks Park boys who I grew with went on to make the grade as a professional footballer and that was another close and lifelong friend of mine, Dale Banton, who lived with his Mum and Dad and younger brother Cary (who was a good footballer in his own right) only a stone's throw away from me.

I learnt a lot from footballing maestros like Selvin and Dale and whilst I could never claim to possess even a small fraction of their respective footballing abilities, I finally managed to get picked to play for a football team when at the football trials that were held during my first few weeks at Copland High School, I managed to catch the eye of Mr Hassell, my form teacher in the first year, who managed a team that was a mixture of first and second year boys, with an unlikely piece of skill that saw me glide past four players that put me through with a clear run on goal. In all my years of playing football, I'd never come even close to doing something so spectacular on a football field. Sadly for me though, my brilliant, if slightly fortuitous piece of skill ended in complete anti-climax when the excitement of the moment got the better of me and my lack of composure at the crucial moment caused me to blast the ball way past the post only six yards from goal. Despite that horrendous miss, it was enough to convince Mr Hassell that I was worth a place in the starting line at centre forward alongside my classmate, Stephen Cook, for the first game of the season against Aylestone High School, much to the surprise and consternation of many of the players from the first and second years who attended the trials and failed to make the team, most notably, my own footballing idol and mentor Selvin Campbell. The match itself however from a personal perspective, turned out to be a forgettable and inauspicious debut for me as a combination of uncontrollable nerves, allied to the pressure of having to justify my inclusion in the team ahead of players who clearly had better footballing abilities than my own, led to me having a really poor game and I was substituted at half time.

I had a largely undistinguished footballing career during my teenage years at Copland. I drifted in and out of the side in my first year at school and in the following year, not even making the squad altogether but during the third and fourth years at the school, I had managed to get back into the squad and played a part in the school's only Cup success when the team won the 1975 Brent Cup Final thanks to Glenmore Johnson's glorious twenty five yard strike just outside the Penalty Area in a 2-1 victory over our perennial nemesis and arch rivals, the highly talented Willesden High School.

Every footballer, whether they be professional or amateur, sublimely gifted or otherwise, has at one time or another, had at least one magical performance in them and my finest moments on a football field occurred in the Spring of 1978 whilst playing for the Aylestone Sixth Form in the Brent Cup final against Preston Manor. In the matches leading up to the game, I was unable to hold down a regular spot in the team mainly due to injury and indifferent form but in the training sessions before the final, I had done enough to convince the team's Manager, the Science teacher Hubert Bukari, that I was worthy of a place in the starting line-up and when he handed me the number nine shirt when selecting the eleven players who would start the match, I was determined to give a performance that would justify the Manager's faith.

Our opponents, Preston Manor, were no strangers to me because I had played against the vast majority of their players whilst playing for Copland and given the close nature of all of those games, I knew that the outcome of the final could go either way. Two of their players, the Goalkeeper, Paul Bullard and Midfielder, David Carr, were in my primary school class at Oakington Manor and their exceptional footballing abilities ensured that they were permanent fixtures. Another one of their players, Michael Webster, a talented and gifted footballer who always was a danger with the ball at his feet was Preston Manor's Captain and the cousin of the Captain of our team, Chris Sweeney, who was playing at Centre Half.

As the teams walked on to the cheers of some eighty to a hundred students, I was doing my level best to control the butterflies in my stomach. My playing partner up front was lightning quick and a prolific goal machine, Glenmore Johnson, who scored many a goal when I played with him at Copland High and he continued that same scoring prowess with Aylestone. Preston Manor kicked off to start the game and from the first whistle, they were on the front foot stroking the ball around confidently and with purpose which, allied to intelligent movement of their players both on and off the ball and their constant communication meant that they had complete control of the early stages of the game with Michael Webster at the hub of the team's creative play. By contrast, Aylestone's start to the game could be aptly described by reference to those well-known footballing clichés, "running around like headless chickens" and "chasing shadows." It seemed only a matter of time before Preston Manor's dominance would gain some tangible reward and in the tenth minute, they scored as a result of a neat exchange of passes which was converted by their main striker to give them a fully deserved lead. As the teams were trotting back to line up for the restart, the confident noises coming out the mouths of our opponents signalled their desire to take a stranglehold of the game and score another goal. Their goal was a massive shock to our system and we were disappointed collectively as a team for conceding so easily and early in the game and as our team took up their positions for the restart, we resorted to good old-fashioned clapping and shouting words of encouragement in an effort to get back on level terms as soon as possible.

Chris and the rest of our defenders were under siege trying to repel another assault on our goal and as the ball was whipped in to the heart of our Penalty Area, only the bravery of our goalkeeper, William O'Brien, whose playing style and manner was reminiscent to that of Ray Clemence, the Liverpool and England goalkeeper, saved the day when he managed to punch the ball clear and away from the Penalty Area and immediate danger. Our team were barely hanging on by its fingernails and whilst collectively as a team we couldn't be faulted for effort and determination, all of those attributes counted for nothing if you haven't got control of the ball. After about twenty-five minutes, there was no real change in either the tempo or overall pattern of the game but a misplaced pass by their big Centre Half not only changed our team's immediate fortunes, it also served as a catalyst for the performance of a lifetime.

I was standing some ten yards off that miss hit pass which hit me straight in the midriff but instead of the ball ricocheting away in a different direction, it fell fortuitously only a yard in front of me and all of a sudden, I was presented with a glorious chance to get the team back in contention. I looked up momentarily and noticed that their Centre Half was the only defender protecting the goalkeeper and as he lunged forward in a last desperate attempt to recover his error, I quickly nudged the ball past him and that gave me a clear run in on goal. A mixture nervousness and excitement engulfed me straight away as I entered the Penalty Area, totally unchecked or unchallenged. In front of me stood the opposing goalkeeper who was now on heightened alert and ready to spring into action and trailing in my wake was the Centre Half straining every sinew in a desperate attempt to rectify his error but unfortunately for him I was beyond his reach. I had reached the penalty spot by now and I had to make up my mind of how I was going to convert this opportunity. The goalkeeper who was standing just off of his goal line, then took a quick step forward off it as he tried to make himself big enough to narrow the angle of my shooting opportunities, but as soon he made his move, I had made mine and I placed a firm right foot shot right in the corner of the net by his right hand post before he had the chance to steady himself. I bowed my head and clenched both fists together tightly as a reaction to the immense delight and sheer relief that I held my nerve to equalise and get the team back on level terms. As the team trotted back to the centre circle for the restart, I was greeted with a mixture of hugs and high fives from some of my team mates as the goal gave the team a much-needed confidence boost. The confidence

I personally gained from scoring our first goal saw a dramatic improvement in my overall playing style doing exactly what a Centre Forward leading the line was supposed to do: controlling the ball whenever it was played to my feet or chest and laying it off with precision timing to one of my supporting teammates, winning a greater share of the aerial battles against the Centre Half assigned to mark me during the game who prior to his unfortunate mistake, had the upper hand. There was also a noticeable and significant improvement in my overall movement across the whole of Preston Manor's defensive back four, by making runs that were starting to disrupt and unsettle them to such an extent that they were increasingly becoming more and more unsure of themselves. Whenever I had the ball at my feet facing the opponent's goal, I was playing with an unrestrained, carefree abandon, taking on and beating the opposition defenders time after time as the momentum of the game appeared to be turning in our favour. The game was now simmering perfectly to the boil and there was a ten minute spell when most of the action was being played in our opponent's half. But just as our team were beginning to establish gradual parity with our talented opponents, we suddenly found ourselves two goals down thanks to two well taken chances by their strikers in quick succession to put them firmly in the driving seat before the referee blew his whistle to signal half time. The team trudged off towards the Dressing Room bemused and disappointed that after competing so well how our fortunes had taken such a dramatic turn for the worse.

The minute the team got into the Dressing Room, everyone made a dash for the plastic bags containing sliced oranges and the large bottles of water that were on top of the wooden table in the middle of the room. The collective sentiment was that we were matching our opponents in terms of skill and effort but if we wanted to get back on level terms, we couldn't afford to concede any more goals. Our manager, Mr Bukari, echoed those same sentiments during his half time team talk and he made it clear that we were more than capable of getting back into the game. He added that as a collective unit, we were playing well going forward but not so cohesive a unit when it came to defending from the forwards to the defence and he gave the order to both Glenmore and me to defend from the front which would mean stopping the opposition from playing the ball out from the back to their midfield players and build possession, a tactic which was providing a platform for their dominance.

The Second Half was pure end to end attacking football with both teams really going for it in their efforts to score the next goal which could prove to be an important turning point for either team.

Chances to make that all important breakthrough were coming and going for both sides at an alarming rate and it was only a matter of time before either team scored and just after the half hour mark, that breakthrough fell our way when a clever pass from Arnold Kerliew, our own midfield general, caught the Preston Manor back four who were playing too far up on the halfway line and they could not react quick enough to Glenmore's perfectly timed run which put the speedy goal machine clean through. Glenmore was in a one on one situation similar to the chance presented to me in the first half and like me, wasted no time in dispatching the opportunity to give us a much-needed lifeline. Glenmore didn't celebrate his well taken goal. After he put away the opportunity, Glenmore ran straight past the opposing goalkeeper, eager to get on with the game. Glenmore's actions were a clear sign to Preston Manor that we were right back in the game and with just under twenty minutes to go, we had more than enough time to retrieve the one goal deficit. Preston Manor seemed shaken by that second goal but were by no means stirred and they continued playing their football to the same high standard.

With just under ten minutes to go, our team managed to win ourselves a free kick some ten or so yards outside Preston Manor's Penalty Area. As Preston Manor lined up their four man wall, myself, Arnie and our team captain Chris were standing over the ball having our own private discussions as to which one of us was going to take it. I had never taken a free kick before, but I wanted to take this one. I was playing out of my skin and I insisted to both Arnie and Chris that I was confident that I could put the ball in the back of the net. Sadly, with both the team's Captain and Vice-Captain standing over the ball, my pleas fell on deaf ears. Chris pulled rank and he struck the ball with one of his trademark pile drivers. But alas, in the words of that great Scottish Bard, Robert Burns, "the best laid plans of mice and men," Chris' effort went sailing over the Preston Manor crossbar in a manoeuvre more suited to either code of Rugby than a game of football and he turned away and trotted back to his defensive duties, cursing himself. To his credit though, he didn't let it affect him or his game and he continued to drive the team forward

However, some five or so minutes later, the team won another free kick near the same spot as Chris' lamentable effort. Over the ball were the same three protagonists, myself, Arnie and Chris, pondering the same pressing problem as to which one of us was going to take responsibility for taking the kick and with the sands of time slowly ebbing away, one of us had to come up with something special. Before Chris and Arnie could say anything, I turned to the pair of them and said, "guys, Let me have a go!" The pair of them had no answer this time and with that I bent down slightly and placed the ball with precision and care on the ground with both hands and when I straightened myself, I took no more than six measured paces backwards and paused as I awaited the referee's signal. Once the referee blew his whistle, I ran up to the ball at an angle and curled a right foot shot that cleared the wall and nestled perfectly inside the right hand post, the goalkeeper's despairing dive counting for nothing. I turned away and ran towards the stands and opened my arms out as wide as I could to milk the applause before being engulfed by most of my teammates. As we trotted back to the centre circle, the applause still ringing in my ears above the noise, I saw Chris, who didn't join in the mad celebrations, trotting backwards back into position with a big sheepish smile on his face.

"What are you wearing, Billy's Boots?"

I gave him the thumbs up to acknowledge his sarcastic remark and as a gesture which conveyed the reply, "That's how you do it, my son!"

With the game deadlocked at 3-3 there was everything to play for. On the balance of play, we deserved to be level but in football, a team is at their most vulnerable when they've just scored and a couple of minutes after managing to finally get ourselves back on level terms, the team momentarily switched off and as a result, Preston Manor broke down the other end and scored another goal and their players ran to stands where their supporters were standing wildly celebrating in the belief that they had delivered a decisive blow. I looked around at some of my teammates and for the first time I could see one or two heads drop, seemingly resigned to the fact that the match had slipped through our fingers. Our Manager though, was having none of it. As we lined up to restart the game, he was clapping his hands frantically urging one last effort and to keep going until the last note of the final whistle. With less than two minutes on the clock, the team had no choice than to throw caution to the wind and go for broke. Both teams were becoming increasingly desperate albeit for entirely different reasons. Preston Manor, now only minutes from glory, had adopted the tactic of getting virtually all their men behind the ball and frantically defending their goal as though their lives depended on it, whilst leaving their main goal threat hovering in and around the centre circle waiting for any sniff of a quick counter attack that would put the game beyond our reach once and for all. Aylestone by contrast were, metaphorically speaking, drinking in the last chance saloon as our tactics resorted to the crude and desperate tactic of route one football which required nothing more than simply getting the ball into our opponent's Penalty Area with as many bodies in support in order to create as much panic and confusion in their ranks and hope that the ball would fall kindly to one of our players. Not pretty without a doubt, but when a team is frantically chasing the game, it's probably the best chance a team has of salvaging something and when they conceded another free kick approximately thirty yards from their goal with less than a minute to go before the final whistle, it was time to put that desperate plan into action.

Just after the team won the free kick, I rushed over to where the ball was as I wanted to try and replicate my goal scoring effort only ten minutes previously and given my confident mood that seemed now to be without limit, I saw no reason as to why I couldn't repeat the same feat. But my plans for personal glory were thwarted when Chris bellowed from the half way line for me to leave the ball to our Left Back, Greg Pendle, to deliver the cross and get in the Penalty Area. I wasn't going to argue with Chris given the situation we were in and I quickly ran into the Penalty Area, feinting first to my left and to my right in an effort to try and lose and confuse the defenders designated to mark me but as Greg delivered the free kick, instinctively I decided that given the Penalty Area was crowded, I'd give it a wide berth and took up a position just outside it, waiting and hoping for any chance that could possibly fall my way. My gamble proved to be spot on because the Preston Manor defenders tried to clear their lines with a poorly executed headed clearance which fell perfectly to me at chest height. I controlled it, before allowing the ball to drop to my right foot and then smashed it in the net giving their goalkeeper absolutely no chance whatsoever. I again ran towards the stands where our supporters were standing with both arms outstretched with the pure self-indulgent aim of milking the applause that a strike like that richly deserves. But just before I could put that plan into action, an avalanche of excitable, grateful teammates piled on top me immediately causing me to end up on my back with my arms still outstretched like a windmill. Once we had finished our celebrations, we trotted back to our own half to confront a dejected looking Preston Manor side ready to restart the game and after their second touch of the ball after the kick off, the referee blew the whistle to signal the end of the game.

As both teams trooped off to our respective ends, I immediately began to feel aches and pains all over my body, a product no doubt of the hard, strength sapping ninety minute contest which was compounded by being at the bottom of the pile of my over exuberant teammates. All the players headed straight to our manager and a desperate scramble for whatever was left of the water and oranges we had consumed at half time began in earnest. Given the fact that my lower back was beginning to seize up at this point, I wasn't going to get involved in that particular dogfight and I decided, somewhat ill advisedly, to collapse in a crumpled heap tired, extremely thirsty and worst of all, not knowing how on God's earth I was going to get up on my feet again. The rest of my teammates were also feeling the effects of a gruelling physical contest. Some of them were walking about trying to prevent the build up of lactic acid from seizing up completely, whilst others were like me slumped on their haunches.

In his team talk, Mr Bukari was full of praise for the team's collective tenacity and fighting spirit in refusing to lie down and he made the clarion call for one last monumental effort in extra time and told us that if we kept on playing to the same levels of intensity as we had done in the previous ninety minutes, then he saw no reason why we wouldn't end up with the spoils of victory. But the near moribund state that both myself and some of my teammates were in, another half an hour of extra time playing with the same levels of intensity as we had done over the previous ninety minutes could prove to be one step too far.

In a frantic effort to get ready for extra time, I began pulling both knees to my chest, holding that position for as long as I could before releasing it that somehow managed to provide some respite to my lower back that was tightening with each passing second. Mr Bukari came over to me and asked if I was ok to continue and I replied tentatively that I was ok before finally managing to get myself upright. All of our substitutes were used up by now and playing with a man down was simply not an option. Whatever aches and pains that were torturing my body as I ran onto the field would have to be put to the back of my mind as the prospect of team glory was up for grabs. The team who showed the greater urgency and desire were the ones who were going to grab the spoils and it was Preston Manor who showed that desire when it mattered most when a couple of minutes into extra time, their dangerous centre forward who was a constant menace throughout the entire game was at the end of a counter attacking move which saw him complete his own well deserved hat trick to give his side a crucial lead. That goal was a cruel blow to the team. The last thing we wanted was to be chasing the game once more whilst at the very end of our physical and mental limits. But to the team's credit, our heads didn't drop and we continued to play the type of football that let the opposition know we had no intention of lying down. "We're still in this game," was the message that reverberated around the team as Glenmore and I restarted the game for the eighth time and for the remainder of the half, we tried everything to get back on level terms, going close on a couple of occasions, but the Preston Manor defence were standing firm and refusing to give way. We threw everything including the proverbial kitchen sink at our opponents in a frantically desperate attempt to get back on level terms. Preston Manor were defending their slender lead as if their lives depended on it whilst at the same time were on the lookout for the counter attacking opportunity that would end our valiant challenge once and for all.

With the game rapidly approaching the end of extra time, Preston Manor conceded a free kick some ten or so yards outside of their own Penalty Area as we relentlessly pursued yet another equaliser. Some of the players in their team expressed their collective disgust at the referee's decision to award us the free kick but the referee simply brushed aside their protests and made it clear that he would not change his mind. Preston Manor were now on red alert as the frantic calls to form a defensive wall reverberated throughout their team to summon one last effort to prevent a repeat of conceding another free kick goal at the death. By contrast, virtually all of our players were eagerly hovering around the ball, vying for the honour of being the team's saviour at its hour of need. "I'm taking It!" I boldly declared and given my general performance which resulted in me scoring a hat trick, my declaration was a direct challenge to any of my teammates who harboured any notion that they were going to take it as I barked out the order for everyone to pour forward into the opposition's Penalty Area. As I placed the ball on the ground before walking slowly back a couple of paces, all I could think of was that lightning was going to strike once more and instead of floating the ball into their Penalty Area in the hope that one of my team mates would be at the end of it, I decided that I was going to roll the dice one more time and go for a direct strike on goal.

The Penalty Area was a hive of frantic jostling activity. Players from both sides were desperately either trying to defend, or attack space. The opposing goalkeeper's voice could be heard above everyone else during the frantic confusion, bellowing loudly to his defensive wall clear and firm instructions to stay both strong and alert. Although their goalkeeper was brave and agile, he wasn't exactly the tallest goalkeeper in the world and the only way was to aim for either of the top corners of the goal. There was only one thing on my mind as I approached the ball: hit the target and instant glory would be all mine. I couldn't have struck the ball any better and my attempt easily cleared their defensive wall and the goalkeeper, who took up his position in the centre of his goal, could do nothing other than stand helplessly rooted on his line, a mere spectator as the ball arrowed towards the top left hand upright of his goal post. But in a cruel twist of fate, just as I began to believe that my effort had saved our team yet again, the ball clipped the outside of the post and away for the goal kick, much to the relief of the goalkeeper and the rest of his teammates.

Both myself and my teammates knew that our chance of getting something out of the game was well and truly gone and once the goalkeeper cleared the ball out of his Penalty Area, the referee blew his whistle for the final time which was the cue for wild celebrations of hugs and self-congratulations from the victorious Preston Manor team before players from both sides shook hands and embraced each other for what was truly an exciting and hard fought game. I could barely walk at the end of the final whistle. I was reduced to moving at hobbling pace as we went to receive our loser's medals from the Mayor of Brent, the only tangible reward the team had to show for all that collective skill and effort in what turned out to be a disappointing anti-climax.

On a personal level, I was more than pleased with my contribution throughout the game and the three goals I scored in my so called, "Billy's Boots" performance will live with me to the end of my days. The important and valuable lesson that I took from the game was a lesson that was far more valuable than a mere runner's up medal. No matter how good you are, no matter how hard one may work in terms of commitment and dedication, it will all count for nothing if it doesn't realise your ultimate goals or ambitions because at the end of the day, nobody remembers, or indeed cares, who finished second.

That game of a lifetime was over three and a half years ago and because of the trials and traumas of having to sit as well as retake my A Levels, I never had the time to either play football let alone have the temerity to even think that I was good enough to play the game professionally so why, at the age of twenty one, without the requisite natural ability, pedigree, or reputation to fall back upon, did I suddenly believe that I could make this dramatic transformation from park player to professional footballer? What about those long held cherished dreams I had of being a great and celebrated barrister and all the hard work and sacrifice that I had made up to that point in order to keep those dreams alive? Were they simply going to be cast aside for the sake of an outrageous fantasy that hardly seems achievable? Well that's the whole point about dreams I suppose. Anything in life, even the most unforeseen and most unlikely things can happen – and it could happen to ANYBODY! But if you want to make those dreams and ambitions a reality, no matter how remote, fanciful or unlikely they appear to be, they can only become a reality through the usual attributes of sheer hard work, dedication, determination and not forgetting, that all important large slice of good fortune. My decision to try to become a professional footballer didn't mean that all of a sudden I had forsaken all those long held childhood ambitions to qualify as a lawyer, it was now the case that those ambitions were going to share centre stage alongside another set of ambitions, and only time will tell whether it was possible for these twinned ambitions to become a reality.

The possibility of combining the heavy demands of sport alongside the equally demanding requirements of academic study was not a fanciful one as there were plenty of inspiring examples of footballers at the very top of the professional game who demonstrated that it really was possible. Osvaldo Ardiles, the Tottenham Hotspur legend who won the World Cup with Argentina three years previously qualified as a lawyer in his native homeland. The Liverpool stars Steve Heighway and Brian Hall were themselves university degree graduates before they embarked on their successful footballing careers in the 1970's. Steve Coppell of Manchester United fame made the transformation from Economics graduate at Tranmere Rovers to England international. Paul Power, the Manchester City Captain who led his team to the FA Cup Final the previous season was a law graduate. Even the great Brazilian footballing midfield maestro, Socrates, who was the reigning South American footballer of the year at the time, was a qualified Doctor who managed to continue a top class career as a professional footballer.

It was these role models that I looked to as my source for inspiration when I attended the football trials that were being held at the Polytechnic's Sports Ground in Stanmore. I had a really good game in that trial, even managing to help myself to a couple of goals in the process, but my scoring prowess sadly wasn't enough to get me into the Polytechnic's first eleven and I had to settle for the second string instead. This wasn't the greatest of starts to my footballing ambitions, but I wasn't going to allow the minor setback of reserve team football to be the end of them. The following Wednesday afternoon was the start of the season's fixtures and from my perspective, the perfect platform to show what I can do. Sadly though, my pre-match bravado wasn't matched by my on field performance, failing miserably to convert a host of chances that fell my way, much to my frustration and disappointment, and after the referee blew final whistle, the team were lucky to come away with a draw.

The following Wednesday, the team had to play a Cup match at our home ground in Stanmore. The game was no more than fifteen minutes old when I had a golden opportunity to open my account for the team. I received a glorious pass that put me clean through into the opposing team's Penalty Area, but before I could shoot, I was hacked down from behind by the opposing team's centre half as he desperately sought to prevent me from scoring. I immediately seized the ball and placed it to spot, before taking slow, measured backward steps in an effort to compose myself. Once the referee blew his whistle, I quickened my stride towards the ball, having decided beforehand that I was going to place it high and wide to the goalkeeper's left hand side. I struck the ball in the intended direction, only to see, much to my disgust and horror, the ball sail over the cross bar landing some thirty or so metres onto an adjoining playing field. I wanted the ground to open up and swallow me, but I couldn't dwell on my miserable effort. I had to keep my head up and somehow try to put it to the back of my mind and hope that I would get another chance at some point during the game.

Thankfully, the team didn't let my penalty blunder affect our overall game plan and we continued to take the game to the opposition. After constant and sustained pressure, my teammates presented me with another glorious chance and this time I didn't need asking twice, timing my run to perfection, beating the offside trap which left me in a one on one showdown with the opposing goalkeeper. As he rushed off his line, trying desperately to narrow all possible angles, I shifted the ball quickly which completely wrong footed him leaving me with the simple task of tapping the ball into an empty net to give us a deserved 1-0. It was a massive personal relief to have finally opened my goal scoring account for the team and with the burden of expectation now lifted from my shoulders, all I wanted to do was score more goals and thankfully, I didn't disappoint, adding a further two goals to put us three goals to the good at the interval. Those half time oranges couldn't have tasted any sweeter and I was chomping at the bit to get back on the pitch as our opponents seemed to have lost the will to compete and were clearly there for the taking.

We started the second half just as we had ended the first, imposing our game on the opposition and my thirst for scoring goals was suitably quenched when I added two more goals and the match ended with an emphatic 5-1 victory. It was a wonderful team effort and I certainly couldn't have achieved that personal milestone without the help of my teammates.

As the two teams were walking off the pitch towards the Dressing Rooms, players from both sides came up to me and shook my hand. Inwardly, I couldn't have been more pleased with myself and even though the game was only the first round of a comparatively speaking insignificant College Cup competition as opposed to a game in the English First Division or at the World Cup, it was still nevertheless an outstanding achievement to score five goals in one game, a feat that I will always be proud of.

That five goal haul wasn't the only highlight in terms of my prowess in front of goal on the football field and my goal scoring feats for the second string eventually led to a call up into the college's first eleven by the middle of the second term where I remained an ever present fixture, ending the season having scored a total of nineteen goals. You can imagine all sorts of thoughts and visions were buzzing around in my mind when I reflected on my first season of undergraduate football. I believed that I could translate my goal scoring prowess from the lower reaches of College football, to the rarefied ranks of the professional game. Wildly optimistic I agree, but I was at a period in my life where I believed that even the wildest of all my fantasies and dreams were achievable and nothing, not even the cold harsh winds of reality was going to prevent them from being realised.

Meanwhile, my progress on the second year of my law degree course could best be described as three quarters manageable, with the remaining quarter a constant struggle. Constitutional Law with Jeanette Harden was thoroughly enjoyable, so was the Law of Tort and my non-legal option, International Relations. The one topic on the second year that was proving to be extremely difficult to both understand and come to terms with was the dreaded Law of Property. The lectures and seminars with Angela Sydenham was all a mass of white noise so far as I was concerned, despite her best efforts to make the course as intelligible and interesting as possible. I wasn't alone in my loathing for Property Law. By common consensus, it was the subject that students on the second year detested and there was a collective source of fear in all of us about how difficult a challenge passing the end of year exam was going to be. In spite all the problems I was having with the subject, I still managed to attain a Grade B for each of the three written pieces of coursework, a feat which gave me an overall average of 2:2, which to be honest, was all the more astonishing as it was gratifying as those grades could make all the difference in the final reckoning.

By the beginning of the Easter Term, all the formal lectures and seminars had been completed and from here on in, everything was geared to the end of year written examinations. My revision programme in that time formed the basis of the upturn in my exam success at the beginning of the 1980's and I saw no need to change it. It was a hard, cumbersome slog working some five to six hours per day, every day, and there were times when I felt that this whole effort and sacrifice was just too much. No sooner had those negative thoughts of throwing in the proverbial towel momentarily crossed my mind, they were quickly dispelled with equal measure once I reminded myself of the sole reason why I was doing all this hard work and those positive thoughts in themselves were more than enough to reset and refocus my efforts and get on with those preparations.

I attended the revision lectures in all my subjects, especially those in Property Law where Angela Sydenham had helpfully prepared a small pale green revision pamphlet which managed to condense the course into a palatable, digestible and more importantly, comprehensible form, a form upon which I and I suspect, all my fellow students were pinning all our hopes for success upon. The first of those exams was in Constitutional Law which was followed some two or so days later by Tort and after having sat those papers, I left both of those exams with no undue concerns or worries and felt that my exam objectives were going to plan. The sternest test though was yet to come as the next paper I had to sit some three days later was the one I was dreading most of all: Property Law.

Approximately fifteen or so minutes before the start of the exam, all the second year students made our way to one of the college's Lecture Rooms on the third floor and went to our respective writing desks to be greeted by the sight of the question sheet facing downwards laying neatly adjacent to the answer booklet. At the stroke of 10am, Angela gave the command for all the candidates to turn over the question sheets. I turned over the script and as I glanced through the questions quickly, my first thought was *I think I'm going to struggle here...!* Anxiety quickly turned to near utter panic and I tried to regain some sense of composure and read through the questions again. I noticed from the corner of my eye one of my fellow students followed in rapid succession by at least three to four other students suddenly arise from their seats and head towards the exit only to reappear minutes later, to return to the fray. They must have been overcome, like I was, at the sight of reading the questions and probably needed some respite to relieve the pressure of the situation. I still hadn't come to grips with how on earth was I going to get through the next three hours and without any thought or regard to the fact that time was slipping away all of a sudden, I rose from my desk and headed straight for the exit door for the nearby toilets, not just to relieve myself, but also to help me regain some much needed composure. I returned to my desk a few minutes later, in a much calmer state than I had left it moments earlier and after a few deep breaths, set about reading the questions once more and the panic induced eyes that read the questions initially were replaced by a set of eyes that finally realised that there were questions on the paper that I could answer and I set about the task of answering the questions in the answer booklet with the hundred and seventy or so minutes that remained.

With five minutes left on the clock in the examination hall, Angela reminded all the candidates to allow sufficient time to read over our scripts before the end. Thankfully, I managed to somehow to make up the lost time due to my panic stricken moments at the start and answered the four questions that was required and when I finally left the examination hall, I breathed a massive sigh of relief that the baptism of fire was finally behind me and with fingers crossed, I would never have to encounter Property Law ever again.

There was only one more exam left to face, International Relations, an exam which, in comparison to the other three subjects, wasn't going to present any challenges and after that, I was free. Free to put my law studies on the back burner at least until the landing of the envelope on my doormat containing my exam results and that particular ordeal wouldn't take place until the first week in July. For now, the order of the day was to relax, be happy and enjoy the summer and what a festive summer of fun and enjoyment I had coming my way. Starting in mid July going right up until the last week in August, I managed to secure another stint as a summer Play Scheme Worker on one of the various Play schemes that the Borough of Brent were running throughout the summer. But that wouldn't start for another month or so and with all that spare time on my hands, I had the perfect opportunity to sit back, relax and watch the greatest sporting spectacle on earth that began right in the middle of a hectic exam schedule, the 1982 World Cup in Spain.

The 1982 World Cup was a wonderful tournament with twenty four teams competing ranging from the traditional powerhouses such as Brazil, Italy and for the first time since 1970, England to the minnows such as Kuwait, Algeria and Billy Bingham's Northern Ireland, all vying for the honour of being crowned World Champion on Sunday the 11th of July. The World Cup wasn't solely devoted to simply watching the showpiece spectacle, it was also a time for playing the game itself and Monks Park was no different to any other public park up and down the land, packed with wannabe footballers who like me, were gripped by World Cup fever. These matches were intense and competitive with the players trying desperately to recreate the skills of say, the Brazilian maestro Zico, or the young footballing genius, Diego Maradona, and after the game was finished, there was always lively post match banter about who was the top man. Naturally, I was a part of this footballing obsession which was hardly surprising, after having just come off the back of a highly productive goal scoring season with my college football team. I was determined to display my footballing skills as an outfield player, flatly refusing the demands for me to play in goal as I wanted to prove that my goal scoring prowess was no idle boast. These matches in the park only served to add further fuel to my secret ambition and desire to combine law and professional football. But the wide green open spaces of Monks Park could hardly be described as a football hotspot that would have the top football scouts coming down in their droves to pluck anyone of us from total obscurity to footballing superstardom. Therefore if I was serious about pursuing my clandestine ambition to pursue a career in professional football, then the only possible way to shorten those nigh on impossible odds was to try and play for one of the local semi-professional teams.

There was a high profile precedent to support my line of thinking. Only some three years previously, a local footballer from Brent, Cyrille Regis, who at that time was playing non-league football in the quiet backwaters of Hayes FC was now terrorising First Division defences with West Bromwich Albion and England with his strength, pace and power scoring many a spectacular goal. With Cyrille's exploits serving as a source of inspiration, I decided that joining a non-league club was the best route forward in trying to realise my dreams of professional football stardom. I made those intentions public to some of the Monks Park boys, the response to which drew a mixture of howls of derision and laughter and light-hearted ridicule.

"You? Play professional football?" quipped Mike Sinclair, Junior's younger brother, who was quite a goal poacher himself, on hearing my startling news. "You wouldn't make the sub's bench in your own house!" a remark which was the cue for another round of side splitting laughter from the rest of the lads.

Slightly shaken but not broken, I upped the ante and responded to Michael's witty but stinging barb by declaring, "I'll show my pedigree and four years from now, I'll be playing in the World Cup alongside Cyrille himself."

But Michael was going to have the final and decisive word on the subject and he nearly brought the house down when he replied, "pedigree? The only pedigree I've known you to have is the couple of tins of dog food in your Mum's cupboard!"

Even I collapsed on the floor with laughter at that rapier-like retort. The very notion of Shaun Wallace, Professional Footballer, may be laughable, but for me not impossible. It would remain to be seen who would have the last laugh.

On the Thursday before the World Cup Final, the envelope containing my examination results landed on the doormat. As I bent down to pick it up, all the old ghosts of the summers of 1978 and 1979 began to appear in my mind and those thoughts were accompanied by the pulsating sound of a heartbeat that threatened to jump right through my ribcage. I peeled back the sealed tight flap and slowly pulled out the small slip of paper that revealed the following information;

Constitutional Law – Grade C
The Law of Property – Grade C
The Law of Tort – Fail
International Relations – Grade B

My instant reaction to the news was a strange mixture of disappointment and relief, my sense of delight arising from the fact that at least I was spared the embarrassment of having to repeat all those exams again in the last week of August coupled with all the fears and anxieties having to go through such a terrifying ordeal would entail.

Those feelings of relief though were quickly tempered by the disappointment of yet again failing another exam in the one law paper I thought would give me my best grade. Still, it could have been a lot, lot worse. At least I passed Property Law. With my immediate fate now determined, there were still two glorious summer months left out there to enjoy. My play scheme work wasn't due to start until the third week in July and as such, I could press ahead with my attempt to turn my outrageous fantasy of becoming a professional footballer into reality.

The first week in July traditionally speaking, marks the start of pre-season training where football clubs whether they are professional, semi-professional or amateur, begin the rigorous and intensive fitness sessions in preparation for the new coming season. I decided to try my luck at Hendon FC, a well-established non-league outfit who were playing at the time in the top division of the Isthmian League. I made my way to the club's home stadium at Claremont Road on the first Tuesday scheduled for pre-season and when I walked into the Club House, there must have been at least twenty to thirty guys present, all relaxing and mulling about, all looking forward to the start of a new season and the chance to show what they can do. I only knew two of the faces once inside. I made a beeline for them so as not to stand out like a sore thumb in such a convivial atmosphere. Ian Sutherland, a stylish, tough tackling defender who grew up playing football with me and my close friend at Monks Park and Jeff Tavernier, a talented young goalkeeper from Kingsbury.

"Good to see you, Shaun!" Jeff said, and his high five greeting went a long way to helping me relax a little and feel at ease.

Ian's greeting was equally warm and welcoming and they proceeded to introduce me to the other guys standing close to them. It didn't take long for me to feel that I was one of the guys, becoming more relaxed as well as amused by all the lively football banter. After twenty minutes or so the management and coaching staff walked in which brought about a slight pause to the atmosphere, to announce that everyone should make their way to the Dressing Room for a prompt start for what was sure to be a rigorous and tough training session.

The first part of the training schedule was devoted to fitness work. Everyone had to run ten punishing laps around the perimeter of the expansive park with no cutting of corners. Despite the arduous nature of the run, I was in my element. I was pretty good at cross country running in my younger days having represented Copland many times at the Brent Inter School Championships and by the end of the punishing run, I was not that far off the front finishers. There was very little time to draw one's breath as the session was quickly followed by a series of power fitness exercises, ranging from squat thrusts, sit ups, star jumps and short sprints. All the different exercises devised by the management team were designed to slowly raise a player's general sharpness as well as overall fitness levels, but the sheer intensity of the fitness exercises left the vast majority of the group on the brink of near exhaustion.

After about an hour of non-stop rigorous training, the group was divided in two, with the Manager, Dave Mawson, taking the first team squad alongside some of the fringe players who were close to making the breakthrough into the first team whilst the rest of the group went off with Alan Ackerill, the Manager of the Reserve Team, to an area which he had already laid out with cones designed to work on technique with the ball and mini football pitch for a small sided game thereafter. Right from the start of the session, Alan made it clear that everyone in his charge was starting with a clean slate and how important it was for the reserve team squad selected for the coming season to have the right attitude and commitment and if you were good enough, then there was every possibility of being promoted to the first team. Alan was clearly well acquainted with some of the players in our group as some of them had come up through the ranks of the Hendon Youth Team. The youth players were a close knit, lively group whose constant witty banter throughout the remainder of the session kept the rest of the group marvellously entertained. Two of that group in particular, a wiry seventeen year old left back, Peter Augustine, and eighteen year old left winger, Sylvester Williams, were the main chief protagonists of the sharp and incisive banter flying around and no one was spared their spontaneous and witty put downs delivered without the slightest hint of malice or envy. Their humorous double act would have been more suited to a comedy stage as opposed to a football pitch, but when we played a forty minute eleven-a-side game, it was clear that their Changing Room boasts of being "bad boy ballers" was not an idle one, as their impressive display on the left hand side showed signs of an almost telepathic understanding.

Everyone got their fair share of playing time in that forty minute game and Alan made it clear at the end of the session that he wasn't going to make any snap decisions as to whom was going to be involved in the reserve team squad on the strength of one training session. His decision would be based on those players who attended the training sessions regularly from now until the start of the season, trained well and had the right attitude at all times.

The next pre-season training session came two days after the first and for the next six weeks, the twice weekly training sessions were always fully attended by first teamers and reserve players alike. I trained well during these sessions, scored goals in the practice games and gave as good as I got during the incessant Changing Room banter, frequently clashing with both Peter and Sylvester. There was in the main, a good team spirit and camaraderie that was beginning to develop amongst the reserve team as the countdown to the start of the new season drew ever closer. But twenty good reserve team players unfortunately, cannot fit into eleven starting shirts and in football, no matter what standard one plays at, the man in possession of the shirt (subject to fitness and form), keeps possession of the shirt and just as Alan had demanded (and expected), the competition to be in that starting eleven was slowly but surely, simmering to the boil.

Alan was very fair in ensuring that we all got the same amount of playing time in the six or so friendly matches that we played and although the competition for places was fierce, it was clear there were certain key players who were going to form the spine of the team with the remaining places very much up for grabs. The understanding between Peter and Sylvester on the left hand side allied to their consistently good performances in those friendly games. Ian Sutherland was another player earmarked as a fixture in the team, his small gangly physique betraying his exceptional ability to defend alongside his overall reading of the game. For the rest of the squad, it was a simple case of making the most of your opportunities when you were selected, play well and try to make the spot your own because only consistently good performances would stave off competition from players vying for the same position. As with any sporting set up where there is a big squad of good players, it's hard to keep everyone happy. But ultimately speaking, the manager's decision on team selection is final and the only way a disgruntled player could catch Alan's eye in time for the next friendly, was to train hard, and show the right attitude at the training sessions.

The team swept all before them in those friendlies and I managed to get a fairly decent run in those matches helping myself to a couple of goals in the process. Alan was pleased with my overall performances in the friendly games as well as my attitude and commitment to training. I was naturally delighted to hear Alan's encouraging words that I was in his thoughts but given the standard of the players in the reserves particularly in relation to the attacking options, I couldn't take anything for granted. If I wanted one of the two striking berths available for the first game of the season I'd have to go out and earn it.

In between my footballing exploits, my temporary job with the Brent Play Scheme Services had begun in earnest and I was assigned to one of the Play Schemes at a park in Queensbury, North West London. The Scheme offered a variety of activities designed to keep some fifty to sixty children entertained throughout the long, hot summer. I had a fantastic time working with a group of young children who were by and large no trouble at all and it hardly felt that I was in any form of real employment. Those six weeks finally came to an end in the last week of August and once the three days of hedonistic pleasure at the Notting Hill Carnival had also come to pass, I had to turn my attention to the important matter of a Law of Tort re-sit paper where once again progression onto the next stage of the course was very much on the line.

CHAPTER SIX

A week or so after Carnival, I went to see Sue Knight in her office. She wasted little time in her blunt but straightforward assessment as to why I performed so badly in the Tort exam, an assessment that was almost identical to Judy Newton's no nonsense remarks almost a year to the day. I clearly had not fully appreciated or taken on board both my previous and current failings. Sue's frank discussion wasn't all doom and gloom though. Her final parting words as I was leaving her office gave me some hope that I could turn things around when she said that I wasn't that far off the pass mark and saw no reason as to why I shouldn't progress into the Final year.

The next five days were totally devoted to preparing for the exam. I spent all my time working on the examination style and technique that Sue was looking for in terms of answering problem solving questions when advising the fictitious client by analysing and applying the relevant legal principles to the facts and not simply, reciting chapter and verse on every legal principle or case law under the sun. I took the serious advice on board and I felt ready to tackle the exam.

On the day of the exam, I realised many of my peers were going through the same ordeal, and together we buoyed each other's confidence for the task ahead. Once we were in the room at our respective tables, all calm and settled, Sue went through the customary examination rules before she gave the command for the start of the three hour marathon. I turned over the question paper, which revealed, much to my considerable delight, questions that appeared to pose no real difficulties. I wasted no time at all in putting into practice all the tips and advice Sue had given me in our review meeting and by the end of the three hour test, I managed to answer the four questions as required, an achievement that both pleased and satisfied me no end. Sue asked the examination candidates to leave the answer scripts on the desks for collection and as the small band of re-sit students rose from their seats in order to leave the examination room, the general consensus during the post exam analysis in the corridor outside the room was that although the exam itself was no easy exercise, it could have been a lot, lot worse.

The results of my re-sit exam arrived by post some four days later. As I bent down to pick up the envelope, the proverbial butterflies began flapping incessantly in the pit of my stomach and with a sharp intake of breath, I bit the bullet and tore open the envelope which revealed the following information;

The Law of Tort – PASS (63%).

I'd passed. I've made it into the Final year. My joy however, was tempered by the fact that I would only be given a mere passing grade which meant my score was to all intents and purposes, equivalent to that of a Third Class honours grade. That grade, together with my grades in Constitutional Law and The Law of Property, were the grades that were going to count towards my final degree which in essence meant that if I received similar grades in my final year, I was on course to end up with a Third Class honours award. And that level of degree, or even worse, a graduate degree without honours, was the last thing I wanted to be saddled with after three years. *Surely I'm better than that?* I asked myself. I probably was, but the cold hard facts and statistics do not lie. The reality was that I was heading into the final year on the crest of a slump and whilst there was no doubting the fact that I felt extremely relieved and grateful that I once again managed to survive yet another close shave, I was entering the last leg of my three year legal odyssey under even more pressure than at any other time since I began the course.

The new academic term began in the second week of September with what would be my last ever Fresher's week. I managed to off load my law text books to a couple of the sophomore students whom I knew and was on good terms with and they in turn, were also engaged in their own spot of offloading to some of that year's Freshers intake. My mind flashed nostalgically back to September 1980 when I entered Ladbroke House for the first time as an excited, eager Freshman and now I was beginning the final leg of a three year journey with the priceless spoils of a Law Degree awarded to those who complete that journey at the end. But I as I entered the finishing straight, there was no denying the fact that from my point of view, a successful crossing of that finishing line seemed a long, long way away. If this was the Olympic Games at the point when the medals were being handed out, the gold and silver medals (that being, a First Class or Upper Second Class Honours Degree or 2:1 respectively) were simply beyond my reach. I wasn't astute enough or indeed, studious enough to be able to make such a dramatic transformation in just under a year, but the bronze medal (a Lower Class Second Award or 2:2) was well within my reach and if I wanted to cross that finishing line successfully, then that was the prize that I had to aim for. *I'm not that far away from gaining that medal!* I thought to myself, as I pondered what I needed to do to achieve that feat over the next eight months. It was a goal despite the present state of my grades that I was more than capable of attaining and I vowed that I would do whatever that was necessary to cross that finishing line feeling every inch a winner.

Christopher Champness, the Head of Department at the Law Faculty welcomed all the returning third year students in one of the Lecture Rooms on the third floor and behind him sat the Course Tutors who were teaching the various law subjects that were on offer in the final year. Christopher began his address by congratulating us for having got this far and stressed the need for all of us to continue to work extremely hard in what would be our final year at the College. It was important, he added, that we knew an even greater effort would be required from us for the crucial and important reason that the respective professional law bodies (The College of Law for Solicitors and The Bar Council for Barristers respectively) were now demanding that any law graduates wishing to sit their professional exams would have to have attained at least a lower second class honours degree, a policy change designed to raise the standard of the quality graduates who would be recruited to either branch of the profession, despite the cynical view that the real agenda behind this rule change was that it was an attempt by the respective professional bodies to select entrants more likely to come from the certain educational establishments and more likely, the right social background. Despite the changes, Christopher made it clear that he was confident that every one of us was more than capable of achieving that minimum requirement, but it was an achievement that wouldn't be handed to us on a plate, it had to be earned.

Christopher's address, so far as I was concerned, resonated loud and clear. The minimum target for entry onto The Bar Finals course was a 2:2 degree and anything less than that minimum target would represent complete and utter failure. The rule change only added to my own pressures and overall concerns of firstly, given my present predicament of being outside the 2:2 cut off point, do I really have what it takes to successfully cross the academic finishing line? And secondly, even if I managed to obtain a 2:2 passing grade, would it be enough to get me onto a course that is bound to be oversubscribed? Real concerns, but if I allowed those concerns to dominate my whole way of thinking for the next eight months, it will almost certainly totally undermine all my hopes and ambitions that were still very much within my grasp. The gauntlet had now been thrown down and if I wanted to achieve my stated aims then it was down to me and me alone to pick it up and rise to the challenge.

For the final year, students had to study three Law subjects plus the non-law subject they had chosen from the outset of the course. Two of those subjects, Jurisprudence and The Law of Trusts were compulsory core subjects that all students were required to sit together with several optional Law topics ranging from Employment

Law, Company Law, Social Welfare Law, Conveyancing, Revenue Law and The Law of Evidence. During Christopher's short address about various professional qualification exams, especially those students who had aspirations of going to the bar, two of the main core subjects that a student had to pass either at undergraduate level or The Bar Finals course were the Law of Evidence and Revenue Law, subjects which by their very name suggests, were very formidable subjects in their own right. Christopher was the Course Tutor on the Law of Evidence at the College and if the student grapevine was anything to go by he was by all accounts a very good lecturer whose students invariably performed very well at the end of year final examinations. I weighed up the options as to which of those two subjects would be the lesser of the two evils and eventually came to the view that trying to do both Revenue Law and The Law of Evidence on a one year professional course might be biting off more than I could possibly chew and I opted to get Revenue Law out of the way first and save the "delights" of The Law of Evidence until the following year. I was happy with the options that I had chosen and felt quietly confident that I could get the job done and obtain the grades needed in my quest to get on to The Bar Finals course. With everything now in place, I couldn't wait for the start of my final year at The Polytechnic of North London to finally get under way.

Meanwhile, the 1982-83 football season was up and running and in full swing. I still harboured ambitions to combine professional football with a career in law, but those footballing ambitions seemed to be lightyears away from my present status as a Hendon reserve team player who was struggling to nail down a place in the starting eleven. That previous season, I was in and out of the side managing to score the odd goal here and there whenever the chances presented themselves. Alan was quite pleased with my performances on the whole and my commitment to training during the season. It soon became pretty clear though that my name wasn't going to be amongst the first that Alan would jot down on his team sheet. Despite its non-league status, Hendon was constantly attracting, as well as on the lookout for, good footballers and there was no better place to see how a new player performs than in reserves matches. At times, it was disheartening to see the gradual influx of players being brought into the club and taking positions, but to Alan's credit, he would always have a quiet and reassuring word with player(s) that he had left out of the team and that meant having to go through the delicate balancing exercise of acknowledging a player's obvious disappointment at missing out at being selected for the team whilst in the same breath, dangling the tantalising carrot that in spite of your name being absent from the team sheet you were still very much in his plans.

The reserve team made a fantastic start to the season with one victory after another and that early success was down to three simple reasons: good players, good man management and above all, good team spirit. The Changing Room banter, whether during a training session, or before a competitive game was hilarious and it provided the catalyst for fostering the fierce team spirit that we had. There was never anything malicious or spiteful in the banter. If you were a player who didn't make Alan's starting line up for instance, you'd probably be the butt of incessant teasing but the banter was always without malevolent intent.

The bottom line for any footballer whether playing professionally or amateur is to get into the starting eleven and I was no different. It didn't take long before I grew increasingly more and more frustrated and disillusioned as the season unfolded. I'd put in all that effort in training week in week out just to sit on the bench, getting the occasional run out or even worse, to watch the whole game from the stands.

The season sadly didn't end with the glory of silverware for the team as we only managed to reach two quarter finals in the knockout competitions we were entered for and secured a creditable third place finish in the league. The influx of reserved team players hoping to make the breakthrough proved to be an even harder nut to crack because out of all of the reserve team playing squad that started the season, only two players, the mercurial Sylvester Williams being one of them, made the step up into the first team squad with a couple of appearances towards the back end of the season but for me, the season ended in complete anti-climax. I hardly got any playing time by the season's end and when the referee blew the final whistle for the final game, I decided that it was probably time to move on. Alan was acutely aware of my obvious disappointment and told me that although he acknowledged that I didn't get much playing time during the season, he nevertheless still wanted me to come back for the start of pre-season training at the beginning of July. He could have told me to find another club but he didn't and although his words were not accompanied with any guarantees that I would get into the squad let alone, play more regularly, it was enough to persuade me to stay and fight not only for a place in the Hendon Reserve team but also to keep my increasingly fading clandestine dreams of becoming a professional footballer.

My final year at PNL began in earnest in the third week of September with two academic objectives in mind: firstly, to get the grades in all of my subjects that would get me a 2:2, otherwise I could kiss Bar School goodbye and secondly, to really enjoy and appreciate the remaining nine months I had left on the course. Looking back on those first two years, the only thing I was concerned with was progressing to the next year of the course and nothing more. All I cared about was learning about rules and cases without giving much thought to the reasons why I had chosen the course in the first place which was to train as a Lawyer, to think like a Lawyer and equally as important, to act like a Lawyer. My own lack of insight and to some extent, a lack of academic maturity in not fully understanding or embracing what studying to become a Lawyer was really all about meant that on two occasions, I came within a whisker of losing my place on the course altogether. With hindsight though, those twin hiccups were probably a blessing in disguise as it finally opened my eyes to the importance to adapt and evolve as a student when advancing to the next level. As the great Charles Darwin himself would testify, only the species that evolves and adapts to the constantly changing environment will survive, but my final year was more than just survival. My final year would be solely programmed to the attainment of personal academic success and achievement.

This newfound approach to my studies was slowly but surely beginning to pay dividends as the year unfolded. My prompt and regular attendance in both my lectures and seminars gave me a greater understanding and appreciation of a course that over the previous two years at times I had taken for granted. Even the frighteningly named Law of Equity and Trusts didn't seem as daunting as first appeared in comparison to those really difficult days studying The Law of Property. After every lecture and seminar, I would go over my lecture notes then go to the specific chapter in the relevant text book for more in depth study. My study regime was a perpetual never ending cycle of constant revision that I rigidly adhered to to keep as many principles and cases constantly alive and fresh in my mind. This newfound zest and commitment in my attitude to the course was also reflected in the written pieces of coursework that had to be submitted. The grades I was getting were, much to my surprise, better than I expected, which meant that providing I passed all of my four subjects at the first attempt, I would be on course to gain that 2:2 degree. All I had to do was make sure that I maintained this level of academic commitment right to the very end.

I was in a good place in terms of keeping on top of things with my Law studies as well as my commitment in keeping to a rigid routine of constant revision and study. All of my hard work meant that I could, without a hint of guilt, continue to play football on Wednesday afternoons as my dreams of becoming a professional footballer were still very much in my thoughts even though the reality of the situation was clearly saying otherwise. College football was now the only avenue left open to me to try and realise those fading ambitions once the season was up and running. The bright start I made when I returned to Hendon for pre-season training and in the friendly games leading up to the start of the new season gradually faded though as I found myself competing against the new influx of players both from the youth team earmarked for the reserves as well as those new players who were signed by the management team which meant in real terms, players on the periphery were surplus to requirements. Alan to his credit, never showed me the door but his assurances that I would get more playing time was not so forthcoming this time round and I decided that it would probably be best for all parties concerned if I just left the club quietly, my ego slightly bruised with no hard feelings and more importantly, the self confidence in my ability still intact. College football went a long way to easing the disappointment. The vast majority of the College's first team squad from the previous season were, like me, in their final year and the forthcoming season represented the last chance to leave behind a sporting legacy that we as a team could be proud of. The first team squad remained pretty much intact from the previous year and that meant I was entrusted once more to deliver the goods in terms of goals.

The team was in the First Division (South) of the Polytechnic League and the standard and quality of the teams we were competing against was a very high one. I was determined to start the season just as I had ended the last, scoring lots of goals, and thankfully, I didn't disappoint in that regard. I scored the goals which gave the team a very promising start to the campaign in both the league and the main knock out cup competition.

Having made such a promising start in our first three league games, our next match was the first round of the British Polytechnic Cup at our home ground at Stanmore. As the team were getting changed in preparation for the game, we were all of the collective view that if we got through this match, there would be nothing to prevent us from going all the way in the competition but unfortunately, disaster struck when only minutes after kick off I landed awkwardly after an aerial challenge on my notoriously weak left ankle, and had to be carried from the field. This injury was to keep me out of the game for the next four months.

In the Changing Room, I managed somehow to take off my left boot which to my horror revealed a grotesquely misshapen ankle that had swelled beyond recognition. With my left leg now exposed, the pain in my ankle began to throb incessantly and my immediate fear was that it could be broken. I rose gingerly to my feet and tried to bear weight on the injured ankle. I could stand, but only just, but I couldn't be sure what the extent of the injury was. I decided that I would have no choice but to go to hospital.

With considerable difficulty (I had to point my toes to their limits as opposed to using the sole of my foot and hope that it would keep any further damage to my injured ankle, as well as the clutch, to an absolute minimum), I managed somehow to navigate my way to Park Royal Hospital's A&E Department where I had to sit in the casualty waiting area for the best part of three mind numbing hours for an X-Ray, after which I had to wait a further hour for an analysis with the Doctor. As I hobbled into the Doctor's office, my X-Ray was already on the screen illuminated in the foreground of pure bright light, the outline of my left anklebone clearly visible.

"There's no break in your ankle", he declared much to my considerable relief and joy. "It's more likely that you've strained your ankle ligaments." He went on to add that while I would make a complete recovery, it would take some time to do so. I wouldn't be able to bear weight on it for at least four to six weeks after which time, I would have to go on a course of physiotherapy which I should arrange via my local GP. "As long as you follow the rest and recovery programme," he said reassuringly, "you'll be able to resume playing any kind of sport without any difficulty".

A nurse gave me crutches, medication for the pain, and a Tubi-Grip sock bandage. I thanked her and hobbled with the aid of my crutches to the Hospital Car Park before once again enduring the arduous task of first getting into and then driving my car for the short but challenging journey home.

The day ended on an even more sour note, as later that evening I found out that the team had lost the Cup match and with it went any chance of a League and Cup double. There was a consolation prize however for teams knocked out at this stage of the competition. The losing teams were now in the repechage knockout competition, a far less glamorous competition to win but at least the team had something to play for and all I could do was hope that I would be fit enough to be a part of it.

Despite my injury, it was business as usual so far as my College studies were concerned. I was sticking faithfully to the routine constantly reading and re-reading my lecture notes until the legal principles and case law became second nature. The Michaelmas term seemed to fly by and the first Monday of January 1983 marked the start of the Hilary Term which meant that now I had only four months left as an undergraduate. That very fact caused me to pause and reflect on the last two and a half years at the Polytechnic, astonished and amazed how quickly those two and a half years seemed to have flown by but more poignantly, how much I was going to really miss the place. Being an undergraduate was more than just trying to obtain a degree. It opened up a whole new world for me in terms of the relationships that I had forged with different people from all walks of life and of all ages, whether they be the lecturing staff, or students, all of whom have helped shaped my own overall development both as a student and as a man. I also reflected on the fact that despite one or two hair raising moments in those two and a half years where I almost lost it all, I was still standing with the finishing line clearly in my sights. All that was needed now to cross that line successfully was to really work hard in my studies, harder than I'd ever done before.

I was walking around unaided by the time the Hilary term began in earnest. My left ankle was still very sore and January's freezing cold temperatures wasn't exactly helping to assist in its recovery. I had however arranged my physiotherapy treatment thanks to the efforts of my GP, Dr Peter Brent, and for the next six weeks, I diligently attended the Physiotherapy Department at Park Royal Hospital every Wednesday afternoon so that it wouldn't interrupt my college studies. The sessions initially began with a mixture of ultrasound treatment and gentle manipulation of the ankle to increase mobility in the joint before gradually moving on to ankle strengthening exercises which included standing whilst trying to maintain control on a wobble board, an exercise designed to assist with my ability to improve the ankle's balance and general mobility.

My dedication and commitment to my physiotherapy programme paid off. I had made a complete recovery from my injury by the middle of February and was now eager to get back to playing the beautiful game. But I was a long way short of any sort of match fitness and with two or so months before the end of the season, I was determined to play again. The quickest way to achieve that aim was to go back to my old, but not too recently departed former club, Hendon, for their twice weekly training sessions if they would allow me to do so. I turned up for a Thursday night training session for the first time in nearly four months. As I entered the changing room, I was greeted by the cries, "Lord Lucan Returns!" (a less than flattering nickname provided by my teammates. If ever I had a really bad game, or missed a glaring opportunity in front of goal, they'd call me Lord Lucan on account of the fact that sometimes during a crucial moment in a game, I would be missing in the Penalty Area) and it felt that I'd hardly been away at all. Alan was pleased to see me back and had no problems with me taking part in the training sessions. The team were still doing quite well although most of the playing personnel was barely recognisable from the players I played alongside only a season and a half ago. I was under no illusion as to my chances of getting any playing time at the club given the fact that I lost the bulk of the season due to injury and the reserves now had a settled playing squad. All I wanted to do was train hard and get fit and if I was going to get any playing time at all, then I would have to try and forge my way back into my college team for the end of season hurrah.

My college team's early season momentum had tailed off somewhat during my three and a half month long absence, but I would be the last person to suggest that the team's gradual loss of form was solely down to the fact that I wasn't playing. Other key players, for one reason or another were also missing and by all accounts, the players brought in as replacements were simply not up to scratch and so, the team lost vital ground in our quest to win the League. I decided I was ready to return.

The following Wednesday afternoon, I made my way to the college's Kentish Town site where the team would usually meet up before making our way to the game. I was greeted by all the usual barrage of witty banter before boarding the college bus for another home fixture. We were still in with a shout of winning the League despite lying in fourth place and the following Wednesday, we had an away fixture against Thames Polytechnic in the Plate competition that was now at the quarter final stage.

The team arrived at the ground in confident mood. The banter in the Changing Room was both lively and positive and all the signs suggested that everyone was up for the game. As it was my first game back with the team, our team captain made the call that I would not be in the squad of thirteen, a decision which, given my long absence, I could hardly argue with. The team left the Changing Room and trotted out to our usual playing pitch in unison for a ten minutes warm up prior to kick off and on the surface, the team appeared to be full of confidence. But as is usually the case especially in football, pre-match hype and bravado doesn't always go hand in hand with actual performance and the team made a terrible start to the game by conceding a goal in the first five minutes. I was dying to get on the pitch but there was nothing that I could do except shout all the encouragement that I could from the touchline. The team were desperately hanging on against a well drilled and organised opposition, surviving wave after wave of attacks and we managed, with a combination of sheer good fortune and some desperate last ditch defending, to keep the score to just one but eventually, our luck ran out as midway through the first half, the opposition struck once more in a well worked moved to put them 2-0 in the lead. Now the team were really up against it. That goal seemed to knock the collective stuffing out of us and as the game restarted, we were passing the ball aimlessly without any meaning or purpose. Only divine intervention prevented the team from conceding a third goal and we managed, completely against the run of play, to pull one back thanks to one of Mark Jaggard's trademark right foot pile drivers which gave the team some hope at the half time whistle of somehow getting back in this game.

A few harsh words were said during the half time team talk, with everyone having the opportunity to have his say before embarking on the discussion on how we were going to get back in the game. The team weren't in a position to make any wholesale changes as only eleven players had turned up for the game.

"Have you brought your boots, Shaun?" asked one of my teammates, more in desperation as opposed the hope that I would somehow be the team's knight in shining amour.

"I haven't," was my immediate response. I wish I had brought my boots even though fitness wise I wasn't really ready and in a complete volt face, I asked the lads whether any of them had size eleven boots.

"What have you got for feet, flippers?" came the instant cheeky reply from one of the lads as he lay nearly flat out on the floor and looking seemingly incapable to meet the challenge of the next forty five minutes.

The remarks drew one or two chuckles from some of the players. I was laughing myself the result of which meant that I was in no position to respond to that cheeky one-liner but at least it demonstrated the team spirit and morale was still intact.

The team discarded all their orange peels and water bottles to the side near to the kit bags and took to the field in contrast to the opposition, who were already in formation line up eager to continue their overall dominance in the game. Once more the opposition started the second half on the front foot, creating chance after chance without applying the decisive coup de grace. Our second half display was a vast improvement on the first in terms of the team's style of play and as luck would have it, we somehow managed to scramble an equaliser which on balance was no more than we deserved up to that point. The response from the opposition was both swift and ferocious and once more began to take control of the game. The team were desperately hanging on against an opposition who were virtually playing their game in over half of the pitch, but despite all that pressure, we somehow managed to prevent their winning goal which would have surely ended all chances of winning the League.

The general consensus amongst the lads on the journey home was that we were lucky to get anything out of the game. With only a few games remaining, there was still the outside chance of winning the League but that would mean we would have to win those remaining games and hope that the teams above us would drop the necessary points in order to create such an unlikely scenario. There was still everything to play for and much to look forward to especially with a quarter final at Thames Polytechnic the following next week. *That was going to be our comeback date!* I secretly declared to myself. On the journey back to Kentish Town, all I kept thinking about was the quarter-final tie. The team was on the threshold of doing something special and I was determined to be a part of it.

On the day of the match, the team travelled with thirteen players and none of us, especially me, were certain of a starting place so I decided not to start getting changed unless I was told otherwise. But when the starting eleven was announced by our team captain I heard my name called out.

He went on to add, "we need goals from you today Shaun!"

"Don't worry, I'll deliver!" I was relieved at being back in the side. The only thought that was running through my mind was to justify the faith shown by the team and the only way to do that was to score goals, and if the team as a whole were up for the challenge as our outward confident demeanour appeared to suggest, then that is exactly what I intended to do.

Our captain stressed the need of the team to work hard as a collective unit, constantly communicating and encouraging each other especially in the first twenty minutes of the game and when the opportunities presented themselves at the other end to take them.

His instructions to the forward players were equally clear and unequivocal. "Shaun I want you playing on the last defender and try to time your runs so as not to get caught out offside and when that ball is played up to you, Shaun, you've got to hold up so as to bring others into play."

I nodded in his direction indicating that I had heard what he had said and that I was up for the game. The team then dispersed to various corners of our half of the pitch in order to go through various last minute warm up routines before taking up our respective playing positions in readiness for the kick off. The game got underway and the pattern of early exchanges gave the clearest indication that both teams were both on form and up for the challenge.

I got into the game right from the word go, quickly reprising the almost telepathic understanding I enjoyed with Brendan, the team's midfield maestro, prior to my long enforced lay off. Both sides were creating chances without making the crucial breakthrough but just after the half way point in the first half, Brendan headed a delightful ball which beat their last of defence. I timed my run to perfection as ordered by our captain to meet the pass and give me a clear run on goal. The Centre Half who was marking me and playing quite well up until that point was desperately trying to make up ground but the five or so yards advantage I had on him meant he was never going to recover lost ground I was bearing on the opposition's last line of defence who was determined to stop me from scoring. I reached the penalty area in full control of both the ball and my composure and as the goalkeeper rushed out in order to narrow the angle, in one continuous movement, I feigned my body slightly to my right, causing the goalkeeper to move in that direction before quickly swerving both my body and the ball onto my left hand side, a movement that completely wrong footed him before stroking the ball into the empty unguarded net. There were no wild celebrations on my part when I put our team in the lead although inwardly, I couldn't have been more delighted. Some of my team mates rushed over to where I was standing and greeted me with high fives and pats on the back before we started jogging back towards the centre circle.

We just about deserved to be in front on balance of play but just before the referee blew his whistle for the re-start, our team captain issued the rallying cry for everyone to concentrate and be on their guard. He was right to be wary. Thames by no means were out of it and the combination of sustained pressure on their part and silly mistakes on ours, led to Thames getting back on level terms only ten or so minutes later to leave the game delicately poised. As the game wore on, chances to take the lead for both sides came and went with alarming frequency and it was only a matter of time before one of these chances were taken. Just before half time, I was presented with another golden opportunity in almost identical circumstances as my first goal. I raced into the Penalty Area with the ball hugging the outside of my right foot and my head upright in order to see the goalkeeper who was preparing to advance from his line. As I got closer, he made his move, rushing out to make himself as big as was possible. I shaped up to curl the shot beyond him before swerving to my left, wrong footing him for the second time, and tapping the ball in to give us that precious lead. This time I didn't hold back on my celebrations and I ran to the back of the goal to soak up the adoration of an imaginary crowd before turning to face the real adoration from my teammates. That goal seemed to knock the stuffing out of Thames and by the time the referee blew his whistle to signal the end of the first half, the team walked off and headed for the half time water and oranges well satisfied with our first half exertions.

Just like the first half, the second half was pretty much an open affair with each team trying to gain the ascendency over the other. But as the second half wore on, the initiative seemed to be tilting towards the home side who were gradually beginning to dominate possession both of the ball and the game as our team began to visibly tire and it seemed only a matter of time before the opposition scored. With ten minutes to go, Thames got the breakthrough their constant and sustained pressure deserved with a stunning goal. A frantic and desperate headed clearance from our defence dropped to the feet of one of their midfield players who was hovering just outside our Penalty Area and with one touch, he unleashed a twenty five yard screamer which flew in and nestled in the top right hand corner of our goal. Their obvious delight in having got themselves back on level terms was in stark contrast to the collective despair our team showed at having conceded such a late equaliser. The momentum was now firmly with Thames and at the re-start, our team had the haunted look of a side that knew it was already beaten. Our collective troubles and anxieties then took a turn for the worse because with five minutes to go, Thames took the lead for the first time in the game. Our situation was now all but a lost cause. The ninetieth minute was looming ever closer and the team launched one last hopeful long ball up field into the Thames Penalty Area and prayed that it would somehow save the game and with it our season. The long ball had the desired effect as the numerous ricochets off various body parts from players from both sides somehow ended in our team being awarded a corner kick. Brendan quickly made his way over to the corner flag to take the kick and Thames had virtually everyone back in the Penalty Area. The Centre Half that was marking me was watching my every move as I moved first left and then right just keep him constantly guessing. Brendan stepped up to take the corner kick. As he approached the ball, I made a short diagonal sprint from the Penalty spot to the near post, in hope and anticipation that Brendan's delivery would somehow find me. I made my run a bit too early and by the time I arrived at the near post, the ball sailed over my head right into the area that I vacated. Attacking that space was our long gangly centre half, Adam, who rose majestically with a well-timed leap to powerfully head home the equaliser. All the team, save for our own goalkeeper immediately piled on top of the unlikeliest of footballing heroes as we celebrated as though we'd won the final itself.

The referee's whistle signalling the end of the game could hardly be heard amidst the team's wild celebrations and with the scores deadlocked at 3-3, the teams had to play a further thirty minute period of extra time in order to find a winner.

The first period of extra time was just as competitive as the previous two. Both teams were really going for it even though the players were really tired, but neither team were prepared to give an inch. It was going to take something really special to break the deadlock and that point came during the mid-way point in that first period. As the ball broke to one of our players in our defensive half, he spotted my position on the shoulder of my marker who was one of two defenders trying to hold their defensive positions on the half way line and thus were vulnerable to a pass into space behind them. He delivered a beautifully weighted pass into that space and in anticipation, I timed my run to near perfection to meet the pass, a run that put me completely in the clear and yet another one to one duel with the opposition goalkeeper. I approached the Penalty Area totally unopposed and the goalkeeper took up a position this time in the middle of the six yard box, trying to make himself as big as possible. I had already made up my mind what I was going to do and I smashed it low and hard to his bottom right hand corner to put us 4-3 in the lead. A couple of my teammates rushed over to congratulate me although this time, there was none of the near mass hysteria that followed Adam's late equaliser. The team had the bit between their teeth now that we were back in the lead and this time we were determined not to let it slip. A couple of minutes later, the team won another corner. We had committed quite a few players forward sensing that this could be another golden opportunity to score. Brendan trotted over to take the kick and crossed the ball into the Penalty Area, where players from the opposing side were in a frantic struggle for control of the ball. In the ensuing melee, the opposition failed to clear the ball and in an act of good fortune, the ball ricocheted into my path. Well, I didn't need asking twice given the form that I was in and I smashed the ball in the back of the opposition net for a 5-3 lead. The goal all but knocked the stuffing out of Thames and the lads went wild with excitement.

Despite the luxury of a two goal cushion, there was still work to do before the final whistle. Although they were down they were by no means out and to their credit, Thames never gave up. The team finally cracked in the final minute of the game when Thames scored another goal and the desperate response of one of our players was to hang on to the ball after picking it out of the net in order to waste time. Their goal scorer, anxious to get on with the game snatched possession of the ball from his grasp and sprinted towards the centre circle and placed the ball right on the spot before lining up with the rest of his team mates for the re start. I kicked off for the restart and no sooner had my strike partner played a backward pass towards our defence, we heard the welcoming sound of the final whistle. All the players shook hands with each other in an act which typified the spirit and the manner in which the whole game had been played before heading off towards the Changing Rooms.

The team were on a high after having survived a real baptism of fire, a mood reflected by the constant self-congratulatory back slapping and high fives between ourselves that greeted our hard fought victory. We had made it to the semi-final and now just one game stood between the team and an end of season final. We headed to the Student Bar for a round or two of beers to celebrate as all the players from both teams were chatting amongst themselves about the great game we had all just taken part in. We finally boarded the mini bus for the long journey back to Kentish Town. I was beginning to feel aches and pains in my neck, lower back and legs as I climbed on board but all the aches and pains in the world couldn't take away the feeling of ecstasy in having scored all those goals and being a part of a wonderful team effort. All of us were now looking forward to the semi-final due to take place in seven days' time and the confidence of the team was such that there was no reason we couldn't go all of the way.

The team had to meet at 9.30am sharp that following Wednesday for the semi-final as our opponents were some one hundred and sixty miles up the M1 in Sheffield. The timing of our rendezvous meant that I had to miss a vital Revenue Law lecture and seminar but I was prepared to make that sacrifice to play in an important semi-final. For once, no one in the squad were late and we all boarded the college mini bus in unison for the long and arduous trip North for the game. Once there, our team captain announced that the starting eleven was the same as that which started the quarter final tie.

We didn't know anything about our opponents, but it was fairly obvious that they must have been a good team to have reached this stage of the competition. But we were also a good team and the general consensus was that for us to get anything out of the game, then we had to put in the same effort and commitment that we had shown seven days previously. We then gathered our belongings and all went out together as a team. Our opponents were already out there going through a rigorous warm up routine and were clearly up for the challenge. We placed our belongings close to the touchline before starting our own warm up routine, a routine that was letting the opposition know that we were not here to simply just to make up the numbers. The referee then blew his whistle asking for the team captains to come forward for the toss of the coin. Our captain won the toss and we elected to kick off. From the very first note of the referee's whistle, the team went on the immediate offensive by playing the ball out to our left winger who immediately moved beyond his marker and found himself an open space. This bold and direct approach seemed to catch Sheffield off guard. Our winger attacked the space and got into a decent position which resulted in us winning a throw in deep inside their half. The Sheffield defenders were in a near state of panic, barking out frantic orders for players to be picked up and tightly marked. The ball was thrown back in play and the team kept the pressure on Sheffield, who managed somewhat to scrabble the ball away for a corner with barely a minute on the clock registered. Our team started shouting our own noises of encouragement in an effort to try and make the most of the early pressure whilst our corner specialist Brendan made his way over to take the kick. The Sheffield defence were desperately trying to organise their players to watch the runs from the attackers. I was lurking around in the Penalty Area desperately trying ways to lose the extremely close attentions of a Centre Half, who was sticking to me like superglue. Brendan clipped the ball into the Penalty Area, but its relatively low trajectory enabled a teammate at the near post to flick the ball into space. I instinctively reacted to this slice of good fortune and got in front of my marker and flicked the ball with the side of my forehead past the goal keeper into the back of the net. What a great start to the game for the team. I rushed straight over to Brendan to celebrate another of my goals in which he had a hand in, closely followed by my teammates for another round of hugs and high fives before we all trotted back to our half in order to line up for the restart.

But then our dream like start quickly turned into a nightmare as the combination of Sheffield's attacking prowess and error strewn defensive mistakes on our part saw them race into a 3-1 lead after the twenty minute mark. Sheffield at this time, were in total control of all areas of the game in terms of their organisation and possession and there seemed little that we could do to dent their overall dominance. The fantastic start the team made now seemed to be nothing more than a distant memory as the team conceded possession cheaply time after time. A fourth goal seemed certain on the cards but by sheer good fortune as opposed to design, the team conceded no more goals for the remaining twenty five minutes and the referee's half time whistle when it came provided a welcome relief.

However, the second half began where the first half had left off, with Sheffield continuing to make all of the running in an effort to kill off our team once and for all. By contrast, our team just couldn't seem to get our game together but as the game wore on, the team started creating chances of our own and our efforts were eventually rewarded when we managed to pull a goal back just after the hour mark which put us right back in contention.

As the team relentlessly continued to push forward in the final ten minutes, gaps were beginning to appear in our defence leaving the team both vulnerable and exposed to incisive counter attacking by Sheffield that proved to be the team's ultimate undoing as we conceded two late goals.

The team decided not to hang around for the customary post match drink up in the Student Bar after the game as we all wanted to get back to London as quickly as possible and boarded the minibus for the long and arduous return journey South but thankfully, by the time we eventually arrived back at PNL's Kentish Town annexe, the disappointment of our semi-final defeat had long since dissipated. The following Wednesday was going to be the last game of the season and we all agreed that we'd all be there for one last hurrah. Our hopes of winning the League were virtually over but if we could finish the season on a winning note, then it would be a fitting end for a very good team.

That final fixture didn't turn out to be just one game. Because there wasn't enough time to play our game in hand we had over the other teams, we agreed to play a double header with our opponents, two half hour games with ten minute break in between. In a tale of contrasting fortunes, we lost the first game 2-0, but managed to turn the tables in the return fixture when I scored the second goal in a 2-0 victory which secured a creditable third place finish in the final league standings. We all headed for the Student Bar after that gruelling effort for the last and final time to celebrate not only the end of a reasonably successful campaign but also the end of us playing together as a team.

But the time for indulging in sentimental football nostalgia would now have to take its place firmly on the back burner as my attentions were firmly fixed on my final two months as an undergraduate and my quest to obtain the only thing I cherished above everything else: a 2:2 Law Degree.

CHAPTER SEVEN

My preparations for the most important period of my academic career were bang on schedule despite my continued over indulgent love affair with football. All the written assignments that I had to submit by the end of the Hilary term were handed in on time, leaving me free to concentrate on trying to remember and take in all those principles and cases until they were firmly imprinted in my mind. All my time day in day out throughout the whole of the Easter break was devoted to the ultimate cause of being totally prepared and mentally ready and, as any student will tell you, maintaining one's focus, enthusiasm and commitment during the revision season isn't easy, especially when there's the added distraction of the warm spring sunshine. Despite those potential pitfalls, I managed to stick to the task at hand and by the time I returned to the Polytechnic for the start of the final Trinity term, I'd never felt more prepared to meet the challenge.

The Trinity term was solely geared toward preparations for the forthcoming exams at the end of May. At a specially convened meeting attended by all the third year students in the main lecture theatre, our lecturers announced their respective revision and seminar timetable and lecture seminars for the next few weeks and strongly advised all the students to attend these lectures as the odd subtle hint here and there as to what type of areas we should be concentrating on were more likely to appear on the question paper. I heeded that collective advice and never missed one revision or lecture seminar. Those sessions were enjoyable as they were informative, all of which added to my growing feelings of self confidence that I could achieve overall success. At the same time, the final written pieces of coursework that would crucially count towards those exams were due for submission three or so days after we returned from the half term break and like countless times before in the previous two and a half years, I submitted my final four pieces just before the midday deadline. Those final submissions of coursework also marked the end of an era. The class of 1980 which set out on a collective idealistic odyssey was soon nearing its conclusion and once the final exams were completed, most of the students with whom I shared that journey would be scattered wherever the winds of life would blow us. So to mark the occasion, we headed had an impromptu celebration in the Student Common Room with drinks, farewell hugs and nostalgic musings as in seven days' time, our exams would begin.

The timetable was spread over a two week period and the first of those exams would be the potentially daunting Law of Trusts on the afternoon on the 2nd of June, the timing of which meant that any 23rd birthday celebrations would have to be put on hold. The following Monday was the Jurisprudence exam. Mercifully, there was a three day break before the next exam, Revenue Law, and finally the International Relations exam on the following Monday morning.

I woke up the morning of my first exam in a cheery and positive mood thanks in part to the benefit of having a good night's sleep and not indulging myself in any mad pre birthday party celebrations. The weather was warm and bright and matched my cheery mood as I made my way to Ladbroke House.

The exam itself held no horrors. There were at least five questions that I knew that I could answer with confidence and I breathed a sigh of relief that I wouldn't have to undergo the near total meltdown that I suffered at the start of last year's Property exam. I managed to complete all the questions well within time before the invigilator ordered all the candidates to stop writing on the stroke of 5pm. With the exam now over, all the students began to rise from their own writing desks and I could hear a collective sigh of relief that the first hurdle of our examination ordeal was all over. The post mortem discussions on how the paper went started almost immediately as we all walked out of the examination hall and the general consensus was that the exam wasn't all that bad and could have been a whole lot worse.

The Jurisprudence exam three days later was the last time the Class of 1980 would be together as a group as not all of us were sitting the same optional courses for the remaining set of exams. The Jurisprudence paper went very well so far as I was concerned and with two relatively easy exams left to come, I felt that I was well on my way to accomplishing the main objective.

The last two papers went extremely well and at 5:01pm on 13th June 1983 when the invigilator in my International Relations exam gave the order for candidates to stop writing, it signalled the end of my academic career as a student at the Polytechnic of North London. I paused momentarily to reflect on the fact that the last two and a half years seemed to have come and gone in an instant and soon I would be leaving behind an institution where to all intents and purposes, I had enjoyed some of the best days of my life thus far. All that was left of that career was that all important date of 6th July, the day on which the results were going to be published on the College Notice Board. All I could hope for when that day eventually arrived was that all the ups and downs I endured at the Polytechnic of North London would be totally vindicated.

Now that the exams were over, I could look forward to a well-earned three week break and I was determined to enjoy every minute of it. However, the type of fun and enjoyment I had in mind cost money, so I set about the task of trying to get temporary work with Brent Leisure Services on their summer Play Schemes. I applied as soon as possible, but so as not to put all my proverbial eggs into one basket, I decided to pay a visit to one of the nearby recruitment agencies further along the High Road to see whether there were any other suitable temporary jobs on offer. I scanned the Vacancy Board to see if there was anything that caught my fancy, but the type of employment that was on offer was either beyond my limited capacities or simply too demeaning and I quickly beat a hasty retreat from the Recruitment Agency without any further enquiry. But no sooner had I exited the door, the cold winds of reality began to gather pace to remind me that as of that moment in time, there were no other job offers on the horizon, nor were they suddenly going to fall out of the sky and land on my lap. I had no other choice but to do a complete about turn and go back inside the Agency. Once inside, this time as the reluctant realist who, given the lack of funds, was in no position to turn up his nose at even the most of menial of tasks and with a sharp intake of breath, I began the task of going from one vacancy board to another, each card upon those boards containing descriptions of a variety of different jobs which could hardly be described as awe inspiring together with an hourly rate of pay that bordered on employee exploitation. I had no choice but to bite the bullet and selected a couple of cards and went up to one of the recruitment desks to ask for help. The Recruitment Officer, who was serving me could tell by my half-hearted approach that manual labour wasn't the type of work I was best suited for and she suggested that I should try Recruitment Agencies who specialised in office work. Acting on her advice, I contacted those office recruitment agencies she suggested but alas, there was either nothing suitable or available given my total lack of experience in working in such an environment. For the next few days I spent my time traipsing from one job centre to another in an effort to try and find something, even widening the extent of those efforts to the West End, focusing on vacancies as a shop assistant. But all those miles and miles of walking up and down going from one shop or department store to another eventually come to nothing. As the days went by, the only thing on my agenda was the mind numbing monotony of daytime TV followed by loads and loads of seemingly endless time doing absolutely nothing. But the long boring hours of simply sitting around and twiddling my thumbs were soon about to change when I received a letter which landed on the doormat sent by Brent Leisure Services. I eagerly tore open the letter and a mixture of delight and relief came across my face when its contents revealed the news that I was being invited for an interview for the Temporary Play Leaders post at their offices at 2pm on 6th July. The worries and anxieties of spending an entire summer without any income soon began to melt away. I could rest a little easier now but not too much because two days beforehand, the exam results would be published on the College Notice Board, a decision that would have a profound impact on the next stage of my life's journey.

My date with destiny had now arrived and I woke up that morning feeling a mixture of excitement tinged with apprehension. All my hopes, dreams and ambitions over the last six to seven years hinged on this very day and all I could do as I got myself ready to go to Ladbroke House was hope and pray that the final chapter of my life as an undergraduate would have a happy ending. Despite my optimism however, small nagging doubts soon began to creep into my thoughts which quickly grew into uncontrollable fears that everything could go horribly wrong and that the final chapter would turn out to be a horrible anti-climax. The contrasting emotions of boundless optimism and total negativity were locked in a constant battle in both my mind and my stomach and my attempt to try to keep myself calm and in control was a completely useless exercise.

When I eventually reached the steps to Ladbroke House my thoughts were still dominated by gut wrenching uncertainties, which quickly transferred to my legs which began to shake uncontrollably. I was walking as though I was a man condemned and about to ascend the gallows. Coming towards me at the top end of the stairs were two fellow students of mine on the course and as we got closer, I noticed that they had big smiles on their faces.

"Congratulations Shaun!" they said, excitedly.

"Why?" I asked not really having a clue what they were talking about.

"You got a 2:2!"

"Really?" I felt numb with excitement for a split second but I still couldn't believe what I had just been told. They repeated what they said and added that they also got a 2:2 and that there were some other students still hanging around on the second floor. The three of us then spontaneously engaged in one big celebratory hugging exercise before we parted company and I headed upstairs to the second floor landing with the air of a man who had just been granted a free pardon. The floor was alive with a sea of newly created graduates as well as a few of our former lecturers who were on hand to extend their congratulations on our success. I went straight to the College Notice Board as I wanted to read and confirm with my own eyes what I'd been told moments earlier. The notice read as follows;

"At a meeting held on 5th July 1983, the Board of Examiners for BA(HONS) LAW recommended that the following Degrees be awarded..."

As I scanned through the various classifications, I could see that no one was awarded a First Class Degree. Seven of the students were awarded an Upper Second but it was the Lower Second classification which had my sole attention and as I went down the alphabetical list, I stopped at the antepenultimate name which read SHAUN ANTHONY WALLACE.

I've done it, I've actually done it! Now it was all beginning to sink in. *SHAUN WALLACE BA HONS LAW! SHAUN WALLACE BA HONS LAW!* that's all I kept saying to myself. I'd crossed the finishing line. Maybe not in first place, but I crossed nonetheless. I looked skywards briefly to thank the man upstairs before re-engaging with my surroundings and joining in the many celebrations which were now in full swing on the second floor. Those celebrations provided the perfect end to the final chapter of my academic career at the Polytechnic of North London.

The following day, the College sent me a formal letter congratulating me on the award of my Degree as well as a breakdown of my overall grades for each subject. I got Grade B in all four exams and upon seeing those results it brought about an instant feeling of total satisfaction and a personal vindication of all the past setbacks of my mid to late teens, there was now only one brick left in the wall: success in The Bar Finals Examinations, a task which is easier said than done. The confidence I gained in finally getting that cherished Law Degree made me all the more determined to ensure that at the beginning of September, I would make every effort to try and make that happen. But as one's life ambitions moves ever closer to fruition, another sadly closes as I came to the realisation that my two year fantasy of trying to combine a career both in Law and as a Professional Footballer was going to be what it always was going to be from the very outset, nothing more than just a mere fantasy. Most of the teams had started back with preseason training by this time and if my brief but nevertheless enjoyable stint with Hendon the previous two seasons was anything to go by, the chances of a totally unknown quantity like myself, with no footballing pedigree and/or reputation to talk about reaching the pinnacle of the professional game when I struggled to even make the reserves of a non-league football team were both slim and none. That decision however didn't mean that at the ripe old age of twenty three I was going to turn my back forever on the beautiful game, on the contrary. If anything, it made me want to play even more, but my footballing prowess (if such a thing ever really existed!) would, from now on, only grace the playing fields of the local parks of Brent and its surrounding boroughs and not Old Trafford's Theatre of Dreams!

The following day, I went to Brent Council's offices arriving with plenty of time to spare for the 2pm interview for the temporary post as a summer Play Scheme Worker. The interview could not have gone any better even if I scripted the whole thing myself because as luck would have it, sitting on the interviewing panel was none other than one of my old school teachers from my Aylestone days, Jenny Watts. I wouldn't deny the fact my chances of getting taken on given our obvious connections had shot up immeasurably, but Jenny and the rest of interviewing panel were scrupulous in terms of their impartiality and rigorous with their probing questions in an effort to determine my suitability and that meant that it was by no means a certainty that I would secure the temporary position. Three days later however, I completed a hat trick of strokes of good fortune when I received the letter from Brent Leisure Services offering me the temporary position, with the scheme itself not due to start until the last week in July after the schools had broken up for the summer holidays.

The job offer and the start date was perfect from my point of view because it would allow me the opportunity to spend some quality time with my Aunt Delores who was coming to stay with the family for the first time on a ten day vacation from Florida. Aunty Del as she was affectionately known, is my Mum's only sister. She's very warm and friendly, as well as stylish and glamorous. Mum would often talk about my Aunt when we were growing up and she would visit her whenever she crossed the Atlantic on the occasional trips back home to see her family. Naturally I was extremely keen to meet my Mum's only female sibling as the only other natural aunt that I knew and was familiar with was my Dad's sister, my Aunt Inez who by this time had immigrated to the USA.

I was determined to ensure that, despite the short tenure of my Aunt's visit, her time spent on these shores would be a memorable one but my attempts in trying to achieve such an objective however, didn't get off to the best of possible starts. On her first afternoon in the UK, I asked her whether she would like to go for a drive on a mini sightseeing tour. Despite the fact she was still suffering the effects of jetlag, she seemed up for it. I decided that our first port of call would be Brent Cross Shopping Centre, but as we drove along the North

Circular Road, heading towards Brent Cross disaster struck. I had run out of petrol! What made the situation even more embarrassing was that the traffic was totally gridlocked, a fact compounded by the major road works that were going on near to the North Circular flyover. As we sat in the traffic with cars honking their horns, frustrated by the fact no doubt that my broken down vehicle was adding to the congestion, I wanted the ground to open up and swallow me whole. We were eventually rescued from the embarrassing situation, our saviour coming in the form of a free Recovery truck which towed the vehicle to the petrol station at the Staples Corner roundabout for a quick refill before making the short journey to Brent Cross much to my considerable relief. I managed to atone for that blundering mishap during the remaining days of my Aunt's vacation by taking her on a whirlwind sightseeing tour around London (this time by bus and train!) to all the haunts your typical tourist would wish to see. From Buckingham Palace to the Tower of London, I took my Aunt to every historical and cultural site London has to offer, not forgetting her insistence on visiting virtually all of the major shopping venues form Harrods to Selfridges. I don't know where my Aunt got her energy from during our touring exploits. It was if she had the stamina of a horse whereas I had to spend most nights soaking in a hot bubble bath in order to soothe away the aches and pains of my poor back and feet in preparation for the following day's excursions.

It was fantastic having my glamorous Aunt coming to stay with us, there wasn't a dull moment throughout her entire stay but as always, time always flies when you're having fun and before I knew it, I found myself making the return trip to Heathrow's Terminal 3 taking my Aunt to meet her flight for the return journey home (ensuring this time that there was more than enough petrol in the car!). We hugged each other goodbye and before she exited through to the Departure Lounge I shouted, "I'll come and see you next summer after I've sat my exams... that's a promise!"

To which my Aunt replied, "by which time I'm sure I'll be the proud Aunt of a newly qualified lawyer!"

The following Monday was the start of more fun and good times in the form of my five week stint on one of Brent's summer Play schemes. The scheme I was assigned to was being held at the South Kilburn High School situated on the outskirts of Queen's Park. In overall charge of the day to day scheme was Jenny Watts, which made me happy.

Overall, the scheme went very well with the staff and the forty or so children who regularly attended had a very good rapport and understanding. It was great to see the children and even some of the workers enjoying themselves and having fun. It gave them a chance to let their hair down to relax and be themselves, far away from the vast concrete estate of South Kilburn that some of them call home.

The scheme finally came to an end on the last Friday in August and to mark the occasion we organised an end of scheme party to celebrate the fact that the last five weeks had been an unqualified success. All the staff and children brought their own contributions to the party in the form of sandwiches, cakes, crisps and fizzy drinks and just before we got proceedings underway, Jenny made a short speech thanking both the staff and the play schemers alike for making the last five weeks both memorable and enjoyable. The revelry and festivities that took place thereafter was a perfect end to a perfect summer from a personal perspective and I could not have felt any more content and at ease with myself had the man upstairs granted me the eternal wish of perpetual happiness. I had every reason to look forward to the first Monday of September with newfound confidence and ever flowing optimism as it would signal the start of the final phase of my educational odyssey which, with a bit of luck and a great deal of hard work and effort would finally realise my ultimate ambition.

CHAPTER EIGHT

I arrived at Chancery Lane station a little after 8.30am on my way to the Inns of Court School of Law for day one of the one year Bar Vocational Course. As I walked the short distance on High Holborn towards Warwick Court where the Faculty is situated, I felt a mixture of excitement and apprehension as to what might lie in store for me. At the same time, I couldn't help but feel that I was one of the chosen few because at the time, the Inns of Court was the only Faculty in the country (if not the entire world!), that ran The Bar Vocational Course and I realised how fortunate I was to have got so far, especially when I look back to those difficult and depressing times in my late teens on account of those seemingly endless re-sits prior to my undergraduate years.

When I got to the Law Faculty, I saw some of my old PNL acolytes gathered together looking fairly relaxed. I headed straight towards them and was greeted with smiles and hugs as we chatted amongst ourselves briefly about our expectations of the course and how much we were looking forward to it.

Soon, all the students began making their way inside the Faculty's main building and the vast lecture hall for the formal induction. Each of the lecturers addressed us in turn about all aspects of the vocational course, as well as the standard they expected the students to reach if we wanted to achieve our ultimate aim. The collective message that resonated throughout the induction is best summed up in the following terms:

"This course isn't about how much law you know but how you apply such knowledge..."

The very same message that both Julie Newton and Sue Knight tried to drum into me during my struggles in trying to make the transition from an A Level student to law undergraduate and If I wanted to make the transition from law graduate to newly qualified barrister, then every aspect of the collective message from those lecturers would have to be taken on board.

The course itself was mainly based on two principle objectives that were designed to train and develop students in the aspects of the role of a Barrister in private practice. The vocational aspect of the course had a heavy emphasis in opinion writing, drafting documents and the art of advocacy that are the essential tools which a Barrister must possess if he/she is to survive and thrive in the cutthroat world of private practice. This aspect of the course was mostly taught by lawyers in private practice who were tasked with monitoring a student's progress and to give constructive feedback at the end of each seminar. The academic aspect of the Course involved passing the written exams in the following core subjects: General Papers 1 and 2, Criminal Procedure, Civil Procedure, Evidence, Revenue Law plus one optional subject. I was exempt from sitting Revenue Law on account of already having taken the subject in my final year at PNL and as such, I had the luxury of choosing another subject from the elective options that were available. The subjects I selected were Family Law and Local Government and Planning, the latter seemingly a strange choice on the face of it but from my prospective, it was a logical one to make given my fondness for both Constitutional and Administrative Law whilst studying as an undergraduate.

I settled down pretty quickly as the course progressed. I never missed a lecture or seminar and I quickly excelled in the vocational aspects of the course such as advocacy training and opinion writing and drafting. Such progress was, in no doubt, a reflection of the quality of the tuition I was receiving from the lecturing staff who were always helpful and approachable. But the one aspect of the course that I enjoyed above everything else was the time honoured tradition of 'dining at one's Inn'.

The practice of dining is as old as the profession itself, where Barristers and students alike would 'meet, dine and discuss the law'. It was a tradition that no young aspiring advocate could escape or avoid and even if a student had passed all the written and vocational exams at the end of the year, that student could not be called to the bar unless he/she had sat the minimum number of sittings. My Inn (Inner Temple) required the students to dine at least 24 times. I could have started my dining sittings during my last year at PNL as most of my fellow PNL students who decided to go to the bar had done. But given the touch and go nature of my grades at the start of my last year at the College, I didn't want to tempt fate, which meant that I would have to undergo the process colloquially referred to as "Double Dining" (that is, attending two or more sittings in each term). Whenever I went to dine at the Inn, I would usually go with some of my colleagues from PNL for no other reason other than having somebody there to talk to but gradually, the daunting experience of having to speak to and meet new people became a little easier on each and every occasion. I even brought both my Mum and Dad along with me on one of the special guest days the Inn would set aside which allowed student members of the Inn to invite guests of their choosing. Both Mum and Dad really enjoyed themselves and to see the pair of them sampling one of the profession's most ancient rituals was for me a very proud and wonderful moment.

Before I knew it the start of the summer term was upon us which meant the start of The Bar Final examinations which were due to commence in the last week of May, concluding in the first week of June. All the students were required to sit the core subjects on successive days throughout the first week, with the exams in the optional topics straddling to the following week.

My preparation for those exams was the usual diet of attending revision lectures, incessant drafting of opinions and relevant legal documents as well as the tried and trusted method of timed essays, all of which left me feeling quietly confident that I could cope with both the physical and mental demands for the final and ultimate test that lay ahead. I was so focused on the task at hand that I didn't even have time to watch Liverpool complete their historic treble when they won the European Cup in Rome as I had an Evidence exam the following morning. I had to plead with my brother Steve, himself a diehard Liverpool fan, to tape the game for me and made him promise not to reveal the outcome. I did everything humanly possible to avoid the result of the match the following day, avoiding the newspapers, the TV and radio and stopped anybody in their tracks if they tried to talk about the game. I managed to avoid the result as well as perform well in my Evidence exam and the moment the exam was over, I got home and indulged in the small luxury of watching the taped recording as if I was watching it live before getting back on the revision treadmill in order to prepare for the next exam the following morning.

I managed to emerge from the five day exam ordeal relatively intact, the question papers themselves providing no real horrors or surprises and now all that was required was one last big effort for the Local Government exam on the Monday and the whole ordeal would be over. But the Saturday was my birthday and despite the rigid regime throughout my revision studies and the exams themselves, I was dying to break free from my self-imposed cocoon and let my hair down and celebrate. Those guilty thoughts and pleasures reluctantly gave way to the murmurings of my inner conscience which were nagging away at me and telling me to stay focused. So in deference to those murmurings of conscience, I decided to spend my twenty fourth birthday locked in my bedroom with the bright summer's sunshine piercing through my window, surrounded by my Local Government textbooks, lecture notes and past exam papers for one last Herculean effort. The only luxury I afforded myself that day was to take two hours out in the afternoon to watch England's last International game of the season against the Soviet Union at Wembley on my small black and white TV. The England team were about to embark on a three match tour to South America which had been arranged as a consequence of the team's failure to qualify for the European Championships that were due to be held in France later that month. England were looking to end the season on a high to make amends for their failure to qualify for the tournament, but despite their best efforts, England were comprehensively beaten by a technically more gifted Soviet team who were worthy winners in a 2-0 victory.

The rest of the weekend involved the never ending cycle of eat, sleep, revision and even though the last exam was now only a day away, I'd reached the end of my tether. I wanted to do something, anything just to get away from the monotony of constant revision. The cycle of constant reading and trying to retain the information was making me go stir crazy. I tried my best to maintain a 100% focus but by the time Sunday evening had arrived, my cup had finally runneth over. I'd had enough of this incessant concentration and soon the "focused aspect" of my inner thoughts and conscience had finally succumbed to guilty pleasures and I decided that I was going out to celebrate my birthday, albeit belatedly and with my lonesome self. I headed off to Shoreditch High Street and one of my favourite night club haunts, Night Moves, where for a couple of hours at least I could relax and enjoy myself without a care in the world. That minor transgression seemed to do the trick. The following morning I woke up feeling all the more invigorated and went to the final exam that afternoon with my focus realigned and committed to the task at hand which paid dividends. On the stroke of 5pm, I rose from my seat at the end of my final written paper and breathed a deep sigh of relief. The results of those Bar Finals exams were due to be published in both The Times and the Daily Telegraph in the second week of July which in the infinite wisdom of the Faculty happened to be Friday the 13th. Now was not the time to dwell on any superstitious concerns. There was a whole summer out there to enjoy and if everything went according to plan, it could turn out to be the best summer yet.

Even though it seemed that I had all the time in the world now that my exams were over, that well-earned luxury didn't mean that I was going to lounge around putting my feet up and allow the world drift on by. My immediate priority was to try to find temporary employment as soon as I possibly could. Just as important, if not more so, was the need to secure that all important rite of passage that all newly qualified barristers must undertake before they can practice professionally: the twelve month training period under the watchful eye of an experienced barrister known as Pupillage. However, such an exercise is easier said than done as trying to secure pupillage was on par with trying to find the proverbial needle in the haystack, an exercise made all the more arduous if you weren't from a particular social background or didn't attend the 'right' University. Those apparent obstacles would have to be overcome if I wanted a career in private practice but I decided to begin my search in earnest once I knew the outcome of my exams.

My first port of call in my efforts in trying to find temporary work for the summer was a visit to the Brent Leisure Services. Whilst I was filling in the application form, the receptionist at alerted me about a temporary position on the Chalk Hill Estate in Wembley. The news was music to my ears. I managed to get an interview that very afternoon with the person in charge of running the Project, John Bradford, at the Project's main site on the Chalk Hill Road deep in the heart of the estate.

The interview itself was relaxed and informal, with John appearing impressed not only with my play scheme credentials, but also with the fact that I was a young black man trying to do something positive with his life. At the end of the interview, John made it pretty clear that, subject to the obligatory checks on my background, the temporary position was mine if I wanted it. I walked out of John's office feeling on cloud nine. I was determined to justify as well as repay all the faith he had shown in me.

From the daily routine of supervising as well as engaging the children on the variety of schemes organised by the Projects throughout the Estate, to the light-hearted banter with it came to an end. I will always remember my short stint there with the fondest affection as it provided me with another opportunity to enhance and develop my interpersonal skills. All that wonderful work experience, however, would pale into insignificance if my results didn't go my way.

The day of reckoning had finally arrived. I tried to remain as calm as I could throughout the train ride to get my results but I couldn't help feeling like the train itself: entering a dark tunnel with only a flicker of light at the end of it, totally unsure as to whether or not the light represented successful progression to the next stage in my life or if the light was really an oncoming train speeding towards me in a sort of academic train crash.

By the time I arrived outside the College Courtyard, the place was a sea of Bar students who like me were anxious to know whether they had passed or failed the final academic hurdle. I managed to locate some of my old PNL classmates amongst the expectant crowd and their outwardly cheery optimism as we waited around together chatting amongst ourselves helped to put me at ease and in a better frame of mind.

Eventually, there was a mass surge towards the gallery of windows at the side of the reception building as the results were finally about to be published. It was like a frenzied scrum as loads of students found themselves huddled over the glazed Noticeboard, frantically searching for either their name or candidate number that was printed in the smallest type print imaginable.

I didn't get involved in that initial mad frantic surge preferring to bide my time and wait for the whole mad rush to die down before going over to see whether or not I had made the grade. It must have been at least ten minutes before I could finally summon up the courage to go over to the window, but as I approached the window the onerous burden of anxiety and worry were finally cast aside when I was greeted by the words of one of my PNL students who had already been to the Noticeboard who told me I had passed.

I could hardly believe it, I had to have confirmation of the astonishing news with my own eyes. I rushed over to the Noticeboard getting as close as I could to where the crowd in front of me were hampering my search, which given the manner in which the results were published was understandable as there were students desperately scanning the published lists in the vain hope that their names were somewhere on there, whilst in other cases, it was a sight of students displaying the contrasting emotions of relief at their success or the bitter disappointment of failure.

Eventually, I got close enough to carry out my own inspection and after scanning the candidate numbers under the Third Class Classification, there it was under candidate number 6810 – Shaun Anthony Linford Wallace. *Shaun Wallace, BA Honours In Law and now a Qualified Barrister!* It took a little while for it all to sink in and when it finally did, I punched the air in an outward expression of delight to reflect that a thirteen year mission, from all its triumphs and setbacks were well and truly accomplished. I re-joined my old classmates who were all in the midst of celebrating their own personal achievements. Every single one of us had passed at the first time of asking and thus sparing us the agonies of having to go through it all over again in the Autumn re-sits. All the talk amongst the group was how much everyone was looking forward to the quasi mystical ritual of being Called to the bar by their respective Inns which in most cases was going to occur at the end of the month. However, that wasn't going to happen in my situation unfortunately. I had only managed to sit eighteen of the twenty four Dining Terms that were required by my Inn, which in turn meant that I would have to postpone my Call to the bar until sometime in the late Autumn.

After having said all my goodbyes to my old PNL classmates, which in most cases would probably be for the last time, I headed back to Chancery Lane tube station for the homeward bound journey only this time, completely and totally devoid of the angst ridden uncertainty that was the dominating feature of my outward bound journey only two hours earlier. Steve was the only person at home by the time I eventually arrived. I walked into the living room where Steve was watching TV and I slumped myself in the middle of the settee with the apparent air of a man carrying the world on his shoulders.

"Well, how did you get on?" my kid brother enquired hesitantly, his hesitance totally understandable given the fact that he had witnessed many a setback and disappointment during my pre-undergraduate years.

I turned to him with a facial expression of a man who was about to deliver the most devastating news and whispered, "yeah bruv... I've done it!"

Steve could hardly contain himself and we celebrated with a round of hugs and high fives before I got on the telephone to call as many friends that I could think of to share the good news. Because Mum wasn't due home from work until later that evening, the pair of us drove to Dad's place in Chapter Road as I wanted to catch him before he started his usual night shift at the Heinz factory. Dad was overjoyed with the news and clearly felt an immense sense of pride that his first born son had finally achieved a lifelong goal. I told Dad that I wanted both him and Mum to be present when I was Called to the bar in the late Autumn and that seemed to excite him even more. Steve and I eventually left Dad's place and headed straight for home where Debbie had recently arrived home from work. When I broke the news to her, she was over the moon. Mum eventually arrived home an hour or so later and as soon as I heard the key turning in our front door, I rushed quickly from the living room into the passage way to meet her the instant she got through the front door.

"Mum... I passed!"

The news seemed to invigorate her obvious weary demeanour. "Tank Gord!" she replied in a drawling Jamaican tone.

I went up to her and she displayed a moment of genuine physical affection rarely seen in my twenty four years; it was a seminal moment. It was a vindication of all the years of unflinching support and sacrifice that Mum had made that made my own personal accomplishment all the more possible. I felt more pleased for her than I did for myself perhaps, for the pure and simple reason that the optimistic hopes and dreams that she had for the infant she so lovingly cradled in her arms all those years ago had come true.

After my memorable short stint at the Chalk Hill Neighbourhood Project had come to an end by the last week in July, the rest of my summer was spent working once again with Jenny

Watts back at the Brent summer Play Scheme at South Kilburn High School for another round of onsite activities, outings and short holidays all crammed into four hectic yet enjoyable weeks. Those summer months of 1984 couldn't have gone any better. I felt like a man that had the world at his feet. I could start to think positively about both my immediate and long term future.

Before I could do anything, I had to secure the elusive twelve month pupillage. For the present however, all such thoughts would have to occupy the proverbial back burner as I decided that I wanted to spend my last two months as a care free student on a grand tour of the Eastern Seaboard. I had to seize the moment because if I didn't take advantage of this window of opportunity now then the opportunity may not present itself again.

I contacted all the family and friends that I hoped to stay with on my travels and once they had all given me the green light, I immediately went to my local travel agent and bought a one way ticket on the recently created Virgin Airlines and left Heathrow on 13th September for John Foster Dallas Airport, Washington for the first leg of my two month grand tour.

After a week of trawling around all the major landmarks in the Capital, the next leg of was a trip North on a Greyhound bus bound for the Garden State of New Jersey and the home of my favourite cousin and boyhood idol Paul Kitson and the rest of the Kitson family. The whole of the Kitson clan had emigrated to the United States in the summer of 1976 from their cramped terrace abode in Langler Road, Kensal Rise, and they seemed to have adjusted quite comfortably to the American way of life.

By this time, Paul had realised his own boyhood ambition of a career as a professional footballer, plying his trade in the (now defunct) Major Indoor Soccer League for a number of years. He remained heavily involved in the game coaching teams both in the United States and Canada right up until his untimely death on 25th August 2005 when after a training session in Toronto, he collapsed on the training field suffering a massive heart attack.

I spent a little over three weeks with my cousins who went out of their way to make sure that I wanted for nothing and they were all clearly very proud of the fact that there was now a qualified lawyer in the family. Paul took me here, there and everywhere, whenever his professional commitments would allow it, taking me to the nearby states of Maryland, New York and Connecticut as well as a memorable trip to Atlantic City and its famous Board Walk. I spent the best part of two weeks in New Jersey before boarding a plane at Newark Airport for the flight South to Miami to see my Aunt Delores thus honouring the promise that I had made to her when she left at the end of her trip to the UK in July of the previous year.

My Aunt arranged to pick me up from the airport and greeted me with a warm embrace. Accompanying my Aunt as part of the welcoming committee was her only son, Peter, who would have been in his mid-teens at this time. This was the first time I ever met Peter but despite the fact we were virtual strangers to one another, we greeted each other as if we had known each other all our lives. We all left the airport and headed for the multi-laned highway for the hour long drive to my Aunt's home, a spacious four bedroomed detached house on the outskirts of the city. I stayed just over ten days in Miami and from the moment I arrived I totally fell in love with the place. Everything, from the glorious sunshine, to Miami's golden beaches was just wonderful. Both my Aunt and my cousin went out of their way to ensure that I had the best time possible and as far as I was concerned, it was more than mission accomplished. For the final leg of my tour, I flew back North to New Jersey to spend some more time with Paul and his family. I didn't want this holiday adventure to end. I tried to think of a justifiable reason for staying in the USA just that little bit longer, but in my hearts of hearts, I knew I had to bring my adventure to a close and re-join the real world albeit with some considerable reluctance. I booked a ticket on Virgin Airlines and arrived back at Heathrow on a cold and rainy day at the end of October which the sobering effect of bringing me out of my holiday mode but if the truth be told, I was glad to be back in good old London Town. I had a lot of things to be getting on with and those things were not going to get done if I was laying on my backside on a beach getting a sun tan. Once I had cleared customs, I headed straight for the Underground and the Piccadilly Line and during the journey as the train rumbled towards Alperton Tube station, my thoughts were dominated by my urgent need to shed quickly the hedonistic mindset that I so lovingly embraced throughout my great American adventure and replace it with thoughts of the arduous task that lay ahead of me in trying to kick start a professional career.

With only four weeks to go before my big day, I managed to obtain some much needed temporary employment as all the money that I earned during the summer months was virtually gone. I was part of a team of temporary staff who were required to sift through and process the thousands upon thousands of applications for shares by members of the public in the British Telecom Company that was about to be floated on the Stock Exchange. The sale of those shares was part of the economic philosophy of the day which advocated pure and undiluted lassaiz-faire economics that was now firmly embedded in the nation's consciousness. The seemingly infinite number of application forms left little room for doubt on how popular the sale of previously state owned institutions was as it provided an opportunity for the ordinary person to be part of the share owning democracy. This temporary employment stint lasted only two weeks but luckily for me, the Employment Agency that I signed up with managed to find me further temporary office work which meant that by the third week in November, I could breathe a sigh of relief that I had managed to attain some form of financial stability. I could now go out and do such things as buy some new clothes, make the final payment for my last Dining Term for Call Night, there was even enough money to allow me to pay for the rental of a wig and gown. In a week's time I was going to be called to the bar, that's all that mattered. All the hard work was about to be vindicated and I was going to make sure that, on the day itself, I was going to savour and enjoy what for me would be a very personal and seminal occasion.

The day, Tuesday. The date, 27th November 1984. The time, just after 7pm. The venue, The Inner Temple Church Hall. The occasion, the day when another generation of newly qualified barristers would celebrate being formally called to the bar by one's Inn. All of the new Barristers to be were resplendently dressed for the occasion in formal barrister's wigs and gowns, each one of us beaming with pride as we posed respectively for the many photos taken by the equally proud family and friends both outside and inside the great hall. As promised, both Mum and Dad were on hand to witness my reward for successfully completing my long academic journey and the very fact that they were there filled me with an overwhelming sense of pride and satisfaction that all their continued love and support was now about to be repaid in full. Despite the seemingly quasi mystique and solemn ritual involved with the ceremony, it was a surprisingly simple and straightforward affair. The actual event itself couldn't have been any less understated or any less dramatic than the grandiose affair that I had conjured up in my own imagination.

The ceremony began with the students walking down the Inner Temple Church aisle to the sounds of organ music playing in the background, followed by officials who were responsible for the governing of the Inn known as The Masters of the Bench. Presiding over the whole ritual were the Treasurer of the Inn, the Reader and other Masters of the Bench who were already in place at the Church altar and their specific role was to formally welcome the newly qualified Barrister to the Inn. One by one, different Masters formally "called" the name of a student to come forward and after a shake of the hand, the Treasurer handed the student a beautifully embossed certificate certifying one's name, the date the student was admitted to the Inn and most importantly, the date the student was formally called. My own seminal moment now had finally arrived when one of the Masters of the Bench "called out" for me to step forward. With a slight pinch of my nose, quickly followed by a sharp intake of breath, I walked towards the altar, each step a measure of my own pride and accomplishment. The Treasurer shook my hand and then gave me my certificate and suddenly an explosion of complete, albeit restrained joy resonated throughout my whole being. No sooner had I walked to join the other newly qualified Barristers, the reality of my newfound status and situation began to take hold. This was, without a shadow of a doubt, the greatest moment of my life up to that point, but as I looked around at my newly called contemporaries, I knew the cold hard reality of such a joyous situation really meant nothing more than a passport to the starting line of a whole new different challenge. I realised this, even amongst the midst of these wonderful and joyous celebrations. The starting pistol marking the start of this new challenge had already been fired and some of my contemporaries were already up and running and if I was not careful, I could easily find myself left behind. At least I had the small but satisfying comfort of being on that start line if not as of yet, fully out of the starting blocks. The one solemn promise I made to myself amidst all the celebrations though was this: no matter what obstacle, no matter what setback, no matter what disappointments I may or may not encounter along the way, this was the journey that I would pursue with total and loyal dedication for the rest of my natural days.

After the formal ceremony was over the Inn held a champagne reception. Whilst the champagne celebrations were in full swing, I broke away from the main group and went to the other side of the hall for a moment of quiet introspection. I looked up and was staring at the various paintings and commemorative plaques displaying some of the professions most illustrious predecessors. *I wonder if my name will be up there one day?* I fantasized to myself as I began to contemplate the shape of my professional career and what may lay in store. *What will I be doing in ten years' time? In twenty years' time?* I asked myself inquisitively, a question I suppose, all young fledgling Barristers ask themselves as they take the first tentative steps along the long at times precarious road to the top of the profession. *It's not going to be easy!* I mused to myself and there was a real possibility I wouldn't get past base camp, let alone conquer the summit! But the one thing I do know for sure is, for however long I last in the profession, I will be at all times professional, committed, but above all – MYSELF!

Although I enjoyed all the fun and celebrations of Call Night, these weren't exactly the sort of celebrations that I had in mind to mark this seminal rite of passage. I wanted to have a party, a good old fashioned rave up. The problem was I didn't know where I was going to hold it. I daren't ask Mum about the possibility of having it at home because I knew in advance what the answer would be - an ear splitting, resounding "NO!!" Mum was one of those typical West Indian women who, when I was a kid growing up, didn't take too kindly to people traipsing in and out of our house unless they were *her* friends. There was no real change in my Mum's attitude even in my teens and early twenties particularly when my friends would call me on the house phone at home and if Mum answered it, she would usually adopt a typically impatient tone and on some occasions, leave my friends hanging on the other end of the phone with the dialling tone ringing in their ears. There were times that I was so exasperated by Mum's behaviour that I would try to take her to task about her forthright manner, but it was an argument I was destined to lose because she would always let me know in no uncertain terms that this was HER HOUSE, she pays all the bills and if I didn't like the rules, then I knew where the front door was.

My clandestine plans to have a house party seemed all but dead in the water but in a fortunate twist of fate, they were suddenly revived when Mum announced that she was going to spend Christmas in Florida and Jamaica. The news of Mum's impending trip overseas was music to my ears. My plans to have a party appeared to be back on track. But those plans had to be kept closely under wraps for now and would only swing into action once I was absolutely sure that Mum was safely out of the jurisdiction.

I dropped Mum to Heathrow Airport a couple or so days before Christmas, my secret party plans still on course in the forefront of my mind with Mum still none the wiser. During the journey to the airport, I was pondering over the difficult dilemma as to whether I should hold a party and say nothing to her at all, or to briefly mention it to her and risk incurring the inevitable cursing and moaning. I decided that it would be probably wise to say something for in the unlikely event of something going drastically wrong, then my life would not be worth living. I decided to bite the bullet and test her reaction.

"Mum...is it alright if I have a few friends over for the Christmas period as I didn't really celebrate passing my exams with my close friends?"

"Wha' yuh whan keep party fa?" was her brusque reply.

"I'm not keeping a party Mum honest!" I said, crossing the two sets of fingers on both of my hands instantly as they gripped the

129

steering wheel whilst at the same time, frantically trying to reassure her that everything was going to be very low key. It was hard work trying to convince Mum that everything would be alright, but eventually, I managed to wear her down and extracted from her reluctant blessing to go ahead.

With Mum safely out the way, it was full steam ahead. I informed Debbie and Steve of my intentions and like Mum, they were dead set against the idea and it took all of my persuasive charm to get their cautious blessing that nothing would go wrong. I wasn't sure what date to have the party, as I was sure how long Mum would be away for. It didn't occur to me to ask her, a glaring blunder on my part which I blamed on the fact that I was so obsessed about the excitement of having a party. I finally decided on Saturday 5th January as that would give plenty of notice to the people whom I planned to invite whilst allowing me to roll the dice and take a calculated gamble that it was unlikely that Mum would be back by then.

The evening of the party had arrived and with the help of a couple of my close mates we moved all the dining room furniture, opening the sliding doors and piled them all up into Mum's sacred front room. In most West Indian households, the front room where the best furniture and all the finest crockery are kept and it was strictly off limits so far as we siblings were concerned. That room and my Mum's bedroom were the no go areas as far as my party was concerned, which left the small back room with the equally small extension attached as the areas where all the main action was going to take place. I spent a modest amount on drinks and food and all the invitees were told in no uncertain terms that they had to bring a bottle and to be fair, most of my guests did bring a bottle of some description. Cheap bottles of wine, the odd spirits and the occasional bottle of Champagne were handed in by my guests but the main drink that people seemed to be carrying with them was that ghastly beverage that was all the rage at the time, the notorious Thunderbird.

I invited around fifty or so people and told them to arrive between 11pm and midnight and I made it clear that the invite was for them and them alone and if they brought anyone who was not on the guest list then they would be left on the doorstep. But sadly, house parties, especially free house parties, are a notoriously difficult thing to keep a secret and before I knew it, people were starting to arrive in their droves, occasionally in tandem with someone whom I neither knew and/or invited and I felt powerless in trying to deny those people entry. By midnight, the whole house was absolutely jam packed. Everywhere, from the hallway to the small narrow first floor landing was standing room only, tightly packed like a tin of sardines. Even outside the front door was packed, with scores of people invited or uninvited frantically scrambling in an effort to gain entry, especially when the harsh winter snow began cascading from the heavens. I had to draw a line somewhere. I plucked the remaining few invited guests who were caught up in the mad rush for the front door and managed to haul them in before slamming the door firmly shut. "THIS DOOR IS NOT TO BE OPENED!" I declared "I DON'T WANT IT OPENED EVERY FIVE MINUTES, IT'S ABSOLUTELY PACKED BOTH INSIDE AND OUT AND IF ANYONE DECIDES TO LEAVE, THEY WON'T GET BACK IN!" Everyone inside got the message and now it was time to get the party started.

The party was, to use a well-worn cliché, Absolutely Kicking!. I was rushed off my feet in terms of trying to make sure that everyone inside was constantly fed and refreshed. I had the assistance of both my sister Debbie and my next door neighbour, Angela Holmes, who on occasions had to resort to going outside the back door and supplying drinks and plastic cups to the tightly packed guests in the living room via the extension window in an effort to ensure that nobody missed out. But aside from the free food and free booze the main reason the large crowd hung around was because the music was first class. My old school mate and close friend, Chris Sweeney and his sound system, "The Winner Road Show" plus another close friend of mine, "DJ Lorraine Martins" were my DJs for the night. They played everything from Atlantic Starr soulful grooves to reggae classics from Bob Marley and the Wailers, which kept the crowd rocking long into the wee small hours. At 7am, the party was still going strong and showing no signs of petering out.

I hardly had time to enjoy the party myself what with all the running around that I had to do, keeping an eye on things and making sure that the whole affair could pass without any real drama or incident. With most of the food and drink virtually gone the ravers that remained were now down to a comfortable size in the main room and I could relax and enjoy what was left of the party. But just as I was getting into the swing of things, the party was brought to an abrupt end when all of a sudden the music went dead.

"THAT'S IT! THE PARTY'S OVER!" my sister Debra declared much to the dismay of the remaining crowd. Debra had gone into the small cellar under the stairs and deliberately flicked off the switch that supplied the electricity to the downstairs plugs. It was a wholly unilateral decision made solely on the fact that she was virtually dead on her feet from all the hard work both she and Angela had done in the kitchen, serving all the drinks and food to some guests whose manners at times left a lot to be desired. Although I was annoyed by the manner of how the party ended, I couldn't argue with the fact that the party had to end sometime and eventually the remaining revellers began to head through the front door into the cold January morning and a scene that said that winter had well and truly arrived. Once most of the revellers had gone I got some of my mates to help me retrieve the living room furniture from the front room and put them back in their rightful places and I decided any inspection as to any damage caused by my unauthorised rave would have to be put on hold until after I had a well-earned rest.

I didn't get that much sleep, managing a mere three or so hours at best and even though I was really tired when I eventually got up, there was still the unwanted chore of tidying up and getting the place back to normal. I went downstairs into a living room cluttered with unarranged furniture and with the aid of the sharp natural light that shone into the extension's windows into the living room, clear and unmistakable evidence of my unauthorised party was plain for all to see and it did not make pleasant viewing. Plastic cups on the floor with its contents seeped firmly into Mum's precious carpet. Folded paper plates with half eaten food still in it left unashamedly on some of the bookshelves. The gas heater with its covering grill virtually hanging off the brackets on the wall, a product no doubt of people either leaning or actually sitting on it due to the chronic lack of space. But the mostly ghastly sight in the living room was all the hand marks and black marks in general which seemed to be everywhere over Mum's cream painted walls. Mum probably would have had several heart attacks if she had witnessed such a scene and I broke into a cold sweat at the mere thought but thankfully, she was thousands of miles away thus giving me a few days' grace to sort those minor problems out before she eventually came home. I painted over the numerous marks and stains on the walls at least three times before I could satisfy myself that all the blemishes were finally gone before having to get on my knees and scrub by hand all the visible stains on the living room carpet. All the repairs were finally completed when one of my mates took no more than a minute or so with his electric drill to tighten the loose brackets on the gas heater and its covering grille. Once when I had removed all traces of a full blown party from the remainder of the house could I finally relax and reflect upon the fact that whilst I clearly had taken an almighty liberty in having a party in my mother's house on such a massive scale, the party itself was a resounding success and a clear case of the ends fully justifying the means and a fitting end to celebrate the end of my days as a student. 1985 would mark the beginning of a whole new chapter in my life in terms of trying to start and build a long and successful career in my chosen profession and I for one couldn't wait to get the journey started.

CHAPTER NINE

My hopes and efforts in trying to obtain pupillage was not as daunting or as difficult as some of the horror stories that were prevalent at the time, but there was no denying the fact that the difficulties in trying to obtain a pupillage were so bad in some cases many of the newly qualified barristers (a lot of whom I knew), were increasingly becoming so despondent and despairing of the problem that they decided to throw in the towel and seek employment in the private sector or local authority work, demoralised no doubt by one pupillage rejection after another by sets of Chambers who could afford to be choosy about the type of pupils they were prepared to take on. The depressingly stark reality of what was happening was that the large percentage of the newly qualified barristers who couldn't find pupillage were probably not taken on because they didn't fit the right social or gender profile, or wasn't educated at a particular educational establishment all of which only sought to reinforce the prevailing view that the successful pupils taken on in the vast majority of the traditional and established sets of chambers were principally drawn from a narrow social grouping mainly, University educated, white, middle class male.

My first effort in trying to obtain pupillage began during one of my double dining terms leading up to Call Night, when on one of those occasions I met a kind and approachable barrister called Peter Latham, who was a Civil Practitioner practicing at New Court Chambers. Mr Latham was more than willing to offer me a first six months pupillage after he had invited me to see him at his Chambers in late December 1984, but he added that any final decision as to whether I would be taken on, would formally rest with the Chambers' Pupillage Committee. He went on to add that he himself wouldn't be a part of that interviewing process but encouragingly, he concluded our brief discussions by saying that if I prepared and presented myself well at the interview then he saw no reason why I wouldn't be successful. Naturally, I was really pleased and grateful for his encouraging words and excited at the prospect of learning Civil Law with such an experienced practitioner but what made the situation all the more exciting was the prospect of being in the same Chambers as one of my legal heroes at the time, the legendary George Carmen QC.

George Carmen QC was probably the most famous lawyer in the country at the time. Originally a practitioner on the Northern Circuit Mr Carmen joined the South East circuit and made his name successfully defending clients in such high profile cases the former

Liberal Party Leader Jeremy Thorpe in the notorious Norma Scott affair trial, where Mr Thorpe was accused of Conspiracy to Murder. He also successfully defended Peter Adamson (aka Len Fairclough of Coronation Street fame), who was found not guilty of the sexual assault of a young girl in a swimming pool and in 1983, secured the acquittal of the comedian Ken Dodd on tax evasion charges. I took everything on board that Mr Latham had told me and prepared myself the best that I could for what would be my first ever formal job interview. With a smart haircut, my best YSL blue silk suit and pair of shoes coupled with well-rehearsed reasons as to why I wanted to be a Barrister and start my pupillage with New Court Chambers, I set off for the interview feeling a mixture of nervousness, optimism and excitement at the prospect of the possibility of being taken on as a first six month pupil.

I agonised long and hard as to whether or not I should remove the gold sleeper earring that I had in my left earlobe but decided that I would leave it in figuring that it was so small they probably wouldn't notice it. However, any such excitement and optimism I may have felt beforehand quickly evaporated the moment I entered one of the rooms in the Chambers where I was confronted by a Committee of five to six expressionless, emotionless and seemingly unfriendly middle aged white males, who invited me to sit on a chair in the middle of the room in the full glare of my soon to be interrogators, a scenario that, quite frankly, would not have looked out of place at the height of the Spanish Inquisition during the Middle Ages. If it was a deliberate ploy on the part of the interviewing panel to create such a scenario then they clearly succeeded, because the actual interview itself turned out to be a very harrowing and chastening experience.

The panel started off the interview, by asking the usual questions like, why did I want to be a Barrister, what areas of Law did I hope to Specialise in, but as the interview wore on I could feel my chances of being taken on slipping away when I was asked questions such as, what University did I go to, and even more strangely, did I ever study Roman Law. *Roman Law? Who the hell studies Roman Law?* I asked myself as the panel continued to probe me with one question after another, questions that I felt had no bearing on either the interview itself or indeed my pupillage application. I began to wonder whether the whole interview process was merely designed for me to fall at the first hurdle or whether they were simply horrified at the thought of taking on a pupil who was wearing an earring. At the end of the interview, the Chairman of the Panel thanked me for attending and told me that I would be notified as to their decision in writing which I would receive in the next few days.

After I said my goodbyes and left the room, I felt as though the die had already been cast. *That did not go at all well!* I muttered to myself with an air of resignation and I walked out of the building and turned left going past Fountain Court Buildings heading towards Temple tube station. Before I got to the bottom of the stairs, I heard a male voice call my name. I turned around and recognised it was an old student colleague of mine from my PNL days Raj Joshi. Raj was a year above me at the college and during our time there, we had got on quite well but I hadn't seen him since he graduated from PNL in 1982. We greeted each other warmly and began chatting and catching up on all the good old days. Raj asked me where I was coming from and I told him that I had just finished what was, to all intents and purposes, a gruelling interview at George Carmen's set.

"What are you doing now, Shaun?"

"Nothing apart from heading home."

"I tell you what…why don't you follow me to the Chambers that I'm at and I'll introduce you to my clerks and some of the barristers who might be hanging around in Chambers".

That was a nice gesture on Raj's part, typical of that old PNL camaraderie spirit that was still very much alive and kicking. Raj had completed his twelve month pupillage and was now squatting at 2 Garden Court Chambers, a liberal, progressive set renowned for championing human rights, civil liberties and equal opportunities but as I was soon to discover, when it came to recruiting prospective pupils and tenants, they could be just as arbitrary and selective in the type of recruit they were looking for. Raj told me that he was unsuccessful in his tenancy application but he seemed to take the disappointment of not being taken on in his stride. He went on to say that trying to obtain a tenancy takes a lot of hard work, patience and perseverance and those pupils who are fortunate to be taken on at the end of the pupillage were either very able or fitted the particular profile that certain Chambers were looking for. I got the impression that Raj didn't seem to be all that bothered whether or not he would be taken on. What was more important to him was gaining as much experience as he possibly could that would provide him with an important stepping stone towards either a tenancy if he was lucky, or other opportunities within the profession itself though not necessarily in private practice. We walked up three flights of stairs leading to the top floor where the Clerk's Room was situated, as Raj wanted to know whether or not there was any work for him the following day. Raj then introduced me to his Clerks starting firstly, with Carol Thomas the Senior Clerk who was affectionately referred to by everyone in Chambers by the affectionate name "Pud" and then the First Junior

Clerk, a young black man named Colin Cooks. The mere fact that two of the most important positions in the day to day running of Chambers were filled by a white woman and a black man was a clear illustration how liberal and progressive Garden Court Chambers were, given the fact that those positions are usually the exclusive preserve of white, autocratic middle aged males.

Both Carol and Colin were very warm and friendly when Raj introduced me to them, a greeting which was a complete and pleasant contrast to the horrendous interview that I underwent at New Court Chambers a mere half an hour earlier, where I sat in the middle of the room as if I was a *persona non grata*. Raj took me to some other parts of the building to see if there were other tenants that he could introduce me to and in one of the rooms was a black barrister who I came to look up to as a mentor, role model and friend over the years.

Courtenay Griffiths was smartly dressed in a pin striped suit with a stiff collar and tie looking every inch of a barrister with a thriving and successful practice. I was impressed. Very impressed. Courtenay was very friendly in a down to earth sort of way, a demeanour that immediately put me at ease. We spoke briefly about obtaining pupillages and tenancies and he recognised how difficult a task it was and he offered kind words of encouragement and told me to persevere in my efforts in trying to secure a place in Chambers before wishing me all the best after which, both Raj and I left the room. As we got onto the landing just outside the Clerk's Room, Raj and I said our goodbyes before heading off in separate directions. For Raj, his destination was the short walk towards the Clerk's Room whereas for myself, my destination was home. As I walked towards the tube station it gave me time to think and reflect on my first real insight into what it's like being in a professional set of Chambers, an experience that turned out to be a vital eye opener that I hoped would stand me in good stead as I continued in my quest to find my first six months pupillage.

A few days later, I received a letter from New Court Chambers in relation to my pupillage application. It was a terse four lined statement of rejection that included the less than sincere line, "wishing you the best in the future!" thrown in for good measure. Naturally I was disappointed but not surprised by their decision, but the nightmare scenario that my rejection by New Court Chambers would be the start of a long list of rejections was thankfully averted as my next attempt at trying to secure a pupillage turned out to be a successful one. Not I hasten to add, through any efforts of my own but came about through the most unlikely of sources.

Mum had finally returned from her trip to the Caribbean sometime in the middle of January. I went to pick her up at the airport and I was genuinely pleased to see her and on the surface, it looked as though her month long holiday had done her the world of good. On the journey home though, Mum immediately reverted to type as one of the first things she took me to task about was the so called "little gathering" I had at the house. Her forthright interrogation immediately put me straight on the defensive as I tried to reassure her that nothing major went on whilst she was away and that there was nothing to worry about, a reassurance on this occasion she was less than convinced by.

"I hope yuh nuh keep no party!" she enquired with a hint of menace in the tone of her voice.

"Look Mum, how many MORE times do I have to keep on saying the same thing? I only had a small gathering of friends."

There was a deadly silence momentarily as Mum fixed her cold steely gaze in my direction in the belief that it would somehow extract the truth as to what really went on. I briefly looked in her direction before turning my attention to the road and didn't say another word, but all time I was thinking, *stare all you want.... you can't prove a damn thing!*

Despite our mini standoff, Mum did ask me how things were going with me in general especially with my attempts to secure a pupillage. I told her that I hadn't managed to find anything as of yet. Then completely out of the blue, she said that she heard (in all probability via local gossip), that there was a barrister that lived on Park View (a road which is at the very end of Monks Park) and that I should give him a try.

"Do you know the address?" I asked her in mild astonishment, but sadly, Mum didn't know. I wondered why Mum hadn't mentioned this before, but then again why would it have occurred to her anyway? I was just grateful that she mentioned it and acting upon Mum's advice, I decided that I had nothing to lose in approaching the barrister directly to see if he could help.

Mum eventually managed to get hold of the details for me, again I assumed, with the assistance of the local gossip network. The name of the barrister in question was Jeffery Yearwood. I submitted my CV, which was accompanied with a letter trying to sell myself as best as I could and posted it through his letterbox and waited on a wing and a prayer that he would reply. It didn't take long for those prayers to be answered, for that very evening Mr Yearwood rang me at home. He sounded very amiable in a tone that had an unmistakable soft Bajan twang as we discussed the contents of my letter. During our brief conversation, he told me that he had been in private practice for nine years primarily in criminal defence and had been a pupil master for a couple of years although at the present time, he didn't have a pupil. I asked him whether I could arrange to see him in order to discuss the possibility of me being taken on as his pupil and he responded by saying that I should come and see him at his home the following evening. To say that I was excited at the possibility of obtaining my first six month pupillage would be a massive understatement and whilst ideally I would like to have obtained a civil law pupillage for my first six months, this particular beggar was in no position to be a chooser and anyway, it was in the cut and thrust of court advocacy where I saw my future and hopefully with Mr Yearwood's help and guidance the opportunity to get my foot in the door was one I was going to grab with both hands.

The following evening, I walked the short distance to Mr Yearwood's home dressed in smart but casual clothes. I knocked the front door which was opened by Mr Yearwood who greeted me with a warm welcoming smile. I followed him into his open plan lounge and sat down in one of his comfortable armchairs. He then asked me whether I wanted something to drink, an offer which I gratefully accepted. Moments after he returned with my soft drink, his wife came into the room and I stood up to shake her hand as the introductions were being made. Garcia and I chatted briefly and she told me that she was busy preparing their four year old twins, Jonathan and Alicia for bed. Out of mild curiosity, I asked Garcia when the children were born and to my complete surprise and astonishment she said their birthday was on June 2nd!

"Isn't that an amazing coincidence, that's my birthday as well," I said. *This must be kismet!* I thought to myself and if I was looking for a positive sign that my fortune on the pupillage front was on the rise, then this was it.

This was probably the most relaxed interview environment that I ever experienced. It didn't even feel like an interview, that's how much Mr Yearwood put me at ease. By the end of our friendly chat, Mr Yearwood offered me an initial six months pupillage to start in the last week of January.

"Thank you, thank you Mr Yearwood!" I said, elated beyond belief.

"That's ok Shaun and by the way.... you can call me Jeffery!"

I started my pupillage with Jeffrey at his chambers, 76b Chancery Lane, in the last week of January 1985. The chambers were a relatively small set with approximately eleven members in total. It was also predominantly a black set partly out of choice and partly because black and ethnic lawyers found it nigh on impossible to be taken on by a so called traditional or established set of chambers in the 1970's and early 1980's. As a consequence, sets such as 76b had little or no option but to set up on their own in order to try and make a living and survive in a profession that wasn't exactly welcoming to them and whilst 76b couldn't exactly be described as a set of chambers whose name was up there amongst the bright legal lights, that didn't mean that the members were lacking the competence and ability needed to succeed at the bar, on the contrary. Because aside from Jeffrey Yearwood, other members of the chambers included, to name a few, the legal veteran Wilton Hill QC, a silk appointed from the Jamaican Bar, Icah Peart (now Icah Peart QC) and a very young (no less talented) Ignatius Fessal. Arguably though, the most essential cog in the wheel in terms of the day to day running of chambers and the person responsible for keeping barristers constantly in work was the barrister's Clerk.

The role of the barrister's Clerk in a set of chambers, if one were looking for a similar comparison or analogy, is similar to the role and duties of an agent working in show business. The Clerk's job primarily is to attract work for the barristers under their charge from solicitors who wish to instruct a barrister for advocacy in the higher courts, at a time when the bar enjoyed an exclusive and total monopoly. A Clerk's other duties also include the management and organisation of the barrister's diary, trying to ensure that barristers in their charge are kept constantly busy in court and trying to prevent if possible, any potential clashes with other cases that a barrister may be instructed in on the same day. Another role of the Clerk, arguably the most important, involves the negotiation and collection of barristers' fees. The Senior Clerk was usually assisted by a junior whose role could best be described as that of an office dogsbody, but whose role was no less vital in ensuring the smooth day to day running of chambers

The role of Senior Clerk didn't need any specialised form of training or qualification. Most of the Senior Clerks who were around at the time when I joined the profession were those who probably left school at an early age without any formal qualifications and started at the very bottom of the pile at a set of chambers before making a slow but gradual rise to the top. That's why, despite their important role in a set of chambers, Barrister's Clerks were sometimes commonly referred to, in somewhat disparaging terms as "East End Barrow Boys" who were blessed with the gift of the gab and the talent to tout for work which the bar's Code of Conduct forbade the profession from engaging in personally.

The Clerks who oversaw 76b when I joined the set as Jeffrey Yearwood's pupil were Errol Taylor in the role of Senior Clerk and his second in command, Danny (Donald) Currie. Errol was from the East End of London, would probably have been in his late twenties early thirties at the time, with Danny slightly older. My pupil master, Jeffrey, was rarely out of Court as brief after brief would frequently arrive in chambers in his name, the main source of his work mainly deriving from a sizeable network of black solicitors' firms scattered around London regularly seeking his services. As Jeffrey's pupil, I was required to be with him throughout the working day and my duties apart from watching and observing would also involve reading his briefs in order to familiarise myself with the case and when required, draft written opinions or advices on evidence. Jeffrey would always peruse my written pieces of work in order to ensure that I was progressing along the right lines and he would always provide constructive feedback when he felt it was necessary to do so. I would also be present whenever Jeffrey had conferences with his lay clients either in chambers, or those clients who were held on remand in prison. I was deeply impressed by the calm yet authoritative manner he always displayed at these conferences that put his client's mind at ease mainly because he treated his clients, irrespective of what crimes they were accused of, as human beings and not mere legal aid representation orders from which he would be paid.

But the arena where Jeffrey showed his real abilities as a barrister was in the courtroom where his all-round ability as an advocate both in terms of his impressive abilities when cross examining prosecution witnesses, or with his closing arguments before jury or lay magistrates invariably won the day. For my first six months as a pupil, Jeffrey never lost a trial, either in the Crown Court or Magistrates' Courts and his abilities as a barrister served as a benchmark that I wanted to aspire to and achieve in the future.

The most memorable of these victories that I vividly recall during that remarkable run was a trial at the Old Bailey where Jeffrey's client was charged, along with others, with conspiracy to rob an armoured van. The prosecution's evidence against all the defendants related to a detailed but covert police operation (a product which, in all probability, was a result of an anonymous tip off), which had the defendants under constant photographic surveillance allegedly watching the comings and goings of an armoured post office van when it was depositing money to a bank. The surveillance operation was conducted over several days, with the police taking what appeared to be damaging photographs of what the prosecution suggested was Jeffrey's client in and around the vicinity of the bank on numerous occasions at the time the armoured van was making its normal delivery. On those occasions, Jeffrey's client appeared to be what the prosecution suggested: dressed in various disguises, his facial features covered with a bandana. Jeffrey's client was adamant that he wasn't involved in any conspiracy and denied that he was the person seen in the various surveillance photographs. The trial itself lasted just under two weeks. The issue for the jury to determine was whether or not Jeffrey's client was the person seen in the surveillance photographs and therefore involved in a criminal conspiracy with others to rob an armoured van. Jeffrey didn't call his client to give evidence during the trial because in his view, the evidence the prosecution was relying upon wasn't strong enough to secure a conviction and it was a viewpoint that proved to be spot on. All the defendants who stood trial were acquitted both to my astonishment and amazement and once we had left court after having said our goodbyes to a mightily relieved and grateful client, we walked the relatively short distance via Holborn Viaduct back to chambers feeling pretty pleased that Jeffrey had secured yet another notch on the victory bedpost.

On another memorable occasion, I watched the combined talents of Jeffrey, Wilton, Icah and Ignatius co-defend in another fairly lengthy robbery trial at Southwark Crown Court. All four of them had their own unique style in terms of Court presence and demeanour. Wilton Hill, the wily Jamaican QC, reminded me of a black version of John Mortimer's eponymous creation, Horace Rumpole of Rumpole of the Bailey fame, with the charisma and charm to match his seemingly infinite talent in the art of advocacy. Icah Peart, whose thoughtful and methodical approach in cross-examination punched huge holes in the prosecution case and gave a closing speech that left me with the unflinching impression that with the right support, he was destined for the higher reaches of the criminal bar. Finally, the least experienced member of the quartet from chambers instructed in the trial, Ignatius Fessal who was about four or so years call at the time but proved throughout the trial that despite his relative inexperience, he was just as capable as his more experienced colleagues. Iggy (as he is affectionately known), was trying to build a career for himself and because his career was ostensibly in its infancy, he was heavily reliant on the work that both Errol and Danny were getting in for him, plus any returns that other members of chambers were unavailable to do themselves because they were booked in another court elsewhere. Errol had given Iggy the defendant who was commonly referred to in a trial as "Tail End Charlie" (that is to say, the defendant who was normally listed last in a multi-handed trial, which is a usual indication that the prosecution takes the view that the evidence against that particular defendant is at its weakest). Iggy didn't have to answer as many questions as the others, but when he did, he proved just as competent and able as his fellow colleagues and clearly had what it takes for a long and thriving career in the profession.

For a fledgling young pupil such as myself fresh off the academic conveyor belt, this was exactly the type of experience I needed to be observing, absorbing and learning from for the sake of my own professional development. It was the perfect blueprint. I wanted to be like them, speak like them, have the same air of confidence like them and it gave me a great sense of pride watching black men speaking just as eloquently in a court of law as their white counterparts, thus clearly demonstrating that it's possible for black barristers to survive as well as thrive in the profession and it's people like Jeffrey, Wilton, Icah and Ignatius who served both as a beacon and inspiration for young aspiring black lawyers like myself eager to follow in their seemingly small but nevertheless trailblazing footsteps.

Those first six months of pupillage went extremely well. I was constantly observing and learning from a pupil master who genuinely had my best interest at heart. The only major drawback during those first six months was that I was hampered with the age old problem that hampers virtually all first six months pupils, the chronic shortage of money. First six months pupils (unless you were one of the fortunate few to have won a bursary or scholarship) earned virtually little or no income and unless there was a personal fortune to fall back on, it was difficult to survive from one day to the next. I for one, was most certainly not in the category of the fortunate few and my only source of income was the odd £20 here and there that Mum would give to me just to make sure that I got by. I knew that I had to generate some form of income in order to keep going.

I went through all the possible options in my head as to how I could earn some money without it interfering or compromising my pupillage with Jeffrey. Suddenly, I had a flash of inspiration - *what about making enquiries to see if there are any vacancies for lecturers at Bar School teaching in their small seminar groups?* I thought to myself. The idea held my attention for a little while but those thoughts were immediately dashed when it dawned on me that the academic year was well into the Hilary Term and the likelihood of there being any vacancies at all were virtually nil and besides, even if such a vacancy existed, I came to the somewhat cynical view that they certainly wouldn't consider a Polytechnic law graduate who passed the bar Finals without any particular distinction. Despite that reality check, the idea of tutoring or teaching nevertheless continued to appeal to me. I still had most of my old lecture notes and books to work with and more usefully, most of the information I was taught last year was still very much fresh in my mind. I saw no reason why I couldn't make the transition from student to teacher, an unlikely poacher turned gamekeeper scenario if ever there was one but a scenario I was more than capable of creating.

The following day, I left chambers and went to the main reception office at my most recent *alma mater,* The Inns of Court School of Law, where I put an advert on the Noticeboard offering home tuition. Afterwards, I scanned the Noticeboard, and my attention was suddenly transfixed on a notice that was a sight for sore eyes. The school was looking for people to invigilate the forthcoming Bar Finals exams. I left my details with the receptionist, before heading back down Warwick Court's short narrow passageway feeling quite pleased with myself that I was making an effort in trying to be as self-sufficient as I possibly could. It is a difficult rite of passage that pupils past and present have gone through and Jeffrey was quite sympathetic to my struggle, due to the fact that he too had to go through the same financial struggles when he first started out. Jeffrey began to recount his own tales of how he used to teach part time with the remainder of his spare time devoted to spending a couple of evenings a week giving free advice at a Citizen's Advice Bureau to help support both himself and his young family. He gave me his full support.

With the firm support of my pupil master, I decided that teaching part time would be the only way forward in terms of keeping things going and thankfully, it didn't take me long to secure my first teaching assignment which arose as a result of the combination of good old fashioned luck and the link of the "old school tie". A few days after my decision, I was with Jeffrey who was about to start a case in one of the Crown Courts in London and whilst Jeffrey was changing into his robes in the barrister's Robing Room, I ran into a fellow pupil who was also in the same court with her own pupil master, Glenda Fontaine. Glenda and I go back a long way. She was a member of the Sixth Form at Aylestone High and like me, had ambitions of wanting to make a career at the bar. Glenda had landed on her feet so far as pupillage was concerned, managing to secure a twelve month pupillage at 2 Crown Office Row, one of the leading sets in London, if not the whole country, at the time with such noticeable leading legal heavy weights as Richard Ferguson QC in their ranks. Glenda's pupil master was the Jamaican born John Perry, a man who rose from humble beginnings to become one of the leading lights at the criminal bar mainly due to his encyclopaedic knowledge of the law and was heavily tipped to become one of the first appointed black QC's. Glenda and I were pleased to see each other and because the cases our respective pupil masters were set down for the next couple of days, we agreed to meet and have a catch up in the bar mess canteen during the luncheon adjournment.

Glenda and I met up as arranged and we began chatting about the good old days in the Sixth Form and how far we had both come. The conversation then steered round to how our respective pupillages were going. Glenda seemed to be loving every minute at the Chambers she was in. I told her that things were going pretty well so far as my pupillage was concerned but I was finding it hard to come to terms with the fact that I had virtually little or no money to survive on and I was hoping to do some teaching as a means of raising income.

"If you're interested in teaching, I've got a friend who's desperately looking for a tutor on the bar Course." Glenda then started to tell me about her friend who was studying for the forthcoming finals exams and by all accounts, was finding the course difficult to cope with.

"Where does she live?" I enquired.

"Not far from me. She lives on Wrentham Avenue in Kensal Rise. You should do it Shaun!"

I asked Glenda to give the person concerned my contact details and to give me a call if they were interested. Glenda said that she would and thereafter, we said our goodbyes before re-joining our respective pupil masters for the remainder of the luncheon adjournment. Later that evening I received a telephone call at home.

"My name is Georgina Linton. Glenda gave me your details and asked me to contact you about the possibility of you helping me with the course".

My initial impression was how polite and well-spoken she sounded but at the same time, I could clearly hear the tone of desperation as she spoke. She told me that she was a 22 year old student from Buckingham University who completed a Law Degree in two years instead of the normal three where she ended up gaining 2:1, an impressive feat by any standards. I then asked her how she was finding the course and she replied that she was finding it tough with all the topics she had to study and really needed help from someone who had done the course before. When she mentioned what she was prepared to pay without me having the chance to tell her what I was going to charge, I didn't need to be asked twice. We agreed to start the following day on a trial basis in order to see whether the arrangement would be mutually suitable for both of us and if it was, then we would take it from there. After our telephone conversation ended, I went upstairs to my room and gather together all my old law books and lecture notes and I paused for a moment and stared at them for a while. *This could be my salvation!* I thought to myself. A salvation, not only in terms of much needed revenue to support myself, but an opportunity to teach as well as communicating information to others, a skill that almost certainly would be a useful tool in the nurturing and development of my fledgling abilities as an advocate.

The following evening, I arrived outside the address of my prospective student for my first ever teaching assignment. That initial session lasted the best part of two hours and at the end of it, Georgina seemed pretty pleased with how it all went and immediately booked me for another session the following week at the same time. Just as I was gathering my lecturer notes, she handed me my well earned and much needed £60.

"Thank you!" I said as I eagerly put the money in my trouser pocket. Georgina escorted me to the front door and after we shook hands she stated that she was already looking forward to our next session. On the journey home I was feeling quite pleased with my evening's endeavours. I managed to secure for myself some form of regular income albeit for the short term, but just as important, my inaugural teaching session demonstrated that I could teach and communicate information effectively in the same manner like my old teaching mentors Mike Cooley and Gordon Small had done back in my days at Aylestone High School and that gave me a great deal of confidence and belief that if I showed the same dedication and commitment as my mentors of old, then it was possible that my abilities as a teacher could be a resounding success.

I continued with those one to one teaching sessions with Georgina right up until the start of the bar Finals of that summer and apart from the odd occasion or two, when I had to take her to task when I felt that her commitment and effort was less than it should be, the tuition sessions were on the whole a mutually beneficial exercise for both parties concerned. Georgina's confidence in her approach to the course had vastly improved from the near rock bottom position it was hovering around when we first started our sessions. Her commitment and dedication to hard work had also improved in leaps and bounds which, allied to her innate academic abilities, left me in no doubt that she had every chance of passing those exams with flying colours. As for myself, those one to one teaching sessions weren't only the financial life saver, it also went some considerable way to providing a major boost to my own self confidence and esteem. With every session that passed, I saw my own gradual improvement in terms of my ability to teach and communicate information in a style and manner that somebody could understand and respond to and because of this, I began to explore the possibility of teaching to a wider audience in a school or further education college, the logic behind the thinking being that teaching a group of strangers would be the perfect platform to overcome my own inherent shyness. Undeterred by my lack of any teaching qualifications or teaching experience, I decided to ring up as many further education colleges as I could to see if there were any part time vacancies available. My inspired gamble paid dividends when two colleges responded by saying that they would be interested. The first of those colleges was Hackney College in Dalston who told me that whilst there were no immediate vacancies available they would nevertheless send me an application form for me to fill in and return as soon as possible. However, it was with the second College, South London College based in Knight's Hill in Upper Norwood where I had much better luck as it gave me the opportunity that I was looking for. I asked the College if there were any immediate teaching vacancies and their encouraging response was that they were looking for someone straight away to stand in temporarily for one of their lecturers and if I was interested, I should come along to their main campus in Knight's Hill for an interview.

I attended the interview the following day armed with my academic qualifications and a reference from Jeffrey and by the end of that interview, I was offered a temporary teaching post at the college, teaching students aspects of the Industrial Revolution in Britain in the Seventeenth and Eighteenth Centuries. Teaching on that period of history presented no problems or fears from my point of view given my long standing love affair with anything historical, even though it was a subject that I hadn't visited or read up on for quite some time. I began to wonder whether I had bitten off more than I could chew in agreeing to take on a challenge in which I had no real experience but if I wanted to overcome my nauseating fear of standing in front of strangers, then it was a challenge that had to be met head on and eventually mastered.

Those first few lessons teaching in a public arena for the first time was every bit as nerve-wracking and daunting as I thought it would be. I could hear myself at times struggling to maintain that much needed authoritative tone that any teacher or lecturer should possess to be taken seriously by your listening audience. There were the all too frequent stuttering words and phrases or even worse, rolling three words into one coupled with the break neck speed at which I was delivering the lecture, whilst at the same time thinking what the students were making of it all. At the end of those first few lessons, I felt a great sense of relief that somehow, by hook or by crook I managed to get through them. But as the lessons progressed over the next few weeks, my fear of public speaking began to subside considerably on account of the fact I was more and more confident even though my diction and delivery still left a lot to be desired.

After my short stint had come to an end, the college thanked me for my efforts in stepping into the breach at such short notice and made it clear that they would welcome me back to teach part time in the future if a suitable teaching post became available. Their feedback was an immeasurable boost to my self-esteem and confidence however, I knew that I needed to vastly improve both my communication and speaking skills if I wanted to get into the teaching profession, but such an improvement could only be achieved if I found myself a regular teaching post. From the perspective of my own personal development, my time at South London College had gone a long way in helping to develop my confidence in general and I was less afraid of standing up and speaking in front of strangers, which will stand me in good stead in years to come.

My run of good fortune in terms of trying to find work to support myself during pupillage showed no signs of abating when I received a letter from the Inns of Court School of Law informing me that I'd been chosen as one of the invigilators to help supervise the forth coming Bar Finals exams. Watching all those candidates scribbling away frantically at their desks evoked all too vivid memories of the seemingly infinite stresses and pressures that I went through when I was in their position and I couldn't help thinking how fortunate I was that I didn't have to do anything like this again.

The best news of all was yet to come so far as those Bar Finals were concerned when just over a month and a half or so later, I received the fantastic news that Georgina had come one hundred and tenth overall in those Finals and was awarded a lower second class honours. From a teaching perspective, Georgina's stunning success was a personal triumph and vindication that I had a talent for teaching students. A talent I hope, that could be of considerable help to others on their own road to success and achievement. The greatest compliment I could be paid being that the successes and achievements of others would go on to surpass the successes and achievements that I have managed to attain in my own life thus far, as it would be the ultimate vindication of my own teaching beliefs and philosophies.

The end of July also marked the end of my first six month pupillage with Jeffrey. I was supposed to start my second six months straight away, but I asked Jeffery for permission to delay the start until the beginning of September, for the pure and simple reason that I needed to earn money to help support me through the second stage of my pupillage. Not for the first time, Jeffrey showed his supportive side and without hesitation or even a hint of complaint, gave his blessing for me to spend another five weeks at the summer play scheme on the South Kilburn Estate for the third consecutive year before starting the second half of my pupillage when I would be allowed to receive briefs in my own name and with it, the opportunity to put into practice all that I had observed and learned during those first six months under Jeffery. With a bit of luck, it could lead to the possibility of obtaining a tenancy at the first time of asking.

CHAPTER TEN

I had every reason at the beginning of September 1985 to be full of optimism. Apart from the excitement and anticipation of looking forward to getting my first ever professional brief, Hackney College also offered me a part time teaching position on Monday and Tuesday evenings. My part time appointment would, apart from allowing me to stand on my own two feet financially, allow me to develop and enhance both my teaching and communication skills to those students in my care with the ultimate aim of helping them realise their own personal future goals and ambitions. I had no doubts in my mind that Hackney College was the type of institution that would provide the platform to help me achieve my own aims and objectives with regards to teaching, a marriage made in heaven from my point of view, and I had every reason to be optimistic that my teaching appointment albeit part time in nature, would be the beginning of a long and hopefully mutually beneficial relationship between us.

I re-joined 76b at the beginning of the second week of September for the start of my second six month pupillage where I was looking forward to being 'let off the leash'. The opportunity, finally, to stand with a wig on my head, a black stuffed gown firmly hugging my shoulders, and address a judge and jury in different courts throughout the land. But my rose-tinted vision with which I saw my immediate, let alone long term, future at the bar was completely at odds with reality. I was a young, newly qualified lawyer who only a year previously had rolled off of the academic conveyer belt with no name, no fame and no contacts and any sudden and drastic reversal of fortune with regards to my total anonymity within the profession would be totally dependent upon my gradual development and progression during that second six month stint as a working pupil, a factor that was also mutually dependent upon how well I was perceived by and/or got on well with, the person who could make or break my career, given its embryonic nature, the all-powerful, the all influential, Senior Clerk.

Because I was now at the stage of my fledgling career of being able to accept instructions in my own name, chambers protocol dictated that all working pupils had to be in chambers between 8:30am and 9am each morning just in case chambers received last minute instructions requiring counsel to be ready, willing and available to go to court. Furthermore, working pupils were also required to be around chambers between the hours of 4pm to 6pm in order to find out whether or not they would be in court the following day. As the only six month pupil in chambers at the time, I had no choice but to abide by the rules and I had to put to one side any feelings of frustration that the progress and development of my career was at the whim and control of others and therefore dangling like a metaphorical puppet on a string and there was very little I could do or say about i. I felt alone and isolated as the only pupil in chambers when I returned to start the second stage of my pupillage but thankfully, that scenario was about to change when Jeffery, who was still acting as my supervising pupil master, took on a new pupil, Lee John-Charles, a 22 year old of Dominican heritage from Ealing in West London. Lee had just passed the bar Finals the previous summer. Naturally, I found it both pleasing and welcoming that there was someone else in chambers of similar calling and standing to me with whom I could readily identify and empathise with and it didn't take long for both Lee and I to strike up and forge a long lasting friendship that continues right up until this day. The pair of us were very similar in so many ways. Apart from the obvious similarities of both being young, black and highly ambitious, Lee was also working to support himself through pupillage by teaching part time at the Langley Education College in Langley, Berkshire.

The reality of those first few was in complete contrast to the glamorous, idealised vision that I had in mind, of the constantly busy young barrister rushing here and there from one court to another. Instead, my days involved arriving at Chambers at 9am on the dot and thereafter, spending the rest of my time hanging around the Clerks Room engaging in friendly and lively banter with Errol and Danny, or in one of the tenants rooms in Chambers with virtually nothing to do other than to wait (more in hope than expectation) for that elusive call for my professional services that sadly never came. Sometimes, in an effort to break up the long and seemingly never ending monotony of the day, I would wander across the Holborn High Road and head towards Gray's Inn Library, or down Chancery Lane and head towards the Common Room at the Middle Temple, just to give myself the sense and feeling that I was doing something worthwhile and constructive given the seemingly never ending time I had at my disposal. The worst part though was towards the end of each working day, the time when the tenants would be popping in and out of the Clerks Room whilst Errol was busy arranging the diary directing which tenant would be going to which Court the following morning and the feelings of bitter disappointment that once again, there was nothing in the diary that was available for me. I felt as though I was trapped in an endless, repetitive cycle of a career that was going nowhere fast and my growing sense of frustration that my development was at best stagnating and at worst going backwards, left me with thoughts that I somehow had to summon the courage to say or do something to see if there were any way in which I could move things forward. This meant that at some point, sooner rather than later, I would have to talk to the Senior Clerk, Errol. It was not a conversation I was looking forward to but was one that I needed to have because not to say anything at all would only stretch my already strained patience.

The following day I arrived at chambers at 9am as usual and as I walked up the stairs towards the Clerks' Room, where all sorts of differing thoughts were going through my mind as to whether it would be sensible or indeed wise, to have a forthright discussion with the Senior Clerk. I was beginning to get cold feet as I approached the door and I nearly abandoned the whole mission altogether. But as I opened the door, the courage of my convictions suddenly returned and I decided to bite the bullet and face up to the issue at hand. I walked into the Clerks' Room trying to remain as calm as I could before giving my usual morning greetings to both Errol and Danny. Inwardly however, I could feel my panicked heart pounding away in my chest as I braced myself to reveal my true intentions.

"Errol," I said, in a nervous, enquiring tone, "when you have a spare moment, could we have a chat about me and the way things have been going?"

"That's not a problem, let's go to the cafe next door and get something to eat and we'll talk there".

We both headed for the Ideal Sandwich Bar right next door to Chambers, a favourite haunt of the Clerks. Errol went up to the bar and ordered sandwiches, one each for both of us to consume on the premises and a take away sandwich for Danny, before we both headed for the only available table and chairs that were cramped in a corner.

We sat down with our respective cups of tea whilst we waited for the sandwiches to arrive and I began to tell Errol what was on my mind. Errol sat back and listened intently as I began to pour out all my hopes, dreams and frustrations in equal measure and told him in no uncertain terms that I wasn't happy with the fact that I wasn't going to court as often as I would like. Errol, to his credit, didn't display any form of contemptuous disregard or cold-hearted rejection of my legitimate concerns. He said that he knew and understood where I was coming from and appreciated the fact that I had the courage to come up and tell him face to face what I was thinking and feeling. Errol started to open up a little and began to talk about his own struggles in trying to establish himself since leaving school and that my own struggles were in reality no different to that of any other person. His refreshing candour about his own circumstances immediately put me at ease before the nature of the conversation reverted back to my own career concerns and what could be done to get things moving. At that point Errol took control of the discussion and straight away he made it clear that I had nothing to worry about in terms of my lack of court action, however he said I had to appreciate and accept that every barrister, even the top QCs at the bar had to start from the very beginning and not even the most keen and eager young barrister starting their second six can expect to be doing one Crown Court trial after another as if such things were the norm. To get to that level takes both time and experience. Errol went on to add, that it was important that I got to know and begin to build relationships with the solicitors' firms who were going to give me that type of work. As a rule, unless those firms get to know and put their trust in you, no matter how talented you are or may think you are, you simply won't get the work.

Errol's carrot and stick approach seemed to do the trick. He wasn't telling me anything new, but at least any lingering concerns that somehow my entire second six months would be condemned entirely to a fruitless existence of no briefs and no court appearances were finally banished from my mind. I had to bide my time and be patient.

Later on that same afternoon, Errol proved to be a man of his word when he called me into the Clerk's Room after having finalized the working diary for the next day to tell me the news that I had been dying to hear for a very long time. I was finally going to get my chance to stand on my own two feet representing my first lay client. I could hardly contain my excitement that after years of toiling away at the academic coalface, I was now going to put into practise all that I had learned during my time watching Jeffrey and the others.

My first brief came in a folded one page hand written back sheet tied up in a pink bow and written at the top the words in big bold capitals **OLD STREET MAGISTRATE'S COURT**. Just below those words had the name of the lay client who I was instructed to represent. In the middle of the brief, the words, "Bail Application for the above Accused/Advance Disclosure Application" were also written in bold capital letters that were sandwiched in between two broadly drawn lines and below that, confirmation that this was a brief in my name with the words, Mr. S. Wallace in block capitals.

"This is where it all starts, Mr. Wallace. You're out on your own now and it's up to you how far you want to go in this profession. Make sure you're at court on time and good luck!"

Reading between the lines I knew exactly what Errol was trying to tell me. He was letting me know in no uncertain terms that although this was an opportunity for me to show what I can do, at the same time any future opportunities to appear in court on a regular basis would not be based out of friendship or pity. It was a right that had to be earned. From now on, everything from my attitude, my general appearance, to the way in which I dealt with clients and solicitors had to be totally professional and if I fell short in any of these key areas then I would not be taken seriously and as a consequence, my fledgling career would be all but over before it even had a chance to get off the ground.

The following morning, I left my home just after 8am dressed as smartly as I could and no less excited at the prospect of my courtroom debut than when Errol first gave me the news, and after a short train journey, I arrived. The building itself was typical in terms of the content and design in line with most of the Magistrates' Court buildings that existed at the time, buildings that in truth were probably no different to the Magistrates' Courts that were built in the late Victorian era, a design that both externally and internally, would not look out of place in a gothic novel. The foyer was nondescript and had a central stone built staircase that led to the next landing and the other courtrooms. The custody cell area was nauseating, with its dank and musty aroma, and was full to the brim with experienced hardened recidivists, the vast majority for whom being in and out of a courtroom and a cell was just a way of life. The courtrooms all contained the imposing wooden dock at centre stage, in which every accused person stood to hear the case against them. Aside from the dock, the most imposing feature within the courtroom was the judicial bench, perched in its mythical like elevated position looking down at the dock, where the Stipendiary Magistrate or Justices of the Peace sit to dispense justice with clockwork military precision as they determine the immediate fate of all the accused persons appearing before them.

As I entered the building, the foyer was a sea of the usual throbbing activity at the start of the day's proceedings. Lawyers rushing around calling out the names of either their clients or legal opponents in order to have a brief discussion about the case they were involved in before going into court, or the various court ushers emerging from their respective courtrooms to call out the names of the defendants whose cases were ready with the aim of trying to ensure the smooth running order of the court in anticipation of the near avalanche of the many cases that were due to be heard that morning. I wandered over to the court's Daily Cause List and scanned it until I found the name of my client before joining in the ritual of calling out for the lawyer who would be my designated opponent. It didn't take that long for my opponent to make himself known and we made our way to a small corner of the foyer so we could have our own brief discussions away from any prying ears.

I asked my opponent whether he was going to serve any advance disclosure and he replied that given the fact that my client had only been arrested the day before, he was not in a position to do so. He went on to say that he would undertake to serve the necessary papers within the next seven days and suggested that the mode of trial proceedings (a hearing which determined where the venue of any trial should take place) be delayed for a period of fourteen days, thus allowing the solicitors time to consider the evidence, take any relevant instructions from the client and make a decision as to whether the Magistrate's Court or the Crown Court would be the appropriate venue for any possible trial. I agreed to my opponent's sensible proposal before I raised the issue as to whether or not he would be making any objections to my client being granted bail. His response unsurprisingly, was that he would be objecting to bail and he handed me a five paged document which contained a list of the numerous previous convictions that my client had recorded against him. After quickly scanning the first paragraph of my client's personal details which also included a fairly lengthy list of the other names and aliases he was known by, I proceeded to flick through the remaining pages of his antecedents and it was patently clear that I didn't stand a cat in hell's chance of getting my client bail. The list of the convictions stretched back to his juvenile days with the vast majority of those convictions more or less identical to the current charges he was facing. Even more depressing though, were the various failures to appear scattered in amongst that long list of antecedents, coupled with the equally damaging possible breach of bail for having committed this new offence whilst he was out on bail for another offence.

My chances of securing my client bail were, to borrow a two-word phrase from the legendary Hollywood film producer, Sam Goldwyn, IM-POSSIBLE! and with an air of resignation, I decided it was time to go and visit my client. I made my way to the vast metal door that served as the entrance to the custody area and once inside, I was pointed in the direction of where my client was being held and moments later, I was outside the door that held my client. There were other people in the cell, so I called out my client's name and one of them came up to the small opening and pressed his face right up against the small opening. My nostrils by this time were just about fully acclimatised to the putrid smell that consumed the whole of custody area including my client's cell. I formally introduced myself before going on to explain to my client that the prosecution was not in the position to serve any evidence today and were seeking a two week adjournment prior to mode of trial proceedings. However, before I had a chance to finish my sentence the client asked in a rather excitable tone, "What about getting bail?" I responded by telling him that the prosecution was objecting to bail because of his previous record and the suggestion that he may be in breach of his bail in having allegedly committed this new offence there was a strong likelihood that he would be kept on remand until the next hearing date. "I want you to apply for bail," my client replied in his increasingly eager and unpleasant tone and he was becoming more and more restless before breaking out in cries protesting his innocence. I tried to calm him down and endeavoured once more to explain to him the difficulties of his position but my efforts only served to fuel his outrage. "I don't want you to represent me in court!" he suddenly shouted. "Where are my solicitors?" At this point I was in a state of near panic and I tried to reassure him that I would make the bail application on his behalf. My last ditch effort to appease my client's incessant demands seemed to do the trick and I managed to persuade him to cooperate with me long enough for me to take instructions from him in relation to his personal antecedents and background that would form the basis of the bail application that I would make on his behalf. I finally managed to get all the information I felt I needed and thereafter, breathed a sigh of relief as I left the cells in preparation for my professional debut as an advocate that I hoped was not going to end in abject humiliation.

The case was eventually called on by the court usher after waiting around for what seemed like an eternity and both myself and my opponent strode forward and took up our respective places on the front bench in the well of the court as my client was being brought into the dock by two burly prison officers for the start of the hearing. The Court Clerk, the court official who acts as a legal adviser to the bench, then identified my client before reading out the charges as my debut as a fully-fledged lawyer began in earnest. My opponent then rose to his feet and informed the court that the prosecution, in agreement with the defence, were seeking a two week adjournment in relation to the mode of trial proceedings. The Magistrates readily agreed to the timetable for my client's next court appearance before going on to ask the prosecuting lawyer what his position in relation to my client's bail position was, to which he replied that there were objections to the defendant being bailed. The bench then turned their attentions to me and asked whether I would be making a bail application and I replied that I would be despite the inward misgivings I may have had. My opponent then rose to his feet and began to outline his reasons for his objections and at some point during his submissions, he handed up to the bench copies of my client's less than attractive previous convictions which they proceeded to scrutinise with considerable care. My opponent's submissions, despite their relative brevity, were concise and on point and once he had finished making them, he sat down no doubt full of confidence that his argument would win the day. The forceful and persuasive manner of my opponent's submissions meant that the odds against my client being granted bail were lengthening with every passing second and in truth, there seemed little point in going through the seeming fruitless exercise at all. But rather than risk incurring the wrath of both my client and more importantly, that of my Senior Clerk, I had no choice other than to make the application. As I rose to my feet in order to respond to the prosecution's objections, I was now the centre of everyone's attention in the courtroom, the sustained and relentless scrutiny had the unsettling effect of making me start to sweat profusely and with a tone that was just about audible, I began to respond to my opponent's objections to bail as best as I could, before putting forward to the court suitable bail conditions which, I submitted, would remove any concerns the court may have with regards to any possible non-attendance and/or the prevention of any future offending by my client. I felt an almighty sense of relief when my efforts of trying to defend the indefensible was over but even that sense of relief couldn't prevent the continuous flow of nervous sweat that was now pouring down my head, neck and torso. The bench decided that they wanted to discuss their findings in private and they retired to their room to deliberate. I went over to the dock to talk with my client briefly about the proceedings generally and to find out whether or not he was happy with the way I had represented him. The client seemed happy enough with my performance but in truth, the only thing he was concerned with was getting out on bail. "All we can do is wait and see," were the only crumbs of comfort I could offer my client in terms of optimism before returning to my seat in silence to await the outcome of the bench's deliberations.

It was nearly a full ten minutes before the bench eventually returned to the courtroom. I couldn't help feeling a small sense of pride and satisfaction that there must have some substance in the submissions that I made and that belief was confirmed when at the start of their giving reasons for their decision, the Chairman of the Bench started off with the words, "We have listened with care to Mr Wallace's submissions as to the reasons why his client should be admitted to bail, however...." when his second phrase started with the conjunction, "however," I knew that my submissions were unsuccessful. My client was remanded in custody by the justices and ordered to be produced at court in a fortnight's time for a hearing to determine the venue of the trial.

As my client was being led away from the dock and taken back to the cells, I stood up and bowed my head towards the bench in line with court etiquette and protocol before heading for a further conference with my client. When I arrived at the cell door, I opened the small wicker gate half expecting a reaction from a client similar to that of a volcano waiting to erupt but surprisingly, his reaction and demeanour in general was the complete opposite. My client thanked me for all my efforts in trying to get him bail and even more astonishingly, asked me whether I would be representing him on the next occasion. I replied that such a decision wasn't one for me to make but if he wanted me to represent him in future, he should inform the solicitors of his wishes the next time they came to visit him. I didn't feel I had either the authority or that it was my place, to tell him that I would be representing him on the next occasion especially at this stage of my career. Only my Senior Clerk or my instructing solicitors could make that call but at least I received a confidence boosting thumbs up from a lay client who seemed to be happy with my services and if the news of how I performed in court somehow managed to filter back to both to my Senior Clerk or my instructing solicitors from a source other than myself, then it would demonstrate that I could be trusted to do their work. I extended my hand through the open wicker gate in order to shake my client's hand before gratefully swapping the musty smell of the custody area for the welcoming fresh air of Old Street and the journey back towards Chambers.

As I walked towards the tube station, it gave me a chance to think and reflect on my first court hearing as a professional barrister standing on my own two feet. There was no doubting the fact that it was a nerve wracking experience standing up in front of a real life court acting on behalf of a real life client, but it was also an enjoyable one and I took a great deal of comfort from the fact that the initial nervousness I felt standing on my feet for the very first time, would have been no different to any other fledgling barrister making their professional debut, even the best and most experienced advocate will suffer the odd occasional adrenalin surge. The only way to bring those feelings of nervousness and anxiety under some sort of control is if I am regularly exposed to the court environment and if the seemingly glowing testimony of my first professional lay client was anything to go by, then I was well on my way to achieving that aim.

My career seemed to be progressing quite nicely by the time my second six months came to an end. Errol was keeping me fairly busy in the Magistrate's Court doing first appearances and bail applications as well as the odd summary trial involving minor cases such as shop lifting and motoring offences and on the odd occasion, there were appearances in the Crown Court doing non-contentious matters such as applying to break a trial fixture in a case, or taking a verdict on behalf of a tenant in Chambers because that tenant was busily engaged doing another case in another court. Even the barrister's fees that I began earning at the start of my second six were beginning to trickle in. I was beside myself with unadulterated joy when Errol handed me my first Legal Aid remittance sheet attached to which was a pink coloured cheque with a sum that was a little over £300.

"I know exactly what I'm going to do with this!" I proclaimed, excitedly.

"What are you going to spend it on?" Errol enquired.

"I'm going to spend it on someone very special!" was my cryptic reply and I refused to elaborate any further despite Errol's incessant probing. He probably imagined that I was going to spend it on some girlfriend or sweetheart, but he couldn't be further from the truth, because the only person I had in mind was the person who was by and large, one of the main reasons why I was holding the Legal Aid cheque in my hand in the first place, my cantankerous and irascible dear old Mum.

As soon as the cheque cleared, I withdrew the entire sum from my bank account and headed towards the West End on the hunt for what I hoped would be the perfect gift to say thank you. I went in and out of the finest stores in the West End looking for that perfect gift that my money could afford. Clothes and jewellery didn't seem right somehow but after a near exhaustive search, I finally chose a beautiful bone china tea set and two crystal decanters. *That would be a welcome addition to Mum's cabinet in her precious front room!* I thought with a wry smile and asked the sales assistant to gift wrap the delicate items before heading home.

No one was home by the time I arrived and I decided to hide Mum's gift somewhere in the front room and surprise her with it at some point later in the evening. I couldn't wait to see her reaction when I gave it to her! I pulled away the large sofa from the wall and put the large carrier bag with its contents behind it before pushing the sofa back as far as it could go. Then with an air of smug satisfaction, I headed for the living room in order to settle down and relax to watch another edition of one of my favourite TV quiz shows, Blockbusters.

Eventually, other members of the household started to arrive home. Steve was the first to arrive and after poking his head through the opened living room door in order to say hello, he headed straight upstairs for the bedroom that we shared to continue the commendable self-imposed study regime he had set for himself working religiously every evening on his Pure and Applied Maths and Economics Studies in preparation for his forthcoming exams that summer, fully conscious of the fact that only hard work and dedication to his studies would get him over the finishing line. Steve had managed to secure a place at Kent University to start in the Autumn and judging by his colossal efforts, he stood every chance of doing very well. Mere words could not express how proud I was of my little kid brother and all I could do was hope and pray that all of Steve's hard work would be suitably rewarded. Debbie was the next to arrive home from her full time job as an Accounts Assistant at the Department of Energy. She too barely had time to say hello before disappearing upstairs into her bedroom that was strictly off limits to everyone in the household for her much sought after privacy. Finally, Mum arrived home after another long and exhaustive shift at the Maida Vale Telephone exchange. She looked as though she was carrying the whole world on her shoulders when she entered the living room and unlike the others after saying hello, she headed towards her favourite armchair and collapsed in a state of near exhaustion. It was gut wrenching to see my dear old Mum in such a weary state. I asked her how her day went, and it was clear from her response that so far as work was concerned, she was physically and mentally close to breaking point. I decided that it probably was not the best time to give her the gifts I had bought for her and settled instead to offer to make her a strong cup of tea in order to help her relax and take her mind off her troubles.

Later that evening after Mum had finished cooking her signature spaghetti bolognaise for the three of us before retiring as usual to her bedroom early enough for rest and peace and quiet in preparation for the start of another long and gruelling shift at the telephone exchange the following day. I decided that it was the perfect time to give Mum the gifts and I went back into the front room to retrieve the large carrier bag from behind the sofa before heading upstairs to her closed bedroom door.

"Mum!" I whispered softly as I knocked on her door to see if she was still awake. "Can I have a word with you!"

There was a slight pause before she responded by saying "Is wha' yuh want?"

"I just want to come in and talk to you for a minute." I opened her bedroom door slightly and poked my head inside before turning the light switch on. Mum was awakening from her deep slumber and she started to pull the covers away from her head. "Mum, I've got something for you," I said, coming into her room with the large carrier bag nestled in my arms.

"What is going on?" Mum asked quizzically still slightly groggy and disorientated whilst her eyes struggled to accommodate the sudden burst of light in her room.

"Mum, this is to say thank you for all you've done."

However, Mum's reaction to my grand gesture was not the reaction I was hoping for. "Weh yuh get de money from?" she demanded.

"I got paid the other day, my first pay cheque as a lawyer and the first thing I promised to do with the money was to buy you something really nice!" If I thought my heartfelt explanation would do the trick, I was sadly mistaken.

"Yuh shouldn't waste yuh money!" Mum replied before switching the theme of the conversation to my so called general lack of responsibility whenever money comes into my possession. Unperturbed by her remarks, I placed the carrier bag next to her on the bed opened it to show her the contents. Mum's attitude softened a little as she picked up the glass decanter giving it a thorough examination. "They're beautiful, Shaun," she said, and with that I gave her a gentle hug in appreciation.

I wasn't hurt by Mum's initial reaction to me spending all that money on her. She has carried the burden of the family on her shoulders for a very long time and for her, every penny really does count and besides, she was dead right in her assessment of me when it comes to anything financial given my "spend it today, borrow it tomorrow approach" to life, leaving Mum in a state of constant worrying about the direction my life was heading.

In an attempt to allay those fears, I declared with bold bravado, "Don't worry, Mum! Once I get my career up and running, there'll be plenty more of this to come." Brave words indeed and only time will tell over the next couple of years whether or not I would be able to make good on that promise.

I finally completed my six month pupillage in the middle of March 1986 and I was now at the point where I had to decide on my next career move. Do I apply to extend my stay at 76b and try to become a fully-fledged tenant, or do I seek my fortunes elsewhere? It was a decision I admit that should have been given proper consideration well before my completion date and my failure to properly address the issue concerning my immediate future left me feeling anxious. Why, I asked myself, did I lack the foresight (or possibly the courage) to line up another pupillage stint in another set of Chambers, just like my friend and fellow pupil, Lee John-Charles had done just before he had joined 76b? Was my lack of activity because I somehow took it for granted that 76b would roll out the red carpet and offer me a tenancy? Suppose 76b asked to leave? Where would I go? If I applied to go elsewhere, would another set of chambers even consider the likes of me given my modest educational background and the lack of a network of contacts or solicitors firms to send me regular work? I didn't really know which way to turn but in the end, I decided that the best thing to do would be to have a chat first with Jeffrey and then have the same sort of discussion with Errol, not only for some much needed advice, but also to find out whether or not the option of remaining at 76b would be open to me.

When I spoke with Jeffrey, his positive response and attitude was exactly the kind of response that I needed to hear. He made it clear that he was more than happy for me to remain at the set for a further six month stint and promised that he would speak to one or two of his network of instructing solicitors to see if they could start to send me a couple of cases in order to help kickstart my career and if I proved my worth and ability, Jeffrey went on to add, then he saw no reason why those firms would not instruct me on a regular basis. Errol was equally supportive and understanding during the separate discussions that we had about my immediate future and by the end of those discussions, it was agreed that I would remain in Chambers as a pupil/squatter for a further six months and at the end of that period, consideration would be given to the offer of a tenancy if my further six months period pupillage was considered to be a success.

It felt as if a heavy burden had been lifted from my shoulders and I approached the start of my six month pupillage feeling a little more settled and secure that I had the real and genuine support from a set of Chambers who were interested in helping me build and develop a legal career. Errol was ensuring that I was going to the Magistrate's Courts as often as possible, sometimes with two or even three different briefs at any given time, as I grew more and more accustomed to the courtroom atmosphere and etiquette, all of which was having both a profound and positive effect on my confidence. Jeffrey also played his part in helping to get my career up and running and it didn't take long for the odd brief or two to start arriving in chambers solely in my name. One firm in particular, Cremin Small, a small but extremely busy outfit based in the heart of Brixton and run by the affable Phil Cremin, became the main source of my work and biggest supporter of my career during my formative days. In spite the fact that I was grateful for all the work I was doing in the Magistrate's Court, it was not enough to prevent the ever increasing restlessness and frustration that I was still no nearer to getting my first Crown Court brief for trial in my own right. From time to time I'd raise the issue with Errol, trying during the course of those enquiries to tread a fine diplomatic line between being seen as a young eager lawyer who was determined to progress and succeed as opposed to that of an ingrate pupil who really has no grounds for complaint. Errol reminded me that I had to be patient and that building relationship and trust with solicitors took time.

Over the next eighteen or so months, it would have been fair to say I was pretty content about the direction I was heading in. Teaching at Hackney College was going very well mainly due to the good rapport I had with both my students and fellow teaching colleagues alike which made the giving up of a couple of evenings of my week all the more worthwhile. My legal career was also progressing nicely under Errol's tutelage as, apart from the summary trials I was doing in the Magistrate's Courts now on a regular basis, I was getting more and more regular exposure in the Crown Courts doing bail applications, and appeals to the Crown Court against sentences imposed by the Magistrate's Courts in accordance with my Senior Clerk's grand strategy, the principal aim being: the gradual building and developing a Crown Court practice for me.

Sadly, the burgeoning professional relationship between myself and Errol was brought to a sudden and abrupt end when in the late Spring of 1987, Errol was relieved of his position as the Chambers Senior Clerk by the Head of Chambers, Reginald Parchment. My immediate reaction upon hearing the news was one of total shock and disappointment and I was at a complete loss as to why the Head of Chambers would take such a drastic step. I tried to find out what little I could about Errol's dismissal from his post and my first port of call was to ask the now newly promoted Senior Clerk, Danny Currie, about what happened but his "sitting on the fence" approach on the subject, coupled with his infuriating cryptic responses to my probing left me no more the wiser. Even my attempts to have discreet one to one chats with some of the more approachable members of chambers to find out what was going on didn't make the reasons for Errol's dismissal any clearer. The one thing that was patently clear from those discreet discussions, that the opinions of the tenants in chambers as to the rights and wrongs of the decision to relieve Errol of his duties was sharply divided and, in the cases of one or two of those members, they were seriously considering whether or not they would remain members of the set.

I eventually managed to contact the man at the centre of the storm, not only to get his side of the story but also to offer what help and support that I could for the way he had been treated. Errol appreciated the fact that I called to see how he was and as we discussed the situation, it was clear that Errol felt aggrieved and betrayed by the decision and pointed the finger towards certain factions within Chambers who were the probable cause for his downfall. I told him how disappointed I was to see him go and in turn poured out my own worries and fears about how his departure could have a serious and unsettling effect on my own progression and development. Errol told me that I had nothing to worry about on that score and promised to speak to firms like Cremin Small as well as other firms with whom he had established a good working relationship with over the years to ensure that the good and steady progress that I was making wouldn't be seriously affected in any way. I asked Errol about his plans for the future. Errol assured me that he had no intention of permanently turning his back on the profession and in all probability he would end up in a criminal law firm for the time being until he decided upon his next move. Errol then asked whether I would provide a written reference on his behalf I agreed to his request without any hesitation. It was the least that I could do, given all the encouragement and support he had shown me throughout my pupillage.

From my own selfish perspective, the cold harsh facts were that with my main ally now gone, I was, to all intents and purposes, back to square one and facing the agonising dilemma of either sitting tight to see how things develop under Danny's leadership, or to jump ship and start to look elsewhere. This was not time to procrastinate and worry about what to do. A decision had to be made sooner rather than later. Such a seismic upheaval at Chambers can go one of two ways. One way is that the Chambers digest and absorb a disruption of such magnitude and simply carry on as normal. The other, is that the disruption is so profound that some members feel they have no option but to move on. Sadly, in the case of 76b, it turned out to be the latter, and over the next three or so months, three significant members made their decision to seek pastures new. The first of those members to announce his departure was the talented Icah Peart. Icah had just been offered a place at 2 Garden Court to work alongside the likes of notable criminal heavyweights such as Ian MacDonald QC, Ken MacDonald and the rising star of the Criminal Bar, Courtenay Griffiths. It was an offer that was too good to turn down and in truth, it was the perfect union between a top set of chambers and a barrister destined for the very top. Even my usually unflappable pupil master, Jeffrey Yearwood was considering his position and eventually, both he and Ignatius Fessal tended their resignations. One by one, the cream of chambers talent was walking out through the door despite Danny's best efforts in trying to persuade those members to stay. He could do little to prevent the haemorrhaging of such talent whilst at the same time, attempt to keep the Chambers functioning as a viable entity amidst all the unsettling chaos.

I'd already decided to leave 76b by the time the exodus had reached its height but with no firm exit strategy in place, I felt as if I was about to jump off a mountain with no safety net to fall back on. Whilst these were extremely worrying times, it was not the time for me to be sitting around and wallowing in self-pity because if I allowed anxiety and procrastination to take hold of the situation, then it would almost inevitably lead to my fledging legal career sliding inexorably towards the legal exit door and in all probability, to a point of no return. Thankfully though, that possible nightmare scenario did not manifest itself and the combination of good fortune and true friendship helped paved the way for my eventual departure from 76b by the summer.

Lee John-Charles and I were still constantly in touch with each other despite him being now based at Mitre Court chambers and in the middle of his second six month pupillage. Lee seemed to be doing quite well and by all accounts, was being kept constantly busy. I told Lee about all the unsettling upheavals that was going on at 76b and confided to him about all the usual worries and concerns that I had in relation to my own future. Lee's response to my anxieties was both blunt as it was supportive: "Shaun, you've got to get out of there!"

"That's easier said than done!" I replied in a resigned and defeatist tone.

"Listen to me!" Lee retorted authoritatively. "Send an application into Mitre Court Chambers. The set's extremely busy and they regularly take on pupils. Send your CV in. What have you got to lose?"

Lee's encouraging words of support was just the boost my flagging demoralised spirits needed and I decided I would apply. Not long later, I received a letter from Mitre Court Chambers inviting me for an interview. To help me prepare for that interview, I contacted Lee for help and advice on the best way to sell myself to the interviewing panel and without hesitation, Lee duly obliged, his helpful guidance covered everything ranging from the type of questions I was likely to be asked, to the manner and form the interview was likely to take. Lee's help and advice was worth more than its weight in gold and I arrived at Mitre Chambers for my interview on the appointed date five or so minutes before the appointed time accompanied with the usual mix of optimism and nerves. One of the junior clerks invited me to sit down and relax on one of the nearby chairs, whilst he notified the interviewing panel of my arrival. Moments later, the doors to one of the rooms in the Chambers opened and a man emerged from the open door before inviting me to come in. I shook his hand by the open door and then walked into the small room which was dominated with a large writing desk stacked high with legal briefs. I was somewhat taken aback by the fact that it was only the pair of us in the room as I was half expecting to be interrogated by a panel of expressionless and hard to please interviewers but instead, my immediate fate was going to be determined by only one individual.

"Good afternoon, Shaun. My name is David Farrington and I am the Head of these Chambers. Tell me about yourself." David's relaxed demeanour as well as the informal nature of the whole process immediately put me at ease. I began to state my case as to the reasons why I would be a worthwhile asset to the Chambers by describing my personal circumstances, educational background and my work experiences to date.

David then began to talk about the history of the Chambers from its humble origins in and around the Temple, to the near eighteen strong criminal prosecution and defence team, before going on to give an outline of the Chambers' policy of expanding its membership and that the Chambers were in the process of moving to a much larger premises on the ground floor at Garden Court by the end of the summer, to complement their objectives. If I were to be offered a place, then I would join a large pool of at least seven to eight pupils and squatters, all of whom were kept constantly busy with either prosecution or defence work in both the Magistrate's and Crown Courts. He also told me that all working pupils taken on by Chambers would have his/her application for a tenancy fairly and properly considered at the end of that pupil's probationary period.

I felt a sense of relief that David's interrogation, however mild, was now over and by and large, I felt that I had given a good account of myself. David then escorted me to the small reception area and the exit door as I turned to shake his hand for the final time, I noticed a faint smile. Almost immediately, a ridiculous and irrational thought popped into my head, *He's not smiling because he thought my performance in the interview was laughable was he?* However, no sooner had that ridiculous thought popped into my head it was swiftly dispelled and replaced with a much more optimistic train of thought. I was sure I hadn't done too badly.

I didn't have to wait long for an answer as only three or so days later, I received a letter from them.

"Dear Shaun, on behalf of Mitre Court Chambers we are delighted to inform you that your application for a pupillage with a view to a tenancy has been successful."

"I got in! I got in!" I exclaimed wildly to myself and began punching the air in triumphal delight. To make sure that my eyes were not deceiving me, I read the first few lines again as I gradually calmed myself down from the heights of near ecstasy before continuing to read the rest of the letter's contents. I felt as if I had been pulled clear from the edge of a gaping chasm and I immediately rushed to call Lee and tell him. Lee was just as pleased as I was that I'd be taken on and that we would be linking up once again once more.

That night, as I lay awake in bed, I began to think about the best time to start with my new chambers, but the more I thought about the starting date, the more uncertain I was as to what to do next. *Do I start straight away...? Do I put the starting date back a bit?* That was all I could think. *Should I hit the ground running straight away? If I join Garden Court now, could I count on the small pool of solicitors who had instructed me at 76b?* The state of my finances was another primary consideration and in the end I knew I needed to spend the summer working if I was going to succeed in my new Chambers. The abject state of my financial situation had won the argument in my mind.

My soon to be Senior Clark, John Gutteridge, was delighted to hear I was accepting their offer of pupillage and said the six months could commence when they had moved to their new premises at 2 Garden Court.

Then, as I was on my way to 76b to inform them of my departure, fortune smiled on me once again, when I bumped into an old school friend of mine from my Alyestone High schooldays, Juene Guishard. Almost immediately, we began chatting about all sorts of things, ranging from reminiscing about our school days to how things were going with regards to our respective careers. Juene was working as a teacher for Brent Council's Family Service Unit, but her ultimate ambition was to qualify as a Clinical Educational Psychologist to Doctorate level. I told her how things were going for me generally and how tough I was finding it all. I then began to tell Juene how I was delaying the start of my pupillage for financial reasons, but I was nervous because I didn't have any work set up yet. Then, out of the blue, to my utter astonishment and delight Juene made me the following offer, "Why don't you come and work on the Play Scheme Unit that I'll be running throughout the summer?"

Of course I was delighted at the opportunity to work in another Play Scheme for the summer, as I had done so many times before. I applied for the role and was duly accepted, then had to face the somewhat daunting task of finally informing 76b that I was leaving.

I eventually arrived outside the front glass door of chambers and with a sharp intake of breath, I pushed it open and started walking up the stairs, clear in my mind as to how I was going to play the situation. I walked into the Clerk's Room where Danny was sitting at the desk once occupied by Errol on the phone chatting away to one of the solicitors. I waited until he finished his call before dropping the bombshell.

"Danny, I've decided to leave Chambers. It's nothing personal against you, but with all that's happened in the last month or so, I felt I had no choice but to move on, I'll be leaving with immediate effect."

Danny seemed genuinely disappointed by my announcement and he tried to win me over with his natural charm, but it was apparent that I wasn't going to change my mind. We shook hands and I turned and walked out of the Clerk's Room. As I did so, I couldn't help but feel a tinge of sadness at leaving behind the place that had given me my first big break, a ground breaking opportunity that I will forever be grateful for, but the time was right now to move onto pastures new. I finally reached the bottom of the stairs and opened that glass door for the last time and when I pulled it firmly shut behind me, it was a clear statement of intent that one stage of my career was now closed and two months from now, the doors to 2 Garden Court would begin stage two.

The remainder of that summer was solely devoted to my now all too familiar alter ego: the "big kid". This scheme was no better or worse than any of the other play schemes that I had been involved with before in the past as both Juene and I worked tirelessly to ensure that all the children under our care really enjoyed themselves throughout the whole summer. My short two month stint working with Juene was exactly what the doctor ordered given all the stresses and upheavals surrounding my departure from 76b. The relief in having secured a place in a set of Chambers that seemed destined to be going places also put me in a good frame of mind. By the end of August, I felt completely reinvigorated and reenergised physically, mentally and financially, and hopefully I was now ready to demonstrate and prove to the powers that be at 2 Garden Court, that I would be worthy of a permanent place in Chambers. I've done it once before and there's no reason why I couldn't achieve the same feat again.

CHAPTER ELEVEN

That first Monday of September 1987 heralded the start of yet another quest in trying to secure that holy grail of a tenancy. As many a successful practitioner would tell you, an important contributing factor to a successful career at the bar is a long and unbroken association with the Chambers where they practise their trade. Virtually every successful barrister at the top of the profession has been associated with the same set of Chambers since their pupillage days and overseeing the gradual rise through the ranks is the Senior Clerk, ensuring that the constant volume and the quality of work they attract on behalf of the barristers in their care will help realise profession ambitions. Moving from one Chambers to another would be seen as an anathema by most successful practitioners, for the plain and simple reason being that it would not provide the important ingredients of continuity, mutual trust and respect and mutual confidence the Senior Clerk and a barrister must have in their respective abilities, which can only develop and blossom over a considerable period of time.

It's the same philosophy that I have tried to follow and embrace with regards to my own development and ambitions but alas, my efforts to secure a tenancy at Garden Court chambers was to end in disappointment. This resulted in my career following a pattern over the next twelve or so years that could best be described as an unsettling nomadic odyssey, as my membership or association of six different sets of Chambers during that period would bear testimony to. Equally frustrating, and no less disappointing, was the fluctuating stop/start development within those twelve or so years of myself as a barrister and the type of cases I was instructed in. During that time, I experienced the thrill of successfully defending clients on many occasions, even managing to go through an entire calendar year on two occasions without losing a single trial, to complete and utter despair of going days and sometimes weeks on end when I would spend my time watching daytime TV due to the fact that there was nothing in my professional diary, leaving me feeling both professionally and personally drained and constantly wondering whether I should turn my back on the profession altogether.

It would be easy to point the finger of blame on various external factors that contributed to the stop start nature of my career development. One such factor was the passing of The Courts and Legal Services Act 1990 which removed from the bar its centuries' old exclusive monopoly of the right to appear in both the Crown and High Courts as well as the courts at Appellate level. The rationale and thinking behind this seismic change to the legal profession was the government of the day's determination to open up the legal market to greater competition in order to give the consumer more choice. The bar fiercely opposed these changes arguing that they threatened not only the bar's independence, but also its very existence and it lobbied hard in its attempts to derail or at the very least, slow the pace of reform but despite the bar's protestations, the die was cast. By the end of the decade, solicitors were not only doing more and more of the advocacy themselves in the Magistrate's Courts but, increasingly, in the Crown Courts as well, which had a profound effect in terms of the volume and the quality of the primary source of work barristers like myself were totally reliant upon. A notable effect of this paradigm shift saw solicitor firms begin a policy of actively recruiting members of the bar to do their advocacy in the courts in order to keep the work "in house", a policy that in the longer term could threaten the very existence of an independent Bar.

Another external factor inextricably linked to my seemingly endless professional struggles was the government's determination to get to grips with the annual spending of the Legal Aid budget, which by the mid-eighties and early nineties, was running into hundreds of millions of pounds. The combination of political and public misgivings working in tandem with the constant media backlash and criticism of the so-called "fat cat lawyers" earning seemingly endless fortunes from the public purse eventually led to the government radically overhauling the way barristers, doing publicly funded criminal work, were paid with the introduction of the Graduated Fee System, a system designed ostensibly to provide greater efficiency and transparency in how the legal profession are paid as well as the overriding objective of value for money. The long term effect of these reforms not only saw a significant reduction in the bar's earning power but subsequent rule changes to the Graduated Fee System led to even further reductions in barrister's fees resulting in an overall reduction of nearly 40% since the scheme's introduction.

I need hardly tell you how devastating an impact those factors/reforms had on the type of cases I had been involved in as well as my overall earning power during my first twelve years in private practice, but all the factors in the world couldn't really hide or disguise the ultimate reason why my career wasn't making the steady constant progression that I was hoping for and that reason was: the man in the mirror that I have to look at every day. I and I alone must bear ultimate responsibility for the way things were developing and if I was brutally honest with myself, the dire nature that the state of my career was in at the beginning of 1999 was exactly the place it deserved to be. On reflection, my difficulties stemmed from the idealised romantic view I had (and continue to have), of the profession and my role within it, an idealised view which bore little to no resemblance to reality. From my perspective, the principles and ideals that have driven my career are based on three main tenets: first, how you prepare for a trial, secondly, how you relate to the client and finally, how you perform and conduct yourself in court. I have always strived to maintain the highest standards the profession demands and if you tick all the boxes and win the vast majority of the cases like I was doing during those first twelve years, then one would be forgiven for thinking that your career is heading in a positive direction. In my case sadly, those first twelve years of my career were characterised by good, steady progress that gradually descended into near terminal decline which I couldn't, despite my best efforts, seem to be able to arrest. It begs the obvious question - if I was this archetypal barrister who followed the rules and won cases then how was it possible my career was one endless struggle? My honest response to the charge would be that, I just couldn't (and at times wouldn't), maintain relationships with the solicitors who have instructed me in the cases that I have conducted. Not because I thought that cultivating and sustaining such relationships was somehow beneath me, but because of my stubborn and steadfast refusal to either grasp or indeed appreciate the fact that you can't simply rest on your laurels and expect cases to flock in just because you win trials. No one has the God given right to briefs, and developing and sustaining a successful career requires more than just winning trials. Forming and cultivating relations with the powers that be is just as important when it comes to the choice solicitors make.

My own personal mantra and philosophy, rightly or wrongly, was that I wanted my professional abilities to be judged on the quality of service I provide as a professional and no other arbitrary reason, an idealistic one sided view that to all intents and purposes was tantamount to professional suicide. As for networking, the lifeblood for many a barrister's practice, I simply wasn't cut out for it. On the few occasions I would attend such functions like Chambers' events when solicitors would be invited for drinks and canapés, where barristers would engage in convivial conversation in a relaxed and chilled atmosphere, I would usually either be seen standing on the side lines. Blame it on my inherent shyness or in truth, my total lack of interpersonal skills, that left me both ill-equipped and ill-prepared to deal with situations like these.

It was a never ending cycle of kowtowing, not knowing whether or not your efforts will pay dividends. If you're not prepared to "play the game" in some way shape or form you won't get anywhere in the profession no matter how talented you are and during those first twelve years, it would be fair to say that my rose-tinted quasi-maverick approach to my career saw it almost sink without a trace.

I spent just over fifteen months at Garden Court and when I started my first day at the Chambers, it was patently clear that I had joined a set that was leagues above 76b. The twenty strong members of the set were a mixture of experienced practitioners and busy juniors who were kept constantly busy by a clerking team consisting of the Senior Clerk, John Gutteridge and his junior, the amiable Paul Richardson, to the mutual benefit for all parties concerned.

The set didn't have any practicing silks at the top end of the pecking order but names such Sally O'Neil (now Sally O'Neill QC), Stephen Holt, Graham Trembath (now Graham Trembath QC), Paul Dodgson (now His Honour Judge Dodgson), Vincent Coughlan (now Vincent Coughlan QC) who was my de facto pupil master, and the rising star and driving force alongside the Head of Chambers, Andrew Mitchell (now Andrew Mitchell QC), were doing trials that were not far off silk standard and it was no surprise when years later, they were appointed to the highest rank within the profession or at the very least, a full time judicial appointment.

At the junior end, barristers like Jon Swain and the two with whom I became good friends with as time went on, Nicky Merrick and David Bentley (now David Bentley QC), were doing back to back Crown Court trials despite being no more than five or six years call. The remaining personnel in practice at Garden Court was the group I and my old mate Lee John- Charles was a part of. The role of the working pupil was clear and simple. Their primary role was to cover all the cases in either the Magistrates' or Crown Courts for tenants who were involved in other cases elsewhere. It was at the Senior Clerk's discretion as to whether or not that working pupil retained that brief and if that was the case, then it was a good indicator of the confidence the Clerks had in your abilities which would be an important factor taken into consideration when the Chambers Tenancy Committee met to decide which of the current working pupils (if any) would be elevated to full membership.

There were about eight working pupils when I first. Because we were technically still pupils, each working pupil was assigned a pupil master, a titular appointment in truth whose role was to "monitor" that working pupil's all round abilities and would give his or her views to the Tenancy Committee on the day of reckoning. There was a good camaraderie amongst the group of working pupils such as Lee, Allan Goh, Ed Fizpatrick, Sherry Caddle and a young Charlie Sherrard (now Charles Sherrard QC), to name a few. Although all the working pupils were competing for tenancy places available on a level playing field, a crucial factor that could give a working pupil the edge on the tenancy stakes was the number of solicitors who regularly instructed them, especially those contacts that came from a source that was independent from Chambers. In terms of my own pool of contacts, the only regular source that I could only rely on was Phil Cremin and his staff at Cremin Small, which paled in comparison to the contacts and support my fellow pupils and rivals had at their disposal. However, only a bad workman blames his tools and I wasn't going to use the excuse of the lack of a vast network of solicitor contacts as a reason as to why I could not secure a tenancy position at Garden Court. If I wanted to be one of the chosen few in terms of being offered that tenancy, I would have to convince the powers that be that I had all the attributes they were looking for both in and out of court.

During the next five months, my professional career was still making the good and steady progress that I was happy with. By day, I was a practising barrister going to different courts in and around London doing summary trials defending as well as prosecuting the lists on behalf of the recently created Crown Prosecution Service (CPS), appearing in the Crown Court doing bail applications, appeals against conviction or sentence and occasionally, the odd noting brief, taking notes on evidence on behalf of some of the tenants involved in major criminal trials. My frequent appearances in court were helping the development and perfection of my abilities as a barrister and contributed greatly to my increasing confidence. I was more than happy with the way my career was progressing but despite such contentment, the one missing piece in the jigsaw from that continuing development, was that elusive Crown Court trial brief and my biggest concern, apart from my disappointment in not having made the much hoped for breakthrough in that regard, was that my lack of Crown Court trial experience could count against me when it came to the Chambers' Tenancy Committee's decision as to whether or not I was deemed worthy enough to be offered a tenancy.

By night, I was still teaching part time. The teaching and educating of others had now become a personal mission statement of mine. I was totally dedicated and committed to teaching those students who were equally committed to giving up an evening in their week in their quest to attain an educational qualification that would go a long way towards improving their own life chances both personally and professionally. I have always been a firm believer that people who have a special talent and ability to help others succeed should always use that talent and ability. That belief and philosophy stretches back to the days when teachers like Gordon Small and Mike Cooley taught me at Aylestone High School.

Any student who shows a real commitment and dedication to study, must as a consequence, be prepared to make sacrifices in order to achieve those aims and that means regularly attending lectures, doing all the necessary background reading and research on the topics covered during the lecture and finally, submitting all written pieces of coursework, especially those pieces that counted towards their end of year exams by any designated deadline. The students under my charge were left in no doubt of what I expected and demanded from them. That philosophy was made abundantly clear to them before the course began in earnest that myself as the lecturer and every student on the course, had to give the same level of effort and commitment from the beginning right through to the course's end in order to achieve the successful outcome both lecturer and student desired.

The vast majority of my students responded positively to my approach and they were well aware that they would be placed firmly in the spotlight if they hadn't read the handouts the designated reference books, as any such failings would be ruthlessly exposed at the start of the next lecture. I would choose one student after another at random asking them questions on either the topics covered in the previous lecture or aspects of the homework or research that I asked them to do in time for the next lecture. For my students, there was no hiding place.

Towards the end of February, rumours were circulating around Chambers that decisions had been made with regards the new tenants who were going to be recruited. Those rumours turned out to be true as Chambers made a total of six new appointments in the form of three highly experienced and highly regarded practitioners from outside of the Chambers and three chosen from their pool of working pupils. Sadly for me, I wasn't amongst the chosen group of new tenants, a decision that came as no real surprise if I was brutally honest, but that didn't mean that I felt any less disappointed by the news. I was genuinely pleased for those former working pupil colleagues of mine who had been elevated to the status of full tenants, but the decision of Chambers not to offer me a tenancy meant that I was facing an uncertain future. I had to act quickly and try to secure a place to continue my career at another set of chambers because the last thing I wanted was to be perceived as a discarded squatter who had nowhere to go, hanging around Chambers like a musty smell.

Any lingering fears that I may have had concerning Garden Court's decision not to take me on was going to result in me being ushered out through the exit door in an instant were quickly allayed when a day or so later, I was asked by John to follow him into one of the rooms for a brief discussion. Also present in the room was the Head of Chambers, Andrew Mitchell, and my de facto pupil master, Vincent Coughlan. Collectively, all of them expressed their regret that my application wasn't successful and they made it abundantly clear that my non-appointment had nothing to do with either my ability or general conduct. The most reassuring words that emerged though was still to come when they informed me that I was under no pressure to leave Chambers, clearly acknowledging and appreciative of the fact that it could take some time before I found somewhere else to practise and until that day arrived, I would still be an active working pupil. I couldn't tell you how relieved I felt that I didn't have to leave Chambers straightaway.

I had a bit of breathing space, but with no prescribed time limit on my extended stay of execution, it was still nevertheless imperative that I got back on the treadmill of circulating my CV to as many tenancy committees at different sets as quickly as possible. As the barristers left the room to attend to other matters, John came up to me and handed me another bundle of papers. Thinking that they were additional papers for a hearing I was doing tomorrow, I asked him what these papers were about and his surprising response were the most pleasant sound for the sorest of ears, "You've got a trial coming up in the warned list at Knightsbridge Crown Court from a client that wants you to represent him. Paul will be speaking to the solicitors to arrange a conference in Chambers towards the end of this week." I was so overjoyed by the news, my initial reaction was to give my Senior Clerk one big hug, but as approachable a person he may have been, I don't think that form of expression of gratitude would have gone down too well. Finally, after three years to the day when I was formally called to the bar, three long years of waiting, of frustration and, at times, bitter disappointment, at long, long last, I was going to get the chance to do what I've been craving to do: represent a client in a Crown Court trial.

The circumstances that led to my first Crown Court trial brief came about in a most unexpected way. I was at Marylebone Magistrate's Court, discussing matters with my client. He soon became anxious and agitated and it was clear that he felt a sense of injustice at being in court charged with an offence he steadfastly maintained he did not commit and if anything, he felt he was the victim. It was clear from a quick glance at the papers CPS had served me that my client was no stranger to the courts. He had a number of minor convictions in the mid 1980's for Theft, Possession of an Offensive Weapon and Offence of Violence albeit, of a relatively minor nature, but it was clear from his initial outburst that he was going to vigorously contest the allegation of Actual Bodily Harm on the basis that he was acting in lawful self-defence. To back up that assertion, my client then produced photographs which on closer inspection showed evidence of injuries to his teeth and mouth which he stated he suffered as result of the incident, injuries that were examined by a Forensic Medical Examiner back at the police station. The more my client spoke, the more plausible his account was beginning to sound and just before I was about to leave him to book myself in with the usher for our court, my client turned to me and asked, "Will you be representing me at trial?" I didn't know how to reply to his question, conscious of the fact that the case was Chambers work and the final decision as to who would be conducting his trial wasn't mine to make. "Only if you want me to," was my tentative reply. My client said he would tell his solicitor he did want me to, as he was happy with the way in which I dealt with him. He proceeded to tell me about his previous dealings with lawyers who had represented him and his frustration and despair in not having the same lawyer every time he went to court as these different lawyers either didn't know what they were doing or didn't care.

My client turned out to be a man of his word, the consequence of which resulted in me representing him at the final Committal hearing stage before the case was committed to Knightsbridge Crown Court for my client stand trial on a date to be notified. Even at that stage, I still wasn't taking it for granted that I would be the actual trial counsel and it was only when the Crown Court brief was handed to me with my own name on the front of it and the subsequent conference that I was finally convinced that I really was going to be Defence Counsel at trial.

On the 29th of February 1988, the Chamber's Junior Clerk, Paul Richardson, informed me that my trial was going to be heard the following day, news that I greeted with a mixture of excitement and apprehension in equal measure. The following morning, I arrived at Knightsbridge Crown Court nice and early on order to have a last minute conference with my client. I had left no proverbial stone unturned in terms of preparing the case for trial that included, a conference that I had with my client in Chambers and not forgetting, the seemingly infinite number of times that I read the brief in order to give me a clear understanding of the main issues as well as create a clear, vivid picture of the incident in my mind that I hoped would assist me in the way I would conduct the trial. I even went to the scene where the incident had taken place with the sole aim of helping to reinforce my understanding of the important issues of the case, but all the preparation in the world wasn't going to eradicate any nervous apprehension and tension that was sure to play some part in my debut as a Crown Court advocate, but I suppose that comes with the territory. I'd talked the talk for a long time, now it was up to me to prove that I had what it takes to walk the walk.

The trial was scheduled to be heard at 10.30am and after one final conference with my client, I made my way to the advocate's robing room in order to find my opponent. I called out for the prosecuting counsel in my case and a response came from the corner of the room by a man who was in the middle of discarding motor cycling gear which he was folding up to place in a wooden locker and exchanging for his professional attire. Once he had finished changing, I went up to him and introduced myself and was greeted in a very gracious and friendly way. My opponent in my very first Crown Court trial was Richard Atchley, a youthful looking, but vastly experienced barrister who practiced at Chambers somewhere in Gray's Inn. I was pretty sure that he could sense straight away that I was a rookie when we were discussing the case in general but to his eternal credit he never sought to take advantage of any shortcomings I may have shown. His fair minded approach during those discussions made it clear from the outset that he was not the "win at all costs" type of opponent and that the trial was going to be conducted in the manner that all adversarial proceedings should be conducted.

All parties were told to go to Court 2 via the court's Tannoy system. Once inside, I spoke to my client, promising I would use my very best endeavours to secure an acquittal and my words seemed to reassure him and we wished each other good luck before we went to our respective positions, my client in the dock and myself in the seat on the second row within touching distance of the jury panel. Moments later, there was a loud knock on the door behind the judge's bench which then opened and the judge entered the courtroom at which point everyone in the room rose to their feet in accordance with court protocol and etiquette. Just before he took his seat on the bench, he nodded his head slightly towards trial counsel to which both Richard and myself responded in kind. Richard then rose to his feet and formally introduced the parties in the trial. The trial judge, His Honour Judge Oppenheimer QC smiled and nodded in my direction which went a long way to settling the raging butterflies that were flapping incessantly in my stomach. Moments later, the jury panel were led into court by one of the court ushers and the fifteen potential jurors assembled by the door as the court usher approached the clerk and handed her the cards that contained the names of those jurors. The clerk then proceeded to shuffle the cards which she is required to do by law in order to ensure that the selection process was totally random before reading out the first twelve names one by one as the jurors took their seats in the jury seating area. Once the potential jurors were empanelled, the clerk asked my client to stand and offered him the soon to be abolished right of challenge which allows a defendant standing trial to ask for up to three jurors to be removed from the panel before that juror takes the oath without giving the reason for that challenge. I turned towards my client to indicate to him not to make any challenges and he nodded acknowledging that instruction. The clerk then read out the charges on the indictment and my client pleaded not guilty to the substantive count and the same plea to the alternative charge of common assault. The trial was now formally under way and the trial judge invited Richard to open the case to the jury.

The prosecution's case against my client related to an incident which occurred on the 17th of April 1987 at approximately 4.30pm on a number 8 bus travelling along Oxford Street. Prior to the start of the incident, my client was walking along the north side of Oxford Street in a party containing his wife, sister, his young son who was asleep in his pushchair and a family friend. The party decided that they wanted to look at some other stores further up Oxford Street towards Tottenham Court Road but because they had spent a considerable amount of time walking nonstop, they decided to board a bus. After boarding the bus, my client, with the assistance of both his wife and sister, carried the pushchair containing the sleeping infant onto the open platform. Upon seeing this, the Bus Conductor whom the prosecution allege was the victim of the incident, approached my client who at this time was alone with his son on the open platform and asked him to fold up the pushchair as it was creating an obstruction, which could potentially cause an injury to other passengers. The Bus Conductor also informed my client that if he allowed this to continue, he could get into serious trouble with his employers. My client was then alleged to have pleaded with the Bus Conductor that his party were only travelling a couple of stops and folding up the pushchair would mean disturbing his sleeping young son. My client's request was refused and the Bus Conductor insisted that my client either fold up the pushchair so as not to cause an obstruction, or leave the bus altogether. Thereafter, a heated verbal exchange ensued between the Bus Conductor and my client that resulted in my client, according to the prosecution, losing his temper and instigating an unprovoked and sustained attack on the Bus Conductor who after the attack, managed to escape to the front of the bus to alert the driver who radioed for police assistance. The police arrived on the scene quickly and their collective account was that my client's demeanour was verbally threatening and abusive particularly towards the Bus Conductor before he subsequently turned his anger towards them noting that he was bleeding profusely from his mouth. Because of what they were told at the scene, the police arrested and cautioned my client for Actual Bodily Harm and according to the arresting officers, my client continued with his abusive and threatening behaviour, conduct that eventually resulted in my client having to be restrained with handcuffs before being placed in a police van and taken to Paddington Police Station. During the journey to the police station, my client was alleged to have made a series of unsolicited comments all of which were recorded by the police officer who sat next to him in his notebook in which he denied either assaulting or verbally threatening the Bus Conductor steadfastly maintaining that it was he who was in fact the victim of an unprovoked assault and he went on to state that he only struggled with the police officers at the scene at the time of his arrest because he was surprised and angry at the fact that the police officers had arrested the wrong person. My client was examined by a police surgeon who had made a note of all his visible injuries to his mouth and despite being eventually charged with ABH, my client was never, prior to being charged, formally interviewed by police under caution.

In so far as the injuries suffered by the Bus Conductor, the written report of the police surgeon's examination of him revealed only a bruise and a small cut to his right index finger with no other complaint being made. However, during our pretrial discussions in the robing room, Richard handed me a further statement from the Bus Conductor dated almost ten months after the incident in which he stated that he suffered injuries to his knees, an injury that was not noted in the police doctor's report which caused him to be laid off work for a period of nine months. The final part of Richard's opening remarks dealt with a summary of my client's case on account of the recorded unsolicited comments that he made after his arrest. In summary, he told the jury that my client's account of the incident was in direct contrast to that of the Bus Conductor, in that he stated that after he was given the ultimatum, he decided to leave the bus and as he bent down to pick up the pushchair, he felt a tap on his shoulder. He turned around and felt "a sharp powerful blow" to his mouth which he maintains was totally unprovoked and resulted in him bleeding profusely all over his clothing and sleeping young son. After the unprovoked assault, my client immediately got off the bus bleeding and in pain and whilst he accepted that he was angry and abusive towards the Bus Conductor, that was because of the Bus Conductor's threatening demeanour and it was my client who, according to him, demanded that the police be called to the scene. The issue to be decided by the jury therefore was, who was the real aggressor throughout the entire incident and it was for the prosecution to prove my client's guilt to a standard that the jury must be sure before they could convict him.

The trial got under way and after the Bus Conductor had given his evidence in chief it was my turn to cross examine him, in a calm but determined manner, with a series of sustained and measured questions that challenged every aspect of his testimony. During cross examination, I showed him the album of photographs which showed the injuries my client sustained during the incident, my client's medical report from the Police Surgeon's examination of him and finally, a medical report detailing his injuries from St Mary's hospital, before proceeding to asked him whether he was responsible for causing those injuries and if he was, would he accept my suggestion that it tended to demonstrate that he used a disproportionate amount of force in causing those injuries due to his aggressive conduct. The witness vigorously rejected that assertion and replied that any injuries sustained by my client on that day, was as a direct result of him trying to defend himself from the unprovoked and sustained attack that was instigated by my client and that he used what he believed was reasonable force given the circumstances he was facing. I asked him about the injuries to his knee and the fact he made no complaint of such a condition during his medical examination by the police surgeon, or in the witness statement that he made some considerable time after the incident. The reason for that glaring omission, as I suggested to him most forcefully, was that his account was an exaggeration at best, or at worst, a total fabrication of the true nature and extent of the injuries he sustained on that day. The Bus Conductor's response to that suggestion however was to steadfastly maintain that all the injuries he suffered that day was a result of my client's initial unlawful aggressive conduct.

After Richard had called his remaining witnesses, he closed the case for the prosecution. The trial judge turned to me and asked whether I would be calling any evidence and I rose to my feet and informed him that I intended to, but I would request, subject to his consent, a short adjournment in order to speak to my client before I began the case for the defence. The judge paused momentarily and gazed in my direction, a time delay that from my rookie perspective, seemed to last for an eternity before he finally granted my request and thereafter, he rose from the bench and retired to his chambers.

My client and I left the courtroom and went to a quiet corner in the foyer to discuss the trial's progress. My client was happy with the way I was representing him and felt that the trial was going well, but amidst the air of cheery optimism, I uttered the following salutary words of caution, "We're only at the half way stage and the jury have not yet heard your version of events. It's now your opportunity to calmly look the jury in the eye and tell your side of the story. The prosecution will have their opportunity to cross examine you and you'll be facing a very experienced and able prosecutor. When he cross examines you, the one thing I want you to have in mind, at all times, is that no matter how persistent the line of his questioning, no matter how tempted you may be, you must not, under any circumstances, suggest or call any of the prosecution witnesses liars because if you do, your previous convictions may be put before the jury and it could go against you." My client nodded in response. He gave his wife a final hug and we both returned to court for the start of the case for the defence.

My client was called to the witness stand and during his evidence in chief, he did everything that I asked of him. However, it was during my client's subsequent cross examination by prosecuting counsel that he found himself presented with an entirely different challenge as Richard used all his know how and experience with his persistent, but fair line of questioning, that had the principal aim of gradually undermining the composed demeanour my client had previously shown. In an effort to break up the rhythm of Richard's sustained questioning, occasionally I would object that my opponent's line of questioning were an attempt to goad my client which the trial judge politely, but firmly, rejected each time. Eventually, Richard's persistent probing paid dividends as he finally got the response he was looking for when my client, despite all the warnings I had given to him beforehand, was finally trapped when he said that the evidence given by the Bus Conductor was a wholly untruthful and lying account. That response prompted Richard to inform the trial judge that a "matter of law" had arisen and he requested that the jury be withdrawn from the courtroom while those legal discussions took place. The trial judge acceded to that request and once the jury were safely in their retiring room, Richard rose to his feet and then placed his Archbold, the essential criminal practitioner's guide book on the wooden lectern in front of him, its long red ribbon already at the relevant page citation. The substance of Richard's submission was that my client's evidence directly impugned the character of the witnesses for the prosecution and under s.1(f) ii of the Criminal Evidence Act 1898, he had lost his protective "shield" which precludes an accused's previous convictions being put before the jury without leave of the court. Richard went on to submit that my client's previous conviction for violence, albeit for a minor assault, as well as his previous conviction for an offence of Dishonesty, were relevant to the issue of my client's credibility as a witness and it would be unfair, from the prosecution's point of view, for my client to attack the character of a prosecution witness without the jury being made fully aware of the true nature and background of my client's character. The trial judge then turned his attentions to me and asked whether I wished to respond to the prosecution's submission. I rose to my feet with a fair degree of trepidation, not knowing what to say. Richard very kindly passed over the wooden lectern together with his Archbold. In essence, the main thrust of my response to Richard's submissions was that the persistent nature of his line of cross examination served merely to entice or goad my client into attacking the character of the main prosecution witness. However, if the court were of the view that my client, by virtue of his attack on the character of the prosecution witness had indeed lost his protective shield, then the court I submitted, should exercise its inherent discretionary powers to exclude evidence of my client's bad character not solely because of its lack of probative worth, but also because of the prejudicial and adverse effect on the admission of such evidence would have on the trial proceeding as a whole.

Unsurprisingly, the trial judge accepted Richard's submissions and when the jury returned, Richard was given leave to put those previous convictions to my client, but not even that potentially damaging state of affairs prevented him sticking doggedly to his account to his eternal credit and he returned to the dock after completing his evidence bruised but unbowed. My client's witnesses, in the form of his wife and family friend, gave evidence on his behalf, the effect of which corroborated his version of events.

The trial was now into its third day and after all the parties had reassembled in court, the trial judge invited Richard to begin his closing address. He delivered his closing speech in a calm, confident and persuasive manner rarely referring to his notes on account of the fact he was focusing his gaze on the jury panel throughout thus setting a benchmark that could prove hard to match let alone surpass. It was now my turn and despite the beads of sweat that were beginning to gather all over my forehead as I rose to my feet, I was ready for the challenge. I turned my wooden lectern to face the jury panel and I began to utter my first ever words of a closing speech in a Crown Court trial. In my attempt to emulate my opponent's forceful and persuasive closing submissions, I also adopted the tactic of looking the jury squarely in the eye as I was speaking despite having to look down at the outline that I had written for my speech with greater frequency than Richard had done.

I grew more and more confident as my speech developed, confidence which I can only put down to the fact I had a complete and total understanding of the evidence and the issues the jury would have to decide upon. As I began to sit down, my shirt totally drenched in gallons of sweat, I turned my head slightly towards the dock in order to gauge my client's reaction to my performance and his thumbs up was a reassuring sign that he was more than happy with my efforts. The penultimate part of the trial process was the judge's summing up, reminding the jury of the salient parts of the evidence during which he made certain remarks which were so remarkable, so unexpected, but the net effect of those remarks was a massive boost to my confidence.

"As Mr Wallace said to you in his excellent closing speech..."

It was the best compliment that I'd ever had bestowed on me, ever! The overwhelming sense of pride that a rookie barrister like me felt hearing those complimentary remarks coming from an experienced judge was immeasurable, and if there were any lingering doubts as to whether I have what it takes to survive and thrive within the profession then the trial judge's comments dispelled them in an instant. Richard leant over towards me with sentiments that were equally complimentary and he went on to add that I conducted the trial very well and in his view, the delivery and content of my closing speech meant that the outcome of the trial was now hanging in the balance.

A little over two hours later, the jury had reached their verdict. I spoke briefly with my client and shook his hand and told him not to react in any way irrespective of the result. The trial judge then entered court and sat on his seat before ordering the jury to be brought back and they filed into court one by one.

The Court Clerk asked the question whether the jury had found my client guilty or not guilty. The foreman replied that the jury had found my client guilty. My initial feelings of disappointment at the verdict though would momentarily have to be put to one side as I had to turn my attention to the sentence my client was likely to receive. Because of the fact my client was convicted of an offence of violence on a public employee, a custodial prison sentence was an inevitable consequence and he could not expect to receive any reduction or discount in terms of the length of any sentence on account of the fact that it was a contested hearing, the length of any custodial sentence in criminal cases would only be reduced if there had been a guilty plea by a defendant at the earliest opportunity.

I rose to my feet in an effort to try and mitigate an already difficult situation and I began that plea of mitigation by first asking the trial judge not to sentence my client immediately, submitting that a social enquiry report should be prepared by the Probation Service in order to look into my client's personal background and circumstances which, I argued, could be of some considerable assistance to the court at the sentencing hearing even if only to help the sentencing court determine the length of the appropriate term of imprisonment. The trial judge appeared to be in no mood to postpone what he regarded an inevitable outcome, but he nevertheless acceded to my request. My efforts to try and persuade the trial judge that my client should have his bail extended pending the preparation of those reports though was flatly refused and my client was taken downstairs for his first ever taste of life behind bars as he was remanded in custody until the date of his sentence hearing.

I felt a degree of sympathy for my client and his disappointment and his subsequent remand was all the more visible when I went see him in the cells afterwards. Despite his incarceration, my client nevertheless thanked me for all my efforts and asked whether there was any chance of appealing the jury's finding. I told him that in my initial view, there may be a possibility of an appeal and that I would set about the task of preparing the appropriate grounds and send them to him via his solicitors. Before I left the cells, I shook my client's hand for the final time and assured him that I would represent him at his sentencing hearing.

My client appeared in court a month later before a different judge due to the fact that the original trial judge was not available, and he received a sentence of six months imprisonment. As promised, I prepared and submitted a written advice and grounds of appeal on my client's behalf to challenge his conviction in the Court of Appeal (Criminal Division), on the principle that the trial judge had erred in law by allowing the admission of my client's previous convictions before the jury during the trial. However, despite my best efforts to persuade the Appellate Court that there were strong and cogent reasons in those written submissions, the application to seek leave to appeal my client's conviction was rejected.

That first Crown Court trial was the breakthrough my career desperately needed and it went some considerable way to reinvigorating my own sense of purpose and optimism that there was a future for me at the bar. My performance in that trial didn't go unnoticed, as over the next six or so months leading up to the beginning of Autumn, there was a considerable increase both in the volume and the quality in the type of cases I was doing, especially in terms of prosecution work. From the monotony of prosecuting the long and uninspiring lists of traffic offences at far flung courts such as Feltham Magistrate's Court or the afternoon lists at the Magistrate's Courts in Ealing, I was suddenly doing bail applications and opening the facts on behalf of the prosecution at sentencing hearings, as well as Crown Court trials prosecuting low level offences ranging from Shoplifting, to Offensive Weapon and securing convictions on every occasion. The regular exposure and experience I was gaining prosecuting trials was proving invaluable in terms of developing my capabilities of being able to conduct both prosecution and defence work and by the late autumn of that year, I was instructed by the ever loyal and supportive, Phil Cremin of Cremin Small, to co-defend in a five day trial at the Inner London Crown Court. Because it was my first trial co-defending with other lawyers in the Crown Court Phil gave me the client where the evidence against was the weakest. I would be working alongside a pair of experienced Crown Court defence advocates, Mark Wyeth and Andrew Hill, with whom I struck up a long-standing friendship.

The case against the three young defendants, all of whom were of previous good character, related to their arrest outside enclosed premises at an industrial unit estate in an area of South London that had been broken into moments before they were arrested by police who arrived quickly on the scene in response to the activation of the alarm system. The defendants who were facing trial claimed that they were on their way home and were walking through the industrial estate which provided a convenient short cut to their respective homes. All three defendants accepted that they noticed that the premises was broken into and that they could clearly hear the alarm. The three defendants also accepted that they each approached the open door of the premises and at least two of the defendants stepped inside before deciding to leave the scene and make their way home. Police Officers quickly arrived on the scene and immediately apprehended and detained the three defendants and thereafter, they were separated from one another and questioned by those officers at the scene. All three strongly denied that they had anything to do with any unlawful break in. Despite those emphatic denials, all three were formally arrested and taken to a police station close to the scene where they were separately interviewed in the presence of a designated legal representative. During their respective interviews, each of the defendants in turn exercised their right not to answer any of the questions that they were asked. All three defendants were jointly charged with Attempted Burglary. The prosecution's case at trial would be entirely based on circumstantial as opposed to any direct form of evidence and in their opening remarks to the jury at the start of the trial, counsel for the prosecution submitted that there was "an irresistible inference" to be drawn from their immediate presence in and around the time when the alarm was activated and their admission at the scene to the police officers that two of the defendants actually entered the premises, their reasons for being on the premises was not an innocent one and as such, their joint presence in the premises was for one purpose and one purpose only and that was, to jointly attempt between the three of them to burgle the premises in question.

Despite the apparent "strength" of the prosecution's case, Mark and Andy's methodical and incisive questioning of the police witnesses during the trial set the tone for gradually dismantling it whilst myself, as the Tail End Charlie of the defence team who had the least difficult case to defend, it was as a simple case of observing, learning and working alongside experienced advocates in a Crown Court trial that could only be of considerable benefit to my own long term career development. After nearly five long hours of deliberations on day five of the trial, the jury finally returned to court after having reached their verdicts and as they settled into their respective seats, the inscrutable blank expressions on their faces giving nothing away, the adrenalin in my system began its slow and gradual rise to an excitable level which in turn caused me to replay the whole trial in my mind and begin to wonder as well as question whether all the collective efforts of the defence team had done enough to tip the balance in our favour. The unbearable tension that I was feeling was hiked up another notch or two as the Court Clerk asked the jury foreman to stand and deliver the verdicts. I turned my gaze towards Mark and Andy but the *sang froid* expression on their respective faces suggested that they had seen it all before. There was no doubting the fact that given the way the prosecution and defence had put their respective cases, the jury foreman's first verdict was going to set the tone for the whole outcome of the trial.

"Members of the jury... Have you reached any verdict in relation to any of the defendants upon which you are all agreed?"

"Yes we have"

"In relation to the first defendant, do you find him guilty or not guilty?"

"Not guilty!"

"In relation to the second defendant, do you find him guilty or not guilty?"

"Not guilty!"

It was now my client's turn to learn his fate. The nervous tension was reaching ridiculous levels, so much so, that my customary wing tip collared shirt was so saturated with sweat it clung to my torso like wet cling film.

"Finally, in relation to the third defendant, do you find him guilty or not guilty?"

"Not guilty!"

If I felt as if I was on top of the world ! Then for some inexplicable reason, I began to rise to my feet, not knowing the reason why I was doing so or indeed, what I was going to say. Thankfully though, any potentially embarrassing situation was swiftly averted when Mark got to his feet before me and with his right hand, gestured slightly in my direction which had the desired effect of curbing my over exuberance before applying to the trial judge for his client to be formally discharged from the dock. Andy then rose to his feet to make a similar application and then finally, I stood up feeling rather sheepish, fully aware is if I didn't already know, that the courtroom is neither the stage or indeed, the forum for any brazen display in terms of victory celebrations. With my composure intact, I completed the defence team's requests for my client to be released and he left the dock with his good name and reputation intact and any lingering thoughts concerning my unscripted aberration was all forgotten when in the foyer the three acquitted defendants were hugging each other and jumping around in unrestrained joy. All three of us went over and they showed genuine gratitude when thanking us for getting them off before they gleefully walked towards the main swivel door and FREEDOM!

It was all smiles as we congratulated each other on a job well done and despite the merciless ribbing I continued to suffer at the hands of my more experienced colleagues, it was an important milestone that filled me with a great deal of pride and satisfaction. I finally had the experience and the ability to win a Crown Court trial especially in front of my professional peers who appear to acknowledge and respect that fact. This first and much cherished victory as a defence advocate was a long time coming and with the right support (allied to a degree or luck and skill) it could be the start of many more to come.

With the end of the year now fast approaching, I decided that the time was now right to try and build on the gradual but encouraging signs of my career development and the only way I could achieve this would be to move on to pastures new. Thankfully, yet again, Dame Fortune came in the guise of my old mentor and pupil master, Jeffrey

Chasing the Dream

Yearwood. I bumped into Jeffrey in the robing room in one of the Crown courts in London. It was the first time I'd seen him since he left 76b the year before last. We greeted each other like long lost acquaintances and Jeffrey seemed especially pleased by the fact that I seemed to be finding my feet at the bar. Jeffrey told me that he had now moved to 54 Fleet Street at the chambers of Edmond Alexander and that he felt more settled since the problem and upheavals since leaving 76b and that he was far busier than he had ever been. Then, completely out of the blue, Jeffrey suggested that I should apply to join him at his chambers adding that I would make a welcome addition. The opportunity to be reunited with my old pupil master was not one I was going to let pass me by and we arranged to meet at his chambers later on that day so I could meet the Head of Chambers and Senior Clerk as well as any other tenants who may be available.

Events were now moving at a rapid pace and by the end of that informal meeting, the Head of Chambers Mr Alexander himself had offered me a tenancy. I asked him whether there was any scope for compromise in terms of my commencement date, the 1st of February of the following year was the date that I had in mind, putting forward the reason that I wanted to see out the final two months of the year with Garden Court followed by a short break before joining them. Edmond said that he didn't have a problem with that arrangement and with a cordial handshake, the deal was sealed.

The following morning, I informed the clerks at Garden Court that I was leaving at the end of the year, having secured a tenancy in another set. They seemed pleased by the news and wished me the best of luck for the future. Although my quest to become a member at Garden Court failed to materialise, the two positive things I took away with me when I said my goodbyes were, firstly, I left the set on good terms and secondly, I gained invaluable experience that can only stand me in good stead in the long term. With my first proper tenancy firmly in my pocket, a future in the profession seemed all but secure.

CHAPTER TWELVE

There was method to my madness when I asked Edmond to start the beginning of my tenancy three months after he had offered it to me. No sooner had he given my request the green light my quick-thinking mind saw this as the perfect opportunity to take another short but carefree sabbatical and the one place I had in mind was the place I've always wanted to visit ever since I was a little boy, the ancestral home of my parents, Jamaica. However, such an ambitious plan costs money and lots of it and if I wanted to make those pipedreams to become reality, then it would mean working hard for the remaining two months of the year both in my teaching and legal practice and saving up every penny that I earned so I could make my intended five and a half weeks adventure all the more enjoyable and worthwhile.

By the time Christmas arrived, everything was now in place and after spending Christmas Day in the company of my immediate family and close friends, I headed for the South Terminal of Gatwick Airport to meet up with my old school friend, Winston Davis, who was a seasoned traveller to the island. He was sure to provide the perfect companionship for my inaugural visit which bore all the hallmarks of being a holiday to remember.

Of all the guys I grew up with, Winston is the one whom I consider to be my best friend. It's a million dollar question as to why Winston and I are so close. He wasn't even part of the original Monks Park boys and our first encounter during the first few days as a freshman at Copland High didn't get off to the best of possible starts, when he and one of his classmates tried to barge past me as I waited in the queue for school dinners wearing for some strange reason a trilby hat and displaying the type of hubris and bravado as if he owned the place. I took umbrage to his actions and I stood my ground before letting him know that he wasn't getting in front of me. My actions stopped him dead in his tracks and the next thing you know we were pushing and shoving each other as well as exchanging the odd word or two before the storm in a teacup eventually died down. We were in different classes throughout our time at the school but gradually over time, I got to know him more and more and as a consequence our friendship grew ever closer. This bond was probably due to the fact that we've got a lot in common, for instance, we were born six days apart in the same hospital (Winston arriving in the world first and if I was laying generous odds, probably in the same ward). We even share the same middle name, Anthony. Our best friend status was well and truly cemented when, at the age of twenty-five, he asked me to be the best man at his wedding (a union which, sadly, for one reason and another, didn't last that long). His most enduring and stand out quality is his charming but cheeky demeanour, particularly during our school days when Winston was seen as the joker of the pack, popular with guys and girls alike. Winston's greatest gift though was his remarkable knack of always managing somehow to wriggle out of trouble, especially with the teaching staff, much to the dismay of myself and the boys we used to hang around with as we invariably had to carry the can for misconduct that Winston was usually at the centre of. By the time we had reached our mid-teens, he was a fully paid up member of the Monks Park crew when we were heavily into raving at nightclubs and house parties. When it came to chatting up the opposite sex, there was no greater exponent of the art, his fit, well-built frame and persuasive patter the clear stand out reasons for his high success rate. Sadly though, as the years have passed, whilst his cheeky, charming demeanour has remained intact, his once well-built frame is now a shadow of its former glory and the young man that I knew that was so quick over 100 metres would only move so quickly if there was a free cheeseburger on offer.

The agreed itinerary for my trip of a lifetime was clear and simple. Using his parents' house in Retreat in the parish of St Thomas as a base, we intended to hire a rental car and travel around the island's fourteen parishes, stopping off along the way to visit relatives on both sides of my family and availing myself the opportunity to finally see for myself some of Jamaica's iconic landmarks. My old pal Glenmore Johnson used to wax lyrical about the delights of places such as Dunn's River Waterfalls in Ochio Rios, or the world famous Negril Beach. But the reality of my exciting adventure with Winston was nothing like what I hoped for or envisaged.

It took almost a whole day before I finally recovered from the rigours of the plane journey and accompanying jet lag, but now I was ready and raring to go to tour and explore the whole beautiful island, an attitude that was in stark contrast to my so called travelling companion who seemed more or less content to amble around the aptly named Retreat where we were based as if he hadn't a care in the world. This clash of attitudes was becoming an increasing source of irritation and frustration so far as I was concerned during those first few days on the island and it was also becoming increasingly apparent, that Winston was trying to cut every corner he could especially when it came to hiring a car. I was desperate to explore this wonderful and beautiful island but it seemed, by contrast, that Winston simply wasn't interested.

By day three, I was at the end of my tether and I let him know in no uncertain terms that if he wasn't prepared to share the costs of hiring a car, then I'd hire one myself and go my own way. Winston then used his old persuasive charm to assuage my raging mood and told me that he had already made arrangements for us to have a car. There was a sting in Winston's long and barely convincing tall tale as the car that he was referring to was situated in a place called Santa Cruz, over one hundred and thirty miles way. When I asked him why we had to travel so far just to pick up a car when it would be easier to go to numerous hire car companies in Morant Bay, Winston gave his usual "cast iron" assurance that everything would be fine and to stop my constant whining. My so called "whining" sadly turned out to be totally justified because by the time we arrived at our destination after having spent a mini fortune hiring a taxi for the journey, the vehicle that was supposed to take both Winston and I on our grand tour around Jamaica was on a ramp with its bonnet wide open whilst a man who I assumed was a mechanic was apparently working on the engine. We spent the best part of nearly three hours waiting around for the car to be repaired before the mechanic broke the hardly surprising news that the car was not ready which meant another long and expensive return journey back to our base in Retreat. But the straw that finally broke the camel's back was when, without telling me where he was going or what he had planned, Winston dropped me off at his parents' place and disappeared. When I woke up the following morning, he hadn't returned from his mysterious walkabout, an absence which extended to the afternoon, evening, night and into the following day.

To say that I was incandescent with fury and rage would have been the mother of all understatements and my initial reaction to Winston's unexplained and prolonged absence was to simply pack my bags and head for the North Coast all by myself, that's how angry and disappointed I felt. But for a mere rookie to the island like myself, travelling solo was not appealing and, despite my strongest reservations, I had no choice but to sit and wait for Winston's eventual return.

However, just when I thought that I would have nothing to look forward to other than endless rides in dangerously overladen taxis from Retreat to Morant Bay town centre and back again, I heard a honking horn just outside the security gates. I rushed out to see what it was and standing outside was a sight that soothed the sorest of eyes, a Hertz rented Toyota Starlet and sitting in the driver's seat was not my missing best friend Winston, but my school old pal Glenmore Johnson. I was fully aware that Glenmore was going to be on the island at the same time as me but when I told him that I was coming to the island with Winston, his raised arched eyebrows told its own story, a reaction of dismay that probably stretches back to our schooldays when the pair of them didn't exactly see eye to eye. I told Glenmore about the issues I'd been having and he was unsurprised. His instant response was that I should pack enough clothes in a small holdall and hit the road with him. I didn't need asking twice! Just before I left, I said my goodbyes to Winston's mum and thanked her for kind and generous hospitality and within a blink of an eye, I was in the front of Glenmore's hired car which couldn't get away fast enough.

From my new base in the Red Hills area of Kingston in the parish of St Andrew, the home of one of Glenmore relatives, we began to plot our travel itinerary in earnest. Because we were in "town", the first place I wanted to go above all else was 21 Covey Avenue, Kingston 5, the home address of Mr Emerson Carter, my maternal grandfather. That visit was a seminal moment for me, not just because I was meeting one of my grandparents for the very first time, it also gave me the chance to see for myself where the young Millicent Carter had spent her formative years growing up in the 1940's and 50's before her migration to England. Although frail, my grandfather still had his wits about him and he was proud as well as overjoyed to see his "lawyer grandson" of whom he had heard so much about from his eldest daughter. Glenmore could see how much this first ever meeting meant to the pair of us and he told me that he would go back to Red Hills so that I could spend some quality time with my grandfather and resume our travel plans in the morning.

Glenmore picked me up the next day and we headed west in a clockwise direction passing through the parishes of St Catherine, Clarendon and Manchester, stopping on every occasion to take a photograph at the official signpost welcoming visitors to the parish. The latter two parishes were where my father was born and raised.

We made sure that we did all our travelling by day as the country at the time was in the midst of an extremely bi-partisan general election and the last thing either of us wanted was to be caught up in the wrong place and at the wrong time especially at night where stories of roadblocks involving masked gunmen leaping out of the bushes and either robbing or killing drivers on the road were both frequent and all too real. Because none of my Dad's parents were alive at this time, for some inexplicable and I must confess, unforgivable reason, I never asked Dad for the contact details of any of his vast extended family much to my eternal regret and shame and the only plausible explanation I could possibly put forward was that I wanted to see all of the island and not get bogged down moving from one relative to another. After leaving Black River, we headed for the parish of Westmoreland and the world famous Negril Beach where we chilled out at Rick's Café during the day and raved at one of the legendary beach parties at night. The next day we were on the north coast via the parish of Hanover and the island's second city, Montego Bay. Our stay was only a fleeting one though as I was anxious to head towards the parish of St Ann's, some eighty or so miles along the north coast, and a tiny little village way up in the hills called Mount Zion where Mum was born and incredibly, where my maternal grandmother affectionately known as Aunt Cora, was still alive and kicking.

With all the family and relatives I needed to see now seen, it was time to hang out with Glenmore's family and relatives which meant heading back along the north coast westwards and his home parish of Trelawney to a place just outside Falmouth where his parents were now living since their retirement to the island some five or so years earlier and they were just as pleased to see me as I was to be there. After a good night's rest at the Johnson household, the pair of us set out as early as possible for the last leg of our circumnavigation of the island. There were only two more parishes left to visit on my checklist. We got to the first, St Mary's, sometime in the afternoon as the tourist in me wanted to go to Port Maria and see for myself Ian Fleming's Goldeneye retreat as well as the place where Noel Coward had built his sumptuous holiday home. By dusk, we finally arrived at the fourteenth and last of the parishes on this wonderful island, the parish of Portland way out on Jamaica's north eastern coast. Glenmore was especially anxious to be in Portland because waiting for him at her parent's house in a secluded area a few miles outside the parishes' main town of Port Antonio was his fiancée Charlie (pronounced with a phonetic "Sh" sound) Johnson who had been on the island for just under a week and thankfully, had given Glenmore "permission" to link up with me so in some indirect way, I owe her an enormous debt of gratitude. The reason why Charlie had come to the island, apart from wanting to spend some quality time on holiday with her partner, was that she was making the necessary arrangements for her marriage to Glenmore in her hometown parish in late December of that year.

I spent the weekend in the parish with the pair of them. There was so much to see and do on my whistle stop tour of Portland. To the South, there were the tall and imposing Blue Mountains which contrasted sharply with the peace and tranquillity of the magnificent Blue Lagoon, but one of my favourite highlights of my all parish island tour was when Glenmore and Charlie took me on was a two hour leisure cruise on a long bamboo made raft on the Rio Grande indulging ourselves with a mini picnic of fried fish and festival and a selection of fruits for dessert, sipping a chilled cocktail of alcohol flavoured coconut water from an actual coconut with the aid of a straw, whilst the soothing sounds of the best of Bob Marley and other well-known reggae artists were playing in the background on my beat box. The following day we spent the morning visiting the wonderful natural geographical waterfall features of Reach Falls and Somerset Falls, sites that equal (and some would argue even surpass), the more illustrious and well known tourist attraction, Dunn's River Falls in Ocho Rios. The remainder of the day was spent relaxing at one of Glenmore and Charlie's favourite sites on the coast, Boston Beach, and just before sunset rather than head for home for something to eat Glenmore suggested that we head towards the nearby Boston Jerk Centre. There was even time to squeeze in a bit of history and culture with a brief visit to the Maroon Cultural Centre before a trip to an area in the parish named Nanny Town in deference to a female leader affectionately known as "Nanny", a Jamaican national heroine who led her Maroon native peoples to a number of great victories in the series of Maroon Wars in the Nineteenth Century in the same way that Joan of Arc had symbolised French resistance in their power struggle with England some four centuries previously. It wasn't that long though before we returned to more hedonistic and leisurely pursuits with another day of lazing around on the beach, this time at the popular Frenchman's Cove whilst at night (with Charlie's blessing!), Glenmore and I raved the night away at one of Port Antonio's premier nightspots, The Roof Club.

In total, it took just over ten days to visit all fourteen parishes on the island. I'd just about run out of the clean clothing I had with me at the start of the journey so I decided it would make sense to pick up the rest of clothing and luggage that were still at Winston's parents' house, so both Glenmore and I headed south for Retreat where my circumnavigation of fun and adventure on the island would be complete. Winston was at his parents' house by the time we arrived and we briefly said hello as I was gathering the rest of my belongings. I don't know what was going through his mind during my brief visit but from my perspective, there were no hard feelings and he was still my best friend, but so far as the remainder of the holiday was concerned he was *persona non grata* and I told him to enjoy himself and I'd see him in the UK upon my return before jumping in the passenger seat for another tour of Jamaica, this time in an anti-clockwise direction once trying to check out as many sites as we could.

Glenmore only had five more days left on his vacation and before he left, he made arrangements for me to stay at Charlie's relatives in the Red Hills area of Kingston as well as transferring the hire of the rental car into my name so I could get around the island that I was becoming more and more familiar with. I couldn't thank him enough for not only preventing my inaugural trip to Jamaica from being a near disaster but also making it such an exciting sense of adventure and fun that would live with me for a lifetime. Forever the modest type, Glenmore replied that he was glad that he was in a position to do what he did and the only thing that he demanded from me in return for chaperoning me around the island was the promise that I would return to the island eleven months hence for his wedding to Charlie, a promise I had no intention of breaking.

I was greeted by the good old cold wind and rain when I eventually arrived back at Gatwick Airport on the last day of January 1989 with my travel luggage overladen with alcohol, foodstuffs, souvenirs and photos, and my thoughts equally overladen with a host of wonderful memories. When I finally arrived home later that afternoon, cold, tired and very, very hungry, I decided to have a good long soak in the bath, a luxury that I was rarely afforded on my recent travels and whilst all the stresses and aches and pains began to gradually melt away, it afforded me the opportunity not only to reflect with fondness of my recent travel exploits, but also to look forward with excitement and anticipation that I was going to become a new tenant at 54 Fleet Street the following day.

But those immediate plans of commencing my tenancy were about to be put on hold for a further three weeks. The following day I found myself once more heading towards another fantastic adventure of a lifetime.

I had called my friend, Asad Zoberi, to let him know I was home, and he informed me that his younger brother, Ather, who was also a good friend of mine, had gone with his cousin and close friend on a three month tour of Brazil. My reaction to what Asad told me was a potent combination of complete seduction coupled with a large slice of envy and despite the fact that I had just come back from my own fantastic holiday, the fact that Ather and his friends were about to live it up in a country that I've dreamed of visiting ever since I was a little boy, made me even more desperate and determined to join them.

No sooner had I ended my conversation with Asad I was calling Ather and in my brief conversation with him, he had totally convinced me that Brazil was the place to be. Despite my tenancy situation, my thoughts were firmly fixed ongoing to Brazil. I still had plenty of money, well over £3000 in cash and traveller's cheques, left from my Caribbean trip and aside from a few dirty clothes, my suitcases were virtually unpacked, so in theory, there was nothing to prevent me from going to South America. In reality, could I really justify embarking on another long and expensive trip a day or so after having returned from one? And how could I justify to the Chambers that I was about to join, for a position I fought so hard to obtain, that I wanted to go on another trip? Would I be putting my tenancy in jeopardy? Those were the immediate dilemmas that were racing through my mind in the aftermath of my telephone conversation with Ather. In the end, despite those difficulties and conundrums, I came to a decision. I was heading off to join Ather and his travelling companions in Brazil for the Carnival celebrations and to hell with the consequences.

The following morning I left my home bright and early suited and booted for what was supposed to be my first day as a practicing tenant as 54 Fleet Street. My intentions though were not to await instructions from my new Senior Clerk as to which court in London he was going to be sending me to, but to try and offer some plausible reason or excuse as to why I wanted to postpone the commencement of my tenancy for a further three weeks. By the time I arrived outside the building's main front door, I still hadn't thought of what to tell him, but as I climbed the seemingly endless set of stairs leading to the third floor where chambers was situated, my mind was firmly fixed on achieving my stated aim.

The Senior Clark, Harold Ezzidio, greeted me warmly and welcomed me on board. Despite Harold's warm greeting, I felt a twinge of guilt at what I was about to say. I took a deep breath and announced in a rush that I wanted to postpone the start of my tenancy by some three or so weeks, relying upon the ad hoc and extremely vague reason that, "There are matters that I need to attend to". Harold didn't have a problem with me delaying my tenancy. I was well aware that if I was joining any other set of Chambers, the likely outcome would have been very different, so I was lucky and very grateful to have someone like Harold as a Senior Clark. We agreed that I would be ready to accept my first set of instructions on Monday the 20th of February.

I went straight to a travel agency and booked my flight to Brazil, and a further internal flight so I could travel around with ease. Not long after I was walking out, my travel documents in hand, which confirmed that eleven hours hence, I would be going to Rio de Janeiro. I had to pinch myself. It seemed hardly conceivable that I was actually going to Brazil.

With my luggage more or less packed, everything was now in place before I headed off for another adventure of a lifetime. There was just one more hurdle to overcome, a hurdle I wasn't particularly looking forward to facing and that was breaking the news to Mum. In the end, her reaction, much to my relief as well as surprise, was minimal, although she did go on a bit (mercifully, not too much!) about me wasting money that I should be saving. Before leaving for the airport, I attempted to give Mum a goodbye hug which she did her very best to avoid. Steve at least, was more forthcoming with his goodbyes and he gave me a good luck high five before helping me with my luggage into the taxi waiting outside for the journey to Heathrow Airport Terminal 3 and flight to Rio de Janeiro.

Although the eleven hour night flight was mind numbingly long, and I was relieved when the aircraft eventually landed at Rio's Geleao International Airport just after 8am local time. Once I'd retrieved my suitcases and cleared both Immigration and Customs Control, I made my way to the Varig Airline Desk and with the use of my internal flight pass, booked the next available flight to Recife, a journey which took just over three hours. I finally arrived at Recife's local airport after having undergone almost fifteen hours of nonstop travelling feeling desperately tired and very, very hungry. I pushed the trolley carrying my suitcases through the Arrivals Hall and saw a smiling and heavily tanned Ather, his cousin, the suave looking Faisal Sartaj, and the third member of travelling trio, the dreadlocked Hassan Hajjaj. All three of my soon to be travelling amigos were looking completely chilled and relaxed and seemed totally assimilated and in tune with the Brazilian language, culture and general way of life.

Once all four of us got outside the airport with temperatures in excess of thirty degrees, Ather called for a taxi speaking in near fluent Portuguese which took the four of us back to the hotel we would be staying at for the whole of the five day festivities. The lively demeanour and spirit of my travel companions seemed to re-invigorate and re-energise my body and mind that was still suffering the effects of travel fatigue and by the time I managed to freshen up and have something to eat and drink back at the hotel, I felt brand new, raring to go and more than ready for the nonstop partying and revelry that was going to begin in earnest that very evening.

The Carnival celebrations in Brazil is an annual event of huge proportions renowned and revered throughout the entire world. The Rio Carnival is by far the most famous and well known of all the carnivals taking place throughout Brazil, drawing vast crowds not only from Rio itself, but from all over the world. So far as my travelling companions were concerned, the Rio Carnival, despite all its fame and popularity, was far too "commercial" for their liking and taste and for them, the real meaning and flavour as to what the Carnival is all about and represents can best be found in towns and cities beyond Rio de Janeiro. I had no reason to doubt that particular point of view as the styles of Carnival no doubt, vary from state to state in Brazil and irrespective of whether you're in a major city like Rio, or the remotest village deep in the Amazon, taking part in the Carnival would represent, for the uninitiated like me, a never to be forgotten, once in a lifetime experience which I was looking forward to with great excitement and anticipation.

The "Pernambuco Style Carnival" named after the state of which Recife is the Capital where the four of us would be based throughout the festival period, has its own unique style that sets it apart from any other. The main feature of the Recife carnival is the "Galo da Mandrugada" which literally means "Rooster of the Dawn" and involves a street parade that begins at the start of the day and is dominated by the main musical rhythms and sounds that are a dominant feature in this part of Brazil, the Frevo, which is a rhythm/beat synonymous with the state of Pernambuco and the Maracatu, a wonderful rhythmic blend of music of African origin and local Brazilian sounds.

That first night, the four of us together with some of locals, partied nonstop and it wasn't until way after six o'clock the following morning that the celebrations finally came to a halt. I had the time of my life but in the end, the rest of the guys had to help me to my feet after they saw me slumped by a doorway, my mind and body completely worn out after being awake in excess of twenty-four hours. We eventually got back to our hotel and my bed was a welcome sight for my weary and tired eyes. All I wanted to do was to get as much rest as I possibly could. There was still another four days of nonstop carnival left to go and if the first night was anything to go by, then I would have to pace myself otherwise I would either be too tired, or too burnt out to appreciate and enjoy the whole Carnival experience.

No one else seemed to need the rest however, and they were ready to go again the next night. I don't know how the three of them managed to remain upright for so long without getting a wink of sleep. I had barely recovered my strength after what I'd been through during the previous seventy two hours and I was beginning to have reservations as to whether I wanted to be jumping up and down listening to the same music, pleasant as it may have sounded, arriving home at some ungodly hour, only to find that there's no time to rest because the festivities have started again once more. The rest of the guys could sense my less than enthusiastic response to another round of Carnival revelry, but my pleas for moderation and restraint were constantly drowned out by the collective good natured teasing and taunting by the others who found it hilarious that I would travel all that way to be part of a once in a lifetime experience, yet the only thing I seemed to be concerned with was trying to get a good night's sleep.

The mild-mannered taunting made me feel like Killjoy's younger brother with all my griping and complaining and eventually, I succumbed to the pressure my travelling companions were exerting on me and got myself ready for the second instalment of the carnival celebrations.

The next night we went to the State's old and historical capital, Olinda. The festivities in this part of Brazil was on the face of it, no different to any other form of Carnival celebrations which begin in a place in the city called "Os Quatro Cantos" which roughly translated means, "The Four Corners", with a seemingly endless parade along the narrow cobbled streets dominated by large brightly coloured effigies swaying to and fro to the constant Frevo beat that is associated with the city. There's an old adage which says that it's hard to replicate precisely those special moments you once enjoyed and whilst the whole Carnival spectacle was enjoyable, that enjoyment was tempered by the physical aches and pains to my lower back which was rigid stiff with pain, a pair of sore feet acquired as a result of too much jumping up and down to the constant musical beat, all of which was compounded by my physical and mental exhaustion as a result of being awake for another ten or so hours all because my travel companions simply didn't know when to call it a day.

By day three, I still hadn't sufficiently recovered to be ready for another long night of Carnival fun and festivity and I decided that this time I was going to have the night off. I tried to justify my stance by saying that "once you've been to one Carnival, you've been to them all' but that didn't seem to cut much ice with the others who reignited their good natured taunts, referring to me as "Grandad" as well as promises to "tuck me in" before they went out to party. Despite the relentless barrage of protestations by the others over my steadfast refusal to join them for another long night on the cobbled streets of Recife, I stuck to my guns and in the process managed to earn myself some much-needed shut eye. I didn't make it out again until the final night on the festival.

With the Carnival festivities well and truly behind us, the four of us spent the next four days winding down and indulging in more relaxing and gentler activities ranging from playing beach football or beach volleyball with the local residents to more aesthetic cultural pursuits when we revisited the old historical town of Olinda in order to view the number of impressive historical and old colonial buildings. Having seen and explored the best that the state of Pernambuco had to offer, the four of us decided that it was time to move on to pastures new.

So far as I was concerned, it clearly wasn't feasible both from a practical and financial point of view for me to visit all the major cities within the vast country and after much discussion and debate between us, we decided to visit the Brazilian state that would serve as a complete antithesis to the hustle and bustle of the carnival celebrations, we were heading northwest towards the country's largest state, Amazonas and the heart of the Brazilian jungle. Once we made all the necessary inquiries and put all the arrangements for the journey in place, we flew out two days later landing at Eduardo Gomes airport in the state's capital of Manaus for an exciting but no less intriguing journey into the unknown. Our seven day journey through the vast expansive jungle terrain was done entirely on the various interweaving tributaries that are connected to that great and mighty river that runs right across mainland South America from the Peruvian coast in the west, all the way to the Atlantic coast in the east, the River Amazon. We hired an experienced boatman who knew how to navigate the river and its tributaries like the back of his hand and we placed our complete and utter faith in him. We knew he was going to take all four of us on a voyage that not only was going to be an eye opener, but on a voyage of discovery that was sure to leave a long lasting memorable imprint on our minds for the rest of our lives.

During the early morning and late afternoon, our guide would take us on a gentle cruise along the river, giving us the perfect opportunity to view and gaze in awe at the diverse exotic plant and animal wildlife species, many of which are not to be found anywhere else in the world. On other occasions cruising along the river, we even indulged in a spot of fishing for piranha and other types of fish and we managed to catch a fish so large that we took a photo of it before devouring it as part of a celebratory hearty meal later that evening.

Another fascinating aspect of the journey was observing and meeting some of the local indigenous peoples who have had a long history of occupation and settlement along the Amazon River and the surrounding basin for thousands and thousands of years. The indigenous natives have tried to maintain the same language, customs and traditions and day to day organisation of their daily lives just like their forefathers before them and for these peoples, the rainforest is a sacred place to be revered because not only has it provided a safe haven and means of protection from the outside world, the entire habitat has provided a sustainable existence in terms of shelter, food, clothing and medicine which to a great extent has allowed them to maintain a way of life that they love and feel comfortable with. However, ever since the arrival of the Europeans to the continent some five centuries ago, these indigenous peoples have seen their once flourishing numbers virtually wiped out by almost 90%, firstly by diseases brought by those Europeans against which they had no protection, secondly, those same Europeans who proceeded to drive the indigenous peoples from their lands, seizing it for themselves and in many cases, enslaving them to work on the vast sugar or coffee plantations they created with which to enrich themselves and finally, the general exploitation of the rainforests in the late Nineteenth and Twentieth Centuries by companies in search of valuable commodities such as timber and oil which threaten not only the eventual destruction of the entire rainforest within the Amazon Basin but with it, the natural habitation of all the plant, animal and indigenous human beings of a way of life and existence that could never, ever be replaced.

There were other types of activity that all four of us took part in during our Amazon adventure that were also enjoyable and memorable. There was a half day hike in the jungle as well as a bit of tree climbing. There was also a visit to an animal sanctuary where we got close up and personal to some strange and weird looking creatures, so close in fact that I got to hold a heavy non-poisonous snake and wrap it around my neck as if I was wearing a scarf.

As the time honoured saying goes, all good things, no matter how enjoyable and memorable they may be, have to come to an end and before we disembarked the vessel that carried us on our amazing week long journey, all four of us in turn hugged and vigorously shook the hand of our tour guide to express our gratitude for leading us on our wonderful river odyssey of exploration and discovery and for keeping the four of us safe from harm. The whole experience had made us truly appreciate the things we can take for granted an the luxuries we are lucky enough to know in our everyday lives.

I had only just under a week left before my Brazilian adventure would come to an end and there was only one city I wanted to spend the remainder of my time in Rio de Janeiro. Set on the western strip of Brazil's Atlantic coastline, Rio is the country's second largest city in terms of both size and population behind Sao Paulo but it remains Brazil's most famous city. Geographically speaking, the city is divided into four main zones or districts. The Central Zone is the city's main historical and cultural area with wonderful buildings and museums and like London's Square Mile or New York's Wall Street, is also the main financial centre. The North Zone is the area which best sums up the two polarised extremes of the city's social and economic divide where the most affluent *cariocas* or residents who originate from Rio are affectionately known by live in the middle class residential areas which contrasts sharply with the shanty towns or *favela* inhabited by the poor and the destitute. The larger West Zone serves principally as the industrial heart of the city but if any visitor to Rio was principally looking for fun and an exciting time, then you would look no further than the South Zone which is the city's commercial and tourist centre and home to some of the most iconic and well known beaches on the planet such as Ipanema and Copacabana. With our hotel base understandably in the South Zone and with so little time left, me and my travelling companions tried to strike the right balance between visiting as many iconic landmarks in the city that I wanted to see and having as much fun as I possibly could in the city's main hotspots and there's no prizes for guessing in which favour the balance was struck. After a quick viewing of the massive Christ the Redeemer Statue in its awesome splendour perched on top of the Corcovado Mountain, with the same amount of time devoted equally to viewing the iconic Sugar Loaf Mountain and the legendary Maracana Stadium which is based in the North Zone, we spent the vast majority of time chilling out, alternating between the Copacabana and Ipanema beaches, indulging ourselves in the usual hedonistic activities such as lazing around on sunbeds, or playing beach sports with some of the locals who were more than happy for us to join in whilst at night, we went to one or two of the local nightclubs especially on Valentine's night where we partied with the same level of intensity and enthusiasm just like we did back in Recife during the carnival celebrations.

That week in Rio virtually flew by. The passage of time always seems to go that way especially when you're having the time of your life and the day before I was due to return to England, I took a little time out whilst on the beach away from the rest of my travelling companions to go up to the beach's shoreline. As I gazed out at the vast horizon of the Atlantic Ocean, I reflected momentarily on the fact of how lucky and fortunate I was to be sitting on a beach in one of the world's greatest cities and for a split second or so, I wished I could stay here forever, but I couldn't and even if I had a magic wand at hand to make such a choice, in both my heart and mind I know that it would be one that I wouldn't choose because awaiting for me across the vast Atlantic Ocean lay an even greater desire and prize to be gained. A prize that is far more real and obtainable than any hedonistic fantasy of simply travelling the world chasing the sun's golden rays. The days of all play and no work would soon be behind me now and I couldn't wait to get back home and prove to the world as well as to myself that I was more than just a pleasure seeking playboy.

CHAPTER THIRTEEN

It is often said that the best and most carefully laid out plans do not always come to pass and there was no better illustration of that principle than the set of circumstances which led to the delay in commencement of my tenancy at 54 Fleet Street by one full day and for that, I must bear full responsibility.

I woke up on my last full day in Rio groggy after another long night on the tiles, and decided, with a 10:30pm flight, and my bags more or less packed, to spend the day on the beach. Like every day, before we left the room we locked our valuables away in the safe in our room, and I pocketed the key, then we made for Copacabana beach. The whole day was glorious – but then disaster struck. The key to the safe which held, of all things, my passport, fell out of my back pocket.

When I realised it was gone, we combed the sand frantically to try to find it. We must have traced and retraced that area dozens of times, scanning the sand, but alas, our collective efforts were to no avail. The key was lost forever and after about thirty or so minutes, the search was abandoned. My friends assured me the hotel would have a spare though, so with relatively high spirits we returned and informed the staff at the hotel reception of the mishap. The response I received left me in a state of shock and panic. The Reception Manager on duty informed me that there was no duplicate key for any of the safes in the hotel and given the fact that it was early Saturday evening, there were no locksmiths shops that would be open at this time either. Now I was in full panic mode. My return ticket, passport and money were all locked in the safe and because of an act of carelessness entirely of my own making, I could not get to them. With more than a hint of desperation in my voice, I asked the Manager if there was anything that could be done given the fact that in a little under four hours, I had to be at the airport for my return flight home and he replied that he would call a member of the hotel maintenance staff to see if they could gain access to the safe. However, he made it clear that if there was any damage caused to the safe in trying to get it open, then I would be entirely responsible for the cost of any repairs. With no other option available to me, I gave the Manager the go ahead to get the safe open and I went with the others back to my hotel room on a wing and a prayer that that the safe would be opened fairly quickly without too much damage caused so that I could retrieve all my personal belongings inside and make that flight.

However, the safe proved to be a far tougher task to prise open than I'd bargained for as the drills the maintenance man was using to try and gain entry were hardly making a dent on the thick, seemingly impregnable safe door and lock and after over two hours of constant drilling, I was no closer to retrieving the safe's valuable contents.

Now I was really under pressure. I had to be at the airport. The taxi that was ordered on my behalf in anticipation that I would have retrieved my travel documents and money had been hanging around for nearly half an hour and it was at that point that my patience snapped and I turned to Ather and told him and the rest of the guys that I couldn't wait any longer and that I was going to the airport to explain to Varig airlines about the situation concerning my passport and see whether they would still allow me to travel. Ather, Faislal and Hassan didn't respond to my ridiculous declaration, but the common consensus must surely have been that I had lost all sense of reason. They agreed nevertheless, more out of pity than anything, to ride with me in the waiting taxi as I headed to the airport with my suitcases, plus the commemorative souvenir hunting bow draped over my shoulder that I had acquired from my trip in The Amazon, hoping against the faintest of hopes that I would be able to persuade the airline personnel that I should be allowed on the flight despite my lack of travel documentation. Those faint hopes (unsurprisingly) were dashed as soon as I arrived at the Check-In desk and was told, in no uncertain terms, that unless I had all the relevant travel documents, I would not be boarding the plane. If I was bitterly disappointed by that response, even worse news was to follow. Not only had the airline refused to let me board the flight, but I was also informed that I would have to purchase a brand new ticket and the next available flight to London was on the Monday evening. I felt totally dejected, and with my head bowed and feeling subdued, I headed back with Ather, Faisal and Hassan to the hotel only to discover that the maintenance man had finally managed to open the safe after almost four hours of prolonged and sustained drilling. The gamble that the safe could be opened with minimal damage had not paid off – I was slapped with a bill for the eye-watering sum of $200!

The rest of the guys tried their best to raise my spirits by suggesting that we go for a cable car ride up Sugar Loaf Mountain and go to a nightclub thereafter but I really wasn't in the mood for such revelry. The only thing I wanted was to be on a flight heading home to England and I was beginning to have real concerns in my mind as to when that was going to happen.

The following morning, after a restless night's sleep, the only thing on my mind was that I had to find a way to leave the country as quickly as possible, but given it was now Sunday and all the travel agents in the city were closed, I had no way of knowing when that was likely to be. Ather told me that he would do all that he could to help me and I told him how grateful I was. The $200 to replace the hotel's safe had made a sizable dent in the money that I left over but luckily, I still had just enough for a one way ticket. Ather suggested that rather than incur any further unnecessary and additional hotel expense by making telephone calls from our hotel room, the best way to ensure that I got a flight later that night would be to go the airport and find out from the airlines themselves whether there were any available seats. We did so, and Ather's suggestion had paid off as I managed to secure a seat on Air France.

And so, I said my final goodbyes before flying out a little after 11pm local time for the long and uncomfortable eleven hour flight to Paris, stopping briefly for an hour and a half at Charles De Gaulle Airport before boarding a connecting flight to Heathrow that finally touched down at Terminal 3 late in the afternoon. I emerged from that long and arduous flight exhausted, hungry and virtually penniless but mightily relieved that I was finally back on home soil. With my near eight week holiday adventure firmly behind me, all that was left was to look forward to the commencement of my tenancy at 54 Fleet Street and the start of a new and exciting chapter in my legal career.

The following morning I arrived at 54 Fleet Street a day later than originally planned and as I walked into Chambers, I was slightly apprehensive about the type of reception I would receive Those fears, thankfully, were immediately laid to rest as Harold's warm and friendly greeting in welcoming me to the fold put me immediately at ease, and also made me feel that 54 Fleet Street would be the perfect environment for me to develop and thrive in for a very long time to come.

54 Fleet Street had approximately twenty members and was the near perfect blend in terms of ethnicity, gender and experience. It was mainly a mixed Common Law practice specialising principally in the fields of Criminal law, Family law and Immigration law. Some of the more notable members of the set, aside from Edmond Alexander and my old pupil master Jeffrey Yearwood, were Sylvia Allen, who was called to the bar in 1982 whose soft, husky tone of voice very much complimented her superb abilities as a criminal defence advocate. Michael Cogan, Sailesh Metha, Nalla Lawrence (now His Honour Judge Lawrence) and the irrepressible, and very affable, Kevin Metzger, were other barristers of note who had thriving and busy practices, all of whom represented tangible proof that, with the right support, my own career could really take off.

I didn't have to wait long for that support to materialise when at the end of my first full day in Chambers, Harold handed me a Crown

Court brief to appear at Wood Green Crown Court the following day on an allegation of shoplifting. The barrister in Chambers who was initially instructed to conduct the trial was unavailable on account of the fact that he was part heard in another case and whilst my first ever Crown Court brief at 54 Fleet Street could hardly be described as the most challenging of cases, it nevertheless provided the opportunity for me to demonstrate my capabilities as an advocate and I was determined to take it. The trial itself only lasted one day and my client, a person of good character, steadfastly maintained that there was no dishonest or deliberate attempt to conceal an item of clothing found in her carrier bag when she was apprehended by a security guard after she left the store, her case being that it was a genuine mistake. The jury accepted her version of events and she was acquitted of the charge. Understandably, my client was very pleased to have come through what for her was a worrying and strenuous ordeal and she thanked me for all my efforts for keeping both her good name and reputation intact. I was equally pleased with the outcome, not just for my grateful client, but also for myself. I got my career at 54 Fleet Street off to the best possible start. That was a view shared by Harold when I informed him of the verdict upon my arrival back in Chambers and his response to my first win was that he would get me better quality work to help build on the promising start that I had made. Harold was as good as his word as that inaugural acquittal was the beginning of a remarkable run of success right up to the middle of the October of 1989 where I won every trial I was instructed in, and if I was to include the trial that I conducted alongside with Mark Wyeth and Andrew Hill before embarking on my two month holiday sabbatical, that meant that I went through a entire calendar year without losing a contested trial.

I was winning cases ranging from Drugs Supply, to Robbery, to Serious Assault, the most memorable of all those acquittals taking place at the Inner London Crown Court where my client, a young amateur boxer was charged with Actual Bodily Harm after having punched his then girlfriend after a heated domestic argument. The jury accepted his account at trial that, because as a boxer he is trained to protect himself at all times, he used reasonable and proportionate force to defend himself from his irate and angry former partner who was about to hit him with the object she was holding in her hand. My client steadfastly maintained that he prevented her from hitting him as a result of a single pre-emptive punch.

Chasing the Dream

My Baby Book

No matter how often
You measure and weigh...
There's more "bounce to the ounce"
In the darling each day!

RECORD OF GROWTH

A family tree is something
That no child should be without,
And here is one your little Son
Can feel really proud about!

Baby's Family Tree

Baby's Name _____

207

These highlights of his progress
All play a happy part
In making Father prouder still
And warming Mother's heart.

First Takes Notice
Coos 9 weeks
Sits Up 6 months
Crawls 9 months
First Tooth 6 months
First Steps Aug 8th 1961
First Words

When your Son
is a little older,
He may enjoy a look
At the loving
"facts and figures"
Set down in this Baby Book.

HIS FIRST PICTURE

Now here's a handsome little Son
With such endearing ways
You can "picture" all the happiness
He'll bring in coming days.

What an exciting moment...
Bet your hearts were filled with joy.
When the doctor beamed upon you
And announced "You have a BOY!"

Date 2 6 60
Hour 12 10 am
Hospital CENTRAL MILDMAY ROAD
Doctor 1st Visit
Nurse Sister Lima
Birth Certificate filed at CENTRAL
MILDMAY ROAD LONDON
Number DL 048 EXX

208

Family portrait, 1968

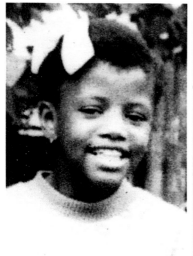

My sister Debbie (above)

And me, aged 9 (below)

My mum

Camp America, Summer
1981

Me and John Jackson, Camp America Summer 1981

Chasing the Dream

NPL Graduation,
November 1983

Bar Graduation,
November 1984 (below)

Bar Graduation Day, 27th November 1984

Travelling in 1989

(Left) Amazon Forest

(Below) Copacabana Beach (and losing that safe key!)

That run of success finally came to an end however when a teenaged client whom I was defending at the same Inner London Crown Court was convicted alongside two other co-defendants of a street robbery which occurred in broad daylight. An elderly victim had had her handbag snatched in Coldharbour Lane in Brixton. The principal pieces of evidence relied upon by the prosecution that helped secure the convictions were overwhelming identification evidence and most damning of all, fingerprint evidence of at least two of the defendants which were found on the discarded handbag. That loss brought to an end an astonishing run of success that not even I could have envisaged or hoped for even in my wildest of dreams. It was a platform that with the assistance of a very supportive Senior Clerk, enabled me to put into practice all that I observed and was taught during my pupillage and was now beginning to pay dividends. One positive aspect of all that hard work and continued success was reflected in the dramatic increase of the fees that I had earned from all those trials which I was receiving on a more regular basis and those fees, together with the salary I was receiving from my part time teaching, meant that I had greater financial freedom and independence that seemed nigh on impossible only two years previously. I could now afford to buy essential things like smarter clothes and shoes, up to date text books including my very own Archbold, the criminal practitioner's equivalent to one's very own right arm. My newly found financial freedom also meant that I could afford to trade in the old mini I had been forced to run around in after my beloved VW Golf was written off and exchange it for a sporty Ford Fiesta XR2. Even holidays were on the agenda that included, a fortnight in Greece and most notably, a trip to Jamaica in the late December to attend Glenmore's wedding.

My greatest achievement during this golden period of financial prosperity was, together with my brother Steve, who by this time was working in his first full time post as a computer programmer at Total Oil after graduating from Kent University, buying back the family home from Brent Council. This was the least that either both myself or Steve could have done, given all that Mum had done for us in the past. Mum was naturally overjoyed by what we had done, but Mum being Mum, was equally anxious about how the pair of us, especially in my case, given how notoriously fickle the nature of my profession can be, were going to be able to regularly pay the mortgage. The nightmare scenario so far as she was concerned would be that of her beloved home being made the subject of a repossession order, a scenario that for her would be far too much of a cross to bear. Both Steve and I immediately sought to allay her understandable fears by reassuring her that all was well so far as our respective careers were concerned and that we both would work hard enough to ensure that her fears would never become a reality. Our combined words of reassurance seemed to have the desired effect and the taut worry lines that were visible on her forehead appeared to recede a little. Given the more than encouraging start that I had made to my first ten months at 54 Fleet Street, it made me all the more determined to banish Mum's worry lines once and for all.

At the start of the new decade I felt safe and secure that my career was finally heading in the right direction. I had a great working relationship with a Senior Clerk who was doing everything in his power to help me and the respect of my fellow tenants who were equally supportive and encouraging. However, not everyone in Chambers was entirely happy with my progress and that person was none other than my own Head of Chambers, Edmond Alexander, whose constant murmurings, snide comments and even more disappointingly, blatantly untrue accusations over the following six months that I was deliberately hijacking his long standing solicitor contacts sadly, led to an irreconcilable breakdown in both our professional and personal relationship, a difficult state of affairs that led ultimately to my inevitable departure form 54 Fleet Street in the Autumn.

The problems that arose between myself and Edmond can be traced back to the middle of January 1990. It was my first day back in chambers from my trip to the Caribbean for Glenmore's wedding and Harold asked me if I would be up to doing a three day trial in Bristol. My first reaction to the offer was less than enthusiastic, my reticence based purely on the fact that it would mean travelling over a hundred odd miles to a place I've never been to before, let alone conducted a trial in. Harold though, with his calm and persuasive tone reminded me of the importance of building new contacts with all of the solicitors who instructed Chambers and if I performed as well as I had been doing thus far, then not only would it benefit me personally in terms of getting more cases, but also be of considerable benefit to Chambers in the long term. He was right. This was a golden opportunity to impress a new set of solicitors and after Harold had handed me the brief, I headed straight for home to prepare for my first ever trial outside London where, to all intents and purposes, I also would be on trial and as such, I was determined to make the right impression.

The firm who was instructing me, Robinsons, were, in terms of sheer volume of work, one of the leading firms in the West of England. The firm was sending a sizeable amount of work to Chambers, with Edmond being the major beneficiary of that work on account of the long standing relationship with the firm who had instructed him in serious heavy duty cases in the past. The matter I was instructed by Robinsons to appear in was nowhere near in the same league as the type of cases Edmond would normally be instructed in by the firm but it was still, nevertheless, a serious enough matter in its own right.

The client who I was instructed to represent was facing a single charge of Grievous Bodily Harm, the circumstances of which related to an argument in the toilets of a pub between my client and the complainant, that escalated into a full blown physical confrontation, resulting in the complainant sustaining a fracture to the jaw. My client readily accepted having caused the injury. However, he explained that the other man had torn the metal paper towel dispenser from the wall with the intention of striking my client with it, therefore my client was defending himself. There were no independent eye witnesses to the incident but the alleged complainant rushed out of the toilets after he was struck and claimed to all who would listen that he had been assaulted. The police were quickly called to the scene and after speaking to the alleged complainant, arrested my client who despite protesting his innocence, was taken to Central Police Station in the City Centre where he was later interviewed under caution. During that interview, my client strenuously denied being the aggressor throughout the incident and maintained that the initial argument started because of the racial insults he was subjected to and the single punch was thrown because he genuinely believed that he was going to suffer serious injury.

The trial was scheduled to last two to three days at the city's main Crown Court situated at Bridewell Street. I walked into the court's main foyer area and found the representative from Robinsons, a young man with whom I would go on to forge a long standing professional as well as personal relationship over the forthcoming years, called Paul Whitcliffe. Standing next to him was the client whom I would be representing. After all parties had formally introduced themselves, the three of us headed off to find a conference room in order to discuss the case before the trial began in earnest. The trial was being presided over by HHJ Boothman, who Paul had informed me beforehand was an extremely fair and impartial judge.

The trial itself went according to plan after it got underway and I cross examined the alleged complainant in a controlled but forceful manner. I mentioned my client's defence that the argument was racially motivated, and Counsel for the prosecution strongly objected to my line of questioning and sought a ruling from the judge in the absence of the jury that my client's previous convictions in the past for ABH should be revealed to the jury because my suggestion that the alleged complainant may have been racially motivated amounted to an attack on his character. I argued that my line of questioning did not amount to an attack on character and was instead a necessary part of my client's defence. I also argued that the admission of my client's previous convictions before the jury would have both a prejudicial and detrimental effect on my client's case that would far outweigh the probative value of admitting such evidence and if the judge allowed the admission of such evidence, it would have an adverse effect on the fairness of the proceedings. Judge Boothman had to decide in the context of the trial which of the respective submissions advanced by counsel for the prosecution and defence respectively was both correct in law and the most persuasive in the context of the overall fairness of the proceedings as a whole, for whosever side succeeded with the argument, that party would have a crucial advantage in determining the final outcome of the trial. As the judge delivered his decision, everything Paul Whitcliffe had told me about how scrupulously fair he was came to pass as he ruled in favour of the defence and refused to allow the prosecution to adduce evidence of my client's previous convictions. The judge's ruling was a partial victory for both myself and my client but in the context of the case as a whole, the judge's favourable ruling did not mean that either myself or my client could now rest on our laurels, a fact I was at pains to remind my client about at the end of the first day. All the evidence in the case had been heard and I forewarned my client that the nature and the line of questioning he would be facing under cross examination by prosecuting counsel would be just as tough and relentless as the one endured by the alleged complainant and before we parted company for that day, I told my client that as long as he looked the jury squarely in the eye when it came to his turn to give evidence and did not fall into the trap of impugning the character of any prosecution witness by calling them liars, then he stood a fairly even chance of winning the trial.

Just before luncheon adjournment on day two of the trial, the prosecution closed their case and the early finish to the day's proceedings meant that I could spend some valuable time preparing my client in a final conference before it was his turn to give his account from the witness box in his own defence. I gave my client the best pep talk that I possibly could, and he seemed to be ready. Later that afternoon, the defence case began and I called my client to the witness box for his examination-in chief where he gave his version of events in a calm and controlled manner, doing his utmost to look at the jury panel throughout resisting the temptation to focus his attention on the person asking the questions. I took my time in trying to ensure that I covered the sequence of events in painstaking detail and to his credit, my client didn't waiver or hesitate in responding to my line of questioning. Then it was the turn of prosecuting counsel to cross examine my client who, despite the sustained and forceful line of questioning by my opponent, withstood the ordeal and by the time he eventually returned to the dock, I was more than satisfied that he had given a good account of himself and I could not have asked any more from him. With the defence case now closed, it was down to me in my final closing speech to try and persuade the jury of my client's innocence. Just prior to giving that speech, I suffered the usual bout of butterflies in my stomach and increasing nervous tension, but once the trial judge had invited me to reply to prosecuting counsel's closing submissions, that fleeting bout of tension and nerves disappeared in an instant. I looked the jury panel firmly in the eye, in the same manner I instructed my client to do, only referring to my handwritten notes unless I was specifically quoting passages from the evidence.

After just over forty or so minutes my closing submissions were complete and I sat down in my seat, the customary and obligatory sweat saturating both my shirt and torso, but I was completely satisfied that I had said all that I could on behalf of my client. The jury hadn't arrived at a decision by the end of the day so they were sent home for the night and had to return the following morning in order to continue. Once I had gathered my belongings and thereafter had left the courtroom, my client approached me shook me vigorously by the hand as a way of expressing his gratitude for the way I conducted his trial. His gratifying remarks made me feel ten feet tall as there can be no greater endorsement that you have done your best as an advocate. Sam Joseph, that day's representative from Robinson's, echoed my client's sentiments when he too said that he was impressed by my handling of the trial and without any prompting by me, went on to add that, irrespective of the outcome of the trial, he would see to it that I would be doing a lot more work on the Western Circuit.

The following day the case resumed with the re-swearing of the jury before they retired once more to continue their deliberations. They had been out over three stomach churning hours before they finally came back into court with their verdict and they unanimously acquitted my client of the charge. Outwardly, I showed little emotion to the jury's decision other than nodding slightly in their direction as an expression of thanks, but inwardly, I was jumping around for joy that my client had been cleared.

After the hearing, my client once again thanked me profusely for my efforts and I responded to his gratifying words with my own salutary words of advice that was steadfastly becoming my signature phrase after having defended clients in criminal cases, "Try and make these appearances in court your last because if you don't, all you'll be doing is making lawyers like me rich at the expense of your own liberty."

When I got back to Chambers, Harold was more than happy with the feedback he received from the firm and they told him that they would be instructing me in the future, but Edmond's attitude was, mystifyingly, the complete opposite.

"I hope you're not trying to steal my work," he remarked as he stood in close proximity clearly eavesdropping on the seemingly harmless discussions that I was having with Harold about the case.

My initial thoughts concerning Edmond's comment were that they were uttered in jest, but I was soon to discover that those comments were masquerading his real belief that somehow I was some sort of threat to him. I was bemused as well as mystified by Edmond's unwarranted remarks and I tried to brush them aside when I responded by telling him that he had nothing to worry about, but nevertheless, I was still surprised that someone with Edmond's seniority and experience would have made the comments that he had. So far as he was concerned, and I suppose the same is also true for the vast majority of barristers in private practice, the valuable network of solicitor contacts that he had carefully nurtured and developed over the years are contacts that are to be fiercely guarded and protected at all times and are not to be shared with any potential rivals.

As the volume and the quality of the work I was getting from Robinsons increased over the following six months, there was a corresponding gradual decline in my relationship with Edmond who, by this time, was barely acknowledging my existence whenever our paths crossed either in Chambers or at court. It wasn't a pleasant situation to find myself in, an experienced practitioner feeling threatened by a comparative rookie, and whilst his apparent lack of respect towards me was at times somewhat unpalatable, I was determined to try and rise above Edmond's silent treatment and not to let it affect me. Sadly though, my strategy of trying to sweep this apparent problem between myself and Edmond under the proverbial carpet in the hope that things would settle down and eventually resolve itself proved ultimately, to be ineffective which meant that a showdown between the pair of us became inevitable as Edmond graduated from his cold shoulder treatment towards me to a policy of making various indiscreet remarks that eventually got back to me concerning how I managed to get all the work I was getting which included the blatantly untrue suggestion that I was "sleeping my way to the top." I was both furious and extremely disappointed when I heard about these ridiculous, slanderous remarks coming from a man who didn't have the courage to say those comments to my face, let alone discuss any "issues" that he had with me in general. I felt that I had no other choice but to confront Edmond and try to resolve this issue once and for all.

I headed straight for Chambers to have those discussions with Edmond sensibly managing to calm myself down as the last thing I wanted to avoid was completely losing my cool by saying or even worse, do something that I would later regret. Edmond was alone in his room at the time and I politely knocked the door before I was invited to come in. Once inside the room, I did all the talking, letting Edmond know straight away how bitterly disappointed I was by his attitude. I also let him know in no uncertain terms that he was totally out of order for the remarks that he had made to other people and while I was prepared to continue as a member of Chambers, if we couldn't resolve this problem between us, then I would have little or no choice but to move on. Edmond was noticeably ambivalent throughout our whole discussion which led me to come to the conclusion that he couldn't care less whether I stayed or left. The only one contribution to the discussion he made was that that if I decided to leave, then I had to give three months' notice or otherwise pay three months' rent in advance.

I knew that I had no other choice but to leave 54 Fleet Street but because I hadn't anywhere else lined up to go, I wasn't going to simply resign on the spot. My priority therefore was to move on as quickly as possible before the situation between got worse. Harold was at his desk as usual arranging the Chamber's Diary for the following day's work for the tenants when I left Edmond's room. He could sense that something was not right and he asked me if there was anything wrong. I told him that now was not the time or the place to talk about the situation and that I'd let him know what was going on in due course. Forever the diplomat, Harold respected my stance and didn't push the matter any further and as he handed me my brief for my court appearance the following day, he told me that if I needed to talk to somebody then he was always at the end of the telephone, a gesture that was typical of the kind and thoughtful man that he is. However, the last thing I wanted to do was to put him in the middle of this "war of attrition" between myself and Edmond. I decided to discuss my ongoing problems with Edmond with one of my colleagues in Chambers, a decision which turned out to be an extremely wise choice because, putting his discretion and candour to one side, the colleague in question had also come to the conclusion that it would be in his best interests so far as the progress of his career was concerned to move on to pastures new. Michael Cogan, the friend and colleague in question, had been fed up and disgruntled for some time about certain aspects of 54 Fleet Street, especially in the way the Chambers was being run, and he had told me in confidence, that he had been accepted as a tenant at a set of Chambers at 6 King's Bench Walk (6 KBW) in the Temple. When I told Michael about Edmond's attitude and conduct towards me particularly over the last six months, he seemed hardly surprised by my revelation and urged me to leave 54 Fleet Street as quickly as possible. He then asked me if I had anywhere lined up to go to and when I told him that I hadn't, he immediately suggested that I should send my CV to the set he was about to join as they were looking to take on one or two new tenants. I wasn't going to look a potential gift horse in the mouth and I sent off my application letter together with my CV the following day. I didn't have to wait long before I was invited to attend an interview at the Chambers, an interview that went very well and a couple of days later, I received the letter from 6 KBW offering me a tenancy.

One of the first people I told about my good news was my soon to be erstwhile Senior Clerk, Harold, who tried everything in his power to persuade me to stay and continue our successful relationship but on the other hand fully accepted and understood the reasons why I had to leave. I didn't leave straight away. I decided instead to give Edmond the three months' notice period option in writing rather than pay him the three months' rent, partly because I didn't have such a sum at my disposal and the other reason, was due to the fact my continued presence at his Chambers would have annoyed Edmond a great deal and after all the unwarranted and at times, disgraceful treatment that I had to endure from him, I was determined to leave 54 Fleet Street in a timing and manner of my own choosing as opposed to be driven out by a man who was determined to see the back of me.

I stayed on at 54 Fleet Street for a further two months during which time Harold saw to it that I remained constantly busy right up until the end of my tenancy that ceased on the last day of September of 1990 and after I had said all of my final goodbyes which also included a final handshake with Edmond himself. I left the chambers with a hint of sadness that I was leaving behind some good colleagues, especially my excellent Senior Clerk, but I was leaving with my head held high that I had made great strides so far as the development of my career was concerned. In situations like these however, it's time to look forward with optimism, not backwards nostalgically, and I couldn't wait to make even further progress in a completely new environment.

6 KBW was a set which had over twenty members, the vast majority of whom mainly had their legal practice in Civil as opposed to Criminal Law, specialising in areas ranging from Housing law, Immigration law, Employment law and Judicial Review, practiced by lawyers who were extremely talented and highly sought after, most notably, Manjit Gill (now Manjit Gill QC), Goolam Meeran, Harjit Grewal, Terry Gallivan, Andrew Zimuto and Sylvester Carrott, to name but a few. Myself, together with Michael Cogan and Robin Howat, who themselves were very able and talented advocates in their own right, were the only practitioners in the set who specialised exclusively in Criminal law and at the head of the set was the highly regarded and respected lawyer, Sibghat Kadri QC, who is widely regarded as one of the leading pioneers of non-white practitioners who were trying to break down barriers in their attempts to gain a foothold in the profession.

The personnel in charge of the Clerk's Room were the Senior Clerk, Gary Jeffrey and his second in command, Janet McGlasson, both of whom had been working at the set since its formation with the third member of the clerking team, Phil Bamfylde, joining the set sometime in the mid 1990's. In order to achieve my stated aim of establishing a busy and successful practice at 6 KBW, I had to ensure that firstly, the one or two firm of solicitors who had kept my practice going were going to continue their support in addition to trying to build and forge new links with other solicitor firms and secondly, to have a good working relationship with my new clerk team.

Just before I left 54 Fleet Street, I contacted some of the firms who instructed me during my time there in order to let them know that I was on the move once more. With most of those firms, I was expecting little or no feedback given the fact that they have been associated with the set for a very long time and they were hardly likely to follow me to my new set despite the good results I may have got for them in the past, but in a firm like Cremin Small, who were one of my biggest supporters since my pupillage days at 76B, I had real and genuine high hopes that our long standing relationship would still continue once I had informed them the whereabouts of the chambers I was moving to. Those high hopes, to my utter disappointment and bewilderment, were brought crashing down to earth following a telephone conversation that I had with Phil Cremin, a conversation that left me in no doubt that his firm's previously loyal support would no longer be forthcoming. When I told Phil the news that I was joining 6 KBW, he seemed strangely disinterested before bluntly informing me that from now on, his firm were only going to instruct three set of Chambers in the future and if a barrister wasn't in one of those designated sets then it was unlikely that cases would be coming their way. Despite my obvious disappointment and bewilderment in his firm's sudden change of briefing policy, the last thing I was going to do was to ask the reasons why, or even more humiliating, beg or plead with Phil to be a part of his firm's new briefing policy and after Phil abruptly ended our telephone conversation, that was the last time we ever spoke to each other. I did have one Crown Court brief left in my pigeonhole from his firm which they allowed me to retain only because the client insisted that I represent him at his trial, a case that resulted in my client being acquitted and since the end of that trial, my relationship with the firm came to an end.

The reason why Robinsons stopped instructing me was also completely unforeseen and unexpected. The firm were being investigated by the Legal Aid authorities over very serious allegations that thousands and thousands of pounds were being claimed under the Legal Aid's Green Form Scheme for giving advice to clients who simply did not exist. Those allegations led not only to the firm being closed down but it also resulted in criminal charges being brought against certain individuals who were deemed to be responsible for the running of the firm, which meant the firm's principal and some of those individuals eventually stood trial (some of whom were convicted), ironically, in the same Bristol Crown Court that they represented many of their clients.

The demise of Robinsons didn't mark the end of my work in Bristol. Friends I'd made in Robinsons set up their own firm and continued sending me work on a fairly regular basis. Despite this invaluable support, it didn't take a genius to work out the fact that I needed to generate more work next year from different sources because failing that, the worries and the stresses that seemed to blight my career in the early years would return with a vengeance.

The beginning of 1992 got off to a good positive start. My first case for the year was a brief involving inmates at the Young Offender's Institution at HMP Pucklechurch, a prison situated some ten or so miles away from Bristol, who instigated a serious riot that lasted a few days, resulting in extensive damage being caused to the prison. Because so many of the inmates were involved in the incident, the court hearings were, in the interests of trial manageability and efficiency, split into five separate trials and through sheer luck and good fortune, my client was not only in the first of those trials but also, his name was the first on the indictment. That fact alone gave me cause for much delight however those feelings were tempered considerably by the news that the person also instructed to appear alongside me in the same trial was my former Head of Chambers and chief nemesis, Edmond Alexander, who seemed to be considerably annoyed and put out by the fact that my client was listed above his own in the indictment pecking order.

The trial was scheduled to last at least two weeks and was to be presided over by one of the most respected judges to sit on the bench at Bristol Crown Court and on the Western Circuit, HHJ Colin Willis. After the jury was sworn in, counsel for the prosecution opened their case describing in outline, the evidence they intended to adduce during the trial and part of that evidence related to showing fairly extensive and potentially damning film footage which showed parts of the prison ablaze with a large number of inmates, their faces concealed occupying the prison roofs hurling roof tiles (and verbal obscenities,) on the prison guards below who were engaged in a desperate struggle trying to regain order and control. The case even made the national news with some of the footage actually making its way onto The News at Ten programme and from a professional point of view, I was excited by the fact that for the first time in my career, I was involved in a trial that had some sort of public profile.

The client I was representing was a very likeable young man and in the conferences that I had with him prior to trial, he was steadfastly maintaining that he took no active part in the riots. Despite those protestations, his long gangly frame and distinctive frizzy hairstyle appeared to betray those steadfast denials of guilt as one of the disguised inmate closely resembling his appearance and build could clearly be seen on the prison rooftops hurling roof tiles on the besieged prison guards below.

It soon became apparent after day four of the trial that the six defendants in the dock were facing an uphill task to exonerate themselves from the charges. So far as my client was concerned, at least three prison officers who had given evidence in the trial were adamant that even though my client was wearing a tied handkerchief across his face, my client's tall gangly build and distinctive frizzy hair left them in no doubt that my client was on the prison roof actively involved in riotous behaviour despite my best efforts in suggesting the contrary view during cross examination. After listening to such damning evidence, I came to the firm view that there was only one verdict the jury were going to arrive at once all the evidence was heard and that was guilty, a verdict that would mean every single one of the defendants were facing the prospect of lengthy prison sentences on top of the existing sentences they were already serving. Judge Willis recognised that fact despite his complete impartiality throughout the whole trial process and at the end of day's proceedings, took the unusual and astonishing step of offering significant discounts in terms of the prison sentence he would impose to any defendant who decided to change his plea and to ensure that no defendant who was standing trial would feel any undue duress or pressure by his sudden pronouncement, Judge Willis said that all parties would be given overnight to consider their respective positions. Everyone was caught by surprise by Judge Willis' extraordinary offer and for the defence barristers especially, the offer presented a professional as well as ethical dilemma. What was of greater importance? Acting in the best interests of your client? Or persisting with a seemingly hopeless trial knowing full well that it will be financially rewarding? From my own professional and personal point of view, the situation was a no brainer. The interests of my client would always take priority as I believe wholeheartedly that it is detestable for any lawyer to put his own professional and personal interests ahead of that of his/her lay client.

The following morning, all the defendants on trial, through their respective advocates, asked for the charges to be put again and one by one, starting with my client, they all pleaded guilty. My client received a sentence of three years imprisonment, a sentence that my client, my instructing solicitor and myself were more than happy with given the circumstances. Judge Willis' bold and innovative intervention had a positive knock on effect on the follow on trials arising from the riots in terms of drastically reducing the length of those trials that would make considerable savings made by the public purse. Whatever the rights and wrongs of how the case came to an abrupt end to this day in my mind, it was clearly the right and proper one to take.

I continued to make what I considered to be good and steady progress at 6 KBW over the next two and a half years. I managed to retain the support of my small but vitally important network of contacts working in those solicitors firms who were instructing me and even though some of these contacts were not legally qualified, they nevertheless wielded a considerable degree of flexibility and autonomy to instruct counsel of their own choosing. So far as my practice was concerned, the volume of my work was totally dependent on their continued support. The good progress I was making was also reflected in the type of cases those contacts would occasionally send to me which represented a serious step up in class of the type of cases that I would normally do. I won my first ever Rape trial at Manchester Crown Court in September of 1992, thanks mainly to my former Junior Clerk at 54 Fleet Street, Claire Brazier, who at the time was working for a firm of solicitors in her home town city of Liverpool. There was also a couple of Drug importation trials heard at Isleworth and Croydon Crown Courts respectively the following year that were sent from one of my old law students from Hackney College in the early years, Shade Agibeda, whilst working for a law firm in Stoke Newington, and the not guilty verdicts that I managed to secure in both of those trials demonstrated that I was more than capable of winning serious and important cases. But as I was soon to discover much to my professional detriment, once those professional contacts began to dry up, or in some cases, cease altogether, the impact of the loss of that regular support had on my practice as a whole was without a doubt, a totally devastating one.

By the beginning of 1995, the only firm I could really rely on was Hugh Norman Solicitors in Bristol where both Paul Whitcliffe and Rodney Wilson of Robinson's were endeavouring to qualify as solicitors in their own right. Against that increasingly difficult backdrop, I soon began harbouring thoughts of leaving 6 KBW and continuing my practice elsewhere. Sometimes I even considered the nightmare scenario of quitting the profession altogether. The cold reality of my situation was such that there was nowhere else I could go and if I was being brutally honest, virtually every Chambers in private practice were looking for something more than mere talent in any prospective and potential member seeking to join them. Most Chambers would be interested to know what a barrister wishing to become a member would bring to the table in terms of their own independent network of contacts, thereby helping to contribute and expand the Chamber's portfolio of available work, as opposed to taking on a barrister with no viable or sustainable contacts, who contributes very little or nothing to the Chamber's pool of work and may be viewed somewhat disparagingly as the proverbial blood sucking leech.

I spoke to my Senior Clerk, Gary Jeffrey, about my fears and he promised he would do what he could to help me. Gary was true to his word in terms of ensuring that I was working constantly appearing in court but the type of cases he gave me were not always of the quality and levels of seriousness that I had in mind. Even though my overall success rate in Crown Court trials had improved that year in comparison to the previous couple of years, the number of trials I had conducted over the same period had fallen significantly. The only serious trial I was involved in that year was my first ever Murder trial at the Central Criminal Court (The Old Bailey), a case I was instructed in only because the defendant facing trial specifically requested that I represent him. Although that request was welcoming as it was flattering, I knew that I lacked the necessary experience, let alone the expertise, to undertake such a daunting challenge of being the lead defence counsel at the trial, but that didn't stop me from being excited at the prospect of being junior counsel in a murder case and I was determined to put in all the hard work and preparation for my potential leader in order to demonstrate that I was more than capable of being involved in cases of this magnitude.

At the preliminary level stage, I conducted the committal proceedings that were held in the Magistrates' Court which lasted over the best part of three days where I had the opportunity to cross examine the main witnesses whom the prosecution were intending to rely upon at trial in the Crown Court and the vast majority of those accounts were, at best, confusing, and at their worst, totally unreliable, and although the proceedings served as a dress rehearsal for the main event, I felt that I had made significant inroads into lessening the strength and veracity of the prosecution's case which would be of enormous benefit to the defence in the way the case would be presented at trial. After the case was committed to the Crown Court, I wrote a lengthy advice to the Legal Aid Board requesting that they extend the legal aid certificate for an experienced leading counsel to conduct the defence, not by Queen's Counsel as would normally be the practice in cases of this seriousness, but by one of the best leading juniors at time who was a silk in all but name, Courtenay Griffiths. The Legal Aid Board granted my request and from a professional and personal standpoint, I couldn't have been more thrilled and excited of working with as well as closely observing a real rising star of the criminal bar.

The prosecution's case against our client related to an incident at a Community Centre close to where I live. What started out as a verbal dispute escalated into a serious confrontation which resulted in the fatal stabbing of a young man. There were a number of witnesses to the incident, some of whom stated that our client produced a knife during the course of that argument and deliberately stabbed the deceased before fleeing the scene. Our client claimed that he had been surrounded by a group of young men which caused him to flee from the Community Centre getting only as far as the gates where the pursuing group of men cornered him and were making serious threats to do him grave and serious harm. One of the surrounding group, according to our client, produced a long knife. Our client somehow managed to disarm that youth and during the ensuing melee, he accidentally fatally wounded the deceased before fleeing the scene out of fear and panic. Our client was arrested some three days later when he voluntarily attended the local police station and was subsequently interviewed under caution, an interview in which he made no comment which was perfectly permissible prior to the change in the law in April 1995, which allowed for adverse inferences to be made by a court for any suspect who had not given an account during that interview but had given an account at any subsequent trial and thereafter, he was remanded into custody at a Young Offender's Institution.

The trial took place in May 1995 before the Recorder of London. Our opponents on the formidable prosecution team were Joanna Korner, another rising star at the criminal bar who was renowned for doing high profile prosecution cases, and Nicholas Hilliard. Although the case wasn't the easiest to defend, it was nevertheless going according to plan from the defence point of view with some of the prosecution witnesses either showing a real reluctance to give their evidence at trial or in some cases, giving accounts that were becoming increasingly unfavourable to the prosecution's that bordered on becoming hostile. On day four of the trial however, disaster struck as the jury trying the case had to be discharged by the trial judge because they inadvertently heard inadmissible (and potentially prejudicial) evidence, a decision which, given our client's age, caused him some considerable distress as it meant the trial would not be heard until the last week in September. Both Courtenay and I went to see our client in the cells afterwards in an effort to reassure him that despite the four month adjournment, the case would eventually be heard, and we would both redouble our own efforts when the time arrived in order to achieve the desired result for him.

The trial eventually got under way in the last week of September and the prosecution, just like in the first trial, were once again hampered by some of their own witnesses who seemed somewhat reluctant to give the same accounts they initially gave in their original witness statements, thus allowing Courtenay, with his incisive and devastating method of cross examination, to seriously undermine the prosecution case as a whole. After the close of the prosecution case, it was then our client's turn to go into the witness box and he gave his evidence which he had done in exactly the way that both Courtenay and I had advised him to. After all the evidence was called, counsel on both sides were required to make their closing speeches to the jury with Courtenay as the defence barrister having the final address and what a closing address, a speech delivered with all its usual eloquence and commanding authority that are the hallmarks of his unique style and practice. Despite Courtenay's brilliant effort, the trial was still nevertheless delicately poised to go one way or the other, but there was no doubting that after the jury retired to consider their verdict, the manner in which Courtenay had conducted the defence had given our client more than just a fighting chance.

The jury were out deliberating for just over a day before they finally reached their verdict late in the afternoon on day eight of the trial. I was sitting behind Courtenay as the jury filed into court one by one and therefore was unable to see whether his facial expression betrayed any sort of emotion although I suspect, that he was probably taking it all in his stride, having been in this situation many times during his professional career. In stark contrast, this was a novel experience for me. It was my first murder trial verdict and my heart was racing faster than it had ever done in any previous Crown Court trial that I've been involved with. I glanced briefly towards the dock where our client was situated and winked as a sign to wish him good luck and he nodded his head slightly by way of response. The moment of truth had finally arrived after the jury had settled down in their seats, the Clerk of the Court asked the jury foreman and then our client to rise to their feet before turning his attention back to the jury foreman.

"Members of the jury, can you confine yourselves to simply answering my next question yes or no. Have you reached a verdict upon which you are all agreed?"

The foreman replied, "Yes we have"

"Do you find the defendant, guilty or not guilty?"

"Not Guilty."

I turned straight towards the dock and saw that our client was in floods of tears with his head bowed presumably in a mixture of joy and relief. Courtenay, with his usual sangfroid demeanour, then rose to his feet to formally ask the trial judge for our client's release from the dock which he granted before he rose from the bench and left court. As Courtenay began gathering his set of papers, I gave him a well-deserved pat on the back for a job well done before the pair of us were congratulated by our opponents, Joanna and Nick.

With all our papers safely gathered, we left the courtroom with the aim of heading straight to see our client who, once all the administrative paperwork was completed, would become a free man. Our client was still in a tearful and emotional state by the time the pair of us got to see him and he couldn't thank us enough for our collective efforts in setting him free. I told our client that it was Courtenay who should take all the credit due to his excellent performance throughout the trial but Courtenay would have no such talk and he made it clear that the not guilty verdict was a team effort as the work I had done during the committal proceedings in the lower court contributed greatly to the defence's ultimate success. After we left court, Courtenay ordered a black taxi to take the pair of us back to our respective chambers and before I alighted from the vehicle, he repeated the genuine sentiments that he had made earlier that my hard work prior to the main trial had played a crucial and significant difference to the outcome of the trial and it helped make his task all the more easier, and for a rookie doing his first ever trial of that nature, to receive such a glowing endorsement from a man whom I greatly admired both professionally and personally, it swelled me with a great sense of pride. But after I alighted from the taxi cab and headed towards 6 KBW, I couldn't help feeling the contrasting bitter/sweet emotions. Sweetness because of the hard work and effort I had put in had contributed, in some meaningful way, to a successful outcome for my client, but the bitter after taste that would be left behind after such a fantastic victory was that it would be probably a long, long time before I'm involved in a case of that seriousness again.

A year had passed since Gary and I had our chat with regards to the progress of my career at 6 KBW. I was ten years call now and at a stage that if I wanted to make real progression up the career ladder, then I had to be doing, or at the very least, be involved in, the type of serious quality cases that went hand in hand with the upward progression that I had in mind. I felt as though an invisible and impregnable concrete ceiling was hampering that upward progression, not a ceiling that was put there by my Senior Clerk I hasten to add, but a ceiling that seemed to be giving a clear and unmistakable sign that there may be a defined limit to my career ambitions, and whilst Gary was doing his utmost to keep me busy, I was coming to the slow but inevitable realisation that if I wanted to shatter that ceiling then it would be best for me to move on. But where could I go? Or more importantly, which set of Chambers would actually take me on given my seemingly desperate predicament of having only one or two instructing solicitors who remained loyal to my practice despite being ten years call? Do I stay at 6 KBW and hope that my "patience" would be rewarded in an upturn in fortunes that has so far failed to materialise, or do I cut my ties with 6KBW and take my chances elsewhere? Both my head and my heart were saying the same thing. I had to take my chances and look to move elsewhere even though finding a set of Chambers that was prepared to take me on as well satisfy my long term career ambitions was not going to be an easy task to achieve. By the spring of 1996, I finally found the courage to bite the bullet and I was on the move once more, a situation that came about as a result of the combination of being at the right place at the right time and the reconnection of a relationship with an old and valued friend whose help and support provided for me a professional lifeline.

Rosemarie Phillips is that old and valued friend I'm talking about who came to my rescue at that critical time. I first met Rosemarie in the early 1980's at the immensely popular nightclub and one of my favourite haunts, Night Moves on Shoreditch High Street. On the numerous occasions that I would see her there, she was usually in company with her sisters, Vivienne, Sharon and the youngest of the Phillips siblings, Yvonne. I would occasionally ask Rosemarie for a dance and she would always accept, but not once when dancing with her, did I ever ask what her name was, did I even try to chat her up and worst of all, to my eternal shame, I never even bought her a drink at the bar. I don't even think that, apart from the whispered words, "May I have this dance?" or "Thank you!" at the end, that I even spoke to her so you can imagine my complete shock and surprise when Rosemarie walked into the Clerk's Room when I was a pupil at 76B with a couple of briefs in her hand and speaking to my clerks, Errol Taylor and Danny Currie in a manner that suggested that the three of them had been friends and colleagues for a very long time. Rosemarie also seemed slightly taken aback to see me in this environment and we shook hands and smiled at one another after Errol formally introduced us.

Rosemarie had been a Senior Clerk in her own right since the late 1970's and it would be fair to say that she was a pioneer in her own right as she was probably the only woman of colour to occupy a position that was almost exclusively the preserve of the white male. She was the Clerk at the Chambers of John Roberts at 2 Stone Buildings in Lincoln's Inn and John, who has had a long and distinguished career at the bar, created his own piece of history in 1988 when, alongside another black veteran at the bar, Len Woodley, he became the first appointed Queen's Counsel of African descent and it would also be fair to say that the hard work that Rosemarie put in behind the scenes as the Senior Clerk was, in no small way, a contributing factor behind that significant and ground breaking milestone. Over time, Rosemarie and I became good friends after that first formal introduction, going out for drinks, even the odd dinner date or two, but our friendship never extended beyond the realms of a professional relationship and whilst that relationship could so easily have crossed the threshold and turned into something much more personal and intimate, with the benefit of hindsight, I'm so glad that it didn't because aside from the fact that it's never a good idea to mix business with pleasure, the fact that the pair of us never crossed that romantic line has meant that I have a person in my life who I will always consider, given all the help and support she has been to my career in the subsequent years particularly when my career was at its lowest ebb, to be a selfless and lifelong friend.

By the mid-nineties, Rosemarie had left Lincoln's Inn after the Chambers had dissolved and was appointed to the position of Senior Clerk at Somersett Chambers, a set that was relatively new at the time that were situated at 52 Bedford Row. I was totally oblivious to the fact that Rosemarie had moved onto pastures new because even though we were good friends, we only kept in contact from time to time at this stage and it was only when I saw her one morning as we passed each other on the escalators going in opposite directions at Chancery Lane station and she gestured to me to contact her, I found out that she was plying her trade in a new set. It was during our conversation as we sought to catch up on both past and present times that I told Rosemarie about my situation at 6 KBW and how increasingly disillusioned I was becoming. Her immediate unprompted response was to suggest that I come and join her at Somersett Chambers, an offer that had the immediate and instant effect of raising my flagging spirits. She told me that I knew most of the members in the set and suggested that I stood every chance of being taken on if I sent in a written application addressed to the Head of Chambers together with my CV straight away. I couldn't thank her enough for her encouraging words of support.

With nothing to lose, I submitted my application to the Chambers the following day and it didn't take that long before I was seen by the Head of Chambers, a man whom I knew quite well in private practice, Lanre Oke, for an interview that was very relaxed and informal, at the end of which Lanre offered me a tenancy. Naturally, I was extremely pleased at being offered a place, however I had not yet informed 6 KBW of my intentions to leave and I must admit, it wasn't a conversation that I was looking forward to. I had spent five and a half years at 6 KBW and despite the ups and downs, by and large they were good years. It would be a wrench to leave 6 KBW but I had to make what I believed would be the right call for the sake of my own career and with both my head and my heart singing in harmony from the same hymn sheet, the time had now come to move on.

Gary seemed to be both surprised and disappointed by my announcement that I was leaving and told me that I would be a considerable loss to the criminal team at Chambers and he would be sad to see me go. Later that day, I spoke to my Head of Chambers and he too expressed genuine sentiments that he was sad to see me go and also offered his best wishes before giving his consent in allowing me to leave without giving the usual three months' notice period, a gesture for which I was extremely grateful. Gradually, the news of my impending departure circulated around Chambers and two or so days before I finally left, some of my soon to be erstwhile colleagues clubbed together and presented me with a couple of leaving presents and a card signed by everyone wishing me all the best in my future endeavours. Their unexpected gesture in giving me such a send off was tangible proof that I had the respect of everyone at 6 KBW both on a professional and personal level and I could leave the Chambers, despite my disappointment that things didn't work out as I had wished, on good terms with no feelings of antipathy or animosity. I was on the move once more, joining the fourth different set of Chambers that I've been associated with in the last nine years and despite maintaining the same burning ambition and desire to succeed at the bar, the important common ingredients that always seemed to be lacking in the sets that I'd previously been associated with that being, sustained longevity and stability coupled with real and positive support was without a doubt, clearly hampering the progress that I was hoping to make. If I wanted to turn that ambition to succeed as a barrister at my next port of call, those common ingredients had to be present and working in tandem with one another. Maybe this latest tenancy would be the place to provide the longevity, stability and support that my career so desperately craved and hopefully, serve as the launch pad of getting my career heading in the right direction.

Named in honour of James Somersett, an 18th Century Black Slave who was the plaintiff in a landmark case which held that slavery was not recognised by the common law of England and Wales and therefore no slave could be removed from England and Wales against his will, Somersett Chambers was a relatively small set in terms membership, the vast majority of those tenants I have either known or have worked alongside with at various times during my career. Eddie Cofie, Charles John-Jules and Cedric Thompson, a contemporary of mine when we were students on the bar Finals course back in the mid 1980's, my former co tenant from my 54 Fleet Street days, Stephen Fletcher, were some of the names who would be my new working colleagues and I for one was looking forward to the prospect of working alongside them in the same Chambers. Even more exciting though was the prospect of working alongside my new Senior Clerk Rosemarie Phillips. If there was one person who could inject that much needed impetus and support, motivated only by the genuine desire to see me do well and succeed, it was Rosemarie. But I couldn't take for granted that with Rosemarie as my Senior Clerk, all of a sudden I would be inundated with an avalanche of cases. In truth,

I was starting with a clean slate and Rosemarie made it clear that I would have to earn that right to have a busy and thriving practice and prove that I was good enough.

Because I had no outstanding cases for trial in my own professional diary by the time I moved to my new set of chambers, my next appearance in court would be dependant entirely on the whim of my Senior Clerk. I felt somewhat uncomfortable by that thought as it would mean that I had no control of my own immediate destiny despite the fact that it was a good friend of mine who had that initial control. The only way I could regain that control was to prove my worth in the courtroom when the chance came my way. Thankfully, I didn't have to wait that long to be given that chance when Rosemarie gave me my first three day trial as a fledgling tenant at Croydon Crown Court. This was the opportunity I had been waiting for and admittedly, it only came about because one of the barristers in Chambers who was originally instructed to conduct the trial was unavailable to conduct it. I had to recognise and accept that being the newest member of Chambers, I wasn't going to be, nor did I expect to be, first choice when it came to work distribution but this was my *carpe diem* moment and I wasn't going to let this opportunity to show my worth pass me by.

The case I was appearing in related to an allegation of a man in his late fifties and of good character who, according to the prosecution, was knowingly concerned in trying to smuggle large quantities of cannabis inside cakes in one of his suitcases on a flight from Kingston Jamaica. My client's proposed defence at trial would be to the effect that whilst he accepted that he was the person responsible for packing his suitcases prior to his departure, he was completely unaware and had no knowledge that the cakes that contained the cannabis in question were inside his suitcase at the time of his departure and that he never gave his consent, expressly or impliedly for those cakes to be placed in there. On the face of the papers, it looked as though I was going to have a tough task on my hands in trying to convince a jury of the veracity of my client's account, but the reality of the matter turned out to be the complete opposite during the actual trial itself, as both my client as well as myself rose to the challenge that confronted the pair of us and against seemingly overwhelming odds, my client was found not guilty by the jury, much to the trial judge's complete and utter astonishment as it was to my own complete and utter delight. Even Rosemarie seemed somewhat taken aback by the surprise verdict but nevertheless she was pleased with the trial's outcome for the simple reason that it vindicated both her professional assessment and judgement that I was more than capable of doing those types of cases.

Over the next six months, I was to prove myself to be more than just a legal super sub because within that period, in almost an exact carbon copy of how I began my career at 54 Fleet Street working in tandem with Harold Ezzidio, I never lost a single trial either in the Crown Court or Magistrate's Court. It was an amazing period of professional and personal success that I enjoyed because of a combination of a large slice of good fortune, hard work and preparation that was intertwined with an ever growing sense of self confidence and belief. But the major contributing factor to that success was having in your corner a supportive and loyal Senior Clerk. Sadly though, that extraordinary run of success turned out to be the high point of my time at Somersett Chambers because by the end of the October of that year, my gradual good progress began to take a dramatic turn for the worse when the Chambers first decided to suspend, then eventually dispense with, the services of the one person who was by and large responsible for those successes, Rosemarie Phillips, for reasons that could be described at its best, harsh, or at its worst, grossly unfair.

The sequence of events that led to Rosemarie's suspension and ultimate dismissal, I myself inadvertently played a minor part in, something I still regret to this day. I had returned to Chambers after having finished a case in court and was one of only two barristers who had nothing in their diaries the following day once Rosemarie had allocated the work for the barristers that afternoon. Then, as is often the case in a busy set of chambers, Rosemarie received a late telephone call from a firm that usually instructed Chambers to find out if there was anyone available to cover a first appearance hearing at Tower Bridge Magistrate's Court. I was in the Clerk's Room at the time of the call and after briefly placing the call on hold, Rosemarie quickly asked me if I wanted to cover the hearing. I nodded my head in agreement initially, but then promptly changed my mind, for the purely selfish reason that I wanted a small break from the seemingly endless toil of working in the courts during the day before heading off to teaching at Hackney College at night. Rosemarie returned to the call and informed the solicitors that there was no barrister in Chambers available cover the matter. But there was someone in Chambers available to cover the hearing and that person was none other than the Head of Chambers himself, Lanre Oke. Rosemarie who was later to argue in her efforts attempting to justify the decision that she took of not informing our Head of Chambers at a subsequent Disciplinary Hearing, said that the reason why she didn't consider instructing the

Head of Chambers was that she didn't think that a first appearance at the Magistrates' Court was a matter deemed worthy of the Head of Chambers standing, especially when compared to the serious cases that he was accustomed to doing. Whether Rosemarie made the right judgement call in not informing the Head of Chambers about the case will always be open to debate and conjecture but the following morning when she arrived at Chambers, she was told by her Junior Clerk who happened to be sitting in Rosemarie's seat at the time, a deliberate, provocative act according to Rosemarie which made her incandescent with rage, that the Head of Chambers wished to speak to her in his room the moment she arrived as a matter of urgency. Rosemarie had no idea what Lanre wanted to speak to her about, but she could tell by the slightly dismissive tone of her second in command that it was no trifling matter.

Rosemarie went straight to Lanre who explained to her what she was accused of. Lanre made it clear that her decision in refusing to accept the case not only let the Chambers down, but also had the potential to cause consternation and disquiet to the solicitor firm that send him a considerable amount of work. Then, quite unexpectedly and to Rosemarie's complete astonishment, Lanre handed her a letter informing her that she was suspended from her duties for a period of two weeks with immediate effect for what was considered to be a gross breach of conduct. After the two week period of suspension had elapsed, her position would be reviewed by an internal Disciplinary Panel convened by Chambers who would thoroughly investigate and ultimately adjudicate on the matter. Rosemarie was already due to take her annual leave during those two weeks having booked a fortnight's holiday to Jamaica, but to do so whilst under a period of suspension with the real possibility that she may lose her job on her return was hardly going to do wonders for her morale.

I was very disappointed by the decision to suspend Rosemarie but there was little I could do to influence or try to change a decision that was already a *fait accompli*. All I could do was hope that when Rosemarie's suspension from chambers was over and the Chambers Disciplinary Panel had carried out their investigations, that she would be back in the Chambers hot seat where she belongs.

Those faint hopes though were ultimately dashed after she returned from her holiday as the Disciplinary Panel, which consisted of the Head of Chambers himself plus two prominent members of Chambers, decided to formally dismiss her. She walked out of the hearing clearly hurt and angry not just by the decision, but also by the fact that no reference or mention was made in terms of any financial settlement that she may be entitled to especially, any outstanding clerking percentage fees for the professional services she provided to Chambers. Despite the decision, Rosemarie made sure that she walked out of the Disciplinary Hearing with her head held high and her dignity intact. I could tell when I spoke to her, that she was clearly in the mood to renew this bitter dispute with Chambers and she vowed that she was going to take them to court for a claim of wrongful dismissal and a claim for the outstanding clerking fees that she believed she was entitled to. My initial knee jerk reaction on speaking to her was to tender my resignation and walk out in protest at the treatment she suffered, that's how strongly I felt about it. Rosemarie though advised against making such a reckless and foolhardy decision reminding me, as if I needed reminding, that I had nothing lined up and if I was thinking of making such a move, then I should bide my time and only do it once I had definitely secured a place to go to.

After Rosemary left, I was doing the odd sporadic trial here and there but not with the same regularity as before under the clerking regime that was now in place which I found to be both mystifying as well as disturbing and I couldn't help but feel an overwhelming sense of a subtle, but deliberate campaign to gradually marginalise me from Somersett Chambers altogether. I had no choice but to address the increasing alarming situation and I tried to have a chat on a couple of occasions with the person who was now in charge of clerking duties as to why there appeared to be a gradual decline in my court appearances. What I got in return in terms of a reply, were unconvincing assurances that nothing sinister or untoward was being done to detrimentally affect my practice and that the situation would soon improve.

That "assurance", despite the rhetoric from the now newly installed Senior Clerk, turned out to be an extremely hollow one to such an extent that by the beginning of spring 1997, my lack of regular court appearances was also beginning to have a detrimental effect on me financially as well. I was finding it increasingly difficult to find the means to pay my Chambers rent when it became due and even more worryingly, my share on the mortgage on the family home. I was finding it very hard to make ends meet and to prevent myself from sinking even further into the financial quagmire, I had no choice but to take up another teaching post. Even finding myself another part time job wasn't enough to keep the proverbial wolves from the door and if it wasn't for the emergency bail out loan from my brother Steve to the tune of over £1000 which I used to reduce the ever growing arrears on my monthly rent liabilities to Chambers, then I really would have been in a dire financial situation that I may not have been able to keep control of. I knew that I had to leave Somersett Chambers as quickly as possible and, in an effort to achieve that aim, I sent out an application letter and accompanying CV to as many established criminal sets that I could in the hope that I would get some sort of response but sadly, all I received in return was one rejection letter after the other. I was now at my wit's end as to how I was going to break this seemingly never ending cycle of frustration and despair that was threatening to leave me in a state of professional and financial limbo.

There was some form of temporary respite after the Easter break when I did a series of back to back Crown Court trials which came about, not because of any dramatic and sudden levels of support from the Clerk's Room, but as a result of the combined factors of clients who were specifically requesting that I represent them at their respective trials that coincided with the support by the small but loyal network of solicitor contacts like Paul Whitcliffe and Rodney Wilson.

A particular case that stays in my memory which I appeared in as a result of the client specifically requesting my services was an allegation that my client had a vast quantity of Class A Drugs, namely, crack cocaine, that were found in various rooms of a house that he had been renting in the Harlesden area of London. My client, a Jamaican national and a man of good character, steadfastly maintained that the drugs did not belong to him, nor according to him, was he aware of their presence on the premises at the time police executed a search warrant. My client maintained that the drugs belonged to another man who was also renting a room at the premises at the time and he had been set up. The trial was a memorable one from my point of view mainly because my opponent appearing on behalf of the prosecution, James Doyle, was a friend of mine from our days when we were on the same course at the Polytechnic of North London. The trial this time took place at the Inner London Crown Court and lasted just over four days and from the straight forward and professional manner in which both James and I presented our cases on behalf of our respective clients, neither of us could be sure how the jury would ultimately decide the case right up until they delivered their verdict. My client was convicted by way of a 10-2 majority verdict and thereafter was sentenced to a period of imprisonment totalling six years.

That trial and others I received from my dwindling but very loyal contacts provided both a welcome and much needed shot in the arm to a career that was way down in the doldrums, but given the minimal level of support I was receiving in the Clerk's Room, it now became a matter of extreme urgency that I moved on in order to build upon and maintain those green shoots of recovery. I continued with my applications to different sets hoping against hope that I would make that all important breakthrough and be offered a place at a good and established set but sadly, those hopes failed to materialise. Despite those setbacks, there was one set that was prepared to offer me a place to practice criminal law unconditionally, an offer that had been on the table for at least two or so months before the beginning of May of 1997. The reason why I was in no great rush to take up the offer, despite all the problems and difficulties I was encountering at Somersett Chambers at the time, was that I had major doubts as to whether I was making the right career move. On the plus side, if I took up the offer, at least I would be in the position to make another fresh start, as well as reprise the successful working relationship in a completely new environment with the set's new Senior Clerk, the ever dependable, ever reliable, Rosemarie Phillips.

Named after the street on which it was situated that was a stone's throw away from Farringdon Train Station, Britton Street Chambers was a relatively small set that only established itself at the beginning of 1997. At its head was Marvin Gederon, a veteran practitioner whom I first met way back in the mid 1980's when I was a law student. Marvin had been practising at the bar for a many number of years at a set of Chambers based in Lincoln's Inn where he specialised mainly in civil law, but the Chambers decided to dissolve which resulted in Marvin and some of his fellow tenants getting together to form and establish their own set of Chambers which they hoped would develop and expand over time. If anyone could achieve those stated aims for the Chambers, then it was Rosemarie Phillips, but with a membership of just only nine tenants, the Chambers needed to attract a fair number of good quality lawyers, coupled with a proper financial investment in the Chamber's infrastructure, just to make those ambitious aims realistically achievable.

After Rosemarie was appointed to become the Chamber's Senior Clerk in the spring of 1997, she contacted me to see whether I would be interested in joining her at Britton Street and she invited me over to the Chambers in order to have a chat with both her and Marvin about a potential move. When I arrived at the second floor where the Chambers were situated, I was pleased to see my good friend back in an environment where her talents and abilities were best suited, a feeling that was in stark contrast to the Chamber's physical environment in terms of its basic and spartan appearance that was less pleasing to the eye.

I made it clear that while I was receptive to the idea of reprising our working relationship, without trying to appear disrespectful, ungrateful or indeed, without trying to come across that I was in any way far too good or superior for Britton Street, I felt that I would be taking a retrograde step in joining a Chambers so lacking in gravitas. Rosemarie fully understood where I was coming from and made it clear that she did not take offence to my frankness and honesty for wanting to aim my ambitions as high as possible and while she recognised that Britton Street Chambers may not be the Chambers ultimately for me to realise those ambitions, she pointed to the obvious fact that moving to Britton Street Chambers, even for a short while, would be a far better proposition than remaining in an environment that had no interest whatsoever in helping my career. Rosemarie's advice and general observations were spot on as usual and any such comments and or observations were made ultimately, with my best interests at heart.

Over the following week or two, I agonised and debated day and night as to what was going to be my next career move. Do I remain at Somersett Chambers and allow my career to wither on the vine and die? Reunite with Rosemarie in the hope that, like the proverbial mythical phoenix, my career would somehow rise from the ashes? Do I consider the possibility of looking to practice criminal law outside of London or perhaps, even outside England all together and finally, given the topsy turvy nature of the way how my career has fluctuated over the last four or so years, do I give up on chasing the dream and turn my back on law for good? The first of those options was never an option. I had to leave Somersett Chambers and the sooner that divorce took place, the better, but I was indebted to Chambers in terms of rent arrears and with the Chambers requiring the usual three months' notice period, if one includes paying three months' rent up front thus enabling me to terminate the tenancy agreement prematurely, the amount of money I would be liable to pay to Somersett Chambers would be well in excess of two thousand pounds. I never had that amount of cash at my immediate disposal to pay off my outstanding debt right away which meant I would have to come to a mutually acceptable arrangement with the Chambers to eventually clear the arrears. Despite being saddled with that burdensome debt, crippling arrears, the one thing I was sure of in my mind was come hell or come high water, I was definitely leaving Somersett Chambers. In terms of the last resort option of leaving the profession completely, I must admit that in weighing up all my options, it was something that I had given real consideration to. After nearly thirteen years at the bar, I felt that my career was following an unsettling pattern of one step forward three steps backwards as the lack of consistency and stability in my career to date was stifling all that hope and optimism that had been the driving force keeping me both focused and motivated. As I approached my 37th birthday, I found myself, not for the first time, in a position of having to ask important and deep soul searching questions. Was the only reason I was still at the bar solely because in reality, there was nothing else I could possibly do? Was the bar my one and only life raft, and if I were to loosen my grip, even for a nanosecond, then both myself and my career would sink without so much as a trace in life's stormy seas? Those questions may sound over the top and melodramatic, but there were times when I considered alternative career options at my disposal if the bar was no longer a sustainable or viable option and aside from the possibility of a full time career as a college lecturer, an option that in truth, was hardly an appealing one, let alone rewarding in terms of my own personal goals and ambitions, those options in reality, at best were extremely limited and at worst, wholly non existent. Given the stark choices in front of me, a life without a career at the bar without doubt, would be a life barely worth thinking about.

The only realistic and sensible option open to me in the circumstances therefore was to join Rosemarie at Britton Street Chambers, but even that option in itself seemed to leave me somewhat underexposed. I had to consider a back-up plan. I also thought about the possibility of looking to practice beyond the confines of the London Bar and moving further afield possibly in Manchester, Bristol or Birmingham or maybe, moving away from England all together. America perhaps? Practising law in either New York or California? The American option would involve the arduous task of having to undergo a further course of study over a set period of time and thereafter, sitting a whole raft of exams which at the ripe old age of 37, I had grave doubts whether I had the motivation or indeed, the desire to commit myself to all the long hours of intensive study and preparation necessary to pass those exams. What about Jamaica and becoming a member of the Jamaican Bar? That seemed to be a more appealing and achievable option since the regulations for being called to the Jamaican Bar exempted practitioners with my years of call from having to sit further exams. However, in order to claim exempted status, I would have to be the holder of a Jamaican passport. I knew a couple of colleagues of mine at the bar who made the switch from the English Bar to practising law in Jamaica and after having made the switch, never regretted it. One of those ex pats, a barrister with whom I got on quite well with before leaving these shores in 1992 was Sandra Graham (now practising professionally under her married name Bright). Despite having emigrated, Sandra would still come back to England occasionally to visit her family and catch up with old friends and acquaintances and it was during one of Sandra's flying visits in the late spring of 1997, that I bumped into her by chance in High Holborn on my way to Chambers. Things seemed to be going quite well for Sandra but when she asked how things were going for me, my pessimistic tone and negative demeanour said it all as I told her about my ongoing difficulties at the bar and how disillusioned I was becoming with it all. Sandra, being the straight forward talking person that I have always known her to be, pulled no punches in lambasting me for wallowing in self-pity and told me in no uncertain terms that my problem was and probably always has been, that I have allowed those feelings of self-pity to prevent me from taking firm and decisive action with regards to the direction of my career. After taking on board Sandra's straight talking no nonsense comments and observations, I floated the idea to her that I was thinking about emulating what she and her husband had done and relocating to Jamaica. I asked whether she could advise me as to the best way to get the ball rolling. Without wishing to come across as though she was trying to dissuade me from the whole idea, Sandra's frank and forthright response gave me a much needed reality check as she made it abundantly clear that it was just as hard to get a foothold in Jamaica as it was at the English Bar, especially at the Criminal Bar where legal aid as we know it barely existed. It could, she went on to add, take a very long time to make any sort of breakthrough at the Jamaican Criminal Bar because firstly, I was a foreigner and secondly, I was a complete unknown. Despite her frank and forthright advice, Sandra did not completely pour cold water over my plan as she went on to say that if I was really serious in wanting to pursue the option of applying to become a member of the Jamaican Bar, she would do all that she could to help me with that aim and with that, she gave me her business card and told me that we should keep in regular contact. Sandra's frank yet sensible words and advice had given me food for thought and as we went our separate ways, the Jamaican option, although on the face of it was a long shot, was one that I was nevertheless intent on pursuing despite the obvious lack of firm guarantees that anything concrete would arise from it. It was an option I felt that I had to consider because if things didn't work out with Rosemarie at Britton Street Chambers, then it was vital for my own piece of mind that I had an alternative back up plan in place to fall back on.

With my mind now firmly made up on my immediate short term plans, I contacted Rosemarie to inform her that I would join her at

Britton Street providing the offer was still open and I would come over to see both her and the Head of Chambers, Marvin Gederon, to discuss the matter. Rosemarie was clearly pleased that we would be working together once again and so far as she was concerned, saw no reason why our working relationship would not be just as successful this time, if not more so, than it was the first time around. From my own point of view, I too saw no reason to doubt the sincerity and sentiment of Rosemarie's words despite my persistent and nagging doubts about the actual location of the Chambers itself, its actual physical state, its general set up and also, doubts about my prospective new fellow tenants whom I barely knew. But if I wanted my tenancy at Britton Street Chambers to be a success, all these doubts and concerns as well as the ridiculous irrational prejudices I seemed to harbour about the Chambers and its whole set up had to be firmly put to one side and superseded by positive thoughts. My principal focus and aim, apart from developing my own practice in joining the set, would be making a positive contribution to Britton Street's gradual growth and development.

I formally joined Britton Street Chambers on Monday the 2nd of June, my 37th birthday. On my first day, still feeling nervous, I asked Rosemarie about the growth and development of Chambers both in the immediate and the long term. Rosemarie responded by saying that she was confident that Britton Street would be adding to its membership in the very near future as the Head of Chambers had received a number of applications from barristers expressing an interest to join and it was a question as to whether or not those applicants would prove to be a suitable fit in terms of what Chambers was aiming to achieve both in its short term as well as long term aims. Bold and confident words from my Senior Clerk which, taken at face value, sounded really convincing, but in reality that's all they were, just words, and my insecurity remained at rock bottom.

"Stop worrying so much Shaun!" Rosemarie admonished me. "Go home and enjoy the rest of your birthday and give me a call later in the afternoon as usual and I'll let you know if you're working tomorrow."

In truth, I deserved to be at the receiving end of Rosemarie's mild admonishment given that my seemingly endless griping and whingeing, ever since I agreed to renew our professional working relationship, appeared to be calling into question, the veracity of what she had been telling me. If there was anyone who needed to ensure that the pair of us were singing from the same hymn sheet it was myself, not Rosemarie, therefore it was up to me to make sure that both my mind and my attitude was right for the challenges that lay ahead for there to be any hope of successfully reprising our working relationship.

My work situation began to gradually improve throughout the summer months of 1997 just as Rosemarie said that it would. I was going to court on a regular basis and although I was winning my fair share of Crown Court trials, it wasn't with the same freakish regularity when I was working with Rosemarie the first time around, but the main thing was that my practice appeared to be on the move again and with cases such as the multi-handed conspiracy that Martin Walker had sent me for trial at Swindon Crown Court, or the junior brief for the murder case I was instructed in from Rodney Wilson, I had a lot to look forward to. The Chambers was also making efforts to improve. With all due respect to the Chambers, Britton Street wasn't going to be the type of set that would attract your run of the mill high ranking heavyweight practitioner. It was the kind of set that would attract the young, hungry upcoming practitioner looking for their first tenancy who saw Britton Street as the type of place where they could cut their teeth and act as a stepping stone for bigger and better things, or practitioners whose practices were either stagnant, or drifting aimlessly along seemingly on the road to nowhere. I could hardly describe myself as either young, hungry or up and coming anymore, more like a man who was on the cusp of middle age, full of world weary cynicism, who if I wasn't mindful, could easily find myself ending up drifting aimlessly into the latter category.

Some six or so weeks after becoming a tenant, Britton Street took on three new tenants all of whom were young, ambitious, up and coming and exactly the type of fresh injection of potential talent that was needed to improve the quality of Chambers personnel. Ayesha Savage, Razak (aka Zack) Atunwa and Olajide (aka Jide) Lahleilin were the new recruits in question and the three factors that the new recruits all had in common was firstly, they were at least three years call at the time. Secondly, this was the first proper tenancy at a set of Chambers for the three of them and although Britton Street didn't have the same kudos as say, a Garden Court or Tooks Court or indeed, Cloisters Chambers where Ayesha, Zack and Jide respectively had spent their formative years doing their pupillages, Britton Street was a place that would provide all three of them with the stability and continuity that is vital for any young and inexperienced practitioner starting out in their career. The final factor that was common to all three of the new recruits was that they each possessed an infectious enthusiasm and a burning desire to succeed in their new surroundings.

All three new recruits settled into Chambers' life pretty quickly and it was apparent from the outset that the three of them, particularly in the cases of Zack and Jide, would not be dependent on the Senior Clerk for their main source of work as they had their own independent regular and reliable network of solicitor contacts that were keeping them extremely busy and what was even more astonishing and refreshing, was that they were more than happy to allow other members within Chambers to cover their cases if they were unavailable. I got on extremely well with all three of the new tenants and treated them as my equals despite the ten year gap between us in terms of professional experience. The genuine levels of respect I had for those young practitioners was also derived from the fact that all three of them represented the next generation of young black advocates trying to make that all important breakthrough in the profession, just like I had tried to do all those years ago and if there was anything that my near thirteen years call could help them to achieve that breakthrough, then I would be more than willing to be on hand to do so, a sentiment that all three of them appreciated a great deal. Those mutual levels of trust and respect between all four of us had a tremendous beneficial effect on our respective professional and personal relationship. Zack and Jide's altruistic and unselfish attitude in terms of their willingness to share their network of contacts was self-evident as they would always put my name forward to cover for them in trials, which led in one instance, to me conducting a series of back to back trials in Birmingham that summer at the city's Crown Court both of which ended in not guilty verdicts for the clients that I represented. My involvement in those cases would not have been possible but for Zack and Jide, an altruistic act of kindness that I will never forget.

I had been at Britton Street for the best part of nearly four months now. My work situation had improved considerably since the turn of the year, the majority of the credit for that dramatic upturn in fortune must go to the diligence and hard work behind the scenes Rosemarie was putting in just to make it happen, not solely for me, but Britton Street Chambers as a whole and there are no words that exist that could truly express my genuine gratitude and thanks for all she was doing for me. Yet despite all that welcoming steady progress, despite Rosemarie's unwavering support, and despite the high levels of respect and admiration I was receiving especially from some of the more junior members in Chambers, I still felt strangely dissatisfied. Even though I was far happier both from a professional and personal point of view than I had for a very long time, I still found it difficult to change my opinion of Britton Street, the perception that Britton Street was somehow a third rate establishment that no self-respecting practitioner would even consider becoming a member of, unless they had been rejected by every other set of Chambers in existence. Britton Street was a Chambers which teemed with competent, hard-working individuals who were proud to have their name associated with the place, but I couldn't see it that way. My shallow, self-inflated, self-absorbed perception was that the entire set up of Britton Street was somehow beneath me and that I deserved to plying my trade in a set of chambers that was infinitely better. I felt deeply ashamed that I had the temerity to think of Britton Street in such a demeaning and disparaging way, especially when it was the only set of Chambers that was prepared to throw me a much needed lifeline amidst the sea of constant rejection. But try as I might, I couldn't (or indeed wouldn't) discard or erase such disloyal, negative, disparaging thoughts from my mind, the continuance of which would ultimately pave the way for my eventual and inevitable departure.

Over the next couple of months right up until the end of the year, I appeared to be caught between the devil and the deep blue sea as I procrastinated and agonised over my next decisive move. One of the options that I had in mind that I had kept ticking over on the proverbial front burner was my desire to get myself admitted to the Jamaican Bar, a desire borne out of those brief discussions that I had with Sandra Bright on Holborn High Street. It was an option that I had given serious consideration to during the subsequent months that followed that chance meeting and to demonstrate how serious I was about the idea, I made it a point of duty to keep in regular contact with Sandra in order to seek both her advice and guidance as to how to go about turning that pipe dream into a reality. Whenever I called to have a chat with her, Sandra would always provide helpful advice and support and by slavishly adhering to every aspect of that advice, I applied for and eventually obtained a Jamaican passport, certified copies of all my educational and legal qualifications and an up to date Certificate of Good Standing from the Inner Temple, the three important documents that were essential in my claims for exempted status that would make it easier for me to be admitted to the Jamaican Bar. All those documents would then have to be prepared in the form of a legal brief, which I would have to submit together with the relevant Jamaican Bar Council application form that Sandra had sent to me on request. I duly completed the form post haste, before sending all the documentation to her as she agreed that she would check my application thoroughly prior to formally submitting it to the Jamaican Bar Council on my behalf. With virtually all of the formalities being completed by late November, all that was left for me to decide was when I would go to Jamaica and make the final part of the application in person. The only window that I had available was a two week period from the end of December to the end of the first week in January.

I was pleased that I had acted firmly and decisively in giving myself an option by applying to become a member of the Jamaican Bar, instead of wasting all my valuable time and energy sitting around thinking about it and in the end, doing nothing. Despite giving myself that option, I was under no illusion that moving to Jamaica in order to live and work was always going to be a last resort, an option to fall back on if all else fails. The $64,000 question I had to ask myself given the fact that I was fully committed to my intention of leaving Britton Street Chambers was, where would I find this suitable place to practise law given the previous places that I thought were suitable turned out to be, for one reason or another, less than so? It was a question I always found nigh on impossible to answer. Not for the first time in my career, I was at a complete loss as to how I was going to achieve that desired aim, but once again, Dame Fortune was to play a helping hand and it was a chance meeting with an old colleague that was to provide the catalyst for making that dream become a real possibility.

Rosemarie had sent me up to Birmingham to conduct a trial that was scheduled to last a couple of days at the beginning of December. While I was getting changed into my robes, I ran into John Rowbotham, a barrister and long standing acquaintance of mine. I had first met John when he was just starting out at the bar and I used to get him to cover some of my teaching sessions at Hackney College for me back in the early nineties because, as with most pupils who were struggling to support themselves during those early testing years at the bar, he was finding it difficult to make ends meet financially. As we began to swap accounts about what each of us had been doing since we last laid eyes on each other, John told me that like me, he had become fed up and increasingly disillusioned with the stop start nature of his career at the bar in London and he decided to take the plunge and make a fresh start in Birmingham, a decision that from a professional point of view, he has never regretted. John went on to say that since relocating to the Midlands, he has managed to build up a thriving practice doing good quality work derived from a network of solicitors' firms in the city who have remained both loyal and supportive of his practice ever since. John made it clear that if he hadn't taken the bold step in to relocating his practice to Birmingham and had continued to remain in London, then it would have been a near certainty that his whole career at the bar would have gradually sunk without a trace. After listening to John's tale of redemption and re-invention, I proceeded to relay to John my own frustrating tales. John immediately suggested that I seriously consider taking the same gamble that he had done and relocate my practice to Birmingham. John then went on to add that his Chambers, Victoria Chambers who were based in Corporation Street, a stone's throw away from the city's Crown Court, were always on the lookout for practitioners with my level of experience and if I wasn't doing anything at lunchtime, I would have nothing to lose by accompanying him when he popped into Chambers where I could see for myself whether it was the kind of place I would consider joining. I was slightly taken aback by John's selfless offer and sentiment and the pair of us met outside on the steps of the Crown Court at lunchtime before making the short two minute journey to his Chambers. John gave me a quick tour of the set up before he introduced me to some of his colleagues without disclosing the real purpose of my visit. My initial first impressions of the place were that it appeared to be the type of set up I could envisage myself joining even though on the surface, there seemed hardly any difference between John's Chambers and the Chambers I was so intent on leaving. That initial impression caused me to pause for thought and ask myself, not for the first time, a series of soul searching questions as I began to contemplate whether I was making the right decision in leaving behind the familiar surroundings and safety net that Britton Street Chambers would provide and swapping it to join a place of the unknown. Would it be the classic case of jumping out of the frying pan into the fire if I did decide to relocate my practice to the Midlands? Furthermore, would the task of seeking out and building new relationships with solicitor firms in this part of the world be any less difficult and challenging than the difficulties that I always seem to have in terms of first forging, then trying to sustain those relationships in London? Would the relocation of my practice to Birmingham mean having to sell up and look for a home in the Midlands, or would it make sense to commute? Those were just a few of the various conundrums that were racing through my mind as I considered the feasibility of relocating my professional practice which on the one hand, could offer a new and exciting challenge whilst on the other, would be a massive gamble that could turn out to be a complete and utter disaster. I decided that it was wise to keep my own counsel and not commit myself one way or the other until I considered all the alternative options that might be out there for me.

As the pair of us were about to make our way out of the building in order to grab ourselves a spot of lunch, entering the building at the same time was John's Head of Chambers, Lee Masters. John and I stopped momentarily to speak to Lee and after

John had formally introduced us, he unexpectedly disclosed the fact that I was sounding out the possibility of joining a new set of Chambers. I was caught slightly off guard by his unprompted, but well-meaning revelation. Lee's reaction to John's disclosure though was as cordial as it was inviting and he told me that he would welcome any application made by me to join his set.

I was in a fairly good place towards the end of 1997. Only the man upstairs knew how grateful I was that I had a person like Rosemarie working in my corner because without her unwavering support, I have no doubt whatsoever that my career would have reached a point of no return. The immeasurable gratitude that I owed my Senior Clerk though was not going to deflect me from my committed determination to move on from Britton Street, even if that meant spelling the end of a professional relationship that on two separate occasions has worked to perfection. Despite my tremendous sense of loyalty and respect towards Rosemarie, above all else, I owed it to myself to try and find a place to practise where I felt comfortable with the environment I was working in. The time for any heartfelt sentiments or procrastination had to be put to one side now and I made a promise to myself that in 1998, I was going to pull out all the stops in making sure that any positive changes that I needed to make for the sake of my career were going to be made and that would only come about once I made the break from Britton Street Chambers. To show that I meant business, I decided before the Christmas break, to grab the proverbial Bull by the horns and submit my letter of application together with my CV for a tenancy at Victoria Chambers in Birmingham.

After spending the Christmas festivities in the company of family and friends, I flew out to Jamaica for my first trip to the island since my pal Glenmore Johnson got married there just over eight years previously and accompanying me on my travels once more, was the person who I still considered to be my best friend, Winston Davis. Thankfully this time around, Winston made sure that he had more than enough money in his possession thus ensuring that the holiday aspect of our joint visit to the island would not mirror his embarrassing cost cutting antics that put paid to our first trip nine years previously. Although I was looking forward to enjoying some much needed rest and relaxation, the main purpose of my visit was to try and get myself admitted to the Jamaican Bar and once the New Year festivities were out of the way and everything on the island had returned to normal, I made my way to the Jamaican Bar Association's main headquarters on Old Hope Road in Kingston, armed with all the relevant documentation that Sandra Bright's firm had helpfully prepared on my behalf before duly submitting the documentation to The Bar Association official on duty.

I was getting more and more excited by the fact that I was within touching distance of becoming a member of a legal profession in another jurisdiction. That initial excitement though was given an instant reality check by the official dealing with my application when she told that despite the documentation that I submitted being in order, there was still the small matter of the ceremony of being called to the bar that I had to undergo before I could be formally admitted and the next available date for that formal call ceremony would take place in the parish of Portland sometime in the Spring. To say that I was massively disappointed by what I was told would be a massive understatement. I knew that I would not be able to come back to the island by that time given my court and teaching commitments, but at least I was comforted by the fact that the formality of the call ceremony to the bar was the only outstanding hurdle that was left to be overcome before my quest to become a fully paid up member of the Jamaican Bar was completed and after my fortnight stay on the island had come to an end, I headed back to England more or less secure in the knowledge that if I failed to make any progress or further development of my career back home, there was at the very least, a viable alternative option that I could potentially fall back on as a last resort.

I was back at work by the start of the second week in January full of optimistic belief that this year was going to be my year. Quite a few defence briefs had arrived in Chambers for me whilst I had been away, more than enough to keep my practice ticking over nicely well into 1998. On the horizon, there was the important matter of the forthcoming murder trial that my friend and colleague from Bristol, Rodney Wilson, had instructed me in to act as the junior defence counsel that was scheduled to take place sometime in the second week in February to look forward to. However, even though matters were ticking along nicely in Chambers, nothing had changed so far as my desire and determination to leave Britton Street and that would be sooner rather than later. So you can imagine how pleased and excited I was when, awaiting my attention amongst the pile of correspondence on the hall table when I returned home from the Caribbean, was a letter from Victoria Chambers inviting me to attend for an interview.

I didn't speak to Rosemarie about my plans to my eternal shame and if I had, I probably wouldn't have persisted with my blinkered, narrow, steadfast determination to leave a set of Chambers that was doing a very good job of rebuilding my career, instead of allowing fatuous and superficial reasons like the physical makeup of the building coupled with its location, to be the constant overriding factors that were behind my reasons in wanting to leave. Rosemarie's good counsel and wise words probably would have persuaded me at the very least, to consider all of my options a bit more carefully instead of allowing myself to be consumed by those irrational reasons that were clearly clouding my judgement.

I went into Chambers a day or so after I received the invitation letter and invited Rosemarie for lunch. She knew something was wrong and questioned me on it. I blurted out the news that I had an interview for another set of Chambers in Birmingham before adding that if the Chambers made me an offer, I was, in all likelihood, going to accept it. Rosemarie reacted calmly to my announcement and in fact, she hardly seemed surprised given my persistent grumblings in the past. She did however express her disappointment in my determination to leave especially at a time when the work in the Chambers was really beginning to pick up. Rosemarie made it clear she didn't think I was making the right decision. "Sometimes in life,' she said, 'you have to be careful what you wish for!" Rosemarie however, knew that I had made up my mind to leave and even though she didn't want to see me go, she nevertheless made it clear that my decision to leave Britton Street would not in any way affect our current working relationship, nor would it affect the mutual respect we would always have for one another before finally adding, that no matter where I ended up in private practice, I could always count on her continued support for my career, which considering what I had just told her, was a sentiment that I really appreciated.

The interview with the Head of Chambers, Lee Masters, was a relaxed and informal affair conducted on a one to one basis where we discussed a number of matters ranging from my reasons for wanting to relocate my practice to Birmingham, my professional experience which included the types of cases that I been involved with in the past as well as cases that were currently pending, my network of solicitors, and finally a discussion about Victoria Chambers in general. By the end of those discussions, Lee had offered me a tenancy and because he had given such a very good sales pitch coupled with the fact that within that sales pitch, he made me feel both wanted and valued, I was left in no doubt after we both shook hands that Victoria Chambers was going to be my next port of call and we agreed between us that I would commence my tenancy at the beginning of March. After the interview, Lee introduced me to some of the other tenants who were in Chambers at the time and also to the members of the Chamber's Clerking Team and the warm and friendly manner in which I was received, reinforced my belief that I had made the right choice.

To celebrate my offer, John invited me for drinks, and we were soon joined by one or two his solicitor contacts. After the introductions were made, John wasted little time with his sales pitch extolling my virtues and qualities as an advocate although this time, he did so without going too much overboard in a way that would have made either myself, or his contacts, feel embarrassed or indeed obligated in any way. John's impromptu "getting to know you session" was a nice and thoughtful gesture on his part in his efforts to gradually introduce me to all the people and personnel who are an integral part of the Midlands legal scene, the type of people who could mean the difference between my decision to relocate my practice north of the Watford Gap ending in success or failure.

Despite my adverse dislike involving anything to do with networking, it was something that I had to wholeheartedly embrace and come to terms with if I wanted to develop and sustain a practice in a whole new environment. Being so far removed from my normal professional comfort zone without the benefit or security of really knowing anyone in a new and unfamiliar surroundings, if my relocation to the Midland circuit was to stand any chance of success, there would have to be a complete paradigm shift both in terms of my attitude and approach towards the art of networking, in my attempts in trying to strike the right balance between embracing the concept in its entirety and not coming across as an overbearing individual who was clearly desperate for regular work. As with all new chapters and stages, I had to remain positive and optimistic in my belief that I made the right judgement call in deciding to relocate my practice to Birmingham and with all things being equal, I was going to make a real effort to ensure that the move will turn out to be a resounding professional and personal success.

I still had a number of important cases to attend to in the time I had left at Britton Street, the most important of those case above all was the murder trial at the Old Bailey. I was excited at the prospect of being Junior Counsel in a murder trial for what would be only the second time that I been instructed in such a matter in over thirteen years at the bar and in addition, I was also excited at the prospect of working alongside the barrister who I had specifically requested to be my leader at trial, Joanna Greenberg QC, a leading silk from 3 Temple Gardens.

It is the expert opinion of the team leader that decides how any defence will be conducted at trial and in Miss Greenberg's view, while she did not believe that our client intended to kill his attacker with the screwdriver he was holding in his hand at the time, his conduct amounted to an act of Manslaughter, not Murder, and if any agreement could be reached between the prosecution and the defence resulting in the murder change being substituted for a charge of Manslaughter, such a charge would be a true reflection of our client's culpability. Miss Greenberg went on to add that she would try to find out which counsel would be representing the prosecution at trial as any such discussions as to the relevant and appropriate charge should take place between trial counsel themselves on an informal, without prejudice basis, either prior to trial, or on the day of trial itself and if, or until those discussions take place, Miss Greenberg made it clear that the defence team must be ready and prepared for trial. That one to one discussion between Miss Greenberg and her opponent eventually took place before the trial and her judgement call that a Manslaughter charge was the more appropriate charge proved to be spot on as the prosecution agreed to drop the charge of Murder. For our client, the decision to accept the prosecution's offer was a no brainer and he accepted Miss Greenberg's advice and changed his plea to guilty of Manslaughter. The court proceeded to sentence our client once he entered that plea and after Miss Greenberg had completed her mitigation submissions to the court on his behalf, our client was both pleased and relieved by the sentence of six years imprisonment that he eventually received. As Junior Counsel, I was also pleased by the sentence that our client received, but the sentence in itself was not going to preclude me from exploring the possibility of examining whether there were any possible grounds to appeal that sentence and while my initial view was that no such grounds existed, I prepared, on Rodney's specific instructions, the appropriate Advice and Grounds of Appeal and sent them both to Rodney and Miss Greenberg well within the time limits allowed as to whether there was any merits to those submissions. I received the following reply:

THREE TEMPLE GARDENS

Tel:
Fax:
LDE: Box No. 0064

3 Temple Gardens
Temple
London
EC4Y 9AU

Rodney Wilson Esq
Harrison Glover
64-68 Stokes Croft
Bristol BS1 3QX

Faxed to

24th February 1998

Dear Rodney

RE:

Thank you for sending me a copy of Shaun's draft Advice on Appeal.

I am just about persuaded that it is worth at least letting the single judge consider an application for leave to appeal against sentence. I do not hold out a great deal of hope, as the authorities which support our argument are (in sentencing terms) quite old and the current climate with regard to offences of violence has hardened considerably since 1993 when the cases Shaun relies on were decided. Furthermore, they do not provide any strong support for an argument that the sentence is more than marginally high, rather than being manifestly excessive. However, I have concluded that it would be unfair to Mr ▬▬▬▬ to deny him the opportunity to have the single judge consider the merits of an appeal.

Shaun's advice in favour of appeal is excellent. All that is needed is a minor amendment to Line 4 of paragraph 1. It should be amended to read "Mr Justice Gage." It is a matter of personal taste as to whether Shaun combines his Advice & Grounds of Appeal in one document or whether he drafts a separate Grounds of Appeal document.

I must urge you to tell Mr ▬▬▬▬ that an appeal is unlikely to succeed and that, if leave is refused, I do not consider that he would be wise to take the appeal further.

I hope you are well.

Yours sincerely

JOANNA GREENBERG QC

257

I hardly need tell you how pleased I felt when I read the contents of Miss Greenberg's letter. It was a fantastic boost to my professional self-esteem which had taken a bit of a battering in recent times and to be acknowledged for your efforts by lawyers at the very top of your profession, was not only satisfying personally, it served as a perfect reminder that not only I do belong in this profession, I still retain the ability to succeed in the profession with the right support and good fortune and as I prepared to undergo yet another period of transition, endorsements like the one I just received will also serve to ensure that my inner self belief, no matter how difficult or trying the circumstances may be, will never be irretrievably broken.

My time at Britton Street Chambers was now coming to an end and while its always sad to move on, on this occasion it really was going to hit me quite hard on account of the fact that it was going to spell the end of a very special working relationship which I know no matter how long I last in the profession, will never be replicated. There is no doubting the fact that I owe Rosemarie a great deal first for rescuing, then steadfastly supporting, my professional career over the last two years, a period during which, I had probably some of my biggest successes as an advocate.

On my penultimate day before leaving, Rosemarie asked me to come into Chambers late in the afternoon after I had finished court and when I arrived there nearly all the members of Chambers including the Head himself, had made themselves available for my send off, an event I had neither planned for, or indeed was expecting. Marvin led the tributes and his kind, but succinct address brought an emotional lump to my throat when he described the important contribution that I made since I joined the set and that my imminent departure was a considerable loss to Britton Street Chambers. He ended his short speech by wishing me every success in the future before handing me a large envelope that contained a farewell card signed by all of the members together with a small oblong shaped gift wrapped which had contained within a beautiful fountain pen (that I still treasure to this day). To say that I was almost overcome by the genuine sentiments of appreciation and respect by my soon to be erstwhile colleagues would be a massive understatement. I kept my own valedictory address equally short and succinct, thanking everyone present for giving me such a memorable send off, struggling throughout to keep my emotions in check with every word that I uttered before the impromptu gathering ended with a round of applause. Some of the members of Chambers came up to me afterwards to offer their own best wishes, personally especially Zack and Jide, who both made it clear how much they were going to miss my presence in Chambers. They even said they would still put my name forward to their solicitor contacts as first choice cover of their respective workload in the Midlands, more so now that I was going to actually be based in Birmingham, a parting gesture that was so typical of the pair of them which I more than gratefully received as the subsequent hugs and high fives between the three of us bore testimony to. Rosemarie, the person responsible for arranging my wonderful unexpected send-off was now sitting at her desk and I went up to her and planted a big kiss on the side of her cheek as a means of saying thank you, for so many things, but most of all for the special working relationship that we had and the immeasurable positive effect that she has had on my career, genuine heartfelt sentiments which she appeared, as usual, to take in her stride.

I formally joined Victoria Chambers sometime during that first week in March with all the feelings of optimism and goodwill that usually goes hand in hand when making a new or fresh start. So I could keep to my teaching commitments, and complete some outstanding cases in London, I suggested to my Clerks that I would contact Chambers every afternoon in order to find out what I would be doing the following day and if there was a case for me to cover either in the Midlands, or anywhere else within the Midlands catchment area. My Clerks were happy with those proposals and for those first four months my efforts in trying to maintain and sustain the right balance between my legal and teaching commitments in the south whilst at the same time trying to build a practice in the Midlands seemed to be working. But by the end of the summer sadly, the gradual steady development that I appeared to be making at Victoria Chambers was about to undergo the sternest of tests when John Rowbotham, the person who was one of the main influences in my decision to move to the Midlands, announced that he was leaving Chambers and moving to one of the top sets in Birmingham. His decision to leave Chambers was, to use the well-worn cliché, like a bolt out of the blue and whilst I was pleased for John in that he appeared to be moving in the right direction, from my own professional and personal perspective, it left me in an exposed and vulnerable position of being bereft of my main conduit to the vital network of solicitor contacts that I was gradually building a stable, professional rapport with. However, with John now moving on to pastures new, following him through the door no doubt, would be the very same network of solicitor contacts the potential success that my career at the Birmingham bar was by and large dependent upon. The stark yet real haunting worry and fear that I had to face was that I would have no firm guarantees that I would still be in the thoughts of those solicitors John introduced me to. It didn't take long for the clouds of uncertainty to gradually reappear over my horizon and with no real close friends or colleagues on hand to turn to for advice and support, the main worry that started to dominate my thoughts was, with the lack of any consistent and proper support, how on earth was I going to be able to sustain a long term and worthwhile career in the Midlands? For the umpteenth time in my rollercoaster career I was facing yet more uncertainty, and, unlike the previous episodes of crisis, this time, I really was on my own, without the aid of a safety net of say, a Rosemarie Phillips or Harold Ezzidio, the type of individuals who were always on hand to catch my fall and serve as vital a springboard to help me get my career on an even keel.

Over the course of the final three months of the year heading into the first two months of the following year, the cases I was doing in the Midlands had dwindled to virtually nothing and if it wasn't for one or two of my loyal solicitor contacts in the South who sent me the odd trial or two, my practice would have collapsed completely. Unsurprisingly, the old demons of despair and despondency reared their respective ugly heads to occupy and dominate my thoughts as my career at the Birmingham Bar appeared to be heading inexorably on a downward trajectory and I was unable of arresting that sad development. My big Midlands adventure was a complete and utter disaster and the bottom line was that there was no one to blame for my predicament, save for the reflected image of the mirror that I gaze into. There seemed little point in continuing the journeys up North either by car or rail for cases that were neither challenging let alone, cases that ultimately were mine to retain and keep, or to continue to persevere with chasing the solicitor contacts that I was trying to foster and develop in the Midlands in the hope that they would honour their promises of support, promises that in the long run, turned out to be empty and hollow. My levels of despondency and disillusionment had now reached an all time low and I had reached the point where I wanted to turn my back on anything and everything that connected me to law. I felt that I had given my all to the one thing I craved above everything else in life, a successful career in law but it simply wasn't happening for me. My seemingly defeatist attitude was also telling me that there seemed little point in applying to join another set of Chambers either in London or anywhere else for that matter. Even the option of relocating to Jamaica to practise law that I spent all that time and effort putting together as an option to fall back on if all else in England failed had lost its once alluring appeal. I reached the end of my tether.

I contacted Chambers and spoke firstly to Lee Masters and thereafter, to the Chambers' Clerks to inform them of my decision that I was going to terminate my tenancy with immediate effect, a decision in truth, that hardly took anyone by surprise and after reaching an amicable agreement that I would settle all the outstanding debts that I owed to Chambers by the end of that month, I ended my short, but ultimately disastrous year long stint in the Midlands with best wishes from both my Head of Chambers and the Chamber's Clerking team for the future which at that point was already looking decidedly bleak. Precisely what that future was going to entail, both in the immediate and the long term, with no alternative plans in place or indeed, no safety net to catch my impending free fall was worrying to say the very least. Given my increasingly desperate situation, I was prepared to do or try anything, absolutely anything, rather than endure the perpetual and never ending cycle of frustration and despair that seemed to have blighted my career over the last few years and with my fourth decade looming large on the horizon, I had reached the point where I felt that I needed to do something completely different with my life if I wanted to make the sort of impact on the world that I've always dreamt about, the sort of lasting impact that I hoped my career as a barrister would make which, barring some farfetched miracle, is unlikely to ever materialise. Maybe the enforced sabbatical I was about to take from practising law would help me evaluate my life in general and also help to gather my thoughts as to how to go about making this sudden and momentous change that had to be made if I wanted to salvage the dreams of making the worthwhile impact I hoped that I could make.

My long term plans and objectives appeared to have stalled considerably and unfortunately, I had no real idea or definitive Plan B as to how I was going to get those plans and objectives back on track. All I could do was to hope and pray that whatever I chose to do over the next couple of months, it would get me moving in the direction I want to be heading and help kick start my low levels of self-confidence and boost my virtually non-existent self-esteem. The choice I eventually settled upon after nearly three months of contemplation and procrastination (besides the "life changing" decision to change my hairstyle from the boring out dated flat top style to small dreadlock plaits!) was to try my luck as a contestant in the highly competitive world of TV game shows.

CHAPTER FOURTEEN

My interest and passion for quizzing, whether it be in the form of watching television quiz shows, playing quiz type board games, taking part in quiz competitions, either as a solo player or as a member of a quiz team, goes back a long, long way, almost as long as my passion for the law or the beautiful game. Back in the late 1960's, despite my tender years, I was a devoted watcher of *University Challenge*, hosted by the inimitable Bamber Gascoigne on BBC2, my stand out favourite out of all the quiz shows that were on our screens at the time. Other quiz shows that I enjoyed included *Top of the Form*, a sort of school's version of *University Challenge* hosted by Geoffrey Wheeler, or Robert Robertson's Ask The Family, and even though I couldn't answer any of the questions on these shows, they were part of my own personal "must see" television programmes whenever the opportunity arose, not purely for its exciting entertainment value, but also because of the fact that I found it awe inspiring watching clever people on TV and I wanted to be just as clever when I was all grown up. Other television quiz show that formed a part of my essential viewing included the programme that was billed at the time as "television's toughest interrogation quiz", BBC's *Mastermind*, or Jimmy Tarbuck's *Winner Takes All*, that began broadcasting towards the end of the decade on Friday evenings on ITV, *Bullseye*, the extremely popular darts and general knowledge quiz hosted by the comedian Jim Bowen, and the teatime quiz show that both myself and my brother Steve liked watching on a regular basis, *Blockbusters*, hosted by Bob "Can I have a P Please?" Holness. By religiously watching all these different types of quiz shows over time, gradually my all round general knowledge began to noticeably and significantly improve across a wide range of different subjects, an increase, I would readily admit, hardly seemed conceivable a few years earlier, and it became increasingly apparent that these quiz shows, aside from their entertainment value, were an important and valuable source of learning that would go on to serve me well in later years.

Although I loved watching those quiz shows on TV at the time, I didn't take part in any form of quiz competitions either during my teenage years or early twenties and although a big part of me harboured a secret desire to appear on one of those shows, my all round general knowledge, despite the improvement I had made, was still not at the required standard to do myself justice. Another reason why I was somewhat reluctant to take part in television quizzes was also because I was young and still painfully shy and I know in my heart of hearts, that if I had taken part as a quiz show contestant at that point in time, I would have performed like a startled rabbit caught in the headlights. So unless or until I managed to overcome my all round lack of self-confidence and shyness in general, the very idea of Shaun Wallace taking part in television quiz shows was totally out of the question.

Even though I had dismissed out of hand the mere thought of appearing as a television contestant on a game show, I was still nevertheless keen to test myself in some form of quizzing format and the chance to see how good I could be as a potential quizzing maestro presented itself in the late spring of 1981 when I happened to be listening to Capital Radio Station's popular *Breakfast Daytime Show* hosted by Graham Dene. There was a segment on the programme called, "Which Month of Which Year?" where Graham would give a series of clues based on certain events and play well known hit records of the time and the first contestant who phoned in with the correct answer won themselves a Capital Radio sweatshirt. On this occasion, one of the clues to the month and year that Graham had mentioned was the death of the legendary French singer Edith Piaf. At an instant, the date October 1963 flashed in my mind. I was 100% certain that was the right month and year because I remembered reading about her death in the one and only encyclopaedia that we had in the house. I was the only member of my family (as far as I am aware) who actually took the time to read the encyclopaedia and I was so fascinated by its contents, that I would read it over and over again until I knew the book like the back of my hand. I rushed to the bookshelf inside the living room in order to see if my hunch was correct, a big broad grin came over my face as my recollection of Edith Piaf's death proved to be spot on. Knowing the correct answer though is one thing, the chances of calling up the radio station and being lucky enough to get through to Graham Dene is an entirely different position altogether. There seemed little point to my mind in even trying as my chances were minimal at best, so I decided to simply carry on listening to the show in the belief that it would only be a matter of time before another listener came up with the right answer. However, after the near umpteenth caller had given the wrong answer and with Graham Dene, despite his increasingly exasperated tone, encouraging listeners to call the radio station, I had a complete change of heart and decided to try my luck and make the call as I had nothing to lose. Then, to my complete surprise and astonishment, I somehow managed to get through to speak to one of the show's production assistants instead of being confronted with the endless engaged tone

one normally encounters when thousands of others call in at the same time to enter these types of competitions. The person at the other end of the line asked for my name and the area where I came from before asking me for my answer. After I had given my answer, I was asked to stay on the line and to turn off any radio that was close by to prevent feedback as I was going to be put through to Graham Dene live on air as soon as the record that I could hear faintly in the background had finished playing. My heart started to beat a little faster than usual as I waited to be put through to the studio and as soon as the record had finished playing, I could just about hear Graham Dene as he returned to the "Which Year Which Month?" conundrum that had yet to be resolved. Graham then announced that he had "Shaun Wallace from Wembley" on the line. My big moment had now arrived and with butterflies fluttering away in my stomach, Graham asked me for my answer and once I had replied, "October 1963," I was greeted by the show's fanfare jingle that would denote that a contestant had given the right answer amidst Graham's cheery congratulatory tone. I had to stay on the line to give the station details of my home address and my preferred sweatshirt size which was the prize that I won for my endeavours and it was sent to me by way of registered post a couple of days later. It was the first thing that I had ever won in my entire life, a tangible reward for a talent and ability in terms of general knowledge that I clearly possessed and while the sweatshirt that I won was an item that was not going to last forever, for as long as it lasted, it was a prize that I was going to savour and treasure.

It was during the middle of the 1980's that my ability and confidence as a quiz competitor really increased in leaps and bounds and that was due in no small part to the board game that was a popular global phenomenon during this period, the irrepressibly addictive Trivial Pursuit. The first time I ever played the game was when I enjoying a convivial evening with some of my American colleagues on the Camp America summer Scheme way back in 1981. Despite some of the questions having a slight North American bias, especially on the Entertainment and Sport and Leisure categories, I managed to correctly answer the questions on those areas that happen to fall nicely for me. There was however, one particular question on the History category during the keenly contested game that was memorable not only for the fact that it paved the way for my eventual victory, it was on an area of American history that my competitors were simply completely taken aback that somebody from England would know. The question was: *what was the name of the newspaper that the victorious President Harry Truman was holding in his hands after the 1948 Presidential election with the headline*

'Dewey Defeats Truman'? I knew the answer to that one straight away on account of the fact that apart from my near obsessive passion for the history of the English Monarchy, I also had a keen interest in American history, especially American Presidents, and I remember an occasion when I was reading about US history, when I saw a picture of President Truman with the broadest of grins on his face holding aloft the newspaper in question to celebrate his re-election which confounded all predictions of the pollsters that he would suffer a resounding electoral defeat. There is no rhyme or reason as to why that image remained buried in the deep recesses of my mind that I could somehow retrieve at an instant. This uncanny ability must have something to do with the fact that I found that piece of relatively trivial information interesting and without hesitation, I calmly answered, "The Chicago Tribune," to leave my quizzing rivals both astonished and bewildered as I reached for the yellow coloured History segment to place in my six segmented playing piece on my way to my inaugural and memorable win playing Trivial Pursuit on foreign soil.

I used to play the game on the odd occasion after I qualified as a barrister mainly against some of my old school friends from Aylestone High School, with whom I was still very much in touch and hung out with a great deal at the time after they graduated from the various universities that they attended. Jacquie Nedd, the "Two Heathers" Thomas and Daulphin (Heather T and Heather D) respectively, and not forgetting the irrepressible (DJ) Loraine Martins who went to Warwick University with Jacquie and Heather D, were just some of the names who formed the core of these occasional Trivial Pursuit evenings that were not only a great deal of fun and thoroughly entertaining, they were also extremely competitive mainly due to the fact that I always played the game with an arrogance, swagger and belief that I was head and shoulders above the rest of the others, an attitude that quite understandably, was usually met with the hostility and contempt it deserved. It was an attitude that, unfortunately for my competitors, was usually vindicated in a hard fought but inevitable victory which I would celebrate with a bout of nonstop, over the top self-congratulation against the background of a cacophony of boos from my vanquished opponents.

Despite my egotistical belief that I was a player without an equal, there was one person who, no matter how many times we played each other, no matter how hard I tried, would always beat me. Not, you may think, a winner of the quiz show Mastermind past or present, nor a reigning or former champion of the equally tough radio quiz, Brain of Britain. No. My ultimate nemesis of my favourite board game was none other than my equally smug and equally condescending little kid brother, Steve Wallace.

Although Steve never shared the same morbid obsession for TV quiz shows like I had done, he did like watching the teatime daily quiz show Blockbusters whenever the mood would take him, and it wasn't long before I realised that his general knowledge was, in fact, better than I had given him credit for. It was only when he became an undergraduate at Kent University that he really began to fancy himself as a bit of a quizzing aficionado, especially at Trivial Pursuit. He caught the bug for the game whilst playing against his fellow students and, according to him, he would always emerge as the top man. It seemed inevitable therefore that a showdown between the two rival "champions" would have to take place to unify these imaginary titles that existed in our respective warped egos, but the real title we were playing for was the right to be called the undisputed quizzing champion of the Wallace household, which so far as myself and Steve were concerned, was the most valuable prize in competitive quizzing.

We both agreed to contribute equally to the purchase of the board game which remained unsealed until the day we played each other and the build up to our inevitable quiz showdown was akin to those highly publicised big unification boxing bouts of the 1980's and 1990's as the pair of us went through the pretence of press conferences, signing contracts, even the wholly unnecessary and at times somewhat distasteful trash talking that seems to go hand in hand in mega sporting showdowns of that nature. After all the pretence and hullabaloo, the contest got under way and as expected, it was a fiercely competitive confrontation, with each correct answer given by either one of us celebrated to excess in an unsporting nauseating manner that was the complete antithesis to the Corinthian spirit in which the game should have been played, but given it was two over inflated egos competing against each other, that was never going to be an option.

There was nothing between us throughout the epic struggle and eventually it all came down to the final question, a question which annoyingly Steve answered correctly, giving himself the spoils of victory, a victory made even worse by his completely over the top post match celebrations pacing up and down our living room punching the air with nauseating delight that was accompanied by constant taunting that was barely tolerable to be on the receiving end of. Likewise, there was nothing gracious or humbling in the manner in which I handled such a devastating defeat, resorting to accusing my gloating conqueror of everything, from unsporting unfair gamesmanship, to the slanderous and totally unwarranted allegation of cheating! The cold hard facts told a different story. I lost to the better player on the day and being the sore loser that I clearly was, I immediately demanded a re-match, an entitlement I tried to argue, because of the re-match clause inserted into our imaginary "multi million dollar" contract. The newly unified title holder simply brushed aside my constant whining when he declared in an extremely dismissive tone that contenders like myself had to "wait in line" and had to earn the "right" to challenge him and it would be then and only then that he would give consideration to giving me another shot at the title.

The humiliation and disappointment of losing a game of Trivial Pursuit to my younger brother was a defeat that was very difficult to take especially, when he would drop the odd reminder or two from time to time as to who was the champion of the Wallace household and as with anyone in his position who has the upper hand, he made me wait for the opportunity to rip the title from his grasp. Unfortunately, when my brother granted me the opportunity to gain revenge, the outcome was the same: a victory for my condescending kid brother. He repeated this feat on the three other occasions during that decade, resounding and comprehensive victories in his favour, defeats that were so devastating and soul destroying that I found it difficult to come to terms with it, and since that last occasion when I lost to him, I have not played either Steve or the board game itself since.

Throughout the late 1980's and early 90's, whilst I still retained my passion and enthusiasm for TV game shows and quizzing in general, it was placed on the back burner, because building my fledgling career at the bar alongside my teaching commitments was my main priority. Just about the only quizzing that I took part in during that period was in the summer of 1988, when my good friend and fellow pupil, Charlie Sherrard, asked me to be a part of a quiz team that he had put together and had entered for a quiz night involving quite a large number of teams mainly from the legal world that was held at the Ye Old Cock Tavern on Fleet Street, which we ended up winning much to our considerable delight. That period coincided with the early stages of my legal career as it began to scale the heights of success and it was only when the slow but painful reversal of fortune in my career began in earnest in the mid 1990's, that my interest in TV game shows and quizzing was slowly rekindled. Days, sometimes weeks, would go by when I had no work at all most notably, after Rosemarie got her marching orders from Somersett Chambers, when my appearances in the courtroom were becoming more and more rare. I felt an acute sense of embarrassment and shame during those frequent spells where there was barely any work in my diary and it was equally depressing to wake up the following morning with no real sense of purpose or direction. My days were usually spent doing nothing more than sprawl myself over the living room sofa watching hours upon hours of daytime television. It was a miserable and monotonous routine that continued right up until 3.45pm when the teatime quiz show programmes would begin. Those quiz shows provided the perfect platform (and comfort) to help me to momentarily escape from the depressing despondency that was my real world. Those programmes, especially, the Channel Four quiz show *Fifteen-To-One*, also gave me the opportunity to demonstrate my quizzing prowess and ability, albeit to a solo audience, and whenever I watched the programme, I would play the game as if I was an actual contestant taking part in the show, trying to answer the questions, no matter how easy or difficult they were, before the answer was revealed and I would always have a pen and paper on hand in order to keep an accurate record of how well I performed. I took the whole business of watching of quiz shows very seriously indeed and always played the game strictly according to the rules and even though there was no one else present, I would never, ever cheat. More often than not, I performed very well when testing myself by this method, and to to improve my knowledge, I would pay greater attention to the questions I didn't know, as it was those wrong answers that I considered most important in helping develop and expand the depth and breadth of my general knowledge. Furthermore, by answering questions in such a random manner, it was also a valuable exercise in that it helped to develop and enhance the speed in which I could retrieve and answer questions quickly from my mind.

I became so dedicated and committed to watching quiz shows as a means of building the breadth and depth of my general knowledge, that to ensure that I never missed a show I would pre-set my VCR to record them. I recorded programmes like *University Challenge, The People Versus* on ITV, *100%* on Channel 5 and of course, my favourite of all the afternoon quiz shows, *Fifteen-To-One* hosted by William G. Stewart. I watched all those recordings religiously, sometimes way beyond the midnight hour, constantly answering question after question *ad nauseum.* Over time, I managed to build up an extensive recording library of quiz shows that contained hundreds upon thousands of questions, questions so diverse not only in terms of the topics they covered, but also in terms of their varying degrees of difficulty and I would watch all these shows with such regular, almost religious devotion and dedication, that my general knowledge coupled with my ability to combine speed and lateral thinking when answering those questions correctly was constantly improving all of the time.

Because of the great strides I was making, I began to harbour thoughts of applying to become a contestant on a quiz show as it would be the only way to really discover how good I was. I was under no illusion as to the difficulties and challenges of being a contestant on a game show. It's all well and good having the talent and ability to answer questions correctly sitting in the comfort of one's sofa or armchair. The true test and measure of those talents could only be properly tested in the environment of a real TV studio, with the cameras rolling, and the glare of the studio lights, being interrogated by a real television quizmaster, coupled with the butterflies flapping incessantly away in the stomach as you constantly struggle to keep your nerves under control. However, even though I kept telling myself that I was ready to take the plunge and apply to go on one of these shows, I never resolved to do anything about it and instead of taking positive and decisive action, procrastination and inertia would always rear their ugly heads thus preventing me from making that achievable aim a reality.

Over the next couple of years, I still retained a deep-rooted passion and interest for TV quiz shows despite having no real objective, reason or defined purpose to aim for other than watching the shows themselves. Deep down, I knew that I had the potential to be a good quiz player, but instead of pitting my as of yet untried and untested quizzing credentials against the seasoned or more experienced quiz competitor, my regular quizzing opponent at this time was a lifelong friend of mine who at times, was a reluctant participant when watching teatime quiz TV.

Anthony Patrick Clifford, or Nipper as he is affectionately referred to by anyone who knows him, was my quizzing opponent in question and whilst Nipper could hardly be described as a Quiz opponent in the ordinary sense of the word, his contribution to my gradual development into a TV quiz competitor of some repute should not be understated. Nipper lived a couple of streets away from my home and I have been friends with both him and the other members of his family, his parents Patrick and Maureen who are now retired and his elder brother Kevin (who now lives and works as an Accountant in Newcastle) for well over thirty years and throughout that time, I became a frequent and welcome visitor to the Clifford household. Nipper is, and has always been, an extremely popular and likeable individual. You would be hard pressed to describe Nipper as an individual who was gifted academically, having left school aged 16 with only a handful of O Levels, but he was a shrewd, quick witted individual who was nobody's fool.

Nipper's availability during those miserable and depressing days when there were considerable gaps in my working diary were from my own selfish point of view, an absolute godsend because at the very least, I had a friend that I could turn to and Nipper's convivial company would always provide a welcome respite whenever I felt isolated, lonely or just plain bored sitting at home watching daytime TV. Whenever I went to his house for that much needed company, I would always time it to coincide ten or so minutes before the start of Channel Four's teatime quizzing zone with *Fifteen-To-One* commencing at 3.45pm followed straight afterwards by *Countdown* hosted by Richard Whitely a half an hour later. Not everyone that I knew would have been so accommodating as Nipper, nor would they have indulged my compulsive desire for watching *Fifteen-To-One* on their own television set when they could have been watching something else or indeed, doing something else with their free time. Furthermore, I would have been hard pressed to have found anyone that I knew who would have allowed themselves to be commandeered into being the token sacrificial opponent answering questions on a game show that they either simply didn't know the answer to, or weren't quick enough. Nipper never got remotely close to beating me whenever we played *Fifteen-To-One*, not even when we introduced a handicap system where he would get a twenty, sometimes thirty point head start, a head start that invariably, I would surpass either by the end of the first round or, by the end of round two by which time, a demoralised Nipper would simply sit back and leave me to play the remainder of the show by myself giving me an easy victory over my hapless opponent. Those quizzing battles between myself and Nipper was not always a one-sided affair as Nipper would invariably gain some measure of revenge for the regular quiz drubbing he received *playing Fifteen-To-One* when we played against each other in *Countdown*. Nipper was on far safer ground with this type of game show format, as he always seemed to have the knack for spotting longer words than I could during the word games, and his natural flair for figures also gave him a distinct advantage in the numbers round.

This ad hoc arrangement of going around to Nipper's house and testing my quiz show skills lasted on and off for the best part of three years and my general knowledge improved steadily with each passing year. Intermittently during those three years, I would say to Nipper that I was thinking of taking the plunge and becoming a contestant on a quiz show and his response was always one of genuine positive encouragement that I should do so although I suspect that a small part of him, or maybe even a large part of him, was saying that because he had probably had enough of being shanghaied into competing with me in *Fifteen-To-One*.

Given the fact that by February 1999 I was in a state of professional limbo, there was nothing preventing or standing in my way from fulfilling my dream of becoming a game show contestant. The problem was – I couldn't decide which quiz show I wanted to appear on. After a lot of dithering, I eventually settled on a quiz show that I had been avidly watching ever since its first broadcast the day after the launch of Channel Five on the 30th of March 1997, *100%*. Billed as "The Game show without a host", *100%* was presented by the former Thames Television newsreader, Robin Houston. At long last, after years of talking the talk, I was going to finally walk the walk when a couple days after my 39th birthday, I posted my application to the *100%* Production team offices in Central London. The response from the Production team was just as swift and I was invited to attend an audition on one of the various audition days that were available and given the fact I had so much spare time on my hands, I chose the first date available. My debut as a quiz show contestant was now a tantalisingly real possibility.

I attended the Pearson Television Company Offices situated just off Tottenham Court Road and I couldn't have been more excited at the prospect of competing for a place on a real TV quiz show. I arrived at the studio and thankfully, I didn't have to wait all that long before I was greeted by a member of the show's production team and introduced to the other auditionees. The first part of the audition involved all of us having to complete a written test paper that contained thirty questions before we were divided into groups of four where we would be competing against each other on the buzzer. The written part of the audition presented no problems for me whatsoever and the second part went even better on account of the near lightning speed I displayed on the buzzer, not giving any of the opponents I was competing against a look in. The audition was becoming so one sided that after a while, the person in charge of the auditions asked me to refrain from pressing the buzzer for the remainder of the audition, a request that caught me off guard momentarily and for a nightmarish split second, led me to believe that I'd blown my chances. After I had finished my audition, the producer who made the call came up to me and explained his reasons for his intervention. He started off by apologising profusely for the unexpected intervention before going on to say that he was hugely impressed with both my general knowledge and speed in dominating the audition. Such domination however, he went on to add, meant that my fellow contestants hardly got a chance to shine and he wanted to see how they would react on the buzzer. He reassured me that I shouldn't think for one moment that his intervention harmed my chances of appearing on the show and that I would definitely be hearing from them. I could not have felt any happier on how my audition went and as I headed for home, I felt sufficiently confident in believing that I'd done more than enough to make my debut as a serious TV quiz competitor.

A week or so later I received a letter informing me that I had successfully passed the audition and I was requested to attend the same studios on 26th June 1999 to record the show. I was excited but nervous. Performing well at an audition or in the comfort of one's sofa at home is one thing, performing on a TV quiz show with the lights, cameras or the occasional studio audience, is an entirely different proposition altogether. Whether I really had what it takes to perform well on a game show was about to be put to the ultimate test and I could not wait to find out the outcome.

On the day, I arrived at the studios in plenty of time and was escorted to the green room where my other two contestants were waiting. The introductions between all three of us were both pleasant and friendly despite the fact that pretty soon, all three of us would be in direct competition for quiz show glory. My fellow competitors were Michelle Raffle, from Luton, and the returning champion, David Lever, who hailed from Manchester. Moments later, a member of the production team came in to explain the competition's rules. Once the three of us had confirmed that we agreed and understood those rules, we were then required to report to makeup. As I sat in the make-up artists' chair, I suddenly felt a sharp, adrenalin surge. *This is it, Shaun!* I said to myself. *Just remain as calm and relaxed as you possibly can… you can do this!*

The show's format as its very name suggests, consisted of one hundred questions, which in turn, were divided into ten questions on a specialist topic. The first round was General Knowledge and the other categories in the following rounds could be any number of things. The last twenty questions of the show always concluded with a General Knowledge round and at the end of the show, the player with the highest score would win one hundred pounds in addition to the option to return on the next show to defend their title.

All three of us went to our respective positions on the studio's set and I could not have felt more relaxed or confident. Unfortunately though, I didn't get off to the best of starts in the first round as I only scored 50% and found myself languishing in last place. Michelle was one question ahead of me on 60% and the returning champion, David, had managed to score a very respectable 80%. The next two categories were Film and then Space, and once again my performances in those rounds were hardly setting the world alight as I returned scores of six out of ten and five out of ten respectively. My score had improved slightly enough for me to be in joint third place with Michelle on 53%, but David had stretched his lead and was way out in front on a score of 67%. This was not the blistering and positive start to a TV quizzing career that I had envisaged.

I was hoping for a more favourable category in round four but sadly that was not to be, as the next category was on the topic of Scotland and all things Scottish. Once again, I performed poorly, managing to answer only four questions correctly with the most embarrassing point in the round coming with the final question, the True or False question, where I selected the option False, to the question that the Lord Advocate was the official responsible for all Public Prosecutions in Scotland. Hardly inspiring quizzing given the nature of my profession and if I continued with that lamentable level of performance, my television debut was well on the way to becoming a disaster. The final category before the break was on Literature and for the first time in the contest, I managed to get off to a perfect start by answering the first five questions correctly, but that ideal start was tempered by the fact that David was matching my efforts stride for stride. On the sixth question within the round, I managed to take a slight advantage in that I was the only contestant to correctly answer the question concerning the gift sent by the Dauphin of France to King Henry V in the Shakespeare play of the same name. I knew the answer was Tennis Balls straight away out of the choices of Fine Wines or Nintendo 64, a fact I remembered from my student days of reading Henry V when studying (and ultimately failing as you may recall) O Level English Literature. My apparent good form in the round even continued with the following question where once again, I was the only contestant out of the three who knew that E.M. Forster's novel, A Passage to India, was published in the year 1924. Just as I was beginning to believe that I had really turned the corner, all my efforts during my mini revival were quickly undone when I answered the final three questions in the round incorrectly, with the most embarrassing of those wrong answers being the penultimate question, which asked for the nationality of the first winner of the Nobel Prize for Literature. I knew that the Frenchman Sully Prud'Homme was the first winner of the award in 1901 out of the three options that were on the screen, but for some inexplicable reason, I pressed the option for American. It was silly little mistakes like that which summed up my less than impressive performance up to that point, a performance that was not only threatening to undermine my chances of winning the show, but was also making considerable dents on my confidence.

In stark contrast, my main rival in the show, David, was pushing further and further ahead with his score, consistently giving one correct answer after another and his near flawless performance was threatening to take a complete stranglehold on proceedings. The show had now reached the halfway stage. Michelle had 52%, I was a mere one question ahead of her on 54% and David was way out in the lead with a healthy score of 68%. The high hopes I had of a debut victory coupled with a strong and impressive performance to match was, at this stage of the contest, looking extremely misplaced and hollow. The short interval couldn't have come any quicker so far as I was concerned as it provided the perfect opportunity I needed to compose myself and try to figure out what was needed to dramatically improve on what was at best, an extremely average performance.

The sixth category was on World War One. *At long last*, I said to myself. *A subject I know something about.* This was a category that I hoped would provide the springboard for an improbable comeback. David and I both answered the first three questions correctly. On the fourth question though, I managed to gain a slight advantage over David in correctly selecting the right answer, the Battle of the Somme, as the battle which began in July 1916, as opposed to David's selection, the Battle of Passchendale, but that initial advantage was quickly surrendered within the next two questions as David was the only contestant to know that Serbia was the allied Balkan State in question that was overrun by the Germans in 1915, as opposed to my choice of Romania. David then continued to demonstrate his vast and impressive general knowledge with the penultimate question by selecting the correct answer, The Battle of Caporetto, as the battle in question where the Allies suffered a major defeat in 1917. Despite those successive setbacks in my so called favourite round, I still managed to score an impressive eight out of ten. My performance was improving, but if I wanted to win the entire contest, I had to maintain a high scoring average in the next round, which, Robin revealed, was Religion. This category proved to be a real competitive tussle between David and myself. David scored an early advantage with the second question being the only contestant who knew that the Cowley Fathers was the common name for the Society of St. John the Evangelist. The initiative then swung back in my direction with the next question, as I was the only contestant who knew that it was the Angel Gabriel who revealed the Koran to the Prophet Mohammed. I slipped up again sadly though on the seventh question, a question that I should have known the answer to which, much to my annoyance, David knew, in that it was Lilith who was Adam's first wife in the Bible. By the end of that round, I still managed to score a respectable seven out of ten, but despite the improvements in my performance, after the first two categories in the second half of the show, David remained infuriatingly consistent with his scoring and still retained a sizable and healthy lead.

Round eight was on Food and Drink, a category which caused me to raise my eyebrows skywards in apprehension, as it is a category that I would hardly consider to be one of my strongest subjects, but I managed to score a very impressive eight out of ten. In stark contrast, David managed to score only two out of ten and his unexpected collapse raised the faintest of hopes of the possibly of me beating him. At the end of the round, Robin gave an update on the scores. Michelle was a distant third on 48%, my score had now improved considerably to 60% and David's seemingly healthy lead was now reduced to a score of 65%. Slowly but surely, my performance was improving. I was now in with a real shout of surpassing David's score and possibly going on to win. I felt that the momentum was clearly with me now and could only hope that, despite his consistently strong performance throughout the show, David would somehow eventually crack under the pressure. David was still in the driving seat, but the way I was now performing meant that the game was there for the taking.

With everything to play for at the start of the final General Knowledge round, I needed to get off to a good solid start, but sadly for me, instead of maintaining my impressive second half form, I reverted to the indifferent form I displayed in the first half of the quiz by answering the first question incorrectly which, given the choices that were on offer, was a poor mistake to make. After the first ten questions of that final round, David answered seven correctly, whereas I managed to answer only six correctly, the only question that I managed to get the better of David in that category was knowing that it was the Bridgewater Canal, as opposed to David's choice of the Grand Union Canal, that was the first canal built in England. With only ten questions remaining, I now needed something just short of a miracle to stand any chance of victory. However, those chances of a remarkable comeback went up in flames when I answered the first two questions incorrectly, whereas David got them both right. By the ninety-fifth question, the contest was effectively over bar the shouting. I couldn't catch David even though two questions later he answered incorrectly the question which I definitely knew the answer to which was, that King George II was the last British King to lead his troops on the field of battle. Over those last ten questions, David scored eight out of ten, thus proving himself to be both a worthy winner and champion. He won with a final score of 68%, with Michelle coming in a gallant third on 48%. My final score was a respectable 63%.

After the show had finished, all three of us congratulated each other on how well we had performed. David really was a deserved and worthy winner although I could sense that he was clearly relieved that he had come out on top in a very close contest. I said my final goodbyes to everybody involved in the show and made my way to Tottenham Court Road tube station. I was naturally disappointed in having lost such a close contest although I nevertheless felt justifiably proud of my debut as a television quiz show contestant and my performance only served to whet my appetite to be a contestant on as many game shows as possible.

Despite my understandable desire to continue my TV quizzing career, there was a much more pressing dilemma on my immediate horizon that needed to be resolved: my future employment status. Over four months had passed since I left Victoria Chambers without any plans as to what was going to be my next move. Another major dilemma was the dwindling state of my finances. I just about managed to survive financially, thanks mainly to surrendering two long term savings plans that I had cashed in not long after leaving Chambers, much needed funds that enabled me to pay off some crippling long term debts in the form of Chambers rent arrears not only to Victoria Chambers, but also to Somersett Chambers who, given the age of the outstanding rent arrears, had to resort to issuing legal proceedings against me to recover the aforementioned, a claim that eventually was settled amicably out of court when it was agreed between the parties that I would pay an initial lump sum payment with the remainder of the debt paid off by direct debit payments. I was still receiving outstanding legal fees that was owed to me for previous court appearances although those payments were becoming more and more sporadic, a reflection no doubt, of how often I actually appeared in court during my ill-fated stint in the Midlands. My only other income stream was my part time teaching salary, but even that source was going to be the subject of drastic change as I was informed by Hackney College, just before the start of BTEC final examinations at the end of May, that they were not going to renew my teaching contract for the new academic term in September, a unilateral decision by the College that sadly, would bring to an end a fourteen year association with the institution that had given me my first employment break. The never-ending worry of trying to get back into full time employment was compounded by the additional dilemma as to what form that employment was going to take. Do I go back into private practice and try to rebuild my career, or do I go down the route of trying to obtain a job with the security of a regular pay cheque at the end of each month, knowing full well that the chances of anyone employing a dreadlocked thirty nine year old, whose adult working life has been confined to the very narrow field of criminal defence advocacy, are not all that good? My employment dilemma however thankfully resolved itself and it happened at the most unlikely settings one could ever imagine, at the funeral of a dear friend.

In early August of 1999, I heard the sad news that Kevin Metzger, my good friend and erstwhile colleague at 54 Fleet Street had tragically passed away at the young age of 42. I was extremely shocked and saddened by Kevin's untimely passing and one of my first thoughts upon hearing the news was thinking that the legal profession as well as the world at large, would be all the more poorer at the loss of Kevin's cheery and amiable character, a demeanour that went hand in hand with his undoubted talent as a lawyer, and given the nature of our long standing friendship, there was no way on earth I was going to pass up the opportunity to pay Kevin my final respects. The funeral service itself as you would expect for a man as popular as Kevin, was packed to the rafters, many of whom were my fellow colleagues who I hadn't seen for some time. One of those colleagues who was present both at the church service and the wake that followed was Wilf Foster-Jones whom I hadn't laid eyes on since we co-defended together successfully in the multi-handed trial at the old Knightsbridge Crown Court some seven years previously. Wilf was now the Head of the relatively small but successful set of Chambers based at 1 Middle Temple Lane and as the pair of us were catching up on old times at the wake, he asked me what I was doing as he had heard on the legal grapevine that I had left the bar altogether. I told him that I was "taking a break" and was currently "in between Chambers". Then Wilf told me that if ever I was thinking of coming back to private practice in the foreseeable future, then I should contact him straight away as the Chambers had moved to bigger premises at New Court Buildings in the Temple. Wilf's magnanimous offer was a lifesaver and I wasted very little time in telling him that I would be in touch with him within the next day or so. I couldn't have felt more relived that the uncertainty surrounding my next move had fallen by the wayside and that meant that I could turn my attentions to plotting my next appearance on a TV game show.

The next TV quiz show appearance I was aiming for was, of course, Channel Four's legendary *Fifteen-To-One*. I posted the obligatory postcard to the programme's main offices in Wandsworth, South London requesting an application form which I duly filled out and returned post haste. I didn't have to wait all that long before I received a letter inviting me to attend an audition for the show that was going to be held at the Wandsworth Town Hall sometime in the middle of August 1999. When I arrived for my audition at the appointed time, I was greeted by a scene of what appeared to be hundreds upon hundreds of eager wannabe contestants like myself, milling round in a scenario that resembled a crowded cattle market. The sheer volume of the people present inside the Town Hall in itself was a testament to *Fifteen-To-One's* enduring popularity.

Once everyone had finally been registered, another member of the production team then appeared from behind a large red curtain on the stage. He began his address firstly by immediately apologising for the chaotic nature of the audition and even he seemed to be taken aback by the sheer number of people in attendance. He then went on to explain the logistics of how the audition was going to be conducted and he asked for volunteers to step forward in groups of fifteen in an orderly fashion and so on and so on, until the end of the session. No sooner than he finished his short address, people began to surge forward. *At this rate the audition is going to take all day*, I thought to myself so I too joined the surge of people, displaying equal determination not to be at the audition any longer than was necessary.

The auditions themselves lasted no longer than ten minutes on average on account of the fact that there simply wasn't enough time given the sheer weight of numbers that were present, all the more reason no doubt, to answer the questions that one would be facing correctly otherwise the chances of getting on to the programme could non-existent. I eventually stepped, managing to answer four of the questions I was asked correctly and after my audition, I made my getaway as quickly as possible. A few days later, I received a letter with the welcoming news that my audition was successful and the date for my recording would be on the 5th October 1999 at the *Fifteen-To-One* Studios in Wandsworth.

This was the quiz show above all quiz shows that I wanted to win the most. I had firmly set my sights on trying to win one of the two ancient artefacts that are awarded to the contestant who finishes top of the Leader Board at the end of the series, with the main prize going to the contestant who ultimately becomes *Fifteen-To-One* Series Champion. I wanted to give myself the best possible chance of doing really well on the show, so I went out and bought a number of quiz books prior to taking on the arduous task of reading the whole of the Encyclopaedia Britannica from A-Z that I managed to borrow from the local library because, although I felt that I was a good quiz competitor, there was still vast gaps in my knowledge. Going through all those encyclopaedias was every bit as arduous and daunting as I had expected, but in saying that, I had such a fascinating time learning about so many new different things on subjects, which years ago, I never had an interest in, let alone cared about, such as Classical Music, Science and Astronomy, and the more I read those encyclopaedias, the more I wanted to learn about something new. It took me the best part of six weeks to go through all those encyclopaedias by which time we were approaching the end of September 1999. With all my preparation now complete, sure in the belief that I had left no stone unturned, I was ready to take on the challenge of *Fifteen-To-One*, full of confidence, my sights firmly set on not just winning the Fifteen-To-One episode that I was appearing in but winning the Grand Final itself.

The day for my appearance on Fifteen-To-One had finally arrived, and I woke up that morning with a feeling that all the hard work and preparation that I had put in over the previous two months was going to pay handsome dividends as I could not envisage anything else in my mind other than a complete and comprehensive victory. I left my home and made my way to Stonebridge Park tube station for the sixty or so minute journey to Wandsworth tube station on the District Line via Paddington as I was required to be at the Wandsworth Studios for mid-day. Because I had arrived at the studios half an hour early, I had no inkling of the terrible tragedy that had occurred earlier that morning at Paddington's Main Line Station, where all those poor people lost their lives in the rail disaster. I was totally unaware about the details of the disaster until after I had returned home from the studios later that afternoon and such an awful and terrible disaster really put into perspective the things that really are important in life. That sentiment was self-evident especially in the light of my own lamentable performance in a contest in which I had set my hopes so unrealistically high.

Once I arrived at the studio, I met with my other contestants, and we had to draw lots to determine where in the line up we would appear. I drew lot number two. Once the lot drawing formalities had been completed, the production assistant then went on to explain the rules of the show, rules which all fifteen contestants probably knew better than their own names. The rules of *Fifteen-To-One* are as follows: all fifteen contestants start off with three lives and in the first round, each contestant faces two questions. To survive, a contestant had to answer at least one of their designated questions correctly but if a contestant got both their designated questions wrong, then they would be eliminated from the game.

Once all the fifteen contestants had been seen by the makeup department, we all reconvened back at the green room as the recording before ours was just about to finish. Moments later, all fifteen contestants were escorted onto the studio set and our respective positions on Contestant's Row where we were approached by a number of the studio's technicians who began the process of wiring all of us for sound.

Once we were all settled down and all in place, the show's legendary host, William G. Stewart, made his entrance onto the studio set, confidently bestriding the studio stage like the quiz colossus that he is. William briefly chatted to some of the contestants before he addressed all fifteen of us with some sensible advice which was, to relax and enjoy the whole experience and not allow ourselves to be put off by the glare of the bright studio lights or the presence of the camera.

The Studio Floor Manager then asked for complete silence on the set before he began a five second countdown to the start of the show. The show's familiar theme music started to play heralding the start of the show before William began his usual piece to camera by giving an update to the millions of watching viewers with regards to the progress of the Leader Board. In order to make it onto the Leader Board, the winner of our recording only had to equal or surpass the relatively modest target of one hundred and forty three points. Prior to the start of our game, William talked briefly about one particular previous winner, Bill McKaig, a Minster from Glasgow who sadly had been eliminated on the recording before our show. The reason William made special reference to Bill was because in a previous edition of the show, he was the first (and so far only) contestant in the long history of the show to achieve the maximum achievable score of four hundred and thirty three.

Before he asked the first question, William reminded the contestants as he does at the start of every edition, that we would each be facing two questions in the first round, and only one correct answer was needed to survive to progress to the second round. William launched into the first question which was correctly answered and now it was now my turn to face the first of the two questions which I hoped would be a fairly routine and straightforward one which I would answer correctly and help settle any nerves and ensure that I survive to progress into the second round.

"SHAUN, PLEASE, BUSINESS AND COMMERCE. WHICH MOTORING ORGANISATION ENDED ITS NINETY-FOUR YEAR HISTORY AND AN INDEPENDENT COMPANY OWNED BY ITS

MEMBERS WHEN ITS SALE TO THE UTILITY COMPANY, CENTRICA, WAS APPROVED IN SEPTEMBER?"

I wasn't entirely sure about the correct answer to the question but It was clear from the question's construction that I had a 50/50 chance of getting it right as it could only be either the RAC or the AA. In situations like these where the correct answer is narrowed down to only two choices, I would normally go with the option that first pops into my head because nine times out of ten, your first instinct is the correct instinct. Because a contestant only has approximately three seconds in which to give their answer, I replied rather hesitantly and without any real confidence or conviction, "The RAC?" However much to my disappointment I heard the sound that I didn't want to hear, the sound of the incorrect buzzer. I rolled my eyes skywards in dismay but I was determined not to let it affect me as I still had one more chance to progress into the second round. Out of the rest of the contestants, only four people answered their question correctly.

I was very disappointed with myself in getting the question that I faced wrong and as is always the way in these situations, I could answer virtually all of my fellow contestant's questions but failed miserably in answering my own. *Only William G Stewart and the man upstairs know what's coming next, it could be on anything!* I said to myself and I started to become increasingly apprehensive. My chances of surviving the cut now relied on a wing and a prayer and all I could do was hope that all those hours upon hours of hard work and preparation spent both at home and in the library would somehow come riding to my rescue.

William seemed to breeze through those first fifteen questions and before I knew it, he began asking the second set of questions for that first round. The first contestant answered his question incorrectly but once again, I knew the correct answer to his question - that Persia was the country where the legendary army "The Ten Thousand Immortals" originated from in ancient times. But answering other contestant's questions was going to provide no help or assistance whatsoever as I prepared to face my second question.

"SHAUN, PLEASE, OPERA. WHICH VERDI OPERA IS BASED ON THE ALEXANDER DUMAS PLAY, THE LADY OF THE CAMELLIAS?"

I raised my eyebrows skyward in sheer desperation thinking to myself "*Opera! Of all the questions to be facing at this critical time, Opera!* Although my knowledge of Opera music had vastly improved, it was the sort of question that I was far from knowing. Once again rather unhelpfully, two conflicting options immediately sprang to mind and in truth, they were the only two Verdi operas that I really knew anything about, Rigoletto and La Traviata, but which one do I go for? Another nerve wracking 50/50 choice that I had to make, but with my immediate future in the game hinging on that choice, I had to trust my instincts and hope that within the three second time limit allowed to give my answer that it would be the answer to see me through to round two. After yet another slightly hesitant pause I eventually replied, "Rigoletto?" BZZZZZ! That depressingly onomatopoeic sound confirmed that my answer was incorrect, the correct answer being La Traviata. I was gutted, totally gutted. I was forced to sit down as the rules of the show demanded. I sat down in my seat with my head bowed and as my personal studio light faded to total darkness, I listened to the remaining thirteen questions while at the same time wondering where it all went wrong.

I was not looking forward to the embarrassing moment at the end of the first round of questions when the studio announcer lists the names of the contestants eliminated in the first round as I knew my name was going to be the first to be called. Once the second set of questions in the first round had been completed, William announced the even more depressing statistic, "SEVEN DOWN, EIGHT TO GO!" and out of the eight contestants who survived, only one managed to keep her three lives intact. Myself, together with the six other eliminated contestants, had to leave the set and make our way to the gallery where I had sit and watch the remainder of the show from the side lines and as the second round began, the only matter that dominated my thoughts was, why did I perform so badly? I was desperate to be a part of the contest that was being played out before my very eyes, but my swift exit meant that there was very little that I could do other than sit, observe and suffer in silent agony. At the end of a non-eventful second round, only three made it into the Final. There was a short interval before the final round began, during which time, all fifteen contestants were required to assemble to take a team photo with the show's host, as a treasured memento of the day's events and despite my best efforts, I found it almost impossible to raise a cheery smile.

After the end of the recording, I left the studio as quickly as I could, totally consumed by my disappointing performance, especially after all the effort and hard work that I had put in preparing for the show. Looking back with the benefit of hindsight, if I was brutally honest with that assessment, I suppose hubris, coupled with a large dose of misplaced self-confidence, were the main reasons for my abysmal, abject performance. Despite such a comprehensive defeat, my embarrassing performance on *Fifteen-To-One* only served to strengthen my resolve to succeed in the tough, sometimes unforgiving environment of TV quizzing and it made me even more determined to redouble my efforts and give it another go in my relentless quest to try make some sort of impact in the world of television quiz shows.

CHAPTER FIFTEEN

Amidst all the hard work, preparation and excitement that surrounded my fateful appearance on Fifteen-To-One, I made the arrangement to meet up with Wilf Foster-Jones at New Court Chambers to discuss the possibility of me returning to the fold of private practice as a full time tenant. Just before I entered the building, my thoughts momentarily travelled back in time to the last occasion I had a reason to come to New Court Chambers which was for my ill-fated "interview from hell" in my attempt to secure a first six month pupillage at George Carmen QC's Chambers in January 1985 and how bitterly disappointed I was by the whole chastening experience. By the time I left New Court Chambers after my discussions with Wilf on this occasion, my good mood contrasted sharply to the miserable mood when I left the building on that last visit after the pair of us had shaken hands on the deal in which I agreed to accept Wilf's offer of a tenancy. There was no doubting the fact that I was extremely pleased and relieved that I had returned to the world of private practice but at the same time, I was under no illusion that this latest "fresh start" was going to see an immediate and dramatic upturn in my fortunes. After having turned my back on the profession nearly six months previously, I had effectively severed all ties with all the loyal solicitor contacts that had kept my legal career going. My return to the fold meant that, in essence, despite being in my fifteenth year as a barrister, I was effectively having to start from scratch once again and that would require me to develop and forge new relationships with solicitors as well as reprise old long standing relationships with solicitors who have supported my career in the past. I knew full well given the countless setbacks that I have endured in the past that the rebuilding process of my professional career was not suddenly going to be transformed overnight. It was going to take some time to get my career back on track and was going to require a considerable amount of effort on my part and a considerable amount of support and goodwill on the part of the solicitors that I have a professional working relationship with.

Although New Court Chambers was a relatively small set, it was an extremely busy set that had the right blend of young practitioners who were up and coming, a group that was to include, my young proteges Zack Atunwa and Jide Laleilen, who joined New Court some two or so months after my arrival and good, experienced barristers such as Dominic Roberts and Kevin Metzger (no relation to the late Kevin Metzger that had recently passed away). However, as with the previous occasions in the last nine years when starting out at a new set of Chambers, the one individual that I had to rely on initially in terms of helping me to rebuild my career from scratch, was the Senior Clerk who in the present case, was the rather youthful looking Brian Peters. I went straight to him to discuss my future there, and during the fruitful discussions that I had with him after joining New Court, I had every reason to feel hopeful and optimistic that in time, he would play an integral and positive role in the revival of my career.

Sadly, from that point in August 1999 to the end of year celebrations that ushered in the year 2000, my career didn't enjoy the resurgence I had hoped for. Once again I started to seriously call into question whether it was worthwhile persevering in a profession that was causing me nothing but stress, disappointment and an enduring sense of frustration. But I knew, this time, throwing in the towel and opting once again for exile was not an option. I simply had to be patient and persevere.

Those ongoing difficulties that my career was experiencing was not enough to put me off my ambitions of winning a TV quiz show and the programme that was next in line on my quizzing radar was Channel Five's *One to Win*, another teatime quiz show hosted by Paul Roseby. I applied for an audition to appear on the programme towards the end of January 2000 and after successfully passing that audition that was held at the same venue where the quiz show *100%* held their auditions, I was formerly invited to appear on the programme a week or so later back at the same studios.

The show's format consisted of four contestants who, in the first round, had to answer general knowledge questions on the buzzer, with the aim of trying to achieve a target of nine points in order to progress to the second round. In the second round, each contestant had to try and answer a sequence of four correct answers in a row within a sixty second time limit. If in attempting to build that sequence for four correct answers, a contestant answered a question incorrectly, that contestant would have to start again from scratch. At the end of those sixty seconds, the best correct answer sequence recorded by a contestant would count as their final score and at the end of the round, the top two contestants who recorded the highest sequence of correct answers would progress to the final head to head showdown. In that final round, both contestants would face a series of questions in the form of clues, with four points awarded to the contestant who answers the more difficult clues within the shortest period of time, right down to one point for the easiest clue. The winner is the first to reach twenty-one points.

I arrived at the studios on the day of the recording relaxed, in good spirits and above all, confident that at the very least, I couldn't perform any worse than my last abysmal showing on Fifteen-To-One. After I presented myself to reception, I was escorted to the green room by a production assistant where my fellow contestants were. All of the competing contestants in the room were given a general briefing about the show that was quickly followed by a detailed explanation of the show's rules before we were invited to help ourselves to the light refreshments that were on offer. Thankfully for me, I was spared the mind numbing ordeal of having to hang around the studio for hours on end because I was selected together with three other contestants, for the first scheduled recording of the day. After all four of us were wired for sound, we were directed to take our place at our respective podiums before the show's host, Paul Roseby, made his entrance onto the studio. Paul then got the contest under way with the utterance of his standard catchphrase that was synonymous with the programme: "WE KNOW WHO YOU ARE, WE KNOW WHY YOU'RE HERE, SO LET'S PLAY, ONE TO WIN!"

Once the show got underway, my strategy for the first round was to make a fast start as a way of letting my fellow contestants know that I intended to stamp my authority all over the contest. My forthright and determined tactics immediately paid the handsome dividends I was hoping for as I managed to storm my way through that first round with room to spare. My lightning performance in that first round gave me the advantage I would have first pick of the various categories on offer in the second round and as luck would have it, one of those categories on offer was Sport which apart from History, is one of my favourite subjects. With that slight advantage at my disposal, there was no denying the fact that I felt that I stood a real good chance of building a sequence of answering four correct questions in a row to put myself in a strong position to progress to the final head to head round.

"SHAUN, YOUR TIME STARTS NOW!" Paul declared as he launched the start of the second round in earnest. As the round progressed, I appeared to be having very little difficulty answering my questions correctly but unfortunately for me, I got the next question wrong, a mistake which meant that I had to go back to square one and begin a new sequence. On my second attempt to build a sequence of four correct answers, I built up a sequence of four correct answers – or so I thought. I barely had time to revel in my achievement before the show's producers changed their mind and told me I had got the fourth question wrong.

The question I was asked was: which Olympic sport contains the disciplines where competitors have to Ride, Shoot, Swim, Fence and... before Paul had finished asking the question, I interrupted him with the quick response, "PENTATHLON, MODERN PENTATHLON!" The show's producers took issue with the fact that I had given two answers and insisted that he had to accept my first answer. Paul was extremely apologetic and said that he had to be strict at this stage of the competition. I thought the decision in refusing to allow the response that I gave was somewhat harsh, but rules are rules and as a result of the producer's decision, I was deemed to have posted a score of three, as opposed to four correct answers in a row. I had an anxious wait for the remaining two contestants to have their turn to see if they could either equal or surpass my score. At the end of that second round, my fellow two contestants also managed to score three correct answers in a row and the rules dictated that all three of us had to go into a three way play off to determine which two contestants would go through to the final round. Paul then began to explain the rules for the tie-breaker and for some inexplicable reason, my focus and concentration seemed to drift, an ill-timed lapse in concentration borne no doubt, as a direct result of the fact that I was still dwelling on my disappointment in being overruled by the show's producers in my split second attempt to change my answer. My lapse in concentration and focus at such a critical stage of the contest was in stark contrast to the steely focus and determined attitude of my two fellow competitors, a costly state of affairs that was to manifest itself throughout the tie-break decider that sadly resulted in my eventual elimination.

I was escorted off the set and directed to the part of the studio where the audience were seated where for the remainder of the show, I watched on helplessly as yet another final stage of a quiz show that I had competed in was taking place without me. This was yet another frustrating and disappointing performance which left me wondering whether I was ever going to make that all important, but increasingly elusive, quiz breakthrough. There was nothing left for me to do except gather my belongings together before walking out of the studio exit door, my head bowed and subdued heading in the direction of the tube station for the long, miserable journey home.

My situation at New Chambers was not improving, but this time, I was going to make a real effort to explore as many avenues and options that were available in my ongoing quest to achieve professional stability and longevity that seemed to constantly elude me. I was willing to try anything that was worth pursuing in the hope that it would bring about a real and positive long lasting transformation in my fortunes. Over the next three to four months, I endeavoured to put this new proactive approach into practice, an approach ranged from, making active enquiries that resulted in firstly requesting, then filling in, application forms with a view to seeking employment working for local authorities or government departments, to actually going as far as applying to the Lord Chancellor's Department to become a part time judge, and while in this latter instance, my application ultimately turned out to be an unsuccessful one, that application surprisingly got further than I thought possible. Out of all the options, the one that I actively pursued and persevered with, was my decision in March 2000 to enrol on an intensive two month course at the BPP Law School in Holborn that would result in me taking The Qualifying Legal Transfer Test (QLTT) which, if I passed successfully, would enable me to re-qualify as a solicitor. Out of all the options that I was actively pursuing at the time, It was by far the best option available for the simple reason that if it came to the point that there really was no future for me at the bar, then at least by qualifying and retraining as a solicitor, I would still be able to remain as a lawyer in every sense of the word as opposed to the nightmare scenario, of not being in the legal profession at all. Once again for the umpteenth time, I had reached an important crossroads in my chequered professional career and if I was going to succeed in my efforts of securing a real future, then over the next couple of months I was going to have to really work hard, giving total commitment to my attendance on the course and totally commit myself to the requisite preparation and study. Anything less than those minimum requirements would not only result in failure, it would in all probability, be the *coup de grace* both to my career and my confidence; a devastating blow from which it would be extremely difficult to recover from.

The course was open to all qualified lawyers who practiced either in the UK or other foreign jurisdictions. However, in order to be eligible to sit the test, all candidates had to obtain from the Solicitors Regulation Authority, a Certificate of Eligibility, a certificate, that would determine the subjects the candidate would be examined on which were, Property, Litigation, Professional Conduct and Accounts and The Principles of Common Law. The course itself consisted of three lectures lasting three hours each on a designated Saturday that were evenly spread over the duration of two and a half months. A student could apply to sit the examinations either in June or September and a candidate had to achieve a minimum target score of fifty per cent to successfully pass the paper they were being examined on. If a candidate passed all the requisite papers as determined by their individual Certificate of Eligibility, then it would only be valid for a period of three years.

I applied for and received my Certificate of Eligibility through the post before I began the course in earnest and I was only required to sit the Professional Conduct and Accounts exam paper because I had already passed the principal core subjects on the course when I sat the bar finals exams sixteen years ago. That stroke of good fortune in only being required to sit one exam didn't automatically mean I was going to have an easy time on the QLTT, on the contrary. If anything, I was going to have my work cut out for me to pass the exam, especially the Accountancy module. I could hardly describe myself as an individual who had an aptitude or a knack for numeracy or figures and as this would be the first time that I have studied such a daunting subject, I knew from the outset that I would be facing an extremely difficult challenge, but I also knew it was a challenge, given what was at stake, that I was more than capable of meeting.

It felt slightly surreal that after nearly sixteen years since I sat the last of my examination papers for the bar exams and previously having taught for over fourteen years as a part-time lecturer at Hackney College, I was reprising the role of an eager, willing to learn student, but as the old adage says, "you never stop learning irrespective of your age or circumstance" and myself, together with my other fellow students were there for that very reason. That first lecture aside from being interesting and informative, also provided a real insight into the amount of hard work and effort that I would have to put in away from the lectures theatre, the message that resonated loud and clear from the lectures was that the more you practiced the important and relevant accountancy techniques required to pass the exams, the more comfortable and familiar you will be with them and it would be only a matter of time before those principles and techniques become second nature.

Despite my lecturer's sound advice as to how I should approach the course, it could not completely overcome my irrational dislike for, or subdue my general lack of confidence in, all things numerical. I was going to need a great deal of help and assistance from people who were specialists in this field, people that I knew and could trust in helping me overcome these real difficulties. Fortunately for me, that unconditional assistance and support was readily available firstly, in the form of my Accountant of some eight years standing, Maureen Penfold, whose accountancy firm, Kingston Smith, had been preparing my annual accounts and VAT returns ever since I have been in private practice. When I told Maureen that I was studying Accounts as part of my attempts to re-qualify as a solicitor, she didn't hesitate in offering her assistance readily giving up her free time for a couple of hours on a Saturday teaching me accountancy techniques and practice that was invaluable in helping prepare me for the final written exam. Another source of help and assistance came from another good friend and long time acquaintance, Dele Ogun, a person who I have known since our undergraduate days at the Polytechnic of North London back in the early 1980's. Dele was a year below me at PNL, but he was one of the brightest and unassuming students throughout the entire Law Faculty. Although he passed the bar finals in 1985, he decided against forging a career at the bar, enrolling instead to sit and obtain qualifications in Accountancy before going on to re-qualify as a solicitor and by the year 2000, he had managed to build up a very successful practice based on the City Road. When I approached Dele for assistance, he too was more than willing to help me with getting to grips with the principles of Accountancy. He invited me to his home in Mill Hill and like Maureen, showed extraordinary understanding and patience during our one to one tuition seminars as I struggled to digest and comprehend the accountancy techniques and practices that I needed to know. It took some time admittedly, for the proverbial penny to drop despite the expert tuition I was receiving but gradually over time, the accountancy techniques, rules and practices that I needed to understand and master were becoming more and more easy, with each passing lecture at the BPP and the one to one seminars sessions with Maureen and Dele, all made possible because I took on board the sound advice of the people who were teaching me. The more I practiced those accountancy techniques and practices, the more I understood and the more I understood, the more confident I was becoming in my belief that I could do well in the forthcoming exams.

After I attended the second of the scheduled course lectures sometime in mid April, the course providers sent out the timetable for the forthcoming examinations and as if destiny or fate had ordained it, the date set for my one and only exam was on Friday the 2nd of June 2000 at 2pm, my fortieth birthday! I never thought in a million years that I would have to spend such an important milestone sitting an exam. I had always envisaged spending my fortieth birthday lying on some exotic beach, or throwing a massive outlandish party like the one I had in celebration of my thirtieth birthday at a time when my career appeared to be flying high. But just like Icarus in Greek Mythology, I had fallen from those lofty heights and, passing that solitary Accountancy and Professional Ethics paper offered me one last shot at redemption. The 2nd of June 2000 was going to be a day that would have a much greater significance for me than a mere milestone in my life. It was going to be a day that would either signal the start of a bright new beginning or confirm that the slow and gradual decline that I have endured over the last few years have reached the point of no return, with a once promising future firmly behind me.

I woke up early on the morning of my fortieth birthday excited by the prospect of the day that lay ahead of me. My bed was covered with the books and revision notes I was pouring over the previous evening and I intended to do some further revision prior to having a nice long celebratory birthday soak in the bath before getting myself ready and mentally prepared for my three hour exam later that afternoon. Those immediate plans had to be put on hold temporarily due to the succession of telephone calls that I received from family and friends wishing me a happy birthday and, in some cases, wishing me the best of luck for my forthcoming exam. The calls were matched by the countless number of birthday cards that greeted me on the doormat when I eventually went downstairs, a sight that caused me to break out in the broadest of smiles and as I gathered the pile of cards, I decided, despite my obvious delight, that now would not be the time to open them. I decided to wait until after I had returned home from sitting my exam later that evening when I would have all the time in the world to relax and celebrate.

Just a little after half past twelve in the afternoon, I declared myself finally ready and fully prepared for whatever may lay in store and I left my home a few minutes later, carrying my bag that contained all my revision notes and materials. I strolled leisurely along the length of my road enjoying the sun's warm summer rays penetrating the pores of my skin in a state of relaxed contentment. Once I arrived at the BPP Law College, the adrenalin that had laid dormant in my body started to rise a little. I tried to calm my nerves and made my way to the examination hall where we were given permission to enter and sit at a desk of our own choosing. Once all the candidates were seated and settled in their seats, the principal invigilator gave a short address concerning the rules that would apply throughout the three hour examination and it was at that point I felt another adrenalin surge, a surge of the type that I have not felt or experienced since I sat the last of my exams sixteen years ago. I was practically bursting with curiosity in wanting to know what questions were on the face down test paper and the waiting seemed to last an eternity before finally, the invigilator uttered the words I hadn't heard since my days as a law student, "Your time starts now," a forthright command that was immediately followed by the synchronised rustling of test papers being turned over in unison that would finally reveal its tantalising secrets.

I took my time reading every one of the questions with care, and I was fairly confident that I could answer four questions within the designated three hours. All my preparation, hard work and planning stood me in good stead, as my methodical approach to answering each of the four questions in turn meant that I was comfortably inside the average time of allowing forty five minutes to answer each question. By the time the exam invigilator announced that there were only five minutes left before all candidates had to stop writing, I used that precious time to read over my whole answer sheet, checking for any spelling mistakes and correcting any grammatical errors and when the final instruction was given by the invigilator to stop writing, I was more than satisfied with my efforts. I rose from my desk along with the other candidates and left the Examination Hall pleased that I had given my all and now I was looking forward to enjoying what was left of my birthday.

As I had nothing specifically planned to mark my birthday, I thought I was going to have a quiet, relaxing evening, but those plans were altered on account of a telephone call that I received from one of my closest friends, Lenworth Hodge (affectionately known as "Len") who told me that he was picking me up at around 8.30pm to take me for a birthday drink at The Iron Bar in Ladbroke Grove. I was initially reluctant to go at first as all I wanted to do was relax and stay at home, but Len was not the type of person to take no for an answer and true to form, he picked me up and took me to the wine bar that on a typical Friday night was packed to the rafters. After we entered the wine bar, Len told me to head upstairs. I did so and, as I reached the top floor, to my complete and utter surprise, there waiting for me was a table of more than twenty of my closest friends who were in on the conspiracy to hold a surprise birthday party in my honour. For once, I was totally gobsmacked and truly touched and I couldn't have asked for a better way to mark the occasion. The exam that I had sat only a few hours ago, as well as all the months of constant stress and endless worry in preparation for that exam, seemed to be nothing more than a distant memory and by the end of the evening when I was in bed lying awake reflecting on my momentous and landmark day, my last thoughts before I eventually closed my eyes for the night was, despite all my ups and downs, I am grateful that the man upstairs had seen to it that I reached such an important milestone and despite the ups and downs that I have been through, life really can begin at the age of forty.

My results came out in the last week in July. I had been fairly confident that all would be well, but as the time drew closer, small nagging doubts began to gradually dominate my thoughts and grew to such an extent, that I seriously started to question whether all that initial self-confidence about the outcome was totally misplaced. It didn't take long during this agonising period of self-doubt before I began to cast my thoughts back in time to my student undergraduate days of the late 1970's and the torturous agonies I would put myself through waiting for the letter to arrive that contained the examination results and remembering all too well, the crushing sense of bitter disappointment when on a couple of those occasions, I failed to achieve the grade I was hoping for. The gut wrenching suspense I was putting myself through as I waited for the result to arrive equalled the sheer torture of the past and I had reached the point where I was desperate to know my fate one way or the other. When at last the letter arrived, it was the first thing that I noticed once I got inside my front door from work and almost immediately, my heart began beating at breakneck speed. I picked up the envelope from the hallway table and I nervously peeled away at the envelope's stick flap and retrieved the letter that was contained inside. I opened the envelope the contents of which revealed the following information:

LAW SCHOOL

67-69 Lincoln's Inn Fields
London WC2A 3JB
Tel: 020 7430 2304
Fax: 020 7404 1389

BPP Professional Development
Fax: 020 7831 4561

DX 35719 Bloomsbury 1
e-mail: law@bpp.com
web site address: www.bpp.com

Mr Shaun Wallace

24 July 2000

Dear Mr Wallace,

Our Ref: 1696

Qualified Lawyers Transfer Test Examination Result

I am delighted to inform you that you have passed the QLTT Professional Conduct & Accounts Exam exam sat with BPP on 2-JUN-00.

The grade you achieved was B.

The grades awarded for this examination are as follows;

A	70%+	Pass
B	60 – 69%	Pass
C	50 – 59%	Pass
F1	45 – 49%	Fail
F2	40 – 44%	Fail
F3	39% and below	Fail

Yours sincerely

Ruth Cohen
Professional Courses Manager

I underwent a mixture of shock, surprise, relief and unrestrained joy when I read the letter's contents. The result was the perfect belated birthday present and a vindication of all the dedication and hard work that I had put in that made the result possible. It was an achievement that ranked alongside my passing the bar finals exams over sixteen years ago. Now that I had passed the QLTT exam, I had to ask myself: what was going to be my next move? Do I make the career switch and become a solicitor where, at the very least, I would have the elusive job stability and security that I've always craved not forgetting, a regular income, even though making such a choice would mean sacrificing control of my own destiny? Or secondly, do I remain at the bar where, despite my fluctuating fortunes, I still believed wholeheartedly, I would eventually be successful? Having those two concrete career options at my disposal was, for once, a nice dilemma to be in, but my choice ultimately, was not a difficult one to make. I chose a reaffirmation and rededication of my childhood ambition that was consecrated by the solemn promise that I made to myself on the day I was called to the bar. I am a barrister first and foremost and despite the welcome boost to my confidence that passing the QLTT exam had given me, unless or until being a practicing barrister really was no longer a possible or viable option, it was my steadfast wish and desire to remain a practicing member of the bar for the rest of my days.

Although my TV quizzing ambitions had been put on the back burner for a while as I tried to sort out the ongoing problems and difficulties that were besetting my legal career, my passion for TV quiz shows and quizzing generally still burned brightly as ever. In between my studies in preparation for the QLTT exam, the normal way I would relax and unwind usually revolved around watching recordings of my favourite TV quiz on my trusty VCR for viewing late at night. I even managed to find the time to occasionally play in a pub quiz team that was put together by my old friend Nipper. The team consisted of some of Nipper's closest friends who I also was friendly with, Patrick "Stan" Bowles (his nickname "Stan" was in homage to the maverick Queen's Park Rangers footballing legend of the 1970's), John "John Boy" Leigh, Michael "Colesy" Collins and last, but by no means least, Robert Harding. Nipper, who was the self-appointed leader of the quiz team made no secret as to the reason why I was recruited to be a part of the team because so far as he was concerned, my general knowledge was a cut above most of the teams that were competing in the quiz. Nipper was desperate for a change in the team's fortunes as the team's repeated attempts to win the modest top prize of thirty pounds had so far eluded them and he believed that my very presence within the team could make all the difference. He was spot on course! The team would win more often than not after I had joined them and although invariably, I supplied the vast majority of the correct answers during the quiz, it would be completely wide of the mark for me to suggest that the team's make up consisted of one stand out player, plus the others (even though there were times that it may have felt that way!) as there were many an occasion when some of my team mates, especially Stan and John Boy, would come up with answers to questions that I didn't know, answers that, undoubtedly, were the difference between the team winning and losing. Winning that cash prize was of no less importance to me than it was to my teammates, but that wasn't the sole reason why I agreed to take part in the quiz alongside them. Above all else, my motivation for taking part was the thrill of the competition, being able to use all my quizzing skills and knowledge when competing that had one sole objective, winning, being number one, and if there was a tangible prize on offer for being the top dog, whether that prize was big or small, then that was just a mere welcome bonus. It is the winning that counts and winning, as any truly competitive individual will tell you, is priceless!

All that involvement in competitive pub quizzing whetted my appetite and desire to return to the world of competitive TV quizzing and the show that I had my sights firmly set on was the quiz show whose popularity had gone stratospheric since it hit the television screens in the summer of 2000, *The Weakest Link* hosted by the acerbically acid tongued, Anne Robinson.

I first became aware of the show's existence sometime in late May 2000 when I was contacted by a production team of the BBC inviting me to take part in a pilot for the show, but I had to decline the invitation as all my energies and focus was solely concentrated on preparing for the QLTT exam. The show was an instant hit and there wasn't a day that went by in its early infancy when *The Weakest Link* wasn't being talked about either in the popular press, or by the ordinary person in the street uttering Anne Robinson's dismissive popular catchphrase after a contestant had been eliminated, "YOU ARE THE WEAKEST LINK, GOODBYE!" It was at least a good six or so months of constantly watching the programme, together with my usual act of prevarication, before I finally decided that I was going to apply to appear on the show.

I didn't have to wait too long before I received a reply and I was invited to attend an audition which was being held in Wells Street Central London in December 2000. Well over sixty people had turned up for the audition which took the form of a written test paper and then playing a mock rehearsal of the game that lasted for about fifteen or so minutes. I managed to score a fairly impressive nineteen out of twenty five on the written test paper and faired even better in the mock rehearsal and a few days later, I received a letter from production team informing me that I would be invited to take part in the show. Naturally, I was overjoyed by the news, but that news got even better when a couple of days before I was due to attend the recording, I received an unexpected call from the show's production team who told me that instead of appearing on their normal weekday programme, they wanted me to take part in one of their prime time midweek specials in front of a studio audience where the prize fund would be increased from its normal £10,000 to £20,000!

I was required to attend the BBC TV Studios on Wood Lane on the 12th of February 2001 for the recording of the show that was scheduled to commence at 7pm. Because I wasn't required to be at the BBC studios in Wood Lane until 6pm, an hour or so before the scheduled recording time, I had virtually the whole day to get myself mentally prepared for the challenge that lay ahead of me. Once I had dealt with a couple of quick matters in court that were concluded well before lunchtime, the rest of the day was mine which enabled me to do all the little, but important things, that would play a vital role my preparation for the show for instance, stopping off at Michael's Shoe Repairs in Holborn to see my close friend, George Papageorgeiou or Goggsy as he's affectionately known, so that he would give the shoes that I would be wearing a last minute pristine polish before heading for my local Drycleaners, Orbit on the Wembley High Road to collect the clothes I was intending to wear. After arriving back home mid-afternoon, I started to go through the long and arduous process of pulling out my hair from its spiky dreadlocks as I wanted to wash it before going to my appointment at 4pm at the home of my hairdresser, Nadine Parris. Nadine was excellent when it came to creating original and different styles and she was the only person that I would let anywhere near styling my hair at the time, but to my absolute horror and despair, when I knocked on her front door for my 4pm appointment with her, she was not at home. I went into a state of complete panic. After I had pulled out the plaits my hair resembled that of an unkempt, overgrown, petrified forest and I couldn't think of any hair stylist off hand who had either the skill or the expertise to make my hair look presentable. With time slowly ticking away before I was required at the studio, I began to weigh up my options and I decided that instead of going to a local hair salon, I headed towards the Goldhawk Road just off Shepherd's Bush Green, less than a mile away from the BBC studios for an emergency visit to see my close friend and erstwhile barber, Jeffrey Walters, at his Headlines 2000 Barber salon and virtually pleaded with him to do something with my hair, anything that would prevent me from becoming a laughing stock on national television. Jeffrey's remedy was to cut off a fair few inches off the top of my hair, much to my considerable anguish and settled on my old signature flat top hair style that I had consigned to the past. Whilst I wasn't exactly enamoured at the thought of a return to my old look, I was grateful for the fact that at least my hair looked presentable for my impending TV date and thanked Jeffrey profusely for sparing me the ultimate humiliation of a bad hair day disaster.

I walked the short distance along the Goldhawk Road via Shepherds Bush Green towards Wood Lane struggling with a bag that contained a load of quiz books precariously balanced on one shoulder and my dry cleaned clothes in my other hand. Just before I arrived at the studio, I noticed a queue beginning to form of the audience who were going to watch the recording that I was going to appear in and waiting patiently in that queue was my Father, courtesy of the ticket I had requested from the show's production team. Dad was an avid follower of the programme and when I told him that I could get him a ticket to watch me appear on the show he was, to use the hackneyed cliché, "over the moon". I called out to him and as soon as he saw me, he became really excited, excited not just at the prospect of being in the audience of one of his favourite TV shows, but also by the fact that he was going to be witnessing his eldest son actually take part in the show which I'm sure, filled him with an immense sense of pride.

I eventually arrived inside the studio's main entrance and once inside, I was immediately greeted by a member of the show's production team who had been waiting around in the foyer area, together with some of my fellow contestants who had already arrived. Once all the contestants were present, our first port of call was to be escorted to our respective dressing rooms so that we could deposit our belongings before we were taken to the green room, the same green room that is featured in the show's opening titles. Once all eight of us had more or less settled in the green room, it didn't take long before we all began chatting amongst ourselves, getting to know one another, in a convivial atmosphere that was relaxed and friendly. During the course of those friendly discussions, my attention was drawn to the small TV monitor perched on the wall as it was showing the final stages of the recording that was taking place before our show at the point where the two remaining contestants were about to embark on the five question shoot out to determine the overall winner. I was particularly interested in the outcome of that final showdown because one of those two competing finalists was a young woman called Emma who was at the same December auditions that I attended. Emma and I got on quite well at that audition and I remember her telling me that she worked as a Barmaid at the time and that she had a passion and fondness for competing in quizzes, a passion that was clearly evident by her impressive performance in having made it all the way to the final five question shootout, a performance I hasten to add, given her equally impressive performance at the December auditions, that came as no surprise. Unfortunately for Emma though, she lost the final and after the recording had finished, both her and the eventual winner joined us in the green room. Once inside the room, Emma immediately recognised me and I gave her a consolation hug, which given the huge disparity in our respective sizes, meant that she had to get on her tiptoes in order to make such a feat possible. I told her that she performed brilliantly and was very unlucky to lose. She responded by shrugging her shoulders before replying, "That's life!" Despite her obvious disappointment in not going all the way, Emma then went on to say that she was pleased with her efforts and proud to have reached the final. With one final hug, we said our final goodbyes and she wished me good luck before making her way to the dressing room, our paths sadly, unlikely to ever cross again. It wasn't going to be that long now before myself and my fellow competitors were going to be escorted into the glare of the studio's bright lights, a live studio audience and having to face being questioned by one of the most daunting and fearsome of all quiz hosts, Anne Robinson, the self-styled "Queen of Mean."

All eight of us were escorted into the studio and directed to stand behind to our respective podiums on the set. As we all stood patiently at our respective podiums waiting for the show's host to make her entrance, our respective levels of nerves and tension had undoubtedly, began to increase a little and as we were being wired for sound, Anne Robinson finally made her entrance into the set dressed in her trademark satanic black outfit. Before taking her place at her podium in the middle, Anne briefly spoke to us in a very friendly and pleasant manner but once those pleasantries were dispensed with, she seemed to undergo a complete transformation morphing into her on stage persona the moment she received her cue from the Studio Floor Manager as she fixed her steely glare into the camera.

"ANY OF THE PEOPLE STANDING BEHIND ME IN THE STUDIO THIS EVENING CAN WIN UP TO £20,000. THEY DON'T KNOW EACH OTHER, HOWEVER, IF THEY WANT THE PRIZE MONEY, THEY HAVE TO WORK AS A TEAM. BUT SEVEN OF THEM WILL LEAVE WITH NOTHING AS ROUND BY ROUND WE

LOSE THE PLAYER VOTED THE WEAKEST LINK! LET'S MEET THE TEAM."

My fellow opponents in the team were as follows: on the first podium was Craig, aged twenty five, a teacher from Bedford. On podium number two was Myra, aged sixty two, a retired teacher from Conway in North Wales. Next to Myra at podium number three, was Glyn, aged thirty, a Hotel Consultant from Colchester. On podium number four was Susan, aged twenty six, a Research Assistant from Cumbria. I stood next to Susan on podium number five, introducing myself as a forty year old Lawyer and part time Lecturer from Wembley. To my left on podium number six was Linda, aged thirty nine who worked as an Accountant in Belfast. On podium number seven, was Peter aged sixty eight, a retired Freelance Stage Manager from Horsham in Sussex, and last but no means least, at podium number eight was Liz aged forty three, who was employed as a Local Government Officer from Morpeth in Northumberland. After we had all introduced ourselves, the Queen of Mean then went on to explain the rules of the show.

"IN EACH ROUND, THE AIM IS TO ANSWER ENOUGH QUESTIONS CORRECTLY TO REACH THE £2,500 TARGET WITHIN THE TIME LIMIT. THE FASTEST WAY IS TO CREATE A CHAIN OF EIGHT CORRECT ANSWERS. IF THERE IS AN INCORRECT ANSWER THEN THE CHAIN IS BROKEN AND ALL THE MONEY IN THAT CHAIN WILL BE LOST. BUT IF A CONTESTANT SAYS "BANK", THEN THE MONEY IN THAT CHAIN IS SAFE AND IS CARRIED FORWARD AND A NEW CHAIN IS STARTED FROM SCRATCH. AT THE END OF THE ROUND, ONLY MONEY THAT IS BANKED WILL BE CARRIED FORWARD. THE TIME FOR THE FIRST ROUND IS TWO MINUTES AND THIRTY SECONDS AND AFTER EACH ROUND TEN SECONDS IS DEDUCTED FROM THE TIME. THE FIRST CONTESTANT IS THE ONE WHOSE NAME IS FIRST ALPHABETICALLY, WHICH MEANS THAT CRAIG YOU FACE THE FIRST QUESTION. START THE CLOCK.."

The first two questions were answered correctly in turn firstly by Craig and then by Myra, but the chain was unfortunately broken when Glyn got his first question wrong. Susan was next in line to face her first question which she managed to answer with consummate ease before Anne turned her attentions in my direction. Despite the team managing to answer three out of the four questions asked correctly, Glyn's incorrect answer in the middle of that sequence of questions meant that the team had not built a decent enough chain of correct answers and as I faced my first question, it was imperative that I answered that question correctly in order to help the team start to build that chain.

"SHAUN, COMPLETE THE TITLE OF THE 1969 HIT BY MARVIN GAYE I HEARD IT THROUGH THE…?"

Without any hesitation, I immediately answered, "GRAPEVINE." I was pleased as well as relieved to have been asked such a relatively straightforward question as it went a long way to settling the inner tension and nerves that I was feeling before the show. The team had now started to build a tidy sum with three successive correct answers in a row and just before Craig faced his question, he sensibly banked the accumulated sum on the money chain that at that point, had reached £1,000. The chain then began again with Glyn who finally managed to open his account with his correct answer of Bob Geldof to the question that asked him for the name of the lead singer of the Boomtown Rats. Susan's subsequent correct answer to her question meant that the money chain had now reached the sum of £500, a sum that tactically, I elected to safely bank before I faced my second question.

"SHAUN, IN MEDIEVAL LEGEND, THE CHALICE USED BY CHRIST IN THE LAST SUPPER WAS KNOWN AS THE HOLY WHAT?"

"GRAIL," I replied with the ever increasing confidence of a player who was beginning to feel more and more comfortable and at ease not only with the glaring bright lights of the studio, but with the competition as a whole. Linda, Peter and Liz also gave correct answers to their questions, building up another healthy chain which Craig again sensibly banked thus adding an additional £500 into the pot which brought the sum of money banked to a very respectable figure of £2,000 only £500 short of the maximum target. It was a good job that Craig banked that £500 as he passed on the question that asked for the name of the shoe that shares its name with an animal similar to a donkey (the answer, for those who are not sure, a mule). That question may have seemed like an easy one to have passed on, but under the glare of the camera and lights, the presence of a studio audience, not forgetting, the pressure of being subjected to rapid, quick fire questions from a formidable and daunting quiz presenter like Anne Robinson, it's easy to get even the simplest question wrong. With only seconds to go until the end of the round, Glyn once again, answered another of his designated questions incorrectly after which, a short piece of the show's music denoting the end of the round resonated throughout the studio thus depriving me of the chance to answer the question that Anne was about to ask me.

Anne informed the team that we won £2,000 in that first round and despite being only £500 short of the maximum target of £2,500, her subsequent observations and comments left the team in no doubt, that she was less than suitably impressed.

"WHO CAN'T COPE WITH THE PRESSURE? WHO IS OUT OF THEIR DEPTH EVEN AT THIS EARLY STAGE? THIS IS AN OPPORTUNITY NOW TO SLING THE STUPID! AND DITCH THE DIMWIT. IT'S TIME TO VOTE OFF THE WEAKEST LINK."

All eight of us then set about the task of casting our votes which we were required to do by writing the name of the nominated candidate on the screen in front of our respective podium, as opposed to writing one's nomination on the oval board that is normally used in the weekday edition of the show. Once Anne had asked the team to reveal their nominations, the voting was unanimous with Glyn's name coming up on all the podiums save for his own.

"TEAM, IN THAT FIRST ROUND YOU ANSWERED THIRTEEN CORRECT QUESTIONS IN A ROW WHICH MEANT THAT YOU COULD HAVE EASILY REACHED YOUR TARGET IF YOU HAD BANKED INTELLIGENTLY AND STAYED AWAKE!"

The only person other than Glyn to be nominated was Myra, but the first member of the team to feel the full force of Anne's acerbic put downs was Craig. Craig to his credit, remained calm in the face of such a relentless onslaught before giving his reasons why he voted for Glyn which was because he got two questions wrong. Anne then turned her attentions to Liz who, despite trying her level best to keep as low a profile as possible, was failing miserably with those efforts and she echoed Craig's reasons for nominating Glyn. Finally, Anne turned her steely gaze towards the unfortunate Glyn.

"HOW EMBARRASSING!" she haughtily declared. "DID YOU COME TO THE RIGHT STUDIO?" she asked him in a cruel, teasing manner, a remark that raised titters of laughter from the watching studio audience. "I THINK IT'S PRETTY UNANIMOUS. I THINK WITH SEVEN VOTES YOU OUGHT TO GO. YOU ARE THE WEAKEST LINK, GOOD BYE!"

Glyn wandered off past Anne towards the camera on that dreaded Walk of Shame, back to the green room where all of the discarded weakest links would record their final piece to camera in a short, concise utterance about their experience on the show.

"ROUND TWO, £2,000 IN THE BANK OUT OF A POSSIBLE £2,500. SEVEN OF YOU LEFT AND WE ARE NOW TAKING TEN SECONDS OFF THE CLOCK. WE'LL START WITH THE STRONGEST LINK THE ROUND – THAT'S YOU SUSAN! – LET'S PLAY THE WEAKEST LINK – START THE CLOCK!"

Susan had answered her designated question without any difficulty and now it was my turn.

"SHAUN – COMPLETE THE TITLE OF THE E. NESBIT NOVEL PUBLISHED IN 1910, THE RAILWAY...?"

"CHILDREN," was my immediate positive response to another relatively straight forward question. Linda and Peter who followed me, also answered their respective question correctly before Anne swivelled her podium in the direction of Liz who sensibly decided to bank the accumulated sum of £500 before facing her question, a decision that turned out to be a wise choice on account of the complete *faux pas that* she made in attempting to answer what on the face of it, appeared to be a relatively simple arithmetic question.

"LIZ, IF THERE ARE SIX GLASSES IN ONE BOTTLE, HOW MANY ARE THERE IN TWELVE BOTTLES?" (the answer of course being 72). Liz's incorrect answer was the beginning of the start of a run of incorrect answers when first Craig, then Myra, also got their questions wrong. Susan mercifully, broke that mini sequence of incorrect answers to continue her impressive start to the game and I decided, given the nature of the poor start that the team had made to the round, to take no unnecessary chances and banked the sum of money from Susan's correct answer which sadly, only yielded £50 before facing my next question.

"SHAUN, COMPLETE THE NAME OF THIS CHILDREN'S PARTY GAME: PIN THE TAIL ON THE...?"

"DONKEY." Although I was pleased that I was matching Susan's 100% success rate of correct answers, I was under no illusion that the nature and standard of the questions would be just as easy and straightforward as the rounds progressed. In acknowledging that fact, it didn't mean that there would be any change in terms of strategy so far as my own overall game plan was concerned, a game plan that was as simple as it was straightforward and that was, when facing a question, make sure that you answer it correctly! There was a subsequent chain of three correct answers after my own, but that successful run was eventually broken by Craig with an incorrect answer that cost the team £500 when he went the wrong way on one of those horrible 50/50 type questions, by not knowing that plants do in fact, secrete hormones. Both Myra and Susan answered their respective questions correctly in their efforts to rebuild the money chain before once again, it was my turn.

"SHAUN, AS WELL AS BEING PART OF THE HUMAN BODY WHAT WORD DESCRIBES THE CALM AREA AT THE CENTRE OF A HURRICANE?"

"EYE." There appeared to be just enough time for the team to face another round of questions, but as I looked up at the studio clock, I noticed that there was only a couple of seconds left before the end of the round. Ann was about to ask me another question, but instead of waiting for her to complete the question, I shouted the word, "BANK", a decision which earned the team a further £100. The total amount that would be carried over to the next round was £950, a figure Anne described when she reviewed the team's performance in that round with one solitary word: DISAPPOINTING!

"WHO, QUITE FRANKLY, SHOULD NEVER HAVE VOLUNTEERED TO BE HERE TONIGHT? WHO HAS GONE FROM DIM TO DIMMEST? TIME TO VOTE OFF THE WEAKEST LINK."

The nominations by the team to vote off the weakest link for this round were as follows; Craig voted for Myra, Myra voted for Craig. Susan voted for Linda. Myself, Peter and Liz voted for Craig and finally Linda voted for Peter. Once we had declared our votes, Anne then turned her steely gaze in my direction.

"SHAUN, HOW'S IT GOING FOR YOU?"

My own risible attempt to remain under the radar to avoid Anne Robinson's legendary verbal putdowns had failed miserably and in a somewhat muted tone I responded, "I could be doing better than I am..."

Fortunately for me, Anne's response to my deliberately muted reply was neither harsh or insulting when she said, "YOU'RE HUMBLE AT LEAST, WHY CRAIG?"

Again trying to maintain a softly spoken, humble demeanour I responded, "I thought that he was a bit unfortunate with the questions that he got!"

"IS HE STUPID?" she asked, trying her level best to goad me into saying something disparaging to a contestant who was about to be ejected, but I wouldn't rise to the bait and I said, "NO!" and reinforced that view by means of shaking my head before Craig as with all the weakest links at the end of a round, was unceremoniously ejected from the show.

"ROUND THREE, OUT OF A POSSIBLE £5,000 YOU HAVE £2,950 IN THE BANK, AND WE'RE DOWN TO SIX PLAYERS! THERE ARE TEN SECONDS COMING OFF THE CLOCK, GIVING YOU TWO MINUTES AND TEN SECONDS. WE'LL START WITH THE STRONGEST LINK, THAT'S YOU, SUSAN. LET'S PLAY THE WEAKEST LINK".

Susan once again was the strongest link for the second time in the contest but on this occasion, she got off to an unexpected bad start by answering her first question in the round incorrectly. I was next in line.

"SHAUN, COMPLETE THE TITLE OF THE SHAKESPEARE PLAY LOVE'S LABOUR'S...?"

"LOST!" I replied with confident ease. Linda, Peter and Liz also got their questions right thus making four correct answers in a row, which meant that the prize fund was now up to £1,000. However, Myra broke the money chain and as a consequence, lost the money earned with a costly incorrect answer. Susan then managed to regain her impressive form with another correct answer before I faced the next question.

"SHAUN, IN WHICH FICTIONAL, SMALL AMERICAN TOWN IS THE 1987 FILM ABOUT THREE WITCHES SET?"

"EASTWICK." There was no doubting the fact that the questions and answers were falling my way and even though I was playing very well up to that point in the game, there was also the added danger that I was making a rod for my own back in that my fellow competitors would probably see me as the player to beat and would not hesitate in seizing on the opportunity to vote me off the show were I to make even the slightest mistake.

When Linda answered the next question incorrectly, I was now the only member of the team not to have got a question wrong and as the round progressed, the performance of the remaining members of the team fluctuated between the sublime and the downright ridiculous particularly, the previously impressive Susan whose indifferent performance in that round made her extremely vulnerable to the threat of ejection as once again, she answered a question incorrectly. Matching Susan in the vulnerability stakes though was Myra, who, despite banking £200 during the round, had also answered two of the questions she faced incorrectly, the last of those incorrect questions resulting in the team losing another £500. In stark contrast to the rest of the team, I appeared to be having no such difficulties as I prepared to face my final question in the round.

"SHAUN, THE 27th OF FEBRUARY 2000, MARKED THE ONE HUNDRETH ANNIVERSARY OF WHICH UK POLICITAL PARTY?" to which I replied, "THE LABOUR PARTY," for my eighth correct answer in a row.

At the end of that third round, Anne's comments were very scathing   indeed.
"YOU UTTERLY EXCELLED YOURSELVES! YOU BANKED A PATHETIC £350! I URGE YOU, LIGHTEN THE LOAD, DROP THE DUNCE, DITCH THE DEADWOOD! YOU NEED TO BE RUTHLESS TO BE RICH. TIME TO VOTE OFF THE WEAKEST LINK!"

The team's nomination for the weakest link in that round were as follows; Myra voted for Liz, Susan in turn voted for Myra, I voted for Liz, and the remaining members of the team all voted Myra.

Anne turned her attentions to Susan and as usual, did not hold back in her critical put down of her performance in that round. "HAD YOU SIMPLY WANDERED OFF IN THAT ROUND?" Susan quite sensibly, was in no position to argue and readily accepted Anne's scathing assessment, conceding that her overall performance in that round was poor, but argued with some justification, that her performance was no better or worse, than Myra's. Anne then fixed her steely gaze on Myra, teasing her incessantly about her earlier reference to having recently become a member of her local historical society. "WELL," Anne said mockingly, "THE HISTORICAL SOCIETY IS GOING TO HAVE ITS WORK CUT OUT." a reference no doubt, to the number of history questions that Myra answered incorrectly during her time on the show and with her fate sealed, she became the third member of the team about to embark on the Walk of Shame.

"ROUND FOUR. IN THE BANK THERE IS £3,300 OUT OF A POTENTIAL £7,500. THERE ARE FIVE OF YOU LEFT. IN YOUR WISDOM, YOU HAVE CLEARED ONE SIDE OF THE SEMI-CIRCLE. WE ARE NOW TAKING ANOTHER TEN SECONDS OFF THE CLOCK. WE'LL START WITH THE STRONGEST LINK, THAT'S SHAUN. LET'S PLAY THE WEAKEST LINK, START THE CLOCK"

"SHAUN, ARE THE ISLANDS OF IONA AND STAFFA SITUATED OFF THE COAST OF SCOTLAND, IRELAND OR WALES?"

"SCOTLAND!" was my correct reply that on this occasion was said with a tone laced with dismissive arrogance. There appeared to be no apparent weakness in my impressive quizzing armoury. With yet another correct answer in the bag, for a brief moment, I allowed myself momentarily, to harbour thoughts of distinct possibility of going through the entire show without getting a single question wrong. Counting one's chickens before they hatch though, especially in such a cut throat game like The Weakest Link, can be fatal if you're not careful and that was something that I was about to experience to my ultimate cost as I underwent a sudden and complete reversal of fortune.

"SHAUN, IN AUSTRAILIA, WHAT IS THE STATE CAPITAL OF VICTORIA?"

On the face of it, this should have been another routine question that I should have answered correctly, but for some inexplicable reason, I was gripped by hesitancy and confusion, and without really thinking, I blurted out the answer, "NEW SOUTH

WALES," which is another Australian State and not a State Capital. "NO", Anne replied tersely, "MELBOURNE." That was my first incorrect answer but unfortunately for me, I was the only person to give an incorrect answer up until that point in that round and for the first time in the game, I appeared to be vulnerable to the possibility of being nominated to be the next in line to be voted off. I didn't have to wait long before I faced my next question, my answer to which was a clear and unmistakable sign that my apparent aura of invincibility was gradually slipping away.

"SHAUN, IN MARINE BIOLOGY, BY WHAT NAME IS THE SEA STAR MORE COMMONLY KNOWN?"

Another question to be fair that could hardly be described as difficult, but the calm and composed manner that was an important feature of my game up to that point seemed to have deserted me completely and without giving any real thought to a question that clearly contained a subtle clue, I said the first thing that came into my head and blurted out the answer, "STINGRAY."

"STARFISH!" Anne replied in a sardonic tone.

My chances of remaining in the game were now hanging by the slenderest of threads and apart from Linda and Liz who each got their respective questions wrong, the remaining members of the team were answering their questions correctly. To even have a slither of a chance of progressing to the next round, I had to answer my final question within that round and hope that my previous strong performance would somehow keep me in the game.

"SHAUN, WHAT B IS A UK CITY THAT APPEARS IN THE SAME TITLE OF A BONEY M HIT?"

The game was now well and truly up for me as I didn't have a clue. I couldn't even draw on the inspiration of the fact that one of the female members of the Boney M line up had a sister who attended the same secondary school as me. I had to place my faith in the man upstairs and also rely on inspired guesswork and hope that somehow it would lead me to the right answer. "BIRMINGHAM," was my frantic, desperate reply but alas, the correct answer was Belfast. Only a few seconds remained before the two minutes had expired and the team had only managed to bank the relatively modest sum of £700. It didn't take long before feelings of utter dismay and disappointment began to surge right through me. I knew my time was up and like the condemned man awaiting the inevitable end whilst on the gallows, I prepared myself for the dreaded Walk of Shame.

"WHO NOW IS CLEARLY A PASSENGER? WHO IS TOO BEMUSED AND BEWILDERED FOR YOU TO HAVE ON THE TEAM ANY LONGER? IT'S TIME TO VOTE OFF THE WEAKEST LINK".

I could feel the eyes of my fellow team members firmly fixing their gaze in my direction, especially Peter who was making no attempt to disguise his intentions. As the team began the process of casting their votes, it didn't take a genius to work out that I was going to be the next in line to be voted off. Would my previous good performance save me? Not a hope in hell! As the team revealed their choices, it was no surprise that my name was the one unanimously selected for ejection and if the programme's rules would have allowed it, even I would have voted myself off the show, but my token vote for ejection for what it was worth, was for Liz.

Anne turned to Linda and asked her why she was voting for me. Linda replied that she was aware that I was getting my questions wrong and as a result, she had no money to bank. Anne seemed totally unconvinced with that reply. "IT'S ONLY THIS ROUND. SO IT WOULD BE QUITE GOOD FOR YOU TO GET RID OF HIM NOW!"

"Possibly, possibly." Linda frankly admitted.

Anne then turned to Liz and immediately set about the task of trying to undermine her confidence once more by reminding her of the simple arithmetic question she got wrong in the second round. Anne asked Liz what she did for a living, "a government officer," she replied somewhat sheepishly. "THAT'S ALL THE MORE WORRYING," Anne responded spitefully before going on to ask her why she was voting for me. Liz gave the same reasons as Linda which, given my lamentable performance, I could hardly disagree with.

Anne then fixed her steely gaze in my direction before going on to say, "SO SHAUN, SMILING IS NOT ONE OF YOUR HOBBIES IS IT?" seizing on the poker face persona that I attempted to maintain throughout the competition.

Her comment caused me to smile momentarily before I replied, "no, not really," as I braced myself for Anne's oncoming verbal onslaught before my inevitable ejection.

"OH, YOU'RE SMILING NOW. IT'S THE FIRST TIME I'VE SEEN YOU SMILE"

I replied, "Well I'm about to take the walk"

"YOU ARE INDEED. DID YOU JUST GIVE UP?" she enquired, sneering.

"No, I just had a poor round. It was unfortunate how the questions came, that's how it goes," I responded, trying to maintain my dignity whilst at the same time, adopting a resigned, philosophical approach to my impending demise.

Not content with that response, Anne then turned her attention to my old fashioned flat top hair style, "DID YOU HAVE YOUR HAIRCUT ESPECIALLY FOR THIS EVENING?"

I tried in vain to explain to her that my regular hairdresser was not available to do my hair in the style that I wanted, but that risible explanation sadly, fell on deaf ears. I was standing under the proverbial trap door that was soon about to give way.

"I THOUGHT THAT YOU WERE JUST FRIGHTENED," were Anne's final parting words and whilst I tried in vain to refute that suggestion, my remaining presence in the contest was finally over. "SHAUN, WITH FOUR VOTES, YOU ARE THE WEAKEST LINK, GOODBYE!"

With Anne's cruel dismissive words resonating in my ears, I began the dreaded Walk of Shame, trying to be as calm and dignified as I could. I walked off set towards the camera on my way to the green room for my individual piece to camera that ended up sounding like rambling, incoherent assessment on where it all went wrong for me.

"I was very disappointed because I thought I could win. But if you don't answer your questions, then you can't expect to win. I didn't answer my questions, it's as simple as that."

After my piece to camera, I joined Glyn, Craig and Myra and we were chatting about the game and our respective performances before collectively, we attempted to predict which of the remaining contestants would emerge victorious. The four of us were subsequently joined in the green room by Peter and finally, Liz leaving Susan and Linda to battle it out in the final five question showdown that Susan eventually won 4–2 and in the process, bagged herself a deserving £5,700.

I waited around in the green room for the plucky finalists to arrive to congratulate the pair of them on their performance, managing to exchange contact details with the runner up Linda in the process, before I finally left the green room to make my way back to my dressing room in order to pick up my belongings. As I was walking along the corridor, I saw my diminutive tormentor in chief, Anne Robinson, who in the absence of her on screen clothing, looked totally different and appeared to be in total wind down mode after her hectic three show recording schedule.

I went up to her and said, "Thanks Anne for a great time," and I bent down to give her a hug to which she willingly responded in kind.

"I thought you were going to win," she said as we ended our short embrace.

"So did I at one point, but that's the brakes," I ruefully replied before we both went our separate ways.

I finally left the BBC studios and met up with Dad who from his animated facial expression, clearly enjoyed the whole game show experience despite his initial disappointment that I did not win the contest. Nevertheless, Dad told me how proud he was of my performance and so far as he was concerned, the only reason I was voted off was because the other contestants considered me to be a threat. That may or may have not been the case, but it couldn't disguise the cold harsh reality of the situation. I answered three questions wrong in a row and that was the simple reason why I did not win. Despite my disappointment that once again, I had failed to live up to my own high expectations, I was nevertheless pleased that my overall performance on the show was a vast improvement on my previous two outings and that was something from which I could draw comfort from at the very least. There was no doubting the fact now that if I continued to show those continued levels of improvement, then it would only be a matter of time before I eventually landed that elusive win. That inaugural breakthrough might not be on the next show or even the show after that, but the one thing I was certain of was that it will happen one day.

I was at home one afternoon in early April of 2001, when I received an unexpected phone call out of the blue.

"Hello, is that Shaun Wallace?"

"Yes," I replied in a somewhat bemused and quizzical tone.

"I'm from the production team that produces the quiz show, *Greed*."

I was naturally surprised to have received the call because I hadn't formally applied for the show and as I wracked my brain as to the reasons why I was contacted by the production company, I came to the conclusion that the production team must have obtained my details from the previous application forms I had filled in when applying for other shows. On those various application forms, I would always tick *yes* to giving my consent to having my details circulated to other television production companies.

The caller went on to say, "We were wondering whether or not you would be interested in being a possible contestant on our show."

Well, an ambitious TV quizzer like myself didn't need asking twice about an opportunity to take part in another television show and I readily agreed. The caller then said she was going to ask me thirty multiple choice questions to test how good my general knowledge was and out of those thirty questions, I only got three wrong. The caller at the other end of the line seemed quite impressed with my efforts. I then asked the caller for some details about this new show, but the response I received could only be described as cryptic at best. All I was told was that Channel 5 were launching a brand new and exciting game show in the next couple of weeks called "Greed" where the contestants who were selected to take part on the show could potentially win for themselves one million pounds. The caller then thanked me for taking part in the quick fire test over the telephone and said that I would be hearing from the production team in a couple of days by letter.

A few days later the letter duly arrived on my doormat and it contained the following information:

Pearson Television
1 Stephen Street
London W1T 1AL

Tel: 020 7 691 6000
Fax: 020 7 691 5208

Congratulations!

Following your recent interview for 'Greed', you have been shortlisted as a possible contestant for the series to be recorded during May 2001. **However, this is not a guarantee that you will be used on the show.**

We have shortlisted around 400 possible contestants from all over the UK and we will be using around 250 of these on the show. Due to the nature of the game we never know exactly how many contestants will be used on the series as this depends on how well each group does. We therefore obviously shortlist more contestants than we need.

In order to make our final selection of contestants for the show, we need to know a lot more about you. We are enclosing a shortlist questionnaire for you to complete **in as much detail as possible.** Please make sure you do not leave any sections blank and feel free to add extra sheets if you need more space.

The questionnaires will be used to write a short biography on each contestant for the host of the show so that he can decide what to talk to you about on the programme. So the more information you can give us the better – but do not tell us anything that you would not want to share with the audience at home! Also remember that the show will have a family audience, so please don't tell us anything rude, gory, or involving bodily functions!

We appreciate that this questionnaire will take some time to complete but it is worth spending the time on it if you want to be on the show. Please complete in black biro and write clearly – we need to be able to read your writing!

Successful contestants will be contacted by telephone during April and May so don't give up hope if you don't hear straight away. When we call, we will give you a recording date, confirm everything in writing and send you a detailed Information Pack.

Please return the completed shortlist questionnaire to:

'Greed' Shortlisted Contestants
Pearson TV
1 Stephen Street
London W1P 1PJ

ALL FORMS MUST BE RETURNED BY FRIDAY 6TH APRIL

Please do not telephone us to find out whether or not you are on the show as we will be in touch with you again in due course to let you know if you have been successful.

Greed had burst onto our television screens at the beginning of May 2001 and was hosted by the irrepressible King of television trash chat shows, Jerry Springer. The first part of the show was an elimination round in which six contestants are asked a question which requires a numerical answer and the contestants have approximately five seconds to tap in their answers using the keypad provided. Those elimination questions could be very difficult but they were a great leveller. An example of the kind of question is: how many panes of glass are there in the MI6 building? The contestant who was closest to the correct answer would become Team Leader. The contestant who was second closest to the correct numerical answer was designated to sit in the £50,000 seat, the third closest in the £25,000 seat. The fourth, in the £10,000 seat, the fifth contestant occupying the £5,000 seat whilst the remaining contestant would sadly, be eliminated. The Team Leader sat opposite all other players and was by far the most important player in the game, as he/she had to decide whether or not to accept any given answer by a fellow contestant. The Team Leader's position on the set also had another distinct advantage because he/she had a clear and unrestricted view the other members of the team and could therefore, gauge their reactions, in contrast to the rest of team who were prevented, by virtue of the way the studio set was designed, from seeing each other. If a team member sitting in one of the designated prize money seats answered a question correctly, all the team would share the money equally. However, it remained the choice of the Team Leader to decide whether to play on, or to stop playing and if the latter choice was made, the money accrued by the team up to that point would be equally shared between them. If the team successfully managed to answer the £50,000 question correctly and the Team Leader decided to play on, at that stage of the game, the team would be introduced to a large prop that dominated the studio set called, "The Tower of Greed", where sums of £100,000, £250,000, £500,000 and the ultimate jackpot sum of one million pounds were there to be won and lost. Also introduced at this stage is the concept known as the dreaded "Terminator." This consisted of a random light flittering from contestant to contestant and once that flickering light lands on a contestant, the host would offer a £5,000 cash sum to challenge any of his/her fellow contestants (that challenge could also be made to the Team Leader as well) for their share of any prize fund on a head to head round. The winner of the head to head would win the loser's share for the remainder of the game whilst the loser of that showdown would sadly be eliminated. After the Terminator showdown, the team had to face the £100,000 question and in order to win that eye watering sum of money, the team had to give four correct answers from a possible choice of six, each surviving member of the team would then have to give their answers in turn. At this point, the host would give the Team Leader a "Freebie Card," a card which if chosen to be used by the Team Leader, would eliminate an incorrect answer from one of the multiple choices, but care and judgement in the use of that Freebie Card by the Team Leader had to be exercised wisely as the card could only be used once throughout the remainder of the game. Once all answers had been chosen by the team, the host would then reveal those answers in turn and if three of those answers were correct, the host would then offer the Team Leader a "buy out" consolation prize, a sum of money that represented 10% of the potential prize fund before the fourth answer is finally revealed. If the Team Leader was not sure that fourth answer selected by the team was correct and accepted the 10% buy out consolation offer, the team would equally share that sum and the game would be over, but if the Team Leader rejects the buy out offer and the fourth answer was correct, then the team share £100,000 between them. Finally, if the Team Leader rejects the buy out offer and that fourth answer turns out to be incorrect, then unfortunately, the team would lose everything. If the £100,000 cash sum was won by the team, only The Team Leader could decide whether or not to quit, or continue up the Tower of Greed and if The Team Leader decided to proceed, the Terminator roving light would once again select a player who would be offered £5,000 to challenge any of the remaining players in another one question showdown, the winner of that showdown winning once again the loser's share for themselves. The surviving team members then had to select four correct answers from a multiple choice of seven options in order to win £250,000. If the surviving team members managed to progress to the £500,000 question, then they would have four correct answers from a multiple choice of eight options to choose from and for the final one million pound question, any surviving members of the team would have to select four correct answers from a multiple option choice of nine.

I was an avid viewer of the show from the day of its first transmission. It was a show that I was desperate to be involved in, as I imagined myself as the Team Leader leading the rest of the team to glory, but unlike the three other TV quiz shows that I had previously appeared in, there were no firm guarantees, as the letter I received in the post made abundantly clear, that I would actually be selected to take part in the show. For that to happen, a lot was going to depend on the content of the application form that I submitted which I hoped would be good enough to grab the attention of the people charged with the task of selecting the contestants. Even after having submitted my application form, I would still have to undergo the nail biting process of having to wait for that all important telephone call from the production team inviting me to come to the studio. I was going to need a huge slice of luck and good fortune to go my way before I could even think of the possibility of quiz show glory. All I could do was to sit, wait and hope that Dame Fortune would smile on me.

The slice of good fortune that I was hoping and, indeed, praying for finally came to fruition when, after five weeks of waiting, the call duly came with the wonderful news that I had been selected to be a prospective contestant on the show. I could barely contain my delight when I heard the news. I had to attend the Fountain Studios in Wembley on the 27th of May. However, even though I was selected to attend the recording of the show for that day, there was still no firm guarantee that I was would actually be selected as a contestant on the show. That possible fly in the ointment was at that point in time, the least of my worries. I was in with a shout of appearing on the show and for now, that's all I could ask for.

The day that I was required to attend the studios had finally arrived and I woke up that morning feeling very excited and full of optimism that the day itself could be a day to remember. Despite my boundless optimism and enthusiasm, a number of important variables really had to go in my favour, the main variable being, that I had to be chosen as a contestant in the first place even though the odds of being chosen were a bit of a long shot. I had no choice but to rein in that boundless optimism because as the initial letter and information pack that I received made abundantly clear, not even the show's production team themselves knew precisely how many contestants would be required for any particular recording schedule, or indeed, the selection criteria the show's producers would apply when determining the actual make up of a team. The only thing I could think of to try and increase my chances of appearing on the show was to ensure that my general appearance in terms of the clothes that I intended to wear and especially, the way I intended to style my hair would be so noticeable, that it would somehow make the people who would have the final say on the contestants sit up and take notice.

With a plaited hair style standing rigid and upright like a set of antlers on a stag courtesy of Nadine's creative hairstyling endeavours, a brand new brightly coloured open neck pink shirt that displayed a trendy looking brown beaded necklace, a black pair of trousers freshly dry cleaned with razor sharp creases from my regular dry cleaners, and finally, a pair of black shoes pristinely polished by

Goggsy, I strolled into the foyer of Fountain Studios, looking like a male fashion model strolling down the catwalk at London Fashion Week and with a demeanour that oozed supreme confidence, I was determined to demonstrate that I have all the necessary ingredients to be a stand out contestant on the show.

After I arrived at the studio, I knew I'd made the right decision, as we were all informed that the production team were looking to select contestants with interesting and lively personalities in addition to having a good standard of general knowledge. A team of production assistants were going to go around the room carefully observing all of the prospective contestants and take note of how people were conducting themselves generally and interacting with fellow prospective contestants, before reporting their findings back to the main producers who would have the final say.

With the selection criteria fixed firmly in my mind, I straight away started to mingle and interact with as many of my fellow prospective contestants as was possible and those efforts paid handsome dividends because before I knew it, I found myself pulled to one side by one of the production assistants who silently whispered in my ear the news I hoped that I would hear, I had been selected to take part in the show. I was escorted by the production assistant from the room to one of the wings by the set and standing there were five other contestants who like me, were also selected. They were, Maz Foley, a Housewife from Gateshead, Angela Hill, a Debt Collector from Leicester, Ted Beaumont, who was Retired and came from Grantham in Lincolnshire, Rob Palmer, a Sales Manager from Nuneaton in Warwickshire, and finally, Alison "Pooee" Pitman, a Directors' Chef from Waltham-On-Thames. Although all six of us were naturally excited and delighted to have been chosen out of the hundreds of wannabe hopefuls, even at this stage there were still no guarantee that we were actually going to get onto the show because the team from the previous show were still playing and were about to begin their ascent up the Tower of Greed. The six of us could do nothing more than wait patiently in the wings as hopeful standbys who could be summoned on to the set at any moment.

As the six of us stood in the wings, we could see Jerry Springer entering on the other side, where he was greeted by the rapturous applause of the live studio audience and after the applause died down, Jerry began the show in earnest with the following opening remarks:

"GOOD EVENING LADIES AND GENTLEMEN, WELCOME TO GREED. IT IS A SHOW WHERE ONE MILLION POUNDS IS AWAITING SOMEONE WHO DARES TO CLIMB ALL THE WAY TO

THE TOP OF THE TOWER OF GREED. THE TEAM START AS FIVE PEOPLE PLAYING TOGETHER, HOWEVER, ALONG THE WAY, THEY WILL BE TRYING TO KNOCK EACH OTHER OUT IN THE HOPE OF GRABBING THE MONEY ALL FOR THEMSELVES. THAT'S WHEN WE FIND OUT WHO TRULY FEELS THE NEED FOR GREED."

Jerry summoned the next team of players to enter the studio and with that clarion call, the five of us all marched in behind Maz and headed towards our respective positions on Contestant's Row and stood in front of our individual keypads. Jerry barely had time to exchange pleasantries before he announced that all important qualifying round question that not only would determine which of the five of us would be taking part in the game but more importantly, determine which would claim the coveted position of Team Leader.

"ACCORDING TO THE SCOTTISH TOURIST BOARD, HOW MANY GOLF COURSES ARE THERE IN SCOTLAND?"

The team had approximately ten seconds in which to tap in their respective answers on the keypads. I thought to myself, *there are at least five Golf Courses in and around where I live. Scotland's the home of Golf, a country which makes up roughly one third of mainland UK.* Taking those factors into consideration, I tapped in the number 432 on my keypad and hoped that my estimate would be closer than the others thus allowing me to claim the coveted role of Team Leader. A sound resembling a bell rang out to denote that the time was up which was the cue for Jerry to reveal the correct answer.

"THE CORRECT ANSWER IS, 351. OOOH, LOOK AT ALL THOSE FACES. SOME OF YOU ARE NOT TOO HAPPY. WELL LET'S FIND OUT, WHO AMONGST YOU WAS THE CLOSEST TO THE CORRECT ANSWER?"

The same bell sound rang out once more before Jerry announced, "SHAUN, YOU ARE THE TEAM LEADER. CONGRATULATIONS!"

I couldn't have felt more excited and happy at the news that my guess of 432 was the closest and I triumphantly made my way to the Team Leader's seat. Jerry then continued to reveal the names of the other contestants who else would form part of the team. It went, in order: Angela, Ted, Rob and Pooee.

Jerry revealed that Maz's choice was 60 before going on to say that it was a shame that a contestant with such a booming personality as hers could not take part in the show and he hoped that she would be selected as a contestant on any future series. The line-up was now complete and the game was ready to begin in earnest.

Jerry was clearly intrigued by my hairstyle. "I KNOW THAT YOU'RE EXCITED, BECAUSE I CAN TELL BY YOUR HAIR. DID YOU PUT YOUR FINGER IN AN ELECTRIC SOCKET?" His remarks drew howls of laughter from the studio audience as I was trying to explain my reasons for choosing this style, but I didn't mind being the target of such light hearted mockery. My outlandish spiky hairstyle had the desired effect that I'd hoped for. It got me noticed by the show's powers that be and ultimately, got me selected. Jerry then reminded me of my responsibilities as the Team Leader and the crucial advantage that I had. I could see my fellow team mates, but because of a series of dividing partitions in between each of them, they couldn't see each other and if I was unsure about any answer given by a team mate, then to help me reach my final decision, I could gauge the reactions of the other members of the team before making my final choice.

Jerry turned to Pooee to ask her the £5000 question. "IN THE NURSERY RHYME HEY DIDDLE DIDDLE, WHO JUMPED OVER THE MOON? THE CAT, COW, DISH OR LITTLE DOG?"

Pooee's question was a nice and easy one to start the game off with and Pooee gave the expected answer, Cow, which I duly accepted and secured the team an equal share of £5,000. As the Team Leader, I elected to go up the next level where Rob was sitting in the £10,000 seat.

Jerry then asked Rob the £10,000 question. "WHICH OF THE FOLLOWING COUNTIES IS OFTEN REFERRED TO AS THE GARDEN OF ENGLAND? CORNWALL, SURREY, KENT OR CUMBRIA?

I could tell from the confident look on Rob's face that he knew the correct answer was Kent which he duly gave and I accepted, winning for the team an equal share of £10,000. As the audience applauded Rob's correct response, I smiled and gave him the thumbs up sign to let him know how pleased I was with his answer.

"WE'RE ON A ROLL," Jerry exclaimed excitedly and he turned to me and asked whether or not I wanted press on to face the £25,000 question. I turned momentarily towards the team to find out whether they wanted to play on and for making that enquiry, I found myself on the receiving end of mild admonishment from the host. "WE'RE NOT TAKING POLLS HERE. YOU'RE THE LEADER." Jerry wasn't telling me anything I didn't already know. I had no intention of quitting at this stage and I told Jerry that I wanted to move on to the £25,000 question.

Jerry turned his attention to Ted. "WHICH OF ENID BLYTON'S FAMOUS FIVE WAS NOT HUMAN? JULIAN, TIMMY, DICK OR GEORGE?"

Ted was in like a shot with the correct answer, Timmy. "DO YOU ACCEPT HIS ANSWER, SHAUN?" Jerry asked enquiringly. "OF COURSE I DO," I confidently replied and when the answer was revealed, Jerry exclaimed excitedly, "TWENTY-FIVE THOUSAND POUNDS!" a somewhat over the top reaction that was the cue to a round of wild and enthusiastic cheering from the studio audience. "THIS TEAM HAS MOMENTUM!" Jerry proclaimed with increasing enthusiasm and excitement before he turned to me and asked whether I wanted to continue. Quitting was not an option and when I told Jerry that it was my intention to go on, Jerry responded by saying, "I LOVE YOUR ATTITUDE."

Jerry turned his attention to the £50,000 seat where Angela was sitting and it was apparent straight away that she was a bag of nerves, a demeanour Jerry immediately seized upon and with that, he tried to reassure her that I was there to help her with the answer.

"WHICH PERFUME MANUFACTURER INTRODUCED A FRAGRENCE CALLED PLEASURES? ESTEE LAUDER, CALVIN KLEIN, YVES ST LAURENT, CHRISTIAN DIOR OR ELIZABETH ARDEN?"

I looked somewhat anxiously over towards Angela in order to try and gauge her reaction to the question and to my initial disappointment and dismay, she appeared to be recoiling at the question in sheer and utter terror. Angela's initial reaction to the question was the first mini crisis that the team had encountered in the game up to this point. I certainly didn't know the answer to the question and both my male team mates, Ted and Rob, were looking equally nonplussed. In an act of increasing desperation, I switched my attentions finally, to the last remaining team member Pooee and my initial worry and concern that the team may not be able to answer the question were lifted considerably by virtue of the encouragingly confident signals that Pooee was making, either with the nodding or shaking of her head, at the five options before finally pointing her index finger firmly and decisively at the option, Estee Lauder. I turned my attention back towards Angela once again in the hope that by this time, she had managed to calm herself down a little.

Angela's moment in the spotlight had now arrived and after Jerry prompted her to reveal her choice, she eventually replied, "I'M NOT ABSOLUTELY SURE, BUT I THINK IT'S ESTEE LAUDER." With that committed response, I immediately switched my attentions back towards Pooee who responded to Angela's answer by giving me the positive thumbs up sign. As the Team Leader, I now had to make the crucial decision as to whether or not to accept Angela's choice, a crucial decision that would determine whether the team had won for themselves an equal share of £50,000. I rocked back and forth on my seat momentarily, agonising over whether or not to take the gamble and in the end, I decided that Pooee's firm thumbs up meant that there was a high probability that Angela had in fact made the right choice.

"I'M GOING TO GO FOR IT!" I boldly declared. "I'VE GOT CONFIDENCE IN HER." Angela's response to my bold declaration was to put both her fingers into her mouth as if she was biting her fingernails way beyond the quick because despite her selection, she was still unsure whether she had got the answer right.

"FOR £50,000, IS ESTEE LAUDER CORRECT?" Jerry nervously enquired. A solitary note from the studio bell rung once more before he declared, "FIFFTY THOUSAND POUNDS! FIFTY THOUSAND POUNDS!" The audience once again burst into life with wild and sustained spontaneous applause. I pointed both index fingers in Angela's direction as if to say, *yo, Angela, you really are The Girl!*

However, no sooner had Jerry had confirmed the correct answer, Angela was already making cut throat signs in my direction, pleading with me to stop the game there and then, but I was paying no such attention to her desperate pleas. I was determined to play the Terminator game and start the team's ascent up The Tower of Greed and the only thoughts that were running through my mind at this point was hoping and praying that the flickering random light would eventually land on me because if it did, not only was I going to accept the £5,000 to challenge one of my team mates, but the team mate who I had fixed firmly in my sights was Angela.

"LET'S PLAY TERMINATOR!" Jerry exclaimed enthusiastically before pushing the big red button on his podium setting off the flickering light as it moved rapidly throughout the team member to another and as it was doing so, I closed my eyes in silent prayer hoping that when the spotlight finally stopped, I would be the lucky beneficiary. The random light flickered past the team for what seemed like an eternity then suddenly and without warning, it halted its tantalising journey. "IT'S POOEE!" Jerry revealed. Jerry then offered Pooee £5,000 to accept the challenge of trying to seize the share of one of her team mates and she wasted no time in accepting Jerry's offer and selected Ted for the one question showdown. After Pooee had made her choice, Jerry escorted the pair of them across the vast studio set to the Terminator Zone, where they stood face to face at their respective podiums. Jerry then explained the rules of the one question showdown.

"I'M GONNA ASK YOU A QUESTION, AS SOON AS YOU KNOW THE ANSWER HIT THE BUZZER. THE FIRST PERSON WHO HITS THE BUZZER, I'M GONNA IMMEDIATELY ASK YOU FOR AN ANSWER. IF YOU ANSWER CORRECTLY, YOU WIN THE OTHER PERSON'S SHARE, IF YOU GIVE ME AN INCORRECT ANSWER, OR YOU FAIL TO GIVE ME AN ANSWER STRAIGHT AWAY, YOU LOSE. ARE YOU READY? HANDS ON THE BUZZER." Jerry then read out the question on the card he retrieved from the side of his podium. "WHICH ACTRESS, AFTER LEAVING THE CAST OF EASTENDERS, WENT ON TO STAR IN THE WEST END PRODUCTION OF MY FAIR LADY…?"

Both Ted and Pooee pressed their respective buzzers whilst Jerry was reading the question, but it was Pooee who was a nanosecond quicker. "MARTINE MCCUTCHEON," Pooee replied with a great deal of trepidation.

"YOU'RE RIGHT!" Jerry confirmed that Pooee had won the first one question showdown, a victory that meant Ted was eliminated and he had to leave the set. To the victor go the spoils and Pooee gleefully picked up the £5,000 that Jerry had left for her by the side of her podium before the pair of them made their way back across to the main part of the set as the team prepared themselves to face the £100,000 question.

Jerry then sought to increase the tension that had slowly been creeping up to almost unbearable levels. "YOU HAVE JUST WITNESSED A VERY TENSE MOMENT IN THE SHOW AND NOW POOEE, YOU'RE PLAYING FOR £45,000 WHICH EQUALS YOUR SHARE OF £20,000 PLUS TED'S SHARE OF ANOTHER £20,000 PLUS THE £5,000 THAT YOU ACCEPTED FOR TAKING THE CHALLENGE, WHEREAS SHAUN, ROB AND ANGELA, YOU'RE PLAYING FOR £20,000 EACH!"

I looked across towards where my fellow team members were sitting in order to try and gauge their respective levels of confidence or nervousness before we faced that important question. Pooee's visible demeanour was a positive sign of sheer delight and it was evident to me that aside from myself, she was the one team member who was clearly up for the challenge. Both Rob and Angela were showing signs of nerves and frantic apprehension respectively. But this was neither the time, or indeed, the place to concern myself with their increasing anxieties or fears. All I was interested in was answering the next question with the help of the rest of the team correctly.

Jerry turned to me and asked, "ARE YOU READY?"

"I'M READY," I responded with a confident tone.

"OK THEN, HERE'S THE £100,000 QUESTION."

The question itself appeared on the screen on the console in front of me before Jerry had started to read it out and from the moment I saw it, I knew that it was a question that was there for the taking. *I think that we've won £100,000!* I said excitedly to myself.

Jerry proceeded to read out the following question. 'WHICH OF THE FOLLOWING FOUR WOMEN HAVE BEEN BLUE PETER PRESENTERS? VALERIE SINGLETON, SUSAN STRANKS, LESLEY JUDD, ANTHEA TURNER, JENNY HANLEY, AND FINALLY, DIANE LOUISE-JORDAN."

As the options were being read out, I looked over at the rest of my team mates for any positive or negative reactions to the question and it was clear from their collective body language, that they all knew who the four presenters from the show were with Angela especially, appearing to be the most keen and animated about the real possibility of the winning £100,000.

Jerry then reminded the whole team of what we had to do in order to win the life changing sum of money. "THERE ARE SIX CHOICES. FOUR ARE CORRECT. I'M GOING TO MAKE IT EASIER FOR YOU. THIS IS A FREEBIE CARD!" Jerry held up the card. "YOU CAN USE IT NOW, OR AT ANY TIME BETWEEN NOW AND THE END OF THE GAME IF YOU GO ALL THE WAY UP TO ONE MILLION POUNDS. IF YOU USE IT, I'LL ASK THE PRODUCERS TO REMOVE ONE INCORRECT ANSWER. DO YOU WANT TO USE YOUR FREEBIE?"

"NO," was my firm and confident reply.

"SAVING IT FOR LATER. OK GOOD FOR YOU!" Jerry then began to ask each of my remaining team members in turn to provide an answer from the options that were on offer.

Pooee picked Diane Louise-Jordan. Rob chose Anthea Turner. An excitable Angela went for Lesley Judd. And finally, I, somewhat dismissively, in the full knowledge we were about to win a cool £100,000, chose Valerie Singleton.

"THIS IS A VERY CONFIDENT TEAM" Jerry declared. "LET'S SEE IF YOU'RE RIGHT." Jerry then started to go through the answers, starting with Rob's choice, followed by Angela's then my own, all of which were correct and with every correct answer declared, Jerry was doing his level best to build the suspense, but we knew we were onto a winner. Once the three correct answers were confirmed, Jerry then offered me the buyout consolation prize of £10,000 to split between myself and the rest of my team mates if I was not totally sure that Pooee's answer was correct.

"YOU CAN KEEP THAT, JERRY!" was my emphatic response and I politely pushed away the comparatively paltry sum in the full and confident knowledge that the team were on a pay out that would represent ten times that amount. Jerry made a vain and ultimately, futile attempt to try to get me to change my mind by pointing out the fact that Pooee was the only team member who was certain to go home with at least £5,000 if her answer turned out to be incorrect. However, Jerry could see that as far as I was concerned, there was no going back. "FOR ONE HUNDRED THOUSAND POUNDS IS DIANE LOUISE-JORDON THE CORRECT ANSWER?"

It is! I whispered to myself and when Jerry confirmed that we had won the money, my three team mates sprang to life with a mixture of relief, happiness and joy but no sooner had the team started celebrating in earnest, Angela was once again, making frantic cut throat signals in my direction imploring me to stop the game.

Jerry came over to shake my hand, but by this time, I was enjoying myself so much that I celebrated the team's good fortune by bumping fists with him. Angela's hand signals meanwhile were growing more and more frantic and intense, signs that were imploring me to call the game to a halt there and then. Even the normally ice cool Pooee, who at this point was sitting on a tidy sum of £45,000 was also signalling to me to call it a day. Rob was now shifting even more nervously in his seat and beginning to show the clear and unmistakable sign that the pressure was starting to get to him. It was those collective signs of anxiety from the rest of my team that got me thinking straight away that this could be the perfect time to exploit their varying degrees of anxiety if I elected to play on and move up to the next stage of the Tower of Greed where we would be playing for a quarter of a million pounds, a stage that no previous team throughout the entire series had successfully managed to achieve.

"DO YOU WANNA BECOME THE ALL TIME HIGH WINNER?" Jerry asked me teasingly.

As I was weighing up my options amongst the backdrop of the near deafening sounds of the lively and raucous studio audience, a group who themselves were equally divided as to what my next move should be, my fellow teammates were still frantically signalling to me to stop and quit whilst we were ahead. I glanced up and down the team one more time and the decisive factor in terms of my next move was Angela's desperate signals for me to call a halt that convinced me to play on as the chance to win a quarter of a million pounds was far too tempting an opportunity to let pass by.

"ANGELA IS BEGGING FOR YOU TO STOP. SO IS ROB!" Jerry declared stating the obvious. "LET'S SEE WHAT THIS WOULD MEAN, IF YOU DECIDED TO GO AHEAD. POOEE, YOU WOUD WIN £105,000 JUST FOR YOURSELF, AND ROB AND SHAUN, NO SMALL CHANGE FOR YOU, AS YOU WOULD WIN £50,000 EACH." After Jerry had finished explaining the various possibilities, I took one final look at the rest of the team who were still frantically appealing to me to stop, with Angela in particular, acting as though she was praying for divine intervention at the altar.

Jerry then turned to me and asked me to reveal my final decision.

"I ALWAYS SAID THAT IF I SAT IN THIS CHAIR THAT I'M GOING TO ... GAMBLE!"

The studio erupted into wild applause over my decision and as they were doing so, I immediately turned my attention to the rest of my team who collectively, looked shell shocked by my decision. Pooee reacted to my momentous decision by rolling her eyes skywards towards the heavens and as for Angela, well, as the old proverb goes, "if looks could kill...." Jerry responded to my decision with the comment, "SIGNIFICANT UNHAPPINESS FROM ANGELA, ROB WOULD PULL YOUR HAIR OUT, AND POOEE, SHE'S JUST NERVOUS.... NOT ANGRY, JUST NERVOUS!" those last two words of his observation prompted Pooee to use her £5,000 cash winnings as a fan in an effort to keep her cool her from the mounting levels of tension and stress threatening to engulf her. "YOU'RE VERY COURAGOUS SHAUN!"

"THAT'S THE NAME OF THE GAME!" I replied but I wasn't interested in Jerry's platitudes. All I was interested in was playing the Terminator game and hoping that this time, I would find favour with Dame Fortune thus enabling me to take full advantage of my team's increasing anxieties.

Jerry then pressed the Terminator button for the second time and as the flickering random light danced its way around all the members of the team, I closed my eyes once more in deep, silent prayer hoping, praying that my wish to be chosen would ultimately be granted. The random light finally stopped its merry dance before Jerry revealed, much to my bitter disappointment, the identity of the lucky recipient was Pooee again! Jerry offered Pooee another £5,000 to accept the challenge and after pausing for a short while to consider her options, Pooee's shrewd and calculating instincts rose immediately to the fore. She was fully aware that she had a confident Team Leader, but more importantly, from her point of view, she was in the perfect position to take full advantage of Angela's ever increasing nervousness. She accepted. The whole team applauded her decision, but the one team member that was clapping less enthusiastically was Angela because she realised, just like King Belshazzar had done in the Book of Daniel in the Old Testament, that the writing was firmly on the wall.

"WHO WOULD YOU LIKE TO CHALLENGE?" Jerry enquired.

"ANGELA!" Pooee responded, steeled and determined.

As Jerry, Pooee and Angela made their way over to the Terminator Zone across the other side of the studio floor, I began to rock back and forth in my chair in complete and utter disappointment and frustration that once again, I was not chosen by the elusive random flickering light. Over at the Terminator Zone before the one question showdown, Jerry handed Pooee another £5,000. Even if Pooee were to lose her one question showdown with Angela, she would still have a handy sum of money to take away with her. Pooee though, had her eyes firmly fixed on a far greater prize and there was no doubt in my mind that she saw her nervous opponent as nothing other than a mere stepping stone on her way to earning herself a small fortune.

"YOU KNOW HOW THIS GOES, AS SOON AS YOU KNOW THE ANSWER, HIT THAT BUZZER, YOU'RE BOTH PLAYING FOR A POSSIBLE £150,000 HERE! HERE'S THE QUESTION. WHERE IN GERMANY IS THE ANNUAL BEER FESTIVAL THE OKTOBER...."

BZZZZZ! Not for the first time in the contest, Pooee was in like grease lightening before Jerry had even finished completing the question. "MUNICH" Pooee answered in a soft but no less certain tone.

"YOU'RE RIGHT!"

Pooee put her head in her hands, a reaction no doubt, to the sheer joy and relief she felt in having dismissed her hapless opponent, a reaction, that was in stark contrast to the utter disappointment and dejection on Angela's face as it finally dawned on her that her histrionics and frantic pleas to stop the game had cost her big time and she too, like Ted before her when challenging Pooee, was sadly dispatched to the side lines.

For the second time in the contest, Pooee marched triumphantly back to her seat only this time, she was waving two wads of £5,000 in each hand, clasping the cash as if she was holding the world's most expensive fans to keep her cool.

"BOY, POOEE, YOU ARE TOUGH. KNOCKING THESE PEOPLE OUT. ALRIGHT HERE'S WHAT WE'VE GOT, THE £250,000 QUESTION. IF YOU ALL GET IT RIGHT, POOEE YOUR

SHARE WILL BE £160,000 JUST FOR YOURSELF WHICH INVOLVES YOUR SHARE, TED AND ANGELA'S SHARE, PLUS THE £10,000 YOU WON IN THE TERMINATOR, AND SHAUN AND ROB, NO SMALL CHANGE - YOU'LL EACH GET £50,000."

I was preening in my seat like a proud peacock, really looking forward to the exciting prospect of sharing with my two remaining team mates a quarter of a million pounds. Before the question was revealed, I immediately turned my attention to my team mates, Pooee and Rob, and gave them the clenched fist sign of support and encouragement, hoping that it would somehow inspire them to collectively rise to our impending challenge. "HERE'S THE £250,000 QUESTION." Once again, as with the previous question, the question and the various options flashed up on my screen before Jerry had read it out aloud. *Well, that's £250,000 in the bag,* I said to myself as it was the type of question that I could answer in my sleep.

"WHICH FOUR OF THE FOLLOWING WON THE BBC SPORTS PERSONALITY OF THE YEAR IN THE 1990'S? GARY LINEKER, LINFORD CHRISTIE, NIGEL MANSELL, FRANK BRUNO, MICHAEL ATHERTON, DAMON HILL OR LIZ MCCOLGAN."

The money was all but ours. However, to be absolutely certain that we would win the record breaking sum of money, either Pooee or Rob had to give at least one correct answer between them because if one of them were to give an incorrect answer, then as the Team Leader I could alter it, but if they both gave incorrect answers, then it would not be possible to win the £250,000 prize and I would be left with no option other than to accept Jerry's buy out consolation prize of £25,000 and share the relatively paltry sum of £8333 between us.

After Jerry finished reading the question, he reminded me that I still had the Freebie Card that I could use to eliminate an answer I wasn't sure about. I turned my attentions towards Pooee and Rob who were now looking more and more anxious and concerned with each passing second that was in stark contrast to my own supreme confidence that the team were only one correct answer away from getting our hands on a quarter of a million pounds. In the midst of the game's ever increasing tension, I decided it was time to have my own bit of fun and in the process, ratchet the tension up a notch or two when I declared after Jerry asked me if I would like to use the Freebie Card, "I'LL KEEP THE FREEBIE!" It was a bold and bullish declaration that took even the usually unflappable Jerry Springer completely by surprise. "YOU'LL KEEP IT? OK YOU'RE A VERY COURAGEOUS GUY. IT SEEMS TO ME THAT YOU'RE PRETTY CONFIDENT OF WHO THESE FOUR PEOPLE ARE."

"OH YEAH!" came my instant cocksure reply. I looked over towards my team mates and Pooee reacted to my cocksure declaration with a visibly nervous smile which she complimented by crossing her fingers on both of her hands in the style of the National Lottery logo sign whereas Rob on the other hand, pretended that he was fainting at the daunting prospect that the team were about to face.

"WE'LL START WITH YOU POOEE, GIVE ME ONE OF THE CORRECT ANSWERS!"

The moment of truth had now arrived, all Pooee had to do was give one correct answer and her life would change forever.

"I'M FAIRLY CONFIDENT OF DAMON HILL!" As she said that, I nodded approvingly in her direction because there was no doubt about it, we had definitely won the money.

"ROB, WHAT SAY YOU?"

Rob replied, "I'M FAIRLY SURE IT'S LINFORD CHRISTIE."

Finally, Jerry turned to me and asked, "SHAUN WHO DO YOU PICK?"

I replied, "LIZ MCCOLGAN," in the full knowledge that she had scooped the award in 1991 for her gold medal victory in the 10,000 metres that was Britain's only medal at the World Athletics Championships in that year.

There was one choice left to be made. As Team Leader, I had to decide who made that final, important choice.

"I'LL CHOOSE IT," I replied, and I selected the 1992 winner, Nigel Mansell.

"THIS IS A SEMINAL MOMENT IN TELEVISION. TO BE HONEST IT IS THE SINGLE MOST EXCITING MOMENT I HAVE EVER HAD IN TELEVISON. I HAVE NEVER BEEN AROUND PEOPLE WHO ARE ABOUT TO WIN OR LOOSE THIS AMOUNT OF MONEY, SO I'M PRETTY EXCITED."

Jerry read out the question again before going through each of our first three answers, revealing each one was correct to the frantic delight and joy of the whole team and the audience combined.

Before the team's fourth and final answer was revealed, Jerry asked me if I wished to change any of the declared answers, but not even the man upstairs himself could have persuaded me to change my mind. Jerry then offered me the £25,000 buyout consolation prize if I was unsure as to any of the four answers declared was correct but given the fact that I was supremely confident that the quarter of a million pounds was all but ours, I decided that I wanted to continue having my own bit of fun as means of relieving the relentless tension. "CAN I HOLD IT JERRY?" I asked mockingly, referring of course, to the large wad of cash that was stashed in his podium. He handed it to me. Once I took possession of it, I began to mockingly caress the large wads of cash as if I was caressing the sexiest woman in the world. "OOH! THATS A LOT OF MONEY," I said jokingly as I continued to fondle and caress the fake bundles of cash with even greater intensity before abruptly ending the pretence by shoving it firmly back into Jerry's hands. "YOU CAN HAVE IT BACK." I declared.

"THAT'S THE FIRST TIME I'VE EVER SEEN A LAWYER GIVE ME BACK MONEY!" Jerry responded with his razor sharp wit which drew fits of laughter from the studio audience.

"THAT'S A SLUR AGAINST MY PROFESSION." I responded in a joking manner.

Jerry was clearly enjoying our harmless verbal exchange and had the last word when he said, "IT CERTAINLY IS, BUT I'M ONE TOO, SO THAT'S OK. LET'S GET BACK - ARE YOU WILLING TO BET EVERYTHING ON YOUR ANSWER?"

"EVERYTHING!" I replied adopting a far more serious tone realising that the time for jocular frivolity was over.

"OK THEN, FOR £250,000. IS LIZ MCCOLGAN THE CORRECT ANSWER?" There was a momentary pause designed solely to increase the already limitless tension, then finally, the familiar sounding note that I knew was coming, the sound that denoted a correct answer. "A QUARTER OF A MILLION POUNDS, A QUARTER OF A MILLION POUNDS!" Jerry shrieked in a slightly concerning high pitched tone that was threatening to do untold damage to his vocal chords.

The studio audience reacted by breaking into wild applause and I reacted instantly to that sustained cheering by rising to my feet in the style of an ancient Roman Emperor as he milks the applause of his adoring crowd. After milking the acclaim of the studio audience, I sat back down in my seat and my attention was immediately drawn to my team mates Pooee and Rob who were trying to get my attention by making frantic signals begging me to quit, but in truth, they needn't have bothered. I had already made up my mind to stop because although we were playing a game called "Greed", I for one, AM NOT GREEDY. There was no way I was going to continue to proceed up The Tower of Greed any further, not even with the Freebie Card still intact, because somewhere in the back of my mind, I believed that there was a potential banana skin in the offing just waiting to undo all the team's hard work.

Despite having already made up my mind to stop playing and call it quits, I still wanted to continue having a bit more fun by prolonging the agony and suspense.

"CONGRATULATIONS! THAT'S THE MOST MONEY EVER WON ON THIS SHOW!"

"IT'S CONGRATULATIONS TO THE WHOLE TEAM!" I steadfastly insisted.

"YOU'VE WON A TON OF MONEY! NOW, I'VE GOT TO GIVE YOU THE CHANCE FOR £500,000. YOU'VE GOT YOUR FREEBIE CARD TO HELP ELIMINATE ONE OF THE INCORRECT ANSWERS TO THE NEXT QUESTION, IT'S YOUR DECISION, IT'S ALL ABOUT GREED."

I was completely and totally relaxed, and I decided that now was the perfect time to have the little bit of fun and games that I had in mind. Instead of turning to my extremely anxious and concerned team mates for advice, I turned my attention towards the audience to ask for their assistance and they responded by shouting the words, "GAMBLE!" and "QUIT!" in equal measure that seemed to mesh into an incomprehensible cacophony of white noise. I turned to face Pooee, who by this time was wagging her finger at me in a forthright, no nonsense manner and teasingly, I responded by pointing to my chest as if to say, "I'm in charge of the situation, not you." This exchange between us went on for a few seconds, but the moment had now arrived as Jerry pressed me for my decision. By the expression etched all over his face, even he was looking somewhat apprehensive and unsure as to what my final decision would be. Jerry then asked for hushed silence from everyone in the studio as I embarked on revealing my final choice.

"THIS IS A ONCE IN A LIFETIME CHANCE FOR ME, BUT I'VE GOT RESPONSBILITIES TO MY TEAM MATES, AND I'M GOING TO TAKE THE MONEY!" As soon as I revealed my decision, I gave the thumbs up to both Pooee and Rob and both they, together with the studio audience, greeted my decision with delirious applause.

Jerry walked a few paces towards me and shook my hand and judging by his reaction, he seemed to be more relieved than anyone else in the studio that I made the only decision that any sane and sensible person would have made in those circumstances. "CONGRATULATIONS TO THE THREE OF YOU, EXCITING GAME. SAVE THE MONEY, SPEND THE MONEY. WHATEVER YOU DO, DO IT WISELY AND WITH CLASS. YOU'VE BEEN WONDERFUL, WONDERFUL GUESTS AND WHAT A WONDERFUL WAY TO END THE SHOW."

"AND IT'S MY BIRTHDAY!" I declared despite the fact that my 41st Birthday was six days away, but the team's record breaking win made it feel like that it was and my slightly misleading declaration only served to increase the already sustained enthusiastic audience applause.

After the show had finished, Pooee, Rob and myself took some pictures with Jerry. After the happy picture snaps were taken, the show's producers asked us to take part in an epilogue during which Jerry discussed with the three of us how we felt after the game.

"I HAD MAJOR CONFIDENCE IN THIS MAN, HE'S PRETTY AMAZING" Pooee declared, complimenting my performance and I gave her a peck on the cheek in response to her unexpected but, nevertheless, welcome kind words. Rob admitted that although he wanted to go for the million at the outset, once he started seeing those life changing figures, he just had to stop but most poignantly, Rob also revealed that his big win had come at the right time as he was about to be made redundant, a revelation that drew a heartfelt round of applause from the studio audience. Then Pooee, without giving away so much as a hint of her secret intentions, did something completely out of the blue that had taken everyone in the studio completely by surprise when in an act of pure altruism, she declared that she was going to give Ted and Angela £5,000 each from her winnings. Ted and Angela then came onto the stage looking totally gobsmacked by Pooee's extraordinary gesture and all five of us proceeded to embark on a spontaneous victory team hug. During that team embrace, I turned to Angela and immediately apologised for the seemingly aggressive and ruthless way I played the game and she responded by giving me a tender touch with her hand on the side of my cheek and told me not to worry.

"WE'RE ALL WINNERS HERE, WE'RE ALL WINNERS HERE!" I triumphantly declared.

Jerry asked me what I was going to do with my winnings and I told him I needed to cover some debts but otherwise it was for my family and friends. Before the closing credits began to roll, Jerry's final remarks were that he thought we were a wonderful team and that we all played the game with style and class. He went on to add that he hoped that whether we saved the money or spent it, that we should all enjoy the rest of our lives before delivering his parting shot that he directed towards me: "GET A HAIR CUT!"

Afterwards the whole team joined the production team and the rest of the prospective contestants who were not selected for the show, in one big celebratory party, but amidst all the celebrations and hullabaloo, I decided that I didn't want to hang around as I was going on holiday the following day and after such an eventful day, all I wanted to do was to go home, pack my suitcase and thereafter, put my feet up and relax. I said all my goodbyes to everyone, who seemed really disappointed that I was leaving so soon but before I left the studio, I needed to satisfy my burning curiosity that would have nagged away at me for an eternity if I didn't make an enquiry about it, what was the £500,000 question and the multiple choice answers that went with it? I asked one of the more senior members of the production team, and she told me (from a choice of eight options) the question was, "From an American prospective, what were the most important events of the 20th Century?" I gave the question some careful thought before coming up with the following answers. The Bombing of Pearl Harbour in 1941, The Assassination of President Kennedy in 1963, Man's First Landing on the Moon in 1969, and finally, The Watergate Scandal of the 1970's. Perfectly good answers one would have thought and I for one would have been more than confident with those options if I had decided to continue up the Tower of Greed for £500,000 and had no reason to doubt that the team would have been in with a real shout of winning that massive sum. However, to my complete and utter surprise, the production assistant declared, "You would have lost the money with those options."

"Really?" I replied in a curious and bewildered tone. "What was the missing event?" I asked intriguingly.

"The Assassination of Gandhi," she replied.

I thought she was joking at first but her facial expression told a different story. There are not many things in life that completely stop me in my tracks, but that was surely one of them. I didn't even bother to ask which one of my four choices had not made the list and with a shake of my head in sheer utter disbelief, I said my final goodbyes before gathering my belongings in readiness to leave the studio.

The following day, I arrived at Heathrow Airport to meet up with the rest of the guys I was going on holiday with, looking forward to having a hilarious as well as relaxing time. Before boarding the plane, I decided to take a leisurely stroll around one of the various Duty Free shops at the airport and whilst browsing at the Perfume section, I noticed displayed on one of the shelves, the product, Pleasures from Estee Lauder in cream form. I immediately grabbed the product from the shelf despite the fact it was for women and took great pleasure in rubbing its contents all over my body whilst I was on holiday, as it served as a poignant and memorable reminder that at long, long last, I finally managed to make an emphatic quizzing breakthrough.

CHAPTER SIXTEEN

Five or so weeks after my breakthrough win on *Greed*, the spoils of victory finally landed on my doormat in an envelope. I opened the letter and contained inside with the *Greed* logo on its background, was a cheque which read as follows, "Pay Shaun Wallace £50,000." That's right, £50,000! In all my years on this planet I've never seen such a potentially life changing sum of money, let alone, been the proud recipient of such a vast amount of cash tax free! I don't think that I had ever earned that amount of money over a period of two years throughout my entire working career, let alone in one go. It really was a gift that was heaven sent but the dilemma that I was faced with, albeit a nice dilemma to have was, what on earth was I going to do with it? Do I invest it? Do I follow in the legendary footsteps of the 1960's football pools winner Viv Nicholson and Spend, Spend, Spend? Or, do I do what said I was going to do - settle my debts (which were continuing to mount), and look after after family and friends (in that order)? There was also another potential dilemma on the horizon. Because of the very public nature in which I won the money, there were a number of "friends", acquaintances and hangers on who were hell bent to get their sticky fingers on a share of the spoils, coming up with hard luck stories, tales one of how financially desperate they were coupled with the "sacred promise" to swiftly repay any loan or loans I would advance them. As the age old saying goes, "A fool and his money are easily parted" and in a blink of an eye, I found myself on the receiving end of one hard luck story after another, the net result of which was that my healthy bank balance was lighter to the tune of over £3,000, monies that unsurprisingly, took a great deal longer to get back that I had envisaged or indeed, had been promised by the seemingly "hard up" borrowers who had the bare faced cheek to ask me to lend it to them in the first place. The financial loans that I made to these so called "friends" was a mere drop in the ocean, as I was asked to lend out £40,000 (yes, £40,000!) by the one person who in truth was the only person (save for my own mother) in the whole world that I would have absolutely no hesitation in lending such a vast sum of money to. That person was my kid brother, Steve. The reason why Steve needed to borrow all that money was, unlike those hard luck tales of financial woe that I foolishly succumbed to when making those aforementioned loans to so called friends, my brother's need was borne out of an urgent and genuine necessity. He was in the process of selling his house, but he hadn't quite managed to do so within the time frame that he had envisaged. Steve and my lovely sister-in–law, Lavinia, had set their heart on buying what they considered to be their "dream home" in Kew, but they were in danger of losing out altogether if they didn't come up with a sizeable deposit. Steve asked me to help him out and promised to pay me back from the proceeds once his house was sold. When he told me of his dilemma, I agreed to loan him the money without a moment's thought or hesitation. I love my kid brother dearly and I never forgot his unwavering support of me over the last three difficult years I had to endure, riding to my rescue financially on many an occasion. When some of the clothes that I wore to work were looking the worse for wear, Steve would often lend me the money to buy myself the odd new suit or two, or occasionally, give me one of his expensive cast offs. We used to have an ongoing joke between ourselves that whenever I looked smart in a suit, it was mainly because I was wearing one of his hand me ups! Those frequent acts of altruism were not the limit or extent of Steve's unfettered love and generous support of his elder brother. Towards the end of the previous year, at a time when I didn't have a car of my own to run around in, especially over the Christmas period, I had the unlimited use of my brother's pride and joy at the time, a red two seater Alfa Romeo convertible, without so much as a hint of reticence or complaint on his part. So as a consequence, if my brother needed anything and I mean, absolutely anything, then he could have it, because I know that in both my heart and mind, if the proverbial shoe was on the other foot and Steve had won that money, if I needed it, he would have lent it to me unconditionally and the one thing I could always count on so far as my kid brother is concerned is that he is a man of his word, if he says that he would give me back the money by a certain time, then it is as good as done.

Steve paid me back the £40,000 in full by the middle of September, just like he said he would, which meant I was also now able to completely remove the burdensome millstone of indebtedness that had hung constantly around my neck, weighing me down, and for the first time in a very long while, I was financially in the black, financially stable and more importantly, indebted to no one. However, just because I had that vast sum of money in my bank account, it didn't mean that I was going to go on some mad and wild reckless spending spree. £30,000 might seem like a lot of money but if one is not careful, it's easy to fall into a situation where you find yourself constantly withdrawing some monies here, and some monies there from the account without realising that you're doing it and before you know it, that vast sum of cash that you thought could last you for an eternity has all but gone. I did however treat myself to one particular item that on the face of it, could be construed as an item of pure hedonistic luxury, but so far as I was concerned, it was an item of absolute necessity. I bought a second hand, left hand drive, two-seater, racing green Mercedes SLK 200 convertible. It was the first car I had owned since my old trusty BMW finally ended up on the scrapheap some eighteen months previously. Not having my own means of transport and having to rely on the kindness and goodwill of others in order to get around, sometimes felt demeaning and the fact that I now in a position to own my own vehicle, thanks to my incredible winnings, meant that I didn't have to put myself in the somewhat awkward position of having to beg a lift, or borrow other people's vehicles. I can't even begin to tell you how extremely satisfying and gratifying it felt after almost a year and a half of having to resort to relying on different ways and means of getting around, of being able to regain my independence and freedom of getting from A to B whenever I liked. It was money well spent and the bottom line is that, I spend my hard earned cash on how I see fit.

I still had a considerable sum of money left over despite buying the car and I still hadn't decided what I was going to do with it so when Steve asked me for another advance, almost two months after paying me back the original loan, this time, to the tune of £20,000, once again, I never wavered or hesitated in advancing him that second substantial loan. Steve never told me what he needed it for, nor indeed, did I feel it was my business to ask him. I didn't have any real use or plans for the money at that point and even though I had lent out a substantial amount of money for the second time in two months, I was comfortable and secure in the knowledge that my money was once again in the safest of hands.

I was at home one afternoon towards the end of October when I received an unexpected telephone call from a person calling on behalf of 12 Yards Productions, an independent production company that regularly made and commissioned television programmes. The caller told me that the reason for the call was to find out whether I would be interested in becoming a possible contestant on a brand new game show that was going to be screened on the BBC sometime in the Autumn. To say that my response to the offer was nothing less than sheer and utter excitement would be a massive understatement and I made it abundantly clear to the caller that I was more than interested. The caller went on to briefly explain that the show was called *The Waiting Game* and it was hosted by the comedienne Ruby Wax. My initial thoughts, as the caller began discussing the show in outline, was to draw immediate parallels with the last memorable occasion a television production company got in touch with me in such an unexpected manner, an act of serendipity that resulted in my highly successful appearance on *Greed* some five months previously, and I couldn't help thinking that this latest unexpected telephone call from an unexpected source was, quite simply, a classic case of history repeating itself.

I was tested on my general knowledge, and then invited to attend an audition later that afternoon with a partner. The caller's request momentarily halted me in my tracks I could think of no one I could pick to be my partner. So in order to buy myself some time I asked the caller if I could have at least half an hour to speak to one or two people beforehand and see whether they would be willing to accompany me to the audition. The caller agreed to that request and said that she would contact me again in half an hour for a progress update. I started to think long and hard about who could be a possible partner in terms of their all-round general knowledge and personality to accompany me on the show. Then, as if struck by a bolt of lightning out of the blue, I said to myself, *What about one of the Thomas sisters, Sandra or Heather? I wonder if either of them would be up for this?*

I went to Aylestone High School with Sandra and Heather, and they were exceptionally bright students. I also used to play Trivial Pursuit with both of them where they displayed an impressive range of general knowledge that invariably gave me a real run for my money. I contacted the elder sister Sandra first. When I put the suggestion to her of accompanying me to the audition later that afternoon, she declined my invitation on account of the fact that she already had a prior engagement that evening, a reason that, despite my initial scepticism, I had to accept, considering I was making the request at such short notice. All my hopes of taking part in the audition were now totally dependent upon whether her younger sister, Heather, would be ready, willing and available. After I got off the telephone to Sandra, I called Heather straight away. Heather, thankfully, was immediately sold on the idea of appearing on a game show and made it abundantly clear in no uncertain terms that she was up for the challenge. I gave Heather the contact details of the production company for her to speak to them directly and confirm that she was going to be my playing partner at the audition. Heather called me back some thirty minutes later and told me that her general knowledge telephone test went very well, a revelation that in truth, came as no real surprise to me, and the pair of us arranged to meet outside Top Shop in Oxford Circus at 5pm so that we could attend the audition together at the production company's offices in nearby Livonia Street.

I had made the perfect choice of playing partner in Heather. We have been good friends for a very long time, and to my mind, the combination of her striking beauty, poise and intelligence, together with my proven quizzing ability would be the perfect recipe for success. After the pair of us met up at our designated *rendezvous*, we walked the short distance to the production company's offices.

The main aim of the show was all about trying to wait **as long as possible** before answering a question. Three teams would compete in the first round. One team member would press a buzzer on the designated podium in front of them that would allow the other team member, who stood directly behind, to answer the question. The time that was taken to answer the question would be translated into points. The number of points that could be accumulated by the team within ten seconds were, one point, three points, five points, eight points, twelve points, and a maximum total of fifteen points, if any of the teams waited long enough before deciding to press the buzzer. That required the team player pressing the buzzer to show ice cool judgement, tactical awareness and an impeccable sense of timing. It was a skill that was just as important as a team's ability to correctly answer questions on general knowledge and the team that could combine both disciplines well was the team that was going to win the game. Only the team who accumulated the most points would go through to the final where they would be competing against the clock, trying to accumulate as much money as they could by answering questions correctly with the aim of trying to reach the jackpot cash prize of £30,000. Any team with ambitions of progressing to the final end game would not be able to achieve that aim by simply relying on displaying a good level of general knowledge. Equally as important, the competing teams would also have to display good levels of concentration, judgement, tactical nous and cunning, whilst on the one hand trying to lure the opposing team(s) into thinking that they were about to press the buzzer when the team's real objective was to try to build up as much seconds/points as possible, a tactic that a team would resort to and adopt if the team member pressing the buzzer was confident that a correct answer would be given by his/her team mate.

The three couples present at the audition were asked to take part in a mock rehearsal based on the rules of the show where both Heather and I took to the game like a duck takes to water, playing the required alternative roles of each team member during the game to near perfection. At the end of the audition, all three teams were told that we would be notified by post as to whether we had been successfully selected for the show. As we were making our way towards Oxford Circus tube station for the train journey home, Heather and I were more than satisfied with the way that we both performed at the audition and it was no surprise when a week or so later, the pair of us received the letters through our respective front doors proudly inviting us to become contestants on The Waiting Game.

November 2001

Dear Shaun

HAT TRICK
PRODUCTIONS LTD

Congratulations! We are very pleased to tell you that you and your partner have been selected to take part in The Waiting Game on Friday 9th November 2001.

The recording of the show will take place at:

The London Studios
Upper Ground
London
SE1 9LT

Pre-filming with Ruby
All the contestants will be filmed having an introductory chat with Ruby before the show (at The London Studios) and you have very kindly agreed to come in tomorrow for this. For this pre-filming, we have arranged a car to collect you from home at 11.05am and you will both need to be at main reception of The London Studios for 12.05pm. Please wait in Reception and somebody will come and meet you. We hope that this will finish by 12.40pm and there will be transport arranged to take your home.

Recording of the Show
On your studio day, we have arranged a car to collect you from home at 10.15am. You will both need to be at the studio for 11.15am. On arrival please go to main reception and give your names to the receptionist.
We will also arrange for your transport home, and if you have incurred any extra costs, then please bring all receipts with you.
You have probably already discussed your travel arrangements with one of the researchers, but if you have any questions please give us a call. We have sent this letter to your partner if you live at different addresses, and we have also enclosed a map for you.

If you have any problems on either day please phone Harriet Methuen on 07939 139 915

The day will be quite long and will include rehearsals, a full game and studio briefing and some food! The show is recorded in the evening, so you will be at the studio until about 10.15pm

All the successful selected contestants had to go for a pre-recorded interview with Miss Wax that was held a couple of days before the actual recording of the show and that pre-recorded segment was going to be inserted into the beginning of the show as a means of introducing the teams to the viewing television audience. For that pre-recording, I decided that I wanted to create the distinct impression that I was some flash, brash know it all who thought he was the "hottest thing since sliced bread with the brains to match," a strategy I knew that would make me an instant target of Ruby's legendary put downs. To ensure that I would get Ruby's complete and utter attention on the matter, I even went to the extreme lengths of bringing with me to that pre-recorded interview, a picture of myself completely and utterly stark naked wearing nothing other than a barristers' wig on my head and a cheeky smile whilst posing on a white rug. When I showed the provocative image to Ruby during our pre-recorded interview, she grabbed the bait immediately by mockingly dismissing my brazen display of self-indulgent narcissism. Ruby's response to my provocative image was the perfect reaction that I was hoping for thereby setting the stage for an inevitable mouth-watering clash of egos between a cocksure contestant, and a host well renowned for her legendary acerbic putdowns.

Two days after the pre-recording, we had to go to the television studios at the Southbank complex in London. The production company sent courtesy cars to collect both Heather and myself from our respective homes as we had to arrive at the television studios for approximately 3pm. One there, we had a briefing session followed by two mock rehearsal games. Once again, Heather and I played those mock rehearsal games to near perfection, making it all the way to the final end game and going on to win the £30,000 jackpot prize. The three competing teams were then escorted back their respective dressing rooms in order to get changed into the clothes that we would be wearing on the show, and as we emerged from our dressing rooms, I noticed that Heather was wearing a stunning gold jumpsuit. She looked absolutely fantastic and from her confident demeanour it was clear that she was ready to make a major impact on the show. In terms of my own choice of clothing attire, I went for the smart casual look wearing a fawn coloured suede jacket, pale blue shirt, black trousers with a black pair of shoes so expertly polished by Goggsy that I could just about see my own reflection in them. With a simultaneous nod of approval we both gave to each other, I looped my right arm through which Heather stylishly slipped her left arm and we strolled with a graceful yet confident swagger back to the green room in order to relax and take a couple of commemorative photographs with the other two competing teams.

The first of the two teams were two friendly and pleasant ladies called Hela and Annie who jointly owned a company just off Oxford Street curiously named Snog The Agency, whilst the other team consisted of a pair of taxi driving brothers called Alan and Billy, who were equally pleasant and friendly. After all the introductions and pleasantries were completed, all three teams were escorted team by team onto the studio set where we took our respective positions to the polite applause from the live studio audience. Once all the competing teams were relaxed and settled, the Studio Floor Manager began the countdown to the start of the show that was immediately followed by the short, but exciting announcement, "WELCOME TO *THE WAITING GAME* – AND HERE TO GIVE IT AWAY, THE LITTLE LADY WITH THE BIG HEART, RUBY WAX!" and as the inimitable Miss Wax confidently strode onto the set, the polite applause that greeted the teams turned into a rapturous one, more than enough I would imagine, to compliment, as well as satisfy, Ruby's big on screen presence and matching personality.

Ruby wasted no time at all in pointing both barrels of her verbal shotgun in my direction when she had a playful dig at my hairstyle, which was slightly less flamboyant and outlandish than the spiky creation that I wore for my previous TV appearance on *Greed*. But it was clear from that relatively harmless opening salvo that Ruby was merely warming to the task given the vast array of the acerbic comments and withering put downs that she had in her extensive repertoire which were surely going to be heading my way. I had no intention whatsoever of taking umbrage with any such dismissive treatment at the hands of Miss Wax. I had deliberately engineered any verbal onslaught that could potentially be heading my way from the outset and whether I lasted on the show until the end of the first round or the final end game itself, I was determined that I was going to thoroughly enjoy the whole experience.

Ruby asked the competing teams to decide which member of the team was going to press the buzzer first and who was going to provide the answers, as those roles would have to be reversed if a team progressed to the next round. Heather and I had already decided beforehand that she would be on the buzzer for the first round. With Hela and Billy chosen to press the buzzers for their respective teams, the stage was set for the first of the series of eight questions of the first round.

"QUESTION ONE, IN WHICH STATE WOULD YOU FIND SILICON VALLEY?"

As the time began ticking away, with brilliant judgement and timing, Heather pressed the buzzer and managed to amass for our team a very creditable eight points.

"WHY DID YOU PRESS THE BUZZER?" Ruby enquired.

"BECAUSE SHAUN KNOWS THE ANSWER!" Heather replied with a confident, gleeful tone in her voice, which she complimented by doing an impromptu mini Cha, Cha Cha on her podium.

"SO SHAUN KNOWS EVERYTHING?" Ruby further enquired with more than a hint of sarcasm in her voice.

"HE'D BETTER!" Heather replied in a forthright, no nonsense tone in the full knowledge and confidence that the points were in the bag.

Ruby then read out the question again.

"CALIFORNIA," I instantly replied in an exaggerated, cheesy, high pitched tone and the moment Ruby confirmed that the answer was indeed correct, both Heather and I had already resorted to our pre-rehearsed stage routine of a rhythmic low/high five which served the purpose of not only celebrating a correct answer, it's other desired effect was to act as a potential target for Ruby's celebrated acerbic put downs.

"QUESTION TWO, IN SUE TOWNSEND'S NOVEL, HOW OLD WAS ADRIAN MOLE WHEN HE STARTED HIS SECRET DIARY?"

I knew the answer to that one (13¾). I knew that Heather knew that I knew the answer but Billy, in an effort to get his team into the game, buzzed in far too quickly only managing to amass for his team three potential points in the process. Ruby then turned to Alan for the answer and he responded with the incorrect answer, 13 ½. Unfortunately, incorrect response meant conceding points to the remaining teams, but that concession for Alan's team at this stage of the round wasn't too costly. Ruby then switched the focus of her verbal attack on Alan and Billy with the taunting comment that she was surprised given their occupations as Taxi Drivers, that they would make such an elementary mistake about figures especially, she went on to imply, when it came to giving change back to the customers after the fare had been paid

Ruby then proceeded to read out the next question. "QUESTION THREE, WHO IS THE QUEEN'S ELDEST GRANDSON?"

Another straightforward question that I was hoping to get the opportunity to answer, but that opportunity was solely dependant on whether my canny teammate would be first in to press the buzzer.

Heather meanwhile, was trying to use all of her tactical nous and cunning in balancing the need to raise the points level sufficiently high enough to press the buzzer before the other teams, whilst at the same time, trying her level best to out psyche Hela and Billy by feigning that she was about to press it. Billy, whose initial nerves beforehand appeared to have settled down considerably, managed on this occasion, to beat Heather to the punch by pressing his buzzer exercising in the process, almost perfect judgement as he accumulated for his team twelve possible points. Alan made no mistake this time as he provided the correct answer (Peter Phillips) which meant that his team were firmly back in the hunt and ahead of our team by a single point.

"QUESTION FOUR, WHICH IS THE MOST ABUNDANT GAS IN THE UNIVERSE?"

As the time started to tick away, I could see Heather was desperately trying to gain control of the situation, but once again, she could not overcome Hela's even greater determination to press her buzzer in order to get her partner Annie into the game. Hela had accumulated five potential points and Ruby asked her whether she was confident that Annie would give her the correct answer.

Hela replied, "ANNIE'S ALL SEEING AND ALL KNOWING."

Sadly for Hela though, her complete and utter confidence in her playing partner was totally misplaced as Annie incorrectly said Oxygen as opposed to Hydrogen, a costly mistake that resulted in the girls conceding a full five points to the other teams.

"QUESTION FIVE, WHO PLAYED JENNIFER HART IN THE TV SERIES, HART TO HART?"

I was willing Heather on to press the buzzer who, because of the show's strict rules, could not turn around and look at me as the team member pressing the buzzer was required to face forward at all times. Any anxieties that may have been running through my mind were proved to be unfounded as Heather played this particular question to perfection and pressed the buzzer and managed to accumulate a very respectable total of eight potential points.

Ruby turned her attentions to Heather who clearly sounded relieved that her buzzing skills were back on track. "WHY WOULD SHAUN KNOW THIS?' Ruby asked Heather in a typical sarcastic tone. "DOES HE WATCH TELEVISION, OR DOES HE DRESS LIKE PEOPLE ON TELEVISION?"

Heather appeared to be standing rigid like a statute the moment after she pressed the buzzer which unfortunately for her, was the cue for yet another cutting remark from Ruby who suggested that the way Heather was standing gave the impression that she was in a state of rigor mortis.

Heather though was not shaken or affected by Ruby's cutting remark and her total confidence that I knew the answer prompted her to responded firmly with the reply, "HE'LL KNOW THIS."

Ruby asked the question again and I replied quietly, but no less confidently, "STEPHANIE POWERS," a correct answer that was the cue for Heather and I to instinctively break into in our rhythmic low/high five routine. Our act of celebration was like waving a red rag to a raging bull because no sooner had Heather and I finished our routine, Ruby aimed her verbal double barrelled shotgun firmly in my direction, expressing surprise that my hair somehow managed to stay in one place after such a brazen display of wanton exhibitionism.

Surprisingly and without warning, Ruby suddenly switched the focus of her attentions to Hela and Annie by asking them why they seemed to be lagging behind the other teams. That verbal attack on the girls was immediately offset by Ruby's reassuring comments that it was still possible for them to progress to the next round as the rules were about to change slightly for the remaining three questions in the round. For the remaining three questions, she explained, any team who gives an incorrect answer to a question from now on would give away a full fifteen points to the other teams.

"QUESTION SIX, IN WHICH EUROPEAN CITY WOULD YOU FIND THE SAN SIRO STADIUM?"

I desperately wanted this question. I knew that both Alan and Billy knew the answer and if Heather could beat Billy to the buzzer, we would, barring a complete disaster, virtually secure our passage into the next round. Heather did the team proud by buzzing in for a potential five points, much to Billy's frustration and annoyance.

"THIS WOMAN IS HOT TONIGHT!" Ruby exclaimed excitedly, echoing sentiments that I was already thinking.

Heather hadn't a clue where the stadium was but she knew that I would know the correct answer because of my mad passion for football. "M-I-L-A-N!" I said, gleefully.

Heather seemed unsure whether I was correct, but when Ruby asked her if she thought I'd given the right answer she replied, "I TRUST HIM."

"OH MY GOD," Ruby exclaimed. "YOU'RE RIGHT"

Ruby's confirmation that I had for the third time in the round given the correct answer set both Heather and I off on our now familiar low/high-fives routine, but this time such blatant showing off was the last straw for Ruby.

"CAN I GIVE YOU A TIP, SHAUN? WOMEN ARE LOOKING FOR MR RIGHT, NOT MR ALWAYS RIGHT!" Ruby's biting remarks was met with enthusiastic approval and applause from the studio audience but as far as I was concerned, her taunts and acerbic putdowns were falling on deaf ears. Our team's points tally now stood at a healthy twenty-nine, but despite that correct response, it was not enough to make us completely safe from the potential threat of elimination. Alan and Billy were still on seventeen points, with Hela and Annie's plight becoming more and more desperate as they were still stuck on only three points.

"QUESTION SEVEN, WHAT TYPE OF ANIMAL WAS DYLAN IN THE MAGIC ROUNDABOUT?"

This time, Hela made sure that this was going to be their question and she buzzed in where the accumulated points total was on five and this time, Annie made no mistake with the correct answer, rabbit, a correct answer that just about kept their slim hopes alive of remaining in the game.

It was now the final question in the round and there was still everything to play for. "QUESTION EIGHT, A MAGNUM OF CHAMPAGNE IS EQUIVALENT TO HOW MANY STANDARD BOTTLES?"

All three players on the buzzers were frantically jockeying for control for the crucial and final question for the round and the time seemed to drag on for an eternity before Hela was the first to react in pressing her buzzer. However, her valiant efforts were all in vain because the eight potential points which had built up before Hela had pressed her buzzer were agonisingly, so far as the girls were concerned, not enough to threaten Alan and Billy's score and consequently, Ruby informed the girls that they had been sadly eliminated from the game.

At the start of the semi-final, both Alan and I swapped positions with Billy and Heather respectively which meant that we were now in sole control of operating the buzzer on behalf of our respective teams.

Ruby wasted no time in fixing her attentions in my direction. "SHAUN HOW ARE YOU FEELING? WHY AM I ASKING YOU, OF COURSE YOU'RE CONFIDENT!"

I gave Ruby a cheeky wink and smile before replying with the totally unexpected response, "I'M IMPOTENT!"

"WELL! Ruby replied, whilst the audience broke into in fits of laugher, "ALL THE WOMEN IN THE AUDIENCE WILL BE HAPPY TO HEAR THAT." She then asked me, "HOW DO YOU THINK HEATHER IS GOING TO DO?"

I replied somewhat clumsily, in my risible attempt to scale down my erstwhile cocksure demeanour, "HOPEFULLY, I THINK SHE'LL DO WELL."

Ruby was quick to admonish my hastily, ill thought remarks, with the accusation that I was far too condescending with such a response. Ruby was trying her best to knock me off my stride, but I was having none of it.

"DO YOU HAVE ANY PROBLEMS COUNTING TO TEN?" she asked mockingly.

"ONLY IN ENGLISH!" I replied, showing her that my cocksure bravado was still intact.

Ruby then turned her attentions to Heather and asked her whether I would be the type of person that would blame her for any mishaps that could befall our team during the course of the semi-final, to which Heather retorted firmly with the words, "HE'D BETTER NOT."

Alan and Billy did not escape Ruby's withering put downs, even when she suggested, rather cuttingly, that they both resembled a pair of Pillsbury Dough boys. Ruby asked Alan about Billy's areas of expertise, but Alan, like me, was all up for giving as good as he was getting when he instantly came out with the amusing response, "THE M40, THE AIRPORT AND BACK AGAIN."

And with that, it was time for question one. "QUESTION ONE, IN FORMULA ONE, HOW MANY POINTS ARE AWARDED FOR WINNING A RACE"

As Alan and I vied for control of the question, I found that I didn't have the same coordination and timing that I showed in the mock rehearsals prior to the show, let alone, coming even close to matching Heather's accomplished performance on the buzzer in the previous round. Alan, by contrast, was in like a shot and he openly admitted in explaining his reasons for pressing the buzzer quickly when he declared, "I JUST WANTED TO GET SOME POINTS ON THE BOARD!" Billy responded with the correct answer that earned his team three points and resulted in the pair of them embarking on their own form of celebration with their own less animated version of the high five.

Instead of castigating Alan and Billy for their celebratory moves, Ruby wasted little time in focusing her attentions on me. "WHAT WENT WRONG THERE? I BET THIS IS A FIRST."

My response to Ruby's teasing was a cross between sounding rather sheepish, slightly subdued and downright pathetic. "I WAS BEATEN TO THE DRAW."

I tried my level best to reassure her that I was ready and focused and I sought to visibly demonstrate that fact, by appearing to perch over my buzzer like a coiled spring ready to pounce. "UNCLENCH YOUR BUTTOCKS!" Ruby remarked dismissively to derision from the audience. "I CAN FEEL THE TENSION FROM HERE!" Ruby then read out the next question: "QUESTION TWO, WHAT IS THE CAPITAL CITY OF AUSTRALIA?"

I tried to put my new focused approach on the buzzer into action, but before I even had a chance to do so, Alan again buzzed in with lightning speed, this time only managing to gain a solitary point. Once again, Ruby sought to make a mockery of Alan's premature speed in pressing his buzzer, only to be countered by Alan's rapier like wit. "I KNOW I'M QUICK, JUST ASK MY WIFE!"

Billy gave the correct answer, Canberra, and the team earned one point.

"QUESTION THREE, ART GARFUNKEL'S UK HIT BRIGHT EYES WAS THE THEME TUNE TO WHICH 1978 ANIMATED FILM?"

As the ten seconds began to tick away, I knew that I had to make this question ours otherwise our team could be facing a real mountain to climb and on this occasion, I managed to combine the requirements of both judgement and timing and pressed the buzzer thus managing to secure five possible points for our team. Heather answered correctly as I knew she would with Watership Down, to give us a slender lead. Our celebrations this time were less flamboyant than they were in the first round. I simply extended my arms backwards and Heather delivered a somewhat subdued and completely understated low five.

After the third question and answer was completed, Ruby explained that there was going to be a change in the rules that was similar to the rule change towards the end of the previous round. For the final three questions, any incorrect answers that were given by a team would incur a full fifteen-point penalty which they concede to the opposing team.

"QUESTION FOUR, WHO WAS THE FIRST PRESENTER OF THIS IS YOUR LIFE?"

I seemed to have regained my buzzing mojo and once again, I buzzed in just before Alan had a chance to react. Ruby turned to me and asked, "WILL HEATHER KNOW THIS?"

"SHE'LL KNOW!" I replied, confident in the knowledge that Heather's response was going to put the team even further into the lead.

"A WAVE OF ARROGANCE IS COMING FROM OVER THERE!" was Ruby's response as she pressed Heather for an answer and once again, my brilliant team mate responded confidently with the correct answer, Eamon Andrews, that put us 10-4 in the lead and one step closer to a place in the final end game.

"QUESTION FIVE, IN A CALENDER DATE, WHAT DOES THE LATIN PHRASE, AD STAND FOR?"

I could clearly see the determination on Alan's face in trying to win the question for his team, but with the game still hanging in the balance, I decided that I was taking no chances and took a leaf out straight out of Alan's book and pressed my buzzer that yielded a mere three potential points on offer. Three points may not seem a great deal but with the contest delicately poised, I was interested in one thing and one thing only and that was, getting points for our team on the board. Alan expressed his disgust at being beaten to the buzzer once again by uttering an unexpected expletive which drew howls of laughter from the audience, but there was little that Alan could do about the fact that our team were gradually gaining control of the round and were one tantalising correct answer away from progressing to the final end game.

As expected, Heather gave the correct answer, Anno Domini, which extended our lead over Alan and Billy to nine points, and barring an unexpected turn of events, Heather and I were, to use a horseracing metaphor, all but home and hosed.

Just before she revealed the final question, Ruby offered Alan and Billy words of encouragement reminding them that even though they were behind on the scoreboard, it was nevertheless still possible for them to qualify for the final end game. In the midst of the heightening tension, Ruby proceeded to read out the sixth and final question,

"QUESTION SIX, IN JUDO WHAT COLOUR BELT IS WORN BY A BEGINNER?"

A simple and straightforward question on the face of it. I knew the answer and I knew that Heather knew the answer as well and one would have thought that armed with all that information, it was a simple case of me pressing the buzzer immediately because by doing so, there would have been no way back for Alan and Billy, but I didn't. For some strange, inexplicable reason, I allowed my mind to drift off focus at such a critical moment in the contest as the seconds ticked away long enough for them to reach a total of twelve potential points at which point, Alan calmly pressed the buzzer to secure the question for his team. The sound of Alan pressing his buzzer had the immediate dramatic effect of shaking me out of my semi dream like stupor at a time when my mind should have been fully focused and alert to the situation at hand. Once I realised the enormity of my momentary lapse in concentration, it was too late, far too late. It was at that point that my wandering thoughts transported themselves back in time to our Sixth Form days at Aylestone School and our free activity period on Wednesday afternoons where invariably, I would either be playing Football on the school's playing fields or Volleyball in the school gymnasium. Heather's main activity pursuits, aside from her involvement in the Sixth Form's amateur dramatics society, included Badminton and Volleyball and her other favourite sporting pastime, Judo. Because of my lamentable lack of focus and concentration at the wrong time, it seemed that I managed to somehow snatch defeat from the certain jaws of victory, a truly demoralising and depressing state of affairs that was solely down to only one person in the team, me.

Heather and I could only helplessly stand by and watch as Billy began to explain that he used to do judo as a kid, and that the beginners belt in Judo was white.

"YOU'RE RIGHT!" Ruby replied in a tone of clear astonishment and surprise as both brothers began to hug each other both in celebration and relief as they advanced to the final with the chance of winning the potential jackpot of £30,000. Their happy and joyous mood was in stark contrast to my feelings of immense disappointment, not only for myself, but also for the fact that I had let Heather down. I turned around slowly to face my brilliant teammate knowing full well that our unexpected loss was all my fault. What could I say to her? What could I say to make the situation better? The answer is nothing at all.

Heather, being the type of person that she is, took our surprising defeat in good grace and refused to blame me for my monumental error even though inwardly, I'm sure she must have been very disappointed. I then turned around to face Ruby whilst at the same time attempted to brace myself for the verbal onslaught that was clearly heading in my direction.

"SHAUN, I'M STUNNED. I MEAN, WHAT HAPPENED?"

I tried to offer some sort of excuse as to why we fell at the final hurdle, but the more I tried to explain myself, the more pathetic I sounded, so I decided to remain silent and keep my own counsel.

"YOU LOOK AS IF YOU'RE GOING TO BURST INTO TEARS." Ruby lamented. Her parting shot to me before both Heather and I exited stage left was, "THERE ARE A LOT OF CRIMINALS WATCHING YOU ON TV TONIGHT...AFTER THAT PERFORMANCE THEY'LL PROBABLY USE ALAN!"

In the final round, Alan and Billy went on to win a mouth watering and well deserved £14,000 for themselves and amidst all the congratulations and celebrations In the green room after the show, I couldn't help but think that yet again, another golden opportunity had slipped through my fingers. A few days later, I received another letter from *The Waiting Game* production team.

November, 2001

HAT TRICK
PRODUCTIONS LTD

10 Livonia Street
London
W1F 8AJ

Telephone
020 7434 2451

Fax
020 7287 9791
020 7439 2170

www.hattrick.com

Dear Shaun

Thank you very much indeed for taking part in *The Waiting Game* and for being such fantastic contestants.

The series is due to be shown on Saturday nights in BBC1's Winter schedule, so your 15 minutes of fame will hopefully be broadcast very soon! You should receive a letter notifying you of the date your programme will be shown but if you have not heard from us by December, then please call Hat Trick and speak to Georgina O'Connor.

We are very sorry you did not manage to win any money but we hope you still enjoyed the experience, and it was a pleasure to spend the day with you.

With regards,

Harry , Jess, Jon + Nici

The Waiting Game production team

It didn't take that long for me to get over the disappointment of my slipshod performance on *The Waiting Game* as a week or so later, I was contacted by Endermol Productions and invited to attend an audition at their offices in Shepherds Bush as they were looking for contestants to appear on a brand new ITV game show called *Shafted* that was to be hosted by Robert Kilroy-Silk.

The main tenet that defined the show had more to do with the display of the two polar extremes of human character, selfishness and selflessness, as the two finalists in the show's final were left with the agonising decision as to whether to display selfless altruism and share the accumulated prize fund, or whether to display complete and utter ruthlessness and keep any prize fund for themselves. Before making that decision, the two remaining contestants are required to make their final submissions that would involve them squarely looking each other in the eye, in an effort to sound as believable and convincing as to the reasons why they would share that accumulated prize fund. But those seemingly heartfelt sentiments need not necessarily reveal their true intentions or motives and in making those final submissions, the two finalists had to exercise a great deal of nerve and considerable judgement as to whether they could believe the sentiments of the fellow finalist. Once the remaining finalists had locked in their decision on the designated keypad in front of them, Mr Kilroy-Silk would reveal their choices. If a finalist declared that he/she would "Share" but the other finalist elected to "Shaft," the finalist who elected to Shaft would get to keep all of the accumulated prize fund for themselves. If both remaining finalists elected to Shaft, then the finalists both lost out and the accumulated prize money would be forfeited. If both finalists elected to Share, then the prize fund would be shared between them equally. It was a format that would bring into sharp focus the moral and ethical dilemma as to whether there are any justifiable reasons or circumstances for people to deliberately lie to the detriment of others for the sake of potentially huge financial rewards all in the name of entertainment.

However, this novel but controversial attempt to push back the boundaries of quiz show formats to a new and interesting level attracted an unprecedented wave of fierce criticism and opposition from certain sections of the media, to religious groups who strongly objected to a programme that actively promoted and encouraged dishonesty, duplicitousness and sheer naked greed. In the face of such mounting criticism, the show's credibility and more importantly, its continued existence, was facing an uphill struggle.

I did very well in my audition, managing to make it all the way through to the final and when it came to my final choice on whether to

Share or Shaft, I elected to Share any potential proceeds as did my fellow finalist and given the fact that there was no real money at stake, it was the perfect ending to the audition. Whether I would make that same decision if I managed to get to the final in a real life game situation though, would be an entirely different proposition. Endemol contacted me by telephone a couple of days later to inform me that my audition was a success. I would be required to attend Elstree Studios in Borehamwood on Sunday, the 25th of the November 2001, as a contestant on the show.

The object of the game in round one was for the contestants to try and answer correctly as many questions as possible within sixty seconds and for every correct answer given, points would be awarded that would then be converted into pounds for the later rounds. It was important for contestants to try and accumulate as many points as possible because the contestant in the lead at the end of the round, had the choice of selecting any one of the contestants for permanent eviction from the show. That selected contestant would then have ten seconds to plead their case as why they should not be evicted and why they would be a benefit to the team.

The questions came thick and fast during those sixty seconds and unfortunately for me, I wasn't quick enough on the buzzer and managed to only answer two correctly. I could and probably should have answered more, but I was no match on the buzzer to another competitor, a Teacher by profession. She was just that little bit quicker than me, especially on the popular culture questions, and by the end of that round, she was the competitor who had accumulated the most points and as a consequence, earned the right to nominate any of her fellow competitors for eviction. I stood at my podium expecting the worst and it came as no surprise that I was the first person nominated by her for eviction. In the briefing session before the show, all the contestants had to rehearse what they were going to say in the event eviction. I launched into my impassioned plea setting out the reasons for my retention on the team, but I knew in my hearts of hearts that I was wasting my time. The person making the selection for eviction was required to give their reason(s) for making their choice, and in my case, one of the reasons she gave was, "Well Shaun's a lawyer, he doesn't really need the money." I was evicted after the first round and there was nothing that I could do about it, other than to put on a brave face as Mr Kilroy-Silk thanked me for being a contestant on a show that I had to leave with great reluctance. With my head bowed and my mood subdued, I left the set.

I didn't hang around to see how the game that I was freshly ejected from ended, nor did I bother to find out thereafter, because

Shafted was taken off air prematurely due to the insurmountable waves of public criticism the programme was attracting as a result of the public and humiliating distress suffered by some of the contestants who ended up getting shafted, in some cases, for huge sums of money that made the programme's continued transmission increasingly indefensible. From my own selfish point of view, it was just as well that I was spared the embarrassing experience of seeing the edition that I took part in being transmitted, because my entire presence on the game show lasted about as long as it takes to show the length of an advert break!

I made one last attempt to become a contestant on a TV game show before the year's end when I applied for an audition to become a contestant on a game show ITV had intentions of bringing back to our screens, the popular *Play Your Cards Right*. I approached my childhood friend, Hugh Christie, who had also appeared on a couple of TV game shows in the past. When I put the suggestion to Hugh about auditioning for the show, he responded by saying that he was more than up for the challenge and the pair of us attended the audition the show's production team held at a hotel in Bayswater in the second week of December. The audition consisted of playing the game itself against other auditioning teams and Hugh and I gelled really well together as a pairing, even managing to come out on top against the team we were playing against, but sadly for the two of us, our hopes of being selected for the show were dashed once our audition was over. We faced what could only be described as a rigorous interrogation by the show's production team who seemed to be more interested in the number of previous game show appearances that we had made between us, as opposed to the reasons why we both wanted to appear as contestants on the show. I got the feeling that the panel perceived the pair of us, somewhat unfairly I would argue, as a pair of seasoned quiz show hustlers, the usual suspects whose faces are seen on most of the game shows on our TV screens and NOT the types of contestants a show like *Play Your Cards Right* was looking for. My intuition proved to be spot on because a couple of days later after that audition, I received a letter in the post confirming the fact that we had not been selected as contestants on the show, the first rejection letter that I had ever received in the two and a half years that I've been applying, auditioning and appearing on those types of programmes. Despite that setback, overall 2001 was a really good year in terms of my burgeoning career as a TV game show contestant, especially with my breakthrough win on *Greed,* and I had every reason to be optimistic that 2002 would be the launch pad that would propel me to even more TV game show appearances and with a bit of luck, even greater successes.

I had taken a summer sabbatical from my private practice to be a Summer Play Leader on another play scheme. Sadly, on returning, I found that the state of my legal career was the same as I had left it, a clear cut case of more downs than ups, wondering and worrying where the next brief was going to come from and even more worrying, no real plan of action in terms of how I was going to turn things around. In the months leading up to the end of the year, I had to endure the demoralising professional diet of one trial here and the odd trial there, a situation that once again caused me to call into question whether it would be in my best interests to leave New Court Chambers once and for all. Those difficulties were compounded by another major problem that I had to contend with at the time which involved long standing issues concerning my physical wellbeing, mainly, ongoing problems with my ankles and toes that resulted in me having to undergo a number of medical operations which took me a very long time to recover from. Those long-standing physical problems can be traced directly back to a game of football that I had played in September 2000 for my beloved Sunday morning side, Cool Oak Rangers from Kingsbury, North London, who despite our location, played in the Wandsworth and District League against very good footballing teams that were mainly based south of the River Thames. I started playing for Cool Oak towards the end of 1988/89 season after a six year hiatus, the first time I had played any form of meaningful competitive football since my ill-fated attempt to combine law with professional football in the early 1980's. I had joined a team who had already enjoyed considerable success having already won two league championships, four cup competitions and were without doubt, a team that was very much in the ascendancy. The success of the team was from a combination of having the calm, authoritative and at times, ruthless management style of the team's manager, Kim Wade, who, like the self-appointed "Special One" Jose Mourinho, had had no footballing pedigree to boast about as such but nevertheless, commanded the utmost respect from his players. Even though Kim's role as manager was an integral part to the team's overall success, the same sentiment was also true with regards to the team's playing personnel. Some really good footballers have played for Cool Oak Rangers both before, as well as during, my time at the club, a list that is far too long to mention if the truth be told, but as with any successful football team, Cool Oak's successes was built on the foundation of an ever present, strong and experienced spine that galvanised the team. From the goalkeeper, Jeff Tavernier who I knew and played alongside from our time together at Hendon FC who could easily be described as an amateur version of the legendary Peter Schmeichel of Manchester United fame, that is to say, his excellent goalkeeping skills were just as important to the team as his organisational skills, his constant vocal presence could always be heard and resonated throughout the game. In defence, there were the Smickle brothers, Bryan and Ian, who were like an impregnable wall in terms of the way they invariably nullified the threat posed by the opposition's attack and their no nonsense approach to the art of defending was often the springboard upon which the team would launch its own attacking threat that invariably brought with it a great deal of goal scoring success. Dictating the game from the hub of our midfield was our Captain and team leader, Clayton "Dougie Fresh" McClaren, a player whose main playing strength was his limitless ability to drive the team forward for the full ninety minutes and like the team manager, Clayton's leadership qualities always commanded the respect of his teammates who played with him. In attack, Cool Oak Rangers had always been blessed with a whole host of match winning strikers that have come and gone over the years, none less so, than the prolific Lenworth ("Len") Hodge, my good friend and initial strike partner in attack when I first joined the team who was invariably, in the running for the club's leading goal scorer for the season both before and during, my time at the club, right up until the point a horrific knee injury in 1994 resulted in Len severely rupturing his knee ligaments that sadly brought an abrupt end to his playing days. The mere fact of having a good set of players and a good manager doesn't in itself automatically guarantee sustained and continued success. An insatiable hunger for success coupled with fantastic team spirit is just as important. In terms of team spirit, that always manifested itself in the lively dressing room banter where you had to have a very thick skin and be mentally strong enough to be able to dish out as well as take on the chin, the witty and at times, vicious verbal banter that may be heading in your direction, all of which helped to bond and galvanise the team but once the eleven players crossed that white line, our focus was on one thing and one thing only and that was winning the game. After the game, irrespective whether the team were playing home or away, we would always head to one of our favourite cafes on the Harlesden High Street, spending a couple of hours in each other's company, tucking in to a post-match fry up as well as indulge ourselves further in even more lively and witty banter.

Those aforementioned factors and ingredients laid the foundations for even greater success for the club, success that on occasion, turned out to be a bittersweet experience from my own playing point of view. Starting in 1991, the team won a cup competition playing on the hallowed turf at Wembley Stadium, a match that I played in from the start, thus enabling me to fulfil a long held personal lifetime ambition of mine, but sadly, my fifteen minutes of footballing fame came to a premature and abrupt end when I injured my ankle midway during the second half, an injury that was so bad I found it impossible to continue playing and I was eventually substituted. The team repeated the feat of winning at the grand old stadium in the same competition four years later but on that occasion, I was no more than a disgruntled and frustrated non-playing substitute, who played no actual part in the team's triumph on the field. The team won another cup competition the following season, another cup final, that I was forced to watch from the stands on account of the fact that I was dropped by the manager for not having the correct and proper footwear when we played one of the earlier rounds of the competition on Astroturf and I was unable to regain my place as the team steadily progressed to the final. We won our third league title in 1994, my contribution in that triumph only came towards the latter end of the campaign after I initially walked out of the team because of my frustration due to my lack of playing time. I scored in three successive matches on my return that helped the team win some important games that proved decisive in the title run in. The real slap in the face though occurred at the end of season presentation evening when the team were formally presented with the championship trophy and winner's medals. To my astonishment and disappointment, my name was initially omitted from the list of squad members who were going to receive the commemorative medals and it was only at the insistence of the majority of my teammates who had a word with the manager and reminded him that my contribution, especially towards the end of the campaign, had warranted me right to be awarded a medal alongside the other members within the squad and it was only because of the support of my teammates that I received my one and only league winner's medal. The 1995 Wembley victory was Kim Wade's final game as the team manager, a victory that allowed him fittingly, to retire at the top but it also marked the watershed of Cool Oak Rangers' unprecedented run of success. Since that Wembley win, the team's trophy winning days are but a fading distant memory and even though the majority of the players in the team are that much older and considerably slower, the collective love and enjoyment we still felt in getting up on a Sunday morning, playing a game of football still burned as brightly as ever.

That game in the September of 2000 was the team's first league game of the season and like any other striker in my position, I was looking to mark the start of the season with a goal and despite the fact I was now in my early forties and clearly not the same player that I was in my heyday, I hadn't lost any of my ability to play the beautiful game. I would describe myself as a poor man's Teddy Sheringham, a player who could hold the ball up when receiving it and play an intelligent pass to a teammate but unlike my more famous and illustrious counterpart, I didn't score as many goals as often as I should for a player in my position. But in the first twenty minutes of the game, I produced a performance that even Teddy himself would have been proud of, the highlight of which resulted in me getting on the end of a pass by one of my teammates which put me through on goal and a one on one showdown between myself and the opposing team's goalkeeper and as he rushed out to try close down my goal scoring opportunities, I sold him a dummy by dropping my shoulders one way, a move which totally caught him off balance, before quickly shifting my ageing body to the other side, leaving me with the simple task of rolling the ball into an empty and unguarded net. Scoring a goal like that does wonders for your confidence and I continued playing the game believing I really I was Teddy Sheringham, but just as I was really getting into my stride, I was scythed down by a lunging tackle from behind by one of the opposing defenders and felt a sharp, searing pain in my left ankle. I was in real agony and after receiving treatment and the so called "magic wet sponge", I tried to slowly get to my feet in order to see if I could weight bear on the ankle but it was impossible. The throbbing pain coming from my injured ankle was becoming unbearable with each passing second and I was finding it extremely difficult to hobble, let alone walk. The referee stopped the game momentarily, whilst two of my teammates acted as supporting twin crutches and took me back to the dressing room huts where I showered and changed into my regular clothes with some difficulty before managing, with my ankle now swollen to a grotesque state, to hobble back to the touchline to watch the remainder of the game. I've always had notoriously weak ankles and over the many years of playing the beautiful game, I've either twisted, sprained or landed awkwardly on them and whilst back in my younger days it was easier to recover from such mishaps, at the age of forty plus, acting under the insane delusion that I could still run around like a spring (although some of my team mates would use the less flattering term, headless) chicken, injuries of this kind always seems to take a great deal longer to recover. Foolishly though, I neglected to seek proper medical treatment and advice, believing that this was just like any other ankle injury that I had suffered in the past and in a couple of weeks' time it will heal itself. Only a wise man follows good and sensible advice and a foolish man his own and two or so weeks after suffering the injury, I was back playing football (albeit in goal this time), still going for my normal thrice weekly training runs, the rationale behind such foolhardy thinking was the belief that keeping myself fit was the best way forward in terms of my long term rehabilitation and recovery. As the cold chill of the Autumn winds morphed into an even colder Winter, I found myself at the mercy of constant aches and pains coupled with occasional swelling to my left ankle joint that was causing me so much discomfort, I was left with no other option but to seek urgent medical help. I eventually went to see my GP who, after an examination of my grossly misshapen ankle, arranged for me to have it X-Rayed, the results of which showed that there were no breaks, fractures or other abnormalities. I saw my GP a week or so after that and he promised to arrange a course of physiotherapy treatment for me from which he hoped, I would make an eventual recovery. I faithfully attended the sessions which were spread over a two month period and when I completed the sessions, it felt as if the ankle had made a complete recovery which I hoped would enable me to resume all my favourite sporting activities by the summer of 2001 trouble free. However, it didn't take that long before I began to feel sharp pains in my left ankle once more, but instead of going to my GP and having to go through the long drawn out process of waiting to be referred for a further X-Ray coupled with an even longer wait to be referred for more physiotherapy treatment, I decided to pay privately for numerous physiotherapy sessions, separate sessions involving acupuncture techniques. I even resorted to buying a portable TENS machine, a small machine that sends small electrical pulses via pads that are attached to the area needing treatment, but despite all the intensive and different forms of treatment I was receiving, my ankle was not getting any better. There was only one option left in my quest to sort out the problems with regards to my ankle and that was to go against all the steadfast beliefs and principles that I both cherish and hold dear and that was, to pay privately for medical consultation and advice and if necessary, for an operation. Although I didn't have any form of private health insurance, I still had some money left over from my winnings and I couldn't think of a better way to spend some of the savings that I had left other than on my own physical wellbeing. I made an appointment to see a Consultant at the Clementine Churchill Hospital in Harrow and after an extensive examination, I was recommended to make an appointment to go and see one of the best Orthopaedic surgeons anywhere in the United Kingdom who specialised in ankle injuries, Mr Robert Lloyd-Williams.

I went to see Mr Lloyd-Williams at his clinic at Nottingham Place, London, a stone's throw away from the area that is synonymous with the world of privately paying health care, Harley Street, and his calm, authoritative manner throughout the consultation helped put me completely at ease. He left me in no doubt after that consultation, that the longstanding problems with my ankle would be finally resolved. Mr Lloyd-Williams also went on to explain the total cost of the operation if I chose to go private and the figures he was quoting me made my head spin, a figure that easily surpassed five figures before placing the decimal point to the right and given the fact that I had already spent over £2000 in consultation fees, I knew that, even allowing for the savings that I still had in my account, there was no way in the world that I would be able to afford to pay for the cost of the operation. I asked Mr Lloyd-Williams whether it was possible to have the operation on the NHS in an anxious and desperate tone. I have no doubt that Mr Lloyd-Williams could detect the increasingly desperate tone in the sound of my voice and to allay those ever increasing anxieties, he told me that in addition to his private work, he was attached to the University College Hospital in Gower Street and he was more than happy to make the necessary arrangements for me to continue my consultations with him on the NHS. He didn't have to do that. A total stranger who was willing to bend over backwards to help me get my life back on track. So far as I was concerned, it was the ultimate act of true altruism, an act of pure kindness and selflessness that I will never forget and something for which I will be forever grateful.

I went to see Mr Lloyd-Williams a couple of weeks later by way of appointment, at the University College Hospital in order to discuss the results of the X-Rays that were taken at his clinic. He told me that the X-Rays showed that there were floating fragments of bone in my ankle that was probably the main cause of the constant pain I was suffering and that I would require surgery. He went on to add that after the operation, I would need at least six to eight weeks of total rest, during which time, he would oversee the gradual healing process and once I was sufficiently mobile, I would then begin an intensive course of physiotherapy lasting at least two or so months. There was one potential drawback to those plans. Mr Lloyd-Williams was totally frank and up front when he told me that it could be "some time" before I had the operation, but he assured me that he would do all that he possibly could to shorten any delay and that he would keep me informed if an early slot for the operation became available.

Mr Lloyd-Williams proved to be a man of his word when as a little over three or so weeks after my consultation with him, I received a letter from the University College Hospital with the news that the operation on my ankle was going to take place in three months' time in the middle of June 2002. It was at that point I decided that in light of the firm date for my operation, it would probably be the right time to take the bold and decisive step to tender my resignation from New Court Chambers. My court appearances by this time were sporadic to say the least and the knock-on effect of my lack of court appearances was the income I was receiving was gradually declining, the consequences of which would inexorably lead to the nightmare scenario of once again finding myself in danger of falling back into serious arrears with regards to Chamber's rent. With those potential dark clouds looming on the horizon, there was only one realistic option that I could take, it would be in the best interests if myself and New Court Chambers went our separate ways. Bearing in mind what Mr Lloyd-Williams had told me when we discussed how long the whole process, from the operation to rehabilitation was going to take, neither I, nor New Court Chambers in truth, would be suffering any real detriment over my decision to leave and with my mind firmly decided on the matter, I submitted my letter of resignation forthwith so as to ensure I provided three months' notice period and although the Chambers seemed genuinely disappointed over my decision to leave, we were at the very least, parting company on good terms, having reached an amicable agreement that any outstanding fees that I was owed would be used to settle any debts that I owed to them.

Despite feeling a great sense of relief in having made that decision, I was doing so in the full knowledge that there was nothing concrete on the horizon that I could fall back on which meant that once again, I was facing the worrying prospect of an uncertain future. It was an uncomfortable position to be in but despite those uncertainties, the one thing I was not going to do was to throw in the towel and quit the bar and if that meant setting up on my own as a sole practitioner, once I'd made a complete recovery from my injury, that is exactly what I intended to do.

In the spring of 2002, the problems concerning the state of my health and the state of my professional career were temporarily put to one side, when I was presented with the opportunity to redeem myself on the one quiz show that I craved success in above all others, Channel Four's immensely popular, fast paced teatime quiz, *Fifteen-To-One*. The show had reversed its immovable set in stone policy that prevented previous contestants (save for previous winners), from re-applying for the show. I was still smarting from the humiliation of my first appearance on the show three years earlier and I was determined to make a better showing this time around. I formally applied for the show towards the end of January 2002 and was invited to attend the audition that was held once again at Wandsworth Town Hall some two or so weeks later. There was no real difference between this audition and the audition I attended in the summer of 1999, save for the fact that this time around, the audition seemed to be a lot more structured and organised. The audition went extremely so well and it came as no surprise to me when I received the letter from the production team with the pleasant news inviting me for a second appearance on the show that was to take place sometime in early March 2002.

The one major lesson that I learned from my very brief appearance the last time I was on *Fifteen-To-One*, aside from not underestimating the strengths and quizzing abilities of the fourteen opponents, was that *Fifteen-To-One* is a quiz show all about substance and not about style. We didn't have to wait long for the previous show to finish recording before the fifteen of us were required to take our respective positions on the set. Aside from having the ultimate goal of answering the vast majority of my questions in the hope that I would emerge victorious, my other main tactic and strategy was to try to maintain as low a profile as was possible then burst into life once the show was in full swing.

Soon, the show's legendary host, William G Stewart, made his entrance and straight away he began talking to some of the contestants in his usual friendly manner that went a long way to making everyone feel at ease.

After the Studio Floor Manager had completed his countdown, *Fifteen-To-One* began with its iconic signature theme tune with its new jazzed up makeover before William G launched into his usual piece to camera reminding the viewing audience of the progress of the leader board and welcoming back the show's previous winner, Mark Jones. The target score at the bottom of the Leader board which we were all aiming for was 202, not the easiest of targets, but if any of the fifteen contestants didn't think, or indeed believe, that they were capable of matching or surpassing that target, then frankly speaking, they might as well have not bothered turning up in the first place.

William stared straight into the camera to begin the quiz. "TWO QUESTIONS EACH IN THE FIRST ROUND, WITH ONE CORRECT ANSWER NEEDED TO SURVIVE. WE START WITH ERIC MCKEVELEY FROM CHEADLE IN CHESHIRE..."

William G then launched into round one and out of the first six questions that he asked, only three were answered correctly with the previous winner Mark Jones failing to answer his question at his first attempt. Of the subsequent eight questions that followed, there were only three further correctly answered questions before William G finally turned to me with my first question. The only thing I was hoping and praying for was that lightning would not strike twice.

"SHAUN, PLEASE, LONDON LANDMARKS. WHICH BASCULE BRIDGE ACROSS THE THAMES WAS DESIGNED BY THE ARCHITECT SIR HORACE JONES AND THE ENGINEER JOHN WOLFE-BARRY WAS OPENED IN 1894?"

At last, a straightforward question! I felt a mixture of delight and relief and for the very first time after this, my second appearance on *Fifteen-To-One*, I heard the onomatopoeic "PING!" sound that confirmed I had given a correct answer when I replied, "TOWER BRIDGE", thus guaranteeing me a place in the second round.

William then began the second set of questions and it didn't take long before the contestant casualties began to mount up. The previous Fifteen-To-One winner, Mark Jones managed to survive an early exit when he gave the correct answer, Lord Lew Grade to the question of the TV mogul who was quoted as saying that it would have been, "cheaper to lower the Atlantic," in response to the savage criticism the flop, Raising the Titanic, had received. Twelve questions later, it was my turn to face my own second question and I was hoping that it would be the type of question that would give me the perfect two in two start that I was looking for.

"SHAUN, THE UNITED STATES. SUSSEX, MIDDLESEX, ESSEX, SOMERSET AND MONMOUTH ARE IN WHICH US STATE?" I didn't know the answer to that fiendishly difficult question and in trying to make the best educated guess that I could, I opted for the State of New York, applying nothing more other than pure random guesswork. Unfortunately for me though, the contrasting onomatopoeic "BUZZING" sound confirmed that I had given the wrong answer, but my random selection couldn't have been any closer in the circumstances as the correct answer was the adjacent State, New Jersey.

At the end of the first round of questions, the only thoughts that were running through my mind were ones of sheer relief and delight that I had made it into the second round, thus sparing me the awful and humiliating experience I had to endure the last time I stood on Contestant's Row.

William then began the second round in earnest.

"SHAUN, RELIGION. SHINTOISM IS THE INDIGEONOUS RELIGIOUS SYSTEM OF WHICH ASIAN COUNTRY?"

Another straightforward answer and with the correct answer of Japan, I was now in control of the game and I immediately nominated the contestant that for tactical reasons, I had set my sights on from the outset of the game, Mark Jones, because as a previous winner, he was clearly going to be the man to beat. My strategy paid instant dividends as Mark got his nominated question wrong and with only one remaining life left, he was now in an extremely precarious position. I was fully aware that I was adopting a risky strategy in such a cut-throat game like *Fifteen-to-One* because invariably, it's a strategy that could come back to haunt you. This risk was confirmed when seven questions went by and I was nominated.

"SHAUN, GOVERNMENT IN EUROPE. THE LANDTAG WITH JUST TWENTY-FIVE ELECTED MEMBERS IS IN THE SINGLE HOUSE PARLIAMENT OF WHICH EUROPEAN COUNTRY?"

I didn't know the answer, but managed to deduce from the question that the country concerned must be one of the small principalities in Europe either Luxembourg or Lichtenstein, a 50/50 toss of the coin and on a wing and a prayer, I went for Luxembourg. "BZZZZ!", It was the wrong answer. The correct answer was in fact, the other choice that was swirling around in my head, Lichenstein, and with one solitary life left to defend, I knew it was only a matter of time before I faced a nominated question probably, from a contestant who had an old score to settle. I didn't have to wait long to face that question. Mark Jones, who still had one life intact, had just answered correctly the question he was nominated to face and I knew from the look he gave me that there would be no doubt who the next nominated contestant was going to be.

"SHAUN, HUMAN ANATOMY. WHERE IN THE BODY ARE THE LIMBIC SYSTEM, THE THALAMUS AND THE HYPER-THALAMUS SITUATED?"

Another fiendishly challenging question which sadly for me, I didn't know the answer to. In sheer desperation, I latched onto the word, limbic in the question, a word which for some inexplicable reason, I managed to confuse in my mind with the word, Lumber, medical words or terms that are not only totally unrelated in terms of the functions they perform, they also differ in their respective locations in relation to the human body. I gave a hesitant and unconvincing reply, "THE BACK?" "BZZZZ!" It was the unwelcoming sound that I did not want to hear as it signalled the loss of my last life and with it, my elimination from the competition. I had got to the last six this time around and despite my obvious disappointment, at least I could console myself that there was a vast improvement in my performance.

At the end of the second round, time was set aside for a commemorative team photograph to be taken of all fifteen competitors together with William G Stewart and thereafter, I took my seat alongside the other eleven eliminated contestants to watch another *Fifteen-to-One* final which I would not be involved in.

Once the show had finished, I went back to the green room in order to gather all my belongings before leaving the studio for the journey home, still feeling slightly subdued and disappointed, but not too disheartened this time. My failure to make a winning impact on the show led me finally to the sad but firm realisation that my determined quest to win the highly prized ancient artefact from antiquity was to all intents and purposes, well and truly over.

The operation that I had in mid-June of 2002 was thankfully, an unqualified success, and after leaving the University College Hospital a day or so later, I was ordered by Mr Lloyd-Williams to spend the first week at home totally immobilised with my left ankle constantly propped up but for once, I didn't object one little bit, following those orders to the letter. That was because the football World Cup in Japan and South Korea was in full swing at the time and I was kept constantly entertained by the sublime footballing talents that kept me glued to my TV screen, especially the talents of the Brazilian football team spearheaded by the three R's: Rivaldo, Ronaldinho and the one and only goalscoring superstar, Ronaldo, who eventually dazzled their way to a triumphant fifth World Cup. However, once the tournament had finally come to an end on the last day of June, it didn't take long for the onset of boredom and self-pity. The days seemed to drag on endlessly and I could do nothing other than spend my time with my injured ankle propped up watching hours upon hours of mind numbing daytime TV. The rest of the time was being taken up fretting and worrying about my twin concerns as to firstly, whether I would ever make a complete recovery from my injured ankle and secondly, my long term future career prospects. It took the best part of nearly three weeks before I could eventually bear weight on my ankle and a day or so later after reaching that important milestone, I was able to hobble around at home with the aid of the crutches supplied by the hospital and a big protective boot that would not looked out of place on the foot of Frankenstein's monstrous creation.

Now that I was sufficiently mobile, I went to see Mr Lloyd-Williams for the first of a series of regular consultations that I had with him in order to monitor how well I was progressing and his reassuring words always left me with full of optimism that my injury nightmares would soon be behind me. By the end of August, I was finally able to discard the plaster cast, the protective Frankenstein Boot and crutches before embarking on the next stage of my rehabilitation which involved an intensive physiotherapy programme that was scheduled to last for approximately eight weeks. The programme itself involved a number of challenging exercises that included inter alia, balancing on a swivel board in order to help regain both strength and balance in my left leg and ankle, bouncing up and down using my left leg only on a small trampoline, intensive aerobic exercises up and down a small step and various ballet movement type exercises. Those physiotherapy sessions were tough, really tough but my ankle seemed to be getting progressively stronger and stronger after every passing session so much so, that by the time the eight week programme had run its course, my ankle felt as though it had made a complete recovery.

That optimistic but steadfast belief that I had made a complete recovery turned out sadly to be a false dawn because by the middle of October, I suffered an unexpected setback in the form of persistent and nagging twinges in the same left ankle, problems that increasingly became so bad, I was finding it impossible to stand up without any means of visible support. I felt totally distraught, dejected and at my wits end by this unexpected setback. All the hard work and gruelling effort that I had put in during those intensive physiotherapy sessions seemed to count for nothing and I couldn't help but wonder whether my left ankle would ever make the complete recovery that I was hoping for.

I managed to contact Mr Lloyd-Williams a state of distress and without hesitation, he arranged for me to come and see him at the University College Hospital. During that consultation, Mr Lloyd-Williams arranged for me to have a further set of X-Rays on the problem ankle, the results of which confirmed my worst fears that I needed further corrective surgery not only on my ankle, the X-ray revealed that I would have to have surgery on my big toe to prevent the onset of arthritis. Even though the news came as no surprise, it didn't make it any less disappointing or frustrating given the fact that firstly, I had no idea when that operation was going to happen and secondly, after that operation once again, I would have to go through the long and arduous process of recuperation and rehabilitation. Despite my natural concerns and anxieties, Mr Lloyd-Williams was as thoughtful and accommodating as ever and in an effort to allay those concerns, he promised that I would have the operation before the end of the year.

Not for the first time, Mr Lloyd- Williams proved to be a man of his word as no more than a day or so after our consultation meeting, I received a letter from the University College Hospital confirming that the operation on both my left ankle and big toe was going to take place on the 3rd of December 2002. After that operation, Mr Lloyd-Williams came to see me and told me that the operation on my ankle and big toe was successful and that he saw no reason, once I underwent a lengthy period of recuperation and intense physiotherapy, why I would not make a complete recovery. I was no less optimistic about that eventual recovery than I was when I first had the operation six months previously, but if I wanted to achieve my ultimate objective of total recovery, then nothing less than unlimited patience, dogged determination and sheer hard work will do.

That period of recuperation and rehabilitation after my second operation was to last the best part of about four long and gruelling months, but it was also a period that coincided with the start of a memorable and magical run for me that lasted right up to the end of the summer of 2003. Not only was I invited to appear on more game shows, I was even given the unexpected opportunity of the chance to present my very own game show.

CHAPTER SEVENTEEN

The first of those numerous auditions and television appearances began around mid-January of 2003 when I received a letter in the post from Hat-Trick Productions inviting me to take part in a pilot for a quiz show they were hoping to have commissioned by a major TV network. The name given to the pilot for the show was *52* and it was devised by a man with whom I was to forge a good working relationship, David Spicer. I was still recuperating from my second operation at the time and although my ankle and big toe was still feeling very painful and stiff, I was at the stage where I was able to move around with the aid of crutches and my trusty protective Frankenstein Boot. For the audition, I decided to leave my crutches and protective boot at home. I know that I was taking a massive, and some would say, foolhardy gamble by not bringing them with me, running the risk of a possible setback to my recovery. The rationale behind such thinking was I feared that the production company would think that I might not be physically up to the task of withstanding the rigours of the day's activities if I turned up to the audition hobbling around on crutches with a large protective boot on my foot.

The potential risk to injuring my ankle though wasn't the only problem that I had to contend with. My hair was, to put it mildly, a complete and utter mess. I had pulled the plaits out the night before, but rather than going to my hairdresser, I solved my tonsorial problem by covering the tangled mess of uncontrollable hair with an old grey woollen hat.

After announcing my arrival and the purpose of my visit to the person on the reception desk, I was taken to a separate room in the building and present in that room were the three other people who were also going to take part in the pilot. They were firstly, Gary Saunderson from Yorkshire and strange as though it might sound given the fact that he came from that part of the world, he was also a diehard Chelsea supporter. The second person taking part in the pilot was Emma Wilson from Warrington and the final person to complete the quartet was David Semple, a playwright from London. Once we had all made our introductions, the person in charge of the production team briefed the four of us about the day's activities and the easiest and quickest way he ensured that we all understood the rules of the game, was to show us a video recording of the game that was played on a previous occasion.

The show's format consisted of four players who were purportedly going to a clandestine meeting at a seedy location, to take part in some sort of nefarious card game involving large sums of money. Once inside that location, the four players take their seats around a dimly lit table waiting for the Dealer/Quizmaster played by David himself to arrive. After the Dealer/Quizmaster sits down, he then begins to shuffle the deck of playing cards in his hands whilst at the same time, endeavours to explain to the players seated at the round table the rules of the game. The cards that were being shuffled so extensively by the Dealer/Quizmaster was not an ordinary pack of playing cards, the pack contained fifty-two sets of varying questions that could be asked by him during the game. The questions were divided into four suits, each representing a level of difficulty.

The four competing players would start with £1,000 worth of betting chips that would be used by a player to bid for a question. Only one player would get to see that question which would give that player a distinct advantage in deciding on whether to try and answer the question or pass it on to a fellow competitor. In round one, there are eight questions asked by the Dealer which would mean therefore that each of the four competing players would get to see a question twice.

At the start of the End Game, the Dealer would proceed to take the next five cards from the deck and immediately reveal to the players what the questions were. Thereafter, the Dealer would then randomly shuffle the five cards before proceeding to place the cards face downwards, constantly moving the cards around until he was satisfied that none of the competing players would know which card was which. The player who ended the first round in the lead would be given the option to select one of the five cards before being asked by the Dealer if s/he wanted to try to win the money accumulated by the player who finished in second, risking their own share. If the challenge was accepted, the Dealer would read out the selected question and if player one answered that question correctly, then that player would claim all the money of the player in second place, but conversely, if the question was answered incorrectly by player one, then the player in second place would take all the money. If the player who had that first option to select the card decided to pass on that question, then the question on that selected card would be revealed before being discarded from the game, thus leaving the four remaining face down cards from which the remaining players could choose. The opportunity to win a fellow player's winnings would then pass to the player in second place and so on.

After the rules of the game were explained to the four of us in earnest, we were transported by mini-van to the secret location, that in fact turned out to be directly across the road from the main BBC TV Centre in Wood Lane, which at the time was undergoing a major redevelopment programme. As soon as we arrived, we were told to help ourselves to the refreshments that the production team had provided for us and it was whilst I was nibbling on my favourite Prawn sandwich, my attention was drawn to a conversation that Gary and David were having. I listened with keen interest as the pair of them spoke in great detail about their various quizzing experiences and how much they were looking forward to the forthcoming challenge. I decided not to join in their conversation as I was determined not to give too much away about myself. I wanted my fellow competitors to know as little about me as possible even though I got on well with all three of them because so far as I was concerned, if I wanted to do well, even in a pilot show, it was imperative to retain the element of surprise and to save all the talking for when it really matters.

After we had finished our refreshments, one of the members of the production team, Neil Gallery, called us over to the table where the game was to be played. Prior to the start of the game, Neil informed the four of us that we were going to play the game twice initially as a mock rehearsal in order for us to get a feel for how the game should ideally be played but on the third occasion, the game would be recorded and the competitor who came out on top would win a cash prize of £200. During those first two mock rehearsals, my own performance was a complete disaster. My gambling strategy was all over the place as I virtually lost all my gambling chips finishing in last place on both occasions but in saying that, I wasn't too disappointed with my performances in those two mock rehearsals games on account of the fact that beforehand, Neil informed us that it was our performance the third and final game when it would be filmed that would count.

Before the game began in earnest, Neil offered all four of us the following few words of encouragement. "Now that you've got a feel for the game, we're now going to start filming, so good luck everybody."

It was at that point, I reached into my jacket pocket and put on a pair of dark glasses. I chose not to wear them during the two rehearsal games but now we were playing the game for real, my strategy was to try and make it extremely difficult for my fellow competitors to read either my emotions or facial expressions.

David, the Dealer, joined the table, shuffled the cards, then invited the four of us to place the minimum stake of £25. For reasons that were not made abundantly clear during our only briefing session, the rules of the game required that it was to begin in a clockwise direction and David declared that although the first question was for David Semple, I was the person who was going to see the first question of the round. David then passed the question over to me and

I glanced at it for a few seconds before handing it back to him face down. I decided to bid for David's question with an opening bid of £25. The bidding then passed to Gary who decided to pass but when the bid for the question moved to Emma, she decided to up the ante to £50. The bid then passed to David and he decided to bid for his own question by matching Emma's bid of £50. The bid for the question was now back with me and I was more than happy to keep the bid at the same level which Emma decided to match with a further £50 bid. David at this point decided to fold and that left me with the option of either to follow suit and fold, keep the bid for the question at £50, or raise the bid to £75. I decided to leave it at £50 hoping that Emma would continue in the bidding process. Emma was doing her level best to read my facial expression, but she found that exercise virtually impossible because of the dark shades that were covering my eyes. Emma decided to fold leaving me with no choice but to answer the question. I had to answer that question correctly because if I failed to do so, Emma would take all the money accumulated in the pot. I visibly shook my head in disappointment before David Spicer read out the question.

"SHAUN, WHO WAS THE ONLY PRIME MINISTER TO BE ASSASINATED?"

I shook my head once again in apparent, then turned to him and said, "UMMM...I THINK THAT IT HAPPENED IN 1812 AND I THINK IT WAS SPENCER PERCIVAL."

"IT WAS SPENCER PERCIVAL, TAKE THE MONEY!" David replied with a mixture of mild astonishment and admiration. With my shovel like hands, I scooped all the winnings towards me and then proceeded with glee, to stack my accumulated booty in columns.

The second of the eight questions that the four of us were making a bid for was my designated question and as the rules dictated, Gary would be the only person that was able to see it. David passed Gary the question and after briefly glancing at it, Gary decided to bid for the question with an opening bid of £25. Emma quite understandably, decided to pass on bidding for the question given the fact that she was already £125 in arrears. David by contrast, decided to enter the bidding war with a bid of £25. Gary, myself and David again vied for the right to answer the question by making similar bids. On the fifth round of bidding however, David lost his nerve and dropped out of contention which meant that the bidding for the right to answer the question was now with me and there was no way I was going to pull out of the bid for a question that was originally mine in the first place. The ball was now back in Gary's court and he elected to pass, leaving me with no option other than to answer the question correctly otherwise Gary would take the money.

"SHAUN, WHAT IS THE NAME OF THE LITTLE BOY WHO APPEARS ON THE FRONT OF EVERY ISSUE OF MAD MAGAZINE?"

I paused momentarily before looking out of the corner of my left eye via my dark shades in order to see Gary's reaction before replying, "ALFRED E. NEUMAN."

"TAKE THE MONEY!" David replied and I noticed a slight smile on his face.

As I scooped the money towards me for the second successive time, the real pleasure I got from answering the question correctly was seeing the look of sheer horror etched on Gary's face. The third question of the round was Gary's question, which meant that Emma would be the only player to see it before the bidding process began in earnest. After only two questions, the pressure of the game appeared to be affecting David Semple who declined to make a bid for the question. The bidding then passed to me and I decided to turn up the heat on my fellow competitors with an aggressive, no nonsense bid of £50. My aggressive tactics had the immediate desired effect because Gary, like David, appeared to have lost the will to compete as he also dropped out of the bidding. Emma who was the only person to have seen the question also decided to fold which was a clear and unmistakable sign that she didn't have a clue what the answer to the question was. As I was the only player left, once again I was required to answer the question and I really fancied my chances of making it three correct answers in a row.

"SHAUN, WHO WAS THE LAST BRITSH LIBERAL PRIME MINISTER?"

Another question on British Prime Ministers that was right up my street. However, I had to pause for a moment and ask myself *is this a trick question?* The reason for my reticence was that I knew that Herbert Asquith was the Liberal Prime Minister from 1908 to 1916, but I also knew that David Lloyd George, the Minister for War in Asquith's government replaced Asquith as Prime Minister in 1916 at the head of a coalition government. After much agonising, in the end I decided to go for David Lloyd George because, despite being the head of the coalition government, he was still the leader of the Liberal Party. Sadly, it was the wrong choice. David confirmed that the correct answer was the other option I had considered, "HERBERT ASQUITH."

It was the other one! I muttered disappointingly leaving Emma to be the first person other than myself to win any money.

The fourth question of the round was Emma's which only David would get to see. Still smarting from my basic error, I made an initial bid for the question but then inexplicably, I pulled out from making any further bids for it. My decision to fold proved to be a disastrous one because when the question was eventually revealed, I felt totally gutted, as I was the only person who knew the correct answer. David was left to answer the question after Emma rather wisely had pulled out.

"DAVID, WHAT DID MOHAMMED RAZA PALHAVI BECOME IN 1941?"

I gave myself a kick on the shin under the table when I heard what I had I passed on as I knew straight away that the answer was The Shah of Iran. I went into sulking mode temporarily because I knew that I had forfeited a golden opportunity to take David, Emma and Gary to the cleaners. It was clear that the three of them were running scared of me and with the chance to earn more serious sums of money all but gone, I made the conscious decision that after I had seen my last question for the round, I wasn't going to get involved in any subsequent bidding for questions as I already had a sizable enough lead to take me into the final.

For the fifth question in the round, David passed the question to me, which I read swiftly before placing an opening bid of £50. Unsurprisingly, my fellow competitors refused to get involved in bidding for the question leaving me not for the first time in the round, of having no choice other than to answer the question that I had just seen.

"SHAUN, WHICH FOOTBALL TEAM PLAY THEIR HOME MATCHES AT HOME PARK?"

I went through the pretence of appearing to struggle with the question before making the contrived reply, "ERM... I'M GOING TO HAVE A COMPLETE GUESS... PLYMOUTH ARGYLE."

"GOOD GUESS," David said, but in truth, he hardly seemed surprised.

I accumulated nothing more than the stake money that we were obliged to place before the start of each question. It was the third correct answer given by me from five questions and if I needed any further proof that I wasn't going to earn any more money from the other three players then this was it, so I decided that for the remainder of the game, I was no longer going to bid for the remaining questions.

The next question was mine but Gary was the only person entitled to see the question which was: are you wearing socks? On this occasion, Gary, much to his obvious delight and relief, managed to win the accumulated pot and he earned himself £400 taking most of the money off Emma in the process when she elected to fold and invited him to answer the question.

The penultimate question for that round, which only Emma got to see was: who was the prosthetic makeup artist on the harry potter films? Once again, it was left to both Emma and Gary to fight it out for control of that fiendishly difficult question and on this occasion, Emma managed to turn the tables on Gary once she was satisfied that there was enough money in the pot before forcing him to answer the question. The correct answer is Mark Coolier but Gary didn't have a clue and his incorrect response resulted in Emma being able to reclaim the £400 that she had lost to Gary from the previous question.

The eighth and final question in the round that only David had the right to see was: is tiger woods left or right handed? David had no choice but to answer that question on account of the fact that myself, followed by Gary, immediately pulled out of the bidding before Emma forced David to answer the question and, in the process, won for herself an additional £100 when David chose the wrong option, left-handed.

After the first eight question in that round, I was comfortably in the lead with £1,400. The next round was the final in which one of us was going to lose everything on a head to head one question showdown. David proceeded to deal the next five question cards off the deck before reading them out loud one by one.

1. To the nearest thousand, what was the population of Switzerland in 2001?
2. Texas is a state in which country?
3. By how many votes did Neil Hamilton lose by in the 1997 General Election?
4. What is your mother's maiden name?
5. Who was the youngest Marx brother?

As David shuffled the five cards, I had already made up my mind that I was going to challenge Emma for her share as I was certain that I knew the correct answer to three of those five questions. Once David had completed his random shuffling of the cards, he then proceeded to place all five cards face down before moving the cards around so as to ensure no one knew which question card was which.

He asked me whether I would be prepared to challenge Emma for her accumulated winnings and without hesitation, I told him I was up for the challenge. I selected the fourth card out of the five and handed it to the David, and he picked up the card slowly in an effort to heighten the tension, before reading out the question that I chose.

"SHAUN, WHAT IS YOUR MOTHER'S MAIDEN NAME?"

"CARTER" was my immediate truthful reply (despite the fact that neither my fellow competitors or the producers would have had any way of knowing whether the answer I had given was correct).

The game was now over because one of the contestants, as the show's rules demanded, had lost their accumulated winnings. After the game had ended, both David Spicer and Neil from the production team came up to me and congratulated me on what they considered was an astonishing performance. Neil went on to explain that the production team decided that they wanted to re-shoot a different ending for the final. Because I was so dominant throughout the game, they decided that both myself and Emma would pass on our selected choice of questions, leaving either Gary or David to take up the challenge of trying to win their respective accumulated earnings off of each other. In the re-edited version of the recording, Gary elected to challenge Emma but eventually lost out as he chose the Neil Hamilton question, despite making a fairly good attempt with his final answer.

After all the filming had finished, both David Spicer and Neil spoke to me about my performance on the show and it was then that I confessed to them that during the first two rehearsal games that we played, I had deliberately gambled in a reckless fashion so as to give the impression that I didn't know what I was doing even though out of the questions asked in the two rehearsal games that were played, there were only four questions which I didn't know the answer to. Before I left the venue, I received £200 for winning the audition and I asked both David and Neil if they could send me a copy of the audition that was filmed. A few weeks later, I received my own commemorative copy, the edited version containing an entertaining and witty running commentary of the show by the most unlikely of TV double acts, the TV Psychiatrist Dr Raj Persaud and the man who was to gain instant notoriety and subsequent media and social ostracism some sixteen months later, the colourful Ron Atkinson.

A week or so later, still basking in the glow of my successful smash and grab raid on *52*, I decided to strike the proverbial iron whilst it was still hot and applied to become a contestant on Channel Five's *Brainteaser*, the live daytime quiz show whose content was a mixture of solving conundrums, crosswords and general knowledge, presented by Alex Lovell. The viewing television audience also played an integral part of the show in that at various times throughout the programme, viewers were invited to phone in and solve any of the puzzles or conundrums that were posed with the successful applicants winning cash prizes for themselves up to the value of £1,000.

I was invited for an interview somewhere in deepest rural Oxford. The audition itself went well and within the space of two days, I was invited back to the same venue, where the live transmission of the show was to take place on 31st January 2003. When I arrived at the relatively small studio complex, already present were my three other fellow competitors Len, Tom and a veteran of the television game show genre, Rupert Bean, whom I had seen previously perform very well on TV quiz shows in the past and unlike the other two, I was well aware of his quizzing pedigree and capability. I was paired to play against Tom, a first year undergraduate student studying History at Oxford and we were the first pair chosen to play our first round match.

The first game we had to play in round one was called "Scramble," which required the players to solve a conundrum on the buzzer and five points were awarded for every puzzle correctly solved.. I got quickly into my stride in that first game and never gave Tom a look in and by the end, I was in a commanding position of being twenty five points to nil in the lead.

The second game in round one was called "Crossfire," a game that was similar in its construction to a crossword puzzle board. Alex would ask a series of questions, every correct answer scoring a total of ten points for a contestant thus enabling that contestant to retain control of the board. Just like in the previous game, I took complete control of proceedings and by the end of our contest, I won with a convincing score of one hundred and five points to Tom's twenty and progressed to the semi-final where I awaited the winner of the contest between Len and Rupert, a contest which Rupert won convincingly. I wasn't entirely surprised at being paired in the semi-final with Rupert and there was no doubt in my mind that I was about to take part in what promised to be a real titanic battle between two evenly matched contestants.

Aside from the honour and pride of winning an episode of Brainteaser, Rupert had a genuine reason in wanting to win the competition. He was about to get married and declared that any potential prize money won by him would go towards a honeymoon in Mauritius. Neither myself or Tom were asked what we would do if either of us won the potential prize fund in the final, but the winning of any potential prize fund was the last thing in my mind. My focus was on one thing and that was to try and use my best quizzing endeavours to defeat a very determined and very able opponent.

The first game we contested in our semi-final was called "Word Storm." This involved the contestants being shown a letter at the beginning and a letter at the end of a word with missing letters in between. The contestants were required to fill in the gaps with any letters they liked so long as it spelt a properly recognised word. Once the word was declared, the contestant was required to spell the word out loud and if the word declared was spelt correctly, the contestant would be awarded ten points. My pre-match assessment that the semi-final with Rupert was going to be a tremendous tussle proved to be spot on because by the end of Word Storm, our scores were dead level at thirty points apiece. So far as the pair of us were concerned, no quarter or inch would be given or indeed, asked for and as our respective performances in the Word Storm round had clearly demonstrated, both Rupert and I were going to compete and fight for every question in our respective determination to come out on top.

The final game that would decide the semi-final was called "Clued Up." In Clued Up, the contestants were given a category in which up to four clues would be revealed one by one. A contestant didn't have to wait for all four clues to be revealed before pressing the buzzer with an answer but if a contestant buzzed in with the incorrect answer, then that contestant would be frozen out, thus leaving the path clear for the opponent to see the remaining clues. Rupert got off to a flyer in this round, answering the first question correctly. Rupert was lightning fast with his reactions and beat me to the buzzer with the next question but unfortunately for him on this occasion, he gave an incorrect answer, a costly error which paved the way for me to see the remaining clues and I was back on level terms when I gave the correct answer. It was a lucky break on my part but was just the slice of good fortune that I needed to get me back into the game because after that fortunate break, it really was nip and tuck between us.

When the programme's theme music rang out in the studio to signal the end of a titanic contest, I had just managed to sneak home by one correct answer, leaving the final scores of seventy points to sixty in my favour. After such a keenly fought battle, both Rupert and I hugged each other as a mark of the mutual respect we both had for one another and I breathed an almighty sigh of relief as Alex announced that I had made it through to the final – the Pyramid Game.

As the name suggests, the format for this part of the contest required a finalist to solve a word with only one letter revealed in order to win a set amount of cash. With every correct answer given, a cash prize was won, and the competing finalist then had the option to move down the Pyramid where the number of missing letters would increase for the given word with a single letter acting as the only clue. The competing finalist only had forty-five seconds to solve as many correct words as possible as s/he progressed down the Pyramid, with the prize money increasing with every correct answer. The amounts that a finalist could win with every correct answer on the Pyramid were

£100, £250, £500, £750, £1,500 and the maximum top prize of £3,000. A competing finalist could stop at any time after giving a correct word in the Pyramid. However, if a finalist got stuck on a question and the forty-five second time limit expired, then any money earned up to that point would be lost.

I managed to solve the words for the £100 and £250 down the Pyramid before electing to play for the next stage which was the £500 word which contained only five letters, with the letter "M" in the middle of the remaining missing letters acting as the clue. This time I found the going very tough indeed, so tough that after twenty seconds had ticked away, I was no nearer to solving the puzzle and I was starting to fear the worst that I would run out of time and go home empty handed. Alex could clearly see the difficulties that I was having and was willing me on, trying to be as helpful as she possibly could then, with only nineteen seconds left on the clock and with the benefit of divine inspiration, I blurted out the correct word, "Camel." Alex gleefully confirmed that I had given the correct answer much to my own considerable delight and relief. Before Alex even had the chance to ask me if I wanted to continue down the Pyramid, I made it abundantly clear that I wanted to quit whilst I was ahead. If I was struggling to answer the relatively straightforward £500 question, then the odds were even longer against for me to answer the others. Alex seemed quite relieved of my decision to stop the game and she went on to reveal the remaining answers down the Pyramid but in truth, I couldn't care less. I was a winner and that's all that mattered.

I received the cheque for £500 three days later and with those winnings together with the £200 I won on *52*, I decided to go to Jamaica where my close friend and colleague Rodney Wilson was getting hitched to his lovely long term partner Silvia Scott in Montego Bay. I headed to Jamaica for seven relaxing days which, given the two operations that I had, coupled with the two morale boosting wins on *52* and *Brainteaser*, was a holiday that was certainly well earned.

My next attempt to take part in a television quiz show occurred in the middle of April of 2003 when I noticed by chance, a small advert in the Entertainment section of the Evening Standard placed by a television production company who were curiously called Monkey Kingdom Productions. They were looking for contestants to take part in what they billed as "Television's Toughest Quiz," a quiz show with the aptly named title, *Grand Slam*. The show was commissioned to be broadcast during the summer of 2003 and was going to be hosted by the dual presenting team, Carol Vorderman, the numbers polymath from the teatime game show, *Countdown,* and James Richardson, the broadcaster and presenter who would perform the role as the show's studio analyst assessing the performance of the contestants after each round. *Grand Slam* was looking to attract contestants who had been successful on some of the UK's popular quiz shows in the past and the selected contestants, were required to put up £1,000 of their own money to take part in a series of gruelling head to head challenges over a number of rounds, all striving to achieve the ultimate accolade of *Grand Slam* quiz champion and the mouth-watering cash prize of fifty thousand pounds. I was both excited and intrigued at the prospect of pitting my wits against some of the finest quiz players in the country and so I applied as soon as possible. It didn't take long before I was invited to attend an audition at an address just off the Farringdon Road very close to Britton Street where my old Chambers were situated.

After arriving at the location at the appointed time, I met the two other guys who I assumed were there to take part in the audition. I immediately recognised the pair of them as top TV quiz players who had in the recent past either individually, or as part of a team, performed impressively in some of the UK's toughest quiz shows. Olav Bjortomt and David Stainer were the young men in question and despite their relative youth, there was no doubting their quizzing abilities or pedigree. I remember first seeing the two of them as being part of an extremely gifted pubescent quartet who were members of the University of Sussex team that stormed to the semi-finals of *University Challenge* one year. In terms of some of their own respective individual achievements in the TV quizzing world, David had appeared on shows such as *Who Wants To Be A Millionaire?* winning for himself £64,000 in the process and he also won a healthy cash prize on ITV's, *The People Versus*. In Olav's case, he performed brilliantly on *Fifteen-To-One* a performance that led to an appearance in the series Grand Final as one of the youngest, if not the youngest contestant at the time, to achieve that distinction. If the presence of these two young quizzing protégés at the audition was anything to go by, it was a clear indication that the producers of *Grand Slam* were looking for quizzers of the highest calibre and whilst I had the utmost respect for both David and Olav in terms of their quizzing abilities and pedigree, I was neither in awe of, or intimidated by, their quizzing reputation. I had a quizzing pedigree of my own which I believed was no better or worse, than any other competitor on the TV quizzing scene and as long as I maintained a healthy and genuine respect for whoever I was competing against, my philosophy and strategy to competitive quizzing will always be one of belief in my own ability.

The audition that Olav, David and I took part in was comprised of two distinctive parts. The first took the form of a short written test in which we each had to answer twenty five questions in thirty minutes and in that particular test, the results of the final scores between us were very close indeed. Both David and myself managed to score a fairly impressive eighteen points apiece whilst Olav managed to go one better with a winning score of nineteen. The second part of the audition involved the three of us being pitted against each other going head to head on a buzzer facing a series of questions fired at us at rapid speed. I was paired against David for the first of those head to head battles and I saw for myself at close hand just how good a quizzer he really was. During our head to head, I hardly got a look in because David was just far too quick for me and I didn't fair much better when I was asked to take on Olav in a similar head to head contest.

The production company contacted me by telephone approximately a week or so after that audition with the good news that I had been selected to be a contestant on the show and although I was pleased by my selection, those feelings were swiftly tempered by the realisation that I had to come up with the £1,000 entrance fee. The show's producers had given me a maximum period of four days in which to come up with the money as they intended to start recording the first round series of matches, but the plain and simple truth was that I didn't have that sort of money available to risk. I suppose that I could have used some of the money that I had left over from my winnings from *Greed*, but I was using those funds basically to support myself. Furthermore, I couldn't face asking family or friends for such a sum of money. So after two days of going through the torturous dilemma of deciding whether or not to compete on the show, I turned it down as I was not able to raise the necessary funds. Naturally, I was disappointed that I had to pull out of the competition at the eleventh hour but given the precarious state of my finances at the time, in my heart and mind, I knew it was the right and sensible decision to make.

My decision in deciding not to take part in *Grand Slam* turned out, in the long run, to be a real blessing in disguise in view of the calibre of the sixteen contestants who were finally selected to take part in the show, a stellar list that really was the Who's Who of the TV quizzing world and despite the unwavering and unshakable belief that I had in my own quizzing abilities, the sheer quality of any potential opponent that I may have been paired with, coupled with the show's format, would have resulted in my chances of becoming TV's *Grand Slam* Champion a very remote prospect indeed. Virtually all the contestants chosen to compete on *Grand Slam* had appeared in, or had won, most of the premier TV quiz shows in the UK. These quizzing luminaries included players of the highest calibre such as, Michael Penrice, the reigning *Discovery Mastermind* Champion at the time; Gavin Fuller, who in 1993 became the youngest winner to claim the *Mastermind* title; Graham Nash, the Hawaiian shirt wearing *Countdown* Series Champion; Said Khan, who was virtually unbeatable on *Blockbusters*; Dee Voce, another serial *Countdown* winner; Duncan Bickley, the airline pilot whose name will forever be remembered in the TV quizzing world as being the person who lost £218,000 on *Who Wants To Be A Millionaire*, these were just some of the names who would be doing battle to be crowned the quizzing champion.

The series on a whole was highly entertaining. Some of the contests were compulsive and compelling viewing especially, the first round clash between the two quizzing Maths titans, Mark Labbett, the Maths Teacher based in Wales who won £64,000 on *Who Wants To Be A Millionaire* and Clive Spate, another Maths teacher whose notable TV quizzing achievements included inter alia, a sizeable win on *Who Wants To Be A Millionaire*, a winner on an episode of *The Weakest Link*, a *Fifteen-To-One* Grand Finalist on the show's first series, a former series Champion of *Countdown* and to add to that impressive list of notable quizzing triumphs, Clive was also a World Scrabble Champion. The contest between Mark and Clive would have been worthy of the grand final itself especially, in the numbers round where the impressive speed the pair of them displayed in working out different arithmetical problems under pressure was not only a fantastic achievement in itself, but also served to completely and utterly vindicate my decision to withdraw from the competition. Olav Bjorntomt and David Stainer, the pair of young quizzing aficionados who I met and competed against at the audition for *Grand Slam*, were also selected to appear on the show with varying degrees of success. David sadly, fell at the first hurdle whilst Olav managed to go one stage further before he too eventually succumbed at the quarter final stage.

The grand final of *Grand Slam* involved a contest between the two most consistent players throughout the entire series. *Mastermind's* Gavin Fuller, who edged out his fellow *Mastermind* Champion Michael Penrice in a thrilling semi-final, met the formidable Clive Spate who saw off the valiant attempt of Dee Voce in the other semi-final. Both Gavin and Clive were evenly matched in that final contest and they demonstrated why they are quiz champions of the highest order, each of them scrapping and battling for every question as though their lives depended on it. Going into the final round of the contest, the outcome still could have gone either way despite Clive's slight advantage but in the end, it was Clive whose 100% record in the Numbers Round throughout the entire series who emerged to became the Grand Slam Champion and deservedly winning for himself the Grand Slam trophy and a cool £50,000.

The favourable impression that I created on the pilot game show *52* back in January 2003 paid an unexpected, but welcome dividend because sometime during the second week of June 2003, I received an invitation to attend an audition at the offices of RDF Productions in West Kensington for the chance to appear on a game show as a panellist that was broadly similar to the Eggheads format that was given the apt title, *Nobody likes a Smartass*. Whilst I was over the moon that I was presented with an opportunity to appear on another game show, I was mildly curious as to how it came to be that I was nominated to take part in the audition in the first place. That mild curiosity was eventually solved when prior to the start of my audition, I was informed by the interviewer conducting the audition that one of the persons responsible for giving me this chance was none other than the creator of *52* himself, David Spicer.

Before my audition began in earnest, the interviewer gave me a brief overview of the show's format. In short, the producers were looking for a collection of 'Smartass Know All's', with expertise in different subject areas who together would form a collective panel to take on an invited studio audience. I was asked what my specialist topic would be if I was selected as a Smartass, and I chose the only topic that I considered to be not just my favourite subject, but also my strongest – History.

The audition itself was video recorded and I was asked a series of thirty random general knowledge questions that covered a whole range of subjects. In order to ensure that I both looked and sounded the part, I adopted the guise of my quizzing alter ego, a persona that displayed sheer arrogance and supreme confidence as I fired one correct answer after another, showing off the full range of my general knowledge with the precision and frequency of a Rolex timepiece and out of the thirty questions that I was asked, I only answered two of those questions incorrectly. My cocksure strutting performance was thankfully deemed to be good enough by my interviewer and at the end of my audition, I was offered a place as a Smartass panellist on the show.

Seven days later, a courtesy car laid on by the show's production team picked me up from my home address and transported me to the TV studios in Waterloo where some two years earlier, I had recorded *The Waiting Game*. I was pleased, excited and above all, looking forward to having a great deal of fun and frivolity with the show's host and one of my favourite comediennes, Jo Brand.

After my arrival, I was escorted to the green room and already present in the room were my fellow Smartass panellists and the man who played a large part in getting me the gig in the first place, David Spicer, who, judging by the warm handshake and welcoming demeanour he displayed when he greeted me, was clearly pleased that I had made it on to the show. I was introduced to my fellow Smartass colleagues with whom I would be appearing on the show and they were Robin Simon, the Art Critic of the Daily Mail who was the panel's Art Expert. Danny Kelly, the Broadcaster and Journalist who was our expert on Sport and finally, Janet Street Porter the Broadcaster and former Editor whose expertise was The Great English Walks on account of the fact that she had been for some considerable time, the Vice President of the Rambler's Association.

The programme began with the four of us marching on to the studio set floor in single file in a scenario that seemed to resemble an 18th Century bear baiting pit. The team were greeted by a cacophony of good natured boos and hisses from the studio audience who we were playing against who came from the good old Berkshire town of Reading. The show's host, Jo Brand then introduced the Smartass panellists to the studio audience one by one and by the time Jo got to Janet Street-Porter, the two of them began to embark on a mini trip down memory lane as they talked about the "good old days" when they were work colleagues. Janet seized the opportunity to remind Jo that she was her boss in the vain hope that somehow Jo would go easy on her throughout the entire game but sadly, her attempt at pulling some sort of rank was getting her nowhere.

Jo launched into the show in that inimitable style of hers as she explained the rules of the show with the following introductory words. "EACH SMARTASS HAS FOUR LIVES. IF THEY LOSE THEM ALL WHATEVER THEIR SPECIALIST SUBJECT IS, THEY'RE HISTORY."

The first part of the game required Jo to ask each Smartass on the panel a question on their expertise. Robin answered his designated question with consummate ease, knowing that Sir Joshua Reynolds was the first President of the Royal Academy. However, when Danny Kelly he faced his introductory question, he got the year wrong when he was asked when the Premier League was inaugurated. Danny was, agonisingly, a year out with his answer, 1993. I was the next Smartass panellist in line to face his first specialist topic question.

"WHO WAS APPOINTED THE PUBLIC PROSECUTOR IN FRANCE IN 1785?"

It was the type of question that was right up my street and with all the hubris wrapped up in the cockiness that I displayed at the audition, I dismissively uttered the name, "MAXIMILLIAN ROBESPIERRE!" which I immediately followed up blowing on my nails before proceeding to polish on each jacket lapel, a deliberately provocative act which drew a chorus of cat calls and whistles from the Reading audience the moment Jo had confirmed that I had given the correct answer. "ONLY TO BE EXPECTED!" I responded in a haughty arrogant tone amidst the cacophony of derisory boos, catcalls and hisses that were firmly aimed in my direction.

Janet's specialist question was the toughest out of the four questions that were asked which required her to give the name of the footpath that runs from Merseyside to Humberside via Manchester. Janet clearly didn't have a clue and Jo took great delight in informing her erstwhile boss that it was the Trans Pennine trail. At the end of that round, Jo then gave an update of the scores. Both Robin and I still had our four lives intact whilst Danny and Janet had three lives each.

The next part of the game involved the studio audience in which a member of that audience was chosen at random and that individual could select any one of the Smartass panellists to answer a question on any given category, but the rules of the show dictated that a Smartass panellist could not be asked two successive questions in a row. If the selected Smartass panellist answered the question incorrectly, then that panellist would only lose one of their designated lives. If that panellist sought to confer with his fellow Smartass panellist before giving that incorrect answer, then the panellist who was initially chosen to answer the question would lose an additional life. That wasn't the end of the matter though for that unfortunate Smartass panellist, because the studio audience would then be given an opportunity to vote on the correct answer from a multiple choice of three possible answers, if the majority of the audience voted for the correct answer, then that would result in the loss of a further life.

The cockiness and arrogance I displayed in answering my specialist question immediately came back to haunt me at the start of this round because I was selected by Bea Seroon to face the first question which was on Art.

Jo turned to me and said, "ARE YOU READY FOR THIS, SHAUN?"

"I'M READY FOR ANYTHING," I replied in an effort to sustain my cocky and arrogant demeanour.

"OH GOODO!" was Jo's enthusiastic response that she deliberately riddled with witty innuendo as the studio audience roared with laughter.

I immediately sought to backtrack from my previous remark when I said, "I DIDN'T MEAN ANYTHING…"

Jo concluded our brief verbal exchange with the remark, "OH, I'LL UNBOOK THE SUITE THEN." Jo then asked me the following question, "WHICH MASTER CRAFTSMAN CREATED THE CARVED WOODEN FONT ON ALL HALLOWS' BY THE CHURCH TOWER IN THE CITY OF LONDON?"

I didn't have a clue what the answer could be. Reminding myself David told me he was the show's writer, I thought to myself, *That's typical David Spicer!* playfully cursing his name. Given my dilemma, I immediately sought the help of my fellow Smartass, Robin Simon, whose area of expertise this was supposed to be but unfortunately for me, he was no closer to knowing the correct answer than I was. Danny Kelly, the panel's Sports expert, was equally nonplussed, a deepening dilemma which meant that all my hopes were now pinned on Janet Street-Porter who, without being totally sure, came up with the suggestion that the craftsman in question could be the celebrated 18th Century furniture maker, Thomas Chippendale. The Reading studio audience were sensing that the panel were floundering and their incessant booing and cat calls were becoming more boisterous with each passing second. Jo responded to the audience's increasing belligerent mood by pressing me for an answer and I tried stalling tactics, but such futile tactics alas, were to no avail. I felt like cornered prey with no way out and I decided to adopt the policy of attack being the best form of defence and in an act of reckless bravado, I eventually responded to Jo's constant badgering with the words, "RIGHT, NO MORE PREVARICATING!" and with no other option on the horizon, I went along with Janet's suggestion of Chippendale.

"ARE YOU NOW?" Jo responded with a disdainful tone in her voice. "HOW TERRIBLY WRONG YOU ARE!" and with that, a wild resounding cheer resonated around the studio that it threatened, metaphorically speaking, to blow away the studio's roof.

My foolhardy and reckless bravado meant that I had forfeited two of my precious lives and was now in an extremely precarious position of the possible loss of a further life if the studio audience voted by way of simple majority for the correct answer. The multiple choices then appeared on a big wide screen that contained the following names. (a) Henry Cook, (b) Sawrey Gilpin and finally, (c) Grinling Gibbons. The minute I saw the multiple choice answers, I knew in an instant that the correct answer was Grinling Gibbons and almost immediately, I was consumed with a feeling of impending doom, fearing the worst that the intuitive Reading crowd would also come to the same conclusion. The voting patterns of the studio audience revealed the following results; 42% of the audience voted for Cook 21%, for Gilpin, but surprisingly, only 27% for Gibbons. The studio audience by this stage were now in a near state of frenzy as they scented blood, Smartass panellist blood, but their near frenzied state of fevered excitement quickly turned to groans of disappointment when Jo revealed that Gibbons was the correct answer. I knew that I had a lucky escape losing only two of my four lives and from the position of total and supreme confidence that I began with at the start of the programme had all but evaporated and was now replaced by an increasing sense of vulnerability that I wasn't expecting and, most certainly, hadn't bargained for.

The next question was on Sport. Janet was selected to face this particular question, a prospect which, judging by her immediate reaction to hearing her name being called out, filled her with complete and utter horror. The question that Janet had to face was, who defeated Martina Navratilova in the 1994 Wimbledon's women's singles final? Jo might as well have been speaking gobbledegook so far as Janet was concerned because once again, she simply didn't have a clue what the correct answer might be. I looked in Janet's direction to see if she was going to confer, but her apparent state of near paralysis seemed to be preventing her taking any form of decisive action and therefore, I decided to leap into action and confidently declare that I knew the correct answer. I turned to Janet and asked her if she was conferring, and I was met with nothing more than a totally blank expression and without waiting for any sort of response from Janet, I blurted out the answer, 'CONCHITA!" (in reference to the Spanish Tennis player, Conchita Martinez). Danny Kelly, the panel's Sport expert and Robin both gave nodding approval to my suggested answer, an answer that Janet gratefully accepted. Jo begrudgingly accepted the answer, and that served as the cue to another round of boos and cat calls from the studio audience, a fevered reaction that reached a heightened crescendo when Janet promptly grabbed my left arm and raised it in triumph as a means of defiant response. Whilst Janet was doing so, I turned to her and gently reminded her that I had lost two points because of the previously suggested answer that I had adopted from her.

"HOLD ON!" Janet responded indignantly, "THE ART EXPERT WAS NO BLOODY GOOD!"

Once again, the studio audience sensed the possibly of disharmony in the ranks of supposed Smartass solidarity and they wasted little time with their merciless taunting of the panel. Danny, amid all our petty bickering, appealed for unity and calm within our ranks before we faced that next question which was on History. Danny was nominated.

"WHAT WAS THE SUBJECT OF KING JAMES VI OF SCOTLAND'S 1599 TREATISE, BASILICON DORON?"

Danny sought my advice straight away and my immediate response was that it was probably on smoking. My fellow Smartass panellist Robin Simon though was not so sure and he suggested that it was more likely to be the Divine Right of Kings. Robin's eminently sensible alternative suggestion had the instant effect of casting considerable doubt in my mind as to which of the two suggested options on offer was the correct answer. However, after weighing up those two options, my suggestion to Danny was that my answer was more likely to be correct. Robin and Janet were far from being convinced by my offering and it didn't take long for the majority viewpoint within the panel to emerge that the Divine Right of Kings was the more likely correct answer, a viewpoint that not only called into question my supposed expertise, but also served to fan the flames in terms of the derision that was aimed at the Smartass team as a whole, and me in particular, from the studio audience. That collective uncertainty appeared to be reinforced when on the one hand, Danny and Janet were asking Jo to repeat the Latin phrase that was mentioned in the question, whilst on the other, Robin and I were continuing our contentious debate as to which one of our contrasting suggestions should be put forward. Danny, quite sensibly, then reminded both Robin and myself that it was his two lives that were at stake not ours, and he took the bull by the horns and opted for Robin's suggestion, The Divine Right of Kings which, much to Danny's relief, was in fact the correct answer and the studio audience reacted to Danny fortuitous escape with a chorus of loud and audible groans of despair. Robin's timely and ultimately correct intervention had the crucial effect of saving Danny from the imminent threat of expulsion from the game, but the fact that the "so called expert" on the panel had to be publicly overruled in order to achieve that aim had equally put me in a precarious and vulnerable position. The chinks in my so called expert knowledge on all things historical had now been brutally exposed before a studio audience who were on the hunt for a Smartass scalp. There was now no doubting the fact that my previously unshakable self-confidence had been considerably undermined at this point and for myself, and my fellow panellists, there was be no hiding place. The only way for me to restore that dented confidence was to answer the next question I was nominated to face correctly, anything less than that would put me in real danger of an early, unceremonious and humiliating ejection from the show.

The next question was on Janet's specialist subject, Great English Walks. I couldn't get nominated fast enough so I could be knocked from my proverbial pedestal. For the first time in the entire show, I was under real pressure. I was about to attempt to answer a question on a subject that I virtually knew nothing about.

Jo asked me the crucial question. "RUNNING BETWEEN HELMSLEY AND ILKLEY IN YORKSHIRE, THE EBOR WAY CONNECTS THE CLEVELAND WAY WITH WHICH OTHER TRAIL?" My worst fears were about to be realised and, more in desperation than expectation, I turned to Janet in the faint hope that her connection with the Rambler's Association would somehow keep me in the game. Turning to Janet in that manner though was a tactical faux pas on my part, because even if I had given the expected wrong answer, I would have only forfeited one life.

Jo interjected during my increasingly desperate conferring with my fellow panellists, coming out with the wisecrack, 'THE LONGEST WALK THAT I'VE EVER DONE WAS TO WALK FROM MY BEDROOM TO THE FRIDGE," a risible remark that was unwelcome from my point of view given the precarious situation I was facing which nevertheless drew howls of laughter from the taunting Reading crowd.

I felt like a dead man walking at this point and with no option left but to try and guess and hope for the best, with my fingers tightly crossed, I gave the tentative reply, "THE CLEVELAND WAY", having not listened properly to the question.

"CONFIDENT?" Jo teased.

"I'M GONNA HAVE TO BE!" I replied, trying as best as I could to keep the façade of misplaced bravado intact.

"DON'T BOTHER, SHAUN, YOU'RE OFF, GOODBYE!" Jo replied, in a cruel, dismissive tone which would make even the acerbic Anne Robinson sound polite.

I rose to me feet, having lost all my lives and prepared to leave the studio set, trying to show the same poise and dignity that King Charles I must have shown as he ascended the scaffold on his way to his execution. As I stepped off the stage, the air was filled with a cacophony of prolonged wild cheering together with boos and hisses and I responded by defiantly shaking my fists at the frenzied crowd before finally disappearing through the exit door. After my exit, Jo revealed the answer once all the cheering had died down. The trail in question was called the Dales Way.

Although David's reassuring words were a pleasant sound for my sore ears, it was small consolation as once again, I would be forced to look on frustratingly from the side lines as the game entered the final round as Jo announced that there were only three Smartasses left for the "Smartass Showdown." In the final round, the studio audience were all required to stand up and wave the questions that they were holding in the air as if they were MP's debating in the House of Commons waving their ballot papers. The Smartass panel then have to answer ten questions in ninety seconds on the panellists' specialist subjects and those questions will also include the specialist subjects of any Smartass panellist who had been eliminated. If the Smartass panel failed to reach the target of ten correct answers within the designated time allowed, then studio audience would claim victory. On this occasion, my fellow panellists fell agonisingly short of the target as they managed to answer nine questions correctly which made it a disappointing affair all round.

During the journey home, I had the chance to reflect on the thoroughly enjoyable experience that I had just undergone, but those initial pleasant thoughts were tempered by the unpalatable truth that this was another occasion where I failed to last the distance on a quiz show. Somewhat reassuringly though, David had pointed out to me during our brief discussion in the green room in the aftermath of my early elimination, that the only consolation I had to hold on to was the fact that I still had one final chance to put things right on my next appearance on the show in two days' time and it was an opportunity that I was determined to grab with both hands.

The day for my second and final appearance on *Nobody Likes A Smartass* had arrived and I was looking forward to the chance to redeem myself after my disappointing and lamentable showing on my previous appearance. After I arrived at the studios, I was escorted to the green room and present in that room were David Spicer and my fellow panellists, James King, the young, up and coming commentator and broadcaster on music and social trends who was our expert on Music, Stuart Maconie, the broadcaster and television presenter who was our Film expert and finally, Arabella Weir, the comedienne and regular stalwart on the comedy sketch show, *The Fast Show* whose expertise was on the English Literature. Moments later, all four of us were collected by a member of the show's production team who escorted us to one of the sides of the studio set and after we were given the signal by the Studio Floor Manager, we confidently strolled onto the set in single file where a lively and boisterous studio audience from the city of Oxford was awaiting our presence. After Jo introduced the panel, she immediately sought to undermine the collective confidence of the Smartass panel with her cutting put downs. Everyone the panel, rather wisely, refused to take the bait.

Jo then got the show underway by asking us each in turn questions on our individual specialist subjects and, save for Stuart Maconie, the so-called Smartass panel of "experts" got off to the worst possible start, each losing a precious life, much to the gleeful delight of Jo and the partisan studio audience. At the start of the following round that involved the studio audience nominating a panellist to answer a question, the panel collectively as a whole were fairing no better. The Oxford crowd seemed to have me firmly trained in their sights and wasted no time in nominating me to face a rather difficult music question which rather unsurprisingly, I got completely wrong. On this occasion though, despite my blunder, I made the sensible decision not to confer with any of my fellow panellists, having learned my lesson from the last time I was on the show. Thankfully this time around, the studio audience failed to press home their advantage when they had to vote on which of the three multiple choices on offer was the correct answer and their wrong selection meant that I was spared the indignity of the loss of a further life. I was lucky to have escaped even greater punishment, but it still left me in the extremely precarious position of having only two lives left to play with. My fellow Smartass panellist Arabella Weir's position was even more desperate than my own, a situation that came about sadly, because of problems of her own making which arose after she was nominated to face the following film question.

"WITH WHICH FILM DID THE ACTOR DANNY DEVITO MAKE HIS DEBUT AS A DIRECTOR?"

Sadly, and without giving the question any great deal of thought, Arabella leapt in with the answer, the Wars of the Roses.

"NO, THAT'S WRONG, ARABELLA," Jo replied with a hint of glee in her voice, a revelation that prompted a look of sheer horror to descend over Arabella's face which was the cue for the Oxford crowd to start cheering loudly and boisterously in delight at her glaring error.

Arabella immediately realised her mistake and tried to retrieve an already lost cause when she declared, "OH I KNOW, IT'S THROW MAMMA FROM THE TRAIN!" but Arabella's desperate attempts to rectify her unfortunate error was far too late and in her futile attempts to rectify that error, she made her precarious position even worse by blurting out the correct answer. Arabella had virtually gifted the studio audience another of her precious lives as they prepared to cast their vote on the three multiple choice options that were about to be displayed. "I'VE SHOT MYSELF IN THE FOOT THERE!" Arabella lamented ruefully.

Seizing the opportunity to twist the knife even deeper, Jo sarcastically replied, "ACTUALLY BOTH FEET."

Out of the three multiple choices that the Oxford studio audience were required to vote on, a whopping 94% voted for Throw Mamma from the Train, 0% voted for Mafia and 6% voted for Romancing the Stone. Poor Arabella now only had one solitary life left.

"TRY TO CONTAIN YOUR PAIN." Jo added, rubbing even more salt into Arabella's already gaping wound. "WE HAVE A THERAPIST READY FOR YOU AFTER THE SHOW."

The next question was History and James King was nominated to answer it.

"WHO BECAME THE VICEROY OF INDIA IN 1898?"

James decided that he wasn't going to consult with either myself, or his fellow Smartass colleagues and was going to attempt to answer the question by himself. James was clearly struggling with the question and it was just as well that he chose not to consult with the team because admittedly, I didn't know the answer. James decided to throw caution to the wind and went for the unlikely choice of Clive of India, which I knew was definitely wrong on account of the fact that Robert Clive was born nearly a century earlier.

"YOU'RE WRONG, I'M AFRAID," was Jo's expected response and once again, the Oxford studio audience immediately responded to James' incorrect answer with yet another round of wild and frenzied cheering.

James' incorrect answer meant that he too would be vulnerable to the potential loss of a further life if the majority of the studio audience voted for the correct answer from the multiple choices on offer. After Jo revealed those multiple choices, the result of the studio audiences' vote was as follows; Lord Minto 6%, Lord Curzon an overwhelming total of 73% and finally, Lord Chelmsford on 21%.

"THE VICEROY OF INDIA IS MY LOCAL CURRY HOUSE," James ruefully lamented with more than an air of resignation in his voice once the results of the studio vote had been revealed and now he, like Arabella, was sitting uncomfortably on only one life.

Stuart Marconie seemed suitably unimpressed with one of the multiple choices that were on offer. "LORD MINTO? LORD MINTO? THEY MIGHT AS WELL HAVE CALLED HIM LORD TREBOR MINT!" Stuart's protestations may have been justifiable, but in the context of this game, it served to expose him as a target for further ridicule and good-natured abuse.

The studio audience were clearly baying for Smartass blood and it came as no surprise when Stuart was nominated to face the next question on English Literature.

"WHICH FICTIONAL DETECTIVE WAS THE WELL-KNOWN CREATION OF G. K. CHESTERTON?"

It was now Stuart's turn to toy with the audience and with the situation firmly under his control, he replied in a confident, dismissive tone, "WELL LET'S THINK OF THE FICTIONAL DETECTIVE, OR SHALL WE JUST SAY, FATHER BROWN!"

I knew Stuart knew the correct answer to that question and at such a critical stage of the contest, he was the only Smartass panellist who had hardly put a foot wrong.

The next question was on Music and, although half of the audience was baying for my blood, James was nominated.

"WHAT NAME DID ERIC CLAPTON GIVE TO THE BLACK GUITAR THAT HE HAD MADE FROM A GROUP OF STRATOCASTER GUITARS THAT IS STILL HIS FAVOURITE TODAY?"

After Jo had finished reading it, I was almost overcome with a tremendous sense of relief that I was not the panellist chosen to face such a tough question. James bore the haunted look of a condemned man about to take the long and undignified walk to the green room. With nothing to lose, James decided to confer with the rest of the panel. Stuart's initial contribution to the team's discussion was to suggest to James to apply a considered and lateral approach in trying to find the correct answer when he said, "THE WORD BLACK, ISN'T THE CLUE IN THE QUESTION?" before putting forward the suggestion, "BLACK BEAUTY". In terms of my own contribution to this seemingly impossible debate, the suggestion I offered to my beleaguered colleague was that the guitar was probably called "CREAM," in reference to Clapton's one time membership of the Sixties rock super group of the same name. Arabella's contribution to the debate was to suggest that the name of the guitar was probably "LAYLA", in reference to one of Clapton's popular and well known hits, but despite the wild and varied nature of our suggestions, the reality of the situation was that the four of us really didn't have a clue what the correct answer was. The bottom line was that this was James' call and ultimately, only he could decide which of those suggested options he would go for.

Prior to making that final choice, James crossed his fingers in desperate hope. "I'M PREPARED TO WALK! I'M GOING FOR ... LAYLA!"

"GOODBYE, JAMES!" said Jo dismissively.

James now had to suffer the same indignities that befell me a couple days earlier and, like me, he mockingly shook his fists towards the jeering Oxford crowd who took great pleasure and delight in claiming an early Smartass scalp before he finally disappeared from view. After James' untimely exit, Jo then revealed the correct answer which, given the nature of the team's discussions, made it all the more agonising and cruel.

"THE ANSWER, JUST TO MAKE YOU CRY, WAS BLACKIE!"

The next category was Film and given Arabella's precarious position of only having one remaining life left, she was, fairly predictably, the next Smartass panellist in the studio audience's firing line.

"IN WHICH WOODY ALLEN FILM DID DEMI MOORE APPEAR?"

Arabella clearly didn't have a clue and her desperate plight meant that she was teetering on the brink of ejection from the show. Quite understandably, she resorted to stalling tactics, complaining at the same time about how easy she had made it for the Oxford crowd by cheaply giving away the Danny Devito answer earlier in the game. In an effort to offer what assistance that I could, I turned to Arabella and told her that Woody Allen is one of my all-time favourite actor/directors, particularly his earlier films. Arabella responded by asking me if I knew the answer. I said, unhelpfully, that I didn't. However, given Arabella's increasingly desperate situation, I wasn't simply going to just give up without trying to help my beleaguered colleague and with that, I began to trawl through the deep recesses of my mind of all of the Woody Allen films that I could think of in a frantic effort to come up with the right answer.

Suddenly, a flash of inspiration came over me and I turned to Arabella and said to her without any real rhyme or reason, "WHAT ABOUT DECONSTRUCTING HARRY?"

My suggestion was, admittedly, a complete shot in the dark and I offered it solely because I was sure that Demi Moore had not appeared in any of Woody Allen's earlier films. It was good a suggestion as any of them.

With no other plausible suggestion on the table and with nothing to lose, Arabella said, "OH ALL RIGHT, DECONSTRUCTING HARRY."

After Arabella's hurried response, a collective chorus of groans and boos began to resonate throughout the studio audience when to the team's astonishment, Jo begrudgingly confirmed that Arabella had in fact given the correct answer. Even Jo seemed quite shocked that Arabella had managed to survive against seemingly impossible odds and with that, she turned to the studio audience to gently remind them that they should start to be a little wary.

Admittedly, Deconstructing Harry was an inspired piece of lucky guesswork on my part, with a little bit of logical reasoning thrown in for good measure. It was the first slice of good fortune that the team had had in the game and the three of us celebrated Arabella's correct answer by treating ourselves to mini high fives amidst the good-natured jeering and booing from the studio audience. There was no doubting the fact that, as a team, we had an extremely lucky break, a slice of good fortune that we hoped would be the start of the turning of the tide in our favour.

The next question was on History and Stuart was the Smartass panellist nominated to face it.

"WHICH FUTURE PRIME MINISTER BECAME POST MASTER GENERAL IN 1922?"

Stuart wasn't quite sure about the correct answer and immediately turned to me for help and assistance. I began to think about the question and the likely candidates and after some considerable thought, I narrowed the choices down to two possible candidates and offered them to Stuart for his consideration. Those options were, Neville Chamberlain, my own preferred choice, and Stanley Baldwin. During our panel discussions, Stuart mentioned the fact, a fact that I hasten to add, I was acutely aware of, that Stanley Baldwin was the Prime Minister during the General Strike of 1926 before going to ask himself, could he have gone from stamps to prime minister in four short years?

Arabella's contribution to the debate was to suggest the name Clement Atlee, a suggestion that I immediately advised Stuart to dismiss out of hand. Stuart's personal preference appeared to be increasingly leaning towards Stanley Baldwin. Sensing that he was about to make Baldwin his final choice, I intervened and turned to Stuart and told him I really thought it was Neville Chamberlain. Stuart paused momentarily in order to evaluate my suggestion and after a great deal of thought, eventually decided to go with my choice.

Jo turned to me and asked, "DO YOU THINK HE'S RIGHT, SHAUN?"

"I THINK HE IS RIGHT!" I replied with ever increasing confident tone in my voice.

"HE'S RIGHT," Jo confirmed, to yet more groans from the audience.

The sight of seeing an increasingly deflated studio audience was more than pleasing to the eye and my immediate response to another correct answer by the team was to taunt the Oxford crowd by giving them the thumbs down sign. The Smartass panel were now clearly in the ascendancy and were more determined than ever to press home our advantage.

The final question of the round was on English Literature and, surprisingly, and to the audience's disdain, Arabella was nominated. The audience was screaming for me to be chosen, but the man making the decision said it should be Arabella as she had got the last couple of questions wrong. Arabella seemed affronted by this questioning of her intellectual capability, but I did what I could to assure her that she shouldn't let it affect her performance.

"WHICH NOVEL BEGINS WITH THE OPENING LINES, 'THESE TWO VERY OLD PEOPLE ARE THE FATHER AND MOTHER OF MR BUCKET'?"

Poor Arabella! Initially, she seemed to be all at sea and straight away, she sought help from both Stuart and myself. I immediately came out with the suggestion, Willy Wonka and the Chocolate Factory because the name Bucket is synonymous with the story and sought to convince my beleaguered colleague of my suggestion.

Stuart initially appeared to agree with my suggestion, but it didn't take long for nagging doubts to surface in his mind and he began to repeatedly whisper, "I'M SURE IT'S CHARLIE AND THE CHOCOLATE FACTORY."

Arabella, for some bizarre reason, offered Das Kapital as a possible answer, but Stuart was becoming more and more convinced with each passing second that he was right. Arabella by this time was eventually persuaded by Stuart's voice of reason. Arabella, thankfully, managed to regain her composure and boldly declared, with all the confidence and poise of a film expert, that Willie Wonka was the film and Charlie and the Chocolate Factory was the novel from which the film was based on. For the third time in a row, Jo confirmed that the team had given a correct answer that could be heard loud and clear against the backdrop of a totally subdued and silent studio audience.

With the nomination round completed, it was time for the final round and there was no doubting the fact that the momentum and initiative was clearly with the Smartass panellists as Jo set the scene for the final showdown with the following remark, "SO AFTER THAT ROUND, THIS IS WHAT WE ARE LEFT WITH, THREE SOFT

BOILED EGGHEADS READY TO FACE A SMARTASS SHOWDOWN. HERE THEY ARE, THREE OF OUR SO-CALLED SMARTASSES WHO STILL RECKON THEY ARE SMARTER THAN ANYTHING THAT OXFORD CAN THROW AT THEM. LET'S SETTLE THIS ONCE AND FOR ALL."

Jo invited the Oxford crowd to stand up with their questions, which they began waving in the air. "SMARTASSES, YOU HAVE NINETY SECONDS IN WHICH TO RETAIN YOUR REPUTATION BY ANSWERING TEN CORRECT QUESTIONS."

The momentum of the team was now unstoppable as all three of us prepared to face the Smartass showdown brimming with supreme confidence. That collective confidence was more than justified as between the three of us, we answered ten out of the eleven questions we were asked correctly and easily reached our target with thirty-two seconds to spare. At the end of the final round, Arabella, Stuart and myself our rose to our feet in unison, holding hands, making our final bows in a light hearted antagonistic gesture towards a begrudgingly appreciative studio audience. That hard-fought victory turned out to be a crucial one in the long run because in the five match head to head battles between the Smartass panellists against the invited studio audiences, the Smartass teams eventually emerged triumphant with a narrow 3-2 victory.

My summer of TV quizzing didn't end there. Barely a fortnight later, I received another unexpected letter completely out of the blue from Endermol Production company offering me the opportunity to appear on a new TV quiz show called *Beat The Nation* to be hosted jointly by two thirds of the 1960's and 70's comedy trio, The Goodies, Graeme Garden and Tim Brooke-Taylor. *Beat the Nation* was scheduled to replace the "Rolls Royce of Television Quizzes," *Fifteen-to-One* whose long and glorious reign had finally to come to an end in December 2003. This was the first time since I had been taking part in quiz shows that I had been invited to take part without the need of having to attend an audition beforehand.

The night before my scheduled appearance on the show, I drove up the M1 to Nottingham where the studio was. to the designated hotel that was situated on the outskirts of the city. After checking into the hotel and depositing my belongings in my room, I decided to relax by going to the hotel lounge area for a spot of supper. The hotel did not appear to be all that busy at the time, but of the people in the hotel that I had noticed, I had an inkling that they were people were not ordinary hotel patrons enjoying one of those overnight city breaks and were in all probability, in Nottingham as contestants on *Beat The Nation*. Out of all of the patrons staying at the hotel, there was one gentleman who caught my eye in particular after my arrival at the hotel and without knowing why, I was convinced that not only was this man a possible contestant on the show, but that he was a contestant who in all probability, I would be directly competing against and although the pair of us made initial eye contact with each other, nothing was actually exchanged between us other than a polite nod of the head in each other's direction, a nod that seemed to be suggesting something along the lines of, "I know who you are and I know the reasons why you're here."

The following morning, once I had finished a far from strenuous early morning run twice around the hotel's ground that was followed by a quick shower and a hearty full English breakfast, I went back to my hotel room in order to get myself ready. As it was wonderfully hot summer's day, instead of wearing my favourite pink coloured shirt that I would normally wear when taking part on TV game shows, I decided to be daring and go for a complete change of attire by selecting a batique printed orange coloured top called a *bandhani* that my brother Steve had bought for me as a present from his recent trip to India. There was no doubting the fact that my new bright coloured top really suited me and it acted as a perfect compliment to the stylish pair of Ray Ban sunglasses that had been perched on the top of my forehead from the moment I opened my eyes that morning. Anyone looking at me at first glance as I left my hotel room with my small sports bag in tow, would have thought that I was on my way to an all day summer beach party as opposed to a television studio for an important quiz show.

I made my way towards the hotel lobby in order to await the arrival of the courtesy car laid on by the production team for the relatively short journey to Central Studios. Also waiting in the lobby to take her to the same studio was Gina Dunlop, an Editor for a bank from Richmond in Surrey who as it transpired, would be travelling in the same courtesy car. Gina and I chatted away cordially throughout the journey and we both assumed, given the fact that we were travelling together at the same time, that we would in all probability be competing against each other on the show. After arriving at the studio, Gina and I were greeted by a member of the production team who proceeded to escort the pair of us to the green room where, awaiting our arrival, was the third contestant we would be competing against, Mark Gardiner, an IT Project Manager from Edinburgh. The production assistant then briefed Mark, Gina and myself on the competition's rules before leaving the three of us to relax and unwind a little whilst we waited for the previous show to finish recording. About twenty or so minutes later, the three of us were joined by the winner of that show, and the person who entered the green room, was none other than the same gentleman that I had seen in my hotel the previous evening. His name was Phil Porter and he was a Perfumer from Northumberland.

I felt in a calm and totally relaxed state of mind as I sat in the green room alongside my fellow three competitors waiting for our show to start, so relaxed, that I was totally oblivious to the fact that I was still wearing my dark sun shades, a lack of self-awareness that continued right up until the point when sat down in my designated seat in the studio, despite having the presence of mind to carry my glasses case that contained my normal prescription glasses that I was planning to wear during the contest. The minute I sat down in my seat, I simply placed the glasses case on the desk in front of me, acting under the mistaken assumption that I had already made the switch from my dark sunshades to my normal prescription glasses. I don't know what the production team made of the fact that one of their contestants was going to play *Beat The Nation* wearing an outlandish orange coloured top with dark sunglasses, they must have assumed that was how I wanted to be seen on a tea time quiz show looking, quite frankly, totally ridiculous. No one from the production team sought to alert me about my embarrassing fashion faux pas and it was only after Graeme Garden had started his usual piece to camera when introducing the show, that it finally dawned on me that I was still wearing my sun shades but unfortunately for me there was nothing that I could do about it and as such, my only focus and goal from here on in would be to try and use my best efforts and endeavours to beat my equally focused and equally determined fellow competitors.

As the returning champion, Phil was required to sit in seat number one. Seated next to him in seat two was Gina. I was sat in the third seat with the final contestant Mark sitting in seat four. After the sound engineers had wired us all for sound, Graeme and Tim then entered the studio and came over and spoke to all four contestants briefly, wishing us all the best of luck in the process before taking their seats that were directly opposite Contestant's Row. Once he was satisfied that everybody on the studio set was settled and ready to go, the Studio Floor Manager began the final countdown for the start to the show and after the show's theme music had played its last note, Graeme Garden, *Beat The Nation's* principal question master, launched into his usual piece to camera which involved him explaining in outline the show's format.

"ALL THE QUESTIONS ASKED HAVE BEEN TESTED ON A THOUSAND PEOPLE NATIONWIDE, THEREFORE WE KNOW PRECISELY HOW MANY RIGHT AND WRONG ANSWERS THERE

WERE FOR THAT PARTICULAR QUESTION. THE MORE YOU BEAT, THE MORE YOU SCORE."

During the course of his opening remarks, Graeme went onto explain that the top sixteen players who were on the Leader board at the end of the series of heats would return to compete at the End of Series Finals where the ultimate victor in the Grand Final would walk away with the top prize of £25,000.

Round one was the buzzer round, which featured questions that people in the UK generally didn't know the answer to because the polls conducted by the show's researchers told them that less than half of the Nation could answer the questions for this round. So for example, the question *"Who was the sixth President of the United States?" only* 10% of the Nation knew the answer was John Quincy Adams. If a contestant gave the correct answer of John Quincy Adams, that contestant would score ninety points. In order to progress to round two, a contestant had to reach one hundred and fifty points. However, only three contestants could progress from that round and the remaining contestant would be eliminated.

Graeme informed us that the game was about to begin. "CONTESTANTS WITH YOUR FINGERS QUIVERING OVER YOUR BUZZERS, HERE'S THE FIRST QUESTION. WHO COMPOSED THE MUSIC FOR THE BALLET, THE NUTCRACKER...?"

BZZZZZ! I pressed the buzzer before Graeme even had the chance to complete the question and gave the correct answer, Tchaichovsky, for which I earned a surprisingly modest fifty two points.

The next question was a picture question that displayed a UK Road Side Warning Sign. Once again, I was first to the buzzer with the correct answer, uneven road, which this time, earned me a more profitable eighty four points.

"RUPERT MURDOCK ORIGINALLY CAME FROM WHICH COUNTRY?"

On that occasion, Mark was first on the buzzer with the correct answer, Australia, which earned him sixty seven points, a surprisingly high score in my view given how well known a figure Mr Murdock is to the British public.

"QUESTION FOUR, IN ENGLISH LITERATURE, IN WHICH SCHOOL WAS TOM BROWN BULLIED BY...?"

Once again, I was far too quick for my opponents on the buzzer, so quick that Graeme hadn't even finished reading the question. My answer, Rugby, not only earned me eighty two points, it also ensured my comfortable passage into the next round leaving

Phil, Gina and Mark to battle it out for the remaining two qualifying spots.

At the end of that round, it was Gina who became the first contestant to be eliminated but her early exit from the show didn't automatically mean that she would be leaving the contest empty handed. The rules of *Beat The Nation* dictated that a contestant eliminated at the end of any given round would be offered the chance of redemption in the form of a consolation cash prize. The challenge for Gina at the end of the first round was that she had to guess what percentage of the Nation knew the correct answer to any given question, with an allowance of a margin of error of 10%.

The question was, "WHAT KIND OF FRUIT ARE THE BLENHEIM ORANGE, THE BRAEBURN AND THE PINK LADY?"

Gina made up for her early exit and claimed the £100 consolation prize by predicting that 50% of the Nation knew the correct answer, Apple. The actual figure was 40%, which meant that she was just within the scope of the allowable margin of error.

In round two, the three surviving contestants would face only six questions and those same six questions were put to a specially invited guest in a pre-recorded interview. Points would be awarded to a contestant who buzzed in giving a correct answer to any given question, but those points could be doubled if the contestant, having correctly answered the question, could correctly predict whether or not the invited celebrity guest knew the correct answer.

Graeme revealed the image of our invited guest on the screen, David Cracknell, the Political Editor of the Sunday Times, before launching into the first question for the round. "ACKEE AND SALTFISH IS THE NATIONAL DISH OF WHICH CARIBBEAN...?"

BZZZ! The returning champion Phil Porter's lightning quick reactions beat me to the buzzer with the correct answer, Jamaica, earning him initially, a rather generous eighty eight points which he managed to successfully double by correctly predicting that David would know the answer to the question. Phil's lightning speed in answering a question that was right up my street left me feeling slightly embarrassed to say the very least.

"QUESTION TWO, WHICH NOBEL PRIZE WAS WON BY WINSTON CHURCH...?"

BZZZ! Once again I was beaten for sheer speed on the buzzer by Phil whose his confident reply, Literature, earned him an even healthier score of ninety points, a score he successfully doubled for the second time in a row by correctly forecasting that our celebrity guest also knew the answer.

After only two questions, Phil was clearly in the lead with a very healthy score of 356 points that left both myself and Mark floundering in his slipstream. Phil's faultless performance so early in the round had put him in pole position to advance to round three of the contest and if either myself or Mark wanted to join him in the final showdown, then the pair of us had to display the same aggressive speed.

"QUESTION THREE, ON THE FIRST OF JANUARY 1993, THE FORMER REPUBLIC OF CZECHOSLAVAKIA SPLIT INTO THE CZECH REPUBLIC AND..?"

BZZZ! This time, I managed beat Phil to a question with the correct answer, Slovakia, which earned me seventy points that I successfully managed to double by correctly predicting that David also knew the correct answer.

"QUESTION FOUR, THE YORKSHIRE OAKS IS RUN AT WHICH RACECOURSE?"

BZZZ! I seemed to be getting into my stride because for the second question in a row, I was the quickest contestant on the buzzer, but unlike the previous question, this time I came up short on this occasion and gave the incorrect answer, Doncaster.

Sensing an opportunity to capitalise on my mistake, Mark buzzed in for the first time in the round, but he too failed to come up with the correct answer, his response of Epsom (in Surrey), an even more unlikely answer given the course's geographical location. Phil by contrast, simply bided his time and with the application of simple logic, calmly pressed his buzzer and gave the only answer that it could have been in the circumstances, York, which earned him a whopping ninety-five points. Rather surprisingly, Phil failed to double his massive haul of points as he incorrectly predicted that David wouldn't know the answer to the question when he did but that relatively minor slip up didn't matter in the greater scheme of things. Phil had virtually guaranteed for himself a place in the third round.

With only two questions to go before the end of the round, Graeme gave the three of us a timely reminder of the scores. Phil was way out in front with a virtually unassailable lead of 451 points and despite the fact I was in second place with a score of 140 points, Graeme highlighted the fact that I had a relatively slender lead and that it was still possible for Mark to overhaul my score as the three of us prepared to face the penultimate question.

"HOW MANY THREE DIGIT NUMBERS ARE MADE USING THE NUMERALS, 1,2,3 WITHOUT REPEATING ANY OF THOSE NUMERALS?"

Graeme's words of warning turned out to be prophetic ones as the IT specialist Mark was in like a flash on his buzzer with the correct answer, six, which earned him an extremely valuable score of 76 points, a score that had not only firmly put him back in contention to qualify for the next round, it left me in a potentially precarious position of elimination, a position that became even more precarious when Mark managed to successfully double his points tally by correctly predicting that David would know the correct answer to the question.

I was now in last place trailing Mark by 12 points and teetering on the very brink of a disastrous and embarrassing exit. It was now do or die so far as I was concerned and as the three of us prepared to face the final question in the round, I knew that I had to be the quickest contestant on the buzzer otherwise I would be facing certain elimination. With everything to play for, my heart began to pound louder and louder with every beat.

Graeme heightened the tension even further as he prepared to ask that all important and decisive final question. "CONTESTANTS, FINGERS ON THE BUZZER FOR THE SIXTH AND FINAL QUESTION. ANCHORAGE IS THE…?"

BZZZZ! It was my buzzer. I was the quickest by the merest fraction of a second ahead of both Phil and Mark. I was taking a massive gamble buzzing in before Graeme had finished the question, a question that could be going in completely a different direction than the one I was contemplating but to my mind, I felt that the question could only be heading in one direction and replied with supreme confidence, "ALASKA."

Graeme continued to read out the rest of the question. "…THE MOST POPULATED CITY IN WHICH US STATE? IT IS ALASKA. SHAUN, YOU COULDN'T HAVE GOT IN MUCH QUICKER."

I looked towards the heavens breathing an almighty sigh of relief. It goes without saying that he was spot on with his observations. My speed on the buzzer earned me a crucial 68 points that I successfully managed to double by correctly predicting that David would know the answer. I managed, albeit by the skin of my teeth, to qualify for the final head to head round with the returning champion Phil and that was all that mattered.

Graeme announced the final scores for that round. Phil on 451, I ended up with a score of 276 and finally, Mark on 152 points.

Graeme and Tim offered their respective commiserations to Mark on his elimination in a very closely fought contest before proceeding to offer him the chance to go home with the £100 consolation prize providing he could successfully predict who, out of Butter or Margarine lovers, would gain the highest score to the following question. "WHICH SUBSTANCE IS THE DIET OF THE VAMPIRE BAT?" Mark opted for Butter lovers before Tim finally revealed the percentage scores between the two groups, Margarine lovers scored 31% as opposed to 34% for Butter lovers which meant that by a slim margin of only 3%, Mark had deservedly won for himself a consolation prize of £100.

It was now time for the head to head round and before it got under way, Graeme explained the rules to both Phil and myself. "PHIL AND SHAUN REMAIN IN THE QUIZ AND NOW THE PRESSURE IS REALLY ON THEM. IN THIS ROUND, I'M GOING TO ASK QUESTIONS BACK AND FORTH BETWEEN EACH CONTESTANT. YOU WILL START WITH THREE LIVES EACH AND THE CONTESTANT WHO LOSES ALL THEIR LIVES WILL BE ELIMINATED. BECAUSE YOU, PHIL, WERE THE HIGHEST SCORER AT THE END OF THE LAST ROUND, YOU WILL FACE THE FIRST QUESTION WHICH IS A STRAIGHT FORWARD THIRTY POINTER QUESTION".

The first question is, invariably, an easy one to begin with but as the questions alternate between the opposing contestants, they get progressively harder and harder until one of the contestants would give an incorrect answer that would cost that contestant one of their three lives.

"PHIL A THIRTY POINTER. WHICH WARNER BROTHERS CHARACTER IS ASSOCIATED WITH THE CATCH PHRASE, "WHAT'S UP DOC?"

The first question posed no difficulties whatsoever as his correct answer, Bugs Bunny, gave him an easy thirty points.

It was now my turn to be in the firing line as I braced myself to face my first question. "SHAUN A FORTY POINTER. WHAT MEAT MAKES UP THE INGREDIENTS OF A COCK-A-LEEKIE SOUP?"

A fairly straight forward question from the simpler range and I wasted no time in giving the correct response, chicken, but I knew full well that from now on, the questions would get only tougher and tougher.

"PHIL, A SEVENTY POINTER. WHICH AUSTRALIAN OUTLAW WAS FAMOUS FOR WEARING HOMEMADE ARMOUR?"

Phil appeared to pause momentarily after Graeme had asked him the question, and I was unsure whether this was because of any difficulties that he may have had with the question itself, or whether he was simply playing mind games. I suspected that it was probably the latter and as expected, he gave the correct answer, Ned Kelly, which meant that once again, I was forced to face the next question.

"SHAUN, YOU FACE AN EIGHTY POINTER. IMPERIAL AND GOLDSMITHS COLLEGE ARE PART OF WHICH UNIVERSITY?"

I neither hesitated, nor decided to indulge in any pointless mind games and I immediately gave the correct answer, London University, which meant that Phil had to face the next potentially difficult question.

"PHIL YOU NOW FACE AN EIGHTY-FIVE POINTER. ON BOARD A SHIP WHAT IS KEPT IN A BINNACLE?

I knew the answer to that question was a Compass but Phil unfortunately, gave the incorrect answer, food, a costly error that meant he was the first to lose one of his three precious lives.

The rules of the head to head round dictated that a contestant that lost one of their lives would be required to face the next question that would invariably come from the easier range. "PHIL A THIRTY POINTER. WHAT IS THE AVERAGE OF 20, 40 AND 80?"

Once again, Phil seemed to take his time as he considered the answer, a sensible tactic that he adopted more likely, out of an abundance of caution given the fact that he had just lost one of his three lives. That sensible approach paid dividends as it allowed him the time to come up with the correct answer, 40, thus switching the pressure of correctly answering the next question firmly in my court.

"SHAUN YOU FACE AN EIGHTY POINTER. ORIEL AND LANCET ARE TYPES OF WHAT IN A BUILDING?"

It was the type of question I should have known the answer to but unfortunately for me I didn't, and trying to give the best educated guess that I could I replied, "ARCH," instead of the correct answer, window, an error that meant that I too had forfeit one of my three lives. As a result of the loss of that precious life, I had to face the next question that in theory was to come from the supposedly easier range.

"SHAUN, A TWENTY POINTER. SUNDRIED AND SUNBLUSHED ARE TYPES OF WHICH FRUIT?"

The question caught me completely off guard because I had never heard of those types of fruit before and I suppose it was just as well that I had on my dark sun glasses because I was just staring blankly and shaking my head on account of the fact that I was completely stumped. I gave the somewhat half-hearted response, "PRUNE," in the full knowledge that it was likely to be incorrect and when Graeme revealed that the answer was in fact, tomato, I was left in the precarious position of having only one life left which meant that, for the remainder of the round, I had to answer all of my questions correctly otherwise I would be facing elimination.

Getting a relatively easy question wrong at that stage of the game rattled my confidence slightly and as I prepared to face another supposedly straightforward question, the only thing I could hope and pray for was that lightning would not strike twice in succession.

"SHAUN WE'RE NOW BACK DOWN TO THE SIMPLER END, A TWENTY POINTER. WHICH SPOTRSMAN WAS NICKNAMED INTERESTING BY THE TV PROGRAMME SPITTING IMAGE?"

"'STEVE DAVIS," was my immediate reply much to my considerable relief.

The pressure had now shifted to my opponent who had to face the next question that was from the more difficult range. "PHIL, AN EIGHTY POINTER. THE EXPLOSIVE TRI-NITRO-TOLUENE IS MORE COMMONLY KNOWN BY WHAT THREE LETTERS?"

For a question that was supposed to come from the tougher category of questions, I thought that it was relatively easy for a contestant of Phil's ability and stature and his correct response of, "T.N.T," immediately put the pressure right back on my shoulders.

"SHAUN YOU NOW FACE AN EIGHTY-FIVE POINTER. WHICH DRAMATIST WROTE 'LOOK BACK IN ANGER'?"

Once again, without hesitating or prevaricating, I came up with the correct answer, John Osbourne, that kept me alive in the contest thus forcing my opponent to face the next potentially difficult question.

"PHIL YOU NOW FACE A NINETY POINTER. WHAT NAME IS GIVEN TO A QUADRILATERAL WITH JUST TWO OF ITS SIDES PARALLEL?"

Because the game was at a critical stage, Phil, quite sensibly, took his time in considering the question. Graeme began gently pressing Phil for an answer and that prompted him to eventually come up with the response, "RHOMBUS" which unfortunately for him, but fortunately for me, was the wrong answer. The correct answer was in fact trapezium, and that further loss of a life meant that the pair of us had only one life each and as a consequence were both facing sudden death.

With the contest delicately poised, Phil had the slight advantage of facing the first question in the winner take all situation because of his incorrect response to the last question which fortunately for him would come from the supposed easier range. "PHIL, YOU HAVE TO FACE THE NEXT QUESTION WHICH IS A TEN POINTER. WHO TOPPED THE CHARTS IN 1999 WITH MILLENIUM PRAYER OVER FORTY-ONE YEARS AFTER HIS FIRST CHART TOPPER, LIVING DOLL?"

"CLIFF RICHARD" was Phil's expected reply forcing me to face the next question.

"SHAUN, A FORTY POINTER. OPTHALMOLOGY IS THE SCIENTIFIC STUDY OF WHAT?" On this occasion, it was now my turn to take my time before giving my answer in an effort admittedly, to create the impression that I was having real difficulty with the question, just like Phil appeared to have done earlier on in our head to head showdown, but in truth, I knew what the correct answer was all along and I eventually gave the reply, "THE EYE" putting all the pressure back onto my opponent.

"PHIL YOU NOW FACE A SEVENTY POINTER. THE OSCAR WINNING ACTOR RUSSEL CROWE WAS BORN IN WHICH COUNTRY?"

I knew the answer to that question and I was hoping that Phil would succumb to temptation of going for Australia as his answer, but he wasn't a returning champion for nothing and despite the immense pressure he was under, he remained cool and calm throughout and gave the correct answer, New Zealand.

The increasing and intense pressure was all on me now to deliver another correct answer to what was sure to be a real challenging question. "SHAUN, YOU NOW FACE AN EIGHTY POINTER. A STOCKMAN, A PERSON IN CHARGE OF CATTLE AND LIVESTOCK, IS PARTICULARLY ASSOCIATED WITH WHICH COUNTRY?"

I was completely stumped by the question and as I trawled through the possible choices in my mind as to what country it could be, just like he had done to Phil when he faced a difficult question earlier on in the head to head, Graeme began to gently press me for an answer. "YOU'RE DOWN TO YOUR LAST LIFE SHAUN, I NEED HARDLY REMIND YOU OF THAT FACT."

"I APPRECIATE THAT," I replied, doing my level best to stall for as much time as possible as I continued to frantically sift through the various permutations in my mind. I had managed to whittle down those options to two possible choices, the USA and Australia. It could have been any country on the globe so far as I was concerned, the very nature of the question itself providing no real clues. But with time steadfastly running out, I had to make a choice and the option I decided to go for was the USA, for the sole reason that it was the country that had popped into my head first. Unfortunately though, when I heard Graeme's first three words in response to my given answer, I knew that my challenge of trying to beat the nation was well and truly over.

"I'M AFRAID, SHAUN, THAT THE ANSWER IS AUSTRALIA. TOUGH LUCK! YOU HAVE LOST THE LAST OF YOUR LIVES."

Tim also added his voice to the general chorus of commiserations with the following sentiments, "WELL DONE, IT WAS A VERY GOOD CONTEST," before Graeme concluded the head to head with the words, "WELL DONE TO YOU BOTH! BUT IN THE END, PHIL HAS TRIUMPHED ONCE AGAIN. IN A MOMENT HE WILL ATTEMPT TO BEAT THE NATION. BUT SHAUN, NEVER MIND. BECAUSE WE NEVER KNOW WHEN TO STOP GIVING AWAY MONEY ON THIS SHOW, SO I'LL HAND YOU OVER TO TIM."

For the consolation game to determine whether or not I left *Beat The Nation* with £100 in my pocket, I had to play the Fame Game Challenge, a challenge where I would be shown two pictures of well-known personalities and I had to correctly predict which of the two images would be more recognisable by people in Britain. The images that I had to choose from were the veteran DJ Tony Blackburn and the socialite and TV personality, Tara Palmer-Tomkinson. I chose Tony Blackburn solely on the basis of his recent TV success on *I'm a Celebrity, Get me out of Here,* a choice that thankfully was totally vindicated after Tim revealed the nation's percentage votes which were, Tara 45% and Tony 93%, thus allowing me to claim the £100 consolation prize. Welcoming as though that prize was, it could hardly assuage the bitter disappointment I felt at seeing yet another chance of TV quizzing glory slip from my grasp.

"SO, IT'S GOODBYE TO SHAUN, BUT CONGRATULATIONS TO PHIL WHO IS JUST NINETY SECONDS AND TEN CORRECT ANSWERS AWAY FROM WINNING TODAY'S SHOW - THAT IS IF HE CAN BEAT THE NATION."

As Phil took his seat facing both Graeme and Tim in the middle of the studio in preparation for the final round, I took my place alongside the members of the production team who congratulated and commiserated with me in equal measure on my performance. The final round got under way with Tim explaining its rules. Phil was required to correctly answer ten questions in ninety seconds to win £500 in a quick enough time to get him onto the Leader Board where the top sixteen winners would compete against each other in the End Of Series competition where the overall winner would win the main prize of £25,000.

Phil started extremely well in the final round, but when he got to the all-important 90 pointer, he started to struggle with the questions which in the end proved costly and for the second successive show, he failed to answer the requisite ten questions within the ninety seconds. As I sat ruefully on the side lines, I managed to answer ten questions from the different categories well within the time limit allowed and dare I say it, with relative ease but sadly, it did not matter. At least Phil had one more final attempt to redeem himself on the next show, whereas I had to be content with yet another gallant, but disappointing defeat. I managed to speak to the show's co-hosts after the show and the pair of them were very complimentary about my performance throughout the game and expressed the sentiment that I was unlucky to lose my head to head contest with Phil. As I was making my way back to the green room to gather all of my belongings in preparation for the long journey home, I bumped into my head to head conqueror Phil and as we came together, I shook his hand and wished him the best of luck on his final attempt on the next show, a genuine sentiment on my part which he clearly appreciated. Phil responded to those sentiments by saying in a clear, unmistakable Northeast accent, "I heard you're a bit of a pro", a comment which I took as a real compliment in the circumstances and went a long way in lifting the brief gloom and despair that befell me in the aftermath of yet another defeat on a television quiz show.

My final involvement in game shows for 2003 was about a week or so later. I received a telephone call at home from a production company who had close links with the BBC to invite me to audition for a TV presenting role on a game show that was still at its pilot stage and hoping to get TV commission. It goes without saying that I was extremely pleased and excited at the possibility of becoming a television presenter and it didn't take long for my imagination to run amok with visions of myself as the black male equivalent of *The Weakest Link's* Anne Robinson or *Fifteen-To-One's* legendary quiz host, William G. Stewart, and having been presented with this potential opportunity of a lifetime, I was determined to do everything in my power to turn those wildest dreams into a reality.

My contact didn't go into too much detail over the telephone about the audition other than to inform me that I was going to be sent the show's synopsis and script as well as the details of the date, time and venue where the audition was going to take place through the post. I received the documents a couple of days later. Headed at the top of the show's synopsis in bold print was one single word, *Traitor*. The idea for show wasn't entirely an original one as it appeared to have borrowed a number of similar features to a game show called *The Enemy Within*, a BBC1 lunchtime quiz show presented by "Nasty" Nigel Lythgoe, where one of the five competing players is given all the answers beforehand and it was up to the remaining competing players to expose that player at the end of the show otherwise the "enemy" claimed the accumulated prize fund.

Traitor was based around nine people gathered in a studio, seven of whom are called "civilians" who must, at all times, tell the truth when questioned by the host. The remaining two people are the designated "traitors" and their role throughout the game is to deliberately lie and deceive the civilians with the joint aim of claiming the prize money for themselves. If the civilians manage to discover and eliminate both traitors, the survivors share the money between themselves, however, should the number of civilians fall to the number of traitors remaining, it is the traitor(s) who win the prize money.

At any point during the game, any one of the nine members of the group could accuse a fellow member of being a traitor. The accuser would be required to state their reason why they suspected that individual and that accused individual would be given the opportunity to respond to those accusations before it goes to a decisive vote. If there are more "traitor" votes than "civilian" ones, then the accused individual reveals whether they were a civilian or a traitor before leaving the game. If the vote ends in a tie, or there is a majority of "civilian" votes, the accused individual remains in the game.

I read the script repeatedly until it became second nature, practising in every spare moment I had, reciting my scripted parts to my mirror, rehearsing my role with the aid of a camcorder and critically analysing my overall performance on film thereafter. There was no doubting the fact those initial practice runs, whether they were conducted in front of the mirror or recorded on film, looked and sounded like an individual who had memorised the designated scripted lines off by heart and lacked the ability and the confidence to deliver the lines in a relaxed and natural manner. In short, I was terrible. After my umpteenth outtake and hours and hours of practice, there was no real improvement and despite finally managing to deliver my scripted part relatively free from any error, after I viewed the recorded footage in its entirety, it was clear that my TV presenting skills still left an awful lot to be desired. Despite the lack of making any meaningful progress in my presenting abilities, I wasn't prepared to throw in the towel and I continued to work hard on my diction and delivery over and over again until I reached the standard that I believed would, at the very least, give me the opportunity to do myself justice.

The day of the audition finally arrived and despite feeling slightly apprehensive, I was nevertheless determined not only to give it my best shot, but also to ensure that I was looking my absolute best. I picked up my best suit from my local dry cleaners, took my shoes to Goggsy's for their customary polish, then headed to Harlesden High

Street for an appointment with my new hairstylist Donna. I eventually got back home by midday that gave me more than enough time to rehearse and relax before I got myself ready for the journey to the BBC studio in Wood Lane for my date with destiny.

The first person to approach me as I stood on the set was the show's producer who greeted me warmly with a handshake before he introduced me to the people who were going to take part in the game. The producer then gave me a mini tour of the studio set design which mainly had a jungle theme. My big moment was almost at hand. With a sharp intake of breath and a momentary glance skywards to the man upstairs, my audition of a lifetime began. I started by staring intensely into the camera in an effort to engage with an imaginary viewing audience with a short, concise synopsis of the show. That opening piece to camera had to be re-shot at least twice, mainly on account of the fact that I kept fluffing my lines that were on the autocue but once the show was in full swing, I became more and more relaxed and at ease with my role as the host, doing my utmost to strike an intuitive balance between my role as the host asking the searching and probing questions of the contestants when necessary and knowing when to keep silent and let the real stars of the show, the contestants, get on with playing the game. By the end of the pilot, I felt really pleased with how everything went, it was better than I had expected. The producer and some of the members of the production team came up to me afterwards on the set and offered their congratulations on how well they thought I had performed. Even some of the contestants who took part in the show were just as complimentary with their praise especially the way in which I facilitated and interacted with them throughout the show, one or two of those contestants even going as far as to express the wish that they hoped I would be appointed the show's permanent host. Those encouraging words of endorsement and support from the production team and contestants alike, was a considerable boost to my confidence and a tribute to all the hours of practice and hard work that I had devoted to in preparation for the audition. Despite the encouraging and positive feedback, realistically I knew deep down that I was unlikely to be appointed to the role because, despite managing to demonstrate that I had the capability to be a TV presenter, I was a long, long way away from being the finished article. The show's producer bid me farewell and informed me that there were other people who were auditioning for the role and once all those auditions were completed, I would be notified as soon as possible. Just before I left the studio, I asked the producer whether it was possible for me to have a copy of my audition and he replied that he was more than happy to send me a copy and that I would receive it in about a week or so. My request for the audition tape was not motivated by pure and naked vanity of wanting to see myself on screen. I just wanted to see for myself how I looked and sounded as a TV presenter from an analytical and critical perspective with the aim of seeing at first hand what areas of my presentation skills needed improving.

When at long last the producers called me, I was told that although they were impressed with my performance, unfortunately I had not been selected for the role. Naturally, I was disappointed by the news as I genuinely believed that, despite being a complete unknown quantity, I could have been a real success on the show. I did however understand that appointing an unknown quantity like myself with no television presenting experience of any note to a brand new show really would have been a gamble too far. Despite being passed over for the presenting role on *Traitor*, I still believed that the show's format was a very good one and could be a success providing it was transmitted on the right channel. *Traitor* was eventually broadcast the following year with the Editor of the Sunday Sport, Tony Livesey, appointed in the role. I found the show to be lively and entertaining but sadly, it was not re-commissioned which I thought it was a shame really because I believed that the show had all the ingredients to be a real and sustainable success but as the age old saying goes, "that's the breaks!"

The year 2003 had provided me with me several real and exciting opportunities to make the breakthrough into the world of television and despite failing to make the breakthrough that I was hoping for, I had a great deal of fun whilst it lasted. The time had now come for me to put the world of TV quiz shows and auditions on the back burner for a while and return to private practice, with the sole and determined aim of rebuilding my much cherished but seemingly moribund legal career.

CHAPTER EIGHTEEN

After having spent the school summer holidays doing Play Scheme work at the Waterside Project on a council estate in Angel Islington, the first Monday in September marked my return to the legal profession on a full-time basis. I had already made overtures throughout that summer to the small but very supportive core of solicitors who have kept my career afloat in the past of my intention to return to the bar in the hope that between us, we could reprise the professional relationship that we once had despite the fact that I had taken my leave from the legal profession for some considerable time. In those discussions with my old contacts, I sought to convince them that I was fully committed to my career and the profession and asked them to give their full backing and support to my renewed commitment and sense of purpose in rebuilding my career. The general response that I received from those erstwhile contacts about my impending return to the fold was a favourable one, save for the slight, but understandable misgivings and concerns one or two of those contacts expressed with regards to my decision to practice from home as opposed to being a part of an established set of Chambers and the potential practical difficulties that could arise without having the necessary proper administrative infrastructure and support I would need to help manage my practice. The concerns expressed by my old contacts were well founded and I told them quite openly, that the reason why I had to practice from home was from a financial point of view, I simply was not in a position where I could afford to pay the rent on a regular monthly basis as a tenant. I also went on to add that it would take some considerable time before I would be in a position to be able to do so and the only way that I could achieve that aim was to be in court doing cases on a regular basis.

To say that I was immensely relieved and grateful for these offers of help to rebuild my career really would be the mother of all understatements. This was my final chance to reignite my career in law. It would be fair to say that anybody critically examining the state of my career at this point would almost certainly call into serious question, not only my commitment to my profession, but they would also seriously question my professionalism per se. They might see me as an individual who was more interested in the bright lights of a television studio rather than building a legal career and their ultimate judgement on my career would be that it was a complete and utter disaster and that it didn't deserve to be revived or resurrected. I would wholeheartedly refute the charge or accusation questioning both my commitment and professionalism and will continue to do so until my last breath. I have always been totally dedicated and committed to my profession and have always adopted a totally professional attitude, both in and out of court. The fact that I had chosen over the last four or so years to pursue and persevere with my passion for competing on television quiz shows, should not be used as an example to illustrate any lack of commitment or lack of professionalism on my part because my legal career and my passion for quizzing are mutually exclusive of each other. In saying that, however, the one major criticism I will always readily admit to is as to why, after almost nineteen years, I find both myself and my career seemingly back at square one. The truth was, I had allowed the frequent periods of disillusionment and despair that I have suffered as an excuse for not having advanced my career in the direction that I had always envisaged and while it's easy to point the finger of blame in the direction of others for the reasons why things have not gone according to plan, the bottom line is, the buck stops with me and, at the end of the day, I have nobody to blame but myself. But instead of dwelling on all of my disappointments and failings of the past, it was time to concentrate all my energies and realign my focus not only on rebuilding my career, but also on reigniting my belief that it was still possible for me to reach the very top of my chosen field, a belief that may have been severely tested at various times, but a belief that in the deep recesses of both my heart and mind, even in my darkest hour, has never left me.

During the first three months back in private practice, those erstwhile solicitor contacts who promised to support me were true to their word. Rodney Wilson, Fitzroy Lee, Janice Young and Keith Mkanda were those solicitors in question and between them, were responsible for getting me back into the cut and thrust of Crown Court trials, from Sheffield in the North via London, to Bristol in the West. The nature of the legal work I doing on my return to private practice was no longer exclusively confined to the narrow field of criminal law as I decided to widen the scope of my practice a little by taking on immigration cases mainly representing clients who were at risk of deportation and the person responsible for getting that type of work was my dear old friend and former Senior Clerk, Rosemarie Phillips, who at the time was working for a solicitors' firm based in the Surrey Quays area. Those solicitor contacts were not the only persons that I had to be grateful to for keeping my practice afloat. I also owe a considerable debt of gratitude and thanks to my friend, Juene Guishard, who came to my rescue on many an occasion, spending hours and hours of her spare time typing up all my invoices, as well as written legal opinions and documents known as defence case statements (an important document that requires a defendant in a criminal trial to set out in outline the nature of his/her defence). Without the support of those people, there is no doubt in my mind that that my attempts to rebuild my career would have been over before it had begun and at the ripe old age of 43, my professional career would have been firmly behind me.

As 2003 was drawing to a close, I felt that I was in a much better place both professionally and my own personal wellbeing than I have for many a year and this new found sense of optimism was never more poignant and evident than on the last few moments of New Year's Eve when I decided to see in the New Year at home all alone as opposed to in the company of a large and lively crowd at a New Year's Eve party. As I sat in my bedroom with nothing more than a solitary lighted candle for company with midnight fast approaching, the only thing dominating my thoughts was how lucky and grateful I was to still have a viable career that had been handed yet another lifeline, a lifeline some critics would have argued, that was hardly deserved or merited given my inability throughout my years in private practice to make the most of the opportunities that have been presented to me in the past. Admittedly as I had conceded earlier, there may be some element of truth to the assertion that at times, I have been the author of my own career misfortunes, but for the present, those problems are now a thing of the past. I had every reason to be optimistic and positive about the future as I made a wish hoping for great things before blowing out the candle the moment the clock struck midnight. 2004 was going to be my year.

Despite reaffirming my commitment and dedication to my legal career, I hadn't totally forsaken my passion and interest in taking part in auditions with a view to appearing in television programmes in the future. In fact during the first two weeks of 2004, I was invited to attend two vastly different but no less appealing auditions, the former being career specific whilst the latter was an opportunity to fulfil a childhood ambition. Sometime in the early part of December the previous year, I received one of those unexpected, yet serendipitous telephone calls at home from someone working on behalf of Talkback Thames Television. The purpose of the call was to ask me whether I would be interested in taking part in a screen test for a reality television type programme the production company were hoping to get commissioned concerning the day to day goings on in an English court of law. The production company were hoping to recruit professional lawyers and judges as they wanted the viewing public who would be watching the programme to have a real and proper insight into their respective roles in court proceedings. The nature of that screen test required a demonstration of the professional skills of a lawyer in court ranging from the questioning of witnesses to closing submissions. It was an opportunity that I was not going to let pass me by and I readily agreed to attend the screen test.

I arrived at the production company's offices on the 9th of January 2004 for my sixty minute screen test at 2pm. A member of the production team was on hand to greet me and I was escorted to a dressing room where I got changed into my barrister's wig and gown that I was asked to bring with me. Before I got changed, the production assistant handed me a set of instructions that I was asked to familiarise myself with as quickly as possible as they would form part of the mock court case during the screen test. I digested the set of instructions that I was provided with in no time at all, but as I was soon discover much to my bewilderment and disappointment, my screen test amounted to nothing more than simply reading a prepared script that was then followed up with an impromptu piece to camera where I was required to talk about myself and my career in general. The hour long screen test offered very little in demonstrating, in a natural or realistic way, the skills I would employ as professional advocate in a typical courtroom setting, the underlying rationale, I was led to believe, that the programme makers were hoping to showcase. I felt that my chances of being selected for the pilot, after my somewhat lacklustre performance in front of the camera, were virtually nil, despite the initial praise I received from the producers in the studio the moment my screen test had finished. But even a relative TV novice like myself can tell the difference between a good screen test and a not so good screen test and I resigned myself to the fact that if the programme managed to obtain a commission, it was virtually a certainty that I wasn't going to be involved.

As I prepared to leave the studio I heard someone call out in a loud voice, "SHAUN!" from the direction of the upstairs gallery in the studio. I looked up in to see who was calling my name and saw that it was a man who at first I did not recognise. He started to make his way down from the gallery to where I was standing in the studio and walked towards me with his out stretched right hand. He seemed genuinely pleased to see me and as he got closer, he was a person who looked vaguely familiar although I could not precisely remember where, or in what circumstances we had previously met. He told me that he was part of the production team involved in the quiz show *Greed* that I had appeared on some two and a half years earlier and he invited me to have a quick coffee and a chat if I had the time to spare. I decided to accept to his invitation rather than make my usual customary swift exit and the pair of us spent a little over half an hour talking about the hopes and ambitions the production company had for the show and also embark on a trip down memory lane in relation to our time on the game show *Greed*. As for the show itself, I never actually heard from the production company again after my screen test despite their assurances that they would let me know whether or not I would be involved in the show in some capacity, the deafening silence dispelling any faint hopes that may have been lingering in terms of Shaun Wallace becoming a reality TV legal superstar. I don't know whether the show managed to secure itself a commission although I do faintly recall seeing a reality TV show based on the workings of the legal profession at some point during the year but like my own faint dreams, that programme eventually sunk without a trace.

The following week, I had an evening appointment to attend another audition in a hotel just around the corner from Notting Hill Gate tube station, this time to try and become a contender on **THE** most prestigious of all quiz shows, *Mastermind*. As an avid viewer of the show ever since its inaugural late-night screening in September 1972, I'd always dreamed of sitting in the show's famous black chair although I never thought that I would ever get the opportunity. The chances of realising this ambition appeared to have gone forever when the series finally ended in 1997 after a twenty-five year run on account of the fact that the show that previously attracted millions upon millions of viewers seemed somehow to have lost the sparkle that it once had. However, in a sudden reversal of fortune, the BBC decided to re-launch the show in the spring of 2003 with a *Celebrity Mastermind* series that served as a prelude to the start of the main series with a brand new host, the veteran presenter of BBC Radio Four's *The Today Programme*, John Humphreys. I took a keen interest in the new series that mainly featured seasoned TV quiz contestants, most of whom I recognised from their previous quizzing exploits on other television quiz shows as they all vied for the honour of becoming the inaugural Mastermind Champion of the revived series. It really was inspiring to see Andy Page emerge victorious in the Grand Final broadcast in late November 2003 as his almost computer like memory in his specialist subject, Golfing Majors since 1975, held off a strong and determined challenge from his three fellow Grand Finalists to lift the famous glass trophy. Andy's victory was given considerable coverage in all the newspapers over the following days and I was totally captivated by an article in the Independent newspaper as he sat in the famous black chair, proudly displaying his crystal glass trophy wearing the happiest of smiles. As I read the article, my imagination and thoughts began to run amok as I began to fantasise about the unlikely possibility of me sitting in the famous black chair holding the trophy aloft just like Andy. *That's it*, I said to myself. *No more messing around. I'm going apply for the next series!*

At long last, I had finally shaken off the shackles of posturing and procrastination and was finally applying for the show. The opportunity to sit in that famous black chair and be tested in the most daunting of circumstances was a once in a lifetime opportunity and I was going to do everything in my power to make those dreams a reality.

The application form arrived a few days later and I wasted no time whatsoever filling it out. The choices I originally put down for my specialist areas were, Kings and Queens of England since 1066, International Affairs since 1945 and FA Cup finals since 1970. I sent the application form back by return of post and I didn't have to wait that long to receive a reply inviting me to attend an audition that was to be held at The Pembroke Mews Hotel in the Notting Hill Gate area of London on Thursday the 15th January 2004 at 5pm.

I arrived at the hotel some fifteen or so minutes before my appointment in an excited yet confident mood and was greeted by a rather young looking pair of production assistants from the show called Rob and Rachel who were waiting around in hotel foyer. After shaking both their hands, Rob and Rachel escorted me to the deserted bar of the hotel where the audition was to take place. The three of us were engaged in a brief but friendly conversation before the audition formally got under way and at some point during that conversation, Rob asked me how far I thought I would progress in the competition if I was lucky enough to be chosen as a contender on the show.

"Although you need the rub of the green as you do for any quiz," I replied in all deadly seriousness, "I believe I've got what it takes to win the whole competition!"

Rob's facial expression in response to my bold declaration of intent was a slight cynical smile of bemusement that appeared to be saying, "Yeah right, of course you'll win the whole thing.... I've heard that kind of boast a hundred, if not a thousand times before!"

With Rob asking the questions and Rachel acting as the timekeeper and points scorer, the format of my audition was similar to the general knowledge section of the show which required me to give as many correct answers as I could within the two minute time limit. The questions I was asked about covered a range of topics. Some of the questions that I faced were pretty tough, but I thought that overall I put in a fairly good performance. At the end of my two minutes, Rachel informed me that I had given fourteen correct answers out of the twenty questions I was asked, a score that clearly seemed to impress the pair of them.

I was really pleased with the way my audition had gone. I felt pretty confident that I had done enough to finally make my long awaited appearance on the most famous and the most daunting TV quiz shows of them all.

A week or so after my audition, I received a phone call at home from Jon Kelly, one of the producers of the programme who told me the good news that I had been accepted as a contender on the forthcoming series. My initial excitement at the news however, was quickly tempered considerably when he told me that because of the show's very strict rules, I would have to change my chosen subject of the Kings and Queens of England because a previous contender had already covered that subject matter in the last series. Jon asked me whether I had another specialist subject that I could put forward instead but because I was caught somewhat unawares by this news, I asked him for time to reconsider my options. He readily agreed to my request and said that he would allow me until the following day for my final decision on my specialist subjects. I was extremely disappointed with the ruling and my initial thoughts upon hearing the news were that my chances of success had taken a considerable nosedive. I began to consider the type of specialist subjects I could put forward first considering, then immediately dismissing, one topic after another, always bearing in mind as I was doing so, *what's the one topic that I know so well that the programme's question setters cannot get the better of me?* It was a task that even I was beginning to believe was one that I would not be able to resolve then, all of a sudden, the answer came to me as if struck by a flash of heavenly inspiration. *Football! Of course! Football!* Why not choose as a topic the subject you love more than life itself? I already had FA Cup Finals since 1970 as one of my specialist topics and it was just a matter of finding what other areas of football would complement my original choice. After giving the matter some thought, the choices came to me in a true Eureka moment. *What about European Cup Finals and also, England at the European Championships? That's it!* I couldn't have made a better choice of specialist topics to put forward and those three football topics appeared to have the potential to be an unbeatable, winning combination. It made perfect sense to offer football as specialist topic for the three rounds, because aside from my passion for History, I have always felt that I had an extensive array of footballing knowledge and expertise that only a handful of people could equal. My passion for watching football at every opportunity as a young kid growing up, whenever it was League Cup Finals, FA Cup

Finals, World Cups or international matches involving the England football team. There were two other reasons why I chose those specific specialist football topics, first and foremost, my beloved Chelsea, under the stewardship of the current manager Claudio Ranieri, were progressing nicely in the Champions League, the European club football competition that was the lucrative successor to the European Champion's Cup and secondly that summer, the England football team were due to compete at Euro 2004 in Portugal. The more I thought about my proposed specialist subjects, the more excited I became at the prospect of really doing well on the show. I was convinced that I had made excellent choices for my specialist subjects, the only possible fly in the ointment was whether the show's producers would give my choices their firm seal of approval.

Jon called me the following day and asked me what I had chosen. I confidently told him, "European Cup Finals since 1970, followed by the England football team at the European Championships, and for the final, because I live close by to Wembley Stadium, my final topic would be FA Cup finals since 1970." when I told him what I had chosen, he replied that whilst it was somewhat unusual for all three choices to come from one specialist area, but I was ultimately allowed my subjects.

I was now free to begin my preparations for my appearance on *Mastermind* in earnest. To stand any chance of doing well on the show, I had to ensure that my preparation would be thorough and methodical, without interfering or disrupting my professional obligations and responsibilities. I knew full well that it would be a daunting challenge attempting to strike the right balance between those two competing interests but it was one that I was looking forward to with immense excitement, unlimited enthusiasm and fierce determination.

The following day, I made my way to the library to begin my preparation. As I was going through the reference books I found and their well written summaries of the football matches, I started to have vivid flashbacks as if the matches were played only five minutes previously, matches that I watched as a young boy growing up. As priceless as those two books were, they were not the main source of my research material. Another equally vital and invaluable source of information that I intended to use was at the British Library Annexe based in Colindale. It was a library that I knew very well as I used to go there regularly during my days as an undergraduate law student in order to revise and prepare for my exams. The library itself contains the largest collection of newspapers anywhere in the country, with some of those newspapers dating right back to their earliest editions.

Throughout my preparation for my first appearance on the show, I would spend every available spare hour that I had at the library, devoting hours and hours poring over the match reports, making important notes as I was going along so that I covered every little detail of the thirty four year time period of the European Cup Final matches I was going to be tested on. Nothing was left to chance. From the name of the referee, the timing of the first goal, right through to how many players were booked in any one particular match. Those newspaper reports on the matches would cover the gaps that may have been missing in the library book that I borrowed, and it gave me the confidence of knowing that no stone was left unturned.

I also purchased a host of my own books on the subject and was advised that there was a specialist sports bookshop nearby. Acting on that helpful advice, I made my way to the shop in question. The shelves were amply stocked with books, DVDs and videos which catered for all sporting tastes, an Aladdin's cave of precious material that left me feeling like a kid let loose in a sweet shop. I went up to the person behind the counter and asked him whether he had any material on European Cup Finals, explaining to him the reasons why I needed. As I was chatting away with the person who was assisting me about football in general, it became apparent that he was the owner of the shop and he told me that his name was Chris. We quickly struck up quite a rapport and I was very impressed with his knowledge of sport as well as his enthusiastic interest and support in my forthcoming appearance on *Mastermind*. Although I didn't buy anything from his shop on this occasion, I told him that I would let him know how I got on in the heats and if I managed to get through, I would definitely be back in his store to buy some of his books, a promise I genuinely hoped I would uphold.

The regimented way in which I structured my preparation for the first round was as follows. On the days that I was not in court, the mornings and afternoons were devoted to researching my specialist topic and my evenings and late nights were devoted to preparing for the general knowledge round. Given the infinite nature of general knowledge, the way I tried to prepare for it was a combination of an hour or so reading different quiz books and after a short break, watching as many quiz shows as possible, adopting my time honoured and trusted method of answering the questions and keeping an accurate record of my correct answers. That level of preparation even extended to the situation where no matter where I was, or in whose company, I would always have one quiz book or another about my person and my close friends or colleagues would invariably find themselves constantly badgered or press ganged into the role of question master, firing question after question from the same books that were thrust unwelcomingly in their direction. Whilst those friends and colleagues of mine were very accommodating, I'm sure my incessant demands on their time had, on many occasions, stretched the outer limits of their patience, but I was grateful for that assistance and support because without a shadow of a doubt, it played a considerable part in raising the levels of my confidence to an even higher plane as the day for my first appearance in the *Mastermind* heats drew ever closer.

Saturday the 20th of March 2004. The day for my first round heat had finally arrived and as per the letter of instruction that I had received from the *Mastermind* production team, I was required to be at the Granada Television Recording Studios in Manchester at 5pm. Although I would hardly regard myself as a particularly superstitious individual, I saw it was a good omen that I had to record my first round heat on that particular day because it happened to coincide with the 33rd birthday of my sister Sandra's only daughter, my eldest niece Melanie. I was booked on the 1pm train from Euston to Manchester Piccadilly, so I had plenty of time to go through my usual grooming ritual, arriving at the station with more than enough time to spare.

The train departed from the platform on time and as the travelling passengers were walking through my carriage trying to find either seats, amongst them I noticed a young black guy who I was fairly sure I had seen before but for the life of me I couldn't think where that it would have been or in what capacity. The man must have been thinking along the same lines because he too was staring in my direction. As he passed, we nodded at each other.

My journey towards Manchester began without a hitch but when we arrived at the first stop at Watford Junction some twenty minutes later, the train manager announced, much to my considerable dismay, that our train was going to be on the platform for some time due to averse weather conditions. Because I didn't own a mobile at the time, I had to get off the train to telephone the show's producers to inform them that I would not be at the Granada Studios on time. They reassured that my late arrival would not be an issue, which went a long way in putting my mind as ease and I told the production team that I would keep them regularly updated as to my whereabouts whenever the opportunity arose. The train remained at Watford Junction for the best part of an hour before it eventually left the platform, travelling no quicker than the speed of a snail as it stopped and started intermittently. I was beginning to become even more anxious than before but I tried not to let it affect either my mental wellbeing, or my preparations for the show and I continued to browse through the pile of books that I had in front of me. One or two of the passengers who were seated close by were mildly curious as to why I had surrounded myself with a pile of books. I told them that I was preparing for an appearance on *Mastermind* and because they seemed to be quite impressed by what I had told them, I decided rather cheekily, to ask whether they would mind testing me on my general knowledge. A blond haired guy opposite me was more than happy to indulge my request and he began asking question after question from the various quiz books that were plied in front of me right up until the time he got off the train an hour or so later.

After the train finally pulled into Coventry station, the train manager announced that because of the ongoing disruptions to the railway network, the train would have to stop at Wolverhampton train station for an indefinite period of time and that any passengers wanting to travel onwards to Manchester would have to wait on the platform before the train was given the all clear to leave. I alighted from the train immediately on hearing the news and contacted the show's production team to update them of the situation. Once again, I was reassured that everything would be all right and that they would make arrangements for a courtesy car to meet me at Wolverhampton Station that would take me up to Manchester.

The train finally crawled into Wolverhampton at around 5.45pm. I felt totally exhausted and drained from my long and arduous journey and left the station along with my fellow tired and frustrated travellers who were milling around the station like headless chickens, desperately trying to seek reliable alternative forms of transport to take them onto their eventual destinations. Amongst the crowd of people, I noticed the young black guy that I had seen at the start of that eventful train journey also looking frustrated and increasingly concerned as to how he was going to continue his journey.

I went up to him and asked, "Where you going to?"

"I'm going to Manchester," he replied.

I thought I could do with some company up the M6, so I said, "Listen, I'm going up to Manchester as well and I've got a car laid on to take me there. If you want to, you can come with me."

He immediately accepted my offer and together, we found the courtesy car. The pair of us placed all our belongings into the boot and jumped into the back seat for which I hoped would be a delay free, stress free journey all the way to Manchester. Once we had settled, we set about the task of formally introducing ourselves and it was only when he told me that his name was Michael that the penny finally dropped.

"I remember you now. You're Michael Tomlinson who used to live around the corner from me!"

When I told him my name his penny also dropped and like typical long lost acquaintances, we embarked upon a nostalgic trip down memory lane, catching up on old times. Afterwards, I pulled out one of my quiz books and asked Michael if he would test me. Michael readily and kindly agreed. He proceeded to fire question after question during the journey that became so infectious that even our driver who initially didn't know what to make of it all, also joined in the fun by trying to answer some of the questions. Our impromptu quizzing session in the car made a potentially long and mind numbing journey enjoyable and worthwhile. The time seemed to fly by and before we knew it, we were on the outskirts of Manchester's City Centre. Before Michael got out of the vehicle, we bumped fists and I thanked him profusely for his help.

We drove the relatively short distance to the Granada studios where I was by a somewhat relieved looking production assistant who took me straight to the green room where it seemed that everybody was waiting for my eventual arrival. I'd finally made it to the recording studios after all that time and effort then suddenly, I began to feel the onset of fatigue and pangs of hunger and thirst. I felt absolutely drained, physically as well as mentally, so much so, that negative thoughts began to enter my mind as to whether I could get myself physically and mentally up for the challenge and ordeal of sitting in the black chair. I considered withdrawing, but was informed that if I did, there was no guarantee of when I'd be allowed back.

As I was considering my options, there was a flurry of noise and activity and I looked round to see a group of people entering the room, one of whom was John Tweddle, a very good quiz contestant who I had seen previously as a returning previous winner on *Fifteen-to-One*. If he was there, there were certain to be others I knew as well. Seeing John in the green room had the instant effect re-energising me both physically and mentally. I couldn't back out now.

The warm up comic, Ted Robbins was in the throes of finishing the last of his cheesy gags as myself and my three competitors waited patiently before we were eventually called to make our way into the studio and to our designated seats. The sound technicians then came over with their microphone packs to wire us all for sound and almost after they had finished that particular task, the show's host, John Humphreys, entered the studio to enthusiastic and rapturous applause. After the applause died down, John thanked the studio audience for their presence that he followed up with a few witty anecdotal remarks before he walked the short distance over to where we were all seated and with a warm greeting and a disarming smile, John wished us all the best of luck.

With all the last minute formalities now out of the way, the studio floor manager then asked for complete silence in the studio before commencing his countdown to the start of the show. Once the show's haunting signature theme tune, 'Approaching With Menace', began to resonate throughout the studio, the die was finally cast. I was now, officially, after years of procrastinating, years of disappointment and despair, a contender on Mastermind.

John then began his introduction to the show with the following words. "IN THE SPOTLIGHT TONIGHT IS MICHAEL RICHARDS, A RETIRED TEACHER FROM BOLTON WHOSE SPECIALIST TOPIC IS THE LIFE AND TIMES OF LADY EMMA HAMILTON. SHAUN WALLACE, A BARRISTER AND LECTURER FROM WEMBLEY IN MIDDLESEX WHOSE SPECIALIST SUBJECT IS EUROPEAN CUP FINALS SINCE 1970. BETH MCCLURE, A MICROBIOLOGIST FROM HARROW WHOSE SUBJECT IS THE FICTION OF MICHAEL CRICHTON AND FINALLY, EDDIE THORNLEY, A SOFTWARE DEVELOPER FROM RUGBY WHOSE SPECIALIST SUBJECT IS THE LIFE AND MUSIC OF ELVIS COSTELLO. HELLO, I'M JOHN HUMPHREYS AND WELCOME TO *MASTERMIND*. YOU ALL KNOW THE RULES, I HAVE NO DOUBT. TWO MINUTES ON A SPECIALIST SUBJECT CHOSEN BY THE CONTENDERS AND TWO MINUTES ON GENERAL KNOWLEDGE, THE CLOCK IS RESPONSIBLE FOR THE PRESSURE. THE WINNER AT THE END OF THE CONTEST GOES THROUGH TO THE NEXT ROUND WITH THE CHANCE OF THE FINALS AND THE BIG PRIZE, A GLASS BOWL BEARING THE IMMORTAL TITLE MASTERMIND. SO, LET'S GET ON WITH THE SPECIALIST ROUND, MAY I HAVE THE FIRST CONTENDER PLEASE".

Michael was the first contender to make his way to the famous black chair and I listened to his questions intently to see how many of his questions I could answer as a way of warming myself up for my first visit to the chair in about two or so minutes' time. I felt quite pleased at the fact that I managed to answer three of Michael's questions correctly and at the end of his designated two minutes, posted a very respectable score of fourteen points with no passes. As Michael walked back to his seat to well-deserved applause resonating throughout the studio, John then called me to the hot seat. I rose and walked towards the black chair trying to take my time, the adrenalin increasing with each step, hoping to portray an outward air of confidence, whilst a battle was beginning to rage inside me between the contrasting emotions of excitement and nervousness. The moment of truth had arrived and after I made myself as comfortable as I could in the hottest of all seats, I turned to face my inquisitor looking him squarely in his eyes. I sat with both hands spread over my thighs as I wanted to use my fingers as a means of keeping a score of my correct answers. Doubts nagged at me. Would I relax and enjoy the moment? Or would I react like a frightened rabbit caught in the glare of the headlights? In the end, I needn't have worried because those first two minutes in the black chair was probably the best performance to date that I had ever given on a TV quiz show. I rattled off one correct answer after another whilst still managing to keep score despite having to use both my hands twice in order to achieve that feat. When the familiar bleeping sound signified that my designated two minutes were up, John informed me that I got seventeen questions correct with no passes and I returned to my seat with the applause from the audience resonating in my ears. Beth was then invited to take her turn in the hot seat, and when her time was up, she posted a very respectable eleven points and no passes with the final contender, Eddie Thornley going one better than Beth's effort with an equally impressive score of twelve points and just like his fellow contenders, no passes.

To say that I was pleased with my first round performance would be an understatement. What was especially pleasing was that, apart from the fact that nine of the seventeen questions I had predicted that I might possibly be asked about were in fact asked, I did not pass on any of the questions that I faced. That was my main strategy, aside from trying to answer as many questions as I possibly could correctly. Not passing on any question was going to be the main tactic that I was going to faithfully and rigidly adhere to for as long as I remained in the competition. There was no doubting the fact that there was going to be contenders of the highest quality competing in the series, the very presence of John Tweddle in the competition was living proof of that fact and my strategy of not passing on any of my questions could, in the long run, make all the difference between marginal sweet success and agonising narrow failure. I was also fully conscious of the fact that I had performed well in my specialist topic and no more than that as the general knowledge round was yet to come. It was therefore imperative that I had to remain calm and totally focused to ensure that I didn't succumb to the perils of hubris and throw it all away.

Beth was the first contender to revisit the chair for the general knowledge round, and she scored a further ten points with three passes to give her a total of twenty one. Eddie was next in the chair and he scored seven points with three passes to give him a total of eighteen. The penultimate contender, Michael, scored a further eight points with three passes to give him a total of twenty two. This was now the target that I had to beat to ensure that I progressed into the next stage of the competition. John invited me for the final time in the contest to take my place in the black chair, an invitation that was less challenging and daunting than my first visit. John started off by first asking me about my love of football and my interest in coaching young children before proceeding to ask me whether I would like to manage either a top professional club or even possibly, the England Manager's job.

"I'd love to," I replied.

"So, you'd rather coach than be a barrister?" John asked teasingly.

"I'd love to combine both professions if I could because I love football. However, there's more to me than just being a barrister."

John reminded me that twenty two was the score to beat and began asking me my series of general knowledge questions. Once again, I got off to the perfect start by answering the first five questions correctly, a faultless performance which meant that I had equalled Michael's score and had effectively won the heat. Knowing that fact made me relax considerably and out of the fifteen questions that I faced, I got ten right, three wrong and passed on two, but those passes had come well after I had secured the necessary points to secure victory. As I returned to my seat with the sound of the audience's applause resonating in my ears, I felt an immense sense of personal pride. I was through to the next round and a step closer to becoming Mastermind Champion.

We were told we could go to the green room for some refreshment. Once there, I made a hasty beeline towards the one person I wanted to talk to, the *Mastermind* host himself, John Humphreys. John greeted me warmly by shaking my hand before offering his congratulations.

I smiled and said to him, "John, there's an interesting fact that I know about you that I'll wager only a few people in this room are aware of."

"Really?" John replied with mild curiosity. "What's that then?"

Quick as a flash I replied, "Your real first name is Desmond."

"How did you know that?" he asked in a state of mild astonishment, but I never told him.

Although I was immensely tired by the time I got to my hotel room, I was still floating on cloud nine as a result of my win. My mind was still buzzing with excitement and as I lay awake snuggled up under the duvet, I began to reflect on the eventful day that I had from its optimistic beginning, its fraught middle and its glorious end before saying a quick prayer to the man upstairs thanking him for getting me through a somewhat testing ordeal that ended in triumph, and as I began to finally drift off to sleep for a much needed rest, my thoughts momentarily turned to the challenge of the next stage of the competition. I was under no illusion that from now on, the level of pressure, the standard of the questions, as well as the quality of opponent, was going to a step up another level. That would mean that I would have to raise my game in terms of the levels of hard work and preparation if I wanted to remain in the competition, but those battles and problems are for another day. For now, it was a simple case of treating myself to a well-earned good night's rest and to savour the moment of a hard fought and ultimately, well deserved victory.

I woke up bright and early the following morning as I wanted to leave Manchester as quickly as I possibly could after breakfast. My main reason for wanting to get back to London as soon as possible was because it was Mothering Sunday and I was anxious to get myself a decent bouquet of flowers because if I returned home empty handed, which going by previous Mothering Sundays, was more often the case than not, I would never hear the end of Mum's endless moaning.

When I got back to London, I bought the flowers and headed to see my mum. On the way, I bumped into Nipper who was heading towards the shops. Nipper asked me where I had been and I told him that I had just returned from Manchester after having competed on *Mastermind*.

"How did you get on Lej?" (Lej being short for Legend, the nickname that Nipper had bestowed on me on account of my quizzing exploits).

I was somewhat reluctant to answer him because there are times when Nipper is not exactly the most trustworthy person in the world with secrets. "Look Nipper. If I tell you, will you promise that you won't spread it around?"

"I won't tell a soul," he replied in a very convincing tone. "Go on tell me, Lej, how did you do?"

"Ok, I'll tell you. I got seventeen points on European Cup Finals and won the heat with a total score of twenty seven points."

Nipper then nodded his head in approval and he raised his right hand, demanding a high five. I duly obliged. Just as I was leaving I turned to him and said, "Nipper, please keep the news to yourself, do you promise?"

"Of course I will, Lej. Trust me!"

I finally arrived at Mum's, and already present was my brother Steve, my sister-in-law Lavinia and their ten month-old son, Lucas. As I walked inside the living room, I saw the large, ostentatious bouquet that Steve had bought for Mum and it didn't take Steve long to begin to poke fun at the bouquet that I was carrying with his cutting observation, that he had seen a better bunch of weeds growing in the alleyway. Even Mum decided to join in the verbal attack, with a comment of cynical surprise that I actually managed to get her something.

I told Steve in private about my appearance on *Mastermind*, and we broke into excited whooping and congratulatory high fives. I asked him to keep it to himself though because, I decided, the less people who knew the less pressure there was on me. Whilst he didn't entirely agree with my reasoning, he nevertheless respected my wishes and before we left the room in order to join the others downstairs for a Mother's Day Sunday dinner, he took great pleasure in reminding me of the fact that even though I may have won a heat on *Mastermind*, he was still the unbeaten quiz champion in the Wallace household, a fact, given our Trivial Pursuit battles in the past, was something that I couldn't argue with.

Whilst I could rely on my brother Steve to keep things discreet with regards to my appearance on *Mastermind*, the same sadly couldn't be said of Nipper, who proved to be an individual with all the confidentiality skills of Kim Philby, because no sooner had he made me the promise not to tell a soul, I was on the receiving end of telephone calls from most of Nipper's mates like Robert Harding and Colesy, congratulating me on my win. When I next saw Nipper I took him to task as to why he told his mates when I specifically asked him not to and he replied, "I know Lej, I know, I just couldn't help myself. I'm so proud of what you've done, I had to tell Mum and Dad right away, and from there, I told one person and then another. I just couldn't keep it a secret." With that lamentable explanation, whether it was sincere or otherwise, how could I really be mad with him? Still, there was method in my madness in wanting to keep things a secret. The last thing that I needed when competing in a competition like *Mastermind*, was the extra added burden of pressure and the expectation from my family and friends it would bring and it was for that reason that I decided that from here on in, I would keep my own counsel with regards to my appearances on the show in the future and to go about the business of preparing for that round in a low key and understated way.

My increasing levels of confidence that resulted from my appearance on *Mastermind* was starting to have a clear and positive effect on my professional career. I managed to put together a string of good results in the courtroom both in the criminal and immigration cases that I was doing at the time and whilst they were not the most serious types of cases in the world, they were important to the clients I was representing. My career appeared to be heading in the direction that I was hoping it would go and the sources of that regular work was not only coming from the small band of loyal solicitors who were keeping me busy, there was also a noticeable and steady increase in lay clients contacting me directly requesting that I represent them and I would always point them in the direction of my solicitors contacts to ensure that those solicitors would get the Legal Aid Order, the net result being, those solicitor contacts would instruct me to do the case.

One of those cases that I received using that method, was the most important set of instructions that I had received in a very long time. Two days after my appearance on *Mastermind*, I was instructed to attend a preliminary hearing at the Central Criminal Court where my client, an old friend of mine, was facing a charge of Murder. I first became involved in his case when my friend contacted me at home sometime in mid-January and asked if he could come to see me to discuss a very serious matter. He told me that officers from Wembley Police Station wished to speak to him concerning his possible involvement in a shooting that had taken place in Acton where the victim was shot dead whilst waiting in his car. My friend assured me that he had absolutely nothing to do with it and given the fact that I had known him for the best part of ten years, I had no reason to doubt his word. He asked me if I could accompany him to the police station, but I told him that as a barrister, I was precluded from doing so, but I would contact a very good solicitor who would be willing to accompany him. I immediately got on the telephone and spoke to Rodney Wilson and explained the situation to him before handing the phone over to my friend in order for those arrangements to be made and eventually, my friend, accompanied by Rodney, voluntarily surrendered himself to Wembley Police Station. He was formerly arrested, interviewed and eventually charged with Murder (together with another individual who had already been charged) and remanded in custody. Rodney dealt with all the preliminary hearings at Ealing Magistrates Court before the case was committed for trial to the Central Criminal Court.

At the preliminary hearing, a timetable was set for the Prosecution to serve all the relevant papers within six weeks after which time, both defendants would be required to enter their pleas to the charge and they were both remanded in custody until the next hearing date. I went to go and see my client after the hearing to explain to him what had happened in court. He was understandably very disappointed that he was still on remand and that it would be some considerable time before the trial would take place. I tried to reassure him that whilst myself, and the rest of his legal team, would be using their best endeavours to secure his acquittal, I would not be in a position to assess the strength of the evidence against him until I had received the Prosecution's bundle of papers.

The first matter I attended to when I eventually arrived home from court, was to draft legal opinion advising Rodney's firm to apply to the Legal Services Commission requesting the extension of the Legal Aid Certificate, not only to instruct Leading Counsel to conduct the trial, but also to instruct an expert on the issue of cell site evidence as the Prosecution informed the court at the Preliminary Hearing that it was their case that the various phone calls made between my client and his co-defendant prior to the shooting were in their view linked to the murder. Later on that evening, I contacted my friend, colleague and professional mentor Courtenay Griffiths QC at home to ask him if he would act as the Lead Counsel when the case was eventually set down for trial. Courtenay said that he would.

The following day, my preparations for my specialist topic for the next round of *Mastermind*, The England Football Team at the European Championships, began in earnest. A week or so after I began my preparations for *Mastermind*, Jon Kelly, the show's producer contacted me at home in order to discuss my appearance in the next round and the specialist topic I would be covering. Jon informed me that for that specialist topic, I would be required to cover all of England's matches at the European Championships including, all of England's qualifying matches from the years 1962 to 2003 and he concluded our short conversation by telling me that someone from the *Mastermind* production team would write to me in due course with regards to the details of my next appearance and my travel and accommodation arrangements before he wished me the best of luck and how much he was looking forward to seeing me again at that next appearance. A period covering forty years of England matches seems on the surface, a daunting prospect. But this is *Mastermind*, not some second rate quiz show. This was a quiz show that is a cut above the rest, where tasks and challenges demanded from contenders who aspire to ultimate glory get progressively harder. My aspirations and ambitions for the competition were no greater or lesser than any other of my fellow heat winners who had made it to this stage of the contest and if I wanted to take my place in the series Grand Final, then I had to prove over the next coming weeks and months that I was more than capable of raising my game in order to match and if necessary, surpass, the benchmark that the show's producers have demanded. It was a challenge that I wholeheartedly embraced with relish that had one aim and one aim only, a place in the *Mastermind* Grand Final.

My dedication and commitment to my preparation and research for the semi-final heat never wavered over the next two or so months as I stuck to the rigid and repetitive timetable of spending my days researching my specialist topic and my evenings and nights revising my general knowledge that once again, involved me reading one quiz book after another before switching my attention to watching endless TV game shows on my VCR. There was the odd occasion when Nipper, Robert Harding and Colesy (who an excited Nipper had told about my appearance on *Mastermind*. I couldn't be too angry at him, especially after all the help he had given me in the past!), would occasionally turn up at my home out of the blue to help me with my revision that involved them firing questions at me. On one memorable occasion, to make the revision exercise that more interesting, the three of them each laid a small wager to see how many general knowledge questions I could answer selected at random and if I managed to reach a certain target, the wagered sum would be mine. I came out on top time after time in those head to head challenges despite the efforts of my three determined amigos in making the target score that I had to reach slightly more difficult with each challenge. In one last desperate attempt to get the better of me, they decided to set me what they considered to be the ultimate challenge of answering questions on my least favoured topics of their own choosing. Step forward Nipper, who threw down the proverbial gauntlet by wagering £50 that I could not answer correctly twenty out of twenty five questions on one of his strongest topics, popular music. To be fair to Nipper, he is a real music aficionado and would always give me a sound thrashing whenever we played Ken Bruce's popular mid-morning pop quiz, *Pop Master* on Radio 2. Nipper was acutely aware that pop music was one of the few areas of quizzing that was my Achilles Heel and he was determined to take advantage of that fact. However, in true Corinthian spirit, I decided to accept Nipper's challenge and with that, he randomly selected one of my quiz books turning straight to the pop music section before proceeding to ask me twenty five randomly chosen questions. To Nipper's complete and utter surprise and astonishment, I was doing rather well and was well on course to reach my target to claim our £50 bet. There was genuine anxiety on Nipper's face when I was one correct answer away from reaching the magical target. My last question was, Fred Durst is the lead singer of which US band?

"Limp Bizkit," I replied confidently, to my complete and utter joy, in the full knowledge that I had reached the target.

Nipper sat in his chair speechless whilst Robert and Colesy shook their heads in disbelief. In my excitement, I demanded that Nipper should pay up immediately, but Nipper being Nipper began patting his pockets as he launched into his well-worn and familiar rehearsed lines, "If I had it, it would be yours." I took him to task about paying up but deep down, I knew that I was just wasting my breath. Needless to say, Nipper never paid up and, even to this day, I am still awaiting payment.

I eventually received written confirmation from the show's producers that my next appearance on Mastermind was going to take place on the 27th May 2004 on the third scheduled recording for that day just like it was in the last round. The contest was also taking place on the same day my best friend Winston Davis would be celebrating his 44th birthday, just like how my first round appearance and subsequent victory happened to coincide with the birthday of my eldest niece, Melanie and whilst I still maintain that I am not a firm believer in fate or superstition, it was those small coincidences that got me thinking about the possibility that maybe, just maybe I could go all the way.

The day of the next round of Mastermind had finally arrived and this time, my journey up to Manchester was mercifully problem free. I arrived in Manchester mid-afternoon which meant that I could check into my hotel early thus affording me plenty of time to relax in my room and prepare for the contest in a quieter and calmer environment. Granada Studios were only about a mile or so from the hotel so rather than wait for the courtesy car to pick me up and take me there, I chose to take a leisurely stroll taking full advantage of the balmy spring evening and I arrived at the studios at about 6.30pm as my scheduled recording slot was going to take place some two hours later. I was greeted by one of the show's production assistants and she escorted me to the green room where the fellow contenders with whom I would be locking cerebral horns were already waiting. I was pleased about the fact that I was meeting my fellow contenders early as it gave me the opportunity to meet, know and spend some quality time with them, a privilege that was denied me on the last time I was in the studios.

I was informed that, this time, I was designated to be the last contender to sit in the black chair for the first round on specialist subjects, a decision that I was more than happy with from a tactical perspective, because it would give me the opportunity to assess the possible strengths and weaknesses of my fellow contenders before it was my turn to occupy the hot seat. The production assistant told us that the winner would go through to the show's Grand Final which would take place at the BBC Studios in London on 14th June 2004, the welcoming news concerning the venue for the Grand Final had the effect of raising my already sky high levels of anticipation and excitement to an even higher plane because from my own selfish point of view, the fact that the Grand Final was going to be held in London as opposed Manchester or indeed, some other part of the country, made me even more motivated and determined to claim that final berth. It was on par with playing a major soccer final on your own home ground.

A short time after our briefing had concluded, the previous semi-final heat had just finished and all the contenders involved in that show were making their way into the green room. My attention was drawn to one or two people standing around a smiling individual a few yards away from where we were seated. Almost immediately I assumed that the individual concerned must have just won that heat and moments later, he was being approached by other people who were also offering him their congratulations. When I saw the person they were congratulating, it came as no real surprise to me as the individual in question was none other than Don Young, another top class quiz aficionado whose impressive quizzing CV has seen him make numerous appearances on *Fifteen-to-One* including, a couple of appearances in the *Fifteen-To-One* Grand Final where he was the runner-up to the legendary Daphne Fowler. *If he's made it through to the Grand Final, there's a fair chance that John Tweddle has made it through to the final stages as well,* I muttered to myself. Seeing the formidable Don Young win his semi-final heat only heightened my determination to make the Grand Final because given his impeccable quizzing pedigree, he clearly would be the man to beat if I was to stand any chance of claiming the ultimate prize.

The activity inside the green room was becoming more lively and intense and it wasn't that long before another production assistant asked the four of us who were competing in the final heat to gather our belongings as we were going to our respective dressing rooms in order to get ourselves ready to prepare for the show. Once inside my room, I immediately set about the task of removing the same pink shirt and black trousers that I wore in the previous round from the dry cleaner's plastic covering and as I started to get myself ready, my thoughts turned to the important task of trying to secure a place in the Grand Final that lay ahead of me. I was acutely aware that my three fellow contenders craved the same cherished prize as much as I did. Like me, they all had won their respective heats in the previous round heat and as such, this was not the time or indeed the place, to adopt the mantle of complacency. Furthermore, the last thing I was going to do was to underestimate my fellow competitors or indeed, allow myself to be lulled into a false sense of security and get ahead of myself into thinking that my place in the final would be a mere formality on the strength of my previous first round performance. If I was going to make the Grand Final then I had to go out there and earn the right.

As usual, I rounded off my last minute thoughts by going down on my knees and offering a short prayer to the man upstairs, asking him for the strength and the knowledge to see me across the finishing line in victory, and if that wasn't possible, to at least ensure that I did myself justice on such an important occasion. I was as ready as I was ever going to be and moments later, I heard the final knock on the door as the time had now come for me to make my way to the studio. I was escorted to the back stage curtain of the studio where my fellow contenders were already assembled. As we waited for the call by the Studio Floor Manager to make our way onto the studio set, instinctively and very sportingly, we all wished each other the best of luck before we each reverted to our own private and contemplative thoughts, our respective inner tensions and adrenalin surges beginning to rise in the process.

Moments after sitting in our respective seats, the sound technicians were on hand with their microphone packs to wire us individually for sound and as they were doing so the show's host, John Humphreys arrived on the set where he too unsurprisingly, was greeted with the same warm and enthusiastic applause that we were greeted with. With a routine that I assumed is generic at the start of all the show's recordings, John immediately thanked the studio audience not just for their attendance, but also for their patience before making his way over to where the four of us were seated. John then welcomed all four of us back to the studio then wished us the best of luck in the semi-final before making his way to his seat. At that point, I began to feel the proverbial butterflies flittering intensely away around in my stomach whilst outwardly, I was trying to remain as calm and composed as I possibly could for what would undoubtedly be the toughest contest of my quizzing career to date. The Studio Floor Manager asked for silence in the studio before he began his countdown to the start of the show's familiar theme music followed immediately by John's familiar monologue as he introduced the names of the competing contenders.

"IN THE SPOTLIGHT TONIGHT IS IAN COPELAND, A LECTURER FROM EDINBURGH. HIS SPECIALIST TOPIC IS SCOTTISH INFRANTRY REGIMENTS SINCE 1900. DOCTOR

FRANK POTTER FROM THE WIRRAL, AN ANAESTHETIST, HIS IS THE HISTORY OF THE CITY OF LIVERPOOL. ANNA STATHAM FROM LONDON, A RETIRED SECRETARY, HER SPECIALIST SUBJECT IS THE LIFE AND WORKS OF ORLANDUS LASSUS AND FINALLY, SHAUN WALLACE FROM WEMBLEY, A BARRISTER AND PART TIME LECTURER WHOSE SPECIALIST SUBJECT IS THE ENGLAND FOOTBALL TEAM AT THE EUROPEN CHAMPOINSHIPS. HELLO, I'M JOHN HUMPHREYS AND WELCOME TO THE SIXTH AND LAST SEMI-FINAL OF *MASTERMIND*. TONIGHT'S WINNER WILL JOIN THE OTHER FIVE FINALISTS IN OUR GRAND FINAL AND A CHANCE OF WINNING A SPLENDID GLASS BOWL AND MORE IMPORTANTLY, THE COVETED TITLE OF *MASTERMIND* SO LET'S HAVE OUR FIRST CONTENDER PLEASE."

Ian was the first to step forward into the black chair to face his specialist questions and just prior to facing those set of questions, John reminded him of his specialist subject in the previous round, The Life and Career of Cole Porter. Ian initially got off to a bright start with his specialist set of questions but unfortunately, he began to falter considerably from what seemed to be a very tough set of questions that I for the life of me couldn't answer. At the end of his two minutes, Ian managed to score seven points with three passes. The next contender to take his seat in the black chair was Dr Frank Potter who, John revealed, had chosen the Second World War as his specialist subject in the previous round. Frank was calmness personified throughout his designated two minutes and with his soft, yet clearly noticeable Scouse accent, he posted a very impressive score of twelve points with just one pass. I was able to answer three of Frank's set of questions correctly. But if I thought that Ian's specialist subject was unbelievably tough, then the next contender, Anna's, choice of specialist subject, Orlandus Lassus, an individual whose name was just as difficult to pronounce let alone answer questions about, surely surpassed it. In the previous round, Anna had answered questions on Anthony Pole's series of novels, A Dance to the Music of Time, a challenging specialist topic, but her choice on this occasion really was in a league of its own. The questions that Anna had to face were tough, really tough, but despite those challenges, Anna performed admirably eventually posting a score of eight points with three passes before she returned to her seat to the warm applause from the studio audience that was well deserved. John finally called me forward to face my own two minute interrogation. I walked the few short steps towards the black chair feeling slightly more calm and controlled than I felt in my first round heat. I sat down in the infamous black chair before adopting the familiar stance that involved me spreading both my hands across my thighs with the sole aim of using my fingers as a means of keeping a score of the correct answers that I was hoping and praying would result in similar commanding performance just like in the previous round. Those prayers were answered as I managed to answer the first eleven questions in a row correctly. Virtually all of those questions were ones that I had anticipated that I could be asked about, the highlight of which was the eighth question, when John asked me for the name of the Yugoslav player who the England midfielder Alan Mullery had fouled, the consequence of which led him to becoming the first England player to be sent off in an International match (Trivich). My only blemish in my specialist round of questions occurred in the twelfth question when I was asked for the name of the England debutant who set up the equalising goal in the 1968 European Qualifier/Home International Championship match against Scotland at Hampden Park. I knew the correct answer was the Manchester City winger, Mike Summerbee, but for some inexplicable reason, which I can only put down to either nervousness, or excessive over confidence, I blurted out the name, Roger Hunt. As the buzzer sounded to signal the end of my two minutes in the chair, John could see the visible disappointment and frustration I was expressing on account of my less than perfect round. "YOU ONLY GOT ONE WRONG. HOWEVER, YOU SCORED FOURTEEN POINTS AND NO PASSES." I continued my display of frustration and disappointment that was now threatening to border on childish petulance as I rose to my feet in order to make the short return journey to my seat with the applause of the studio audience resonating in my ears.

Although I was in the lead, my nearest challenger, Frank, was only two correct questions and one pass behind me which meant that there was everything to play for in the crucial general knowledge round where anything can happen. Ian was the first contender to be called forward to face his second round question and once again, I resorted to the tactic of limbering myself up in preparation by answering, in my mind, the general knowledge questions of my fellow contenders. Just as I had anticipated, the standard of the general knowledge questions for the semi-final were proving to be a step up in class. I could manage to correctly answer only eight of Ian's set of questions, managing in the process, to beat his own total of five which gave Ian a total of twelve points with two passes. Anna, who was the next to follow Ian into the black chair, faced an even tougher set of general knowledge questions out of which, I could only manage to answer seven correctly and Anna's total was a very respectable fifteen points and three passes. John then summoned Frank to face his series of general knowledge questions and he was now the only realistic barrier between me and a place in the Grand Final, but given his creditable performance in the specialist first round, I knew that the threat Frank was going to pose was going to be a formidable one. I was hoping and praying that Frank wouldn't make the best of starts and those prayers appeared to be answered as he passed on his first two questions, but such an inauspicious start didn't put Frank off his stride because as the round progressed, he became considerably stronger with each question, adding an impressive ten further points to make a total of twenty two points and three passes. As Frank returned to his seat to the rapturous applause of the studio audience, I now knew what I had to do to make it to the Grand Final. Nine points would bring me certain victory and providing I didn't pass on a question or if I did, do so no more than five times, eight correct answers would be enough to put me through. I took my time as I rose to my feet when John called me over to face my own set of questions, I had managed to calm myself down from my over the top reaction from my failure in registering another perfect score. I was only two minutes away from registering one of the best personal achievements in my life thus far. I sat down in the chair trying to remain as calm and relaxed as I possibly could before John began to talk about my performance in the specialist first round.

"RIGHT, SHAUN, YOU HAVE FOURTEEN POINTS IN THE BAG, THE SCORE TO BEAT IS TWENTY TWO POINTS, LET'S SEE IF YOU CAN DO THAT WITH YOUR GENERAL KNOWLEDGE QUESTIONS. YOUR TIME STARTS NOW!"

Once again, I resorted to the practice of gently spreading both hands over my thighs pressing my finger down every time I got a correct answer as a way of helping me to keep score. The importance of the occasion started to take its toll as I got off to an indifferent start. From the first ten questions that I faced, I got the first one right, the second one wrong, the third one right, and the next four in a row wrong. Now the pressure was really on with my chances of progressing to the Grand Final hanging in the balance. I was conscious of the fact that I had to start to put a string of correct answers in a row together, and pretty soon, otherwise my chances of victory would be in danger of a complete and total collapse. My levels of anxiety were increasing with every question and it was a real struggle trying to remain calm and focused. As luck would have it, John asked a handful of questions in a row which I knew the answer to and suddenly I'd moved my score along onto twenty one points and one correct answer away from certain victory. Four questions went by and I didn't get a single one right. This sudden slump in form came at a bad time. I was fully aware that I was rapidly approaching the end of my two minutes and it seemed that my quest for victory was going to fall at the final hurdle.

"AT WHAT AGE MUST A HORSE REACH BEFORE HE CAN..."

BZZZZZ! The buzzer denoting that my two minutes were up had sounded. But one of the show's legendary catchphrases was about to play both a crucial and decisive role in the outcome of the contest. John went onto say, "I'VE STARTED SO I'LL FINISH.... COMPETE IN THE DERBY?"

I momentarily looked up towards the sky by way of thanks to the man upstairs and with an inner sigh of relief I replied, "THREE, THREE YEARS OLD!"

"THREE YEARS OLD IS CORRECT. SHAUN WALLACE, YOU HAD FOURTEEN POINTS, YOU NOW HAVE A TOTAL OF TWENTY TWO POINTS AND NO PASSES!" John confirmed what I already knew, by the skin of my teeth I made it to the *Mastermind* Grand Final. I broke out into a nervous, but contented outward smile but inwardly, I was delirious, ecstatic, and felt an almighty sense of relief before returning to my seat to tumultuous applause of the studio audience.

As soon as I sat in my seat, John began to describe the climax of the contest as the applause of the studio audience began to die down. "AT THE END OF THAT EXCITING CONTEST LET'S HAVE A LOOK AT THE SCORES. IN FOURTH PLACE WITH TWELVE POINTS, IAN COPELAND. IN THIRD PLACE WITH A SCORE OF FIFTEEN POINTS, ANNA STATHAM. IN SECOND PLACE WITH TWENTY TWO POINTS AND SIX PASSES FRANK POTTER AND IN FIRST PLACE WITH TWENTY TWO POINTS AND NO PASSES, SHAUN WALLACE!"

The studio audience reacted to John's pronouncement by bursting once again into applause and for the first time, probably in my entire life, I felt the incredible sense of complete happiness and joy at what I had just achieved. I immediately rose to my feet to shake hands with my fellow contenders before sitting back down and allowing myself another sharp intake of breath for having survived probably the hardest contest that I had ever taken part in.

"SO, SHAUN WALLACE IS THE WINNER TONIGHT AND OUR SIXTH AND LAST FINALIST. HE WILL JOIN THE OTHER FIVE FINALISTS AND MAY, WHO KNOWS, GO ON TO BE OUR *MASTERMIND* CHAMPION. CONGRATULATIONS TO HIM AND THANKS TO ALL THE OTHERS WHO PERFORMED SO WELL.

JOIN US NEXT TIME FOR THE GRAND FINAL, UNTIL THEN, GOODBYE."

Once we arrived back inside the green room, the place was buzzing with excitement. One of the first persons to offer their congratulations was Rob, the production assistant from my original audition for the show. I smiled and winked at him in acknowledgement, but never uttered a single solitary word in his direction for the simple reason that my performance in reaching the Grand Final said it all. I re-joined my fellow contenders and we congratulated each other for our respective performances in such a nail biting contest. Frank Potter then turned to me and said, "For a time there, it was really touch and go, but when you got the question right about the Thyroid being the organ in the human body that stores Iodine, then I knew that you were going to win it." I responded to those comments by shaking Frank's hand. I couldn't have been paid a greater compliment especially, coming from a member of the medical profession.

Despite the green room's lively atmosphere, I was keen to make a hasty retreat and go back to my hotel. Before I could, I was stopped momentarily in my tracks by one of the principal producers of the show who seemed keen to have a brief discussion with me about the arrangements for the Grand Final. After offering his own congratulations on my semi-final success, he told me that he would call me tomorrow to make arrangements for a suitable and convenient day for a camera crew to follow me around for half a day the purpose, which was mentioned at the briefing prior to the semi-final heat, to record a short documentary profiling the Grand Finalists The short excerpts would then be screened just before the Grand Finalist began their specialist round. My immediate thoughts turned to my home and how messy and upside down the whole place was, strewn with unopened envelopes and court papers, especially court correspondence relating to the Central Criminal Court hearing which I was due to appear at on the 7th June. The last thing I wanted was to suffer the public embarrassment of allowing cameras into my home which was also doubling up as my Chambers, to be seen in such an untidy state which to the viewing public, would have been a sore sight for their prying eyes.

I eventually gathered my belongings from my dressing room and left the studio for the short leisurely stroll back to my hotel. I wanted to have my own private celebrations free from the hullabaloo of the green room and I decided to treat myself to a slap up take away meal and bring it back to my hotel room. I ordered a small portion of beef fried rice, a quarter aromatic crispy duck, a prawn omelette and two cans of ginger beer before heading back to my hotel room where the real celebrations began. I plugged in the beat box that I had bought with me and put on a couple of my favourite R&B CDs whilst I was consuming my celebratory feast during which time thoughts of pure happiness and joy were running through my mind as I reflected on realising my childhood ambition of reaching the *Mastermind* Grand Final, a feat that, even in my wildest of dreams, I never ever thought would happen to me. But it did happen and so far as the rest of the evening was concerned, it would all be about wildly celebrating that achievement because the following day would mark the start of my preparations for an even greater challenge, probably the biggest challenge of my life.

CHAPTER NINETEEN

I arrived back at Euston the following afternoon still floating on cloud nine. However, despite that fantastic achievement, I had no intention of resting on my laurels. Instead of going home, I went straight to Chris' Sports Book Shop. I headed straight towards the Football section inside the store and I immediately plucked from the shelf a book entitled 'Wembley FA Cup Finals 1923–2000' by Glenn Isherwood as well as many DVDs that the shop had available on FA Cup Finals matches of the 1970's right through to 2003. It was pleasing for me that at long last, I could finally buy some of this valuable material as I had resisted the temptation to buy them on my previous visits to the shop on account of the fact that I didn't want to tempt fate just in case I failed to progress in the competition.

Later on in the evening at home, I received the telephone call I was expecting from the *Mastermind* production team to organise the interview. As we were discussing the details, the production assistant said that the interview had to relate to my preparation and performances on Mastermind. I had already formulated in my mind some basic ideas as to how I wanted to be portrayed during the interview and I told the production assistant that for the first part of that interview, I wanted the focus to be on my legal career and I suggested to her that it would be a good idea to show me going into court but for that particular scene, she would have to contact Her Majesty's Court Service in order to obtain their permission. Because of my strict insistence in wanting to keep the number of people who knew about my forthcoming appearance in the Grand Final to an absolute minimum, I asked the production assistant not to reveal my identity to the HMCS under any circumstances. For the next part of the interview, I told the production assistant that it would be fitting for me to be seen outside Wembley Stadium, the spiritual home of my specialist subject for the Grand Final despite the fact that the grand old lady was in the middle of a major rebuilding programme, before finishing the interview with a demonstration of the regular football coaching sessions that I ran for the young boys and girls who lived in and around the local community where I lived. The production assistant seemed quite content with my suggested running order for the interview. She told me that she would be sending me a number of parental consent forms that would have to be signed by the parents or guardians of the children granting their permission to allow their images to be used during the show's transmission.

With that sorted, I could now begin to plan my preparations for the forthcoming court hearing and my revision for the Grand Final and although on the face of it I seemed to be facing a heavy and demanding workload, I was determined that everything would go according to plan. As the old saying goes, "If it ain't broke, don't fix it!" and as such, I would be relying on the same strategy and methods in terms of my preparation and revision that had brought me success to date, for one last supreme effort.

The next two weeks was all about my total devotion and adherence to a seemingly endless repetitive structured programme that I affectionately called the "Four R's" which in essence amounted to, Respiration (naturally), Rest and Replenishment (sporadically), Revision (constantly) and finally, Recreation (occasionally), or in layman's terms, Breathe, Sleep, Eat, Work and Play. During the mornings, I would spend my time at the British Library at Colindale, reading and making extensive notes on the match reports either from the hard copy newspapers themselves, or on the papers stored on microfiche film of every FA Cup final dating back to 1970 that I was able to read, thanks mainly to the ever helpful assistance from the library assistant Valerie Howe. I left no stone unturned and given the fact that I could be asked about anything, my Grand Final mantra of "all information is useful information" totally underpinned my revision strategy. Every minute detail, from the name of the referees in the respective finals, to the precise timings of any substitutions during the game would not be overlooked. Nothing, so far as I was concerned, would be left to chance in my attempts not only to try and absorb facts, but also, to try, where possible, to anticipate the types of questions that I could be asked. My afternoons were spent watching and studying the DVD's that I bought from Chris' Sports Book Shop of previous FA Cup Finals in the past, those images perfectly complimenting the information and research that I had obtained from the various newspapers and microfiche films earlier from the library as I sought to absorb and imprint the various sources of important information into my deep subconscious. In accordance with my time honoured meticulous routine, the evenings and late nights were still devoted exclusively to preparing for the general knowledge round in the same way as before.

The hard work and effort I put in with regards to the forthcoming hearing at the Old Bailey and the Mastermind Grand Final was both unforgiving and relentless. My only form of respite and relaxation from that relentless grind came mainly in the form the football coaching sessions and matches that I ran with the group of boys and girls who lived in and around the area of Monks Park and the nearby St Raphael's Estate. Those coaching sessions were a welcome and much needed release from the intolerable pressure that

I felt at times and it was a wondrous sight to see the boys and girls who were in my care having a good time and really enjoying themselves. The *Mastermind* production team by this time had sent me the consent forms for those children who wanted to take part in the coaching session that would be filmed as part of my interview. Just before I began the session, I told the children who were present that the BBC were coming down to film one of our coaching sessions. The children were very excited by the news that they were going to appear on TV. The children were so keen to take part in the filmed coaching session, every single one of them insisted on taking those consent forms home straight away in order to get their parent's or guardian's signature.

The only other day of respite that I allowed myself throughout the entire intensive revision and court preparation programme I set for myself was on the 2nd of June, my 44th birthday. That morning, I woke up in a wonderfully happy mood and I decided that it was going to be a day of self-indulgence in the form of a mini spending spree with my forthcoming appearance in the *Mastermind* Grand Final very much in mind. That morning, I made my way to Brent Cross with the intention of buying a nice smart suit that was well within my limited budget, and after looking in virtually all of the men's clothes shops at the shopping centre that were sadly, clearly beyond my price range, I eventually found the suit I was searching for in terms of style, suitability and price range in the Men's Department in Fenwick's and bought a subtly pinned striped chocolate coloured brown suit. To compliment that purchase, I headed straight to Cecil Gee and bought myself a brand new pink shirt as the one that I had worn in previous quiz shows in the past was looking rather jaded, before concluding my clothing purchases with Tie Rack, where I bought a pair of blue silk boxer shorts as I wanted to wear something smooth in order to keep myself cool for my two visits to *Mastermind's* hottest seat. After leaving Brent Cross, I parked my car by the tube station for the journey on the Northern Line south to Charing Cross for one final visit to Chris's Sports Book Shop where I spoke to Chris about my forthcoming appearance on the Grand Final of *Mastermind*.

Chris turned to me and said "Shaun, I've got an interesting fact that you should try to remember, if you can, about the 1987 Cup Final. Did you know that only half of the Tottenham team who played that day had the Holston Pills adverts on their shirts?"

"Thanks for that piece of information, Chris," I replied before going on to add, "I've got this funny feeling that they're going to ask me a question about whether it was Brian Kilcline or Gary Mabbutt who actually scored the winning goal, because there is always a debate about that." Then I said, "Do you remember which Coventry player supplied the cross for that winning goal?" and in unison, we both replied with a smile, "Lloyd McGrath."

I now had all the material that I needed to revise my specialist topic and it was a case of reading and viewing the material over and over again ad nauseum, wherever or whenever I could, watching Cup Final DVDs on the train on the small portable DVD player that I purchased specifically for that purpose, reading about FA Cup finals from my reference book or the hand written notes I made from the newspapers reports from the British Library whilst waiting to go into court. My revision and preparation for the Grand Final was an uncompromising exercise.

The next seven days marked the start of one of the most important and exciting period of events that has happened to me in many a long while. To begin with, on the 7th June, I had to appear at the Old Bailey with instructions to make a legal submission before The Recorder of London that the murder charge my client was facing be dismissed on account of the fact that on the face of the set of papers served by the prosecution on the defence, there was, in our view, *insufficient evidence upon which a jury could convict him.* The night before the hearing, Rodney and I met at the hotel that he was staying at on the Bayswater Road to discuss and rehearse the finer details of the submission I was going to make to the court. We both agreed that it was unlikely that the submissions that I intended to make were going to be successful on account of the fact that there appeared, despite its somewhat tenuous nature, there was evidence that could implicate our client in the form of a series of mobile telephone calls between our client and his co-defendant whom the prosecution alleged was the person responsible for actually committing the offence, and the deceased victim. The role the prosecution attributed to our client is that he was acting as a conduit, as it is their case that the series of mobile telephone calls between our client and the deceased victim prior to the shooting were made with the sole aim to deliberately lure the deceased victim to the scene of the incident in the full knowledge that our client's co-defendant would be lying in wait. Despite both of us agreeing that on that piece of evidence alone, our client would have to face an eventual trial, Rodney and I both agreed that it was still nevertheless our duty to try everything that we possibly could to get the murder charge against our client dismissed.

The following morning just after 9.30 am, I met up with Rodney and we went straight to see our client prior to the hearing in The Recorder of London's court at 10am. Our client was naturally pleased to see his legal team and despite the nature of the predicament he was facing, he was remarkably in good spirits but at the same time anxious that the allegation, which he insisted had absolutely nothing to do with him, be resolved as quickly as possible. Once again, both Rodney and myself sought to reassure our client that we were working as hard as we could in trying to achieve his stated aim and whilst there was some chance that the application for dismissal that I was about to make on his behalf would succeed, we made it clear to him in no uncertain terms that the likelihood was that the judge would reject the defence arguments and that he would probably have to face a jury trial with his co-defendant sometime in the New Year. On hearing that forthright piece of advice, our client was visibly disappointed but to his credit, he accepted what we had to say and before Rodney and I left the conference room, our client fist bumped the pair of us in turn before wishing me the best of luck.

I arrived outside The Recorder of London's court some ten or so minutes before the appointed time with a view to seeking out my opponent so that we could both have a brief discussion about the case before going into courtroom. I called out for prosecuting counsel involved in the hearing to make themselves known and moments later, I was approached by my opposite number who had just finished speaking with a couple of police officers who were involved in the investigation and when he told me his name, I knew straight away that I was up against an advocate of real substance and quality. Duncan Penny of 6 King's Bench Walk was my opponent in question and one of the legal profession's young rising stars despite the relatively junior nature of his call. Although this was the first time that I had formally met Duncan in a professional setting, I knew of Duncan because his Chambers, a set of considerable professional repute, occupied the same building where I was a tenant at Sigbhat Kadri QC's Chambers some eight years previously. Like myself, Duncan was the instructed junior counsel in the trial and as juniors, we were expected to do all the pre-trial preparatory work such as drafting written advices if required, or attending all of the pre-trial court appearances in advance of the main trial hearing that would be principally conducted by our respective leaders. As this was an application made by the defence, in order of precedence, I went first with my submissions before the Recorder of London outlining the reasons why the case against my client should be dismissed. The Recorder listened with care to the submissions that I put forward on my client's behalf and not once, throughout the entire time I was on my feet did The Recorder interject or make any unnecessary or unhelpful comments. However, once I had finished making those submissions, I knew straight away that they had not succeeded on account of the polite, euphemistic phrase judges tend use on occasions after having rejected counsel's submissions when he turned to my opponent and said, "I needn't trouble you Mr Penny..." The Recorder ruled that there was sufficient evidence upon which my client could face a jury trial despite my best efforts in seeking to persuade him to the contrary. The only consolation we gained from the whole proceedings was that the judge agreed to my request to have the hearing fixed to accommodate the availability of leading counsel for the defence. It was just as well that both Rodney and I had prepared our client as to the likely outcome of the decision of the court as it went some considerable way to cushioning the blow of disappointment our client clearly felt in having to spend further time on remand awaiting his trial. We went to visit our client in the cells after the hearing in order to discuss the situation with him and despite his obvious disappointment, he accepted our joint assurance that whilst it would be almost a year between his initial arrest and eventual trial, it was crucial that he had Queen's Counsel of the calibre of Courtenay Griffiths conducting his defence as it was the type of case where on the evidence he stood a good chance of being acquitted.

With the court proceedings out of the way, I was now free to concentrate all my efforts and energies solely on preparing for the Grand Final and the countdown to my date with destiny began with the fly on the wall behind the scenes interview. For the first part of that interview, I had arranged to meet the show's production team and their accompanying camera crew outside the Royal Courts of Justice in the Strand for 11am as I felt that it would present the perfect window of opportunity to showcase that there is more to the legal profession than the negative and, mostly, unfair perception the profession seems to attract that barristers are just a bunch of elitist, detached money grabbing fat cats. The reason why I chose the Royal Courts of Justice over the Crown Courts that I normally appear in was because I didn't want anyone to know what I was doing or the reasons why I was doing it but as the old saying goes, "The best laid plans of mice and men..." my secret impending appearance in the *Mastermind* Grand Final was nearly exposed when a couple of my colleagues who I knew from the bar had come up to me and asked me why I was being filmed in my full barrister's attire going into court. Instead of explaining to them the real reason I was there, I smiled and simply told them that it was nothing more than a short documentary about the day in life of a working barrister within the legal profession, a half-truth that thankfully my curious colleagues were more than happy to accept. For this part of the interview, I made the following comments and observations, "I have been a criminal barrister for the last twenty years and when you're in court you're put on the spot and you've got to have the ability to present arguments to the court on behalf of your client. It's similar to *Mastermind* because you are in a similar pressurised situation when you are invited to sit in the black chair."

Once we had finished the filming outside the Royal Courts of Justice, myself and the film crew headed for the nearby Temple tube station for the journey north to the destination which would form the backdrop for the next part of the fly on the wall interview that would see me walking down Wembley Way heading towards the iconic, half built Wembley Stadium. As the camera crew filmed me staring in admiration and awe at one of the most famous sporting landmarks in the world, I talked about my reasons for selecting football as my specialist subject on *Mastermind*. "Given the fact that I have lived a mile or so away from the Stadium for the past forty or so years, in all that time I have seen some magnificent matches and that was one of the reasons that inspired me to choose this specialist topic on *Mastermind*."

For the final part of my in depth interview, the camera crew followed me to my home briefly so that I could change quickly into my training clothes for my coaching session with the children at the Monks Park playing fields. Myself and the production crew were greeted by twenty to thirty keen and very excited children, more than the usual number that attend the coaching sessions and given the fact that they were all aware of the presence of a film crew, they were determined to parade their skills that showed them in the best possible light. As the session got underway, I spoke passionately about my fondness for coaching young children as well as my committed desire to try to give something back to my local community. I spoke about how the coaching sessions with the children provides a welcome release from the pressures of the legal profession but also, the pressures of appearing on *Mastermind*.

The last part of the interview was conducted in the relatively relaxed and comfortable surroundings of my home that thankfully, by the time the camera crew had arrived, was spick and span. This part showed me poring over all the reference books and reading material I was using to prepare for the show and during the course of that interview, I was asked whether I was nervous or excited about appearing in the Grand Final and what did I think could be the worst thing that could happen to me in the Grand Final? I replied, in all honesty and seriousness, "Obviously, the worst thing that can happen is if I don't win. When you compete on *Mastermind*, you do get butterflies in your stomach, just like waiting in the tunnel before you walk out onto the pitch, which is similar to sitting in the black chair.

However, once you run onto the pitch, you've just got to focus on the job at hand."

The production team and camera crew finally finished filming just after 7.30pm that evening and I was more than pleased with how the whole day went and I was really looking forward to seeing the final edited version of the interview as I knew it would show the watching public exactly who Shaun Wallace is and what he stands for and believes in: a person who cares passionately about his profession irrespective of the highs and lows that I've been through; an individual who is totally committed to the teaching and educating of others irrespective of their age, gender, colour or background and a contender who was totally focused and totally prepared to grab this opportunity of a lifetime.

In the evening before the Grand Final of Mastermind, I felt that I had done all the hard work and preparation that I possibly could have done and I decided to put all my books and revision materials to one side and settle down in front of the television to watch the start of an event that had played a considerable role in getting me to the Grand Final in the first place. The England Football Team were playing their opening fixture at European Championships against the reigning champions France at Euro 2004 in Portugal. The game itself was a tense affair with England starting off really well by getting off to a flying start when the Chelsea Midfielder and one of the rising stars of the team, Frank Lampard gave England a deserved lead with a header after eighteen minutes, a lead they managed to hang on to until the dying minutes when two goals, one a sublime free kick and a last minute penalty both scored by the French Captain and footballing genius, Zinedine Zidane somehow managed to snatch an unlikely victory from the jaws of certain defeat. Although like any other England fan, I was disappointed by the result, I wasn't too disheartened as the team had given a good account of themselves against a team that was still amongst the best in the world and I was confident that if England repeated that level of performance in their remaining two fixtures in the group stages, then they would have no trouble in progressing to the knockout phase of the tournament.

After the game had finished, I went upstairs to arrange and prepare everything that I intended to take with me to the BBC studios the following day, a selection that not only included the clothes that I was going to wear or a few chosen books for some last minute swotting, but also some of my most treasured mementos which I hoped, despite my lack of superstition, would bring me some much needed good luck and fortune, items such as, the little red rag doll that my nephew Myles had made for me when he was in infant school, my Baby Book and, given the nature and importance of the occasion, the two winners medals that I had won playing football at Wembley Stadium. I decided to bring these precious mementos along with me as they were going to provide the only tangible and visible means of support and comfort to me given my decision not to have, let alone tell, any of my close family or friends about one of the most important days of my life on account of the fact that I almost certainly would have found their presence in the studio audience off putting and nerve wracking. Just before retiring to my bed for the night, I was feeling somewhat restless and agitated which was the last thing I needed to be feeling on the eve of one of the most important days of my life so in an effort to try to bring those feelings under some sort of control, I decided, despite the fact that the time was fast approaching the midnight hour, to get on my bike and ride up to my local church, St. Michael's. I made my way to the steps which lead inside the church. In a scene reminiscent to the one in the classic boxing film sequel Rocky 2 where the hero and protagonist, Rocky Balboa goes to his local church to seek the blessing of the local priest on the eve of his second fight with the seemingly invincible Apollo Creed, in the still dead of night, I knelt down on the church steps by the main door and asked the man upstairs for his personal special blessing, praying that he would give me the necessary wisdom, calmness and fortitude that would bring me the victory that I so badly craved.

I was going to need every ounce of help that was on offer given the formidable challenge that lay ahead of me and as I lay awake in my bed before drifting off to sleep, the only thoughts that ran constantly through my mind was that twenty four hours from now, I would be lying in the same position reflecting on a day that could turn out to be one of the greatest days of my life or one of my biggest disappointments. Whichever of those two extremes of emotions I was going to embrace, the one thing I was determined to ensure was that Shaun Wallace was going to give his absolute best.

After a good night's sleep, I woke up to the beginning of what was shaping up to be gloriously bright and sunny day. I went downstairs with a spring in my step to make myself my customary Weetabix breakfast. As I made my way towards the kitchen, my attention was suddenly drawn to a single solitary letter lying on my doormat. Whilst reading its contents, a big broad smile immediately came across my face. It was a good luck message from my old semi-final *Mastermind* adversary, Frank Potter, a wonderful thoughtful gesture on his part, that was the perfect complement to my ever increasing good mood. Because I had the presence of mind to get myself organised the night before, the only important matter that I had to attend to was to go to the hairdressers as I wanted to make sure that my hair was neat and tidy for such an important occasion. I made my way to Donna's Hair Salon in Harlesden High Street and just as I was about to enter the salon, my second pleasant surprise of the day occurred when quite unexpectedly, I heard someone call out my name. I turned round to see who it was, and saw Heather Thomas, who was out shopping with her Father. I was really pleased to see Heather and we greeted each other with a warm and affectionate embrace as we hadn't seen each other since our appearance together on *The Waiting Game*. After she had introduced me to her Father, Heather and I started chatting away, catching up on old times. Heather then asked me what I was doing today, an enquiry that caught me slightly off guard, I didn't want to alert her to the fact that I was appearing in the *Mastermind* Grand Final later that day.

I responded, "I've got to put a wrong to right," as a totally obscure and wholly irrelevant reference to my costly blunder that denied us both certain victory on *The Waiting Game*. Heather was clearly bemused by my cryptic reply and asked me to explain what I meant, but I managed skilfully, to politely brush her enquiry aside by making out that I was late for my hairdressing appointment and with one final hug we parted company. As I entered the Hair Salon, I couldn't help but smile at the fact that bumping into Heather after all that time, on this day of all days, was some sort of fortuitous omen or sign that today really could be my day and although I keep on saying that I'm not the superstitious type, even I was starting to really believe that bumping into Heather was more than just a mere coincidence. Maybe, there is such a thing as fate after all.

All the Grand Finalists were required to be at the BBC studios in Wood Lane at 3pm, but after I returned home from the Hair Salon sometime in the mid-afternoon I thought to myself, *What's the rush?* After all, it was only a fifteen or so minute journey to the studios and I was determined to arrive at the studios in a happy and relaxed frame of mind and furthermore, as long as I didn't take any outrageous liberties in terms of timing, they could hardly start the Grand Final without me!

The glorious summer sun was at its most brilliant radiance and after packing all the things that I needed to take with me into the boot of my car, I retracted the roof then put on my black Ray-Ban sun shades that complimented the black shorts and the black short sleeved New Zealand Rugby Union shirt with the words, "All Black" and the number Ten emblazoned on the back. With my left elbow casually hanging from the side of the wound down window, I set off on my journey to the BBC studios in cruise mode, the car's CD player turned up to its maximum volume, pumping out tracks from James Taylor's Greatest Hits CD that complimented the glorious day and my mood perfectly. I arrived at the BBC Car Park in the space reserved for me on the fifth floor and I sat in the car still listening to the remaining few tracks of the CD, grabbing for myself those last precious moments of quality time before facing one of my greatest ever challenges. As I reclined my seat in order to relax a little, almost immediately I was totally consumed with feelings of complete contentment with myself, a warm and wonderful feeling that I hadn't experienced or enjoyed in many a long while. I was standing on the threshold of doing something pretty special and the mere thought of that possibility had the positive effect of reinforcing my good mood. After I had given myself one last encouraging pep-talk, I got out of the car and retrieved my belongings from the boot and made my way towards the giant glass swivel doors of the building's main entrance. As I was going through the doors, just in front of me, I noticed a smartly dressed man accompanied by a woman who I assumed was his wife and without knowing why, I knew that he was a fellow Grand Finalist. I turned to the gentleman and introduced myself and he responded in kind by telling me that his name was Michael Kane before proceeding to introduce me to his wife and thereafter, we chatted briefly about various aspects of the Grand Final. One of the production assistants was already in the foyer waiting for us and she took both Michael and I straight to the studio where, already seated, were the four remaining Grand Finalists apparently seated in the order that we would be appearing on the show. As I had anticipated from my first appearance in the heats, John Tweddle had made it to the Grand Final alongside another familiar face that I recognised amongst the four seated gentlemen, Jim Cook, another *Fifteen-To-One* veteran who gave a good account of himself two years previously on *Discovery Mastermind* and by his very presence in the room, I was clearly determined this time to go all the way. I put the clothes that I was carrying to the side and went up to my fellow contenders and shook their hands before being asked to sit in seat number two that was set aside for me whilst Michael took up his position in seat number four. As I sat down, I had a quick look around the auditorium and was momentarily lost in my own private thoughts and started to imagine what the studio would be like a few hours hence where the six of us would be competing for the ultimate quizzing accolade.

A member of the production team who was holding the briefing session explained that there was going to be a mock rehearsal involving the presentation of the trophy and she wanted one of us to step forward to go through the rehearsal of receiving it. Then, totally unexpectedly, the production assistant asked me to be the first of the Grand Finalist to step forward and whilst in the grand scheme of things it would have no real bearing on the eventual outcome, the mere fact that I was the first Grand Finalist chosen to go through this mock rehearsal ceremony had the immediate and positive effect of sending my already high levels of confidence through the roof. I was invited forward to receive the replica trophy from the production assistant and thereafter, asked to make the few short steps towards the black chair and as I sat down holding the replica trophy, the only excited thoughts that were racing through my mind was the feeling that, *in a couple of hours' time, I'm going to be doing this for real!* and even though my fellow Grand Finalists went through the same mock victory rehearsal, so far as I was concerned, the mere fact that I went first was yet another positive and encouraging sign that today was going to be my day!

After the briefing and rehearsals was concluded, all six of us were taken to a room in another part of the studio and it didn't take long before we were engaged in conversation amongst ourselves which I suppose, was a way of getting to know each other and partly, a way of secretly trying to size up the competition. Don Young, who to my mind was the man to beat if I was to stand any chance of victory, was the first of my fellow Grand Finalists to approach me, our short conversation revolving around our respective previous specialist topics and the topics that we had chosen for the Grand Final. Don revealed that he was offering Queen Elizabeth I as his specialist topic and when I told him that my specialist topic was on FA Cup Finals since 1970, he replied that he too was an avid football fan, especially during the times when he followed his beloved Newcastle United and their star player, Jackie Milburn, in their glory days back in the 1950's during which time they lifted the FA Cup three times. John Tweddle and Jim Cook were standing close by engrossed in deep conversation and after my brief conversation with Don, I turned to John and Jim and spoke with them briefly and they revealed that they were offering the specialist topics of The Iliad and US Presidents respectively. I already knew what Michael Kane was offering as his specialist subject for the Grand Final, British Pop Music since the 1960's, on account of the brief conversation that we had after our simultaneous arrival. But the one fellow Grand Finalist that I hadn't spoken to or indeed, knew anything about up to that point, was the quiet and totally unassuming Brent Peeling who was standing by himself slightly detached from the rest of us, engaged no doubt, in his own private thoughts and my first impressions were that he seemed to my mind, to have an aura of calm, stoic forbearance about him. I went up to him and introduced myself and it didn't take me long to discover that he was a sport addict like myself, but of the Cricketing variety. Brent told me that his subject for the Final was on English Test Cricket since the 1880's, quite a wide time period to cover when compared to the time span for my own specialist topic which was a mere thirty four years, but out of all my fellow Grand Final opponents, my instincts were telling me that because of his apparent calmness, because of his totally unassuming demeanour, in all probability, the real dark horse in this Grand Final was standing right in front of me.

Having found out all that I possibly could about my fellow Grand Finalists, I decided that I wanted to take a leaf out of Brent Peeling's book and have some precious quality time to myself away from the others so I left the room we were gathered in momentarily and spoke to a member of the production team to ask whether my desire for solitude was indeed possible. That request was granted and after gathering all of my belongings, I was taken to a dressing room that was so grandiose and spacious with its wall to wall mirrors, it was as if I was in the dressing room reserved for an Oscar winner. It seemed as if my wish to be allowed my own private space away from my fellow Grand Finalists was a positive omen in my quest to claim the *Mastermind* title. I decided to use this priceless moment of solitude to squeeze in some last minute revision on my specialist topic and I began speed reading frantically through all my various notes as well as the FA Cup Finals reference book that I purchased from Chris' Sports Book Shop in the hope that the seeds of information would plant firmly in my mind. As I scanned furiously through the reference book, something was telling me to cast my eye particularly over the two games in the 1990 FA Cup Final between Crystal Palace and Manchester United, paying special reference not just to the goal scorer's over the two games but also, to the various players substitutions that were made. I can't explain the reasons why I felt that I should pay particular attention to this particular Cup Final but whatever the reason, I endeavoured to make sure that I was ready and able to deal with it.

My tranquil and peaceful solitude didn't last long though, because about half an hour or so later, I was joined by the rest of my fellow Grand Finalists before the six of us were escorted to our individual dressing rooms so that we could change before going to make up. Once I was changed, I looked into the surrounding mirrors in the dressing room for a final all point inspection which I responded to by giving my reflection a wink of confidence and one thumbs up seal of approval. I then retrieved all the various mementos that I had brought with me and after careful consideration, selected the three items that would accompany me onto the studio floor which were, the small red rag doll, which I placed in my right trouser pocket and in my two inside jacket pockets, I placed the two winners medals.

Once all six of us were ready (I had even asked the makeup lady to practically give me a manicure so my hands were ready for that trophy!) we assembled together in a corridor waiting to be told to go on. Once we were all seated and wired up, John came on, with his now familiar routine of thanking the audience for their attendance and he went on to add that they were about to witness a very exciting Final.

"TONIGHT, IS THE GRAND FINAL OF MASTERMIND 2004. IN THE PAST, NINETY-SIX PEOPLE HAVE TAKEN THIS SHORT WALK ACROSS TO THE MOST TERRIFYING CHAIR IN THE BUSINESS. ONLY TWENTY FOUR OF THEM GOT THROUGH TO THE SEMI-FINAL AND TONIGHT, JUST SIX OF THEM ARE HERE. ONLY ONE OF THEM WILL WALK AWAY WITH THE TITLE OF MASTERMIND 2004." The show's familiar haunting theme tune began with the thumping sound of the bass drums pounding in rhythm followed by the piercing sound of the trumpet, playing out the next stanza. "THE FIRST FINALIST IN THE SPOTLIGHT IS JIM COOK FROM STOURPORT-ON SEVERN, A FACTORY WORKER WHOSE SPECIALISED SUBJECT IS AMERICAN PRESIDENTS. SECOND, IS SHAUN WALLACE FROM WEMBLEY, A BARRISTER AND LECTURER AND HIS IS FA CUP FINALS SINCE 1970. THIRD, JOHN TWEDDLE FROM MIDDLESBOROUGH, A JOB SEEKER AND HIS SUBJECT IS HOMER'S THE ILIAD. FOURTH, MICHAEL KANE FROM STAINTON, A RETIRED CHEMIST WHOSE SPECIALIST SUBJECT IS BRITISH POP MUSIC SINCE THE 1960'S. FIFTH, DON YOUNG FROM SHAW IN LANCASHIRE, A RETIRED TEACHER AND HIS IS THE LIFE AND REIGN OF QUEEN ELIZABETH I, AND THE SIXTH FINALIST TONIGHT IS BRENT PEELING FROM BILLERICAY IN ESSEX, A FINANCIAL ANALYST AND HIS SPECIALIST SUBJECT IS ENGLISH TEST CRICKET SINCE THE 1880'S.

"HELLO, I'M JOHN HUMPHREYS, WELCOME TO THE GRAND FINAL OF *MASTERMIND* 2004. EACH OF OUR FINALISTS WILL BE IN THE HOT SEAT FOR THE THIRD TIME TONIGHT. THE RULES ARE THE SAME - TWO MINUTES ON THEIR SPECIALIST SUBJECT AND TWO MINUTES ON GENERAL KNOWLEDGE. TONIGHT'S WINNER WILL TAKE HOME THIS BIG PRIZE, THIS SPLENDID GLASS BOWL AND MUCH MORE IMPORTANTLY, THE TITLE OF MASTERMIND 2004. SO, LET US HAVE OUR FIRST FINALIST PLEASE."

449

Jim made his way to the famous black chair and before the start of his own short documentary, John reminded him of his two previous specialist subjects in the previous rounds which were American Manned Spaceflights and British Prime Ministers of the 20th Century. Because Jim's finalist specialist topic was an area that I knew something about, I reverted to my tried and trusted practice of seeing how many of his questions I could answer. At the end of Jim's two minutes he managed to score nine points with two passes and I was quite pleased with the fact that I managed to answer correctly six of the questions he faced. After Jim had returned to his seat, I turned to him and whispered well done.

John Humphreys summoned me to face my own specialist round of questions. As I walked the few short steps towards the black chair, I was trying to remain as calm and composed as I possibly could, trying my level best to blot out everyone and everything around me, save for the man who was about to interrogate me for the next one hundred and twenty seconds. Once I had gone through the time honoured drill of providing my name and occupation, John reminded me of my specialist subjects in the previous rounds before the screening of my short fly on the wall documentary. When I saw the two minute condensed end product, I couldn't have been more pleased with the way that I had been portrayed. John kicked off my series of questions and I got off to a great start by answering the first six questions correctly. The seventh question however, stopped my great run momentarily in its tracks and was without a shadow of a doubt, the only question in my three appearances on the show that had me completely stumped, managing to slip under the radar of my intensive revision programme and even if I had been given all the time in the world to come up with the correct answer, I doubt very much I would have achieved that feat and in a quiz as daunting as *Mastermind*, the one luxury that I could not afford to waste was time.

The question was, "WHAT DID THE SUNDERLAND PLAYERS MISTAKENLY RECEIVE AT THE END OF THE 1992 CUP FINAL?"

I didn't know the answer and I responded with the words, "THE LEAGUE CUP," instead of the correct answer, the winner's medals. I was determined not to allow that slip up to affect my confidence or game strategy, a strategy which has not changed from the outset, make an educated guess, even if it's a wrong guess, but whatever I do, UNDER NO CIRCUMSTANSES WILL I PASS!

I got a further two questions wrong out of the fifteen that I faced. The first of those incorrectly answered questions was slightly disappointing especially in view of the fact it was on the Cup Final I focused my attentions on when I had managed to separate myself from my fellow Grand Finalists momentarily for some precious time to myself.

The question was, "WHOM DID IAN WRIGHT REPLACE WHEN HE CAME OFF THE BENCH TO SCORE TWO GOALS IN THE 1990 FINAL?"

My intuitive hunch that I was going to be asked a question on the 1990 Cup Final turned out to be spot on, but for the life of me, I couldn't remember the name of the player concerned and I just said the name of the first Crystal Palace player that came into my head, Andy Gray, knowing full well it was the wrong answer when in fact, the correct answer, which I remembered the moment, was Phil Barber.

There was one final incorrect answer that I gave which occurred right on the buzzer signalling the end of my two minutes. The question was, "WHAT WAS THE NAME OF TWO PLAYERS WHO PLAYED IN THE 1983, 1984, 1985 AND 1986 FINALS WHO SHARE THE SAME CHRISTIAN NAME AND SURNAME?"

I just couldn't think for the life of me what the answer was. I tried desperately to trawl through the deep recesses of my mind hoping that it would somehow miraculously pop into my head, but time was no longer on my side and John began to press me for a response. I was acutely aware that a non-response would be marked down as a pass so I gave the somewhat hurried reply, "JOHNSON," even though I knew my answer was wrong. My initial disappointment and downright annoyance with my third incorrect answer was compounded even further when John revealed that the correct answer was Gary Stevens, my annoyance stemming from the fact that it was similar to the type of question that I had posed to people like Nipper and the rest of his mates in the past.

John announced that my first round score was twelve points and although I was slightly disappointed with the fact that there were two out of those three incorrect answers that I should have known the answer to, I consoled myself with the fact that despite the enormous pressure I was under, I didn't buckle or capitulate and even more importantly, I did not pass. I walked back to my seat to the applause of the studio audience and as I sat down, both Jim and John who were flanked either side of me congratulated me on my performance and I returned the compliment to John by wishing him the best of luck.

John and the three remaining contenders were now going to have their moment in the spotlight to stake their own claims to the Mastermind title and there was nothing that I could do to influence matters. All that I could do was to remain in my seat and hope that by the end of the first round, I would still be in with a shout.

John Tweddle was the next contender in line to take his seat in the black chair. John Humphreys reminded him of his two previous specialist subjects in the earlier rounds, World Heavyweight Champions and American Presidential Elections, before asking him about his specialist subject for the Grand Final which arguably was the most challenging of all the six specialist subjects that were on offer in the Grand Final. The questions were so difficult, I only managed to answer one of John's questions correctly, that being, Xanthus the name of the horse owned by the legendary Greek hero Achilles, a question which even John himself answered incorrectly.

Another plausible reason why I thought John's questions were so mind numbingly difficult was because during his two minute interrogation in the chair, my focus and attention was drawn away from the contest momentarily for no real reason and was transfixed on the studio audience in the auditorium and as I looked up to my right hand side, I noticed a rather attractive looking middle aged woman seated next to a young girl who was her younger version both smiling in my direction. I immediately acknowledged the pair of them and I responded by winking and smiling right back at them, their lovely smiling faces provided a welcome source of respite and encouragement amidst the tension and drama I was involved in and despite my absolute insistence that I didn't want anybody that I knew to be present in the audience for fear that it could provide an unwelcome source of distraction, I felt that these two smiling strangers were there supporting me in my corner. I continued my visual dialogue by giving them a little wave as a sign to let them know that I appreciated their support and that everything so far as I was concerned was fine.

I managed to regain my momentary lapse in concentration and focus just in time to see the end of John Tweddle's two minutes in the black chair. He managed to post a first round score of eleven points and three passes.

Michael Kane was the next Grand Finalist summoned to the black chair. John revealed before the start of his two minute interrogation that his two previous specialist subjects in the earlier rounds were Buddy Holly and King Charles II. Unfortunately for Michael though, he didn't get off to the best of starts which set the tone for his entire performance and as a result, he posted a rather modest score of seven points with three passes, a score I'm sure, was not a true reflection of his undoubted quizzing abilities. The only question that I managed to answer correctly from Michael's rather challenging set of questions which was really a lucky guess on my part, was that Paul McCartney was the rock star in question who saw a picture of the musician Slim Whitman playing the guitar left handed and believed that he could do the same.

The penultimate contender in the chair was the formidable Don Young whose specialist subjects in the previous rounds were Homer's Odyssey and King Ludwig II of Bavaria. As I was watching Don's short fly on the wall documentary, I couldn't help but notice with particular interest, his final closing remarks when he said, "Since my teens, I've always been one of life's runners up. Always close but no cigar, and if I win, it would make a pleasant change." That surprisingly honest and frank admission by Don gave me some hope and encouragement into thinking that even a very good quiz competitor like Don has weaknesses and vulnerabilities, just like everyone else and it was possible that, despite his quizzing pedigree, he could be beaten. In spite of Don's frank comments, I wasn't labouring under any undue false sense of security that all of a sudden, my chances of winning the Grand Final had gone up a notch or two. Don Young was the man to beat and his two minutes in the black chair only reinforced why he was the favourite to take the title as he gave a near flawless performance by answering fourteen questions correctly in a row, perfection being denied him with an incorrect answer on the stroke of the buzzer.

The last Grand Finalist contender was the man I considered to be the dark horse of the Grand Final, Brent Peeling, whose two previous specialist subjects in the earlier rounds were The Essex County Cricket Club and The Zulu Wars of 1879. My assessment of Brent's quizzing abilities and the genuine threat he posed in his challenge for the championship proved to be spot on as he went on to equal my score of twelve points at the end of his two minutes but crucially, he passed on one question which, I'm not ashamed to admit, came as a welcome relief as it put me slightly ahead of him at the end of an intense and fiercely competitive round of specialist subjects.

John reminded everyone of the scores attained by the Grand Finalists at the end first round. Don was in the lead by two clear points. I was occupying second place with a score of twelve points with Brent only just behind me with the same score in third place by virtue of his single solitary pass. A point behind both Brent and myself in fourth place was John Tweddle, in fifth place was Jim Cook and bringing up the rear but not out of the reckoning, not by any means, was Michael Kane. I was more than content with my placing at the end of a highly competitive first round as it meant that I would be the penultimate contender to sit in the chair for the final general knowledge round, a placing that spared myself the drama and ordeal of having to go last in my efforts to secure victory that was nearly my undoing in the Semi-Final.

As Michael Kane stepped forward to start the final round, I took the opportunity to turn toward my two female supporters in the studio audience and gave the pair of them the sign of a raised fist to let them know that all was well and that I was ready for the challenge. Bad luck and ill fortune blighted Michael Kane's two minute interrogation in the black chair, finding it more or less impossible to shake off his first round malaise, managing only to add a further two more points, four points less than I managed to answer correctly to myself, that gave him a final grand total of nine points with seven passes, a final score that spelled the end of his personal ambitions.

The next contender to follow Michael into the chair was Jim Cook who fared slightly better in his two minute spell in the chair but in the end, posted a score of seventeen points and two further passes in addition to his two passes in the first round, that wouldn't be high enough to pose a serious challenge for the title.

John Tweddle was next in the chair and he too, much to my surprise, suffered a calamitous collapse with his set of general knowledge questions and ended up with a total of fifteen points and five further passes in addition to the three passes he got in the first round. As John returned to his seat and sat down after his attempt to secure the title had also appeared to fall by the wayside, I couldn't help notice the crestfallen expression on his face and deflated demeanour that told its own story of extreme disappointment which prompted me to turn towards him and offer him both my congratulations and genuine commiserations in equal measure for his gallant efforts.

The dangerous Brent Peeling was the next contender in line to lay down a marker in his quest for the title and there was no doubting the fact that he had a realistic chance of posting a high enough score to put him beyond the reach of his two remaining challengers. My focus was now solely on Brent and his performance over the next two minutes and once again, it was no surprise that he began his challenge extremely well with the questions he was asked despite having what I thought were some really tough questions. Unfortunately for Brent, he was unable to sustain his strong start as a string of incorrect answers, coupled with three further passes, meant that his total of twenty one points and four passes was a realistically achievable target to aim for. As Brent was returning to his seat to much deserved applause, I gazed momentarily towards my two female supporters in the audience who were still smiling at me and I gave them a discreet thumbs up sign as a means of reassuring them that I was ready for the most important two minutes of my life.

John Humphreys summoned me to the black chair and I walked the few short steps towards the black chair feeling extremely calm. Just before I sat down, John was busily arranging the question cards that held the key to my success or failure in the next two minutes.

He turned to me and said, "SO, WE MOVE FROM CRICKET TO FOOTBALL BECAUSE THAT CLEARLY IS YOUR GAME, BOTH YOUR PREVIOUS SUBJECTS."

There was no doubting the fact that I was enjoying my moment in the spotlight, grinning incessantly as I responded with the words, "I LIKE PLAYING FOOTBALL; IT'S SUCH A GREAT GAME. IT'S VERY HARD TO EXPLAIN BUT I'VE SEEN SOME EXCITING AND MAGNIFICENT MATCHES OVER THE YEARS WATCHING ENGLAND WIN AND LOSE OR WATCHING CHELSEA WIN AND LOSE AND TEARING MY HAIR OUT 'COS THEY'RE MY FAVOURITE FOOTBALL TEAM."

"WHAT'S THE BEST FA CUP MATCH THAT THERE HAS EVER BEEN?"

I thought about the question for a split second before I replied, "THAT'S HARD. BUT I STILL THINK FOR SHEER EXCITEMENT YOU'VE GOT TO GO FOR THE FA CUP FINAL REPLAY WHEN CHELSEA BEAT LEEDS. I WAS NINE YEARS OLD AND I REMEMBER I WAS CRYING WHEN WE WERE LOSING WITH ABOUT NINE MINUTES TO GO AND WHEN CHARLIE COOKE PUT THAT CROSS IN AND OSGOOD SCORED, I NEARLY BROKE THE CHAIR! AND WHEN WE WON, WELL...! FOR THE LAST FIFTEEN MINUTES, I WAS BITING MY FINGERNAILS TO THE QUICK AND FOR ME THAT WAS THE BEST CUP FINAL, IT WAS REALLY EXCITING!!"

John concluded our amiable dialogue by remarking, "AND AS A CHELSEA SUPPORTER, YOU'VE HARDLY STOPPED CRYING SINCE?" which drew ripples of laughter from the studio audience.

Eager to ensure that I had the final word I replied, "NO NOT REALLY!"

With our light hearted exchange firmly behind us, both myself and John switched our respective attentions to the serious business of the destiny of the 2004 *Mastermind* title.

"RIGHT, TWELVE POINTS YOU'VE SCORED WITH FA CUP FINALS. TWENTY ONE IS THE SCORE TO BEAT. LET'S SEE IF YOU CAN DO IT WITH YOUR GENERAL KNOWLEDGE STARTING NOW!"

As usual, both my hands were spread just above my thighs in readiness to press my fingers or thumbs downwards for every correct answer given and as luck would have it, I got off to the great start I was hoping for answering correctly five out of the first six questions I was asked and by the time I was up to the thirteenth question, I had only given three incorrect answers, by which time I was fully aware and conscious of the fact, thanks largely, to my crude and unorthodox system of keeping tabs on my own individual score, I was now just one correct answer away from equalling Brent Peeling's leading total. My final set of questions were equally as kind and when the final question that John asked was interrupted by the buzzer, I momentarily rolled my eyes skywards in a mixture of gratitude to the man upstairs and relief that I somehow managed to emerge from my two minute ordeal relatively unscathed and in with a real shout of capturing the *Mastermind* title.

The question was, "IN WHICH FANTASY TRILOGY WAS BARN BUTTER THE LANDLORD OF THE PRANCING PONY AT BREE?"

I hadn't a clue as to what John was talking about and I paused momentarily to trawl through all the fantasy novels that I could think of before replying, "AT A COMPLETE GUESS I'M GOING TO SAY ERM, I'M GOING TO SAY … NARNIA!" There was a further bout of eyeball rolling on my part when John revealed the correct answer, Lord of the Rings.

"NEVER MIND HOWEVER, YOU'VE GOT ENOUGH TO PUT YOU AHEAD, YOU HAVE TWENTY-FOUR POINTS."

I walked back to my seat to the tremendous applause from the studio audience resonating in my ears and as I got closer to my seat, I looked in the direction of Don Young and nodded slightly to wish him good luck for his round. I'd given it my best shot to try to win the ultimate accolade, but the situation was no longer in my control. The only thing I could hope for was that Don was beginning to feel the pressure that he only needed eleven correct answers to deny me outright victory which, at this stage of the contest, looked a lot easier to say than to actually accomplish. The first person to congratulate me as I sat down was Jim Cook who turned to me and whispered that I'd given myself a real chance. I looked up into the studio audience towards my two supporters and to see the sheer delight on their faces and when I gave them a little wave as a way of thanking them for their unwavering support, it seemed to delight them even further.

John then summoned Don Young to the black chair with the golden opportunity to become the outright champion clearly within his reach. As John and Don were engaged in a short conversation about

Don's performance in his specialist round, my gaze was fixed firmly on the man who stood between me and eternal quizzing glory, looking for any outward clue or sign of fear or nervousness that could affect his performance in the final round, but to Don's credit, his stony faced expression was giving nothing away.

"TWENTY-FOUR POINTS IS THE SCORE TO BEAT AT THIS FINAL STAGE OF THE CONTEST. LET'S SEE HOW YOU DO WITH YOUR TWO MINUTES OF GENERAL KNOWLEDGE STARTING NOW!"

As John began to ask Don his general knowledge questions, once again I resorted to spreading my long fingers over my thighs to record Don's correct answers. As Don began his quest to win the title, he made the start that I was hoping and praying for, managing to only answer two questions correctly from the first seven, including, even more importantly, a pass on one of those questions. Despite that indifferent start, Don slowly began to show why he is a quizzing aficionado of the highest calibre recovering really well to put him firmly back on track for outright victory but once again, in the next eight or so questions that Don faced, he passed on yet another question, a crucial pass that I felt had swung the advantage slightly in my favour. By the time he had reached the twenty point mark I knew that his two minutes were almost up, but being the great competitor that he is, Don was finishing strongly with a string of correct answers that left me feeling as taut as a snare drum as the destiny the 2004 *Mastermind* Championship hung tantalisingly in the balance.

When the buzzer sounded to signify that the two minutes were up, Don was on a total of twenty three points. It didn't matter whether he got the question right or wrong, the outcome of the contest had now been decided. For the record, Don answered that question, once completed, correctly and after doing so, tried to raise a smile but he knew at that point, the prophetic sentiments that he uttered in his short fly on the wall documentary interview were about come to pass.

"WITH TWO PASSES, DON, YOU'VE SCORED ... TWENTY FOUR POINTS!"

At that point, my mind suddenly went completely blank, totally devoid of any real thought or feeling. Although I could clearly hear the applauding studio audience, the crescendo of continuous noise growing louder and louder, I strangely began to think that I was in a place other than the planet Earth, my body and mind occupying some parallel universe or even more bizarrely, the twilight zone, as time itself seemed to be suspended in disbelief. I just sat there motionless, totally dumbstruck in sheer disbelief. My tear ducts, already full to the brim by this point, suddenly burst their banks and began trickling down

457

both my cheeks at an alarming rate as it finally dawned on me that I had won the contest. A variety of contrasting thoughts and emotions began racing through my mind at a rapid rate. Everything, from the salad days of my childhood, the various setbacks and disappointments that I've had to deal with, particularly all those difficulties in trying to pass my A Level exams and the rollercoaster nature of my career over the last twenty years and now, I'm a *Mastermind* Champion! A black *Mastermind* Champion! A state of affairs that even in my wildest of dreams I would never have envisaged coming to pass and the more I thought about what I just achieved, the more the tears flowed. My tearful motionless expression went on for about a minute or so before two members of the production team came over to me with a box of tissues and a glass of water to help me regain my composure. This went on for another minute or so before they asked me if I was in a fit enough state to continue and I reassured them, after the tears had sufficiently dried from my cheeks, that I was OK.

John was ready to make the announcement of the final results and with my composure now fully restored, I prepared myself in readiness for the impending acclaim.

"SO, AT THE END OF THAT NAILBITING GENERAL KNOWLEDGE ROUND LET'S HAVE A LOOK AT THE SCORES. IN SIXTH PLACE WITH NINE POINTS, MICHAEL KANE, IN FIFTH PLACE WITH FIFTEEN POINTS, JOHN TWEDDLE, IN FOURTH PLACE WITH SEVENTEEN POINTS, JIM COOK, IN THIRD PLACE WITH TWENTY ONE POINTS, BRENT PEELING, IN SECOND PLACE WITH TWENTY FOUR POINTS, DON YOUNG, AND THE WINNER OF MASTERMIND 2004 WITH TWENTY FOUR POINTS AND NO PASSES, SHAUN WALLACE!"

As the studio audience broke into rapturous applause, I shook the hands of both Jim and John either side of me. I then rose to my feet and made my way over to where Michael, Don and Brent were seated, each of them greeted me in turn with heartfelt handshakes before I returned to my seat, my head still spinning in astonishment but with my composure thankfully, fully restored.

In the meanwhile, John Humphreys had left his desk and made his way over to the stand where the presentation of **MY** beautiful crystal bowl was about to take place. "AND TO PRESENT THE 2004 MASTERMIND TROPHY, THE CHAIRMAN OF THE BBC... MICHAEL GRADE."

Michael came onto the set and said, "WHAT A TIGHT CONTEST AND WHAT A GREAT WINNER. SHAUN COME AND RECEIVE YOUR TROPHY."

With a demeanour that was a combination of total composure and delirious happiness, I rose from my seat to embark on the exact same scenario that I had promised I would undergo during the mock ritual some two hours earlier, and as I walked the few short steps towards Michael Grade, I tried to portray the exterior demeanour of a man who was calmness personified but inwardly, I felt an explosion of pure and unadulterated joy. I was greeted by a Michael as he presented my trophy to me.

He then whispered, "IT'S ALL YOURS, GO ON, HOLD IT UP."

As I lifted the trophy, beautifully adorned with the celebrated nine Muses of Greek Mythology, above my head and presented it to the four corners of the studio, it felt as though I was emulating one of my all-time heroes, the late great Bobby Moore, as he held aloft the 1966 World Cup before an ecstatic crowd at Wembley Stadium.

As soon as I finished showing off my trophy, Michael turned to me and said, "A VERY TIGHT CONTEST."

I could only just reply to Michael's comment because I was still choked up with emotion. "IT WAS, IT WAS REALLY, REALLY CLOSE," I said, as I gripped hold of my prized possession with both arms as tightly as I could.

Michael continued his observations by adding, "AND YOU, IF I'M NOT MISTAKEN HAD A TEAR IN YOUR EYE AT THE END. WHAT WAS ALL THAT ABOUT?"

"I DID. IT'S JUST THAT I'M LIVING A DREAM AND FULFILLING A DREAM WHICH I NEVER THOUGHT I COULD EVER ACTUALLY FULFILL. BUT IT'S REAL, AND I'M REALLY ENJOYING IT, IT'S ONE OF THE HAPPIEST DAYS OF MY LIFE!"

After my short address, Michael then said, "CONGRATULATIONS!"

"THANK YOU, MICHAEL!"

The studio audience broke into applause once more as John brought the proceedings as well as the whole series to an end with the final closing remarks, "WELL I HOPE YOU ENJOYED MASTERMIND 2004 AND YOU'LL JOIN US AGAIN FOR MASTERMIND 2005. GOODNIGHT!" and with an escorting gesture with his left arm, John directed me for the final time towards the black chair where I sat down and gave my trophy a triumphant celebratory kiss as the studio audience sustained their applause right through to the show's final closing credits.

There were, as usual, a few minor pickups and mispronunciations that needed to be ironed out before we were given the all clear to leave by the Studio Floor Manager, but instead of exiting the studio, I had what can only be described as my "Pat Cash moment" and immediately made my way into the studio audience where my two supporters were sitting, as they were the only people at that moment in time with whom I wanted to share my moment of triumph with. The reason why I wanted to share it with them was because I couldn't think of any other way to repay or indeed, express my eternal gratitude, for their invaluable support and encouragement during the contest. The minute I got to the pair of them, I gave them a warm and embracing hug and was both eager and insistent that they held the trophy which seemed to delight the pair of them immensely before I let them know in no uncertain terms that it was their warm and smiling faces that kept me calm and relaxed throughout the whole ordeal and without their calming influence, I probably would not have won and with one final group hug, I left the two women and made my way back to the centre of the studio floor.

My only major regret from that special poignant meeting with those two women, and it is to my eternal shame, that it didn't occur to me, was that I never asked them for their names and I can only put that massive oversight down to being caught up in the excitement of the moment.

Once I arrived back in the middle of the set floor, I found myself virtually surrounded by members from the studio audience whose sole intention was to congratulate me on my victory. There was one young black guy in the crowd in particular who seemed even more excited than I was by what he had just witnessed. He asked for my contact details which I readily agreed to give to him on the proviso that he promised not to reveal what he had just seen, a proviso he agreed to comply with even though in truth, I had no right to, or indeed, have no way of enforcing such a promise.

I handed him my trophy to hold as I was writing down my details and turned to him and said, "At least you can lay claim to probably being only the second black person in the entire world to hold a Mastermind trophy."

Eventually, I made my way back to the green room where the number of congratulatory best wishes from practically everyone in the room were coming thick and fast most notably, from Rob and Rachel, the original production assistants from my audition. As I was showing both Rob and Rachel the trophy, in an act of pure spontaneity, I burst into song parodying the words of a well know football chant that was mainly for Rob's benefit.

"I went and won the show,
I went and won the show,
And now you're gonna believe me,
And now you're gona believe me,

> *And now you're gonna believe me,*
> *I went and won the show!"*

That impromptu rendition brought a smile to both of their faces and I left them to hold on to the trophy whilst I headed for the buffet to help myself quickly to some much-needed refreshment. Everyone who was present in the green room were clearly in a celebratory mood but I had no intention of hanging around to be a part of any post production festivities as the only thing in my mind was to head for home. Rachel asked me whether I wanted to stay and watch one of the *Celebrity Mastermind* shows that was about to take place. When I asked her the names of the celebrities who were taking part, she told that one of those participants was my old fellow Smartass panellist, Arabella Weir, a revelation which brought a smile to my face and whilst momentarily I was tempted to stay and watch my erstwhile quiz teammate in action, I decided against it and started to get myself ready to leave the studio. I noticed my fellow Grand Finalist Brent Peeling sitting down with his wife, Beverley, relaxing and chatting amongst themselves. I went up to them both and gave them a hug before letting Brent know how much I respected him as a person and how much I feared him as a quizzer before the contest and it would be nice if we stayed in touch, a request that resulted in the pair of us exchanging contact details. I informed everyone in the room that I was about to take my leave and just as I was about to finally leave the room, someone from the production team hurriedly stepped forward to present me with a bouquet of flowers, a bottle of champagne and a presentation box in which and to keep my trophy. With all these additional items, I had to stop momentarily to rearrange myself and I put the most precious item of all of my impromptu gifts in its presentation box which I immediately tucked safely in my sports bag when I eventually got back to my dressing room to collect the rest of my belongings before heading towards the exit.

The man upstairs chose to smile on me today and once the whole world eventually realises what I managed to achieve has happened, my life would probably never be the same again. I eventually got to the BBC Car Park and after loading the items into my boot, I took my car's roof down as I wanted to enjoy what was left of the evening's warm summer rays and during that short drive for home, I switched on the car's CD player and began singing along to James Taylor's mega hit, "How Sweet It Is To Be Loved By You", singing even more heartily and merrily than ever before. The minute I got home, I headed straight upstairs with all my belongings which I put in my bedroom before making my way to the bathroom to run the bath as I wanted to treat myself to a mega long victory soak. Whilst the bath was filling up, I prepared my favourite tipple, an unusual concoction of strawberry syrup, ginger beer and pineapple and coconut juice with loads of ice, shaken vigorously. I then went to my bath with my drink, some music, and some candles. I stayed in the bathroom for the best part of three hours, celebrating in style like an FA Cup winning team would in those king-sized Wembley baths. I poured the liquid concoction into my beautiful glass trophy and took many a victory sip, in between having a good old sing song to the tunes that were blaring out from the beat box. I must have refilled the hot water in the bath at least three or four times during the course of the evening and by the time I eventually got out of the bath, my skin felt like a worn-out piece of old leather, but the state of my poor old skin was the very least of my concerns. By the time I finally got out of the bath, It was approaching 11pm at night and despite all of my relentless, "madcap partying," I was getting restless for a bit more excitement so after drying myself, I put on a pair of jeans and a top and grabbed the trophy and rushed straight out the door to my car which still had its roof down. Within a blink of an eye, I was gone like the wind heading first for the North Circular and then onto the A40 heading eventually for the West End, driving around aimlessly singing along merrily once more to the beats blaring out from my CD player. There are no words that could do justice in describing my feelings of complete and unadulterated joy. Eventually, I headed towards Wembley but before I got home, I made a quick detour to St. Michael's Church. As I got out of the car with the trophy, I tiptoed my way along the path that led to the steps that I was kneeling on twenty four hours previously and once I got there, I held the trophy aloft above my head with both hands in a gesture of thanks to the man upstairs who had made it all possible. And with that, I decided that it was time to bring my madcap partying to an end. I finally crawled into bed that night, and I am not ashamed to admit, I had my precious trophy lying right beside me. Despite the fact that the day was finally beginning to catch up with me, my mind was still buzzing with happiness and excitement, thinking nonstop about a whole range of things. How were my family and friends going to react to the news? What about my career? What is my life going to be like once the news finally breaks? Loads of differing thoughts and endless questions were racing through my mind and the more I thought about them, the happier I was becoming.

Eventually, I began to I drift off to sleep, my final thoughts resting mainly on the fact that I hadn't told a soul about my *Mastermind* exploits and by the time of the Grand Final's eventual transmission, my family and friends would still be none the wiser with regards to the outcome. That would mean in effect, that my family and friends would have to go through the same stomach churning, nail biting ordeal and tension that I had to go through during all my visits to the infamous black chair, something which, I admit, brought a smile to my face. The only way I could ensure achieving that mean and spiteful objective was to remain totally silent about my *Mastermind* triumph thus guaranteeing the element of maximum surprise and place myself on the missing person's list by the time the semi-final and the Grand Final was transmitted. To execute my devious and cunning plan, it was imperative that I found out from the show's producers exactly when my semi-final and Grand Final performances were going to be shown.

The next morning, I woke up in the same deliriously happy mood from the night before and felt even more relieved to find that my precious Mastermind trophy was still lying in the bed beside me, confirming that this wasn't one of those endless tantalising fantasies I used to imagine in times gone by. The *Mastermind* trophy was real, not some figment of my vivid imagination. The previous night's events really **DID** happen. I rushed downstairs to switch on my TV set because I wanted to watch *Beat the Nation* that was about to begin the first of its twice daily transmissions. I was fairly certain my episode would be on soon.

As I was settling down to watch the programme, someone from the *Mastermind* production team called asking how I was feeling in the aftermath of my victory and the plans that I had for the day. I told her that I was waiting for *Beat the Nation* to start as I was hoping that I was going to be on today's edition. My revelation seemed to alarm her considerably before she proceeded to draw to my attention to *Mastermind's* strict policy that forbids contenders to appear on any recent television quiz shows and any contenders who were deemed to be in breach of this policy may be liable for instant disqualification. Bemused, I told her that I had disclosed the fact that I appeared on *Beat the Nation* on my original application form. She said, to be on the safe side, she needed to speak to other people about what I had told her and promised that she would get back to me later that day. I wasn't worried, not in the slightest. Almost immediately, I began to draw parallels with this bemusing situation to the injustices that befell my all-time hero and role model, Muhammad Ali, when, in 1967, the boxing authorities stripped him of his title at the peak of his boxing career, a harsh and draconian punishment that was later compounded with his subsequent conviction and the imminent threat of a lengthy prison sentence for his steadfast refusal to be drafted into the US Army to fight in the Vietnam war on religious and moral grounds before justice prevailed with his eventual exoneration three years later.

That minor storm in a teacup was all forgotten a couple of hours later, when the same person called me back to inform me that the "problem" was now resolved and she apologised for causing me to suffer any unnecessary alarm or distress. I then asked her when the *Mastermind* series was going to start its transmission. She replied that she did not know but thought it was likely that the Grand Final would be transmitted sometime next year. It didn't make any sense that they would show me winning the 2004 title in 2005, and I told her as much. She went silent for a few seconds presumably because there was no escape from the corner I had backed her into. All she could say to assuage my concerns was that I would be sent written confirmation of the transmission dates for the Semi Final and Grand Final as soon as possible, the letter duly arriving on my doorstep two days later.

BBC   MASTERMIND 2004

Entertainment & Features

Shaun Wallace

16 June 2004

Dear Shaun

We hope you've recovered from your experience in the Mastermind chair! This is to tell you we've now been given transmission dates for the 2004 series.

The first ten programmes will be on consecutive weeknights, BBC TWO, beginning on Monday 21st June at 9pm. The remaining programmes from 5th July are expected to be weekly on Mondays at 8pm. We currently expect your programme to be shown on BBC Two on **28th June 2004 9pm** but please do check TV listings nearer the time, as schedules can change. *Radio Times* should show the Specialist Subjects for each programme in its billings.

After about August, our 2004 Production Team will disband, so in case of queries please address any correspondence simply to Mastermind, BBC, PO Box 27, Manchester M60 1SJ and the relevant member of staff will deal with it.

As you may know, all contestants are free to re-apply for 2005, apart from the six finalists. If you'd like to re-apply, just let us know, but do remember you can't use a Specialist Subject that has been shown in the 2004 series.

Thank you once again for taking part in the show.

Best wishes

Mark Warburton
Asst Producer, on behalf of the whole team

Coincidently, the same day that letter arrived, the edition of *Beat the Nation* that I took part in was finally transmitted, the concerns that the *Mastermind* production team had with regards to my possible over exposure appeared to have been resolved. Throughout the entire series, an episode of *Beat The Nation* was always broadcast twice, but my episode was only broadcast once, a decision made I assumed, as a result of the *Mastermind* production team liaising with the Channel 4 programme schedulers directly to ask for the repeat edition the following day not to be transmitted. I didn't have the time to watch the transmission that afternoon because I had already made plans to meet up with Nipper and the rest of the lads at Royal Ascot for Pimm's, punting and putting into practice the well-rehearsed (in reality, well worn) chat up lines on some eye catching women in their resplendent headgear. I hadn't seen the lads in quite some time and the venue, coupled with the glorious weather, was the perfect setting to continue my clandestine victory celebrations leaving my Ascot companions none the wiser as to the real reasons for my exuberant and happy demeanour. Nipper, who, as usual, was sporting his trademark all white suit he would always wear for these type of occasions, pulled me aside at one point and asked me how my preparations for the next round of Mastermind were going. I responded by telling him that my performance in that next round was, "A bridge too far..." Nipper appeared visibly shocked but at the same time, seemed not totally convinced by what I had just told him and he asked me whether or not what I had just told him was in fact true. "Nipper!" I asserted. "It was a bridge too far!..." whilst at the same time in my mind secretly completing the rest of the sentence. *It was a bridge too far alright... for the others!* For once, Nipper didn't force or press the issue any further and I somehow managed to steer the subject away from *Mastermind*. Given Nipper's track record in the past for revealing confidential information despite his usual cast iron assurances of complete and utter discretion, there was no way I was going to tell him what really happened and my decision proved to be the right one because as no sooner had we had that conversation, Colesy and Robert Harding approached me to offer their commiserations over my unfortunate loss on the show.

A couple of days later, I received another letter from the *Mastermind* production team, the contents of which this time informed me of the exact transmission dates for the Semi-Final and Grand Final that was going be screened respectively on 29th November and 5th December 2004. With those transmission dates set in stone, I could relax and enjoy the next five or so months in relative peace and quiet in addition to affording me, the opportunity to think about the impact winning such a prestigious competition was going to have on my life both in the immediate and long term before the inevitable publicity and enormous interest would come to the fore. Winning *Mastermind* had an immediate positive effect both personally and professionally, my confidence levels seemed to scale even further new heights and for the very first time in my entire life, I felt in complete and total control of my own destiny. All the usual anxieties and stresses that seemed to be a constant and integral part of my life evaporated in an instant and there were times during that six month period prior to the transmission of the Grand Final that I found my achievement in winning the competition so overwhelming that it brought me to real tears of elation and joy. There was lot for me to consider during those six months even though it was business as usual in terms of my daily life and routine. There was many a time that I would find myself asking the same searching questions in my mind. What did I hope to personally gain from it all once my *Mastermind* success was out in the open? What effect will winning *Mastermind* have on my legal career? Will the impact of winning *Mastermind* be as fleeting as Andy Warhol's famous dictum of "Fifteen minutes of Fame," or will my achievement have some longer lasting importance? Not having any real answers to those questions wasn't exactly the worst dilemma that I have had to deal with. Whatever fate had in store for me in six months' time, the one thing I was determined to ensure above everything else was that all the public attention, spotlight and instant fame that was bound to be heading my way would not affect me, or change me as a person and that no matter how high I may go as a result of all that publicity, both my feet would remain firmly wedded to the floor.

I had a taste of things to come when toward the end of June, my first round heat was transmitted and the reaction and general feedback that I received overall was simply amazing. The downside of all that instant publicity and fame would be the constant hassle I was bound to attract in the seven days between my Semi-Final heat and the Grand Final, with the world and his wife wanting to know whether I had prevailed not. I knew full well that I wouldn't be prepared to answer, let alone tolerate, the persistent questioning I'd be confronted with. I was determined to remain in control of events and keep a lid on all the unnecessary hype in the build up to the Grand Final and the only way I could think of to do that would be to go somewhere where no one could find me for the peace and solitude I was going to need before returning to face the world. I was determined more than ever that normality was going to be my watchword that will last up and until the time of the eventual transmission of the Grand Final and beyond.

Chasing the Dream

The time had now arrived for the transmission of my final two appearances on Mastermind and with just under a week to go, I paid one last visit to New Look Travel Agents based on Harlesden High Street in order to pay the final instalment of my week-long trip to Montego Bay leaving on the 28th November. The day before making that trip to the Caribbean was going to be an important seminal milestone in my life as it would mark the twentieth anniversary when I was called to the bar. To honour the occasion, I made my way to the Inner Temple Church and Hall where the Call Ceremony was held to see if I could gain access but unsurprisingly given the fact it was a Saturday, both the Church and the Hall were closed. Unperturbed, I stood outside the church for a while and during that time, I indulged myself on a nostalgic trip down memory lane that took me back to the day I was called to the bar, a seminal moment in my life that seemed as though it happened only yesterday. As I reflected on the evening, I remember asking myself, *what will my life and career in general be like in say ten, or even twenty years from now?* As I stood silently outside the church door, it was a question that now had a clear and definitive answer, an answer that instinctively caused me to look skywards towards the heavens and thank the man upstairs for my astonishing upturn in fortune. The last twenty years really has been a rollercoaster ride, yet throughout all the bad times and the good, I always clung on to the hope and belief that I would make some sort of impact one day but never, not even in my wildest of dreams, did I ever think that I would become a Mastermind Champion, something I was still finding it hard to believe even though it had happened six months previously. But it did happen and soon, the whole world will get to know about it. My life and probably my career will never be the same again once the news becomes public knowledge and that is something that I would have to come to terms with.

After leaving Inner Temple, I made my way to Holborn Station for the short journey to the West End, the sole purpose of my visit was to go the studio of a tattoo artist in Soho on for an appointment that I had arranged a couple of days earlier to have a couple of commemorative tattoos on the top of both my arms to celebrate my Mastermind success. My pre-conceived illusions that getting a tattoo was going to be relatively quick and pain free were quickly dispelled as I had to suffer and endure two very uncomfortable hours under the tattooist's needle. I emerged from that uncomfortable ordeal with two very sore arms but as I inspected the art work carried out by the tattooist, my face immediately lit up with both pleasure and pride with the product. Engraved on my right arm, is an outline of the iconic Mastermind logo that the tattooist had copied from one of the

467

specialist question cards I requested to be sent to me by the Mastermind production team and on my left arm, I had engraved the words, **CHAMPION 2004**. I am not ashamed to admit the fact that the tattoos were an act of pure self-indulgent madness, but I have absolutely no regrets in having them done despite all the pain and discomfort I had to endure as those engravings on my arms will serve as a permanent reminder of a memorable achievement that will stay with me until the day I die.

I finally arrived home that evening and completed the rest my packing for my trip and amongst the items I was intending to carry with me as part of my hand luggage would be my Mastermind trophy which I packed with considerable care. I woke up early the following morning so that I could treat myself to a long hot soak in the bath before eventually leaving home just before 11am for Heathrow Airport in order to catch the 12.30 pm flight on Air Jamaica airlines that afternoon firmly believing that I was giving myself more than enough time to make the flight, but to my horror, there was gridlocked weekend traffic on the North Circular Road. By the time I arrived at the Long Term Car Park for Terminal 3, I had just over twenty minutes before the flight was scheduled to depart. I was now in a complete state of sheer and utter panic. I looked around the near deserted Car Park hoping against hope that there would be a transport saviour who would be willing to drop me outside Terminal 3 and thankfully, those frantic prayers were answered in the form of a small white van that I noticed about to leave the Car Park. I hailed the van and begged desperately for a lift, and the driver, my saviour, magnanimously obliged. After alighting from the van, I asked him to watch out for me on BBC2 the following day at 8pm, without specifying the name of the programme I wanted him to watch, and he replied that he would make every effort to tune in. After getting out of the van, I made a frantic dash for the Air Jamaica Check-In Desk weighed down with my travel luggage and I arrived at just in the nick of time, sweating profusely and out of breath. I presented my passport and travel documents to the Check-In Agent whose face showed frowning disapproval, making an unnecessary, disparaging comment about my sweaty demeanour as she informed me that she was in the process of closing the Check-In counter just before my arrival and it was only the combined factors of my physical tiredness coupled with my sheer relief in having made it to the Check-In Desk in the nick of time, that prevented me from delivering the appropriate verbal riposte in response to her downright rudeness. I had made it to the Check-In counter and that was all that mattered. After I was checked onto the flight, The Check-In Agent then asked me to place all the luggage that was going to be carried in the aircraft's cargo onto the scales and as I was doing so, it suddenly dawned on me that in my frantic haste to get to the Terminal, I left a piece of luggage behind in my car. If I thought that was bad, worse was to follow because without thinking, I placed my rucksack that contained all my spending money, passport and travel documents that had just been presented to the Check-In Agent, save for the only item of hand luggage that was accompanying me on the plane, the cardboard box containing my fragile Mastermind trophy. Because I was initially oblivious to my rucksack blunder, I left the Check-In Desk and made my way towards the Departure Gate feeling mightily relieved. That feeling, however, was short-lived. After I arrived at the end of a very long queue at the Departure gate, it suddenly dawned on me that I had mistakenly given the Check-In Agent my rucksack. For the second time in as many hours, I was once again gripped by the sudden onset of sheer panic before making yet another frantic dash this time, to the head of the long queue to explain my self-inflicted problem to the airline's agents who were busy collecting boarding passes from the travelling passengers, sweating even more profusely than ever before. The attitude of the agents at the Departure Gate to my problem was in stark contrast to the attitude I was confronted with when I arrived in a sweaty frantic panic at the Check-In Desk and they reassured me that I would have nothing to worry about and that they would contact the baggage handlers straight away and ask them to retrieve it. Mercifully, it didn't take the baggage handlers long to locate my rucksack which was probably due in part, to my last minute check in and with my rucksack now safely returned with everything intact, I presented my boarding pass to the Check-In Agents breathing a massive sigh of relief in the process that all the hiccups and possible pitfalls that threatened to scupper my impending trip were finally behind me. There was only one task left for me to do before I boarded the plane and that was, to telephone Mum to let her know that I was leaving the country. The unexpected news understandably took Mum by complete surprise and with an increasingly worried tone in her voice, she asked me why I was going to Jamaica and why I had not told her about the trip. I replied that I just needed to get away for a while and that she shouldn't worry as I was old enough to look after myself and before she could utter another word, I hung up the receiver as the announcement over the Tannoy system called for all Air Jamaica passengers to get ready for embarkation and an eight hour flight to one of the best destinations on the planet, the one and only, Montego Bay.

The week I spent in Montego Bay was just what the doctor ordered. Seven sun drenched days where I did nothing more than relax and chill out and was the perfect place for me to reflect and think for the final time about how I was going to deal with the intense public glare and media interest when I eventually arrived back home. Before I knew it, those seven carefree days were over in a blink of an eye and I found myself back at Terminal 3's Arrivals Hall in the afternoon of 6th December where myself, together with hundreds of tired and travel weary passengers headed towards the Baggage Reclaims Area to retrieve our luggage After standing by the carousel for what seemed an eternity, I eventually managed to retrieve all my luggage which I proceeded to load onto an airport trolley before heading towards the Nothing to Declare Channel. As I was making my way through the Channel, I got the feeling that I was going to be the subject of a customs random enquiry. It was a hunch proved to be spot on as I was approached by a very polite Customs Officer who asked me to accompany him to the nearby bench as he wished to ask me questions about my recent travels. Whilst I obviously intended to fully cooperate with any enquiry the Customs Officer wished to conduct, I decided that I was going to have a bit of fun with him in the process. The Customs Officer asked me a series of general and routine questions about my trip as well as the question as to whether I had anything to declare. I said I wasn't sure, and indicated my large blue sports bag. I then opened the bag and took out the cardboard box and placed it on the bench. I slowly removed the lid from the box to reveal the glass bowl.

"What is it?" asked the Custom's Officer. I picked it up and handed it to him so that he could have a good look for himself and after reading the words at the base of the trophy he turned to me and said, "Mastermind? Are you the bloke that won last night?"

It's started! I said, smiling to myself, and after gathering all of my belongings together I left customs and headed straight for WH Smiths in the Arrivals Hall and bought myself The Times. I frantically flicked through its pages until I came across Giles Smith's column, *Last Night on TV*, which reviewed my performance in the Grand Final and by the time I had finished reading the article, I was left with a smile on my face that was so wide, even the legendary Cheshire Cat would struggle to match it. My thoughts immediately drifted back to just over a year ago when I was reading the Independent newspaper review about the success of my immediate predecessor, Andy Page, and dreaming about the improbable scenario of emulating that achievement, a dream which prompted me to enter the competition in the first place, and now here I was a year later, being feted in the press for realising that same improbable dream. I bought as many different newspapers as I could and at a quick glance through all of them, it was pretty clear that the coverage on my victory, whether they were broadsheets or tabloids, were very complimentary.

A while later, as I was approaching my home, I noticed that there were a couple of people on the pavement outside my front door. I didn't know who they were but I had a pretty good idea as to why they were there. I made my way down the side alley that leads to the back entrance of my house and quietly slipped in through the back door to avoid them. I stepped into a pitch black house because I had closed all of the blinds before leaving for my trip in anticipation that I would be receiving visitors whom I was not yet ready to speak to. I tip toed my way to the front door and picked up a note that was lying on the doormat that was left by a representative from one of the national newspapers asking me to contact them as soon as possible. I crept up the unlit stairs to the bathroom and ran myself a hot bath with a view of treating myself to a long and relaxing soak by candlelight. However, if I thought that I was going to enjoy a long relaxing soak in total peace and tranquillity I was sadly mistaken because the telephone rang virtually nonstop, but no matter how many times it rang, it stood no chance of being answered. It wasn't until close to 11pm that night that I felt sufficiently confident that all the hullaballoo had died down and after peering through the blinds in order to ensure that the coast was clear, I left home to retrieve my car. Because I hadn't eaten anything since travelling on the flight home, I drove to an all night West Indian Take Away, Airey's on Willesden Lane and bought myself a couple of beef patties before returning home to get myself some much needed rest.

The following morning after I had washed and dressed, I picked up my trophy and made my way to see the only person I wanted to see - my dear cantankerous old Mum.

"There she is!" I exclaimed, holding the trophy out towards her. "The only black woman on this earth who has produced a black Mastermind Champion!"

For once, Mum was totally speechless and I could see how much that moment meant to her when I saw the expression of joy on her face, but for me, it meant so much more. I'd gone to great lengths in keeping my Mastermind win to myself because the first person I wanted to show the trophy to, once the news went public, was my dear old Mum. That priceless moment was payback of all the effort, struggle and sacrifice that she went through bringing up three children in a council house and never wavering in her love and support of us, both in the good times and the not so good, and whilst it's true that my *Mastermind* victory will always be my own personal triumph, in many ways it was a triumph for her, my Dad, my siblings and all the people who have ever played an important part of my life and it's with those people I wanted to share my success. After that heartfelt moment, Mum then reverted to type by giving me a mild ear bashing for making her worry. I asked her whether she enjoyed watching me in the Grand Final and she replied that she couldn't watch it because she was far too nervous and she only found out the result on account of the endless phone calls she received from her friends who rang to offer her their best wishes and congratulations. I went into the living room to call my Dad and then my brother Steve and the collective joy when I spoke to them is something that I will always treasure. I then contacted the *Mastermind* production team and spoke to one of the show's main producers, Pam Cavanagh to let her know that I was back in the country. Pam brought me up to speed in relation to the seemingly overwhelming surge of interest my victory was generating and she kindly offered the services of the production team to act temporarily on my behalf as a first point of any enquiry, a kind and welcoming gesture that I gratefully accepted.

I gradually emerged from my self-imposed low profile over the next day or so by making myself accessible to my close friends and acquaintances. The *Mastermind* production team, in the meanwhile, were busy arranging and co-ordinating a hectic and exciting schedule of media interviews as well as appearances on radio and TV which had the beneficial effect of raising my profile to such amazing heights that I never thought was possible. These included numerous appearances on various national radio stations such Radio 4 and Radio 5 Live to local radio. Sandwiched in between were interviews with journalists from the Guardian to the Evening Standard and a memorable day spent with The Sun at their headquarters in Wapping where they arranged a special *Mastermind* Football Challenge where members of the public would put my FA Cup final knowledge to the ultimate test. I was invited as a guest on BBC's Football Focus for a once in a lifetime opportunity to go behind the scenes and meet some of the game's footballing icons such as Gary Lineker, Alan Hansen and, the one and only, "King" Kenny Dalglish who were in the studios to watch and analyse all the Premier League matches to be played that afternoon in preparation for Match of the Day later that evening. Aside from going behind the scenes of the show and meeting those footballing icons, the main purpose for my invitation was to take part in a five question head to head showdown with the King of football commentators, John Motson who, despite my best efforts, came out on top with a resounding 5-2 score line. The best though, was saved till last when completely out of the blue, the show's presenter Manish Bashir announced that the Football Association were offering me two

VIP tickets to the 2005 FA Cup Final at the Millennium Stadium in Cardiff in recognition of "my services" to the FA Cup. Although I knew full well from the moment I won *Mastermind* that my life would change forever, it was a real eye opener to actually experience how recognisable I had become as a result of all the attention and publicity I was receiving and I felt totally vindicated by my decision to use those previous six months before the news went public to think about how I was going to cope and deal with it. People would approach me in the street to shake my hand congratulating me and sometimes I was even asked for my autograph. On one memorable occasion when I was invited onto Geoff Schumann's Sunday night show on Radio London, I was recognised by a group of young men in a car whilst I was in the front seat of the courtesy car taking me to the studio. As both vehicles were waiting for the red traffic light to change on the Marylebone Road I noticed that the window was suddenly wound down in the other vehicle and I heard someone shout out the words, "You're the guy who won *Mastermind* aren't you?" When I confirmed that I was, all the men shouted in unison with compliments such as "Big Up," "'Nuff Respect!" and "Wicked bruv!" and tooted their car horn before driving off. On top of all the media attention that I was receiving, the *Mastermind* production team were receiving a steady stream of letters and cards on my behalf that ranged from messages of congratulations, to invitations to events from various schools and organisations, stretching well into the following year. There was even the odd gift or two from members of the public, the most notable of which was a ceramic replica of the FA Cup together with a note from the sender asking me to keep it alongside my *Mastermind* trophy.

The legal profession also made their sentiments known. I received letters of congratulations at home from the Chairman of the bar and also, from my Inn, the Inner Temple, who very kindly invited me to lunch with the some of the Senior Masters and Benchers at the Inn. But out of all the sincere and heartfelt accolades that I received from my beloved profession, the one that was the most memorable and touching occurred when I had to appear at the Old Bailey for the final preliminary hearing in relation to the murder trial that was due to begin at the end of the following month where most unexpectedly, I received a standing ovation in the Advocate's Robing Room from some of my fellow barristers that were present, an accolade that brought both a lump to my throat and almost a tear to my eye.

Despite the increasingly hectic nature of my media and professional commitments, there were three special people who I made it my personal duty to see as I wanted to thank them for the important contribution they played in my good fortune. The first of those persons was none other than Mr Robert Lloyd-Williams, the surgeon who performed the operations on my left ankle and big toe. I went to his private clinic and when he saw me, he bowed both his head and arms a couple of times. I felt ten feet tall that a man of his considerable stature would see fit to greet me in such a way.

After we shook hands, he said, "Shaun, which two countries went to war over a game of football?"

"Honduras and El Salvador in 1969 after a World Cup qualifying tie and although I don't know what ended the war, what I do know is that El Salvador qualified for the 1970 World Cup in Mexico the following year."

My correct response prompted Mr Lloyd–Williams to embark on yet another short rendition of Kow-Towing before he invited me into his office for a quick chat in private. Once inside his office, the pair of us briefly caught up on old times. After our brief chat, I presented him with a framed copy of a newspaper interview that I had given earlier in the week, where I talked about Mr Lloyd-Williams displaying extraordinary kindness towards me as well as giving me a renewed sense of belief during those difficult times when I had all those ongoing injury problems relating to my ankle. Mr Lloyd-Williams began to feel slightly embarrassed and he responded by saying how grateful he was to receive such an unexpected gift and that it would have pride of place on his desk.

The next special individual in line for a surprise quick visit was Valerie Howe, the kind and helpful Librarian at the British Library in Colindale. As with my unplanned visit to Mr Lloyd-Williams, Valerie was just as surprised but no less pleased by my unexpected visit to see her and I had my Mastermind trophy with me together with a small bouquet of flowers and plants that I bought for her especially as a token of my appreciation for all the help and assistance she had given me before the pair of us posed for photos holding the trophy together that were going to be printed in the Library's In-House magazine.

After leaving the Library, I went to see Chris at his bookshop. He was very pleased to see me when I walked into his shop with the trophy under my arm, which I immediately handed to him. Both he and his colleague said that they were more than impressed with my performance in the Grand Final. Chris handed me back the trophy and went over to the Football Section of his shop and selected at random a book on World Soccer that he said he was going to give to me as a present, a gesture which I found to be very touching indeed. Before he gave me the book however, he picked up a pen from the sales counter desk and inscribed on the inside cover the following poignant words, "To Shaun, Ooh Ahh...Lloyd McGrath!" referring to the discussion that we both had when I was researching and preparing for FA Cup Finals where we discussed the possibility of an FA Cup Final question on the game between Spurs and Coventry in 1987, a discussion which in the greater scheme of things proved to be the difference between becoming a feted quiz champion and returning to the backwaters of relative obscurity.

The media, professional and social commitments I was involved with since I returned from the Caribbean took me right up to Christmas and for once in my life, everything in the garden was rosy. Whilst there was no denying the fact that I was enjoying every moment of this new-found attention, I was determined more than ever to keep my feet firmly on the ground and the six months I had of secret and peaceful solitude prior to all the hype and hullaballoo proved to be the crucial vindication in preparing me for having such a mindset. The rest of the festive holidays gave me the chance to unwind as well as celebrate with family and close friends and as the year drew to a close, I managed to find a quiet moment for myself just like I had twelve months previously, to reflect on a year that began full of all the usual optimistic uncertainty and turned out in the end to be one of the best years of my life. If 2005 was only half as good as 2004, then I was sure to be in for another very special year.

CHAPTER TWENTY

At the start of 2005, my self-belief and confidence could not have been in a healthier state. The seemingly endless invitations, coupled with the ever-increasing requests and demands of my time from various organisations up and down the country, were still coming in thick and fast, showing no signs of abating. In the first week of January alone, I was invited by two different radio stations on successive nights as a guest panellist on the back of my FA Cup Final expertise to take part in a lively debate on the Third Round of the FA Cup. One of my fellow guest panellists on one of those shows was the manager at the time, non-league Yeading's Johnson "Drax" Hippolyte, whose team were drawn against Newcastle United in the third round. I had known Drax (who acquired the nickname on account of his sublime footballing skills striking fear and terror in the opposition), for over twenty years and when we saw each other in the studio, we greeted each other as though we were long lost brothers.

Out of all the numerous invitations that I had received around this time, the most ironic and, I must confess, the one that gave me the most pleasure and satisfaction, was an invitation from the institution who had all but written off my childhood ambitions to become a barrister, my first secondary school, Copland High. The invite requested my presence to help celebrate the school's fiftieth anniversary to be held at the House of Lords on the 15th of July. This wasn't the first time that I had received an unexpected invitation from my old alma mater. That unlikely scenario occurred almost twelve years previously in June 1993. I had been selected, as a result of a recommendation of my friend and colleague, Peter Herbert, who at the time was the Chairman of The Society of Black Lawyers, to feature in an article in the Guardian newspaper to mark the organisation's twentieth anniversary. Unbeknownst to me, the article was read by my old PE teacher, Mr Ian Martin who was somewhat overcome, as he was to tell me later, with a mixture of mild awe and pleasant surprise. Mr Martin was still teaching at Copland at the time and he contacted me, inviting me to get in contact with the school. My immediate thoughts went back to the early days of September 1976 and the day when I walked out of the school gates alongside my old school friend Glenmore Johnson, vowing never to return unless the school itself personally invited me and now here I was, almost seventeen years later, holding in my hand a letter from the very same school that had told me in no uncertain terms that I wasn't going to amount to very much in life, asking me to get in touch with them. *This is as close to a personal invitation from the school that I'm ever going to get*, I said to myself gleefully and without so much as a hint of bitterness or recrimination, I immediately contacted the school and was invited for a visit.

That visit eventually took place towards the end of the school's academic year and as I walked through the school's main entrance wearing my best suit, tie and shoes, I was accorded the treatment of a VIP by a warm and welcoming delegation that contained none other than the school's then Headmaster, Mr Alan Davies and the school's Deputy Head, Mr Richard Noble, and I felt like the Greek hero Odysseus returning to his homeland after his twenty year nomadic wanderings following his victory in the Trojan wars, as opposed to returning like the proverbial Prodigal Son mentioned in Luke 15 11-32 in The New Testament, my life and development in those intervening years had not, since I walked out of the school gates for the final time in September 1976, been a wasteful one.

I spent that morning on a nostalgic tour and as walked through the school with my hosts, it didn't take me long to regain my bearings in a place that I spent the majority of my teenage years. From the large central spiral staircase that I attempted to slide down before being unceremoniously hauled off it by the formidable Mr Rice during my first few days at the school, to the classrooms where I was taught, to the playground area, to the playing fields, my first impressions on my return to my alma mater was that Copland High School seemed to have hardly changed at all over the last seventeen or so years, as if time had somehow stood still, an impression that was reinforced by the fact that some of the teaching staff that taught me all those years ago were still at the school. Teachers like Mr Martin, my old Chemistry teacher. Or Mr (Paul) Knight and Mr Ali who taught Maths and looked as though they had hardly aged at all. Even the school dinners looked and tasted the same.

The fact that I had been personally invited back by the school that once had such a low opinion of me, a school who were now treating me as if I was one of their main success stories, shows I am living proof why it is wrong for a school to write a pupil off as a no-hoper, or to pre-ordain a pupil's future life chances in any negative or unsupportive way, a point that I made most passionately and forcefully during the keynote address I gave when the school invited me back as the guest speaker at their Annual Certificate and Prize Giving Awards Ceremony in January 1994. The highlight of that evening was when the Headmaster informed me that my name was going to be engraved on the school's vast Achievement Board that hung in the Assembly Hall, a truly wonderful honour that brought a lump to my throat and fulfilled a secret schoolboy dream of mine of being honoured as a Copland High student. I had made a significant contribution to the school's long history.

I never reminded the school about the fateful discussion that I had with the Careers teacher about my ambition of becoming a barrister, or of that teacher's curt and dismissive response, nor did I ever bring up the subject of how totally unsupportive the school was of me in general during my time there. I would imagine, in the school's defence, they would argue that the school's negative support of me didn't stop me from realising my ambitions. Their preconceived judgement on my future didn't dent, prevent or irrevocably damage, my ambition in any way, shape or form, and the mere fact that the school sought to recognise my achievements since leaving the school is, and always will be, nothing other than a tremendous personal honour for myself and a wonderful testament to my own determination and perseverance.

Although it was my intention to try and accept as many of the invitations as possible that had come my way, my main priority on the immediate horizon was the murder trial involving my friend and client that was due to start in the last week of January and as such, all the social engagements would have to be put on hold until after the trial's conclusion.

The day of the trial finally arrived and the lawyers acting for the respective parties taking part in the trial were advocates of the highest calibre. Representing the prosecution was the highly rated Treasury Counsel, Aftab Jaffagee QC, ably assisted by his junior, Duncan Penny, and appearing for my client's co-defendant was Michael Corkery QC and his junior, a barrister who I consider to be one of my best friends at the bar, Michael Hall, who was also a tenant at Courtenay Griffiths' Chambers. The prosecution opened their case to the jury on the basis that my client's co-defendant was a major player in serious criminal activity in the West London area, principally in the supply of Class A drugs. There was, according to the prosecution, a long and ongoing major vendetta between the co-defendant and the deceased, who was also heavily involved in the supply of Class A drugs. A vendetta that, the prosecution suggested, culminated in the co-defendant hatching a plot to kill his rival. Mr Jaffagee, in his opening remarks to the jury, went onto suggest that my client had played a significant role in that murder in that it was he who had lured the deceased to the area where he was eventually shot as a result of a series of telephone calls made between him, a third party intermediary and his co-defendant, and those telephone calls, it was alleged, were designed to keep the co-defendant informed as to the deceased's movements and whereabouts in the hours leading up to the murder. As part of their case, the prosecution sought to rely on telephone and cell site evidence that, they claimed, would provide the important and crucial link in my client's complicity and involvement in the murder.

Several witnesses were called on behalf the prosecution, some doing so behind screens to protect their identity. The quality of the evidence from the witnesses left a lot to be desired but most importantly, not one of those witnesses implicated my client. As the prosecution's case began to unfold, it was becoming increasingly clear that there was very little evidence that pointed towards my client's involvement, and in terms of the telephone and cell site evidence that the prosecution were heavily reliant on, it was apparent that the level of contact between my client and the so called third party intermediary, amounted to no more than two very short phone calls. At the end of the prosecution's case, Courtenay made submissions to the trial judge HHJ Barker QC where, in essence, he argued that the case against our client should be withdrawn from the jury because the evidence presented by the prosecution had failed to prove his part in the joint enterprise of murder. Aftab, responding on behalf of the prosecution, gave a forceful and eloquent rebuttal to Courtenay's submissions but, as good as his submission was, the writing was on the wall as trial judge accepted Courtenay's arguments and after they returned to the courtroom, he directed the jury to find our client not guilty.

We went to visit our client in the cells afterwards and there were no words to describe how ecstatic and relieved he felt by the judge's ruling. He could barely express his undying gratitude to the whole of his legal team for the efforts we made on his behalf and it's those touching moments, despite the ups and downs I have experienced during my career, that makes being a barrister both rewarding and worthwhile. Rodney remained with our client in the cells whilst both Courtenay and I made our way to the robing room on the fourth floor. As we were travelling in the lift, I turned to Courtenay and offered him my congratulations on a job well done and he reciprocated by telling me that it was a pleasure for him to have me as his junior. It goes without saying that I will always have the highest professional regard and personal admiration for Courtenay Griffiths QC. His conduct throughout the trial demonstrated, yet again, why he is regarded as one of the bar's top criminal silks and the benchmark for aspiring lawyers like myself who still have both the ambition and desire to reach the very top of the profession.

With the trial now over, I was free to turn my attention to all those invitations, requests and demands of my time from the various educational establishments, institutions and social enterprise organisations which was to last from the beginning of February stretching well into the following year. My travels took me to schools, colleges and universities up and down the country, as well as an invitation to make a nostalgic return visit to my alma mater, The Polytechnic of North London, under its new name, London Metropolitan University. It is difficult to put into words the deep personal honour and privilege I felt in being given the platform at these different events to address so many different people, sharing with them the story of my life's journey. The general feedback I received was always positive from the letters and cards that I received thanking me for attending these events and often, I would be sent, or presented with, gifts or mementos as a thank you, unexpected gifts I will always treasure.

The *Mastermind* production team got back in touch with me at the beginning of April and asked me whether I'd like to be the guest of honour at the 2005 Grand Final where I would present the trophy to the winner. I was also aske if I would be prepared to give an interview that would be shown at the half way point of the Grand Final talking about how winning *Mastermind* had changed my life. I was naturally delighted by such a request and I told the production team that I wanted that interview to take place at my old stomping ground, Hackney Community College, who, by some happy coincidence, were planning to hold a special evening in my honour towards the end of April. Given my long association with the College, it was, after all, the place that gave me my first break at the start of my professional career and I could not think of a better way to show my deep gratitude and appreciation for all the College had done for me.

The most unlikely set of events and circumstances I found myself being involved with at the height of my new-found fame arose as a result of my decision to stand as a MP in the 2005 General Election campaigning as an Independent candidate for the Brent South constituency where I live. A reporter from the Voice newspaper, with whom I was in regular contact with at the time, had called me at home as he was interested to hear my views on the forthcoming election and whether it was an election I would consider standing in. I was slightly bemused as to why he would think I would ever entertain the notion of standing for Parliament and my immediate response was that whilst I had an interest in politics generally, that interest did not extend to active politics and I had absolutely no intention of running for Parliament whatsoever. That apparent cast iron response underwent a complete and dramatic volt face on account of a discussion that I had with my local MP, Paul Boateng, the product of which left me both determined and committed to accept this most unlikely of challenges.

Sometime in early January of 2005, I received an invitation from Paul to have lunch with him at the House of Commons as he wished to personally congratulate me on my *Mastermind* success. Paul and I were in Chambers together at 54 Fleet Street for a few short months just before I left, and I have had nothing but respect and admiration for him. Paul had decided, after almost eighteen years as an MP, to retire from politics after the General Election as he was poised to leave the UK for South Africa in order to take up a diplomatic appointment there.

Traditionally speaking, the Brent South constituency is one of the largest constituencies on the electoral map and a staunch Labour stronghold. Paul had successfully fought the seat on four separate occasions since 1987 when he was first elected returning with a healthy majority usually in excess of five figures and the Labour candidate selected to contest the safe seat, Dawn Butler, who was also present at our luncheon appointment, was odds on to be elected. During our lunch, I happened to mention to Paul in passing about the discussion that I had with the journalist from the Voice about me possibly standing as an election candidate, a comment that was made more in light hearted jest as opposed to any proposition of serious intent. Instead of taking the comment for what it was, Paul's immediate response that was made in a somewhat forthright and dismissive tone, was to let me know, in no uncertain terms, that I didn't stand a hope in hell of winning. *Who is he to tell me that I can't win? I* thought. *I'll show him!* I decided there and then that I was going to take up the impossible challenge of standing in the General Election, allowing my wounded ego and dented pride to get the better of sensible logic and reason.

The campaigning for the election was already in full swing and I only had just over two weeks before the election date to put a campaign together, but I wasn't going to allow the small matter of insufficient campaigning time to deter me from throwing my hat into the electoral ring. I immediately set about the task of getting the campaign wagon rolling with the help of my recently appointed Campaign Manager, Brian Wilson, who was ably assisted by Karen Knowles and Nick Hull-Malhan, from an organisation I was working closely with at the time called the Disability Times Trust and between the four of us, we managed to produce a glossy manifesto and campaign posters which I planned to distribute in the areas of the constituency where I believed I would get a good level of support.

Over the next fortnight, I was going to use every means at my disposal and channel all my efforts and energies to try and obtain the support of at least 5% or more of the electoral vote, a target that would guarantee the return of my £500 election deposit. Given the paucity of the resources that I had at my disposal in comparison to the seemingly limitless resources available to my political rivals from the main political parties, even that target seemed way out of reach but as the old saying goes, "nothing ventured, nothing gained," and until the polls closed on Polling Day, not only was I going to use my best endeavours to achieve my election target, I was also going to have a great deal of fun along the way.

During the fortnight leading up to Polling Day, I did everything that was required of any prospective candidate fighting an election campaign. The first, and most important of those requirements included, an in depth interview with the local press which apart from serving as a launch pad in announcing my candidacy, it also served as the perfect vehicle to get the main contents of my election manifesto across to the whole of the Brent South constituency in a way that my non existent resources and lack of real support structure was unable to achieve.

As with any election candidate hoping to attract as many votes as possible, I took to the streets with a megaphone and soapbox in hand for some good old fashioned electoral campaigning on the hustings that was reminiscent of John Major's electoral campaigning style and methods of General Elections gone by, doing my level best to get the contents of my manifesto across in a concise and persuasive manner, trying to reach out to an electorate who were either bemused, bored or plainly not interested. I concentrated my street campaigning in specifically targeted and well known landmark areas across the constituency such as The Jubilee Clock, situated right in the centre of the one way system of Harlesden High Street, or in the heart of Kensal Rise, after which time, I would concentrate my efforts on door to door canvassing, armed with countless copies of my manifesto and posters in an attempt to drum up as much support that I could.

If I was to sum up my brief foray into the world of election campaigning, my assessment would be that I found the whole experience to be physically exhausting, at times very frustrating, certainly very costly but ultimately, a very rewarding exercise and whilst I'm fairly sure that I might not have made the same choice again if I could wind back the hands of time, I'm glad, despite my reasons for getting involved in the first place, that I had the courage and the conviction to see it through to the very end.

On Polling Day, I cast my vote (for myself naturally!) at my old primary school, Oakington Manor. It was the first time I had voted in a General Election since the Labour Party's electoral trouncing in 1992 before making my way with my Dad and Brian to Brent Town Hall where the election result would be announced. It was an honour and a privilege for me just to be a part of such an occasion as it reminded me of the times I used to stay up and watch election nights in the past as a young whippersnapper in the Seventies with Peter Snow and his eponymous Swing-o-meter as the election results poured into the studio. As the votes were being collated, it was pretty clear that Labour's Dawn Butler was going to win the seat by a landslide, a fact confirmed by the Returning Officer when he announced the following result:

Dawn Butler (Labour) 17,501 votes - 58% of the vote
Jamie Allie (Liberal Democrat) 6,175 - 20.7 %
Rishi Sasha (Conservative) 4,485 - 15.1%
Rowan Langley (Green Party) 957 - 3.2%
Shaun Wallace (Independent) 297 - 1%
Rocky Fernandez (Independent) 288 -1%
Rainbow George Weiss (Rainbow Dream Ticket) 61 -0.2%
Labour Majority - 11,326

My fifth place resulted in the inevitable loss of my £500 election deposit but, despite my failure to reach my own personal election target, I still felt a great deal of personal pride and satisfaction that I managed to attract any votes at all given the fact that I entered the election campaign at a relatively late stage, but what really made me smile, was the vast number of people who approached me in the days and weeks after the election who claimed that they voted for me, a claim which even if it was half true would have probably carried me all the way to Westminster!

Any disappointment that I may have felt in my doomed attempt to enter the House of Commons was immediately put to one side and replaced by feelings of unrestrained excitement and joy in anticipation of my long awaited trip down the M4 to Cardiff's Millennium Stadium and my very first FA Cup Final, courtesy of the Football Association's generous offer that they made following my appearance on *Football Focus*. I'd already promised my eldest nephew Myles that I would take him to the game, an offer that pleased him no end especially because his team, Manchester United, had made it to the final against their fiercest rivals, Arsenal. My beloved Chelsea would not be facing them on account of our defeat in the fifth round by Newcastle United, a result that extinguished all hopes of the boys in blue completing an historic domestic treble. As the day of the game was getting ever closer, I still hadn't received any word from the FA about what arrangements had been made, and I didn't think it appropriate to contact them. Sadly, they never did contact me, and Myles and I didn't get our chance to go. I resigned myself to watching the game on TV at home. As I watched the build up to the big kick off, my disappointment was compounded even further when the commentator happened to mention that the FA's guest of honour was the Swedish referee Anders Frisk, the man who controversially disallowed Sol Campbell's last minute goal in England's Euro 2004 quarter final tie against Portugal, an invite I assumed was the FA's way of apologising for the sustained vitriolic abuse Mr Frisk received from so many England fans who blamed him for the team's eventual exit from the tournament. Although I would have liked to have been there to watch the game live, it turned out to be a blessing in disguise that I didn't travel all that way to Cardiff because the match failed to live up to the billing worthy of such an occasion, the only highlight being the decisive strike by the Arsenal Captain, Patrick Viera, in the equally uninspiring penalty shootout.

The Monday after the game, I received a phone call from a member of the *Football Focus* production team who apologised for the fact that I had not been contacted by either their office, or the FA, with regards to my attendance at the Cup Final. They accepted the blame and promised that they would see to it that I went to the FA Cup Final the following year, an offer I was more than happy to accept.

Just before my appearance on the 2005 Grand Final, I received an unexpected call from an unexpected source. None other than the celebrated former editor of the Daily Mirror, Piers Morgan. At first I thought it was a hoax and I asked him at least three times who he was before I was finally convinced that it really was Piers Morgan on the other end of the line. He told me that the reason for the call was that there was a prestigious quiz competition being held at the weekend and he wanted to put the best possible quiz team together as he was determined to win the competition at all costs. I initially refused Piers' request, citing the reason that after *Mastermind*, I had retired from all forms of quizzing, but Piers Morgan is not the type of man who takes no for an answer and he began to cleverly play on my competitive instincts by dangling the incentive of "putting one over" on some of the competing teams that contained the cream of the media and literary circles, before going on to mention that the quizmaster for the evening was the most formidable television quizmaster of them all, Jeremy Paxman. Piers' stick and carrot approach had the instant effect of awakening my inherent competitive instincts which, allied to Piers' persistent and persuasive charm, finally led me to give in.

Sunday 2nd July at 7pm, I arrived at the River Cafe, and could see Piers standing by the main entrance, looking anxious. I went up to and my very presence seemed to have the instant effect of changing his expression from one of to relief. The pair of us went inside and Piers escorted me to our designated table where he introduced me to the rest my teammates, Connor Hanna, Piers' one time Deputy at the Daily Mirror, Larry Lawrence, a Daily Mirror Librarian, Simon Kelner, the Editor of the Independent and last, but by no means least, Roger Alton, the Editor of the Observer. I greeted all my teammates with a confident high five. I was here to be part of a winning team.

The venue was steadily beginning to fill up with the competing teams that comprised mainly of celebrated and well known personalities ranging from the world of show business to the world of books and letters. As I was settling down in my seat, Piers discretely pointed out to me the table that was directly adjacent to ours that comprised a team from The Guardian newspaper who, according to him, were going to be our main rivals for the title. As Piers and I were having that discussion, their team's captain, Alan Rusbridger, turned suddenly towards our table and began muttering various comments that were audible enough for those words to be heard, along the lines of Piers' team "containing a bunch of ringers". Piers refused to take the bait. He knew he had assembled a good, well balanced team that had amongst its ranks the secret weapon of a reigning *Mastermind* Champion, a fact unbeknownst to the rest of the competing teams. There was just enough time for all of the competing teams to have something to eat after which time, in typical Paxamensque style, the host and quizmaster, Jeremy Paxman, called the competing teams to order for the start of the first of the nine scheduled rounds.

The questions in the first round were pretty routine so as far as I was concerned and my performance throughout the round turned out to be a source of amazement and amusement to Piers and the rest of my teammates, not just because of the speed in which I was answering the questions, but the fact that I was giving some of the answers before Jeremy had even completed the question. Our incredible team effort meant that by the designated half way point, the team was handily placed to be in contention for the top spot, much to the displeasure of the majority of the competing teams who greeted the announcement of our score with derisory groans and cat calls. The thirty-minute interval gave everyone the chance to stretch their legs and mingle with the other teams. I felt like the proverbial fish out of water given the esteemed company that I was mixing with, although I did manage to summon up the courage to approach and speak to one of the participants who was one of my legal heroes, the barrister and Author John Mortimer QC. I also chatted away briefly to Stephen Fry and the acclaimed author, Sebastian Faulkes. Both Stephen and Sebastian were clearly intrigued as to the identity to Piers' secret weapon, but I gave nothing away. My stonewalling had the desired effect. I managed to keep the secret of my quizzing credentials intact and that's how I intended it to remain right up until the end of the competition by which time, if all went according to plan, Piers, with the help of the rest of his teammates, would have achieved his mission of the long awaited and long overdue quiz victory that he so desperately craved.

  As the second half of the competition unfolded, our team were still performing admirably and were well placed for ultimate victory, but at the start of the penultimate round, the team's momentum was in danger of stalling completely as the round involved ten questions on Sudoku. I had never played the game, let alone understood its rules. Piers then turned to Connor, Larry and Roger in turn and asked them whether they could answer any of the questions but the only response he received from all three was a collective shrug. With one final roll of the dice, Piers turned to Simon Kelner and asked him whether or not he had ever played the game. Grinning, Simon said he did, a potentially game changing response that prompted Piers to push the Sudoku questions in Simon's direction and let him to get on with it. In next to no time, Simon completed all of the Sudoku puzzles, a brilliant solo effort that prompted the rest of the team to breathe a collective sigh of relief. We were back on track.

  With everything to play for, the final round was on general knowledge. The battle for the top spot going into that final round was a two way battle between our team who were in second place and the Guardian team. Piers, our team captain, who at this point of proceedings was savouring every moment of an already tense situation, cranked up the pressure even further by announcing out loud that our team were going to play our Joker, giving us double points. Piers' declaration seemed to unnerve Alan Rusbridger considerably who, together with the rest of his team, were beginning to show visible signs of apprehension. Alan had every reason to be fearful because, in that final round, our team answered the questions with the same lightning speed and precision that we collectively demonstrated in the first round and once Jeremy had completed asking the tenth and final question, Piers, together with the rest of his teammates, relaxed in unison into our respective seats, each of us wearing a smug satisfactory smile across our faces, quietly confident that our collective mission of victory had been accomplished.

The moment of truth had now arrived for Jeremy to reveal the answers for the final two rounds as well as the final standings of all the competing teams. Simon's brilliant solo performance in the Sudoku round had virtually put the team level with our Guardian rivals and when the answers to the final round were revealed, I punched the air to celebrate every correct answer the team had given. The team had produced a perfect score for the round. As it became apparent that the final outcome of the quiz was heading one way and one way only, the vast majority of the remaining competing teams began a chorus of good natured booing and hissing in unison towards Piers and the rest of his triumphant team that continued right up until the moment Jeremy formally declared our team as the winners. Jeremy then asked Piers to join him on stage for the presentation and our triumphant team captain made no attempt to disguise the smug satisfaction he clearly felt in finally, after so many failed attempts, managing to put one over his fierce quizzing rivals. Piers gleefully strolled forward to accept the trophy on the team's behalf and throughout the whole of his impromptu acceptance speech, he was once again the target of sustained, good natured booing from the rest of the beaten teams.

Five days after rubbing shoulders with the literary glitterati, my next major engagement was my trip up North to Manchester to present the trophy to the new *Mastermind* Champion on the 8th July. I had planned to travel to Manchester the day before, but those plans had to be immediately shelved on account of the terrible and devastating events of the 7/7 terrorist attacks. Despite the nature and extent of the tragedy and the considerable disruption it caused especially to the transport network in London, the *Mastermind* production team were still keen for me to make it to Manchester that day and they immediately set about the task of making alternative travel arrangements that eventually resulted in me flying up to Manchester instead.

I arrived at the Granada studios just after midday the following day and as I walked through the gates on, I couldn't help feeling like the victorious conqueror returning to the scene of his greatest triumph. I didn't have to wait long I was escorted to the green room where the six Grand Finalists, together with their friends and supporters, were assembled. The atmosphere in the green room had the outward appearance of being relaxed and convivial, but having experienced the pressure cooker type situation only twelve months previously, there was no doubt in my mind that every one of the six competing Finalists were inwardly doing their level best to try to keep any rising tension and inner turmoil they were feeling in check. I recognised Neil

Crockford, the formidable multi *Fifteen-to-One* series winner, and the quizzing legend, Pat Gibson, who had won the one million pound jackpot on *Who Wants To Be a Millionaire?* in 2004, and was attempting to become the second person since David Edwards, to win both the one million pound jackpot and the *Mastermind* title, Derek Moody, a *Mastermind* veteran of some repute who became the series champion on the Channel 4 quiz show, *Number One*, hosted by Krishnan Guru-Murthy in 2001 and Mark Kerr, another top TV quizzer from Liverpool whose impressive TV quizzing CV, aside from the "small matter" of being Pat Gibson's Phone a Friend on Pat's way to winning the million pounds included, winning a quarter of a million pounds for himself on the show (with Pat returning the compliment as Mark's Phone a Friend) and attaining a very creditable third place finish in the Grand Final of *Discovery Mastermind* in 2002.

There was hardly anything to choose between the competing Finalists, and the general knowledge round that would ultimately decide the destiny of the championship was even more competitive and compelling than ever and it was no surprise when Pat Gibson, the last Finalist to face his set of questions in the infamous black chair, despite all of the intolerable pressure and tension, produced a faultless display with one correct answer after another in two minutes, storming through to deservedly take the title. As the studio audience were applauding with all the usual vigour and enthusiasm to reflect Pat's fantastic achievement, John Humphreys, who had moved from his desk to the plinth where the beautiful glass trophy was situated, invited me on to the studio set to present the new champion with his well-earned spoils. *The King is Dead, Long Live the King!* I lamented to myself as I handed over the 2005 trophy to Pat who displayed all the grace and humility that befits a great champion.

I had no intentions of hanging around for the celebrations now that there was a new champion at the helm and I made a swift detour towards my dressing room before changing into more comfortable clothing in preparation for my flight back to London. After gathering all of my belongings, I popped into the green room to say my final farewells. So far as I was concerned, my competitive quizzing days, especially on TV, were consigned to the past and I had no firms plans to resurrect them.

The last of the memorable social engagements that I was involved with during the month of July occurred eight days later when, for the third time in as many months, I was invited to the House of Lords at the Palace of Westminister for a celebration dinner to mark the fiftieth anniversary of the founding of my old secondary school, Copland High. For the occasion, I really pushed the boat out and dressed up to the nines in a smart black Hugo Boss tuxedo suit and black bow tie although in truth, my smart attire was courtesy of my younger brother Steve's hand me ups! The celebration evening really was an exclusive affair which comprised of some (but not all) of the senior current teaching staff that included, the Headmaster Alan Davies, his principal Deputy Richard Noble, and a couple of the teaching staff who were there from my time namely, Sue Dunkley and my old Chemistry teacher Paul Knight. The venue for such an auspicious occasion was fantastic, the food was fantastic, the invited guests were interesting and pleasant to be with, but what made my presence at the event all the more memorable was that, so far as I was aware, out of all of the thousands upon thousands of students, past or present, I was the only one who was invited. I know that such an invite would never had occurred in a million years if I hadn't won *Mastermind* and from a purely cynical perspective, the invite by the school amounted to nothing more than their belated attempts to associate themselves with my success, but whatever lay behind the school's true motives, I saw it as a great and personal honour to have been present to celebrate such an important landmark in the history of Copland High School, an honour that will live with me for the rest of my days.

Towards the end of 2005, my legal career, despite all the endless social engagements and invitations I was involved with was still in a comparatively healthy state, but it had reached the stage where I could no longer continue to practise home. The volume of my work was increasing and it was beginning to create a situation where the cases I was instructed in were starting to clash. It was therefore becoming increasingly clear that I had no real choice other than to join a set of Chambers if I wanted to prevent the possibility of my practice eventually becoming unmanageable. But finding a set Chambers that was suitable wasn't going to be an easy exercise, especially given the various difficulties and disappointments that I had encountered in the past during the course of my career as a tenant and I must admit, the very thought of once again becoming a member of a set of Chambers, to some extent, filled me with a considerable degree of reluctance. Whilst I was hardly in a position to claim that I was spoilt for choice in that regard, there was however one possible option that was open to me and that led me to contacting a dear my old friend and colleague, Andrew Hill who by this time was the Head of Chambers at Farringdon Chambers based in Bermondsey Street, a stone's throw away from London Bridge, in order to discuss the possibility of becoming a full time tenant at his Chambers.

Farringdon Chambers is a set that specialises almost exclusively in criminal defence work and was set up towards the end of the 1990's when Andy, together with his fellow colleagues Ian Henderson, Martin McCarthy, Franco Tizzano and Alex Dunn, decided to set up their own Chambers so they'd have an equal say in the way the Chambers would be run along democratic and egalitarian lines. This modern and innovative approach of running a set of Chambers would be in complete contrast to the way a traditional set of Chambers are normally run in the saturated heartlands of Holborn and The Temple where outright ownership of the building from where a Chambers operates is, in a word, impossible.

With the recruitment of the experienced Clerking duo, Del Edgeler and David Seal from 8 King's Bench Walk as their Senior Clerks, Andy and the rest of his colleagues grabbed the proverbial bull by the horns and set about the task of putting their ground breaking vision of the modern set of chambers in motion, setting up the Chambers in offices on the Farringdon Road before relocating to its present site at the start of the new millennium, growing and blossoming year after year. Farringdon Chambers has come a very long way in a short space of time.

Andy had made tentative overtures to me in the past about joining his set however, for one reason or another I wasn't in a position to take up his offer but when I finally summoned up the effort and contacted him to ask whether the offer was still available, Andy told me that so far as he was concerned, he would be more than happy to welcome me on board, but it wasn't a decision that he himself could make alone. He went on to add that he would make the necessary arrangements for me to have an informal interview with the Management Committee as all tenancy applications, irrespective who they were submitted by, would be decided purely on its merits.

My interview with the Management Committee took place a week before Christmas and it went really well. I didn't have to wait long before I received written notification that my tenancy interview was successful and I made arrangements with Chambers that I would join them at the end of January 2006. The day I formally joined Farringdon Chambers, the members held a drinks party to welcome me on board. It was the perfect convivial setting in which to meet and get to know colleagues some of whom I was meeting for the first time such as, Molly Pinkus, Claire Davies, Gareth Morley, Fergus Malone, Paul Stanislas, Mary Lawrenson and Chris Whitehouse. I also reprised an old friendship with the likes of Charles John-Jules in what would be the third different set of Chambers in which both Charles and I would be working together. By welcoming me into the fold,

Farringdon Chambers offered me the professional security and stability that my practice had not enjoyed since leaving New Court Chambers four years ago. It was an opportunity I was grateful for and I was determined to justify their faith in me and prove my worth. I settled in very quickly to life as a tenant at my new Chambers winning my first couple of trials and that helped set the tone for the remainder of the year. I was really pleased with the progress I was making and that was a view that was shared by my Head of Chambers Andy who played a significant role in helping to secure my tenancy in the first place and my Clerks, Del and David, who were constantly keeping me busy with good, quality work. I had every reason to be full of optimism that Farringdon Chambers was going to be the springboard that would take my career to the next level.

Despite my rededication and commitment to my legal career, my services in terms of both public and media engagements were still sought after although it would be fair to say, it was nowhere near the stratospheric levels of the previous two years. I was doing regular monthly media stints on the radio as guest panellist on the late night shows on Radio 5 Live and in the Autumn of 2007, I was commissioned by Radio 4 to present a programme that traced the history and development of the Dewey Decimal System. The programme itself was quite well received. It even managed to be selected as the "Radio Pick of the Day" in some national newspapers although one notable critic from the Times was not so gracious with his review of my presenting abilities by commenting that, "the story was better than the teller."

In May 2007, The FA finally honoured their promise of two VIP tickets to the FA Cup Final and, although it had been almost two years in the making, it really was well worth the wait. As promised, I took Myles along with me for the first FA Cup Final to be held at the new revamped Wembley Stadium and it was the final we both wanted to see: my beloved Chelsea against his Manchester United. The day itself was a truly memorable affair which began with lunch in the presence of The President of the Football Association, HRH Prince William of Wales and HRH Prince Henry (Harry), alongside well over one hundred famous footballing personalities past and present who have gone down in FA Cup Final folklore. To be in the presence of so many footballing heroes of mine that I idolised as a young boy was an opportunity I was not going to let pass me by and once we had all finished our lunch, I went around the entire room and asked for as many autographs that I could from footballing legends ranging from Bobby Smith, the goal scoring centre forward from Tottenham Hotspur's 1961 Double winning team, to Arsenal's Ian Wright, the goal scoring hero of his team's 1993 victory over Sheffield Wednesday. As for the game itself, it wasn't the classic everyone was hoping for to grace the new stadium but myself and the rest of the Chelsea faithful fans did not mind one little bit because nine minutes from the end of extra time, Chelsea's Didier Drogba and Frank Lampard played a brilliant one-two on the edge of United's Penalty Area, a move that put Drogba through to score the glorious winning goal and give my beloved Blues their second trophy of the season, a victory that not only deprived Manchester United the possibility of landing yet another Premier League and FA Cup Double, it also gave me the pure and unadulterated satisfaction of seeing the look of utter dejection and anguish on my nephew's face during Chelsea's joyful celebrations as the team deservedly paraded the famous old trophy to every part of the newly built stadium.

There was also an opportunity to make my first television appearance in almost two years when I was invited to take part on the BBC2 quiz show, *Identity,* hosted by Donny Osmond, a quiz show that involved contestants trying to correctly guess the identities of twelve random strangers, with each correct answer given allowing the contestant to climb The Money Ladder from an initial cash sum of £250, all the way up to jackpot of £10,000. The identities of the strangers varied from Guitar Player, Carpenter, Opera Singer, to a stranger who had "met their husband on the internet", a Surfing Champion and a stranger who was a Pagan. The identity the contestant had to correctly guess in my case was rather appropriately, a *Mastermind* Champion. Throughout the game the role of the strangers was restricted solely to standing completely still on a podium (I was selected to stand on Podium number seven), without saying a word other than to confirm or refute their identity if they were selected by the contestant and once a contestant had made their choice, they locked in that choice by pressing a button on their podium. The contestant seeking to win the £10,000 jackpot on the show I was appearing on was Lynne McKeone from Staffordshire, who had with her on stage in Supporter's Row, her friends and family in the form of her brother-in-law, Malcolm and close friends Kate and Angie.

Lynne got off to the perfect start in her quest to win the jackpot by correctly identifying the identities of the first seven strangers without resorting to the use of any of her designated lifelines whilst managing to accumulate for herself a healthy £2,000 in the process. Whether it was a case of outrageous good luck or good sound judgement on her part, Lynne was on course to make a clean sweep of twelve correct answers in a row and after she correctly identified the female stranger who had "met her husband on the internet," Donny then turned to Lynne for her next choice and she elected to solve the identity of the *Mastermind* Champion.

Donny turned to Lynne after she made her choice and asked her, "WHO IS EXTREMELY INTELLIGENT UP THERE? WHO COULD WIN *MASTERMIND*?"

After casting her eye over the remaining five strangers on the stage, Lynne made her choice and responded by saying, "I'M GOING TO GO BACK TO WHAT I THOUGHT WHEN I FIRST WALKED ON TO THE STAGE, AND I'M GOING TO SEAL IT WITH NUMBER ONE."

"WHY DID YOU SETTLE ON NUMBER ONE?" Donny asked.

Lynne replied, "I THINK I RECOGNISE HIM ALTHOUGH I THINK IT WAS QUITE A WHILE AGO."

"ARE YOU WILLING TO PUT £3,000 ON THAT DECISION? YOU'RE SAYING THAT THE MASTERMIND CHAMPION IS STRANGER NUMBER ONE?"

With confidence, she replied, "I'M GOING TO SEAL MY ANSWER," and with that, Lynne locked in her choice by pressing her button on her podium.

Donny asked Lynne whether there were any slight doubts with her choice and despite Lynne's honest admission that there were some doubts in her mind, she was still nevertheless happy with her eventual choice. Donny then turned to the stranger on Podium one and asked, "PODIUM NUMBER ONE, *MASTERMIND* CHAMPION. IS THAT YOUR IDENTITY?" For dramatic effect, there followed a three to five second momentary pause intertwined with a short, piercing sound of violins reaching its crescendo. The time had now arrived for the moment of truth and the bespectacled stranger responded to Donny's question with the words,

"I'M SORRY LYNNE, I AM NOT YOUR *MASTERMIND* CHAMPION."

There was a distinctive, deafening silence in the studio that was shattered by audible groans of disappointment as everyone in the studio came to terms with the first incorrect choice Lynne had made in the entire game which, given her faultless display up to that point, was unexpected. As I stood on my podium watching events unfold, the thoughts racing through my mind were that despite desperately wanting Lynne to win the jackpot, I thought it was just brilliant that she chose someone else other than me as the *Mastermind* Champion.

Article in the Guardian, 1993

Return to Copeland High School after they saw my article in the Guardian, 1994

The infamous spiral staircase!

Case History 1
Shaun Wallace --

AT HIS first trial at Bristol Crown Court, Shaun Wallace (above) was mistaken for a defendant. "I still see myself as an outsider looking in," he says.

With his razor haircut, 33-year old Wallace looks more like the footballer he once wanted to be than the identikit, pin stripe suited barrister.

His background, too, is at odds with the Bar's traditional public school Oxbridge image: the son of Jamaican born parents from Wembley, West London, he went to the local comprehensive and on to a law degree at North London polytechnic, qualifying as a barrister in 1984.

"I had great difficulty in obtaining a pupillage, first because my face didn't fit because of my colour and background and because I refused to be a sycophant, and second because of my own individuality. I've had a razor haircut from the year dot and I used to wear a diamond earring.

"I've had some real dark days. I made countless applications for pupillage. I had to serve my apprenticeship in what are wrongly referred to as 'ghetto' chambers — set up by black lawyers rejected by white chambers. Then I applied to a fairly good white set and I was rejected." After "squatting" there for 18 months — allowed to pick up work but not given a permanent place — he became disillusioned and went off to Brazil.

"I came back in 1989 and joined another black set as a tenant. From there my career took off in a whole year, I never lost a trial." But the chambers broke up. "Petty squabbling and in-house fighting led to the members going their own ways.

"I joined my present chambers in 1990 — multi racial chambers predominantly doing housing work. I do crime, employment law and a bit of family law. I'm happy there for now. Because I am ambitious, if chambers don't answer my ambitions I'll be off to pastures new. I want to go to the top.

"We're breaking down barriers now. The colour of your skin shouldn't be detrimental provided you've got that desire to succeed. We have made great strides compared to a generation ago, though we are being wrongly denied the right to practice in certain fields — commercial law, taxation — which seem to be based on the old school tie."

Brent Cup Final, Wembley Stadium

Jamaica trip, 1998

Fifteen-To-One, October 1999

The Waiting Game with Heather Thomas, September 2001

The Weakest Link, 2001

Chasing the Dream

The Weakest Link, 2001

Greed, June 2001

Me and my trophy, and
Mastermind Article,
December 2004

Mastermind Grand Final, 2005

Mastermind's quick answers

BY PAUL KEILTHY

THE limelight found Shaun Wallace in a famous black chair last year and he is reluctant to relinquish it.

Winner of the 2004 Mastermind contest, Mr Wallace meets his next challenge by standing as an independent candidate for the Brent South seat in the General Election on Thursday.

"The one thing the national parties do not do is engage with the local people – they only see them once every four of five years," Mr Wallace told the Times on Friday.

"I'm standing to try and give effective representation as far as the people of Brent South are concerned, and I'm standing on a platform that is dear to my heart – education."

Brent-born, he believes local students are not getting the chance to reach their full potential in an education system that has become financially more risky since the introduction of top-up fees.

He also feels that the large black population in Brent faces a 'financial stranglehold', basing his theory

Shaun Wallace: Need for 'effective representation'

on his experience both as a part-time lecturer and as a black student.

"We've always been at the bottom of the pile," he said.

Wallace is a defence barrister and has worked on cases throughout the borough, an experience which has shaped his 'zero tolerance' approach to crime.

While he has defended a number of youths charged with firearms offences, he recalls seeing one police appeal showing a picture of a victim in particular: "I looked at his poster and took his face out and transposed my own. That could have been me."

This personal touch and local

knowledge should be the envy of any independent, and may well win him votes at the poll.

On Harlesden High Street when we met for interview, Mr Wallace's approach seemed to be gaining support. Jerry Anderson, owner of Hawkeye records, claimed to speak for many in the community when he said he had not voted since 1987, when he had supported Paul Boateng only to be let down when he 'went native' in the political establishment. "We want a politician who'll fight our corner," he said, endorsing Wallace, independent, with a poster in his window.

paul.keilthy@archant.co.uk

2005 General Election Manifesto

LMU Talk, Feb 2005

Shaun
Wallace
wins
Mastermind
2004

Shaun Wallace returns to London Met

THE CHELSEA FAN WHO HAS ALL THE ANSWERS

Game Shaun won't forget

FA Cup Final, 2007

SHAUN'S FA CUP MASTERMIND

1 How many different teams have won the FA Cup?

2 Who is the last player to play in three FA Cup finals at Wembley for three different clubs and lose each time?

3 Former Bolton goalkeeper Dick Pym holds which distinction in FA Cup final history?

4 Who is the youngest player to score in an FA Cup final?

5 Who is the last player to score in every round of the FA Cup?

Answers on Page 35 (below Paper Talk)

BRAD ASHTON

WHATEVER happens in Saturday's FA Cup final, it is sure to live long in the memory of one Chelsea fan.

Shaun Wallace, a lifelong Wembley resident, is an expert on the end-of-season showpiece.

In 2004 he became grand Mastermind champion with his specialist subject being FA Cup finals.

And Shaun is thrilled that the event is returning to its spiritual home.

He said: "One of the things I like about living in Wembley is when you tell people where you live, everyone has heard of it and knows about the FA Cup. It's one of the most famous places on Earth."

Saturday marks the return of the event to Wembley Stadium, following six finals at Cardiff's Millennium Stadium.

And Shaun admits: "I have missed it. The only thing I haven't missed is the traffic."

Shaun, a practising barrister who admits he has "a passion for learning", discovered his fascination with football as a youngster.

He explains: "The first final I watched was in 1967 when Tottenham beat Chelsea 2-1. I didn't really know much about football at the time and just decided to support the team in the dark shirts.

"But from then I started concentrating more on football and watching the cup final every year because almost a religion."

Shaun, a guest of the FA this weekend, is confident Chelsea will score only their second FA Cup victory over Manchester United to gain revenge for the 4-0 drubbing in the 1994 final.

He said: "To me it's the classic final - the last team to win the cup at the old Wembley playing the team that has won it more than anybody else."

MASTERMIND | Shaun Wallace loves the FA Cup

Me and Barry on
Are You an
Egghead?

Dad's 80th Birthday celebrations

Donny turned to the slightly disconsolate looking Lynne and said to her in a soothing, reassuring voice that she was not to worry before reminding her that she still was saved by her first lifeline that allows a contestant to make one incorrect selection and still remain in the game.

Lynne decided to ask for help from her Panel of Experts. Donny asked her which of the remaining identities did she want to solve and she replied, "LET'S STICK WITH THE MASTERMIND CHAMPION."

The Panel of Experts unanimously agreed I was the only one who could be the *Mastermind* champion. Lynne went with their advice, and pressed the button on her podium to lock in her choice.

Donny, with a supporting arm around Lynne's shoulders, turned directly towards me and posed the question that could make or break Lynne's relentless quest for ultimate quizzing glory. "FOR £3,000, STRANGER NUMBER SEVEN, *MASTERMIND* CHAMPION, IS THAT YOUR IDENTITY?"

Once again, the short musical interlude could be heard throughout the studio and with a cold steely gaze that gave nothing away, I finally revealed the truth paraphrasing the programme's most famous catchphrase: "LYNNE, YOU STARTED SO I'LL FINISH. YES, I AM THE *MASTERMIND* CHAMPION!"

Lynne had won herself £3,000 and from that point on she never looked back, managing with use of her remaining lifeline to solve the remaining four identities on her way to winning the £10,000 jackpot.

My appearance on *Identity*, despite not being an actual competitor on the show, had the considerable and notable effect of whetting my appetite for a possible return to competitive TV quizzing and that wishful desire was eventually translated into a firm plan of action when, in September 2007, I managed to assemble together a quiz team of my own to take on a team who has been frequently described as probably, "the greatest quiz team in Britain", the formidable Eggheads from the popular BBC2 quiz show. The Eggheads team were on a long, unbeaten run, the longest unbeaten run in the show's four year history that saw the rolled over prize fund surpass the eye watering total of £70,000! The challenge of toppling the seemingly invincible Eggheads team was a challenge that I felt I could not let pass me by. I needed to find a team of four equally good quizzers who were hungry, competitive and up for the challenge of giving the much vaunted Eggheads more than a run for their money. It didn't take me long to assemble together a set of individuals who matched the criteria I was looking for by virtue of getting in contact with a recent acquaintance of mine, Steven Walker, a solicitor who I first met at a garden party at Lincoln's-Inns Fields in summer of 2005. At the garden party, Steven and one of the partners in his firm, Lee Xavier, noticed me standing alone on the periphery of the event, barely mingling with the other invited guests, which prompted the pair of them to come over to me. For the time I spent in the group's company, we got on like a house on fire, talking on a range of subject from law to my *Mastermind* exploits (Steven and Lee told me from the outset that they had recognised me) to discovering that the group were a pretty formidable quiz team in their own right as a result of having recently retained their title at the annual London Legal Quiz Championship. Then completely out of the blue and much to my surprise and delight, Steven invited me to join both him and the rest of his colleagues to dinner to celebrate their championship victory at Michael Caine's swanky restaurant Lagan's Brasserie the following week, an invitation which I gladly accepted that turned out to be a repeat of the pleasant convivial evening that was the feature of my first encounter with Steven and the rest of his colleagues with their impressive silver trophy taking pride of place at the centre of the dining table.

Steven was clearly up for the challenge when I put the proposal of taking on the Eggheads to him, and he invited me to his offices where I could meet his colleagues, Lee and Phillipa, who would take two other spots on the team. I suggested that Steven should be the team's captain and therefore would be the main point of contact in any dealings with the *Eggheads* production team. We then filled in the *Eggheads* application form and after its completion, I left it with Steven to decide and select the team's final two members. A couple of days later, Steven called me with the exciting news that our team which he decided to call, curiously, The Wrinklies, had been invited for an audition at the production team's offices in the West End. Our audition took place a couple of days later and it was a complete success. A couple of days later, Steven contacted me again to inform me of the exciting news that the team had been selected to take on the Eggheads, the date of our recording to take place on 22nd September. I could hardly contain the near stratospheric levels of excitement I felt at the prospect of taking on the mighty Eggheads and almost immediately, my preparations for the show began in earnest. However, all that hard work and preparation for the team's appearance on the show turned out to be all in vain because only three days prior to our scheduled appearance, Steven rang me at home and revealed the disappointing news that the team had been inexplicably dropped. I asked Steven if he knew why the show's producers had suddenly dropped our team, but he didn't know. After our conversation, which was just as painful and devastating as if I'd been punched on the jaw by Mike Tyson, I attempted to analyse the reasons why the team was suddenly dropped from the recording schedule and after going through all the possible permutations in my mind, I could only come up with one reason: my quizzing credentials. They must have questioned the wisdom of allowing someone with my quizzing pedigree the green light to appear on the show with more than a fair chance of winning a substantial sum of money. But there was nothing I could do about the decision to drop the team because the producer's decision as to who or who may not appear on the show is final. Whatever the reasons behind the producer's decision, there was no disguising my feelings of bitter disappointment in being deprived of the chance of winning a big cash prize, there was also the added disappointment of being deprived the chance to meet and pit my wits against a collection of quiz legends whom I've admired and respected for a very long time.

The disappointment of being denied the opportunity to compete against the Eggheads quiz team was firmly put into real perspective when some six or so weeks later, myself and the rest of my family had to endure a two month period of constant anxiety and uncertainty which I can honestly say was the most challenging and worrying time of my life. Without warning, my 79 year old father had become gravely ill. I had been having growing concerns for some time about Dad's increasing physical frailty, a man who for the last twenty-five years at least, had to cope with, the onset of diabetes. My ongoing concern for Dad's health was brought into sharp focus when I went to see him on one of my regular visits towards the end of October. I was immediately alarmed by the sight of his right eye that all of a sudden had become so grotesquely swollen and misshapen, anyone looking at it would have thought that Dad had just completed twelve rounds with Muhammad Ali. When I took him to task about the condition of his eye, he was his usual reticent self. I was under no illusions that given Dad's age and ever increasing frailty, the grim reaper could strike at any moment and with that nightmare scenario at the forefront of my mind, I told Dad that I was going to take him to hospital right away for an urgent medical examination. Dad, being his usual proud and at times stubborn self, appeared to be in no mood to be dictated to or to be told what to do, least of all from his eldest born son, and in a futile attempt designed to assuage my fears and concerns, he told me that he already had an appointment the following Tuesday and that I shouldn't worry. Dad's feeble attempt to show that all was well with him was anything but convincing and although I was prepared to wait until that hospital appointment, I told him that both myself and Steve would be keeping a close eye on him to make sure that he was all right and I made him promise that he shouldn't hesitate to contact either one of us if he was feeling unwell, no matter what time of day.

I was scheduled to host a Black History Month Quiz Event for Brent Libraries at the Willesden Library which is just under a mile away from Dad's home that following evening and I asked Dad and Steve if they wanted to come and support me, which they readily agreed to.

The quiz night itself was a great success and thoroughly enjoyed by the participating teams, the only slight drawback being that my father and brother only managed to arrive towards the end of the evening. Whilst I was naturally pleased that the pair of them turned up albeit extremely late, the underlying fears that I had for my Dad's physical wellbeing immediately re-surfaced as he shuffled towards me with the aid of his walking stick, looking even more frail and poorly than when I last had seen only twenty-four hours previously. I asked Dad how he was feeling and he replied in a tone that was less than convincing that he was OK. I turned to Steve and asked why they had arrived at the event so late and in an apologetic tone, he replied that he finished work late and couldn't get out in time. Steve then said that he was going to take Dad home who, by this time, was looking extremely tired. I asked Dad if he wanted to come and stay with me for the night but once again, he insisted that he would be OK and I should stop worrying and moments later, both he and Steve left the venue.

I rang Dad the following day at lunchtime as I was anxious to find out how the hospital appointment went but to my dismay, he told me that he didn't go because the Tuesday he was referring to was the following week on the 6th November. After court, I went to visit him that evening to satisfy myself that he wasn't giving me the run around and asked to see the letter concerning his hospital appointment and when he showed it to me, the date for the appointment was indeed for the following Tuesday. So, until the date of the appointment, I would be keeping an ever watchful, ever vigilant eye on him.

In the week leading up to that appointment, both Steve and I would take it in turn to either phone or visit Dad every day and despite his eye still being in the same grotesque swollen state, his general physical state seemed to have improved considerably. However, I couldn't have been more wrong in thinking that. I received a telephone call from Steve who informed me that Dad had collapsed during his hospital appointment and had to be immediately rushed to hospital. I arrived at the A&E Department to find Dad propped up on a bed with saline drips connected to his arms with Steve standing close by. Although Dad was alert, he looked extremely weak. It broke my heart to see my father in that way but I know he was pleased that his two sons were at his bedside. I asked Steve what had happened and he could only reiterate what he had told me earlier on the phone and that the hospital were conducting a number of tests, the results of which were not known yet. Both Steve and I remained at our father's bedside for the next couple of hours by which time, the hospital had decided that they were going to keep him in overnight. Steve and I then went to Dad's flat to collect some of his belongings before returning to the hospital for what we assumed would be just a short overnight stay but the following day, the hospital informed the pair of us that Dad's poor state of health had taken a significant turn for the worse and by the time I went to see him that evening, he was drifting in and out of consciousness and breathing erratically with the aid of an Oxygen mask. I asked the medical staff nursing him for a report and they told me that he began hyperventilating that afternoon so as a precautionary measure, it was decided that Dad should be given an Oxygen mask to assist him and help regulate his breathing. I felt completely helpless when I saw my poorly stricken father lying in his hospital bed in a semi-conscious state, showing visible signs of distress. I constantly tried to reassure Dad that I was there for him whilst I was engaged at the same time in a constant struggle trying to prevent him pulling the mask from his face, a situation that went on for some time until the Staff Nurse assigned to care for him, gave him a dose of medication that had the merciful effect of eventually sedating him. I stayed with Dad until the medication finally took effect and by the time I arrived home later that night exhausted and extremely worried, I was facing up to the real possibility that my father might not be physically strong enough to survive his ordeal and the mere thought of that nightmare scenario caused me to burst into floods of tears. I eventually crawled into bed and the only thing that was racing through my mind was whether I could or should, have done more to keep a constant eye on him and I began to ask myself how would I feel if he didn't make it through this testing time. I spoke to the man upstairs, asking him, pleading with him, that he would somehow find it in his infinite wisdom and help my Dad survive his terrible ordeal.

My increasingly desperate pleas for divine intervention looked as though they were going to go unanswered. At approximately 4.30am that morning, I was awoken by the sound of the telephone ringing. I was terrified, my heart was pounding, I knew I had to answer the telephone, but I could barely gather the strength to do it. When at last I did, it was as I suspected. Someone from Central Middlesex Hospital told me in a calm, quiet voice, that I should make my way to the hospital as soon as was possible because my father's condition was steadily deteriorating and there was a real possibility that he might not survive. The harrowing news immediately shook me out of my disconcerted state and I got myself dressed and rushed to the hospital as quickly as I could. As I approached the Roundwood Suite ward where Dad was being treated, my heart began pounding so hard, I thought it was going to leap out of my chest. The Nurse on duty informed me that Dad had been transferred to the Intensive Care Unit at Hammersmith Hospital. Steve had also arrived by this time and although my father's life was balancing on a knife's edge, I was just grateful and relieved by the news that my father was still alive. The only thoughts in our minds was to get to our father's bedside as quickly as possible. We collected all his personal belongings we had brought in the night before last from his bedside before setting off for the hospital and among those belongings, I noticed the silver St. Christopher pendant and chain that he always wore around his neck, lying next to his Bible on the bedside cabinet. I picked up the pendant and put it in my pocket and whilst doing so, I kept telling myself over and over again in my mind that with the man upstairs' grace and blessing, one of the first things I would do if Dad managed to survive his ordeal would be to put the pendant and chain around his neck myself personally as a mark of triumph and celebration in having overcome the toughest journey of his life.

Once Steve and I had arrived at the hospital, we enquired whether it was possible to see Dad, but we were told that we could but not straight away as he was being attended to by a medical team who were monitoring his progress and that someone from that team would be out shortly to inform us about his current condition. We didn't have to wait long before we were approached by a Doctor who told us that Dad had suffered multiple major organ failure but they were unsure, at this stage, as to the reason(s) for its cause. He went on to add that his team had managed to stabilize Dad's condition. Both Steve and I asked whether we could see him briefly and the Doctor said that we could, but we would have to wear a disposable surgical mask and gown as a precaution. After putting on the equipment supplied, the pair of us walked into the room where we were confronted by the heart breaking sight of our much loved father, lying heavily sedated on a hospital bed connected up to machines and an intravenous drip, wearing an oxygen mask, his upper torso covered with a transparent plastic sheet designed to prevent him from contracting an infection. In all my years on this earth, this scene that confronted me was, without doubt, the worst that I had ever laid eyes on, a sight made all the more worse for the fact that there was nothing that I could do to alter it. My only crumb of comfort was the fact that Dad was still alive and fighting and that was something given the serious nature of the situation that I had to be grateful for. I went up to the side of his bed and gently took hold of his hand, standing silently in prayer for a while as once again I looked skywards to the man upstairs asking him to give my father the strength, courage and fortitude to see him through this most difficult of journeys and whilst I was doing so, Steve was looking on, no doubt, engaged in his own private prayer. With one last gentle squeeze of his hand, I whispered my goodbyes to Dad adding that I would see him soon even though I knew full well that he wasn't able to respond given his heavily sedated state, but I still hoped that my genuine heartfelt messages of love and support would somehow get through to him. There was hardly a word said between my brother and I, a combination of the sheer trauma of the whole ordeal, coupled with the relief that Dad was still managing to cling on to life and after a brotherly hug and a fist bump, we went our separate ways. Feeling extremely tired and emotional, I got home just after 6.30 in the morning but instead of heading for the comfort of my bed, I headed straight for the bathroom and filled the bath tub with piping hot water for a long soak which I hoped would revive as well as re-energise both my body and mind in preparation for the trial I was starting at the Inner London Crown Court later that morning.

I rang my chambers and spoke to our recently appointed Chambers' Clerk of some six months, Michael Bazeley, to inform him of the situation. Michael suggested that if I didn't feel up to doing the trial, he would arrange for suitable cover to replace me. I told him that despite the situation, it would be unfair at such a late stage for my client to see a last-minute change of Counsel and that I would be doing the trial. Even though Dad was gravely ill, there was little or nothing I could do about it. Furthermore, I am a professional with responsibilities both to my client and to my profession as a whole and as long as I felt able enough to do the trial then I would do it and at the end of the day, it didn't really matter how long the worrying situation surrounding my father's short term and long term health issues was going to last. Somehow, someway, I would have to juggle those important competing priorities.

For the next eight weeks, Dad remained in the Intensive Care Unit in a coma, connected to various tubes, wires and drips that were keeping his body, that had now swollen to frighteningly grotesque proportions, barely alive. The daily medical bulletins on his condition varied between stable and critical and on two particularly hair-raising occasions, Dad actually suffered a mild cardiac arrest, but nevertheless managed somehow to survive those ordeals. During this tense and critical time, Debbie, Steve, myself and my elder sister Rose, who by this time had flown in from New York on ten days' compassionate leave, between us made sure that Dad had a strong family presence at his bedside every day. As the news of Dad's illness spread throughout the community, he began to receive a constant stream of visitors as well as numerous messages of prayers and support from members of his church and long-time friends and acquaintances, all of which were gratefully received by the whole of the family. The high volume of visitors and messages of support was a real testament of how well loved and respected my old man was by so many people. Despite Dad being completely oblivious to the constant stream of visitors at his bedside, all of the Wallace siblings were doing everything in their collective power to try and reach the depths of his subconsciousness in the vain hope that he would somehow hear us and know that we were there. Debbie for example, during her visits, would read passages from the Bible to him. Steve would read sections of the newspapers to him on account of Dad's love for keeping abreast of current affairs. Every time I visited him, I would gently take hold of Dad's hand and constantly tell him how much I loved and respected him and that how much the whole family were all looking forward to the day he would make a complete recovery.

Slowly, but surely, Dad finally regained consciousness sometime in mid-December. He was still very ill but nevertheless appeared to be winning the battle for survival. The eight long nightmarish weeks Dad spent in a coma had clearly taken its toll on him, a fact that was evident when his previously grotesque swollen body had changed into an almost skeletal state. After having regained consciousness, the clear and unmistakable sign that Dad was winning his fight for survival came in the form of his increasing ability to recognise familiar faces that were surrounding him and he would try to communicate his acknowledgement by either the flickering of his eyes, or a smile on his face. Sadly at this stage, Dad was not able to verbally communicate with anyone on account of the catheter tube protruding from his throat that was helping to clear all the excess phlegm that had settled on both his chest and lungs.

Once Dad had fully regained consciousness and they were satisfied that his life was no longer in danger, his medical team then set about the task of planning the next stage of his recovery. That next stage involved setting up a carefully structured physiotherapy programme in order to help Dad regain basic physical mobility as his muscles had wasted away to such an extent that everyday things that we would normally take for granted, like sitting in a chair, standing upright or walking even the shortest step, were way beyond his capability. The fortnight leading up to Christmas saw Dad making gradual but steady progress to such an extent, that his medical team took the decision to move him out of the ICU on the second floor up to the fourth floor so that they could continue their careful monitoring of his small but gradual signs of improvement. Christmas Day itself was a special time and the best Christmas present of all was my Dad being around to enjoy it, the highlight of which from my own poignant and personal point of view was when I put his silver St Christopher pendant around his neck as a mark to celebrate the fact that his near life threatening journey was all but behind him. That scenario seemed to be a long way away a few weeks earlier and there are no words and thoughts in existence that would do justice to how thankful and grateful I was that my old man was still here, alive and kicking. I did what little I could in terms of trying to help Dad regain his physical mobility and independence giving him all the support and encouragement when visiting him, like helping him to walk with the aid of his Zimmer frame, or doing leg stretching and other gentle exercises which I always finished off by giving him a full body massage. Steve and I both took the joint responsibility in terms of his general grooming and appearance, the both of us clubbing together to buy him some new clothes for him to wear whilst in hospital and in preparation for when he would be considered well enough to eventually return home. Occasionally, Steve would take it upon himself to shave him, a feat he would always do with particular skill and care, where as I on the other hand, would take responsibility for both manicure and pedicure duties as the nails on both his hands and feet were beginning to resemble claw like talons and there was more dead skin on the soles of his heels than you would see at the local taxidermist.

The constant presence of seeing all his children regularly also played an important and significant role in Dad's eventual recovery, but the real people who must ultimately take all credit for his recovery was everyone associated with Dad medical and aftercare throughout his time at the Hammersmith ICU. Everyone who had been involved with his care at the unit were clearly rather fond of "Our Linford" as he was affectionately referred to occasionally, and if it wasn't for the unwavering dedication and commitment that Dad received from the minute he entered the ICU with his life hanging in the balance from the medical staff to those involved with his aftercare, there is little doubt in my mind that he would not have survived and because of that dedication and commitment, both myself and the rest of my family will always be forever indebted and eternally grateful, to all the staff at the Hammersmith Intensive Care Unit.

Dad remained at Hammersmith Hospital for a further three to four weeks before he was transferred to the convalescing unit at the Willesden General Hospital in preparation for when he would be well enough to go home. The whole family were naturally looking forward to his eventual homecoming, but that joy was tempered by the real and obvious concern that given Dad's age and ever increasing frailty, would he be able to cope living on his own? Steve even suggested that Dad could live with him as he had more than enough room to accommodate his presence that would have the added advantage of my brother being able to keep a watchful eye over him. Despite our genuine and altruistic motives with regards to our father's general wellbeing, the man at the centre of those discussions had other ideas. Dad made the position of his future living arrangements abundantly clear, insisting that despite our best intentions, he wanted to return to his flat for the reasons both Steve and I totally understood and respected. All his friends who would come to visit him and vice versa as well as the Baptist Church that he goes to every Sunday were close by and he would be be isolated from all of that if he moved to my brother's house in Kew. Furthermore, he argued, he had been living on his own for almost forty years and whilst he was proud of the fact that his children were willing to bend over backwards to look after him in his twilight years, he didn't want to be seen to be a burden to anyone, despite such thoughts being the farthest thing from our minds.

Dad's arguments for independence eventually won us over but it was a victory that was not entirely without compromise. Dad was sensible enough to realise that despite his desire to be as independent as possible, he was going to need daily help and support to achieve that aim. Steve contacted Brent Social Services to discuss what help they could provide in preparation for when he eventually returned to his flat and for the daily care and support he would need thereafter. Thankfully, Brent Social Services acted swiftly in response to my brother's request and after carrying out a fairly detailed assessment on both Dad and his home, Social Services set about the task of putting in place an action plan designed to help Dad cope without compromising both his independence and dignity. That help and assistance took the form of cosmetic changes to flat such as an additional hand rail to help Dad climb the stairs to his flat as well as a hand rail to help him in and out of his bath. There was also a daily helper who would clean his flat and bring him meals and a nurse to ensure that he was given the daily medication for his diabetes. With those crucial forms of support firmly in place, Dad was finally allowed to return home towards the end of January 2008, to the relief and joy of the whole of his family and to mark the occasion, both Steve and I accompanied Dad to his Baptist Church on the Willesden High Road for prayers and celebration alongside the rest of his fellow congregation who were equally thankful that Dad had managed to recover from his life threatening ordeal as the Pastor of the church in those thoughts and prayers asked the man upstairs to give our father the ability and the strength to be able cope and manage his life from here on in. Those thoughts and prayers appeared to have been answered because over the next four or so months, Dad was looking as fit and healthy than at any time in many a long while, long enough to celebrate a day which during the tense and worrying months of November and December of 2007, Steve, Debbie and Rose and myself thought that our father would not have been around to have witnessed, the occasion of his eightieth birthday.

The four of us had briefly spoken about how wonderful it would be to have a celebration to mark Dad's birthday during those dark and uncertain times when he was lying in his hospital bed fighting for his life, a wish which given the critical nature of the situation at the time, was more in tune with desperate hope as opposed to expectation. So for Dad to have gone through such a difficult ordeal, survive that ordeal and go on to make a full recovery, the four of us were determined to make the special day of his 80th birthday a day he will always remember.

The 24th of May 2008, as luck would have it, fell on a Saturday, and on that day three generations of the immediate Wallace clan, comprising of his four children, four grandchildren and two great-grandchildren, were all gathered together for the first time on a sunny spring afternoon at Steve's house in Kew for what turned out to be a truly wonderfully intimate family affair. After consuming the wonderfully prepared brunch by my sister-in-law Lavinia in their spacious garden, the whole of the Wallace clan gathered around the man of the hour to sing a rousing rendition of Happy Birthday before adults and youngers alike, spent the remainder of the afternoon having fun in the sun in each other's company all under Dad's watchful gaze in the comfort of an armchair that was strategically placed on the edge of the patio overlooking the garden. I can't begin to imagine how happy and proud Dad must have felt witnessing three generations of his family having fun and enjoying themselves on his special day and to mark the occasion, I arranged for my good friend of mine, Ken Grant, who is an accomplished photographer, to take a series of photographs that captured the joyful mood of the whole afternoon, the highlight of which was the family portrait photograph with Dad as the focal point surrounded by adoring members of his family. A week after the birthday celebrations, Ken put all the photos together in a beautiful leather-bound album which Steve and I later presented to Dad on one of our regular visits. Dad was so chuffed at the gift that it bought a tear to his eye and his reaction and appreciation for his special day brought home to me how much I love and respect my father and what he would always mean to me. I know that one day there will come a time when Dad will leave us for good, which I know will have a devastating impact upon me personally, but until that day arrives, both myself and the rest of my family, will treasure each precious day that he's here.

CHAPTER TWENTY-ONE

A week or so before Dad's birthday celebrations, I was at home relaxing in the afternoon after the case I was instructed in at Harrow Crown Court had fortuitously finished early that morning. That rare moment of tranquillity was interrupted suddenly by a telephone call that came from a completely unexpected but, potentially, life changing source.

"Hello, is that Shaun Wallace?"

"Shaun speaking," I replied.

"This is Nazia Butt from the television quiz show Eggheads. We've been trying to contact you to see if you would be interested in taking part in a competition we're holding called, *'Are You An Egghead?'*"

Nazia went onto explain that the entire filming for the series was going to take place sometime in June with the winner of the overall competition being offered a permanent place on the Eggheads' team. My initial response to Nazia's offer was that it was highly unlikely that I would be available to take part in the competition because of my work commitments, leaving aside the other somewhat childish and fatuous excuse that I told her in that I was still smarting from the disappointment at the last minute decision taken by the producers to pull my team from the show eight months previously. Nazia's lightning response was to apologise profusely before going on to stress the fact that the show's producers were very keen for me to take part in the competition, her flattering comments, I must confess, had the instant effect of softening my initial uncompromising stance in addition to going some considerable way to assuaging my bruised ego that had long since recovered. I told her that I would have to check my diary before making any sort of commitment and I would contact her tomorrow to let her know one way or the other. Nazia, who by this time had sensed that I was gradually warming to the idea of taking part in the competition, told me that she would send me an information pack straight away by first class post and that she was looking forward to hearing from me in what she hoped would be a positive response. Nazia's charm offensive certainly had its desired effect. The thought of coming out of my retirement from competitive quizzing and appearing on the show after our brief conversation was starting to have an irresistible magnetic appeal, but my fantasies of appearing on TV once more began to give way to a dose of cold hearted reality as the chances of me taking up the offer was looking like a nonstarter for two main reasons. Firstly, the competition was going to take place in and around the time when I had some very important trials that had been fixed well in advance most notably, an attempted murder trial where I was due to defend an old standing client of mine that was scheduled to last two weeks at Luton Crown Court and secondly, I had not picked up a quiz book in earnest since the night before the *Mastermind* Grand Final almost four years ago and there were real doubts in my mind as to whether I could reprise the same commitment, dedication, enthusiasm and appetite for the challenge.

The competition's information pack duly arrived the following day complete with invite and an application form to attend an audition at the Holiday Inn Hotel near Great Portland Street. I contacted my Senior Clark about my availability and he told me that I was busy for the first three weeks in June and that there were other cases in the pipeline which were in the Warned List in the last weeks of June. It looked as though it would be unlikely that I would be able to compete in the competition, but I thought there would be no harm in attending the audition because at the very least, I would know one way or another whether I still had the ability to compete as a quiz contestant at the highest level. I contacted Nazia to confirm that I would attend the audition and she asked me if I could be there the following afternoon at 2:30pm.

I arrived at the audition and was soon met by Lucy from the production team, who immediately apologised for a delay as the auditions were running behind schedule. Lucy then handed me a sheet of paper that contained twenty-five general knowledge questions. After taking a minute or so to read the sheet, I knew the correct answers to at least eighteen of the questions which I proceeded to answer in next to no time at all and although I was having some difficulty answering the remaining seven questions, I did so to the best of my ability. As I was filling in the answers on my question sheet, I noticed a woman seated directly in front of me going through the same exercise. Once Lucy had returned to collect our answer sheets, I turned my attention towards the woman and although I recognised her as a TV quiz veteran, despite my usually reliable powers of remembering familiar names and faces, I could not remember who she was, or on what game show that I had seen her previously. The pair of us began chatting away in a friendly and cordial manner. I told her my first name and what I did for a living when she asked me, but I did not go into too much detail in terms of my quizzing pedigree. Despite my scant disclosure, I began to wonder whether in fact she recognised who I was. Once the audition that was ahead of us had finished, Charlotte Gorman, another member of the production team, invited both of us in to the conference room. After myself and my opponent were settled comfortably in our seats, Charlotte told us that our audition was going to be filmed before going on to explain the rules of the competition. The show's format was similar to the normal Eggheads format, the only difference being that the winner of a round would have the option of selecting an Egghead of their choice and that Egghead could be used for help and advice to answer any of the five questions each contestant would face in the final round, however, that Egghead could only be used by a contestant once. The audition itself turned out to be quite a battle, as I initially lost 3-2 after the first five rounds of questions but by the final, I managed to redeem myself by winning the contest sudden death after we each faced our five final round set of questions.

After our contest had finished, both myself and my opponent had to do a short piece to camera where we were required to talk a bit about ourselves and hobbies in general before concluding with what amounted to a sales pitch as to why we would make a good Egghead if we won the competition. Charlotte then told the pair of us that everyone who attended the auditions would be notified within the next week whether their audition was successful. Despite that caveat, I felt that I'd done more than enough to be selected to appear on the show, my only one real concern was whether those dreams would be scuppered by virtue of my professional commitments which, at the end of day, would ultimately take priority. My appetite for a return to competitive TV quizzing had been clearly whetted after such a keenly fought contest but I knew that if I wanted to appear on the show, let alone win such a prestigious competition, I would have to religiously devote and divide my time between constant revision for the quiz and case preparation and even though I had not embarked on such a daunting challenge since the days when I took part in *Mastermind*, it was a challenge that I was looking forward to immensely.

In the meanwhile, I started the first of the series of back to back trials, which I was instructed in on my forty-eighth birthday at Bristol Crown Court. The case involved the supplying of Class A Drugs and the Possession of Criminal Property. The jury's deliberations took nearly two days before they returned a verdict of guilty of the first count of Possession to Supply Cocaine, but acquitted my client of the two remaining charges. My next case was a trial at Luton Crown Court defending one of my old clients, who, together with three other men, was facing two charges of Attempted Murder and Grievous Bodily harm. The trial was scheduled to last two weeks, during the course of which, I had received confirmation from the Production team at Eggheads that my audition had been successful. As I read the confirmation letter, my heart sank a little on account of the fact that the date I was scheduled to appear on the show was right in the middle of the trial I was involved in and not even I would have the temerity to ask the trial judge to postpone the trial for a day all for the sake of an appearance on the TV quiz show. I rang the show's production team the following day and spoke to Charlotte to explain my dilemma. By way of compromise, Charlotte agreed to accommodate me by moving my first round appearance to Saturday 21st June, but she made it clear that the recording dates of 24th and 26th June were set in stone and could not be changed if I managed to progress in the competition. I was grateful for the leeway that the show's producers were prepared to give me, but the latter recording dates presented another potential professional dilemma as I had another trial in a two week Warned List at Isleworth Crown Court starting from 23rd June, which meant that the case could come on for trial at a moment's notice within that fourteen-day period. However, that was a bridge that had yet to be crossed and I decided to bite the bullet and confirm that I would take part in the competition.

Every spare moment that I had was devoted to revision, relying on my old tried and trusted revisions methods that took the form of reading loads of different quiz books before testing myself and watching recordings of old quiz shows from my extensive video library. The level of that commitment to my revision even extending throughout the currency of the Attempted Murder trial in Luton where I would get my trusty quiz book out and read up on a few facts whilst I was waiting to cross examine witnesses, my multitasking skills having no impact on the trial itself whatsoever, which was notable by the fact that my client was the only defendant out of the four defendants who stood trial who was acquitted of all charges.

The day before my first round contest, I felt that I had done as much as I possibly could and I decided to take a break and spend the day at two completely separate and contrasting events. The first of those events involved me attending a graduation ceremony where I was invited to say a few words of encouragement and support on behalf of a friend of mine, who with both considerable courage and praise worthy effort, had successfully completed an extensive twelve week recovery programme from a long term alcohol addiction. I was extremely proud of my friend's determination and courage to seek proper professional help to beat his long standing and potentially, life threatening problem and I promised my friend that I would attend the graduation ceremony to lend what little support and encouragement that I could in support of his efforts and after the graduation ceremony, I stayed on to have lunch with my friend's fellow graduates who had also successfully completed the recovery programme. I couldn't stay for the entire day because I was anxious to get to my second engagement that involved a rendezvous with my old mate Nipper and the boys who were going to the final day of the Royal Ascot. I eventually arrived at the course just before 5pm and met up with Nipper and the rest of the lads where the revelry and merriment was in full swing. I caught the last hour before the last race and thereafter, we left the course and walked the short distance and ended up in a lively Wine Bar where I spent the next hour cornered by two members of Nipper's entourage who were taking me to task with regards to my all round sporting knowledge, a battle where I easily managed to come out on top. After eventually managing to extricate myself, I left the Wine bar and finally arrived home at around 9pm, having thoroughly enjoyed the day's events. The first thing I did when I got home was arrange all my clothes and other items that I would need for the following morning as I was required to be at the BBC studios in Wood Lane at 9am sharp before running the bath and treating myself to a nice long soak as well as contemplating the daunting challenge that awaited me tomorrow.

I woke up early that Saturday morning feeling rather pleased that I managed to save myself from any mad, frantic rushing around trying to find everything that I needed before heading the studio. Because I was so well organised, I was able to go on my regular two mile run that would serve as the perfect way to prepare both my mind and body for my imminent return to the TV quizzing arena, leaving me more than enough time to have yet another long relaxing hot bath before tucking in to my favourite breakfast. As I was getting myself ready for the challenge that lay ahead of me, I felt like the ageing gunslinger coming out of retirement ready and prepared for that final showdown but only time would tell whether after nearly four years, if I was still the quickest gunslinger to the draw. I selected my favourite pink shirts that had served me so well in game shows in the past before proceeding to pick up my suitcase trolley bag that contained, aside from my quiz books, some of the personal treasured mementoes that I had with me at the Mastermind Grand Final which included, the blue silk boxer shorts which hadn't been worn since that memorable night, the two Cup Winner's medals, the rag doll hand made by my nephew Myles and my pair of black shoes that had received their customary pristine polish by my dear friend and shoe carer in chief, Goggsy.

Just before I was about to enter the BBC studio, I heard the sound of a car beeping its horn and my name being called. It was my old mate Drax Hippolyte. We greeted each other cheerfully. We hadn't seen each other since we both appeared on the Radio 5 Live Sports

Show over three years ago. As I approached the swivel doors for the second time, I noticed a tall man with a mini afro hairstyle wearing a purple coloured shirt underneath a green khaki style jacket with its sleeves rolled up, jeans and open toed sandals, in a fashion style that would not have looked out of place in a 1960's Hippie commune, make his way through the swivel doors just ahead of me. His face looked vaguely familiar but because I was not wearing my glasses at the time, I could not precisely remember where I had seen him before, but something was telling me that he was going to be the opponent I would be up against in the first round of the contest. Lucy soon arrived to greet me and as we went through the sliding security panels, the young man whom I initially assumed was going to be my opponent did not accompany us, which immediately made me think that my hunch had been wrong. We headed towards our intended destination with Lucy adroitly navigating our way through a series of seemingly never-ending sets of staircases and a complex maze of corridors, chatting about my up and coming appearance along the way before we eventually arrived at the corridor where the dressing rooms were situated. With a quick swipe of her card key, Lucy opened took me to the green room where I saw the young guy who I had seen earlier, looking even more cool and laid back than before, and a middle aged man whom I discovered was a standby contestant. I went up to where the two men were sitting and introduced myself with a friendly handshake and we chatted amongst ourselves. It was at that point that the proverbial penny finally dropped in terms of where I had seen my first round opponent before. He was Rob Swarbrick from Blackpool who became the biggest ever jackpot winner of the ITV quiz show, *Duel,* that was screened on prime time Saturday evenings from January to April in 2008. Rob's brilliant performance on *Duel* demonstrated that he is an extremely clever young man with the confidence to match his outgoing personality and if I wanted to progress in the competition of *Are You An Egghead?,* I would have to be at the very top of my game. Just before Rob and I were required to go to make up, Charlotte tossed a coin to decide who would answer the first question and because I made the right call, I elected to go first. I did not spend that long being made up and as I was waiting to go back to the green room, Chris Hughes, one of the Eggheads walked into view. I've always been an admirer of Chris's quizzing abilities over the years and like some star struck teenager I approached him to shake his hand. During our short conversation, I asked Chris if he could get for me individual autographs of the Eggheads team and Chris said that he was more than happy to oblige my request. After Chris had left, I noticed on a nearby table, pictures of some of the contestants who were taking part in the competition and the two that caught my eye were Olav Bjortomt and Pat Gibson who represent the crème of competitive quizzing and to my mind, were amongst the clear favourites to win the competition. Their very presence in the competition only served to confirm that the search to find a new Egghead was going to be a highly competitive one and if I was going to stand any chance of winning the series, it would mean me having to get past them. The immediate priority that was facing me was to try and fend off the very real threat to my progression in the competition that Rob was going to pose.

Not long later, we were on the set, and the show's legendary host Dermot Murnaghan was doing his familiar bit to introduce the show.

"HELLO, AND WELCOME TO *ARE YOU AN EGGHEAD?*. OVER THE YEARS WE'VE ASKED WHETHER YOU HAVE THE BRAINS TO BEAT THE EGGHEADS, NOW WE'RE ASKING, HAVE YOU GOT THE BRAINS TO JOIN THEM? WE'VE LAUNCHED A NATIONWIDE SEARCH FOR THE GREATEST QUIZ BRAIN IN BRITAIN AND OVER THE COMING WEEKS, ONE OF THEM WILL EMERGE AS CHAMPION AND WIN THE ULTIMATE PRIZE FOR QUIZ SHOW ENTHUSIASTS, A PLACE ON THE MOST FEARSOME QUIZ TEAM IN HISTORY. SO, LET'S MEET TODAY'S CONTESTANTS HOPING THEY HAVE GOT WHAT IT TAKES TO BECOME AN EGGHEAD."

Dermot kicked off the contest by having a brief chat firstly with both Rob and I respectively about our quizzing credentials before launching straight into the contest by announcing that Geography would be the first of the five specialist categories. As I had won the toss of a coin that took place earlier in the green room, I elected to face the first question.

"SHAUN, IN WHICH EUROPEAN COUNTRY ARE THE DOLOMITE MOUNTAINS. FRANCE, ITALY OR SPAIN?"

A nice and easy question to get me off to a good start and I replied with the correct answer Italy which gave me the early lead. It was now Rob's turn to face his first question.

"ROB, WHAT WAS THE OFFICIAL CURRENCY OF AUSTRIA UNTIL THE INTRODUCTION OF THE EURO, FRANC, MARK OR SCHILLING?"

Like me, Rob also faced a relatively straightforward question and gave the correct answer Schilling to level the scores.

"SHAUN, WHAT IS THE NAME OF THE SEVEN AND A HALF HOUR TRAIN RIDE NICKNAMED "THE SLOWEST EXPRESS TRAIN IN THE WORLD"' WHICH RUNS FROM ZERMATT TO SAN

MORITZ, THE AVALANCHE EXPRESS, GLACIER EXPRESS OR MOUNTAIN EXPRESS?"

I really didn't have a clue what the correct answer could be and I had no choice other than to guess and hope for the best. Eventually I settled on the option, Avalanche Express, but unfortunately it was the wrong guess, the correct answer was the Glacier Express.

"ROB, HOW MANY COUNTRIES SHARE A BORDER WITH FRANCE, FIVE, SIX OR EIGHT?"

I could see Rob trying to visualize the map of France in his head. I was fairly confident that the correct answer was eight, but Rob finally settled with six. Dermot confirmed my initial choice was correct after which he turned his attention to the Eggheads panel and asked whether they could name all of the countries concerned. Kevin Ashman duly obliged and proceeded to list all of the countries bordering France in clockwise order, Belgium, Luxembourg, Germany, Switzerland, Italy, Monaco, Spain and Andorra.

"SHAUN, THE RENOWNED OTAVALO MARKET, WHICH IS KNOWN FOR ITS COLOURFUL TEXTILES, IS LOCATED IN WHICH LATIN AMERICAN COUNTRY, BRAZIL, ECUADOR OR PARAGUAY?"

Another tough question. I tried to apply some sort of logic and reasoning as I was discussing the options out aloud and tried to latch onto Dermot's pronunciation of the place, for some sort of clue to the correct answer and based on that reasoning, I opted for Brazil. For the second successive question in a row, I made the wrong choice which prompted Dermot to turn to the Eggheads to see if they knew which country the market place was situated in and it was left to the excellent kevin to confirm that the market place in question was in fact located in ecuador.

"ROB, THE PLAZA DE CIBELESE, WHICH FEATURES A STATUE OF THE ROMAN GODDESS OF NATURE AND FERTILITY IN A CHARIOT BEING PULLED BY TWO LIONS, IS A FEATURE OF WHICH SPANISH CITY, BARCELONA, MADRID OR SEVILLE?"

Thankfully for me, Rob did not know the answer to the question and just like I had attempted to do with my previous question, he sought to rely on Dermot's pronunciation and he decided, after some deliberation, to go with Barcelona which, much to my considerable relief, turned out to be the wrong choice.

"SHAUN, BEFORE IT WAS RENAMED IN 1963, WHAT WAS NEW YORK'S JFK AIRPORT KNOWN AS?"

At last a question to which I was 100% sure of the correct answer. Idlewild! I replied with a hint of confidence and glee in my voice before going on to add, all Egghead like, that one of the reasons I knew that fact was because Idlewild was mentioned in Martin Scorsese's classic gangster film, Goodfellas starring Robert De Niro. The pressure was now all on Rob as he faced his sudden death question.

"ROB, THE VAST SEMI DESERT REGION KNOWN AS THE KAROO IS SITUATED IN WHICH COUNTRY?"

Rob admitted that he did not know the answer but despite his frank admission I was not taking anything for granted. Resorting to nothing more other than a complete random guess, Rob opted for Egypt, an incorrect answer that wasn't too wide of the mark, but the correct answer was South Africa. Dermot confirmed that I had won the first round and therefore had the first pick from the Eggheads' panel to assist me for the final round and without any form of hesitation or dithering, I went for the best Egghead of them all, Kevin Ashman. Despite my obvious delight and relief in seizing the early initiative in the contest, the truth of the matter was that it didn't really mean a thing. The combination of the standard of the questions coupled with the quality of my opponent meant that it was imperative that I remained focused and alert at all times because if I didn't, I could easily find the entire contest slipping through my fingers.

Dermot announced the next category in the contest was Music, not one of my strongest subjects, especially when paired against someone as bright and contemporary as my young opponent, and it was for those very same reasons why I chose to face the first question.

"SHAUN, TEMPTATION WAS A UK HIT SINGLE IN 1983 FOR WHICH GROUP, DEPECHE MODE, HEAVEN 17 OR SPANDAU BALLET?"

A nice and gentle opening question to the round and I responded by attempting somewhat badly, to sing a couple of the bars of the chorus of the song that I knew for certain was originally sung by the group Heaven 17. Dermot remarked that despite my singing efforts, I wouldn't be getting any extra points before turning his attentions to Rob for his first question of the round.

"ROB, IN WHICH YEAR WAS THE OPERA SINGER JOAN SUTHERLAND BORN, 1926, 1936 OR 1946?"

Rob said that he had heard of the name and went for the year 1926, his reasoning, which had no real rationale behind it, was that she was more "successful historically." It was another random stab in the dark so far as Rob was concerned and despite my hopes that he would make a costly slip up with his choice, I knew full well that he hadn't, a fact Dermot confirmed that made the scores all square.

"SHAUN, THE JAZZ MUSICIAN AND BANDLEADER, CHICK WEBB IS BEST KNOWN FOR PLAYING WHICH INSTRUMENT, PIANO, DRUMS OR SAXOPHONE?"

Chick Webb was a name I had heard of previously in the Jazz world and although I was not 100% sure from the options available, I had a fairly strong hunch that he was more likely to have been a drummer and admittedly with more luck than judgement, my hunch proved to be correct that once again put me back into the lead.

"ROB, A NORTHERN SOUL AND URBAN HYMNS ARE ALBUMS BY WHICH GROUP, THE CHARLATANS, PULP OR THE VERVE?"

No sooner had Dermot finished reading the question, Rob immediately replied that Urban Hymns was a major success for The Verve.

"SHAUN, BY WHAT NAME IS THE SINGER MARVIN LEE ADAY BETTER KNOWN, MEATLOAF, LEMMY OR AXEL ROSE?"

My immediate prayers were answered and like Rob, I was intent on demonstrating my own supreme air of confidence, and answered Meatloaf. Dermot turned to Chris Hughes on the Eggheads panel because he is apparently a big Meatloaf fan and he confirmed that I had chosen the correct answer.

"ROB, ASHOKAN FAIRWELL IS A PIECE OF MUSIC BY WHICH MODERN COMPOSER, JAY UNGAR, JOHN CAGE OR HARRISON BIRTWISTLE?"

What a tough question! I certainly didn't have a clue what the correct answer was and Rob readily confessed that he didn't have a clue either. With that in mind, he decided that the best way to try and answer the question was to resort to employing his so called, "Spider Sense," a tactic that Dermot seemed to find mildly amusing and without any real logic, rhyme or reason, Rob opted for the option, Jay Ungar. Dermot then pressed Rob to explain what this so called "Spider Sense" was all about, but by the time Rob finished explaining the concept, I don't think even he knew what he was talking about. Whatever the logic or reason behind Rob's new secret weapon, it seemed to be working for him because it somehow managed to guide him to the correct answer and with scores deadlocked both Rob and I were once more into sudden death to decide the round.

"SHAUN, A HARD RAIN'S A-GONNA FALL AND THE IN CROWD WERE UK HIT SINGLES FOR WHICH SINGER IN THE 1970'S?"

For the life of me, I just couldn't delve into the deep recesses of my mind and somehow come up with the correct answer. In sheer desperation, I resorted to singing the words of the chorus of that second single in the faint hope that it would trigger some sort of instant recall but sadly my risible singing efforts failed to have the desired effect. Resigned to the fact that I had nothing left to turn to other than resort to pure and simple guesswork, I opted for Gary Glitter, knowing full well in that my answer was completely and utterly wrong. Dermot then turned to the Eggheads to see if they knew and even more surprisingly they were also none the wiser. The only possible suggestion they came up with was that Kevin knew that the first song was a Bob Dylan composition. When Dermot revealed that the answer was in fact Brian Ferry of Roxy Music fame, I could have kicked myself, I knew that I had made a costly slip that could result in me forfeiting the round.

"ROB, LOUIS ARMSTRONG'S NICKNAME "SATCHMO"' APPEARED TO BE A SHORTENING OF WHICH TWO TERMED PHRASE?"

I knew that somebody as good as Rob wasn't going to let such a fairly straightforward question like that slip through his grasp and he calmly replied in his confident and assured tone that the correct answer was Satchel Mouth which meant he clinched the round and earned the right to pick an Egghead to assist him in the final round and he chose the formidable Daphne Fowler.

Dermot then revealed that the next category was Film and Television and with the momentum now swung firmly in his direction, Rob elected to face the first question in the round.

"ROB, WHAT IS THE NAME OF THE CELEBRATED ROAD ON WHICH STARS APPEAR BEFORE SCREENINGS AT THE CANNES FILM FESTIVAL, CORISADE, CROISETTE OR CROISSANT?"

Rob immediately gave the correct answer, Croisette, to give him a lead. Suddenly, I felt as though I was on the back foot and all that was going through my mind at this time was that I had to match my confident, laid back opponent stride for stride otherwise I was going to find it increasingly difficult to remain competitive in the contest.

"SHAUN, WHAT WAS THE NAME OF THE DISNEY CARTOON SERIES STARRING DONALD DUCK'S IDENTICAL NEPHEWS HEWEY, DEWEY AND LOUIE, DUCK DAYS, DUCKTALES OR DUCK TRIALS?"

One would have thought with such an apparently straightforward question, that I would have known the answer right away, especially given the fact that I used to watch the series when I was a young child, but once again, I was hampered by the fact that I couldn't remember the name of the series and for the first time in the game, I was beginning to feel the pressure. Once again, I found myself resorting to the realms of good old fashioned guesswork and I eventually settled on the option, Duck Days, for no other reason other than it seemed the more plausible option than the other two on offer. With that declaration, Dermot turned to the Eggheads' panel to see if anyone of them knew the answer and it was left to CJ to declare his particular fondness for Hewey when he revealed that the correct answer was in fact Ducktales.

"ROB, WHAT IS THE NAME OF THE REAL LIFE PERSON PLAYED BY ANTHONY HOPKINS IN THE 2000 FILM, *THE WORLD'S FASTEST INDIAN*, CHRIS CARR, CRAIG BREEDLOVE OR BERT MONROE?"

As seems to be always the way in competitive quizzing, frustratingly I knew that Bert Monroe was the correct answer. Luckily for me, Rob incorrectly went with Chris Carr.

"SHAUN, WHICH ACTOR PLAYED CHARACTERS CALLED CAPT. ROBERT HATCH, LT. MARION COBRETTI AND SGT JOHN SPARTAN DURING HIS CAREER, ARNOLD SCHWARZENEGGER, SYLVESTER STALLONE OR JEAN-CLAUDE VAN DAMME?"

Once again, I was not 100% sure and I opted for Stallone solely on a wing and a prayer. My totally random selection was right and I was back on level terms, but the initiative still lay with Rob as he faced the third of his questions for the round.

"ROB, WHICH FORMER *NEIGHBOURS* ACTOR APPEARED IN LOST, UGLY BETTY AND 24, ALAN DALE, GUY PEARCE OR STEFAN DENNIS?"

Rob was clearly comfortable with his question declaring that he was a big Neighbours fan that stemmed from the days when he was a young "whippersnapper" who had always watched the show when he arrived home from school whilst having his tea and he gave the correct answer Alan Dale.

"SHAUN, IN THE ORIGINAL SCRIPT FOR RAIDERS OF THE LOST ARK, WHAT WAS INDIANA JONES'S ORIGINAL SURNAME, SMITH, TAYLOR OR WILLIAMS?"

For the life of me I didn't know what the correct answer was, or to use the more apt cockney rhyming slang expression, I hadn't got a Scooby Doo. I had to guess and hope that Williams was the correct choice that would level up the scores. Dame Fortune seemed to have completely deserted me and for the second time in the round, I had made the wrong choice, the consequences of which resulted in the loss of yet another round. Dermot offered Rob the choice of another Egghead to assist and this time, he chose Chris to be part of his increasingly formidable team for the final.

Now I was really beginning to feel the pressure. I felt like a boxer on the receiving end of a barrage of blows who was grateful to hear the bell before proceeding to wearily stagger back to his stool at the end of a punishing round. The contest was now seriously threatening to slip from my grasp . I had to come up with something, anything that would halt his seemingly unstoppable momentum and as luck would have it, Dermot announced the category that I hoped would possibly help me apply the brakes on Rob's seemingly unstoppable march towards victory, my favourite category History. Rob elected to face the first question.

"ROB, IN WHICH CENTURY WAS THE CHINESE STATESMAN AND LEADER, MAO TSE TUNG BORN, 18TH, 19TH OR 20TH?"

Rob appeared to be unsure as to the answer, or at least that was the impression he was giving, but it soon dawned on him that the Mao referred to in the question was Chairman Mao and chose the 19th Century to put him in the lead.

"SHAUN, WHICH JAPANESE EMPEROR REJECTED HIS DIVINE STATUS IN AN HISTORIC RADIO BROADCAST ON 1ST JANUARY 1946, AKIHITO, HIROHITO OR TAISHO?"

A straight forward question for a history aficionado such as myself and I decided to show off a little, in true Egghead style, by explaining that Akihito was the reigning Japanese Emperor and the son of the war time Japanese leader, Hirohito, who was the Emperor in question. Dermot seemed to be quite impressed with my knowledge of Japanese monarchy before confirming that I had given the correct answer to level the scores.

"ROB, THE ENGLISHMAN, EDWARD TEACH, THE NOTORIOUS PIRATE KNOWN AS BLACKBEARD TERRORISED SAILORS ON WHICH OCEAN IN THE 18TH CENTURY, ATLANTIC, PACIFIC OR INDIAN?"

I thought it would be another correct answer for Rob, especially when in the lead up to his eventual answer, he referred to the film, The Pirates of the Caribbean, and mentioned in passing that he just recently returned from a vacation in the West Indies before his appearance on the show. However, to my surprise (and in truth, relief), Rob inexplicably chose the Pacific Ocean. At last, a chance presented itself to take the round and all I had to do was answer correctly the next question.

"SHAUN, WHAT WAS THE NAME OF THE DEFENSIVE LINE KNOWN TO THE GERMANS AS THE WEST WALL THAT WAS CONSTRUCTED TO PROTECT GERMANY FROM ALLIED

FORCES IN WORLD WAR ONE, NIEBELUNG LINE, SIGFRIED LINE OR SASNIR LINE?"

At first sight, this was a home banker of a question for me, but just like Rob had done with his own question, I inexplicably contrived to score an avoidable own goal by ruling out the most obvious and well known of the options available, the Sigfried Line, thinking for some strange reason, that it was possibly a trick question and I went for the option, the Sasnir Line instead. You can imagine my utter horror when Dermot informed me that the correct answer was in fact the Sigfried Line and to rub the proverbial salt into my own wounds, Chris Hughes then treated us all to an off key rendition of the famous wartime song. I had blown the chance to take a precious lead and all I could do was hope that such an expensive mistake would not come back to haunt me in the long run as Rob prepared to face the next question.

"ROB, WHO OWNED THE NICKNAME, UNCONDITIONAL SURRENDER DUE TO HIS TOUGH TACTICS DURING THE AMERICAN CIVIL WAR, ULYSSES S. GRANT, ANDREW JOHNSON OR ABRAHAM LINCOLN?"

Having clearly learned his lesson from his costly error that he made from the previous question that he faced, Rob wisely took his time as he considered the options before the proverbial penny eventually dropped on closer inspection of the first two initials of Ulysses (Simpson) Grant to put him 2-1 in the lead. I had to get the next question right or I too would otherwise have to unconditionally surrender my supposed favourite round and forfeit the choice of selecting another crucial Egghead.

"SHAUN, WHO WAS THE LAST BRITISH MONARCH NOT TO HAVE ANY CHILDREN, EDWARD VII, EDWARD VIII OR WILLIAM IV?"

There would be no silly slip ups or unforced errors on my part this time especially with the British Monarchy being one of my favourite areas of history. Once again, I slipped into show off mode with an elaborate explanation that the unmarried Edward VIII had no children throughout the 325 days that he spent on the throne before his abdication in December 1936. Dermot confirmed that my answer was correct and for the second time in the contest, a round would be decided by sudden death.

"ROB, WHICH NAZI WAR CRIMINAL ESCAPED FROM EUROPE TO SOUTH AMERICA UNDER THE ALIAS RICARDO KLEMENT IN 1950?"

Right away I knew the answer was Adolf Eichmann and was equally sure that my opponent didn't. Clearly clutching at straws, the only name that popped into his head was Wilhelm Hess. I was presented with another chance to claim the round and this time I was determined not to blow it.

"SHAUN, WHAT WAS THE SURNAME OF CLYDE, ONE HALF OF THE INFAMOUS DUO, BONNY AND CLYDE?"

"IT WAS BONNY PARKER AND CLYDE BARROW!" I declared without a hint of hesitation in the full knowledge that I was 100% correct and back on level terms. I elected to choose CJ. I was going to need somebody like CJ in the final round as his strengths mainly centre around all things contemporary. The contest was now delicately poised with two Eggheads apiece between us. Dermot announced the final category in the contest, Food and Drink, not one of my favourite subjects I hasten to add, but with the final remaining judge Judith Keppel up for grabs, I decided to face the first question in order to hopefully, give myself some sort of advantage.

"SHAUN, IN WHICH US STATE IS THE PO' BOY, A SUBMARINE SANDWICH CONSISTING OF A MEAL OR SEA FOOD ON CRISPY FRENCH BREAD TRADITIONALLY SERVED, FLORIDA, LOUISIANA OR TEXAS?"

What a tough first question to be facing especially for someone who had definitely never heard of that particular delicacy. I incorrectly went for Texas, and it was Daphne who supplied the correct answer, Louisiana.

"ROB, THE NAME OF WHICH INDIAN CURRY DISH BROADLY TRANSLATES AS TWO ONIONS OR DOUBLE ONION, DOPIAZA, ROJAN JOSH OR BIRYANI?"

Rob wasted no time in giving the correct answer Dopiaza to put him one up in the round.

"SHAUN, IN BRITAIN NINE IMPERIAL GALLONS IS EQUIVALENT TO WHICH UNIT CAPACITY, BARREL, FIRKIN OR KILDERKIN?"

I knew straight away that Firkin was the correct answer, but the control of the round remained in Rob's hands.

"ROB, WHICH CHEF FAMOUSLY EJECTED THE FOOD CRITIC, A. A. GILL, FROM HIS RESTAURANT AND WAS DESCRIBED BY HIM AS A WONDERFUL CHEF, JUST A REALLY SECOND-RATE HUMAN BEING, RAYMOND BLANC, GORDON RAMSEY OR MARCO-PIERRE WHITE?"

Rob managed to navigate his way through that particular minefield of a question to come up with the correct answer Gordon Ramsey. I now faced my final question in Food and Drink category that I had to answer correctly if only to go through the formality of forcing Rob to face his final question.

"SHAUN, A RUSTY NAIL COCKTAIL IS MADE BY MIXING DRAMBUIE WITH WHICH SPIRIT, GIN, VODKA OR WHISKEY?"

"I know the answer to that one" I confidently declared, "It's Whisky" which prompted Dermot to turn to a fellow teetotaller like me on the Eggheads panel, CJ to see if he agreed with my answer and he confirmed that I was correct. At least by giving that correct answer, I had succeeded in forcing Rob into facing his third designated question, but I was resigned to the fact that given the exceptional form he was showing to date, he wasn't going to blow this golden opportunity to seize the round.

"ROB, BATAVIA IS A VARIETY OF WHICH VEGETABLE, CARROT, CUCUMBER OR LETTUCE?"

Another broad smile enveloped Rob's face and he relaxed back into his chair, calmness personified before giving the correct answer, Lettuce, which enabled him to capture the round and secure the final Egghead, Judith Keppel to complete his impressive line-up.

Now, the pressure was really on and as I turned my gaze in Rob's direction, all I could see was a relaxed and composed opponent who was both ready and determined to go all the way. In truth, I hadn't performed to my best up to that point in the contest, but despite Rob's excellent performance, this is the round where it really counts and if I'm as good as I believe I know I am, now would be the time to prove it.

"THIS IS WHAT WE'VE BEEN PLAYING TOWARDS, IT'S TIME FOR THE FINAL ROUND TO DECIDE WHO IS ONE STEP CLOSER TO BECOMING AN EGGHEAD AND WHO WILL BE ELIMINATED FROM OUR SEARCH. I WILL ASK EACH OF YOU FIVE QUESTIONS IN TURN IN THIS FINAL ROUND AND BECAUSE IT'S THE FINAL ROUND, YOU WILL NO LONGER BE PLAYING ALONE. YOU WILL HAVE THE BACKING OF THE EGGHEADS YOU WON OVER THE COURSE OF THE SHOW. HOWEVER, YOU CAN ASK EACH OF YOUR EGGHEADS FOR HELP ONLY ONCE SO USE THEM WISELY. MAKE SURE YOU DON'T PUT ALL YOUR EGGS INTO ONE BASKET, DO YOU UNDERSTAND?" Both Rob and I nodded in unison to affirm that we understood the rules. "OK THEN, LETS PLAY THE FINAL ROUND."

Rob elected to go first.

"ROB, WHAT DO THE INITIALS P.S. STAND FOR AT THE END OF A LETTER, POST SCRIPT, POST STAMP OR POST STATEMENT?'

Rob quickly answered, post script.

"SHAUN, WHICH WORD DESCRIBES A PERSON WHO, HAVING RISEN SOCIALLY OR ECONOMICALLY, IS CONSIDERED

TO BE AN UPSTART, OR TO LACK THE APPROPRIATE REFINEMENT FOR HIS NEW POSITION, INGENUE, PARVENUE OR RETINUE?"

Just as quickly I gave the correct answer, parvenue.

"ROB, WHO WAS THE ONLY MANCHESTER UNITED FOOTBALLER TO HAVE PLAYED IN BOTH THE 1999 AND 2008 CHAMPIONS LEAGUE FINAL, WES BROWN, RYAN GIGGS OR PAUL SCHOLES?"

Rob took a deep breath as he considered the options before going with Ryan Giggs. *I hope I'm just as lucky!* I thought.

"SHAUN, WHO PLAYED THE ROLE OF ELLIOT NESS IN THE 1950'S AND 1960'S TV SERIES THE UNTOUCHABLES, ROBERT STACK, JACK WEBB OR ROBERT CULP?"

My prayers for an easy and straightforward question were thankfully answered. The Untouchables was one of my favourite TV shows. I wasted very little time in giving Dermot the correct answer of Robert Stack that put me back on level terms.

"ROB, TOKOPHOBIA IS THE FEAR OF WHAT, CHILDBIRTH, GERMS OR KISSING?"

A difficult question on the surface, but so far as Rob was concerned, he seemed extremely comfortable with it, declaring that a close friend of his had just been diagnosed as having a morbid fear of childbirth and that Tokophobia was the technical term that he was led to believe meant just that that.

"SHAUN, WHICH AMERICAN PRESIDENT APPEARS ON THE CURRENT $5 BANK NOTE, THOMAS JEFFERSON, ABRAHAM LINCOLN OR GEORGE WASHINGTON?"

I wasn't entirely sure of the right answer and I tentatively went for Abraham Lincoln, making a big gamble, which ultimately paid off as it was the right answer.

"ROB, IN WHICH FICTIONAL TOWN DID DYLAN THOMAS SET HIS PLAY FOR VOICES UNDER MILKWOOD, LLAREGGUB, LLADOS OR LAUGHHAREN?"

I knew straight away that the answer was Llareggub as it's the word Buggerall spelt backwards. Rob began to weigh up his options as to whether now would be the perfect time to deploy one of his Eggheads with the game so delicately poised. Rob sensibly decided that he was not going to take any unnecessary risks and he chose Judith to assist him in answering the question. Judith answered Llareggub, but she sounded unsure about it. I was hoping that Judith's less than confident demeanour would somehow confuse or unsettle my opponent, but Rob being Rob, he deployed his trusty Spider Sense for inspiration, or to use his own choice of words, "hunching it up to the Spider Sense max!" and went with Llaregubb. Even I could not help but be impressed and feel full of admiration by Rob's steadfast coolness and determination in the fierce heat of battle.

"SHAUN, THE ORIGINAL MASON-DIXON LINE WAS PRINCIPALLY A BOUNDARY BETWEEN PENNSYLVANIA AND WHICH OTHER STATE, MARYLAND, OHIO OR ALABAMA?"

I knew that Kevin would definitely know the answer and immediately, I asked for his assistance and without so much as a moment's thought, Kevin confirmed that Maryland was right answer.

"ROB, IN GREEK MYTHOLOGY, WHICH SORCERESS WAS THE DAUGHTER OF THE KING OF COLCHIS, HECATE, CIRCE OR MEDEA?"

The type of question that was right in my territory but Rob turned to the Mythology expert, Daphne, who confirmed the answer was Medea who eventually married Jason having bumped off his first wife on their wedding night.

"SHAUN, SEBASTIAN MELMOTH AS THE PSEUDONYM USED BY WHICH WRITER, CHRISTOPHER MARLOWE, OSCAR WILDE OR GEORGE ORWELL?"

What a godsend of a question! I knew what the answer was before Dermot had a chance to complete reading the options. Oscar Wilde! My correct answer meant that the contest would have to be decided by the dreaded sudden death, a method that in truth, was only fitting in a way to determine such a keenly and fiercely contested game.

"ROB, WHICH WORD MEANING MODERATE OR SPARING CONTAINS ALL FIVE VOWELS IN ALPHABETICAL ORDER?"

It's definitely Abstemious! I thought to myself. Rob openly declared that he hadn't a clue and sought Chris's advice and he confirmed that my initial thoughts were in fact correct.

"SHAUN, WHICH GERMAN BORN THEOLOGIAN RECEIVED A 1952 NOBEL PEACE PRIZE FOR HIS PHILOSOPHY OF THE REVERENCE BEING EXPRESSED IN HIS WORK, AS A MISSION DOCTOR EQUATORIAL AFRICA?"

I knew the answer was Albert Schwietzer, and for the first time in the game, it was my turn to relax back in my chair and adopt an air of supreme confidence.

"WE'RE NOW DEEP INTO SUDDEN DEATH AND ROB, HERE'S YOUR QUESTION. ONE MORNING I SHOT AN ELEPHANT IN MY PYJAMAS, HOW IT GOT INTO MY PYJAMAS I WILL NEVER KNOW, SPOKEN BY A CHARACTER NAMED CAPTAIN JEFFREY SPALDING, IS A FAMOUS LINE IN WHICH FILM?"

Rob didn't know the answer and lamented on the fact that Chris, who had helped him with his last question, probably knew the answer but that safety net was no longer available to him. Not even his trusty and reliable "Spider Sense" that had served him so well during the contest could save him and in a last, desperate roll of the dice, he went for *The African Queen*. Once Dermot confirmed that he'd given the wrong answer, I stuck my hand up in an effort to attract Dermot's attention, but instead, Dermot turned to Chris, a big Marx Brothers fan, who confirmed that the film in question was Animal Crackers. The pendulum of victory at last swung in my direction and with the advantage of CJ in my corner, I now had a golden chance to advance into the next round.

"SHAUN, IN WHICH PLAY BY WILLIAM SHAKESPEARE DOES JOHN OF GAUNT MEMORABLY REFER TO ENGLAND AS THIS SCEPTRED ISLE?"

I smiled slightly after hearing the question before replying, "IT'S THE OPENING LINES IN SHAKESPEARE'S RICHARD II, AND THAT'S MY ANSWER."

Dermot then said, "TO WIN THE GAME…RICHARD II IS THE RIGHT ANSWER, SHAUN, YOU HAVE WON!" The show's theme music indicating the end of the game resonated throughout the studio and to reflect that fact, I took a sharp intake of breath as a sign my immense relief and joy that I managed to squeeze home. "CONGRATULATIONS GO TO YOU SHAUN. YOU HAVE PROVED THAT WINNING COMES AS NATURALLY TO YOU AS IT DOES TO OUR EGGHEADS, WHICH MEANS YOU ARE THROUGH TO THE NEXT ROUND AND ONE STEP CLOSER TO BECOMING AN EGGHEAD."

Once the recording had finished I went straight over to Rob we both hugged each other. I told Rob in no uncertain terms that I thought his performance from start to finish was of the highest quality and added that I was extremely fortunate to be progressing into the next round. The production assistant Charlotte then came over and informed me that my next match in the competition would take place on Tuesday the 24th June and that she would contact me later on that day with all the details. I was eager to get away from the studio as quickly as possible as I was feeling physically and mentally drained but above all, extremely pleased and relieved that I had prevailed. I had forgotten how physically and mentally draining competing on television game shows can be, especially when you take into account all the waiting around in the green room expending vital nervous energy and tension waiting to compete.

On the following Monday, the day before the second round of the competition, I arrived at Isleworth Crown Court nice and early, fully prepared and expecting that at some point during the day, the trial would get off the ground and if that happened then my continued participation in the competition given the fact that the trial was scheduled to last three days would be over. Naturally, I was keen to continue in the competition but if it came to a choice, the trial would take precedence. Thankfully, I didn't have to face that particular predicament because not long after my arrival at court, I was approached by prosecuting counsel who informed me that the prosecution were not in position to start the trial because two of the main prosecution witnesses who were vital to their had retracted their original allegations. My opponent went on to add that he was seeking a two day adjournment in the case in order to allow the CPS to carefully review the matter before deciding whether they were going to continue or abandon proceedings. I readily agreed to my opponent's proposals and with the trial judge endorsing our joint proposal for the two day adjournment, I was now thankfully, free to compete in the quiz the following day.

I arrived at the BBC studios on Wood Lane at the designated time and whilst I was being escorted by one of the production runners along the now familiar route to the dressing room area, I turned my attentions to my opponent, and saw it was the formidable quiz champion Olav Bjorntomt. My initial thoughts upon seeing Olav, apart from the obvious fact that I was facing an opponent of the highest quality, were that our upcoming contest would have been worthy of the Eggheads Grand Final itself.

I went up to Olav and shook his hand after which, the pair of us attempted to engage in somewhat stilted superficial chitchat, mainly because Olav's general demeanour and body language, a cross between youthful shyness and ambivalent reticence initially made our attempt to converse somewhat difficult. Eventually, Olav seemed to relax a little especially when I started reminding him about our encounter at the Grand Slam audition all those years ago.

After the usual waiting around, the pair of us were summoned onto the studio set to take our respective places before being joined by the Eggheads panel and then Dermot respectively and once everyone was seated and settled, the Studio Floor Manger began the countdown for Dermot to introduce what was sure to be the start of an epic confrontation between two quality quizzers. Dermot welcomed both of us to the show chatting to us briefly in turn before he turned his attention to discussing our respective performances in the previous round. As if I needed reminding, Dermot mentioned the fact

534

that I had lost 3-2 in the head to head contest before the final round, and by contrast, Olav had won his head-to-head contest 3-2 before the final five question showdown, but I couldn't help being surprised by Dermot's revelation that Olav had used all of his Eggheads to help him with three of those questions in that final round, a tactic that he deployed in all probability, to ensure that he would not take any undue or unnecessary risks at such an important stage of the contest but it gave me some food for thought as to whether or not the further deployment of such a tactic could play a crucial role in the outcome of the contest.

The stage was now set for the contest to begin and Dermot announced that the first head to head topic was on the subject, Geography and I would be facing the first question.

"SHAUN, THE CARIBBEAN ISLAND OF ANGUILLA BELONGS TO WHICH COUNTRY, USA, UNITED KINGDOM OR THE NETHERLANDS?"

That was a nice easy question to start off with and after eliminating the options of the USA and the Netherlands and giving my reasons for doing so, I opted for the United Kingdom that was the correct answer. Olav then faced his first question.

"OLAV, THE FLAG OF MONACO IS FORMED FROM WHITE AND WHICH OTHER COLOUR, BLUE, RED OR GREEN?"

Another straightforward question for a top rate quizzer such as Olav who, in reliance of his knowledge of the home colours that the Principality's football team, FC Monaco whose team shirts are White and Red, his correct answer Red made the scores all square. Olav's question momentarily triggered painful memories of when Monaco knocked my beloved Chelsea out of the Semi Final stage of the Champions League in 2004, but I quickly dispelled those negative thoughts from my mind as I prepared to face my next question.

"SHAUN, THE INTERNATIONAL AIRPORT SERVING THE ITALIAN RESORT OF RIMINI IS NAMED AFTER WHICH FAMOUS FILM DIRECTOR, FREDRICO FELLINI, LUCHINO VISCONTI OR ROBERTO ROSSELINI?"

I hadn't even heard of Lucino Visconti and for that reason he was the option that I went for. Dermot then turned his attention the Egghead's panel. "EGGHEADS, IF YOU ASKED FOR VISCONTI AIRPORT IN RIMINI, WOULD THEY KNOW WHAT YOU'RE TALKING ABOUT?" The Eggheads shook their heads in collective disapproval at my choice before resorting to answer in unison that the correct answer was in fact Fellini.

"OLAV, THE RUINS OF THE ANCIENT CITY OF PALMERA LIE IN WHICH COUNTRY, SYRIA, TURKEY OR THE LEBANON?"

Olav confidently declared the answer was Syria to put him into the lead.

"SHAUN, THE PART OF THE ATLANTIC OCEAN, THE PORCUPINE BANK, LIES OFF THE WEST COAST OF WHICH COUNTRY, IRELAND, ITALY OR ICELAND?"

What a stinker of a question and the multiple choices on offer were of no help either because I had never even heard of the Porcupine Bank. Without any real thought, rhyme or reason, I opted for Iceland.

"YOU'RE ONE LETTER, BUT THOUSANDS OF MILES APART I'M AFRAID. IT'S IRELAND."

My worst fears had now been realised as my wrong answer brought a premature end to the round in Olav's favour. Dermot then asked him which Egghead he wanted to assist him in the final round and unsurprisingly he chose the great Kevin Ashman.

Dermot announced that the next head to head category was Music and Olav elected to go second, a choice that according to him, was due to his disastrous performance in the category during his first round match.

"SHAUN, WHICH MUSICAL ENTERTAINER FOUND FAME PLAYING THE ROLE OF SALLY PERKINS IN A TOURING REVIEW CALLED MR TOWER OF LONDON BETWEEN 1918 TO 1925, MARIE LLOYD, GRACIE FIELDS OR FLORRIE FORDE?"

I was more or less certain that the correct answer was Gracie Fields if only for the fact that she was inextricably associated with the song that was to become her signature tune, "Sally".

"OLAV, WHICH MUSICAL NOTATION MEANS MODERATELY SLOW AND DISTINCT, ADAGIO, LENTO OR ANDANTE?"

For the first time in the contest I knew the answer to a question to which Olav seemed unsure of. He initially went for Andante stating correctly that it literally means walking pace, before discarding the choice that I would have opted for, Adagio, Olav instead opted for the choice Lento, his reasoning being that it was similar to the term Largo, a term that according to him, generally means slow. Dermot then consulted the Eggheads who confirmed that Adaigo was the correct answer and Olav's uncharacteristic mistake presented me the crucial advantage that I was looking for.

"SHAUN, GARY LIGHTBODY AND MARK MCCELLAND WERE THE ORIGINAL MEMBERS OF WHICH BAND, TRAVIS, SNOW PATROL OR BELLE AND SEBASTIAN?"

Unfortunately for me, I was asked the kind of question that middle aged old-fashioned quizzers like myself who are not really up to date on contemporary pop music always loathe and dread. I had heard of the first two groups knowing more about Travis as opposed to Snow Patrol and so I opted for Travis. The correct answer unfortunately was Snow Patrol.

"OLAV, SONG 2 AND TENDER WERE UK HIT SINGLES IN THE 1990'S FOR WHICH BAND, OASIS, PULP OR BLUR?"

A small yet confident smile adorned Olav's face after hearing the question and he went on to nostalgically describe how he used to sing along to Blur's 'Song 2' during his days at University also adding for what it was worth, that he didn't care much for the other song Tender.

"SHAUN, PHILLIP GLASS'S OPERA WAITING FOR THE BARBARIANS IS BASED ON A BOOK BY WHICH AUTHOR, J M COOTZEE, SALMAN RUSHDIE OR JOHN UPDIKE?"

In sheer desperation, I started to ramble on incessantly without any real purpose or meaning about the fact that Glass was a minimalist composer and that Cootzee had won the Nobel Prize for Literature in 1999. Without knowing why, I eventually settled on Salman Rushdie. After I declared my answer, Dermot immediately turned to the Eggheads to see whether they knew the answer but even they didn't have a clue and that was the only small crumb of comfort that arose from my incorrect choice. There was one person on the studio set who did know right answer and that was my increasingly confident opponent who after raising his hand to attract Dermot's attention, enlightened all concerned with the correct answer, J M Cootzee..

"OLAV, EVELYN ROTHWELL, THE WIFE OF THE CONDUCTOR JOHN BARBOROII, WAS A CONCERT SOLOIST ON WHICH INSTRUMENT, OBOE, HARP OR CELLO?"

The only reason I knew the correct answer to Olav's question was because I remembered reading about Evelyn Rothwell earlier in the year in the Obituary Section of the Times newspaper, there being a whole page devoted to her and a picture of her playing the Cello. Thankfully, Olav hadn't a clue and instinctively chose the Oboe, which meant for the first time in the contest, we had to go to sudden death to decide who would take the round.

"SHAUN, WHICH EARLY ROCK AND ROLL PERFORMER WAS ORIGINALLY CALLED ELIAS BATES?"

I thought that I knew the answer, but for the life of me it just wouldn't come. Instead of throwing in the towel and simply passing, I gave the answer Chuck Berry. Dermot turned to the Eggheads who confirmed that the answer was in fact, Bo Diddley.

"OLAV, DANA ELAINE OWENS IS THE REAL NAME OF WHICH HIP HOP PERFORMER AND ACTRESS?"

Olav gave the correct answer, Queen Latiffiah, to put him in a healthy and commanding position in the contest. Dermot asked him for his next choice of Egghead and without so much as a pause or hesitation, he chose Daphne.

Now I really had a fight on my hands and I realised that I had to do something fast because Olav was threatening to take a complete strangle hold on the game. My chances of getting back into the contest though were not about to improve as Dermot announced that the next category was Film and Television, another of my relatively weaker subjects.

Olav by contrast, seemed more than happy with the choice of category and elected to press home his advantage by facing the first question.

"OLAV, IN WHICH 1931 CHARLIE CHAPLIN FILM DOES THE TRAMP FALL IN LOVE WITH A BLIND FLOWER GIRL, CITY LIGHTS, MODERN TIMES OR LIMELIGHT?"

Olav gave the correct answer, City Lights, to put him one up for the round.

"SHAUN, IN THE 1988 FILM MIDNIGHT RUN, WHO PLAYED THE ACCOUNTANT WHO STEALS $15M DOLLARS FROM THE MOB, JOHN CANDY, CHARLES GRODEN OR CHEVY CHASE?"

I had to resort to random guesswork in the hope that I somehow landed the right answer with my eventual choice, John Candy. Dermot turned to the Egghead panel for confirmation and not for the first time in this contest, they dashed my hopes of drawing level by revealing that the right answer was Charles Groden.

"OLAV, OVER 51 MILLION VIEWERS TUNED INTO SEE THE FINAL EPISODE OF WHICH US TV SITCOM WHEN IT BROADCAST ON 6TH MAY 2004, FRIENDS, FRASIER OR SEINFELD?"

Olav knew the answer (as did I) that *Friends* was the show in question and as expected, was now 2 – 0 in the lead for the round. I had to stop the alarming rot in my performance somehow as another incorrect answer would bring a premature end to the round, but the truth of the matter was I was simply bereft of any ideas as to how to arrest my alarming decline and for the first time in the contest, I began to think that I was going to get beaten pretty comprehensively..

"SHAUN, BARRY NEWMAN PLAYED THE TITLE ROLE IN WHICH TV DETECTIVE SERIES OF THE 1970'S, BARNEY MILLER, PETROCELLI OR BANACEK?"

I smiled when that question came up because, aside from knowing the correct answer, it was TV legal dramas like Petrocelli that went a long way to influencing and inspiring my ambitions to qualify as a lawyer.

"OLAV, TOM CRUISE RECEIVED AN OSCAR NOMINATION FOR BEST SUPPORTING ACTOR FOR HIS ROLE AS FRANK T J MACKIE IN WHICH 1999 FILM, JERRY MCGUIRE, COLLATERAL OR MAGNOLIA?"

Olav wasted no time at all in selecting the correct answer Magnolia, a response that gave him his third successful round in a row and with it, another choice of an Egghead. On this occasion, he chose Chris Hughes.

The nightmare scenario of Olav having a clean sweep of Eggheads to assist him in the final round was now a very real possibility, but when Dermot announced that the next category in the contest was History, it lifted my spirits considerably. I would always back myself to come out on top in a head to head on the subject of History with anyone, even against an opponent who had a comfortable 3-0 lead and despite my desperate situation, I was nevertheless confident that this would be the round that would provide the springboard for a mini revival.

"OLAV, WHICH ITALIAN CITY WAS GOVERNED AS A REPUBLIC WAS LED BY THE DOMINICAN PRIEST SAVONAROLA FROM 1494 TO 1498, FLORENCE, MILAN OR ROME?"

That question was a gimmee so far as Olav was concerned and in no time at all, came up with the correct answer Florence.

"SHAUN, WHO COMMANDED THE RAF FIGHTER COMMAND IN THE SUMMER OF 1940 DURING THE BATTLE OF BRITAIN, ARTHUR HARRIS, HUGH DOWDING OR SHOLTO DOUGLAS?"

After I had given the correct answer Hugh Dowding, I went on to mention the fact that he was, in my opinion, one of the real unsung heroes of the Second World War on account of the courageous leadership that he and the brave RAF pilots under his command had shown in ultimately repelling the relentless onslaught of the German Luftwaffe in 1940.

"OLAV, WHICH ADMIRAL COMMANDED THE VICTORIOUS BRITISH FLEET AGAINST THE DUTCH AT THE BATTLE OF CAMPERDOWN IN 1797, DUNCAN, RODNEY OR HYDE PARKER?"

Olav gave the correct answer, Duncan, to regain the lead.

"SHAUN, HERE'S YOUR NEXT QUESTION, WHAT RELATION WAS WILHELM II, THE SECOND GERMAN KAISER

DURING WORLD WAR I TO QUEEN VICTORIA, COUSIN, GRANDSON OR NEPHEW?"

Thankfully for me, this was another straight forward question which gave me the opportunity to demonstrate the depth and range of my historical knowledge with an elaborate explanation that Queen Victoria's eldest daughter who also called Victoria, married Wilhelm I who was proclaimed Kaiser after the 1870 defeat of the French in the Franco-Prussian war and their eldest son who became the future Kaiser Wilhelm II, was Queen Victoria's grandson. Dermot then turned to Olav for his final question in the round.

"OLAV, THE ROMAN SETTLEMENT CALLED PONS ELY WAS ON THE SITE OF WHICH PRESENT DAY CITY, DURHAM, CARLISLE OR NEWCASTLE-UPON-TYNE?"

Olav smiled momentarily after hearing the question and without a moment's hesitation, he immediately gave the correct answer, Newcastle-upon-Tyne.

"SHAUN, THE ARMY OF WHICH FRENCH KING WAS DEFEATED BY THE ENGLISH AT THE BATTLE OF AGINCOUR, JOHN II, CHARLES VI OR CHARLES VII?"

I managed to combine an in depth knowledge of French History and Shakespeare's Henry V to come up with the correct answer, Charles VI, that seemed to impress Dermot considerably. My correct answer meant that the round would have to be decided by sudden death and for the first time in the entire contest, I felt that I had a real good chance that I was going to emerge victorious and claim my first round.

"OLAV, WHAT WAS THE NAME OF THE US PRESIDENT ELECTED IN 1908?"

Olav once again was not entirely sure of the correct answer, a dilemma that prompted him to agonise between the options, Theodore Roosevelt and Woodrow Wilson. When Dermot pressed him for his final answer, Olav finally settled on Theodore Roosevelt.

"THAT IS INCORRECT, OLAV. SHAUN, DO YOU KNOW?"

This was my golden chance for payback. "HE BECAME THE CHIEF JUSTICE, AFTER LEAVING OFFICE IN 1913 AND HE WAS THE FATTEST EVER US PRESIDENT, WILLIAM HENRY TAFT!"

"SHAUN, ON WHICH EAST LONDON STREET DID ANTI-FASCISTS CLASH WITH OSWALD MOSELEY AND HIS BLACK SHIRTS ON THE OCTOBER 4TH 1936?"

"THE BATTLE OF CABLE STREET!" I replied confidently. Finally, I had managed to stem the tide of Olav's seemingly unstoppable momentum. From the remaining two Eggheads that were left I chose CJ to assist me in the final round.

The final category before that final round was on the subject of Food and Drink.

"SHAUN, WHAT WAS THE MAIN INGREDIENT OF THE FERMENTED SAUCE GARAM OR LIQUAMEN THAT WAS POPULAR IN ROMAN TIMES, FISH, GARLIC OR MUSHROOM?"

I knew it was fish as a couple of nights previously, I was flicking through my satellite TV channels and happened to stop momentarily on the Discovery Channel which was showing a programme called, *What the Romans Did For Us,* that was focusing on Roman diet and cuisine and how the Romans would make the most elaborate sauces especially with their desserts where one of the unusual flavouring ingredients that they would invariably use was fish.

"OLAV,

WHICH JAPANESE STYLE OF DISH IS MOST SIMILAR TO THE ITALIAN FRITO MISO, SUSHI, TEMPURA OR SOBA?"

Olav had little difficulty in giving the correct answer tempura.

"SHAUN, THE EDIBLE GELATINOUS SUBSTANCE CALLED CALIPASH OR CALIPEE IS TAKEN FROM WHICH CREATURE, OSTRICH, TURTLE OR CAMEL?"

Admittedly, I would have struggled to come up with the right answer if I didn't have the benefit of having the multiple choice answers but ultimately I went for the correct choice, turtle.

"OLAV, "THE INGREDIENT CALLED QUININE USED IN TONIC WATER AND BITTER LEMON IS OBTAINED FROM THE BARK OF WHICH TREE, YOHIMBE, CINCHONA OR JACARANDA?"

"THIS IS A STAPLE QUIZ QUESTION!" Olav declared emphatically. He was right of course and after hearing his question, I knew that there was no way that a player with Olav's impeccable quizzing pedigree was going to slip up on such a straightforward question like that and his correct choice of Cinchona not only levelled the scores, it also returned the pressure firmly back onto my shoulders to come up with another correct answer, particularly with the round so delicately poised.

"SHAUN, WHICH VARIETY OF GRAPE IS THE MAIN CONSTITUENT IN THE TRADITIONAL FRENCH SPARKLING WINE CALLED BLANQUETTE DE LIMOUX, MAUZAC, CLAIRETTE OR ROUSSANNE?"

I hadn't a clue what the answer was. With nothing to go on, I had no other choice other than to hazard a complete and utter guess and went for Mauzac, and as luck would have it, for the second time in the round I somehow managed to come up with the correct answer.

541

"OLAV, THE LIQUEUR KVETCH IS MADE FROM WHICH TYPE OF FRUIT, APPLE, PEAR OR PLUM?"

Olav gave the right answer Plum which meant for the third time in the contest, sudden death would have to decide the outcome of a round.

"SHAUN, THE STRONG SWEET DESERT WINE CALLED COMMANDARIA IS TRADITIONALLY MADE ON WHICH MEDITERRANEAN ISLAND?"

I didn't really have a clue as to what the correct answer could be, but the first island that popped into my head was the largest Mediterranean island of them all. Working on the premise that one's first gut instinct is usually the instinct to follow and with caution firmly thrown to the wind, I chose Sicily. Dermot then turned to consult the Egghead's panel and save for CJ, the rest of his colleagues together replied in unison that the Mediterranean in question was Cyprus.

"OLAV, WHICH STARCHY FOOD IS OBTAINED FROM THE PITH OF CERTAIN PALM TREES PARTICULARLY OF THE METROXYLON GENUS?"

I looked across to Olav and not for the first time in the contest, the expression on his face told the tale of a man who knew that he was about to answer yet another question correctly and his subsequent reply of the foodstuff Sago, paved the way clear for him to select the last remaining Egghead Judith to assist him in the final round.

The only thought running through my mind as I prepared to face the five question showdown were something along the despairing lines of, *How the hell am I going to turn this situation around?* On paper, Olav was the clear favourite to progress with four Eggheads at his disposal to my solitary one, a position that to all intents and purposes seemed to be virtually unassailable. However, despite my situation bearing all the hallmarks of Custer's heroic last stand, the one thing I was not going to do in that final showdown was to simply roll over and accept that I was only there to make up the numbers.

Because Olav had won the last round, Dermot asked him whether he wished to face the first of his five questions and unsurprisingly, he elected to go first.

"OLAV, WHAT WAS THE ORIGINAL CAREER OF F. MATHIAS ALEXANDER WHO ORIGINATED THE EDUCATIONAL TECHNIQUE THAT IS NAMED AFTER HIM, ACTOR, POLITICIAN OR ARTIST?"

There were no visible signs of weakness in either Olav's knowledge or confidence in general and he responded assertively that Alexander was an Australian Actor.

"SHAUN, THE PHRASE, 'WARTS AND ALL', IS SAID TO REFER TO OLIVER CROMWELL'S INSTRUCTIONS TO WHICH PORTRAIT PAINTER TO INCLUDE ALL HIS BLEMISHES, ANTHONY VAN DYCK, PETER LELY OR WILLIAM DOBSON?"

I responded with the correct answer, Peter Lely to level up the scores.

"OLAV, THE FIRST EVER RUGBY INTERNATIONAL IN 1871 WAS BETWEEN ENGLAND AND WHICH OTHER COUNTY, WALES, SCOTLAND OR IRELAND?"'

Olav somewhat surprisingly, was not sure of the correct answer, but what was even more surprising was his decision to use Kevin to assist him. The sight of Olav deploying the use of an Egghead at such an early stage of the final round gave me a massive uplift in confidence because for the first time in the contest, I was beginning to sense that there could be a possible chink in my opponent's otherwise impressive quizzing armoury. Olav's choice of Kevin Ashman to help him answer the question looked as though it was going to backfire as Kevin initially appeared to be having difficulty in getting to grips with the question. Those faint hopes of gaining a crucial advantage were dashed the moment the Master quizzer in chief regained his composure and with his usual impeccable logic and reasoning, Kevin guided Olav to the correct choice of Scotland. Olav was now 2-1 in the lead and with three Eggheads still at his disposal, still retained the upper hand.

"SHAUN, WHICH BRITISH BIRD OF PREY HAS THE SCIENTIFIC NAME MILVUS MILVUS, RED KITE, GOSHAWK OR HEN HARRIER?"

I had a fairly good inkling what the correct answer was but it was by no means, a certain one and at such an important point in the contest, I faced my first major judgement call. Do I ask CJ for assistance or do I back my own judgement? I decided to take no chances and like Olav before me, I turned to my solitary Egghead to help but alas, the assistance I was hoping for would not be forthcoming, a fact that Dermot commented on when he unflatteringly compared CJ to a bird flapping constantly in a state of near panic. CJ genuinely did not have a clue what the correct answer. Without giving too much thought to the question, CJ apologised to me in advance and went for a complete random choice with Hen Harrier. I am glad that he made that choice because I knew right away that he was completely and utterly wrong. It was time for me to demonstrate the unshakeable belief that I had in my ability and back my own judgement.

"I'M GOING TO GO FOR RED KITE," I confidently declared.

Dermot's immediate reaction to my decision to reject CJ's suggestion was one of mild surprise. "SHAUN, YOU'RE OVERRULING YOUR EGGHEAD AND GETTING IT... RIGHT! IT'S CORRECT."

I was relieved that my inkling, judgement, unshakable faith whatever you call it, had paid off. I was still in there fighting, but that fight would have to continue without the safety net of an Egghead to help me If I was going to overturn the seemingly impossible odds and win, I would have to do it all on my own.

"OLAV, ACCORDING TO HOMER'S ODYSSEY, WHO WAS THE FATHER OF THE MAIN CHARACTER, LAERTES, AUTOLYCUS OR TELEMACHUS?"

The questions seemed to be falling Olav's way with another fairly easy question and he wasted no time in explaining that Telemachus was Odysseus's son and his father was Laertes.

"SHAUN, HOW MANY SYLLABLES ARE THERE IN THE SECOND LINE OF THE JAPANESE VERSE FORM KNOWN AS A HAIKU, FIVE, SIX OR SEVEN?"

I knew as an absolute fact that are seventeen lines in a Haiku therefore to my mind, it made more logical sense that the sequence of verses to be 5-7-5 as opposed to any other configuration. Dermot confirmed, therefore, my answer, 7.

"OLAV, WHICH LONDON LANDMARK WAS DESIGNED BY CAPTAIN FRANCIS FOWKE OF THE ROYAL ENGINEERS, BATTERSEA POWER STATION, WESTMINSTER CATHEDRAL OR THE ROYAL ALBERT HALL?"

Olav was lightning quick with his response. "THE ANSWER IS THE ROYAL ALBERT HALL AS HE WON A COMPETITION TO DESIGN IT."

Dermot's response to my opponent's impressive answer sounded to my mind somewhat triumphalist and strangely premature. "YOU'RE GETTING CLOSER TO WINNING THE COMPETITION AND YOU HAVE YOUR THREE EGGHEADS STILL INTACT"

Is he indeed? I said to myself after hearing Dermot's remarks that seemed to give the impression that the contest between us was all but over. *We'll see about that!*

"SHAUN, THE LARGE NUMBER SOMETIMES KNOWN AS A GOOGLE IS WRITTEN IN DECIMAL NOTATION OF ONE FOLLOWED BY HOW MANY ZEROS, TEN, ONE HUNDRED OR A THOUSAND?"

I knew the correct answer was one hundred before Dermot even had a chance to finish reading the question as a similar question was asked on a particularly notorious episode of *Who Wants to be a Millionaire?* I gave my answer and Dermot confirmed it was correct.

Although we had each answered four questions correctly in a row, Olav still maintained the advantage with his three Eggheads intact going into the fifth and final question.

"OLAV, THE SAILING VESSEL, NUGGERS, ARE TRADITIONALLY USED TO NAVIGATE WHICH RIVER, THE INDUS, HWANG HO OR THE NILE?"

What a horrible fifth question! My initial reaction upon hearing the question was one of instant relief that my opponent had to answer it instead of me because I didn't know the answer but even more importantly at such a crucial moment in the game, neither did Olav. He sought the help of his Eggheads and went for Chris on account of his transport knowledge and expertise. Chris, despite such expertise, was not 100% sure, but after some deliberation he eventually suggested the River Nile. Olav was not entirely convinced with Chris's suggestion or logic and his indecisiveness became all too apparent when crucially, he turned to Daphne Fowler and asked for her help. The tension in the studio, which had already surpassed unbearable levels, was now taken up a further notch or two. Daphne really put the cat amongst the pigeons when, to my complete and utter astonishment, she disagreed with Chris's choice and suggested that the river in question was in fact the Indus, her reasoning being, that she always believed that Feluccas were the only sailing vessels that operated on the Nile. Olav was now in a real dilemma and after much agonising, he eventually decided to go with Daphne's choice.

The tension by now had increased tenfold as Dermot prepared to reveal the answer. "THE ANSWER IS…THE NILE." Dermot's revelation seemed to have the dramatic effect of visibly draining the fight out of my once invincible opponent. Olav's incorrect answer could not have come at a worst time so far as he was concerned but suddenly, I was presented with a golden opportunity to turn the game completely on its head. I was now one correct answer away from an unlikely victory.

"SHAUN, THE CONDITION CALLED ABASIA APPEARS AS AN INABILITY TO DO WHAT, SLEEP, WALK OR TALK?"

If I was at home sitting on my sofa hearing that question, I would have screamed out the answer, walk, but under the bright lights of a studio and given what was at stake, even an experienced quizzer like myself was affected by the near intolerable levels of pressure. My heart started beating even faster, excited no doubt, in anticipation that my next response was going to win me the game. "I'M GOING TO SAY, WALK!" and I sat back in my chair with my eyes closed waiting to hear what Dermot was going to say.

"SHAUN, THE ANSWER IS WALK, YOU'VE WON!" A feeling of total relief and elation came over me as the show's theme music started to play heralding the end of the game. "CONGRATULATIONS! THERE MUST HAVE BEEN A POINT IN WHICH YOU THOUGHT, I'M GETTING STEAMROLLERED!"

My reaction to Dermot's astute observations was bullish to say the very least. "IT DID LOOK DIFFICULT ESPECIALLY AT 4-1 DOWN, BUT WHEN IT COMES TO A GENERAL KNOWLEDGE SHOOTOUT THAT'S MY GAME!"

"YOU'RE THROUGH TO THE QUARTER FINALS AND YOU'RE ONE STEP CLOSER TO JOINING OUR QUIZ GOLIATHS!"

Once the show's closing credits had finished and we had been cleared by the Studio Floor Manager to leave the set, I rose wearily from my seat feeling completely physically and mentally drained but those feelings were assuaged by the immense sense of pride and satisfaction in managing to overcome a player of Olav's considerable ability. Charlotte was the first member of the production team to approach me with an initial look of astonishment and surprise on her face before offering her congratulations on my victory before adding, that she would be in touch later that evening to discuss the details for the next stage of the contest. Olav meanwhile quite understandably, had already left the studio before I had a chance to go and speak to him. I was escorted back to my dressing room by one of the show's production assistants so that I could gather my belongings before leaving the studios to go home. At virtually the same time that I was making my way towards the exit turnstile gates, I noticed Olav with his small hand luggage in tow also about to leave the premises. I called out to Olav and asked whether it was possible to exchange contact details and despite still looking somewhat subdued, he nevertheless was more than happy to oblige with my request and after we shook hands for the final time, we went our separate ways. As I headed towards to the BBC Car Park, the unrestrained feelings of happiness and elation resulting from my fantastic victory continued unabated, an emotion that lasted from the moment I got into my car until I returned home. I would be the first to admit that I was extremely lucky to have managed somehow to come through such a bruising contest against a world class quizzer like Olav and but I did which meant that I was now one step closer towards achieving my ultimate objective. My return to competitive TV quizzing, despite one or two hair raising moments in my two contests to date, was still very much alive and kicking.

Later on that evening, Charlotte called with the details of my next match and she informed me that because Thursday would be the last recording date for the whole competition, my potential timetable for that day would begin with my quarter final contest taking place at 9am, with the two semi finals and grand final taking place later on in that same day. A tough and demanding timetable on the face of it but if I wanted to claim the ultimate prize, I had no choice other than to simply get on with it.

My daunting quest of trying to become the next Egghead though was the least of my immediate worries. I still had to go back to Isleworth Crown Court the following day to discover whether the case I was involved in was going to proceed to a full hearing because if it was, there was the real possibility that I would have to withdraw from the rest of the competition.

I received a text message from Olav, which read: "Hey Shaun, thanks for the compliment. Sadly, it can't compensate for how gutted I feel. However, that's the brakes. Anyway, I have crucial news. Mark Kerr knocked out Pat Gibson, so your likely semi-final path and final path is Kerr, then Barry Simmons. Your chances have just risen even more dramatically. Good luck. Olav."

Olav's text message brought an instant smile to my face and I was impressed with how graciously he had taken his very marginal defeat. At the same time, I was also mildly curious as to how he knew so much about the line-up of the remaining competitors particularly in view of the fact when I was told from the competition's outset, that there would be complete and total secrecy.

The following morning I went back to Isleworth Crown Court for the case that had been adjourned two days previously to discover whether the Crown Prosecution Service were going to proceed with the trial. After speaking to my opponent I was informed to my considerable double delight, that the CPS had reviewed the matter and had decided that they were going to offer no evidence, a decision that was not only great news for my relieved client, it also meant that the real possibility of me having to withdraw from the Eggheads competition was now no longer an issue. With the last remaining obstacle removed, I headed for home to immediately immerse myself in the three R's, revision, rest and relaxation.

In terms of my revision, I decided to focus my efforts mainly on the topics of Food and Drink, Music and Entertainment on account of my lamentable performance in those subjects that were nearly my undoing in the previous round. Once I had completed my revision, I grabbed myself a quick bite to eat before heading upstairs to iron my favourite pink shirts before gathering together, all my quiz books and other essential items I was going to need for the following day. After treating myself to the luxury of a long hot soak in the bath, I eventually crawled into bed just after midnight feeling really good about myself and as my head lay on the pillow, my thoughts turned to the forthcoming challenge that lay ahead, thoughts that were nothing other than good, positive ones that my life could profoundly change for the better if everything went according to plan and the mere thought of that prospect immediately bought a big broad smile to my face that was quickly followed by a deep sound of satisfaction as I exhaled my previous intake of breath.

The following morning I woke up just before 6am full of excitement about the day that lay ahead of me, my immediate objective after rising from my bed, was to set myself the strict deadline target of 6.45am by which time I had to leave home. With clockwork military precision, I rushed into the bathroom and turned the hot tap on to a gentle trickle which would give me enough time to rush downstairs to the kitchen in order to prepare a bowl of my usual three Weetabix with loads of sugar as the pot full of cold milk which was already left on the cooker overnight ready to be heated. I quickly changed into my jogging gear and went for a brisk jog from my house to the top of the High Road and back again via the local park that was timed perfectly to coincide with the bath that by this time was now virtually full. I allowed myself the luxury of a full seven minute soak before drying off and rushing downstairs to the kitchen and lit the stove in order to warm the milk in the small pan. I consumed my Weetabix robustly watching BBC's Breakfast TV as I was doing so in the living room before rushing back upstairs where in that time I managed to get myself dressed, gather together my belongings and make my way through the front door with five minutes to spare. Before getting into my car to embark on my early dawn round trip journey, I gave myself a self-congratulatory pat on the back for having kept to my strict time schedule and my good mood was further heightened by the fact that the weather outside was simply glorious. I got into my car and immediately put the roof down and slipped into my CD player, The Best of Steely Dan, and set off for the first leg of my journey.

With the glorious rays of the sun radiating its warmth, my good mood and confident state of mind couldn't have been any higher during my journey to the studios as I sang along merrily to the tracks on the CD ranging from Haitian Divorce and Deacon Blue to my all time favourite Steely Dan track, Babylon Sisters. I arrived at the BBC Car Park with some thirty minutes to spare, time enough to afford me the luxury of being able to recline the driver's seat in order to relax and gather my thoughts for a while. Those thoughts that were constantly drifting through my mind had taken me on a short but wonderful trip down memory lane to June 2004 where I remembered being in a not too dissimilar position, sitting in the BBC Car Park getting myself ready for the *Mastermind* Grand Final filled with a tremendous sense of anticipation that I was on the threshold of doing something extraordinary and now here I am, in the same place and position on the threshold of another significant achievement once more. After emerging from my nostalgic like trance and giving myself one final pep talk, I finally got out of my car and retrieved my belongings before exiting the BBC Car Park for the short 300 yard stroll to the main reception area with a broad smile on my face and a purposeful spring in my step and by the time I negotiated my way through the building's vast revolving glass doors, already waiting for me by the Reception Desk, was the production assistant Lucy. We wasted next to no time navigating our way through the complex maze of stairs and corridors towards the dressing room area where I quickly deposited my belongings in the same dressing room that had been allocated to me on my previous two visits, as I was required immediately, to go to the green room where awaiting my presence, was Charlotte together with my quarter final opponent Terry Toomey, a veteran of a number of TV quiz shows that included, winning an edition of *The Weakest Link*. Charlotte did the formal introductions and after the pair of us shook hands, Terry and I straight away engaged in pleasant, friendly banter that focused mainly on football after Terry had revealed that he was a diehard Tottenham Hotspur fan, a revelation that prompted me to responded in typical partisan fashion by reminding him of Chelsea's impressive run of victories over his team in recent years.

As soon as everybody was settled on set, the Studio Floor Manager began the usual countdown to begin Dermot's opening monologue that was followed by Terry then myself, introducing ourselves to the camera. Dermot then spoke to each of us in turn about our previous appearances before introducing the first category in the contest, Food and Drink. Although Terry had won the toss backstage, he elected that I should face the first question before going on to explain to Dermot that forcing his opponents to face that first question at the beginning of a category was a particular strategy of his.

"SHAUN, WHICH HERB DERIVES ITS NAME FROM THE GREEK WORD FOR IMMORTALITY, ROSEMARY, SORREL OR TANSY?"

I went for Tansy. Dermot turned to the Eggheads panel to see if they agreed with my choice and Judith responded by saying that she believed that the answer was Rosemary. My heart sank a little when I heard Judith's response, but Dermot rode to my rescue when corrected her and confirmed that Tansy was in fact the right answer to put me into the lead.

"TERRY, WHAT TYPE OF FOOD IS A SCOTTISH DUNLOP, CHEESE, BLOOD SAUSAGE OR OATCAKE?"

Without really knowing the reason why, Terry decided to immediately rule out blood sausage before going on to say that out of the two options that remained, the one that seemed more plausible to him was cheese and whether it was by accident or design, he too had somehow managed to get his first question correct.

"SHAUN, THE BEAN'S DISH KNOWN AS FUL MEDAMES IS OFTEN REFERRED TO AS THE NATIONAL DISH OF WHICH COUNTRY, NIGERIA, MOROCCO OR EGYPT?"

With nothing coming to mind, I decided to throw caution to the wind and randomly went for Morocco. Dermot consulted the Eggheads panel and even the great Kevin Ashman agreed with my choice stating that in his view, the name of the dish seemed to suggest that it came from North Africa. Dermot confirmed that Ful Medames did in fact come from North Africa, but the North African country in question was Egypt and not Morocco.

"TERRY, WHAT IS THE DEFINING INGREDIENT IN A DISH KNOWN AS MENRUI SEAWEED, NOODLES OR SALMON?"

The dreaded Japanese cuisine question that has been the scourge of the Eggheads panel on the regular Eggheads series. It was no surprise, that Terry was having the same difficulty and without really knowing the reasons why, he went for Salmon as a complete guess, a choice which, to my relief, was the incorrect answer, the correct answer being Noodles.

"SHAUN, MANCHEGO CHEESE IS TRADITIONALLY MADE FROM THE MILK OF WHICH ANIMAL, SHEEP, GOAT OR COW?"

I shook my head in utter dismay upon hearing the question that prompted me to openly admit that I did not know what the correct answer was. My response seemed to take CJ somewhat by surprise giving his arched eyebrows and once again without rhyme or reason, I resorted to the tactic of random guessing and chose the option, Goat, which sadly for me, was the wrong answer. Collectively, the whole Eggheads panel sought to enlighten me with CJ taking the lead in explaining that it was a Spanish cheese that came from sheep and covered with an orange rind.

"TERRY, WITH A SEATING CAPACITY OF 6,014, IN WHICH COUNTRY IS THE WORLD'S LARGEST RESTAURANT SITUATED. IRAN, SYRIA OR KUWAIT?"

Luckily for me, Terry did not seem to know the answer he sought to rely on an inspired random guesswork and declared that Kuwait was probably the correct answer. You can imagine my complete and utter relief when Daphne revealed that the correct answer was in fact Syria.

"SHAUN, IN FRENCH CUISINE, WHAT IS THE NAME GIVEN TO CHESTNUTS THAT HAVE BEEN POACHED IN SYRUP AND THEN GLAZED?"

I gave the correct answer, Marron Glace.

"TERRY, WHAT IS THE NAME GIVEN TO THE PASTRY TARTLETS FILLED WITH A CURD CHEESE ALMOND AND LEMON FILLING THAT HAS BEEN RUMOURED TO HAVE BEEN CREATED BY ANNE BOLEYN?"

Terry admitted that he hadn't heard of the pastry tartlets and although he gave the answer Bakewell Tart, he did so in the full knowledge that it was incorrect and as a consequence, resigned himself to conceding the round. The sudden death questions were kinder to me than the regular set of questions and when Dermot asked me if I knew the answer, I responded straight away by telling him that they were called Maids of Honour, a response which drew both a smile and a nod of approval from Daphne.

"SHAUN'S OPENED HIS ACCOUNT AND TERRY IS YET TO MAKE A DEPOSIT," was Dermot's assessment after what was in truth, a very poor round, as he invited me for my choice of Egghead and without so much of a hint of hesitation, I immediately chose the infinitely knowledgeable Kevin Ashman to assist me in the final round.

The next was Film and Television and I elected to face the first question.

"SHAUN, WHAT WAS THE FIRST NAME OF RIMMER ON THE TV COMEDY SHOW, RED DWARF, ARTHUR, ALFRED OR ARNOLD?"

I admitted that I had never actually watched the programme,and opted for Arnold which thankfully for me turned out to be the correct answer.

"TERRY, THE TV SERIES, *ALL CREATURES GREAT AND SMALL*, WAS SET IN AND AROUND WHICH SMALL FICTIONAL TOWN, DARROWFELL, DARROWBY OR DARROWDALE?"

Terry said that he had not watched the series but out of the choices that lay in front of him, his gut reaction was telling him that it was more likely to be Darrowby as opposed to the choice that I would have probably gone for, Darrowdale. It was a good job that it wasn't my question as Terry's inkling managed to pay him instant dividends as his selection of the correct answer evened up the scores.

"SHAUN, THE IDIOTS AND DOGVILLE ARE FILMS BY WHICH DIRECTOR, LARS VON TRIER, THOMAS VINTERBERG OR KRISTIAN LEVRING?"

I had never heard of the names of any of these films let alone, the names of Directors. On a wing and a prayer, I eventually went for Von Trier for no other reason other than pot luck that like Terry before me, paid the same lucky dividend. Dermot revealed that Lars Von Trier had in fact directed the films in question.

"TERRY, FOR HIS ROLE IN WHICH FILM DID MARLON BRANDO WIN HIS FIRST BEST ACTOR OSCAR, VIVA ZAPATA, A STREETCAR NAMED DESIRE OR ON THE WATERFRONT?"

Terry knew the answer to this question (as did I) and after eliminating the first two options, he settled for the option, On the Waterfront to put him deservedly on level terms. With the round delicately poised, It was extremely important for me not to surrender the initiative with my next question otherwise a person of Terry's ability and quizzing pedigree was not going to let me off the hook a second time.

"SHAUN, WHICH MAN, KNOWN AS THE PIONEER OF DEEP FOCUS PHOTOGRAPHY, WAS THE CINEMATOGRAPHER ON ORSEN WELLS' CITIZEN KANE, JOHN L RUSSELL, JOHN ALTON OR GREG TOLAND?"

Another question of which I simply did not have a clue. I eventually settled on John Alton in the hope that I had made my third successive lucky guess in a row to keep me ahead in the round, but those hopes were dashed when Kevin revealed that Greg Toland was the cinematographer in question.

"TERRY, WHO PLAYED THE ROLE OF ENA SHARPLES IN CORONATION STREET, VIOLET CARSON, LYNE CAROL OR ANNE REID?"

Terry gave the correct answer, Violet Carson, and with that, he won the round. Dermot asked Terry which of the remaining Eggheads was he was going to choose to assist him in the final round and he declared that he was going to select Daphne.

Dermot announced that the next category was Science and true to form, Terry invoked his tried and trusted strategy of having won the previous round, of putting his opponents in to face the first question.

"SHAUN, IN WHICH PART OF THE HUMAN BODY ARE THE ISLETS OF LANGERHANS LOCATED, PANCREAS, BRAIN OR KIDNEYS?"

I felt on safer ground with Science after the horrors of the last two categories and gave the correct answer, Pancreas.

"TERRY, WHAT IS THE NAME OF THE ECOLOGICAL SAMPLING UNIT CONSISTING OF A SMALL SQUARE AREA OF GROUND WITHIN WHICH ALL SPECIES OF INTEREST ARE LOGGED AND MEASUREMENTS TAKEN, QUADRAT, QUADROD OR QUADRANGLE?"

Terry immediately ruled out Quadrangle as he knew that the word denoted a type of square, but unfortunately for him, out of the remaining two choices on offer, he incorrectly selected the option Quadrod and that surprising error by my opponent presented me with a golden opportunity to extend my lead.

"SHAUN, WHAT NAME IS GIVEN TO A CELL THAT IS ABLE TO ENGULF AND BREAK DOWN FOREIGN PARTICLES, CELL DEBRIS AND DISEASE PRODUCING MICROORGANISMS, SCHWANN CELL, ZYGOTE OR PHAGOCYTE?"

Using my rudimentary knowledge of Greek, I knew that the prefix, Phago, was Greek for to eat and my selection of the option Phagocyte put me into a commanding 2-0 lead.

"TERRY, WHAT TYPE OF CREATURES BELONG TO THE PHYLUM ANNELIDA, ANTS, WORMS OR SPIDERS?"

Terry to his credit, managed to keep the round alive by choosing the correct option, worms, but I still had the advantage as I faced my third question if answered correctly would win for me another round and with it, another Egghead to assist me in the final round.

"SHAUN, WHAT PROPERTY OF A MATERIAL IS A SCLEROMETER USED TO MEASURE, DENSITY, HARDNESS OR CONDUCTIVITY?"

As the old saying goes, "only fools rush in where Angels fear to tread" and instead of taking a step back to consider the options and apply my rudimentary knowledge of Greek to the question just as I had done with my previous question, I would have arrived at the correct answer especially, if I had used as an illustrative example the well known medical condition, Sclerosis of the Liver which denotes the hardening of the organ. But I didn't and instead of securing for myself the important point that would have won me the round, my unforced yet costly error presented a golden opportunity for Terry to level the scores and take the round into another sudden death tiebreak.

"TERRY, A NIT IS A UNIT OF WHAT, THERMODYNAMIC TEMPERATURE, MASS OR LUMINANCE?"

Terry appeared to initially recoil in horror when he first heard the question but to his credit, he managed to pull himself together and after ruling out Thermodynamic Temperature Mass, he settled on Luminance. Dermot then consulted the Eggheads and they all seemed to collectively agree that Thermodynamic Temperature was the right answer, a response that led to think that Terry's apparent incorrect selection had meant that I had won the round as I have never been aware of, or indeed have seen since I have been watching the programme, a situation where the Eggheads panel collectively agree on an answer then proceed to get it entirely wrong. Well, as it turned out, this was one of those situations as Terry had, against all odds, managed put one over the Eggheads to remarkably come up with the right answer. Terry was proving to be every bit the worthy and dangerous opponent I thought he would be and for second time in our contest, we were into a sudden death shoot out to determine the round.

"SHAUN, USUALLY FOUND IN POLAR REGIONS AND SOMETIMES OVER A KILOMETRE DEEP, WHAT IS THE NAME GIVEN TO FROZEN SOIL AND SUB SOIL THAT HAS BEEN AT OR BELOW FREEZING POINT FOR AT LEAST TWO YEARS?"

As I was discussing the options out loud, I almost went for the option, Tundra but thankfully, I just managed to stop myself just in the nick of time by suddenly remembering that the correct answer in fact must be Permafrost, a choice that Dermot confirmed was the right one to make.

"TERRY, WHAT TYPE OF SHALLOW CIRCULAR PLASTIC OR GLASS DISH COMMONLY USED IN SCIENTIFIC EXPERIMENTATION IS NAMED AFTER A GERMAN BACTERIOLOGIST WHO WAS BORN IN 1852?"

Terry kept the round alive with the correct answer, Petrie Dish.

"SHAUN, IN PLANT BIOLOGY, WHAT IS THE COMMON NAME CONTAINING THE MASS OF RAINS THAT CONTAIN THE MALE GAMETES OF SEED PLANTS?"

At first, I was perplexed by the question but after Dermot repeated it, it was not as difficult as it first appeared. I went for pollen, somewhat cautiously, and thankfully, my initial hesitancy and cautiousness proved to be groundless as it was the correct answer that for the third time put the pressure firmly back on the shoulders of my plucky opponent.

"TERRY, IN TERMS OF THE WORKINGS OF THE HUMAN BODY, WHAT DO THE LETTERS CNS STAND FOR?"

As with my previous question, Terry seemed to be stumped on the first reading of the question, but once Dermot had repeated it, it suddenly dawned on him that it could only be the Central Nervous System.

"SHAUN, WHAT IS THE USUAL NAME GIVEN TO DRUGS SUCH AS ATENOLOL THAT ARE USED TO TREAT HIGH BLOOD PRESSURE AND ARRHYTHMIA?"

Thankfully, I knew the answer was beta blockers.

"TERRY, WHICH ELEMENT WITH THE ATOMIC NUMBER 45 IS COMMONLY USED IN OPTICAL REFLECTORS AND THE PLATING OF JEWELLERY?

Terry didn't know the answer and heroically guessed Zinc. I make no apologies for the utter joy and relief that I felt inside when Dermot revealed that the correct answer was in fact Rhodium and after twelve hard fought questions, I finally managed to capture the round, and another egghead. I chose Chris.

Dermot announced that the next category was Sport, a category that Terry and I seemed equally pleased had come up as well as equally determined to win and in my efforts to try and gain some sort of advantage over my knowledgeable and dangerous adversary, I elected to answer the first question.

"SHAUN, WHICH AMATEUR FAST BOWLER FAMOUSLY DEFIED HIS CAPTAIN DOUGLAS JARDINE AND REFUSED TO BOWL THE CONTROVERSIAL LEG THEORY AGAINST THE AUSTRALIANS IN THE 1932-33 BODYLINE SERIES, BILL BOWES, GUBBY ALLEN OR BILL VOCE?"

Out of the choices that were available I was fairly certain that it was Gubby Allen who was the bowler in question and Dermot confirmed that my selection was correct to put me one up for the round.

"TERRY, WHICH DUTCH PLAYER WAS NAMED EUROPEAN FOOTBALL PLAYER OF THE YEAR IN 1988, 1989 AND 1992, MARCO VAN BASTEN, FRANK RIJKAARD OR RUUD GULLIT?"

On hearing the question, I thought it was the type of question that Terry would have gobbled up for breakfast given the fact that like me, he is an avid football fan. However, much to my pleasant surprise and delight, he thought it was Ruud Gullit as opposed to the correct answer Marco Van Basten, who had won the award in those years and with that unexpected slip up by Terry, I had a golden opportunity to press home my advantage with my next question.

"SHAUN, WHICH GOLFER WAS THE FIRST MAN TO WIN THE OPEN, US OPEN, USPGA AND THE US MASTERS KNOWN

AS THE GRAND SLAM, BEN HOGAN, WALTER HAGEN OR GENE SARAZEN?"

I was confident the answer was Ben Hogan, but Daphne corrected my error when she revealed that the golfer in question was in fact Gene Sarazen.

"TERRY, IN WHICH YEAR DID THE POLE VAULTER SERGEI BUBKA WIN THE FIRST OF HIS WORLD ATHLETICS CHAMPIONSHIP GOLD MEDALS, 1983, 1985 OR 1987?"

Terry wasted little time in putting himself back in contention for the round as he declared that he was 100% certain that Sergei Bubka had won his first Gold Medal at the inaugural Championships in Helsinki in 1983.

"SHAUN, WHICH CYCLIST WON THE TOUR DE FRANCE FIVE TIMES BETWEEN 1957 AND 1964, LUCIEN AIMAR, JACQUES ANQUETIL OR LOUISON BOBET?"

I knew the answer straight away and to demonstrate my Tour De France cycling knowledge, I proceeded to list the four cyclists who had won the event on five consecutive occasions or more and who they were. Lance Armstrong, Miguel Indurain, Eddie Mercyx and finally, the correct answer to this particular question, Jacques Anquetil.

"TERRY, IN 2006 THE ENGLISH RUGBY LEAGUE INTERNATIONAL JAMIE PEACOCK SIGNED FOR WHICH CLUB, BRADFORD BULLS, WARRINGTON WOLVES OR LEEDS RHINOS?"

Terry confessed that Rugby League was not one of his favourite sports and his candid admission immediately raised my hopes that he would make another costly error. He went for the Bradford Bulls, and I knew that the round was mine as the answer was the Warrington Wolves. With the round secured, Dermot offered me the choice of an Egghead and out of the two that remained, I selected the one who had been on my side on my two previous appearances in the competition, the inimitable CJ de Mooi.

Dermot then revealed that the final category before the final round would be History, by far and away my strongest subject. I had every reason to believe that the round was there for the taking and purely on that basis, I elected to face the first question.

"SHAUN, WHAT WAS THE NICKNAME OF WILLIAM IV OF GREAT BRITAIN AND IRELAND, THE SOLIDER KING, THE SAILOR KING OR THE FARMER KING?"

Such a relatively easy question for a History aficionado such as myself as it gave me the platform to show how much I knew about William IV, briefly referring to the little known fact that he used to live in Stanmore, North London with his long time mistress, Dorethea Jordan and their seventeen illegitimate children, a detailed explanation that seemed to provoke mild astonishment and amusement of the host and the rest of Eggheads panel. When I eventually got around to giving the correct answer, the Sailor King, Dermot went on to comment that, I must be as mad as the eggheads.

"TERRY, AGAINST WHOM DID THE FRENCH FORCES UNDER NAPOLEON FIGHT THE BATTLE OF MARENGO, AUSTRIA, RUSSIA OR SPAIN?"

Terry was clearly struggling with this question confessing that he wished he could use Chris to assist him. Sadly though, he ruled out the options of Russia, (the correct answer), then Austria, before settling on his final choice of Spain.

"SHAUN, AKHBAR THE GREAT WAS THE RULER OF WHICH EMPIRE IN THE 16TH CENTURY, MAYAN, OTTOMAN OR MUGHAL?"

What a great question as it provided yet another opportunity for me to show off my History knowledge which I grabbed with both hands before eventually settling on the correct answer, The Mughal Empire.

"TERRY, WHICH SOLIDER BORN IN 1788 WAS PLACED IN COMMAND OF THE BRITISH ARMY AT THE START OF THE CRIMEAN WAR, LUCAN, RAGLAN OR AIREY?"

Terry initially went for the correct option, Raglan, as he was aware that he had played a prominent role in the Crimean war but inexplicably, he decided to change his mind and opted for Lucan, a disastrous last minute switch that thankfully for me meant that the round had come to a premature end leaving me with the pick of the last and final Egghead on offer, Judith Keppel.

I now had a healthy 4-1 lead over Terry as we prepared to contest the final round but as I was all too aware, as so perfectly illustrated during my contest with Olav in the previous round, an apparently commanding position is no firm guarantee of outright victory. I was determined to learn from that experience and fully embrace as well as take on board, the wise yet ominous words of Dermot's familiar catchphrase that he utters just before the commencement of the final round of the need for contestants, "TO USE YOUR EGGHEADS WISELY AND NOT PUT ALL YOUR EGGHEADS INTO ONE BASKET." Because I had won the last round, Dermot offered me the choice of facing the first question and given the position I was in, bearing in mind Terry's notorious aversion to going first, I elected to face the first question in the final head to head showdown that mattered.

"SHAUN, WHAT IS FAIENCE? IS IT EARTHENWARE, LACE OR TAPESTRY?'

I wasn't quite sure of the answer but I knew Judith Keppel would on account of her extensive knowledge of all things French. My choice of Egghead to assist me with the question proved to be an inspired one and without any hint of hesitation or prevarication on her part, Judith told me immediately that the correct answer was Earthenware, a clear and confident response that I was more than happy to accept and Dermot's confirmation that my choice was correct gave me a 1-0 lead.

"TERRY, IN WHICH FIELD DID THE ITALIAN-AMERICAN FRANCO MODIGLIANI GAIN EMINENCE IN THE 20TH CENTURY, ENGINEERING, ARCHITECTURE OR ECONOMICS?"

Given his relative paucity of Egghead support, Terry bravely decided to answer the question without the need to resort to assistance because, for purely tactical reasons, he wanted to save his solitary Egghead Daphne until later on in the final round. Terry knew full well that he was taking an almighty gamble at such an early stage in the final round and to his credit, he openly admitting as such. After sensibly taking his time as he deliberated over what was undoubtedly, a really difficult question, Terry finally settled on the option, Architecture. The moment he made that choice, I immediately looked up at the giant screen behind him where the larger than life image of the normally affable Daphne Fowler image was projected. Her normally affable smile had changed into a sad and subdued grimace, a clear sign that Terry had made the wrong choice, a fact confirmed by Dermot who revealed that the correct answer was Modigliani who apparently was a celebrated twentieth century Economist.

There's no denying the fact that I was pleased that Terry had given an incorrect answer so early on in our final head to head showdown especially with the coveted prize of a place in the Semi Final at stake. I appeared, on the face of it, to be holding all the aces with three Eggheads at my disposal, but this was no time to be complacent. If I wanted to progress to the Semi Final, then I had to go out and earn it.

"SHAUN, WHAT WAS THE NAME OF THE PINKERTON AGENCY DETECTIVE WHO INFILTRATED THE SECRET MOLLY MAGUIRES ORGANISATION IN THE 19TH CENTURY, JAMES MCPARLAND, HENRY FRICK OR HARRY ORCHID?"

Once again, I wasn't entirely sure which of the three options was correct and so I decided not to take any unnecessary risk by trying to guess my way to the right answer and instead, turned to the one Egghead in my corner who I felt would be more likely to know the answer, Chris Hughes. After Dermot had read out the question for a second time, Chris responded by saying that he was 60% certain, before adding the caveat that, "wouldn't swear to it", that James McParland was the correct answer as he recalled the actor Sean Connery playing the role of McParland in the 1970 film of the same name. Well, 60% certainty was good enough for me and I decided to accept Chris's advice.

"JAMES McPARLAND IS THE CORRECT ANSWER, SHAUN!" Dermot said. "YOU'RE USING YOUR EGGHEADS VERY WELL."

Terry was about to now face the second of his five questions and from his perspective, it was imperative that he opened his account on the scoreboard sooner rather than later.

"TERRY, WHICH OF THE LONDON THEATRES WAS ORIGINALLY OPENED IN 1818 AS THE ROYAL COBURG THEATRE, ALDWYCH, THE OLD VIC OR THE MERMAID?"

Terry had a slight inkling as to what the correct answer could be but was not entirely sure and he decided to call for Daphne's expertise and assistance because as he candidly admitted, he "desperately needed to put points on the board". Like the super quizzing heroine that she is, Daphne rode to Terry's rescue and came up with the right answer, the Old Vic.

"SHAUN, THE US CITY OMAHA IS LOCATED IN WHICH STATE, NEBRASKA, IDAHO OR OHIO?"

Any faint hopes that Terry may have been harbouring in terms of me slipping up were immediately consigned to the realms of disappointment from the moment I declared to Dermot, that I would be answering the question alone without the need to call for any assistance from my two remaining Eggheads and when I gave the correct answer of Nebraska, I did so by reference to the multi Billionaire financial investor, Warren Buffet one of the world's richest men who is popularly known by the epithet, "The Sage of Omaha".

"TERRY, THE JITTERBUG DANCE IS BELIEVED TO HAVE BEEN NAMED AFTER A SONG BY WHICH SINGER AND BANDLEADER, COUNT BASSIE, DUKE ELLINGTON OR CAB CALLOWAY?"

The air of resignation in Terry voice was clear for all to hear upon hearing the question as once again, he openly declared that he wished that he had saved Daphne to help him answer the question but to his eternal credit, Terry remained both calm and composed, like the experienced quiz player that he is and by clever deduction and cool logic, he managed to come up with the correct answer, Cab Calloway, to keep him very much alive in the contest.

"SHAUN, JOYOUS GARDE, OR AS IT WAS ALSO KNOWN, THE DOLOROUS GUARD, WAS THE CASTLE OF WHICH FIGURE FROM ARTHURIAN LEGEND, LANCELOT, MERLIN OR MORGAN LE FEY?"

As soon as I heard the first and second words of the question, I knew straight away who the character in question was likely to be even though Dermot had not yet revealed the three options and without hesitating, or resorting to the need to call on my two remaining Eggheads, I gave my fourth correct answer in a row with Lancelot. Terry had to answer his next question correctly otherwise the whole contest was over.

"TERRY, WHICH SCULPTOR CREATED THE FAMOUS STATUTE PETER PAN IN KENSINGTON GARDENS AND THE LIONS AT THE BRITISH MUSEUM, JOHN BELL, GEORGE FRAMPTON OR EDWARD LANSEER?"

Terry took a deep breath after hearing the question and as he was doing so, I could see Daphne frantically moving about on the big screen behind him, willing him no doubt, to come up with the right answer. The sharp intake of breath clearly seemed to have the desired calming and positive effect on him as Terry, not for the first time in the contest, demonstrated the qualities of reasoned logic and depth of knowledge that had managed to carry him a long way in the competition. He immediately ruled out Edward Lanseer, correctly surmising that he was the man responsible for designing the Bronze Lions at the base of Trafalgar Square and after vacillating between the remaining two choices, he eventually settled on the correct answer George Frampton, a choice judging from Daphne's reaction on the giant screen behind him, was the source of much considerable relief and delight. All credit to the man! Terry could have easily have buckled under the pressure of having to come up with the right answer but he displayed all the coolness and presence of mind that clearly demonstrated what a really good quizzer he is and although it was virtually certain that I was going to progress to the next round at his expense, at least he had the satisfaction of forcing me to face my fifth and final question.

"SHAUN, THE WORLD HERITAGE SITE OF MACQUARIE ISLAND IS LOCATED IN WHICH COUNTRY SOUTH AFRICA, CANADA OR AUSTRALIA?"

I had a strong inkling that the correct answer was Australia but with so much at stake, I wasn't prepared to take even the slightest risk and I immediately sought the help of Kevin Ashman Kevin's advice was that it was probably Australia, as the island in question was probably named after Laughland Macquarie, one of the nation's first Governor Generals. I decided to act upon Kevin's advice.

Dermot paused for a moment after I had made that choice. "SHAUN, THE CORRECT ANSWER IS INDEED AUSTRALIA! YOU HAVE WON"

I quietly clenched my right fist to reflect my sheer satisfaction and delight with my hard-fought victory as the show's theme music resonated throughout the set heralding the end of the game. Dermot turned his attention firstly to my gallant, vanquished opponent in order to commiserate and applaud him for his magnificent performances on the show before turning to me to offer his congratulations for another victory that put me one step closer to the ultimate prize. I was now just one game away from the Eggheads Grand Final and the only opponent that stood in my way of me reaching that goal was my equally talented, equally determined, opponent, Mark Kerr.

CHAPTER TWENTY-TWO

The moment everyone on the studio set were given the all clear from the Studio Floor Manager, I rose wearily to my feet feeling a mixture happiness and relief with the contest's final outcome and by the time I managed to get myself fully upright, heading towards me across the studio set in what was increasingly becoming a lucky ritual for me, was Charlotte whose first words to me had a welcoming familiarity to it as she once again offered her congratulations on my latest success. Charlotte informed me that the semi-final would not be taking place for at least another two hours. I decided that the best way for me to prepare for the semi-final would be to try and get some much-needed rest but just as I was about to put that particular plan into action, there was a loud knock on my dressing room door. I opened it and there was my quarter final opponent Terry Toomey who came over to say his goodbyes and to wish me luck for the semi-final. After Terry left, production assistants kept coming and going for one reason or another, and I could get no rest. I decided that enough was enough, and I grabbed all the bathroom towels and proceeded to roll some of them up with the aim to create some sort of log pillow whilst I used the remaining larger towel as blankets to cover my head and torso and before I knew it, I was fast asleep. I don't know how long I was sleeping for but the next thing I knew, I was being vigorously shaken from my deep slumber by Lucy who told me that everyone in the production team were worried as to my whereabouts on account of the fact that my dressing room door was knocked a fair few number of times without any response. Lucy then told me that I had to get myself ready as quickly as possible as everything was virtually ready for the start of the contest. I asked her to allow me five or so minutes in order to get dressed and get myself together as I was still feeling slightly groggy. I went to the sink and filled it with cold water before proceeding to douse my face and neck, hoping that it would instantly revive me from my disoriented and groggy like state. After drying my face and neck, I got changed into my clothes next to no time after which, I left the dressing room and found Lucy waiting patiently. The pair of us walked the short distance to the end of the corridor where I saw Mark Kerr wearing an eye catching short sleeved lilac coloured check patterned shirt, waistcoat and spotted dickie bow tie. We both greeted each other warmly by shaking hands as it was the first time that our paths had crossed since we were on the studio set at the end of the 2005 *Mastermind* Grand Final. The first thing I said to Mark was to congratulate him on his victory over Pat Gibson before we endeavoured to catch up on old times as we were making our way to the studio set. Once we were in our places, Mark won the coin toss and elected to face the first question.

Inwardly, my adrenalin levels were gradually increasing with every passing second whilst on the outside, I was trying to give the impression of a man who was both calm and in complete control. This really was going to be the acid test. If I thought facing a player of Olav Bjorntomt's undoubted class was tough, then this challenge was going to be an even tougher proposition. I was facing an opponent who was high on confidence having dispatched the overall favourite for the competition and clearly had his sights firmly set on claiming the scalp of another *Mastermind* Champion. I would have to be at the very top of my game if I wanted to prevent history from repeating itself.

After Dermot had finished doing his piece to camera, he then turned to us in turn, firstly to Mark, then to me as he discussed the history of our respective progress to this stage of the competition. Dermot could see that both Mark and I were, metaphorically speaking, straining on the leash, eager and determined to get the competition under way and Dermot responded to that sense of urgency by announcing the first category of the contest would be Geography.

"MARK, THE CONSTRUCTION OF WHICH CITY'S ROMAN CATHOLIC CATHEDRAL BEGAN IN 1248 AND TOOK, WITH A FEW INTERRUPTIONS, UNTIL 1880 TO COMPLETE, FRANKFURT, TRIER OR COLOGNE?"

Mark seemed pretty at ease when he gave the correct answer, Cologne.

"SHAUN, WHAT COLOUR IS THE SEVEN-POINTED STAR THAT APPEARS ON THE FLAG OF JORDAN, WHITE, GREEN OR RED?"

Not exactly the nice gentle opener was I looking for and was the type of question that was going to require a mixture of thought and logic. I immediately discounted green even though it is the principal colour found in the flags of most Arab nations in the Middle East. Red also seemed unlikely and I tried to visualise what the respective options would actually look like on the star of the Jordanian flag and out of those options, the one that seemed the most feasible, was white which I settled on and whether it was a case of sheer luck or logical deductive reasoning, I managed to arrive at the correct answer to level the scores.

"MARK, WHICH ISLAND GROUP IS GUY FAWKES A PART OF, GALAPAGOS ISLANDS, WINDWARD ISLANDS OR HAWAIIAN ISLANDS?"

Mark reacted to this seemingly difficult question by immediately ruling out Galapagos Islands, his reasoning being that because the Galapagos Islands are situated off the West Coast of Chile, Islands around that area of the world were more likely to have Spanish, as opposed to an English sounding name. Out of the remaining choices, Mark opted for the Windward Islands. Dermot turned to the Eggheads and CJ confirmed it was, in fact the Galapogos Islands.

"SHAUN, FROM 1973 TO 2002 IRIANJAYA WAS THE NAME GIVEN TO THE INDONESIAN HALF OF WHICH ISLAND, FIJI, NEW GUINEA OR EAST TIMOR?"

I immediately ruled out Fiji as I knew straight away that Fiji has never been a part of Indonesia and out of the options that remained, I went for East Timor because I knew that the region had been part of Indonesia before eventually gaining Independence after a long and protracted struggle. But alas, my logic and reasoning on this occasion was completely wrong as the Eggheads confirmed, that New Guinea was the right answer a costly error which meant that I had surrendered my crucial advantage.

"MARK, WHICH SCANDINAVIAN CAPITAL WAS LARGELY REBUILT AFTER A FIRE IN 1808, OSLO, STOCKHOLM OR HELSINKI?"

He first considered and then ruled out Oslo, on the basis that the name Oslo was not in existence in the 19th Century and by making the best guess that he could, he went for Stockholm. Unfortunately for him, the answer was Helsinki.

"SHAUN, CALTON HILL AND NELSON'S MONUMENT ARE FEATURES OF WHICH BRITISH CITY, EDINBURGH, GLASGOW OR ABERDEEN?"

As an educated guess, I chose Edinburgh, and somehow managed to stumble on the correct answer. That slice of good fortune won me the round and more importantly, first pick of an Egghead and once again I chose Kevin. The next category that Dermot introduced was Sport, one of my favourite categories and I elected to face the first question.

"SHAUN, ZINZAN BROOKE REPRESENTED WHICH COUNTRY IN INTERNATIONAL RUGBY UNION, NEW ZEALAND, AUSTRALIA OR SOUTH AFRICA?"

This is more like it! I thought to myself and without any prevarication, I gave the correct answer of New Zealand to put me in the lead.

"MARK, WHICH BOWLER WAS HIT FOR A RECORD SIX SIXES IN AN OVER BY GARFIELD SOBERS IN 1968, KEN HIGGS, MALCOLM NASH OR PAT POCOCK?"

Mark was just as good at sport as I was and he also knew the answer straight away was Malcolm Nash.

"SHAUN, WHICH ATHLETE BROKE THE 110M HURDLES WORLD RECORD ON 12TH JUNE 2008, DAYRON ROBLES, TERRANCE TRAMMELL OR LIU XIANG?"

Although it happened only two weeks previously, it was an event that had clearly passed me by but out of the options available, the athlete I thought logically speaking would have been the most likely to have accomplished such a feat was the Chinese hurdler, Liu Xiang, the reigning Olympic Champion. My so called logical reasoning though was completely and utterly wrong and to add insult to injury, it was left to Judith Keppel, whose least favourite category on the regular Eggheads show is Sport, to put me right when she confirmed with a great deal of certainty and dare I say it authority, that the correct answer was Dayron Robles.

"MARK, DOCTOR REINER KLIMKE WAS THE WINNER OF SIX OLYMPIC GOLD MEDALS IN WHICH EQUESTRIAN DISCIPLINE, CROSS COUNTRY, SHOW JUMPING OR DRESSAGE?"

There were no slips up from Mark this time as he confidently declared that he recalled watching the Olympics Games in the years gone by, a German Equestrian competitor who was virtually unbeatable in Dressage.

"SHAUN, WHICH UNDEFEATED BOXING WORLD CHAMPION IS NICKNAMED 'THE GHOST', SHANE MOSLEY, KELLY PAVLIK OR JERMAINE TAYLOR?"

I knew straightaway the answer was Kelly Pavlik.

"MARK, IN WHICH YEAR DID ROGER FEDERER WIN THE FIRST ATP TOUR TITLE OF HIS CAREER, 1999, 2000 OR 2001?"

Mark decided to opt for the year 2000 and that brought an immediate smile to my face because I knew that the correct answer was 2001, a fact confirmed by Dermot when he eventually revealed the answer. Mark had missed a golden opportunity to win the round and his unfortunate error meant for the first time in the contest, a round together with the valuable prize of an Egghead to the victor, would be decided by the lottery of sudden death.

"SHAUN, WHO, IN 2008, BECAME THE FIRST BRITISH WOMAN TO QUALIFY OUTRIGHT FOR THE LADIES' SINGLES COMPETITION SINCE 1999?"

"AS WE HAVE NOT HAD THAT MUCH SUCCESS IN BRITISH WOMEN'S TENNIS SINCE VIRGINIA WADE AND ANN JONES. IS IT ANNA KETOVANG?" I was not entirely sure that I had pronounced the surname correctly but I was fairly certain that I was in the ball park, a fact Dermot confirmed when he informed me that, "IT'S VERY CLOSE, BUT NOT ACCEPTABLE. IT'S ANNA KEOTHAVONG." I was naturally disappointed that I got so agonisingly close but in saying that, I had no qualms with Dermot's decision particularly in view of the fact that we were at the stage of the competition where you had to be precise and exact with every given answer.

"MARK, EXCLUDING SUBSTITUTES, HOW MANY PLAYERS ARE THERE IN AN OLYMPIC HANDBALL TEAM?"

Given what was at stake, Mark wisely decided to take his time as he considered the question, but it didn't take him long before he came up with the correct answer, seven and with it, the right to choose an Egghead to assist him in the final round. However, it was his subsequent ominous comments after having secured the round that gave me cause me to sit up and take notice with regards to his future intentions and ambitions in the contest.

"I'VE BEEN IN THIS POSITION BEFORE. I ALWAYS LOSE THE FIRST ROUND BUT WIN THE SECOND ROUND AND I ALWAYS PICK DAPHNE, AS EVERY TIME, SHE HAS DONE WELL FOR ME."

With the scores now all square, Mark and I prepared to face the next category, Film and Television, and Mark elected to face the first question.

"MARK, IN 2008, WHICH COMEDIAN PRESENTED A THREE-PART TELEVISION SERIES ON HIS NATIVE LIVERPOOL, KEN DODD, ALEXEI SAYLE OR JIMMY TARBUCK?"

A diehard Liverpudlian like Mark wasn't going to slip up on this type of question and immediately went for Alexei Sayle to put him into the lead.

"SHAUN, IN WHICH DECADE DID DISNEY RELEASE THEIR ANIMATED FILM THE JUNGLE BOOK, 1950'S, 1960'S OR 1970'S?"

It was released the year my brother Steve was born, in 1967. I got the question right, for the easiest point I won in the whole game.

"MARK, 'BE AFRAID, BE VERY AFRAID' WAS THE TAG LINE USED ON POSTERS FOR WHICH 1986 MOVIE, NIGHTMARE ON ELM STREET, ALIEN OR THE FLY?"

Mark eventually chose The Fly from the options, the same choice I would have opted for had it had been my question, providing him with yet another correct answer.

"SHAUN, IN 1955, WHO BECAME THE FIRST PRESENTER ON BBC TELEVISION NEWS ACTUALLY TO APPEAR ON SCREEN, KENNETH KENDAL, RICHARD BAKER OR ALISTAIR BURNETT?"

I was fairly confident that I knew the answer to the question, or so I thought. I confidently said Richard Baker, but the correct answer was Kenneth Kendal.

"MARK, WHO STARRED AS WOODROW F. CALL IN THE MULTI EMMY WINNING TELEVISION SERIES, *LONESOME DOVE*, TOMMY LEE JONES, DANNY GLOVER OR JAMES GARNER?"

Mark immediately ruled out Tommy Lee Jones, believing in his view, that he was far too big a Hollywood A-Lister to be seen slumming around doing a TV mini series. After considering the options, Mark eventually went for Danny Glover, but it was Tommy Lee Jones who was the first actor to play the character on screen. I had been handed an unlikely lifeline in the round but it would all count for nothing with an incorrect answer to my third and final question.

"SHAUN, WHO DIRECTED THE 1944 FILM NOIR, *THE WOMAN IN THE WINDOW*, ALFRED HITCHCOCK, FRITZ LAING OR BILLY WILDER?"

I resisted the temptation of choosing Alfred Hitchcock because it seemed too obvious and instead, I was drawn towards Billy Wilder and simply crossed my fingers and hoped for the best but those hopes were dashed when Dermot confirmed that the correct answer was in fact, Fritz Laing. I had now gone from being 1-0 in the lead to 2-1 behind in the contest. My opponent by contrast, was clearly in the ascendancy and in accordance with his tried and trusted selection strategy that was the hallmark of his previous victories in the competition, he chose Chris Hughes to assist him in the final round.

Dermot announced the next category, a category that I always seem to perform badly in whenever it comes up, Music. Mark sought to press home his advantage by electing to face the first question as he, as he observed, had "momentum on his side".

"MARK, WHICH SINGER HAD A HIT IN THE 1980'S WITH EDITH PIAF'S LA VIEN ROSE, GRACE JONES, DONNA SUMMER OR DIANA ROSS?"

Mark showed how relaxed and confident he was with this question when after quickly discounting the options Donna summer and Diana Ross he said, "IT WAS GRACE JONES WHO SANG THE SONG AND IF I'M WRONG, THEN SHE CAN JUST HIT ME."

"SHAUN, IN WHICH YEAR DID CLAUDE JOSEPH ROUGET DE LISLE WRITE THE FRENCH NATIONAL ANTHEM, LA MARSEILLES, 1692, 1742 OR 1792?"

I told Dermot that 1792 was the year in which the monarchy was overthrown whilst France itself were being threatened by the major European powers that were massing along its borders and La Marseilles was written as a rallying cry in response to the external threat. Dermot confirmed that my detailed knowledge of French History had helped to guide me to the correct answer and put my back on level terms.

"MARK, VESTI LA GIUBBA IS A FAMOUS ARIA FROM WHICH OPERA, I PURITANI, CAVALLERIA RUSTICANA OR I PAGLIACCI?"

Mark explained in some detail that the word Vesti in the question, was the all important clue so far as he was concerned and therefore the correct answer had to be I Pagliacci, an opera that was based on clowns that contained the well known aria, "On with the Motley," as Motley, he went on to further explain, was the type of clothing worn by clowns.

"SHAUN, WHICH ACTOR HAD A UK HIT SINGLE IN 1970 WITH 'I TALKED TO THE TREES', RICHARD HARRIS, PETER SELLERS OR CLINT EASTWOOD?"

I embarked on yet another laborious and detailed explanation as to the reason for making my eventual choice when I revealed that the song came from the film, *Paint Your Wagon*, starring Lee Marvin. In the same film, it was Clint Eastwood who in fact spoke the words as opposed to actually singing the lyrics, a correct answer that meant that the scores were tied for the round.

"MARK, THE BAND LEADER GLENN MILLER WAS KNOWN FOR PLAYING WHICH INSTRUMENT, TRUMPET, TROMBONE OR SAXOPHONE?"

Mark wasted little time in giving the correct answer, Trombone.

"SHAUN, FOR WHICH BAND DID VAN MORRISON SING AND PLAY THE HARMONICA BEFORE GOING SOLO, THEM, CREAM OR MARMALADE?"

I was delighted. Sometimes God does smile on you, because when I was doing some revision on Music and Entertainment before coming on the show I just happened to come across Van Morrison and the group that he was formerly a member of. The band was Them.

"MARK, WHO COMPOSED THE MUSIC FOR THE 1948 SATIRICAL WORK, THE THREEPENNY OPERA?"

"THE LYRICS WERE BY BERTOLT BRECHT AND THE MUSIC WAS COMPOSED BY KURT WEILL," Mark responded confidently.

"SHAUN, WHOSE PIANO SONATA, NO 26 IN E FLAT MAJOR, IS KNOWN AS LE ADIEUS?"

I didn't have the slightest idea as to who the composer could be, so I went for Claude Debussy as I thought Le Adieus sounded French. My thinking couldn't have been further from the mark however, as I learned the answer was Beethoven. For the third consecutive time, Mark had won himself another round and for his third choice, in line with his tried and trusted method, he chose CJ.

Mark was now threatening to take a complete stranglehold of the contest in the same way Olav had done in our encounter and there didn't appear to be a single thing that I could do to prevent it. The fifth and final category was, therefore, crucial to my chances of preventing a potential landslide in Mark's favour and when Dermot revealed that the final category was History, a feeling of instant relief surged right through me and even although Mark had chosen to face the first question in the round, I was quietly confident that it was a round that would be mine for the taking.

"MARK, IN THE LATE 18TH CENTURY, THE LUNAR SOCIETY OF LEADING SCIENTISTS AND INDUSTRIALISTS MET IN WHICH CITY, BIRMINGHAM, GLASGOW OR LIVERPOOL?"

Mark definitely knew the answer to this question Birmingham. He went on to explain that Society derived its name from the fact that it used to meet when it was a full moon as there were no street lights around at the time.

"SHAUN, WHAT WAS FOUNDED BY A VIKING LEADER CALLED ROLLO, THE DUCHY OF NORMANDY, THE KINGDOM OF MANN OR THE COUNTY OF   FLANDERS?"

"IN 911, ROLLO FOUNDED THE DUCHY OF NORMANDY," I answered confidently.

"MARK, THE POEM WHICH BEGINS WITH THE LINES, "'THE BOY STOOD ON THE BURNING DECK WHENCE ALL BUT HE HAD FLED' REFERS TO WHICH OF NELSON'S BATTLES, COPENHAGEN, THE NILE OR TRAFALGAR?"

Mark was not sure about this question, ultimately going for Trafalgar, because of the bloody carnage that he associated with that famous battle. Dermot then turned to the Eggheads panel for confirmation and it was left to Chris to reveal that the deck of the ship the poem was referring to was The Casabianca, a ship that was originally involved in the Battle of Abukir Bay, the alternative name for the decisive naval engagement between Nelson and Napoleon Bonaparte for the control of Egypt, the Battle of the Nile of 1798.

"SHAUN, IN WHICH YEAR DID FOUR TEENAGE FRENCH BOYS DISCOVER THE PREHISTORIC PAINTING PAINTED CAVE NETWORK AT LASCAUX, 1840, 1890 OR 1940?"

Another History question that was right in my comfort zone and once again, I resorted to giving a laborious and detailed explanation of the chance discovery of the caves by a group of schoolchildren that occurred just before, or at the time of the conquest of France by the Germans in 1940.

"MARK, ACCORDING TO TRADITION, WHICH KING OF ROME SUCCEEDED ROMULUS, TULLUS, ANCUS OR NUMA?"

Mark admitted that he did not know the answer and I was relieved when he ruled out the correct answer Numa on the basis that Roman female names usually end in the letter "a", before he eventually settled on the option, Tullus. This incorrect answer meant that I had won the final round and managed finally, to halt Mark's seemly unstoppable momentum. Judith, the last available Egghead left, was now a part of my team and a welcome addition because I was under no illusion as to the size of the challenge that lay in front of me.

There was a short pause before we began the final round, sufficient time to allow me to compose myself, gather my thoughts and focus all of my energies in trying to secure the coveted prize of a place in the *Are You an Egghead?* Grand Final. Just before Dermot was about to begin his usual piece to camera introducing that final round, Mark and I silently nodded our heads simultaneously in each other's direction, a sign of the mutual regard and respect that we had for each other.

"THAT WAS A VERY CLOSELY FOUGHT HEAD TO HEAD, AS WAS TO BE EXPECTED WITH TWO VERY GREAT QUIZZERS. THE BEST OF LUCK TO YOU BOTH, A PLACE IN THE FINAL ROUND AWAITS. LET'S PLAY THE FINAL ROUND. SHAUN, DO YOU WANT TO GO FIRST OR SECOND?"

I replied, "FIRST," without hesitation.

"SHAUN, AFTER WHOM WAS THE NAME OF THE WORLD'S FIRST NUCLEAR SURFACE POWERED SHIP AND ICEBREAKER BUILT IN THE SOVIET UNION IN 1957, V I LENIN, NIKITA KHRUSHCHEV OR KARL MARX?"

I was about 90% sure that the correct answer was Lenin, my reasoning based purely on the fact that it was highly unlikely to be Nikita Khrushchev as he had been appointed to the post of Soviet Leader only two years previously. I went with my gut instinct and it paid off.

"MARK, WHICH MUSEUM STANDS ON TRUMPINGTON STREET IN CAMBRIDGE, THE FITZWILLIAM MUSEUM, THE ASHMOLEAN MUSEUM OR THE BOWES MUSEUM?"

Mark knew for sure that the Fitzwilliam is based in Cambridge.

"SHAUN, PUBLISHED IN 1928, THE NOVEL 'MEET THE TIGER' WAS THE FIRST TO FEATURE WHICH POPULAR FICTIONAL HERO, BULL DOG DRUMMOND, SIMON TEMPLAR OR SEXTON BLAKE?"

I must confess, I had never heard of the novel concerned, so I wasn't about to take any chances and immediately sought to use my lifeline in the form of Kevin Ashman, who gave me the answer, Simon Templar.

"MARK, WHAT IS THE NAME GIVEN TO HIGHWAY SIX, THE ROAD THAT LEADS UP TO THE PALOMAR OBSERVATORY ON MOUNT PALOMAR IN CALIFORNIA, HIGHWAY TO THE MOON, HIGHWAY TO THE STARS OR HIGHWAY TO THE UNIVERSE?"

Sensibly, Mark decided to use one of his Eggheads and called upon Chris Hughes for assistance. Chris appeared think that it was unlikely to be either Highway to the Moon or Highway to the Universe. When pressed by Dermot to make a final suggestion, Chris declared that he was 80% certain that it was Highway to the Stars, a choice Mark decided to go with, and between the pair of them, they managed to come up with the correct answer to level the scores.

"SHAUN, IN WHICH YEAR DID THE BBC THIRD PROGRAMME, WHICH EVENTUALLY BECAME INCORPORATED INTO RADIO 3 FIRST GO ON AIR, 1938, 1946 OR 1951?"

I was virtually certain that I knew what the correct answer was and I decided to keep my last remaining Egghead in reserve for use later on in the round and went for the option, 1946, getting it right.

"MARK, WHICH GROUP'S EPONYMOUS FIRST ALBUM RELEASED IN 1972 FEATURED THE MODEL AND SOON TO BE SISTER-IN-LAW OF MICK JAGGER, KARRIE-ANN MULLER ON ITS COVER, GENESIS, ROXY MUSIC OR QUEEN?"

Mark declared that he had fond memories of the album in question, vividly recalling that he was sixteen years old at the time of the album's release and a young man full of hormones who lusted after the very sight of Ms Muller's beautiful long legs which, according to him, seemed to extend forever. He then gave the correct answer, Roxy Music.

"SHAUN, WHAT FAMOUSLY LINED THE WALLS OF THE ROOM OF THE BOULEVARD HOUSEMAN THAT MARCEL PROUST OCCUPIED FROM THE AGE OF 35 UNTIL HIS DEATH, CORK, MUSLIN OR HEMP?"

I definitely knew the answer to this question, Proust was renowned for living in a cork tiled room.

"MARK, THE GENTLY CURVING SANDBAR KNOWN AS SABLE ISLAND HAS SHIP WRECKED SO MANY VESSELS THAT IS OFTEN REFERRED TO AS THE GRAVEYARD OF THE ATLANTIC, PACIFIC OR ARCTIC?"

"I DON'T KNOW," was Mark's initial reply, "BUT THE IDEAL PERSON TO GO FOR WHEN YOU'RE IN PERIL AT SEA WOULD BE DAPHNE." With her metaphorical quizzing lifeboat launched and ready to sail to the rescue, Daphne suggested to Mark that the answer was the Atlantic because, according to her, the geographical feature referred to in the question was an enclave just off the coast of Newfoundland and if she was sitting in his place, that would be the option she would go for. Mark went with Daphne's advice which luckily for him turned out to be the right choice to make. With the score now locked at four points a piece, the contest was now at the stage where either myself, or my formidable opponent were tantalisingly one question away from a place in the Eggheads Grand Final.

"SHAUN, IN APPROXIMATELY 1622, WILLIAM OUGHTRED IS SAID TO HAVE DEVISED THE EARLIEST FORM OF WHICH DEVICE, CARPET SWEEPER, SLIDE RULE OR ACCORDION?"

What a wonderful question to get at this stage of the game as I knew straightaway the correct answer was slide rule.

"MARK, A PHILOSOPHER GIVING THAT LECTURE ON THE ORRERY IN WHICH A LAMP IS PUT IN PLACE OF THE SUN, IS THE TITLE OF 1766 PAINTING BY WHICH ARTIST, JOSEPH WRIGHT OF DERBY, SIR THOMAS LAWRENCE OR JOHN ROBERT COZENS?"

To his enormous credit, Mark showed no signs of succumbing to either nerves or pressure whatsoever even though his first initial comments after hearing the question were that he knew that Joseph Wright of Derby had a painting called the Anatomy Lesson and the painting referred to in the question was based on very similar lines. Mark initially appeared to raise my hopes of victory when he openly admitted that he didn't really know what the answer was, but nevertheless decided to back his own judgement instead of using his one remaining Egghead and by sticking by his original choice, or to use Mark's phrase, "Taking a chance." Mark's brave but risky gamble proved to be an inspired one and when Dermot confirmed that his answer was correct, I noticed that Daphne momentarily but unintentionally, joyously clasped her hands together before immediately putting her hand to her mouth in an act of self admonishment so as not to appear that she was favouring one contestant over another in any way. Mark's brave gamble showed great courage in the heat of a tremendous battle and his correct answer meant that the pair of us had played the perfect final round after five questions each and therefore, it would take sudden death to eventually separate us.

"WHAT A FINAL THIS IS," Dermot remarked at the end of the designated set of questions. "WE NOW MOVE INTO SUDDEN DEATH. SHAUN, THE FIRST QUESTION IS FOR YOU. THE CHAPEL ROYAL AT ST. PETER ADVINCULA FORMS PART OF WHICH LONDON LANDMARK?"

Thankfully for me, this was yet another perfect question to come my way at such a crucial stage in the contest. I was so confident of knowing the correct answer that I even tried to sing the Tower of London in a tone that could hardly have been pleasing to the ear as I was giving it.

"MARK, WHO DID SIR IAN MCKELLAN PLAY IN THE 1998 FILM GODS AND MONSTERS?"

Mark didn't know the answer to this question and quite sensibly, he decided to call on CJ for help and advice and when I looked up at the giant screen, it was patently obvious by CJ's demeanour that he knew the answer as he appeared to be bursting at the seams hoping that he would be chosen and when Mark elected to use him, the answer, "James Whale" couldn't have come out of his mouth fast enough. The correct answer meant that Mark was still very much alive in the contest but no longer had the luxury of an Egghead to help him from now on.

"SHAUN, WHAT WAS THE POPULAR TITLE OF THE ANONYMOUS POLITICAL PRISONER WHO DIED IN THE BASTILLE IN 1703 AFTER YEARS OF MYSTERIOUS INCARCERATION?"

I wasn't entirely sure what the right answer was but I had a fairly good idea of what it possibly could be. However, given the fact that any mistake at this stage of the contest could prove to be decisive, I wasn't prepared to take even the slightest risk and I called on Judith Keppel to see whether like me, she was thinking along the same lines. Unfortunately for me though, when Dermot turned to Judith for an answer, the pressure of the situation seemed to have an overwhelming effect on her and she declared that she wouldn't provide any advice or assistance whatsoever, her only half-hearted contribution to the debate was to say that the answer would probably come to her "as soon as I gave it!"

On my own now, I went for the Man in the Iron Mask. Dermot, after a cruel, gut-wrenching pause, confirmed I was right.

"MARK, WHICH ACTRESS WAS THE STAR OF THE 1933 FILM BOMBSHELL?"

I knew the moment Dermot completed his sentence that Mark was not going to slip up and his correct answer, Jean Harlow, meant that the pair of us had now answered sixteen correct answers in a row.

"SHAUN, THE RUSSIAN PRINCE ALEXANDER OBOLENSKY REPRESENTED ENGLAND AT WHICH SPORT IN 1936?"

Once again, I breathed an almighty sigh of relief at landing yet another favourable question that was right up my street and I wasted no time in going on the offensive. "HE WAS A FAMOUS RUGBY UNION WINGER, WHO MADE THAT FAMOUS SIXTY YARD DIAGONAL RUN WHICH GAVE ENGLAND A 13-0 WIN OVER THE ALL BLACKS AT TWICKENHAM...AND HE SCORED TWO TRIES!"

"MARK, THREDBO IS A SKI RESORT LOCATED IN WHICH COUNTRY?"

Mark said he had never heard of the resort before. With the proverbial roll of the dice and with nothing to lose, Mark opted for the very clever and educated guess in the circumstances and chose Canada.

The tension was almost unbearable and for what seemed like the umpteenth time in our titanic battle, Dermot paused before he finally revealed that crucial answer. "THREDBO IS A SKI RESORT LOCATED IN AUSTRALIA. CONGRATULATIONS SHAUN! YOU'RE IN THE GRAND FINAL! I'M RUNNING OUT OF SUPERLATIVES FOR THE QUALITY OF THE QUIZZING. EACH OF THESE FINAL ROUNDS SEEMED TO GET BETTER AND BETTER!"

I slumped back in my seat, feeling physically and mentally drained. Dermot turned to Mark and praised him for being the tremendous quiz competitor that he is and with a wry philosophical smile, Mark eloquently responded to Dermot's compliments with his observations as to how fickle competitive quizzing can be. Dermot then turned his attention to me and said, "YOU'RE APPEARING IN THE GRAND FINAL SHORTLY, HOW DOES IT FEEL?"

I humbly responded, "IT'S AN HONOUR TO BE IN THE GRAND FINAL AND NO MATTER WHAT HAPPENS WHETHER I WIN OR LOSE, I'M JUST GOING TO ENJOY THE MOMENT. IT'S BEEN A PLEASURE TO MEET THE EGGHEADS, IT'S BEEN A PLEASURE TO PLAY AGAINST PEOPLE LIKE MARK AND OLAV AND ROB."

Two down, one to go! I said to myself excitedly, as I eventually rose wearily from my seat.

I made my way outside for a cigarette and some breathing space. I rolled my eyes towards the heavens gazing into the clear blue sky. *Just one last effort, Shaun. Just one. You can do this!"* I said to myself, trying to inject myself with as much self-belief and positive encouragement that I could. I was now just one win away from attaining another notable achievement that would rank alongside all the other notable achievements that I have managed in my life to date and with a bit of luck and God's grace, I was determined to complete the mission.

Once back in my dressing room, a sartorial debate started inside my head with regards to the shirt I was going to wear. Should I wear the pink shirt that I had worn throughout my progress to the final, or the pink shirt I last wore on the day I won Mastermind? I must have changed my mind on that issue at least a thousand times before finally, I decided to go with sentiment and nostalgia and chose the shirt that I hadn't worn since that eventful night four years ago and to go alongside that monumental choice, I would also wear the blue silk boxer shorts (since dry cleaned I hasten to add!) that I wore that night in the hope that it would somehow inspire me to achieve a similar outcome. After one final inspection in the mirror and a final prayer to the man upstairs, I turned and headed towards the dressing room door in a relaxed and confident mood.

The question "Are you an Egghead?" was about to be answered.

By the time I arrived onto the studio set my opponent, Barry Simmons, was already present. The atmosphere between us, although understandably tense, was nevertheless, extremely warm and friendly as the pair of us chatted amongst ourselves briefly about the competition in general and how much we were both looking forward to the Grand Final showdown. Charlotte then came over to explain the rules of the Grand Final as they were slightly different from the rules that governed the competition in the previous rounds. The first part of the Grand Final would consist of the usual Eggheads format, save for the fact the Finalists would gain a point for each category won over the five rounds, instead of winning an Egghead to be on their team. What's more, the Eggheads themselves would be setting the questions. The scores gained by a Finalist at the end of the category round would be carried over into the final decisive round where each player would answer questions alternatively and the first player to reach ten points would be declared the winner and the new Egghead. Charlotte then tossed a coin to decide who would face the first question. I won that toss and I elected to go first.

I was beginning to feel a mixture of excitement and apprehension in equal measure as I waited for the contest to get under way. I was potentially just an hour or so away from achieving something truly remarkable and even if I fell short at the final hurdle, I could still justifiably be proud of myself for what I had achieved. I had more than my fair share of narrow escapes on my journey to the Grand Final, but I felt that my performances in those previous four contests had earned me the right to be here. The Studio Floor Manager then gave the cue for the opening titles and the show's theme music before Dermot took centre stage.

"HELLO AND WELCOME TO ARE YOU AN EGGHEAD? SO THIS IS IT. WE'VE REACHED THE CLIMAX OF OUR SEARCH FOR THE GREATEST QUIZ BRAIN IN BRITAIN, SOMEONE TO TAKE THEIR PLACE ALONGSIDE THE MOST FEARSOME QUIZ TEAM IN HISTORY. WELL TODAY, SOMEONE WILL WIN THE ULTIMATE PRIZE FOR QUIZ ENTHUSIASTS, BECOMING AN EGGHEAD. LET'S MEET THE TWO FINALISTS."

Both Barry and I in turn introduced ourselves, staring intently down the camera lens as we were doing so before Dermot continued his opening remarks and it was evident by the tone of his voice, that he was really looking forward to the occasion.

"WELCOME BACK! I'M GETTING TO KNOW YOU VERY, VERY, VERY, VERY WELL INDEED. IT'S BEEN A LONG ROUTE TO THE FINAL, ARE YOU BOTH LOOKING FORWARD TO IT?" Both Barry and I replied almost in unison that we were both keen and ready to do battle. "WELL THERE'S BEEN SOME MAGNIFICENT QUIZZING, I MEAN, BOTH OF YOUR SEMI FINALS WERE QUITE AMAZING. OK THEN BEST OF LUCK TO YOU BOTH, LET THE GRAND FINAL BEGIN!"

"SHAUN, WHAT WAS THE TITLE OF THE MOVE SINGLE THAT WAS THE FIRST EVER SONG TO BE PLAYED ON RADIO ONE, BLACKBERRY WAY, FLOWERS IN THE RAIN OR NIGHT OF FEAR?"

The Music category had not been the kindest of categories to me in any of my previous contests on my way to the Grand Final, but this was undoubtedly, a good question to begin my quest to become the next Egghead. I remembered as though it were yesterday, when explaining the reasons for my answer to Dermot, actually listening to 'Flowers in the Rain', the song played by the first Radio 1 DJ on air, Tony Blackburn in September 1967.

"BARRY, TUMBLEWEED CONNECTION AND MAD MAN ACROSS THE WATER ARE 1970'S ALBUMS BY WHICH SINGER, ELTON JOHN, ROD STEWART OR DAVID BOWIE?"

Barry went through the options and finally decided that the album, Tumbleweed Connection, "rings a bell" with Elton John, a correct answer that also got Barry off to the good solid start he was hoping for.

"SHAUN, IN THE PUCCINI OPERA, MADAM BUTTERFLY, WHAT IS THE NAME OF PINKERTON'S AND CIO CIO SAN'S SON, ANGER, SORROW OR FEAR?"

Although I was not 100% certain of the correct answer, in order to help me make the right choice, I endeavoured to apply logic and reasoning by relying on my basic rudimentary knowledge of the opera's plot that centred mainly on knowing about Lieutenant Pinkerton's final abandonment of his lover the central character Cio Cio San. On that basis therefore, I went for what seemed to be the only stand out choice out of the three options on offer, Sorrow. Dermot consulted the Egghead who was responsible for setting the questions in the Music category, CJ de Mooi and he confirmed that I had made the right choice to put me 2-1 in the lead.

"BARRY, A MASS FOR PEACE IS THE SUBTITLE OF WHICH MILLENNIAL KARL JENKINS COMPOSITION, THE RIVEN WORLD, THE LOUDEST GUNS OR THE ARMED MAN?

Barry admitted that he had not heard of the composition before and just like I had done with the last question, he also resorted to trying to apply logic and sound judgement in selecting the right answer. Barry eventually settled on the option, The Loudest Guns for no other reason other than the title had some connection with war but unfortunately for him, it was The Armed Man that was the correct answer.

"SHAUN, I CAN'T EXPLAIN WAS THE TITLE OF THE FIRST UK HIT SINGLE BY WHICH BAND, THE ANIMALS, THE WHO OR THE KINKS?"

My joyous spontaneous reaction after Dermot had finished reading the question was to jokingly mimic playing the air guitar that was accompanied by yet another dose of woeful, off key singing of the song's chorus. Dermot and CJ seemed to be mildly amused by my playful antics and after Dermot confirmed that my answer, The Who was correct, he asked me who or what was I trying to imitate with my impromptu rendition and I replied, it was a combination of Roger Daltrey and the group's Bass guitarist, the late John Entwistle. With the first point safely in the bag, Dermot announced that the next category was Geography, with all the questions for the round having been set by Chris Hughes. I elected to press home my early advantage and face the first question.

"SHAUN, WHAT IS THE NAME OF THE UNDERSEA TUNNEL THAT LINKS THE JAPANESE ISLANDS OF HONSHU AND HOKKAIDO, SEIKAN TUNNEL, SETO TUNNEL OR NAIKAI TUNNEL?"

My initial response to the question was that I had never heard of the tunnel concerned, but then I suddenly remembered that I had heard of The Seikan Tunnel and on that basis, I selected The Seikan Tunnel as my option which Chris Hughes, who was the Egghead responsible for setting all of the questions in the round, confirmed was the right answer.

"BARRY, APPROXIMATELY HOW MANY MILES LONG IS THE VOLGA RIVER, 2,200, 3,300 OR 4,400?"

Barry knew that the Volga River is the longest in Europe and went on to explain in some detail that the river empties into the Caspian Sea at the Port of Baku in Azerbaijan. He chose 3,300 miles as he believed that the distance of 3,300 miles. However, when Dermot turned to Chris for confirmation of the correct answer he confirmed that its length was approximately 2,200 miles and Barry's unexpected error had presented me with a real opportunity to take a 2-0 lead in the round.

"SHAUN, WHICH STATE OF THE USA IS NICKNAMED EITHER "THE OLD DOMINION" OR "THE MOTHER OF PRESIDENTS", KENTUCKY, MARYLAND OR VIRGINIA?"

The questions seemed to be falling my way and without hesitation, I immediately chose Virginia because I knew that at least four American Presidents were buried there. Dermot confirmed that my answer was correct which meant that Barry had to get his next question correct in order to keep the round alive.

"BARRY, MASHONALAND IS AN AREA OF WHICH AFRICAN COUNTRY, NIGERIA, ZIMBABWE OR ETHIOPIA?"

Barry did not hang about prevaricating with his answer declaring straight away that he knew that Mashonaland is a province that is situated next door to the Matebeleland province, neither of the provinces being situated in either Nigeria or Ethiopia and his correct answer, Zimbabwe gave him a much-needed point.

"SHAUN, ON WHICH RIVER IS THE CITY OF LEEDS SITUATED, AIRE, CALDER OR DERWENT?"

Both Barry and I each broke into a broad smile after my question was revealed given the fact that Barry actually lives in Leeds and in all probability, lives a stone's throw away from the river itself, but as the Egghead Kevin Ashman frequently makes comment on the normal regular Eggheads shows, "That's how the questions falls sometimes" and my choice of the River Aire had given me, not only another correct answer, but also another precious point to put me 2-0 in the lead. The next category was Art and Books, the questions this time were set by Judith Keppel. The momentum was clearly with me

578

at this point in the contest and I saw no reason to change my strategy and elected for the third category in a row to face the first question.

"SHAUN, THE LAKE ISLE OF INNISFREE IS THE POEM BY WHICH AUTHOR, W. B. YATES, ALFRED LORD TENNYSON OR GERARD MANLEY HOPKINS?"

I went with the most likely choice of the three, the winner of the 1923 Nobel Prize for Literature, WB Yates, a correct answer that was confirmed by Judith Keppel to put me one up for the round.

"BARRY, THE 1994 BOOK, CLOSING TIME, IS THE SEQUEL TO WHICH OTHER WORK OF FICTION, PORTNOY'S COMPLAINT, CATCH-22 OR SLAUGHTER HOUSE FIVE?"

I knew the answer to this question was Catch-22 and when Barry immediately ruled that choice out of the equation and went with Phillip Roth's Portnoy's Complaint, I knew that my chances of winning this round had increased considerably.

"SHAUN, WHAT ARE THE NAMES OF SHAKESPEARE'S TWO GENTLEMEN OF VERONA, BERTRAM AND PAROLLES, AARON AND DEMETRIUS OR VALENTINE AND PROTEUS?"

I wasn't going to waste time or try to play mind games with an opponent who is far too good a player to get involved with such subtleties. I gave the correct answer, Valentine and Proteus straightaway.

"BARRY, THE 1826 NOVEL, THE LAST MAN IS AN EARLY WORK OF SCIENCE FICTION BY WHICH AUTHOR, MARY SHELLEY, BRAM STOKER OR JOHN POLIDORI?"

With no real clue as to which of the authors correct, Barry chose John Polidori. Dermot revealed that the correct answer was in fact Mary Shelley and it brought a premature end to the round that resulted in another valuable point in my favour to take forward with me to the final end game. Daphne Fowler was responsible for the next category, Science, and I saw no reason to change my strategy and for the fourth time in the contest, I elected to face the first question.

"SHAUN, WHICH ENGLISH SCIENTIST'S MOST FAMOUS PUBLICATION IS OFTEN KNOWN SIMPLY AS 'THE PRINCIPIA'", ROGER BACON, CHARLES DARWIN OR ISAAC NEWTON?"

A nice and relatively easy question to start the round off. I chose Isaac Newton to put me 1-0 in the lead.

"BARRY, TO WHICH CONTINENT IS THE ACAICIA XANTHOPHLOEA OR THE FEVER TREE NATIVE, SOUTH AMERICA, AFRICA OR AUSTRALIA?"

Barry confidently knew the answer to what seemed on the face of it, a very difficult question as he recalled watching a documentary about the Serengeti Plain with Acaicia trees in the background and his declared choice of Africa, earned him the point to make the scores all square.

"SHAUN, THE UTRICULUS IS A CHAMBER IN WHICH PART OF THE BODY, EAR, STOMACH OR HEART?"

I had not heard of that particular medical term before, but I chose the ear solely on the basis that if it was part of either the heart or stomach, then I probably would have heard of it. Dermot confirmed that my choice, albeit a lucky one, was in fact the correct answer.

"BARRY, THE OXIDIZING AGENT, AQUA REGIA IS A MIXTURE OF TWO CONCENTRATED ACIDS, HYDROCHLORIC AND WHICH OTHER, ACETIC, NITRIC OR SULPHURIC?"

Barry immediately ruled out Acetic Acid as he knew it is the scientific name for Vinegar but even more impressively, he went on to say that Sulphuric Acid was once known as, "The marker for the world's economy", as the vast majority of the world's products in the nineteenth Century contained Sulphuric Acid and the compound was seen as a principal indicator of how the world's economies were doing. Barry knew full well that the answer was Nitric Acid and he concluded his impressive knowledge of all things acid when he added that concentrated Aqua Regis has the ability to dissolve precious metals.

"SHAUN, THE AMERICAN SCIENTIST PAUL ZOLL, WAS REGARDED AS A PIONEER IN WHICH FIELD, CARDIOLOGY, GENETICS OR TOXICOLOGY?"

I'd never heard of the scientist concerned and for the second question in a row, I had to resort to random guessing and hope that I had made the right choice. I eventually settled on Genetics but after Dermot had consulted Daphne who revealed that the correct answer was Cardiology, it was the first time in the Grand Final that I got a question wrong and also the first time I was in danger of conceding a precious point to Barry if he was able come up with the correct answer with his final question.

"BARRY, SOMETIMES USED AS IMITATION GOLD LEAF, DUTCH METAL IS AN ALLOY OF COPPER AND WHICH OTHER METAL, MAGNESIUM, ZINC OR PLATINUM?"

Barry immediately broke into a broad grin when Dermot finished reading the question before saying that he knew (as did I), that Ormolu, the product in question, is used as an imitation form of gold, also contains Zinc. At long last, Barry had earned his first point to haul him firmly back into the contest.

Dermot then revealed the final head to head category, Sport with the questions set by the most formidable Egghead of them all, Kevin Ashman.

Even though Barry elected to face the first question, so far as I was concerned, this was my category and I felt extremely confident that I could win this final point to give me a fairly sizable lead for the final end game.

"BARRY, MIKE HAILWOOD WAS A LEADING NAME IN WHICH AREA OF SPORT IN THE 1960'S AND 1970'S, MOTOR SPORT, SAILING OR ATHLETICS?"

Barry gave the correct answer motor sport to give him the lead in a category for the first time in the contest.

"SHAUN, IN WHICH YEAR DID ENGLAND FIRST PLAY AT THE FOOTBALL WORLD CUP, 1950, 1954 OR 1958?"

I couldn't have been given an easier Sports question to begin with even if I had choice of selecting the question myself and it gave me the chance to demonstrate my extensive football knowledge, with a resume of the history of England's initial dismissive attitude to the World Cup with their refusal to take part in the first three tournaments (1930,1934 and 1938), before going on to mention that the England team flew to the 1950 World Cup held in Brazil as one of the tournament favourites for the trophy. England got off to a good start with Stan Mortensen scoring England's first ever goal at the World Cup Finals with a 2-0 victory over Chile before succumbing to the infamous 1-0 defeat to the USA in their next game. Dermot seemed quite impressed with my rambling, detailed knowledge and even Barry admitted that he wouldn't have minded facing that type of question as he prepared to face his second question in the round.

"BARRY, WHICH AMERICAN FOOTBALLER SCORED THE MOST TOUCHDOWNS IN NFL HISTORY, OJ SIMPSON, WALTER PATON OR JERRY RICE?"

Barry was not quite sure of the answer but I was, and he immediately ruled out the correct answer, Jerry Rice. Barry's incorrect choice presented me yet again with another opportunity to increase my lead.

"SHAUN, JELENA JANKOVIC REPRESENTS WHICH COUNTRY IN INTERNATIONAL TENNIS, SLOVAKIA, SERBIA OR CROATIA?"

I paused momentarily after Dermot had finished reading the question as I was not entirely sure as to which of the options to go for. I immediately ruled out Slovakia and out of the two remaining choices, I thought that Jankovic was more likely to be Serbian on the basis that if she was Croatian, I would have heard of her. My reasoning thankfully, turned out to be correct and it helped to put me firmly in control of the round.

"BARRY, HOW MANY TIMES HAS THE WEST INDIES WON THE CRICKET WORLD CUP, ONE, TWO OR THREE?"

Whilst Barry was correct in his analysis that the West Indies had won the first World Cup, he was unsure as to whether they had won the tournament on any other subsequent occasion. Barry then proceeded go through the list of the previous winners in the hope that it would somehow guide him to the correct answer, but for the life of him, he just could not recall any other World Cup win by that great cricketing team and because Barry could only recall the team's inaugural success, he decided to settle on the option, one. However, first Kevin Ashman then me, declared that the actual answer was in fact, two, as between the two of us, we mentioned the fact that the West Indies had won the first two tournaments in 1975 and 1979 before losing in the final to a Kapil Dev inspired India in 1983. I had won my fourth point out of the first five that were on offer, a healthy lead, but by no means a decisive one and before we headed into the final decisive round that would determine which one of us would become the new Egghead, there would be a short, five minute interval.

Some of the production assistants came over to where both Barry and I were sitting with bottles of water and much needed welcoming words of encouragement. The short interval came at the perfect time as it gave me an opportunity to relax and gather my thoughts in preparation for the final round that could potentially, have life changing consequences. I was now only six correct answers away from winning the whole competition, a tantalising, mouth-watering prospect, but despite having such a healthy and commanding lead going into the final round, I was all too well aware of the fact that in so far as my mission to become an Egghead was concerned, the job was only half done. I looked over at Barry and I could hear him verbally admonishing himself for his first half performance. I consoled him, but make no mistake, there was only one person I wanted to win, yours truly!

For the final time in the entire series, the Studio Floor Manager asked everybody on the studio set to take their respective positions. *This is it!* I said to myself. *Try and hold it together!* as Dermot began his cue to camera announcing the start of the final round.

"SO, THIS IS WHAT WE'VE BEEN PLAYING TOWARDS, IT'S TIME FOR THE FINAL ROUND TO DECIDE WHO WILL BECOME AN EGGHEAD. I WILL NOW ASK YOU GENERAL KNOWLEDGE QUESTIONS IN TURN AND THIS IS HOW IT'S VERY DIFFERENT. NO MULTIPLE CHOICE, I WILL JUST NEED AN ANSWER AND ONE POINT FOR A CORRECT ANSWER AND THE

FIRST PLAYER TO REACH TEN POINTS BECOMES THE NEW EGGHEAD, IT'S AS SIMPLE AS THAT, DO YOU UNDERSTAND? OK YOU START OFF WITH FOUR POINTS SHAUN, YOU START WITH ONE POINT BARRY, THE FIRST TO TEN. NOW IF BOTH REACH TEN POINTS AFTER THE SAME NUMBER OF QUESTIONS, WE WILL THE GO TO SUDDEN DEATH TO FIND A WINNER AS YOU WOULD EXPECT. THE BEST OF LUCK TO YOU BOTH! SHAUN, AS YOU WON THE LAST ROUND YOU GET TO CHOOSE WHETHER YOU PLAY FIRST OR SECOND IN THIS ONE WHAT'S IT GOING TO BE?"

I opted to go first.

"SHAUN, WHICH MEMBER OF TEST MATCH SPECIAL COMMENTARY TEAM HAS THE NICK NAME THE BEARDED WONDER?"

What a tough question to start off with! I really didn't have a clue as to who the person referred to in the question might be. I tried to think of as many cricket match commentators that I could who wore a beard, but nothing sadly was coming to mind and the only commentator I could think of was Jonathan Agnew. I knew that Jonathan Agnew was wrong, but I felt that had to say something. Dermot then turned to the Eggheads panel to see if they knew the answer and the lone solitary voice of Kevin Ashman replied with the correct answer, Bill Frindall to dash all hopes I had of increasing my lead.

"BARRY, MARTIN EDEN IS AN AUTOBIOGRAPHICAL NOVEL BY WHICH CELEBRATED AMERICAN AUTHOR?"

Barry remarked that he probably could have answered my question but as to his own, he had no idea, and he hazarded a guess at Gore Vidal. Dermot revealed the answer was, in fact, Jack London.

"SHAUN, WHAT IS THE SURNAME OF THE INFAMOUS DOCTOR WHO TREATED THE PRESIDENTIAL ASSASSIN, JOHN WILKES BOOTH, AFTER HE SHOT ABRAHAM LINCOLN AND BROKE HIS LEG WHILE MAKING HIS ESCAPE?"

I just could not for the life of me remember the Doctor's surname and the harder I tried to recall the name from the deep recesses of my mind, the more difficulty I was having in doing so, always drawing a blank. In a defeatist tone I said, "I'VE HEARD OF THE DOCTOR, BUT I CAN'T REMEMBER THE NAME SO I'M GOING TO SAY, DR SMEATON, I DON'T KNOW." It came as no surprise when Dermot said that was the wrong answer. He asked Barry if he knew.

"HIS NAME GAVE RISE TO A WONDERFUL ENGLISH PHRASE, 'HIS NAME IS MUD', HE WAS DR MUDD!"

I later came to learn that this origin of that phrase is commonly misappropriated to Samuel Mudd, and Barry was mistaken, in that regard at least. Little good it does me now, though!

"BARRY, WHO WAS IMPRISONED IN 1873 FOR SHOOTING AND WOUNDING THE POET, ARTHUR RIMBAUD?"

Typically, I knew the answer to that question but there was nothing I could do about it and it was at this point, I started to wonder whether I had made the right judgement call in choosing to go first with the set of questions. As he was considering the question, Barry stated that it was a choice between Paul Verlaine and Charles Baudelaire as to who it could be but in truth, I think he was just toying with me. I knew full well that Barry knew the correct answer, a fact confirmed when he went on to say that he knew that Verlaine was Rimbaud's former lover and with the first correct answer in the final round, Barry had closed the deficit to two points.

"SHAUN, THE CONTROVERSIAL PROCESS KNOWN AS AUDITING IS THE CENTRAL PRACTICE OF WHICH RELIGIOUS MOVEMENT?"

My heart sank in despair I had no idea. Desperately searching for an answer, I went with the Mormons.

Dermot then turned to Barry to see if he knew it and once again, Barry did not disappoint. "FOUNDED BY L. RON HUBBARD, IT'S THE SCIENTOLOGISTS WHO BELIEVED THAT WE ARE ALL GUIDED BY PEOPLE FROM THE PLANET THEATON."

"BARRY, CONSTRUCTED BETWEEN 1756 AND 1759, WHAT IS JOHN SMEATON'S MOST FAMOUS BUILDING PROJECT?"

Barry's short and succinct response to the question bore all the hallmarks of a man now playing at the top of his game. "FORTUNATELY, HE WASN'T IN IT AT THE TIME WHEN IT FELL DOWN! JOHN SMEATON CONSTRUCTED THE FIRST EDDYSTONE LIGHTHOUSE!"

"SHAUN, WHAT WORD USED TO MEAN A BOLD STYLISHNESS IN THE ENGLISH LANGUAGE, IS ALSO THE CORRECT TERM FOR A PLUME OF FEATHERS ATTACHED TO A SOLDIER'S HELMET?"

"I'VE NEVER HEARD OF IT," I said shaking my head once more in despair that summed up perfectly my lamentable and demoralising performance. For the first time in the contest, I started to believe that my chances of becoming an Egghead were slowly but surely slipping away. "I'M GOING TO SAY A PREEN. I DON'T KNOW, IS IT PREENING?"

Even Dermot's responses to my eventual answers were beginning to sound depressingly familiar. "SHAUN, THAT'S THE INCORRECT ANSWER. BARRY, DO YOU KNOW?"

"IT'S A PANACHE," Barry responded, with an air of supreme confidence and authority. He was now just one question away from levelling the scores and thereby completing a remarkable comeback.

"BARRY, WHAT NAME HAS BEEN GIVEN TO THE HUGE EXPLOSION THAT OCCURRED ON THE 30TH JUNE 1908 IN CENTRAL SIBERIA THAT FLATTENED OVER 2,000 SQUARE KILOMETRES OF LAND AND AROUND 60 MILLION TREES?"

"THERE'S STILL SOME DISCUSSION OVER THIS IN THE SCIENTIFIC COMMUNITY AS TO WHETHER IT WAS A COMET OR A METEOR," Barry said confidently, "AND I THINK THAT THE PRESENT THOUGHT IS MOVING TOWARDS THE FACT THAT IT WAS A COMET WHICH EXPLODED IN MID-AIR. THE AREA OVER WHICH IT EXPLODED IS CALLED TUNGUSKA."

"WELL, WELL, WELL. IT'S ALL SQUARE, FOUR ALL, AND SHAUN, YOU'VE YET TO SCORE IN THE FINAL ROUND."

The express train that Dermot had likened my performance to in the first half of the contest had now come to a complete halt and there was no indication or sign as to when it would be moving again. If I answered my next question incorrectly, even I knew that any lingering hope of ultimate success would be nigh on impossible.

"SHAUN, IN SEPTEMBER 1955 TWO ROYAL MARINES CLAIMED WHICH ROCKY ISLETS FOR THE UNITED KINGDOM TO ENSURE THAT THE SOVIET UNION COULD NOT SPY ON MISSILE TESTS?"

"IT JUST GOES TO SHOW REALLY. I'VE NEVER, EVER HEARD OF IT," I responded in a deflated, demoralised tone and without giving any sort of thought to the answer I gave the response, Azores. Once again Barry gave the correct answer, Rockall, for me.

"BARRY, IN THE MYTHOLOGY OF THE NATIVE AMERICAN PEOPLES, WHAT IS THE NAME OF THE GIANT BIRD THAT IS SAID TO GENERATE THUNDER BY THE BEATING OF ITS WINGS?"

"I'VE BEEN ASKED THIS BEFORE TWICE AND BOTH TIMES I GOT IT WRONG AND I'M NOW WISHING I COULD REMEMBER WHAT THE RIGHT ANSWER WAS. I'M WONDERING, IS IT THUNDERBIRD OR IS IT MANITOU? I DON'T THINK IT'S MANITOU, I THINK MANITOU IS ANOTHER NAME FOR THE GREAT SPIRIT. I CAN'T THINK OF ANYTHING ELSE OTHER THAN THUNDERBIRD, SO I SHALL SAY THUNDERBIRD."

"THUNDERBIRD IS CORRECT, BARRY, IT PUTS YOU IN THE LEAD. THE THUNDERBIRD IS SO LARGE THAT IT CAN HUNT AND KILL KILLER WHALES IN THEIR NATIVE AMERICAN MYTHOLOGY. SO, SHAUN, FOR THE FIRST TIME YOU'RE BEHIND. LET'S SEE WHAT YOU CAN DO WITH THE NEXT QUESTION. WHICH SOUTHEAST ASIAN FRUIT HAS A SPINY, SPHERICAL SHELL AND IS LOCALLY CALLED THE 'KING OF FRUITS' FOR ITS FLAVOUR, DESPITE ITS FOUL ODOUR?"

I was completely and utterly stumped. Only personal pride prevented me from passing on the question altogether and I gave the answer Lychee just to say anything that would sound even remotely plausible. Dermot immediately turned to Barry who went on to explain that the fruit concerned, the Durian, was recently banned on the public transport system in Thailand for its foul stench despite its sweet sublime taste.

"BARRY, WHAT DOES THE LETTER "B" STAND FOR IN THE NAME OF THE CELEBRATED FILM MAKER CECIL B. DE MILLE?"

Why didn't I go second? I thought miserably as Barry confidently replied, "HIS NAME WAS CECIL BLOUNT DE MILLE," to put him 6-4 in the lead.

"SHAUN, BERYL INGHAM WAS, FOR THIRTY-SIX YEARS, THE FORMIDABLE WIFE OF WHICH ENTERTAINER?"

Yet another question that I did not know the answer to. In desperation, I said Max Bygraves, and this time it was the Eggheads, and Chris Hughes in particular, who enlightened me as to the correct answer – George Formby.

"BARRY, NURSE RATCHED IS A VILLAINOUS CHARACTER IN WHICH 1962 NOVEL?"

I shook my head in complete and utter despair upon hearing yet another question that I knew the correct answer to but was powerless to do anything about it. Barry went on to explain that the actress Louise Fletcher had won the Best Actress Oscar for her role as Nurse Ratched in the 1975 film *One Flew Over the Cuckoo's Nest.*

Dermot noticed the visible signs of frustration and bitter disappointment etched all over my face and, to his eternal credit, he showed a great deal of sympathy and compassion with his kind words of encouragement but in truth, all the best wishes in the world couldn't turn my desperate fortunes around.

"SHAUN, WINIFRED ROBERTS AND BARBARA HEPWORTH WERE THE FIRST TWO WIVES OF WHICH FELLOW ARTIST?"

I attempted in vain to answer yet another question that I simply didn't have a clue about. The name Barbara Hepworth was well known to me, although the only real facts that I knew about the renowned sculptress was her close association with the town of St Ives and her close collaboration with the equally renowned celebrated sculptor Henry Moore and it was he upon whom my faint hopes of a miraculous comeback were totally reliant upon. It was only when Barry gave the correct answer, Ben Nicolson when asked by Dermot did the name belatedly ring any bells.

"BARRY, AN ENGLISHMAN IN NEW YORK, A SONG BY THE POP STAR STING, IS ABOUT WHICH WRITER?"

Barry clearly knew the answer but given how close he was the to ultimate prize, he was determined to take his time. "I DON'T KNOW IF I'M ALLOWED TO SAY THIS BUT HE DESCRIBES HIMSELF AS THE GREATEST STATELY HOMO OF ENGLAND, THE ANSWER IS QUENTIN CRISP." Barry was now 8-4 in the lead and showing no sign of an imminent collapse.

"SHAUN, WHO COACHED THE ITALIAN TEAM TO VICTORY IN THE 2006 FIFA WORLD CUP?"

"AT LONG LAST..." I SAID, "...A QUESTION I FINALLY KNOW THE CORRECT ANSWER TO, MARCELLO LIPPI." I had a point at last but the gap between the scores was far too great for me to close and for that unlikely scenario to happen, Barry would have to undergo a complete and total collapse, and even if I had the assistance of a magic wand to help me, that was simply not going to happen.

"BARRY, WHICH WORD USED FOR LARGE MAMMALS SUCH AS ELEPHANTS IS DERIVED FROM THE GREEK WORD FOR THICK SKINNED?"

There was no way that Barry wasn't going to make a *faux pas* on that question and his swift response, Pachyderm, meant that he was now only one correct answer away from total victory.

Just before I faced my next question, I cheerily began to display good old-fashioned gallows humour when I broke into song with a rendition of "One Wheel on my Wagon and I'm still rolling along."

"WELL," said Dermot upon hearing me singing, "AT LEAST YOU'VE STARTED MOVING. HERE'S YOUR NEXT QUESTION. WHOSE NOVEL, RITES OF PASSAGE, WON THE BOOKER PRIZE IN 1980?"

"WILLIAM GOLDING," I replied immediately in the full knowledge that I was 100% correct, but my mini revival was all too little and had come far too late.

"WILLIAM GOLDING IS THE CORRECT ANSWER, SHAUN, BUT BARRY, THE NEXT CORRECT ANSWER WINS YOU THE GAME AND MAKES YOU THE NEXT EGGHEAD IF YOU GET IT. AFTER SERVING AS SOVIET MINISTER FOR FOREIGN AFFAIRS FROM 1985 TO 1990, EDUARD SHEVARDNADZE BECAME THE PRESIDENT OF WHICH COUNTRY?"

Once Dermot had finished reading the question, I looked over to where Barry was sitting and noticed a broad smile on his face. He knew the correct answer was Georgia and just as he was about to give that answer, I leaned towards him and patted him on the top of his thigh and whispered *congratulations,* before slumping disconsolately back in my chair, consumed with the immense feeling of bitter regret and disappointment that I had fallen agonisingly short at the final hurdle after such a long and arduous day. *I should have gone second, why didn't I go second?* That's all I kept on saying to myself over and over in my mind seemingly lost in my own private world. *I should have gone second. I should have gone second!*

I should have gone second.

Those five haunting words seemed to have the instant sobering effect of pouring a large bucket of ice cold water all over me as I emerged from my trance, my reflection of the ups and downs of the roller coaster nature of my life up until that point. Despite my complete and utter regret in not having gone second in the final round, I could have no real complaints as to how the contest turned out and without a doubt, the best man deservedly triumphed in the end.

The Steely Dan CD had finished playing the last track and that prompted me to look at the clock on the dashboard in my car and it was only then that I realised that I had been sitting in the BBC Car Park for just over an hour. I decided there was little point in lamenting my devastating loss any longer and that it was finally time for me to head for home. As I began to adjust my seat to an upright position in preparation to leave, the dark, depressive mood that had totally engulfed me when I entered the Car Park had been replaced with a more cheery and philosophical one. Ok, so I lost and the disappointment of losing will probably stay with me for a very long time to come. But as the old saying goes, "Time will always be a great healer," and in time, I know that I will emerge from this heart-breaking defeat a stronger and better person. All in all, when I look back on my life's journey thus far, there can be no doubting the great sense of personal pride and real satisfaction that I feel in what I have achieved. Despite that latest disappointment of falling at the final hurdle, I nevertheless remain firm and steadfast in my belief that the best of

Chasing the Dream

those achievements is yet to come and until those achievements and goals are finally realised, I will remain both committed and determined to continue chasing my dreams.

BV - #0014 - 111218 - C20 - 234/156/34 - PB - 9781916440005